Managing Human Resources

Productivity, Quality of Work Life, Profits

McGRAW-HILL SERIES IN MANAGEMENT

Fred Luthans and Keith Davis, Consulting Editors

Managing Human Resources

PRODUCTIVITY, QUALITY OF WORK LIFE, PROFITS

SECOND EDITION

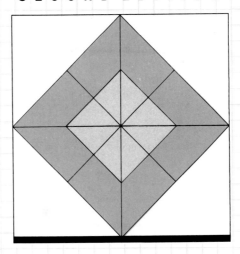

Wayne F. Cascio

GRADUATE SCHOOL OF BUSINESS, UNIVERSITY OF COLORADO, DENVER

McGraw-Hill Publishing Company

New York St. Louis San Francisco Auckland Bogotá
Caracas Hamburg Lisbon London Madrid Mexico Milan
Montreal New Delhi Oklahoma City Paris San Juan
São Paulo Singapore Sydney Tokyo Toronto

MANAGING HUMAN RESOURCES: Productivity, Quality of Work Life, Profits

3 4 5 6 7 8 9 0 D O C D O C   9 3 2 1 0

ISBN   0-07-010377-1

*This book was set in Century Expanded by J. M. Post Graphics, Corp. (CCU).
The editors were Kathleen L. Loy and Linda Richmond; the designer was Joan
Greenfield; the production supervisor was Denise L. Puryear.
The drawings were done by Accurate Art, Inc.
R. R. Donnelley & Sons Company was printer and binder.*

Library of Congress Cataloging-in-Publication Data

Cascio, Wayne F.
   Managing human resources: productivity, quality of work life,
   profits/Wayne F. Cascio.—2nd ed.
     p. cm.—(McGraw-Hill series in management)
   Includes bibliographies and indexes.
   ISBN 0-07-010377-1
   1. Personnel management.   I. Title.   II. Series.
HF5549.C2975 1989
658.3—dc19   88-13353

About the Author

Wayne F. Cascio earned his B.A. degree from Holy Cross College in 1968, his M.A. degree from Emory University in 1969, and his Ph.D. in industrial/organizational psychology from the University of Rochester in 1973. Since that time he has taught at Florida International University, the University of California-Berkeley, and the University of Colorado-Denver, where he is at present Professor of Management and Organization.

Professor Cascio is a Fellow of the American Psychological Association, a Diplomate in industrial/organizational psychology of the American Board of Professional Psychology, and a member of the Editorial Boards of *Human Performance* and the *Academy of Management Review.* He has consulted with a wide variety of organizations in both the public and private sectors on personnel matters, and periodically he testifies as an expert witness in employment discrimination cases. Professor Cascio is an active researcher and is the author of four books on human resource management.

To Dorothy and Joey,

the choicest blessings life has provided; constant reminders of what really counts.

Contents

Chapter 2
Human Resource Management: A Field in Transition   36

Chapter 3
The Legal and Social Contexts of Personnel Decisions   67

Chapter 9
Appraising Employee Performance

PART FOUR

Compensation

PART FIVE

Labor-Management Accommodation

PART SIX

Support, Evaluation, and International Implications

Chapter 15
Safety, Health, and Employee Assistance Programs 549

Chapter 16
Assessing the Costs and Benefits of Human Resource Management Activities 590

Chapter 17
International Dimensions of Human Resource
Management   634

Preface

This book was not written for aspiring personnel specialists. It was written for the student of general management whose job inevitably will involve responsibility for managing *people*, along with other organizational assets. A fundamental assumption, then, is that all managers are accountable to their organizations in terms of the impact of their human resource management (HRM) activities. They also are accountable to their peers and to their subordinates in terms of the quality of work life they are providing.

As a unifying theme for the text, there is explicit linkage in each chapter of the three outcome variables—productivity, quality of work life, and profit—to the HRM activity under discussion. This relationship should strengthen the student's perception of HRM as an important function affecting individuals, organizations, and society.

Each of the six parts that comprise the text includes a figure that illustrates the organizing framework for the book. The specific topics covered in each part are highlighted for emphasis.

Each chapter incorporates the following distinguishing features:

- A split-sequential case. Events in the case are designed to sensitize the reader to the subject matter of the chapter. The events lead to a climax, but then the case stops—like a two-part television drama. The reader is asked to predict what will happen next and to anticipate the impact of alternative courses of action. The case is followed by a new section entitled "What's Ahead." This section shows how the case ties in with the material to be presented and what the flow of topics in the chapter will be. Then the text for the chapter appears, replete with concepts, theories, research findings, and company examples that illustrate current practices. Ultimately we are trying to teach prospective managers to *make decisions* based on accurate diagnoses of situations that involve HRM issues. Their ability to do this is enhanced by familiarity with theory, research, and practice.

At the end of the chapter we continue the case introduced at the outset, to see what happened. This dynamic design allows the student to move back and forth from concept to evidence to practice—then back to evaluating concepts—in a continuous "learning loop."

- Relevant research findings plus clippings from the popular press (Company Examples) provide real world applications of concepts and theories. It has often been said that experience is a hard teacher because it gives the test first and the lessons afterward. Actual company examples allow the student to learn from the experience of others.

- Near the end of the chapter, before the summary and discussion questions, there is a section called "Tomorrow's Forecast," which looks ahead to emerging trends in each area of HRM.

Above all, I have tried to make the text readable, neither too simplistic nor too complex.

New topics in the second edition

- International applications are interwoven throughout every chapter, and, as in the first edition, they also comprise a special chapter (Chapter 17).
- The changing nature of the competitive business environment, and the role and contribution of human resources in that environment (Chapter 1).
- Top management's view of the strategic use of the HR department (Chapter 2).
- 1986 Immigration and Control Act, amendments to the Age Discrimination in Employment Act, and major new rulings by the Supreme Court on affirmative action (Chapter 3).
- New approaches to job design, including telecommuting (Chapter 4).
- Impact of downsizings and restructurings on internal labor markets and human resource planning (Chapter 5).
- Use of computers in recruitment, video résumés, drug screening, and honesty tests (Chapter 6).
- Company examples that illustrate the economic impact of training, plus the plight of displaced workers and corporate social responsibility for retraining them. In short, the economic as well as the human sides of training are presented (Chapter 7).
- Discussion of the "new breed" of chief executive officers, changes in the jobs of middle- and lower-level managers, and cumulative evidence on the relative effectiveness of alternative management development methods (Chapter 8).
- Updated information about the legal implications of performance appraisal systems, court-recommended safeguards against bias in appraisal, computer monitoring of job performance, and guidelines for managing "problem bosses" is presented (Chapter 9).

- The impact of mergers, acquisitions, and downsizing on corporate loyalty, mentoring for women and minorities, and updated research on myths versus facts about older workers (Chapter 10).
- The concept of "flexible pay"—putting more of one's pay at risk—is examined, as are the implications of COBRA, cost-shifting of health-care expenses from the government to the private sector, and the impact of the 1986 Tax Reform Act on benefits (Chapter 11).
- Revised treatment of long-term incentives, in light of the 1986 Tax Reform Act, and company examples to illustrate (1) how long-term incentives are being tied to business strategy, (2) performance-linked pay plans for lower-level workers, and (3) union attitudes toward incentive plans (Chapter 12).
- The effect of mergers and acquisitions on labor relations is explored, as are local versus international union conflicts, management's social responsibility to workers affected by plant shutdowns, and survival tactics of unions—mergers and corporate campaigns (Chapter 13).
- Power tactics by labor (e.g., in-plant slowdowns, "top-down" organizing) and management (e.g., plant-level bargaining, operating through strikes) are discussed in the context of an internationally competitive business environment. Expanded coverage of nonunion grievance procedures and employment-at-will (Chapter 14).
- Examination of job safety and health issues, domestic and abroad, from two perspectives: (1) management's concern with the costs and benefits of job safety and health measures and (2) labor's demand for ethical, socially responsible treatment by management of job safety and health issues. Also new: "right-to-know" rules in the chemical industry, and AIDS and business (Chapter 15).
- Updated treatment of procedures that can be used to determine the costs and benefits of employee absenteeism, turnover, selection, training, and employee assistance programs. Also, the growing use of attitude surveys in personnel research, particularly after mergers and acquisitions (Chapter 16).
- Coverage of the key differences between domestic and international HRM operations in each of the topical areas covered previously. Also, new impact of the 1986 Tax Reform Act on overseas compensation and impact of the Organization for Economic Cooperation and Development (OECD) guidelines regarding codes of conduct for multinational corporations (Chapter 17).

Organization and plan of the book

The figure on the next page provides an organizing framework for the book. It will appear again at the opening of each of the six parts that comprise the book. Each component of the organizing framework will be highlighted for the student as it is discussed. The organization of the parts is designed to reflect the fact that human resource management (HRM) is an integrated, goal-directed set of functions, not just a collection of techniques.

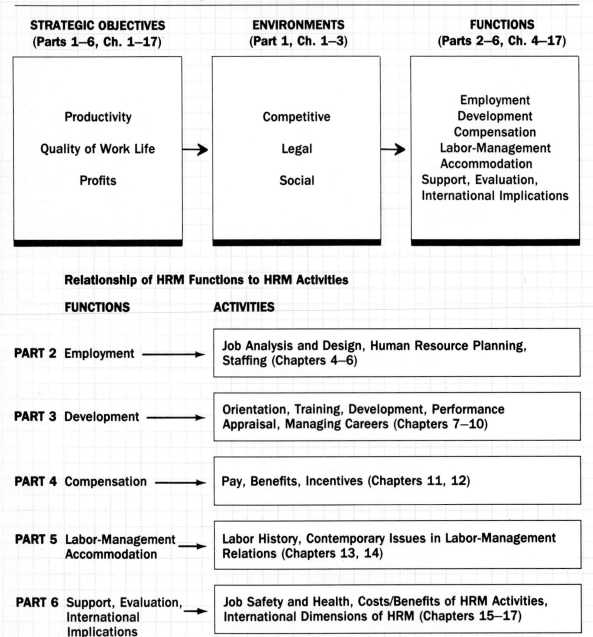

A Conceptual View of Human Resource Management: Strategic Objectives, Environments, Functions

STRATEGIC OBJECTIVES (Parts 1–6, Ch. 1–17)	ENVIRONMENTS (Part 1, Ch. 1–3)	FUNCTIONS (Parts 2–6, Ch. 4–17)
Productivity Quality of Work Life Profits	Competitive Legal Social	Employment Development Compensation Labor-Management Accommodation Support, Evaluation, International Implications

Relationship of HRM Functions to HRM Activities

	FUNCTIONS	ACTIVITIES
PART 2	Employment	Job Analysis and Design, Human Resource Planning, Staffing (Chapters 4–6)
PART 3	Development	Orientation, Training, Development, Performance Appraisal, Managing Careers (Chapters 7–10)
PART 4	Compensation	Pay, Benefits, Incentives (Chapters 11, 12)
PART 5	Labor-Management Accommodation	Labor History, Contemporary Issues in Labor-Management Relations (Chapters 13, 14)
PART 6	Support, Evaluation, International Implications	Job Safety and Health, Costs/Benefits of HRM Activities, International Dimensions of HRM (Chapters 15–17)

The text is founded on the premise that three critical strategic objectives guide all HRM functions: productivity, quality of work life, and profits. The functions (employment; development; compensation; labor-management accommodation; and support, evaluation, and international implications) in turn are carried out in the context of multiple environments: competitive, legal, and social.

Part 1, Environment, comprises Chapters 1, 2, and 3. It provides the backdrop against which to appreciate the nature and content of each HRM function. These first three chapters paint a broad picture of the competitive, legal, and social environments of HRM. They also describe key economic and noneconomic factors that affect productivity, quality of work life, and profits. The remaining five parts (14 chapters) in the book are presented in the context of this conceptual framework.

Logically, Employment (Part 2) is the first step in the HRM process. Job analysis and design, human resource planning, and staffing are key components of the employment process. Once employees are "on board," the process of Development (Part 3) begins with orientation and is sustained through continuing training, performance appraisal, and career management activities.

Parts 4, 5, and 6 are all concurrent processes. That is, Compensation (Part 4), Labor-Management Accommodation (Part 5), and Support, Evaluation, and International Implications (Part 6) are all closely intertwined conceptually and in practice. They represent a network of interacting activities, such that a change in one of them (e.g., a new pay system or collective bargaining contract) inevitably will have an impact on all other components of the HRM system. It is only for ease of exposition that they are considered separately in Parts 4, 5, and 6. Chapter 17 of Part 6, International Dimensions of HRM, is a capstone chapter. That is, each of the topics we considered throughout the book is addressed in the special context of international business practices. It forces the student to consider the broad spectrum of HR activities across countries, across cultures, and across economic systems. The need to "fit" HRM practices to the company and country cultures in which they are imbedded, in order to achieve the strategic objectives of enhancing productivity, quality of work life, and profits, is an important concept for students to understand and to apply.

Acknowledgments

Many people played important roles in the development of the first and second editions of this book, and I am deeply grateful to them. Ultimately, of course, any errors of omission or commission are mine, and I bear responsibility for them. I wrote the second edition while on sabbatical leave at the Industrial Research Unit of the Wharton School, University of Pennsylvania. Wharton provided a rich, intellectually stimulating atmosphere in which to work, while the extensive holdings of the IRU and Wharton libraries allowed me to draw upon a vast collection of information. I am particularly grateful for the support of Dr. Richard Rowan—advisor and friend—throughout this project.

Three people at McGraw-Hill were especially helpful. Kathleen Loy and Mike Morales provided continual support and encouragement. As in the first edition, I found Mike Elia's help to be indispensable. Finally, the many reviewers of various portions of the first and second editions provided important insights that helped to improve the final product. They deserve special thanks.

Eileen Kelly Aranda, Ph.D.
Arizona State University

Professor Brian Becker
SUNY, Buffalo

Professor Randall De Simone
University of Rhode Island

Professor Russsell W. Driver
The University of Oklahoma

Professor Donald Drost
Mankato State University

Professor Robert H. Faley
Purdue University

Professor Charles Fombrun
The Wharton School
University of Pennsylvania

Professor Robert Gatewood
The University of Georgia

Professor Jai Ghorpade
San Diego State University

Professor Joyce B. Giglioni
Mississippi State University

Professor Michael Harris
Purdue University

Professor Stephen W. Hartman
New York Institute of Technology

Professor David Hegedus
University of Wisconsin, Oshkosh

Professor Peter Hess
Western New England College

Professor Wallace R. Johnston
Virginia Commonwealth University

Professor James W. Klingler
Villanova University

Professor John Koziell
Merrimack College

Professor Janina C. Latack
The Ohio State University,
Columbus

Professor Richard Lester
University of Northern Alabama

Professor Kathryn Lewis
California State University, Chico

Professor Fred Luthans
University of Nebraska, Lincoln

Professor Gregory Northcraft
University of Arizona

Professor Len Rico
The Wharton School
University of Pennsylvania

Professor Sara Rynes
Cornell University

Professor Lee Stepina
Florida State University

Professor Cary D. Thorp, Jr.
University of Nebraska, Lincoln

Professor Nan Weiner
The Ohio State University,
Columbus

Professor Arthur A. Whatley
New Mexico State University, Las
Cruces

Professor Kenneth York
Oakland University

Wayne F. Cascio

Managing Human Resources
Productivity, Quality of Work Life, Profits

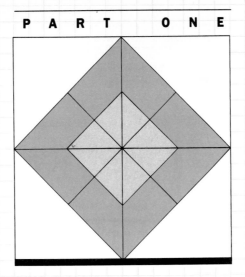

Environment

In order to manage people effectively in today's world of work, it is essential to understand and appreciate the significant competitive, legal, and social issues. The purpose of Chapters 1 and 3 is to provide insight into these issues. Chapter 2 considers the historical development and current status (role, organization, and evaluation) of the human resource management function in organizations.

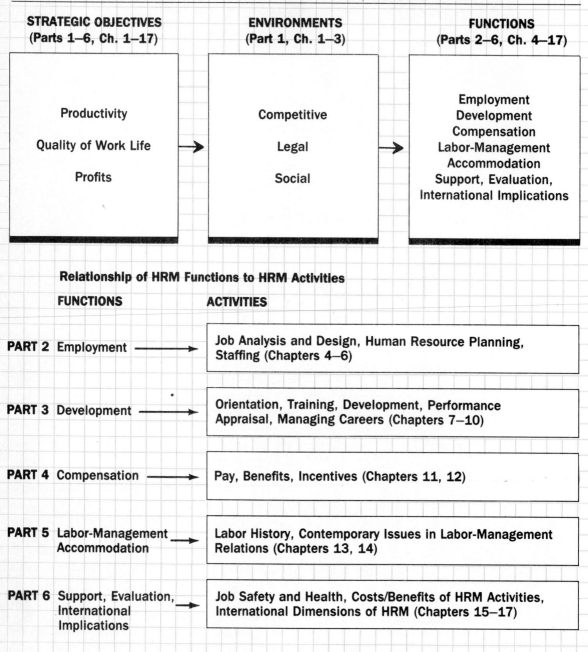

A Conceptual View of Human Resource Management:
Strategic Objectives, Environments, Functions

STRATEGIC OBJECTIVES
(Parts 1–6, Ch. 1–17)

Productivity

Quality of Work Life

Profits

ENVIRONMENTS
(Part 1, Ch. 1–3)

Competitive

Legal

Social

FUNCTIONS
(Parts 2–6, Ch. 4–17)

Employment
Development
Compensation
Labor-Management
Accommodation
Support, Evaluation,
International Implications

Relationship of HRM Functions to HRM Activities

FUNCTIONS

ACTIVITIES

PART 2 Employment → Job Analysis and Design, Human Resource Planning, Staffing (Chapters 4–6)

PART 3 Development → Orientation, Training, Development, Performance Appraisal, Managing Careers (Chapters 7–10)

PART 4 Compensation → Pay, Benefits, Incentives (Chapters 11, 12)

PART 5 Labor-Management Accommodation → Labor History, Contemporary Issues in Labor-Management Relations (Chapters 13, 14)

PART 6 Support, Evaluation, International Implications → Job Safety and Health, Costs/Benefits of HRM Activities, International Dimensions of HRM (Chapters 15–17)

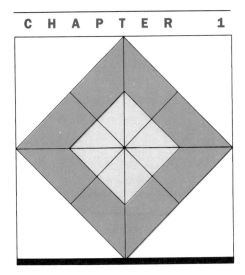

Human Resources in a Competitive Business Environment

Any teenager with a new driver's license is consumed with the prospect of owning a new car. There is delight in the prospect no matter how remote the reality. And it is no different for older folks, no matter how long ago they may have first gotten their driver's license or how many times they may have bought a car, new or used. The auto plays a central role in our culture and in our economy—it represents a major consumer purchase, it is the basis of an enormous industry, it often serves as a symbol of material success, and it is a necessity for living in the suburbs. The auto has been marketed as a payoff for hard work, and we have come to perceive it as such; furthermore, the most recognizable symbol of hard work in an industrial society is probably the automobile assembly line.

In the 1950s most Americans wanted a car that could make a personal statement about them: It would signify their achievement in life and their social standing, indicating how far they had come and where they were going. Today, over 30 years later, our cars still reflect bigness, newness, excess power, and other elements of conspicuous consumption. However, computer-aided design, manufacturing, and on-board controls allow us to continue to enjoy *both power and fuel economy*. Our cars still make personal statements about us, but what they express is our taste, our practicality, and our concern

3

for resources and the environment. Our cars continue to reflect our economic status, the payoff side of the hard-work-pays-off ethic—but what about this ethic's other side, the willingness to do hard work?

In the 1950s and 1960s, assembly line workers, like the majority of the workforce, were mostly married men, sole providers for their families. Not only was the line work difficult and monotonous,[49] but the men were tied to time clocks, their toilet and smoking breaks were monitored strictly, and, in contrast with salaried workers, they were discouraged from using the telephone or even from making light conversation with their fellow workers as they worked. Many Americans would be shocked by the rigidity of the class barriers that separated hourly workers from salaried employees in the automobile industry.

Gradually, the symptoms of worker frustration became more and more visible. Typically this frustration showed up in the poor quality of the products they produced. As recently as the late 1970s, the University of Michigan reported that 27 percent of all American workers—more than one out of four workers—felt so ashamed of the quality of the products they were producing that they would not want to buy them themselves. Fortunately, this perception has changed, for in a 1987 poll by USA Today, 82 percent of workers said that their employers do an excellent or good job in the area of quality products or services.[11]

Not all auto workers are searching for meaning and self-fulfillment in their jobs. But those who are retaliate for the lack of incentives that their work offers; they hold back their commitment, if not their labor. They resent sharp class distinctions between employees and employers. They do not automatically accept the authority of the boss. They want to participate in decisions that affect their work. They prefer variety to routine, they favor informality, and they detest formalism. They want their work to be interesting as well as to pay well.

In short, these auto workers are struggling to revise the work-for-rewards compact in the plant. For them to give unstintingly to the job, they demand in return psychological as well as economic incentives. Just as they demand power *and* fuel economy in their cars, they want *both* good pay and a high-quality work life. These demands make them troublesome to work with, but there is increasing evidence that the work style they prefer may be far more productive in tomorrow's service/information/high-technology economy than the work style of the past would be.[52]

QUESTIONS

1. Both to accommodate these new demands by workers and to improve the quality of the automobile produced, what kinds of people-related management changes would you suggest?
2. What other implications do the changes in the making and buying of cars have for managing people, improving the quality of work life, and boosting productivity in our economy?

What's Ahead

Case 1-1 illustrates that times have changed and that generations have changed over time. To remain competitive, organizations and the people who manage them also must change. This chapter first describes a broad range of changes that have taken place in the competitive and social environments of organizations. It then examines two pressing demands in organizations: (1) pressure for increased productivity and (2) pressure for improvements in the quality of work life. It describes what these concepts mean, why they will continue to be important in the future, and the kinds of changes in management that they demand.

Lesson Number One: People (and Generations) Are Different

Organizations are managed and staffed by people. Without people, organizations cannot exist. Indeed, the challenge, the opportunity, and also the frustration of creating and managing organizations frequently stem from the people-related problems that arise within them. People-related problems, in turn, frequently stem from the mistaken belief that people are all alike, that they can be treated identically. Nothing could be further from the truth. Like snowflakes, no two people are exactly alike, and everyone differs physically and psychologically from everyone else. Sitting in a sports arena, for example, will be tall people, small people, fat people, thin people, black people, white people, elderly people, young people, and so on. Even within any single physical category there will be enormous variability in psychological characteristics. Some will be "screamers," others will be reserved; some will be intelligent, others will be not so intelligent; some will prefer indoor activities, others will prefer outdoor activities. The point is that these differences demand attention so that each person can maximize his or her potential, so that organizations can maximize their effectiveness, and so that society as a whole can make the wisest use of its human resources.

Students of organizations know that the individuals and the organizations they comprise will produce the best results when there is a match between the goals of the individuals and the goals of their organizations. Such a match may have been easier to effect in the pre-1960s world of work than it is today, for the norms of American life are changing as never before. The quest for self-fulfillment is upon us, and we need to understand it so that we can do a better job of managing people at work. Let us consider this movement in greater detail.

appears that there is more to self-fulfillment than self-concern. Indeed, a broader concern with the quality of life is critical to many, if not most, workers. Such concerns may be a source of new economic energy. Efforts to enhance the quality of work life through the effective management of people and organizations provide a continual challenge.

This book is about managing people, the most vital of all resources, in work settings. Rather than focus exclusively on issues of concern to the personnel specialist, however, we will examine human resource management issues in terms of their impact on management in general. Changing norms have forced us to take a hard look at the ways we manage people. Research has shown time and again that human resource management practices can make an important, practical difference in terms of three key organizational outcomes: productivity, quality of work life, and profit. This is healthy. Each chapter in this book considers the impact of a different aspect of human resource management on these three broad themes. To study these impacts, we will look at the latest theory and research in each topical area, plus examples of actual company practices. Let's begin by considering some basic ideas about organizations.

Organizations: Why Do They Exist and How Do They Work?

As our wants and needs grow, so do the ways of satisfying them. Consider the growth of the home-computer industry, for example, and how the firms within it are racing to deliver software—games, puzzles, educational exercises—to meet consumer demands for such products. None of our wants and needs is satisfied randomly or haphazardly. When you go to a store that sells computers, for example, the store will be open, and you can buy the product of your choice even though the salesperson who helped you last time has the day off. In the process of satisfying needs and wants, *continuity* and *predictability* are essential in the delivery of goods and services. In modern society, continuity and predictability are made possible by *organizations*.

Some of the organizations that accommodate our wants and needs are fast-food restaurants, movie theaters, sporting goods stores, hospitals, universities, accounting firms, and antique stores, just to name a few. Each of these organizations exists because what must be done, the task to be accomplished, is too large or complex for one person to accomplish alone. So a number of people are gathered together, and each is assigned a part of the total task. It is most efficient to divide a large task (such as building a house) into its component parts so that specially qualified individuals can perform the subfunctions. *Specialization* by subfunction and *coordination* among all the tasks to be accomplished make the largest-scale task possible.

Although there are great differences among the organizations in our society, they also have much in common. Every organization is (1) comprised of people (2) who perform specialized tasks (3) that are coordinated (4) to enhance the value or utility (5) of some good or service (6) that is wanted by and provided to a set of customers or clients.

In the simplest terms, a formal organization exists by reason of two things: the work it does and the technology it embraces to do that work. However, these are not the only elements of a formal organization. The key elements of a formal organization are related as follows (Figure 1-1). All organizations have objectives (e.g., to provide high-quality goods and services at competitive prices) that are based on some perceived unfilled demand in the outside environment. To attain these objectives, certain tasks must be done (e.g., processing canceled checks, assembling parts of an appliance, checking a patient's vital signs). Indeed, formal organizations are *defined* by the kind of work they do. Technology determines the nature of the work processes since it includes all the aspects of knowledge that are related to the attainment of a firm's objectives (e.g., employee skills, machines, and facilities). Organizational structure supports and facilitates technology by designing jobs and grouping tasks

FIGURE 1-1

Key elements of a formal organization, from specific to general.

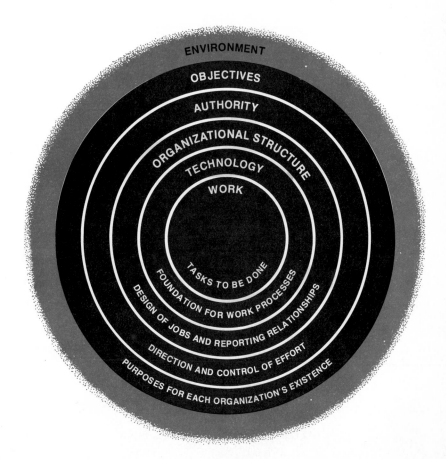

in order to optimize control, coordination, and productivity. This, for example, is why some firms are organized by function—production, marketing, sales, and distribution. To attain the benefits of specialization and efficiency, authority is used to ensure adequate role performance and direction of efforts. Some workers are bosses (in whom authority is formally vested by the organization), while others are subordinates. These concepts are best illustrated by an example.

Case 1-1 described some of the problems associated with assembly line work in the making of automobiles, where the basic technology is mass production. Each worker holds a certain job, does specified actions at a regimented pace, and occupies a certain work station. The specific organizational structure of the assembly line and the content of each job are determined through industrial engineering studies. Once the job is set, the actions of the jobholder are set as well, and the worker must perform what the job dictates; the worker has no discretion to determine whether or not bumpers should be attached to the front and rear of each auto. Technology also limits permissible behavior on the job, for the assembly line worker cannot leave the workstation to take care of "personal business" unless a replacement can be found. In short, technology and organizational structure together place restrictions and requirements on workers' behavior.

When work structure is analyzed with respect to greater specialization for the purpose of producing higher efficiency, little consideration is usually given to the people who do the work and who are thus the substance of specialization and efficiency. This is a serious mistake, as we shall see in later chapters. An organizational structure designed without regard for workers is a structure that dictates behavior to these workers; it will have an adverse effect on their behavior and thus on efficiency. A structure designed with workers in mind affects them so that they contribute more favorably to efficiency. The result is that the workers play an important role in determining the overall efficiency of the organization.

Organizations need people, and people need organizations

Without people, organizations could not function. Even in highly automated plants, such as the one designed and built by Yamazaki to run smoothly using only 12 workers (Yamazaki is a large Japanese company that makes machine tools), people are nevertheless required to coordinate and control the plant's operations. Conversely, people need organizations so that they can satisfy their needs and wants, so that they can maintain their standard of living (by working in organizations), and so that modern society can continue to function. Here are some other reasons for the people-organization partnership.

Demand for productive, efficient use of all resources
In the face of growing worldwide concern over dwindling natural resources (oil, lumber, fish, metals, and clean air, for example), we recognize that nothing exists in limitless

supply. We must abandon our wasteful ways and conserve resources for our own use in the future and for generations to come. But natural resources are not the only types of resources in short supply. What about human resources? As the post-baby-boom generation reaches adulthood, a slower-growing population is propelling the country into a period of labor scarcity that could last until the turn of the century, when the baby boomlet of the mid-1980s will provide a fresh supply of new workers. The problem is compounded by a widening mismatch between the skills that workers have and the skills that employers need. Many jobs in fast-growing service industries, such as financial services, require more education than do traditional jobs in shrinking blue-collar industries, yet more than ½ million students drop out of high school every year, and an additional 700,000 who graduate are barely able to read their own diplomas. As long as employers had a bountiful supply of baby boomers to draw on, these effects were blunted. But now these effects will be costly, leaving few occupations unaffected, as the United States strives to enhance its competitiveness in world markets.[4]

Consumer demand for goods and services   An organization exists to satisfy the demand for a good or service. Without demand for its good or service, an organization cannot grow and survive. In the auto industry, for example, firms such as Kaiser, Packard, and Studebaker went out of business for lack of demand for their products. Conversely, firms like Atari, Apple, and Hewlett-Packard have appeared and prospered *because* of consumer demand for their products.

Global economic competition   In the U.S. auto market, from luxury cars to low-priced cars, foreign and domestic manufacturers compete "head to head." The auto industry is perhaps the clearest example of U.S. organizations' demand for competent, productive workers and of the workers' need for healthy organizations. Since 1973, the year of the Arab oil embargo, foreign-auto sales have grown to about 30 percent of all cars sold in the United States. Product quality, efficient fuel mileage, and low maintenance are key concerns of prospective buyers of U.S. or foreign autos in today's market. To compete in the marketplace, U.S. auto companies need employees who can produce such cars, and the employees need their companies to be healthy. Concessions made by the United Auto Workers since 1981, which resulted from collective bargaining with auto companies, illustrate this fact.

Societal expectations   Americans' values have changed significantly over the past several decades. In the post-World War II era, most families shared in the heritage of the middle class: the guarantee of progress. Most would be promoted at work; most would earn ever higher salaries; most would buy more and better products for their homes. Today, economic turbulence has splintered the middle class. Whereas upward mobility was once a given, middle-class households now find themselves heading both up and *down* the economic ladder.

Economists attribute the increased turmoil to such factors as the deregulation of major U.S. industries, the volatile farm economy, and the growing impact of world trade. The roaring inflation of the early 1980s and the subsequent deflation have also had an unequal effect on many individuals. As one observer noted, "One guy loses his job, while another watches the value of his home double."[18]

But *middle class* represents a way of life as well as a certain income level. While once it was characterized by a broad consensus about how to live and what constitutes success, now there is little agreement. Today the middle class is represented by a single mother with two children as well as by an unmarried couple who do not want children. The middle-class lifestyle can mean pursuing a successful career, moving to the country, or championing a cause.

Sociologists attribute these changes to such forces as the aging of the baby-boom generation—with its anticonformist values—and the increased freedoms afforded by an affluent society. As people are less driven by basic wants, they are more likely to follow different paths. Yet despite these different values and aspirations, one can argue that America will always be a predominantly middle-class society. For under a more classic definition, *middle class* refers to a section of society that is self-reliant. The poor are those who cannot support themselves, and the rich are those who do not have to.[19]

The changes in the outlook, expectation, and attitudes of women are especially striking. At the turn of the century less than 20 percent of women worked outside the home. Today more than two-thirds do, and by 1990 women will make up almost half of the U.S. labor force. To a large extent, these changes are due to the decreased demands of housework, the decline in the birth rate, the growth of jobs that require less physical strength, and the pull of higher wages and salaries for women. In the earlier, postwar period, women worked outside the home to improve their families' standard of living. Since the 1970s, however, as the earnings of many husbands declined, women increased their work effort to maintain their families' standard of living.[46]

While they may need the money, women derive great pleasure from their jobs, just as men do. Both sexes say that job satisfaction is the most important thing about a job, more important than job security, money, or future opportunities. Among those who view work as a career, not just as a job, 79 percent in one study said that they liked work a great deal.[11]

An inescapable conclusion, however, is that the gains for women have come at great social and psychological cost. In a study of male and female corporate officers, 82 percent of the women interviewed said that they paid with personal sacrifices. One in five had never married; only 0.7 percent of the men had never wed. One-fifth of the women were separated or divorced, 5 times the male rate. More than half were childless; 95 percent of the men had children, and the average man had three.[20]

Striving for the "good life"   America has always been viewed as the land of opportunity. Today, television brings the "good life into our homes, and we see people driving fancy cars, wearing fine clothes, eating well, and having

- Demand for productive, efficient use of human talents

- Consumer demand for goods and services

- Global economic competition

- Societal expectations

- Striving for the "good life"

FIGURE 1-2

Organizations need people and people need organizations. Organizations are staffed by people (left); however (right), organizations compete for qualified people (note the diploma in the right hand of the job applicant), and employed people provide a market for the goods and services that organizations produce (note the money and credit card in the applicant's left hand).

lots of leisure time and lots of money to spend during that time. Our TV characters seem to have "made it" in some ideal sense, and they serve as inspirations for some of us whose worlds seem bleak. In addition, instant credit and job availability have a way of making the good life seem just a step away.

In summary, organizations need people and people need organizations for all the reasons shown in Figure 1-2. The point is that people make organizations go. How the people are selected, trained, and managed determines to a large extent how successful an organization will be. As you can certainly appreciate by now, the task of managing people in today's world of work is particularly challenging because of the changes that have occurred in the value systems of workers, young and old, and one of the most pressing concerns that organizations face is productivity improvement.

Productivity: What Is It?

A popular buzzword in American industry today is "productivity." Although people talk about it as though they know precisely what it means, productivity is surprisingly difficult to define and measure, especially in highly diversified firms. How can or should we compare the productivity of a secretary whose boss dictates letters that take hours to edit against one whose boss produces clean copy? How can we measure accurately the productivity of a salesperson who fills her order book every day, but with customers whose subsequent service requirements far outweigh the investment returned?[35]

In general, productivity is a measure of the output of goods and services relative to the input labor, material, and equipment. The more productive an industry, the better its competitive position because its unit costs are lower. Improving productivity simply means getting more out of what is put in. It does not mean increasing production through the addition of resources, such as time, money, materials, or people. It is doing better with what you have. Improving productivity is not working harder, it is working smarter. Today's world demands that we do more with less—fewer people, less money, less time, less space, and fewer resources in general. These ideas are shown graphically in Figure 1-3.

The United States had led the world in annual rate of productivity improvement for decades, but at the end of the 1970s its productivity stopped

FIGURE 1-3

More productive organizations get more goods and services out of a given amount of labor, capital, and equipment than do less productive organizations.

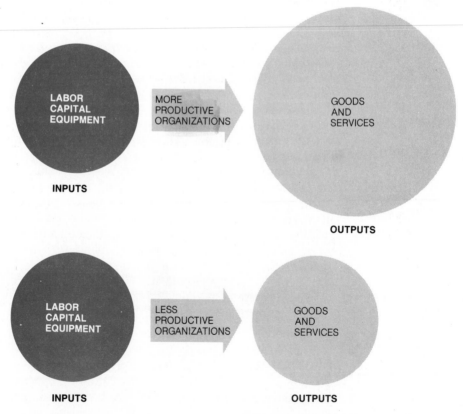

growing and slipped into reverse, while Japan and other industrial nations kept gaining. Later we will consider some of the reasons for this decline, but let's first consider what it implies.

In terms of output per hour of work, U.S. manufacturing productivity grew by just 0.6 percent between 1972 and 1982. During the same time period, however, Japan's grew by 3.4 percent, West Germany's by 2.1 percent, and France's by 3.0 percent. These are significant differences that can lead to unpleasant consequences. Beginning in the late nineteenth century, for example, the yearly rise in the productivity of England, then the world's foremost industrial nation, was just slightly less (1 percent) than that of its industrial rivals, mainly the United States and Germany. But by the mid-twentieth century that seemingly small difference proved to be enough to tumble England from its previously undisputed industrial prominence.[51]

Fortunately, U.S. manufacturing productivity has turned upward again, with increases averaging just under 4 percent per year from 1982 to 1987. Using a mathematical model, economist John Kendrick predicts a 2.5 percent annual productivity growth rate through 1990.[17] This growth is possible because many of the factors that made the United States inefficient in the 1970s are now improving. Oil prices and inflation have moderated. Increased investments in research and development are producing technological advancements. And finally, the 20 million young workers of the baby boom who entered the labor force in the 1970s have now become more skilled, and thus more productive, as a result of their increased job experience.

Outside the realm of manufacturing, however, productivity increases have come more slowly. Indeed, the greatest drag on productivity growth has come from the ever-expanding service sector. Many service firms, from bank holding companies to hospitals, insurance companies, and the government, have been frustrated, trying to squeeze more output from less input. Since 1979, output per hour in service-related industries has risen less than 0.5 percent per year.[36] Figure 1-4 shows this trend over the 1986–1987 period.

Some of the increase in blue-collar productivity is undoubtedly due to widespread automation in the factory, but some of the increase may also reflect the fact that it is easier to measure the output of the blue-collar sector than it is to measure the output of the people who work in marketing, engineering, human resources, and the rest of the white-collar population, where outputs may be less tangible. For example, Tandem Computers, Inc., of Cupertino, California, has cut the average design time for its semiconductors to just 4 weeks from 14 by installing several million dollars worth of computer-aided design equipment. But Tandem cannot identify similar savings for its largest white-collar investment, an information network that links marketing, engineering, and manufacturing divisions at 200 locations in 35 countries.[36] And it is the white-collar segment of the workforce that is growing most rapidly.

Just 10 years ago a typical manufacturing company's workforce was made up mostly of blue-collar workers. Today white-collar employees make up about 50 percent of a manufacturing company's workforce—about 70 percent of its

FIGURE 1-4

Productivity gains in services (shown as "Total nonfarm") have lagged behind those in manufacturing. (Source: Reprinted from August 17, 1987, issue of Business Week *by special permission, copyright © 1987 by McGraw-Hill, Inc.)*

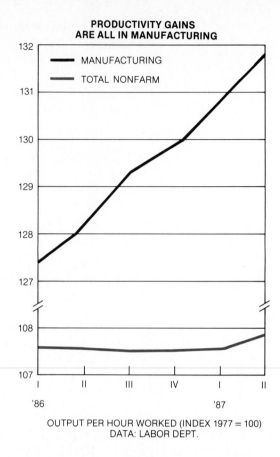

PRODUCTIVITY GAINS
ARE ALL IN MANUFACTURING

— MANUFACTURING
— TOTAL NONFARM

OUTPUT PER HOUR WORKED (INDEX 1977 = 100)
DATA: LABOR DEPT.

payroll. Both percentages are expected to increase in the years ahead. The American Productivity Center predicts that by 1990, nearly 90 percent of all employed Americans will be working either in white-collar jobs or in service-sector occupations. In view of these trends, meaningful measurement of white-collar productivity is an urgent priority.

Productivity measurement

Although in theory a total productivity index that relates all inputs (capital, labor, material, and energy) to final outputs might appear more accurate, there are reasons why this index is not as meaningful as it could be. The companies that have programs to develop meaningful measures of productivity are finding that using productivity measures of *each* of the components of an organization provides more useful information than does a total productivity index. For example, Kaiser Aluminum and Chemical Co. measures labor productivity, material productivity, and energy productivity separately for each of its plants.

These productivity measures are then combined into a productivity index for each plant, so that the firm's plants can be measured against each other. Beatrice Foods found the following productivity measurements most useful:

- Employee productivity measured as output per blue- or white-collar employee or per worker hour: unit sales per payroll dollar and units of output per worker hour
- Equipment productivity measured as output per asset dollar: unit sales per asset dollar and units of output per asset dollar
- Energy productivity measured as product output per unit energy input: units of product per cubic foot (gas), units of product per gallon (oil), units of product per kilowatthour (electricity)

White-collar productivity   Certainly any company is at a competitive disadvantage if its white-collar productivity is substantially below that of its competition, whether domestic or foreign. As Drucker has noted, "The only competitive advantage the U.S.—and every other developed country—can have lies in making productive its one abundant resource: People with long years of schooling who are available only for white-collar work. For the rest of this century—and far into the next one—the competitive battle will be won or lost by white-collar productivity" (ref. 6, p. 30). Yet managers in many firms are surprisingly unconcerned about white-collar productivity. Their excuse: "No one knows how to measure it." This is not true. While the yardsticks available are crude, they are nevertheless accurate. White-collar productivity requires (1) goals to shoot for and (2) means to monitor progress toward those goals.

Westinghouse concluded that the only meaningful way to measure white-collar productivity is to focus not on the individual employee (or on the corporation as a whole, of course), but on the individual department, evaluating each department in terms of its own objectives. That is, the engineering department is measured for the engineering it produces, the marketing department for its marketing, and personnel for personnel. Once each function of the corporation is measured against its own objectives, then "performance ratios" for the total operating division can be established. Here are the top three performance ratios developed by the engineering, personnel, and marketing departments of Westinghouse:

- *Engineering.* Dollar value of reported cost improvements, number of overdue shop orders, and cost of engineering errors
- *Personnel.* Average time to fill employee vacancies, average time to process insurance claims, and number of lost-time injuries
- *Marketing.* Increased market penetration, field sales performance, and forecasting accuracy

The experience of companies using productivity measurement plans has provided the following five practical lessons:[45]

1. Specific plans must be developed to make productivity information routinely and easily available.
2. Do not be disappointed if you cannot develop perfectly accurate measurements of productivity.
3. To devise meaningful productivity measurements, get direction and technical help from the company coordinator of the program or from an outside expert.
4. Realistic, relatively simple, and understandable measurements work best.
5. Even the attempt to measure productivity will improve it, simply because the attempt itself makes employees aware of opportunities for productivity gains.

Organizations have only recently begun to realize the gains to be achieved from increased productivity of white-collar workers. While office automation presents opportunities for increased productivity, there is greater potential for increased productivity through improvements in the workers themselves. Getting people to work smarter, not necessarily merely harder, is the greatest challenge facing management today.

To evaluate how to increase productivity in America, let's first consider some of the reasons why it declined.

Productivity: What Ails It?

The causes of the decline in U.S. productivity lie deep within our value, economic, and political systems. However, some of the measurable causes cited by economists include:

■ In many industries, the ability to improve productivity through further improvements in technology declined.
■ The supply of labor that can be directed from inefficient productive activities, such as outdated steelmills, to more productive endeavors, such as electronics or health care, has shrunk. Lacking the necessary skills and trained only as steelworkers, these people are "structurally unemployed."
■ Complying with environmental and safety laws, as well as with other government regulations, adds costs to production but does not increase it.
■ Increasing dishonesty and crime generate costs which are reflected in increased production costs but which do not increase productivity.
■ Outlays by business and government for civilian research and development are a smaller share of the economy in the United States than in other countries (Figure 1-5).[4]
■ Capital spending on new plants and modern equipment has been reduced.

While it is relatively easy to describe the obvious causes of productivity decline, economists admit that they cannot explain all the reasons for the decline in terms of common economic measures. In the following sections, therefore, we will consider four other causes: (1) the quality of management; (2) the govern-

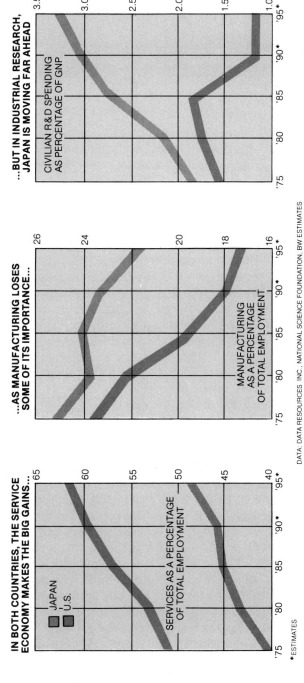

JAPAN BUILDS FOR THE FUTURE WHILE THE U.S. LAGS BEHIND

IN BOTH COUNTRIES, THE SERVICE ECONOMY MAKES THE BIG GAINS…

JAPAN
U.S.

SERVICES AS A PERCENTAGE OF TOTAL EMPLOYMENT

…AS MANUFACTURING LOSES SOME OF ITS IMPORTANCE…

MANUFACTURING AS A PERCENTAGE OF TOTAL EMPLOYMENT

…BUT IN INDUSTRIAL RESEARCH, JAPAN IS MOVING FAR AHEAD

CIVILIAN R&D SPENDING AS PERCENTAGE OF GNP

* ESTIMATES

DATA: DATA RESOURCES INC., NATIONAL SCIENCE FOUNDATION, BW ESTIMATES

FIGURE 1-5

Building for the future: United States versus Japan. (Source: Reprinted from July 13, 1987, issue of Business Week by special permission, copyright © 1987 by McGraw-Hill, Inc.)

19

ment; (3) short-term planning; and (4) the growing numbers of "paper entre-preneurs," those who capitalize on legal and financial opportunities for profit rather than on improved methods of production.[7]

The quality of management

In 1977 a Motorola plant in Tennessee was producing color television sets that regularly experienced defects at the rate of about 150 to 180 defects per 100 TV sets. Then a Japanese firm took over the plant. By 1980 the defects had dropped to only 3 to 4 per 100 TV sets produced. What changed? Not the workforce, since 80 percent of those working at the plant before 1977 were still working there in 1980. The ways people were managed, however, changed drastically. Worker participation in decision making, greater individual re-sponsibility for quality control, and improved communication between man-agement and the workers were the primary factors involved in the improve-ments in product quality. Consider another example: After the Toyota–General Motors joint venture opened its New United Motor Manufacturing, Inc. (NUMMI) plant in Fremont, California, it found that its cars made in the United States were just as good as the ones made in Japan.[2] Does this mean that the NUMMI workers in California are different from those who turn out "low quality" U.S. economy cars? No, the workers are all members of the United Auto Workers. The differences are in job design, worker involvement, and management (the quality control inspector reports to a higher-level manager in Japan and has the power to shut down the plant).

While it is true that the most productive American auto plants are those which have paid the most attention to blurring the class lines between man-agement and labor (as we shall see in the conclusion to the scenario described at the beginning of this chapter), when it comes to making steel, a positive employee attitude is not as productive as a basic-oxygen furnace. On the auto assembly line, no amount of team spirit will make a door fit more closely than it was designed to fit. When Japanese steel productivity soared during the 1970s, it could have been because workers and management felt a personal commitment to the economic welfare of their nation. But most likely it had more to do with the dozens of new mills—with continuous casters and electric furnaces—that the Japanese installed. "It's as simple as two able, willing work-ers, one with a power saw, and one with a hand saw," says Senator Lloyd Bentsen of Texas. "Which one do you think is going to turn out more work?" With knowledge workers (those who produce ideas and information rather than tangible products), however, it is very difficult, if not impossible, to replace worker decision making with improved technology. Besides, innovation is a social process.[48] Creating and deploying new technologies is not merely a sequence of mechanical events; it is inherently a social process that depends heavily on human factors as well as machines. Whether we are analyzing the conduct and management of research, the dissemination and marketing of new technical products, or the implementation of new manufacturing processes at the shop-floor level, we must be sure to consider the social and organizational influences involved. Social science informs us of the influence of these social and organizational factors. Human resource management focuses on how to apply them.

The government's role in productivity decline

By building inflation into the economy through such practices as cost-plus contracting, automatic cost-of-living increases in government spending, and big deficits to fight recessions, the government has been a drag on business's flexibility and on its capital investment in new plants and equipment.[7] Individually some of these steps make sense, but together they serve to increase inflation. Increased inflation discourages capital investment, which leads eventually to reduced productivity.

In addition to government-induced inflation, there are government regulations. General Motors claims that it now spends $1.9 billion per year to comply with government regulations through retooling for new safety equipment and emissions controls, reducing air and water pollution from its plants, and the unproductive activity of filling out forms to comply with regulations.

Short-run planning

Neither capital shortage nor government obstruction has prevented U.S. industries from being more profitable than foreign competitors. The problem is that a firm's continuing success depends on long-term productivity rather than on short-term profitability. Here is an example that illustrates the kinds of difficulties that a short-term outlook can cause.

The Amdahl Corporation, a computer manufacturer based in Sunnyvale, California, recently enjoyed a boom that is impressive even by the standards of this volatile industry. In 1976, its first full year in the market, Amdahl's revenues were $92 million. In 1978, they were $320 million. Between the end of 1976 and 1978 its workforce increased from 770 to 3000 employees.

As Amdahl's sales of computers soared, do did its demand for semiconductor chips. Early on, it bought chips from two suppliers, Motorola and a firm called Advanced Memory Systems, or AMS. Amdahl required a custom-designed chip and tried to convince the suppliers that they would quickly recoup the cost of retooling for production. AMS chose not to produce the custom chip and to end its business with Amdahl, which then was forced to look elsewhere for its second supplier. "If they had stayed with us," said Gene White, the chairperson of Amdahl, "our purchases with them would be equal to their entire sales at the time they left. But they couldn't wait." The new supplier that has enjoyed this surge in business? A Japanese firm.

One solution that may allow some firms to have their cake and eat it too is flexible manufacturing. Such systems emphasize shorter production runs and response times instead of economies of scale (lower production costs per unit as the number of units produced increases). Specifically, flexible manufacturing systems would let manufacturers customize one product line and then shift quickly from product to product with virtually the same equipment. If flexible manufacturing works, it should permit makers of specialized, high-value products to match the cost-efficiency of mass production. Yet there are risks. Flexible manufacturing departs radically from conventional production techniques, such as those used by AMS, that permit little variability in the product. The initial investment is costly, and success depends on cooperation from labor and a steady policy environment from the government.[4] Despite these risks, the use of flexible manufacturing encourages long-term planning for enhanced productivity instead of preoccupation with short-term results. If it had been available to AMS, then AMS might still be Amdahl's second supplier of custom-designed chips.

The imperatives of the financial markets focus the attention of American firms on the short-run instead of on the long-run. In the example described earlier, AMS could not wait long enough to recoup the costs of retooling to produce custom-designed chips for Amdahl. "Today's financial measurements are biased against the long term," says Senator Bentsen. "When you have to make this year's annual report look as good as possible, why [should you] engage in market entry pricing in East Asia? Why accept losses for two or three years to build volume and brand recognition? I can assure you that our competition in the world of trade is more than ready to make market investments that may not pay off for a decade. They are willing to spend years positioning themselves to conquer global markets."[7] Too many American firms behave like AMS, too few like their Japanese replacements. While the Japanese, Germans, and Koreans are making significant inroads on American markets, many American industries have shown an absolute inability to look toward their welfare in the long run.

Paper entrepreneurs

The term "paper entrepreneurs" was first expressed by Robert Reich, director of the Office of Policy Planning at the Federal Trade Commission. His theory is that economic life has yielded more and more of its prizes to those who can work the legal and financial angles or who can guess right in speculation rather than to those who work at improving a product or making a sale. According to Reich:

> Paper entrepreneurs—trained in law, finance, accountancy—manipulate complex systems of rules and numbers. They innovate by using the system in novel ways: establishing joint ventures, consortiums, holding companies, mutual funds; finding companies to acquire, "white knights" to be acquired by, commodity futures to invest in, tax shelters to hide in; engaging in proxy fights, tender splits, spinoffs, divestitures; buying and selling notes, bonds, convertible debentures, sinking-fund debentures; obtaining government subsidies, loan guarantees, tax breaks, contracts, licenses, quotas, price supports, bailouts; going private, going public, going bankrupt. (ref. 7)

Paper entrepreneurs provide the necessary grease for the wheels of the capital system, but they do not, by themselves, add to production. The government is dominated by lawyers; financiers rise to the top of many of the largest corporations; many of the best students are drawn into law and business schools, and from there into consulting, accounting, and lobbying rather than into production itself. Consider that out of every 10,000 citizens in Japan and in the United States, the following are found:

	Japan	United States
Lawyers	1	20
Accountants	3	40
Engineers and scientists	400	70

In short, there is a serious "brain drain" from genuine innovation in production, marketing, distribution, and sales to paper entrepreneurialism. Consider the ways that executives are compensated, for example. Many companies follow the practice of the auto industry, in which executives are given substantial bonuses in profitable years. In theory the bonuses reward those who have been pulling their weight, but in practice so much of the business is done internally that the profit and loss for each division depends mainly on the "transfer prices" charged on purchases from other divisions of the organization. Since the financial staff sets the transfer prices, they have become quite powerful.

Several years ago, two General Motors plants were producing virtually identical automatic transmissions. The Chevrolet transmission plant "sold" directly to the Chevrolet division. The Hydramatic division sold to Oldsmobile, Cadillac, and other divisions, including Chevy. The transfer price for the Chevy transmission was $130; Hydramatic's was $185. Actual production costs at the Chevrolet plant were $7 less per transmission than at Hydramatic, but the way the financial staff allocated the profits meant astronomical bonuses for the Hydramatic officials. One year Hydramatic's manager received $250,000 in salary and bonuses. The manager of the Chevrolet plant got $80,000—for doing exactly the same job but doing it more efficiently.

Lessons we have learned

Many factors contribute to a decline in productivity (Figure 1-6). So what can we conclude regarding the causes of and possible solutions to our productivity decline? We can say that we need:

■ Solutions designed to have some definite payoff in the long run, whether or not they pay off immediately
■ Steps by the government to allow and to encourage businesses to make capital investments and to be more flexible as a result of less government regulation

FIGURE 1-6

Many factors contribute to a decline in productivity. It's hard to single out any one factor as the primary cause.

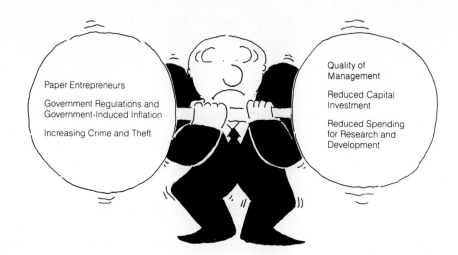

Paper Entrepreneurs

Government Regulations and Government-Induced Inflation

Increasing Crime and Theft

Quality of Management

Reduced Capital Investment

Reduced Spending for Research and Development

- ■ To make workers aware through their unions, and managers as well, that their rewards ultimately depend on production
- ■ To promote greater social value on production

Greater productivity benefits organizations directly (e.g., it improves their competitive position relative to rivals), and it benefits workers indirectly (e.g., improved job security and pay). But many workers want to see a tighter connection between working smarter and the tangible and psychological rewards they receive from doing their jobs well. They want to see significant improvements in their quality of work life.

Quality of Work Life: What Is It?

There are two ways of looking at what *quality of work life (QWL)* means.[25] One way equates QWL with a set of objective organizational conditions and practices (e.g., job enrichment, democratic supervision, employee involvement, and safe working conditions). The other way equates QWL with employees' perceptions that they are safe, relatively well-satisfied, and able to grow and develop as human beings. This way relates QWL to the degree to which the full range of human needs is met.

In many cases these two views merge: workers who like their organizations and the ways their jobs are structured will feel that their work fulfills them. In such cases, either way of looking at one's quality of work life will lead to a common determination of whether a good QWL exists. However, because of the differences between people and because the second view is quite subjective—it allows, for example, that not everyone finds such things as democratic decision making and enriched jobs to be important components of a good QWL[24]— we will define QWL in terms of employees' perceptions of their physical and mental well-being at work.

Components of quality of work life

The Work in America Institute identified 11 areas that were the most important QWL issues of the 1980s. These include:[39]

Pay (77 percent of workers surveyed listed this area as number 1)

Employee benefits (the most frequently mentioned issues were health care, dental care, and retirement)

Job security

Alternative work schedules

Job stress

Participation in decisions that affect them

Democracy in the workplace

Profit sharing

Pension "rights" (with major problems seen in social security and "double dipping")

Company programs designed to enhance worker welfare

The 4-day workweek

It may appear that this list covers every major issue that labor has fought for in the last 10 years or so. In fact, collective bargaining has played an important role in addressing QWL issues.[14, 26] The first QWL agreement was reached in the 1973 contract between the United Auto Workers (UAW) and General Motors (GM), and it has become the model for all others. Nowhere in the agreement did the word "productivity" appear; management would seek its rewards from such improvements as higher product quality and lower absenteeism. The agreement also stated that all QWL undertakings were to be strictly voluntary, and none would be used unilaterally to raise production rates or to eliminate jobs. Since that agreement, local disputes and grievances—one barometer of labor relations—have dropped dramatically, and over a fifth of the nation's organized workers have signed national labor agreements committing themselves to plans for bettering QWL. Also, according to UAW leaders, virtually every slate of union officers who campaigned by supporting an established QWL effort has won. This trend may well continue as long as there are clear benefits to workers, management, and unions.[3]

Participation: The essence of quality of work life

The common denominator of QWL experiments is joint worker-management participation for the purpose of identifying problems and opportunities in the work environment, making decisions, and implementing changes. Results of these undertakings are beginning to appear in the literature (e.g., ref. 28). Critics say that participation will not work over time because it requires managers to give up too much power; this is why 75 percent of all such programs in the early 1980s failed.[41] On the other hand, advocates point to a study which examined 101 industrial companies and which found that the participatively managed companies outscored the others on 13 of 14 financial measures.[41] The advocates argue that we are just beginning to understand what is required in order to bring about large-scale social change in organizations.

There has been widespread interest in worker participation in management decisions among U.S. organizations in the 1980s. This interest is not so much motivated by concern with how an organization affects the people who comprise it. Rather, it is motivated by an increasing recognition that American firms are facing a productivity crisis that threatens both our way of life and the very existence of many of our basic industries. Fearful for their own competitive viability, American business leaders are taking a close look at alternative management approaches. Japanese management style in particular has caught the attention of many of our business leaders. Japanese management has been described as highly participative and consensus-based.[33, 34, 44] Employees are treated with respect and concern, and in turn they are ideologically and culturally inclined to act in the best interests of the company.

Some American businesses (e.g., General Electric) are hoping that if they adopt the participative management practices of Japanese organizations, the U.S. employee will respond in a manner similar to the Japanese employee, thus reversing the trend toward declining productivity. In general, five broad types of participative methods can be identified:

1. Quality circles and other types of employee problem-solving groups
2. Union-management cooperative projects and problem-solving ventures
3. Participative work design
4. Gain sharing, profit sharing, and Scanlon plans
5. Worker ownership or employee stock ownership

The following gives a brief description of these methods, and their effectiveness is then discussed in the section "Does participation work?"

Employee problem-solving groups Of the many forms that this method takes, one is the quality-circle format that is popular in Japan. A *quality circle* is a group of employees (4 to 10) from the same department who meet on company time to solve work-related problems. These groups tend to focus on organizational efficiency issues, such as waste, damage, or equipment maintenance; on work context issues, such as facilities; and on communication problems. Sometimes a group will make changes in job design, such as at Westinghouse, where assembly line workers developed a way to reduce defective products to 1 percent of output from 16 percent. The same group also increased productivity by 30 percent.[37] In other situations, unfortunately, changes were suggested but not implemented in the work setting, and the groups became demotivated.[22, 23]

Union-management cooperative projects and problem-solving ventures
These methods explicitly recognize the need to bring two conflicting groups together to identify areas of mutual concern and to reduce the level of adversarial behavior in the work setting. Union-management committees often serve as sounding boards and attempt to prevent potential problems from occurring or escalating. In addition, a joint union-management committee may identify opportunities, solve problems, and guide union-management task forces dealing with specific problems.[47]

Such "jointness" efforts have spread far and wide. For example, since 1982 as many as 40 percent of Ford Motor Company's 109,000 hourly workers have taken advantage of the programs. Similar efforts are being made at General Motors, with impressive results. At its Toledo, Ohio, transmission factory, GM shaved $20 million off its production costs in 1987, and quality improved so much that the number of rejects dropped 90 percent. Certainly part of these gains resulted from GM's joint program, but without controlled research it is not possible to say exactly how much.[43]

Participative work design   In this method, a team is put together specifically to redesign a job by analyzing its technical and human requirements. Jobs designed in this way have been found to be particularly effective in work settings where tasks are highly interdependent and employees have high personal growth needs.[13] A frequent outcome is the development of semiautonomous work teams. Each team is given primary responsibility for planning, doing, and controlling the quality of a major component of the work, and team members are cross-trained to do more than one job.

Semiautonomous work teams have been especially successful in conjunction with new plant start-ups, for they create an organizational setting quite different from that in the traditional plant.

Gain sharing, profit sharing, and Scanlon plans   These are methods for sharing profits with employees, based on some formula. They are particularly effective in situations in which workers can affect the major factors that influence economic performance, such as labor hours, materials, or damage. Not surprisingly, workers tend to focus their attention and energy on the factors that are included in the formula for determining the payout; nevertheless, the results can be impressive. At Barnes Hospital in St. Louis, for example, all 5500 employees participated in a gain-sharing plan begun in 1986. One year later, the plan resulted in payments to employees of $4.3 million and in financial gains to the institution of over $4.7 million.[5]

Some plans, such as the Scanlon plan, build in several layers of committees to ensure the implementation of ideas and include training in problem-solving.[30] These plans have been found to be highly successful in affecting productivity in manufacturing organizations, for their use assumes that productivity can be measured accurately and compared from year to year.

Employee participation in the ownership of a company The participation ranges from (1) partial ownership through the acquisition of company stock by employees to (2) complete ownership by employees. More than 8000 firms in the United States now share some ownership with over 10 million employees. In at least 1000 companies, employees own the majority of the stock. Employee ownership can be found in every industry, in firms of every size, and in every part of the country.[38] In terms of bottom-line performance, companies that are mostly employee-owned generate 3 times more new jobs than do their competitors, and high-tech companies that share ownership grow 2 to 4 times as fast as those which do not. Publicly held companies that are at least 10 percent employee-owned outperform 62 to 75 percent of their competitors, depending on the measure used.

Worker ownership originally occurred in rather desperate situations, such as when workers purchased a plant rather than allow it to be sold or to go out of business. More recently, it has resulted from concessions by unions during collective bargaining (e.g., with the airlines) or has been initiated by management for financial, tax, or motivational reasons.[9]

Does participation work?

Although it is still premature to state which approaches are definitely effective and which are not, it is possible to detect trends in the emerging literature. Some of these are as follows:[29]

1. Worker participation programs that are tied directly to financial incentives for employees tend to result in productivity increases for the organization. For example, of 72 companies using Improshare[8]—production standards based on time-and-motion studies, plus a sharing of productivity gains 50/50 between employees and the company—38 companies were nonunion, and 34 were represented by 18 different international unions. The average gain in productivity over all companies using the plan after 1 year was 22.4 percent. Productivity gains tended to be larger if workers were provided with training and information; gains tended to be smaller, or none, or negative (that is, productivity deteriorated) if workers perceived that there was "nothing in it" for them. Reports show that a program intended to get workers to improve productivity without sharing with them the financial rewards of that gain will take 1.5 to 3 years to establish. And, of course, gains in productivity, specifically, and in labor relations, in general, will not be seen until after that time. In contrast, consider the following situation, as reported by Fein, in which workers will share in the financial gains that come along with gains in productivity:

> In a meeting called by the management of a highly mechanized machine shop to discuss the introduction of an Improshare plan, operating managers and union committee representatives were present. In response to a question posed by the

plant manager as to how long it would take for an Improshare plan to start operating in one of the large machine departments, a union steward replied, "15 minutes." This was not a flippant remark but a considered statement by a knowledgeable worker of how long it would take him to turn up his production—if he wanted to. (ref. 8)

2. Participation programs are generally perceived positively by those who directly participate but negatively by workers who do not.[27, 31] In one case nonparticipating union members pressured management to terminate a large union-management work redesign effort because of perceived salary inequities.[12]

3. Participative strategies that alter the job itself tend to have a lasting impact on attitudes and productivity if the new job involves substantial increases in responsibility and autonomy. Worker participation in problem solving that does not alter the job itself or job rotational schemes that do not add responsibility and challenge tend only to motivate employees over the short term.[22]

4. Worker participation programs die out eventually if the organization does not change in a manner consistent with the democratic values and behaviors of the participation programs. Here are some of the ways to kill worker participation:

- Middle and upper management cease their responsiveness to worker suggestions after the initial enthusiasm, if there was any, is over.
- The pay system fails to acknowledge the new activities and contributions of workers.
- Supervisors resent the increased attention to workers and undermine the program by not cooperating with the groups.
- Participating workers develop distorted perceptions of their own promotability and value to the company, and they become disillusioned when they do not advance.

Many American organizations embody a hierarchical, departmentalized structure, a set of management assumptions, and a set of norms that discourage employees from taking initiative, accepting responsibility, and cooperating with one another.[32, 34] The unlearning of these assumptions and norms requires a conscious attempt to alter the culture of the organization, something that organizations such as Honeywell, Cummins Engine, and Westinghouse are systematically setting out to do.

5. Many participative programs underestimate the amount of training and learning necessary to support worker involvement. Workers need exposure to problem solving, group processes, and business concepts. Managers need training in the listening and feedback skills necessary to work with groups of workers who are taking responsibility for decision making. Both workers and managers need to learn the basic interpersonal skills necessary to treat others with dignity and respect.[1] Participation as an effort to improve QWL requires that managers treat lower-level employees as mature individuals, for participation implies a redistribution of power within the organization.

6. Workers sometimes reject the participation program. Often this reaction reflects the official position of a union, which sees a threat to its long-term strength in dealing with management. Union and nonunion employees often perceive participation programs as management manipulation in which workers are expected to contribute something for nothing.[15] Managers frequently perceive a participation program as something they are doing "for" the workers. Workers detect this attitude and judge it to be patronizing at best and deceptive at worst.

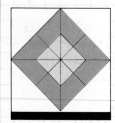

Impact of Improved Productivity and Quality of Work Life on the Bottom Line

The rewards from a successful effort may well be worth it. Consider the potential financial gains associated with an Improshare program.[8] Since an Improshare plan shares productivity gains 50/50 between employees and the company, the gain to both is the same. Using an hourly wage rate of $7.00 as an example, a 1 percent increase in productivity is worth $70 per year per employee [$7.00 × 0.005 (one-half of 1 percent) × 2000 hours per year]. An increase of 10.3 percent, when shared at 5.15 percent to the employee, increased hourly earnings by 36 cents, or $721 per year. With a 24.4 percent increase (12.2 percent to the employee), the gain is 85 cents per hour per employee, or $1708 for the year. The savings for the company equal the total savings for the employees. For a plant of 500 employees, a 10.3 percent increase in productivity will save $360,500; at 24.4 percent the company saves $854,000. Since employees are guaranteed not to make less than their regular earnings, no one can lose under the plan.

A study by the General Accounting Office of productivity sharing plans found nonmonetary benefits as well. Improved labor relations were reported by 80.6 percent of the companies, 47.2 percent reported fewer grievances, 36.1 percent had lower absenteeism rates, 36.1 percent had reduced turnover, and 47.2 percent reported other benefits.

> The vast majority of firms expressed satisfaction with their productivity sharing plans and believed that the current benefits to the firm from their plans warranted their continuation. Officials at 22 of the firms said that the benefits originally anticipated were realized. . . . For the most part, firms . . . believed that their productivity sharing plan gave them a competitive advantage in marketing their products or services. (ref. 10)

**CASE 1-1
Conclusion**

*Changes in the
making and buying
of cars*

General Motors has developed a new approach to managing auto workers, and it is trying it out in several plants that were suffering from low productivity and poor morale. In these experimental plants, the old norms governing assembly line work and the rigid separation of workers and managers have been replaced with new guidelines, such as these:

- The people on the line who assemble the cars may have ideas about how to improve productivity that managers do not have; management should actively seek out their input and listen to what they have to say.
- Workers should have a voice in decisions that affect their jobs; if heeded, productivity and product quality might improve.
- At least some workers should have their jobs made as challenging and interesting as possible—and they should share the rewards of success.
- Workers should be treated with dignity; class lines between management and labor should be blurred.

These experiments based on the value system of self-fulfillment seekers have now begun to pay off. The GM plant in Tarrytown, New York, for example, represented everything bad about labor relations (contentiousness, mutual suspicion, and resentment) before a QWL program was installed. As union members were invited to provide more than brute labor, their innovations improved the quality of the product, and their commitment transformed the atmosphere of the plant. Grievances against management fell from 2000 to 30, and absenteeism fell from 7 percent to 2.5. Now Tarrytown is one of GM's success stories. Based on these results, General Motors has vastly expanded its QWL efforts even to the corporate level, and it is promoting the executives who helped to make them work.[42]

Results such as those at the Tarrytown plant suggest that Americans who are concerned with QWL issues may in themselves be a potent source of new economic energy.

Summary

As Case 1-1 illustrated, vast changes have occurred in Americans' social values over the past years. The self-fulfillment seekers are changing the old giving-getting compact in every one of its dimensions—family life, career, leisure, the meaning of success, and relationships with others. But Americans seem to be evolving toward a new ethic of commitment, of connectedness with the world, seeking a whole new set of psychological satisfactions from their jobs. The challenge of managing people effectively has never been greater.

One of the most pressing demands we face today is for productivity improvement—getting more out of what is put in, doing better with what we have, and working smarter, not harder. Some reasons proposed for the decline in American productivity are: workers with nonmarketable job skills as a result of the economic decline of their industries, excessive government regulations, dishonesty and crime, reduced spending on research and development, and reduced spending for capital improvements that would cut labor costs. However, noneconomic factors have also played a role: lazy workers and indifferent managers, a growing number of paper entrepreneurs, and an inability of American business to plan for the long run. While the effects of some of these factors are exaggerated, the solution is probably a mixed approach that includes improvements in all the preceding areas. Clearly, though, increased productivity does not preclude a high quality of work life (QWL).

QWL may be defined and operationalized in terms of employees' perceptions of their physical and psychological well-being at work. It includes virtually

---

TOMORROW'S FORECAST

In the remaining years of the twentieth century, four key trends should unfold:[16]

1. The American economy should grow at a relatively healthy pace, spurred by a rebound in U.S. exports, renewed growth in productivity, and a strong world economy.

2. Despite its international comeback, U.S. manufacturing will be a much smaller share of the economy in the year 2000 than it is today. Service industries will create almost all the new jobs and wealth in the coming years.

3. The workforce will grow slowly, becoming older and having more females and more disadvantaged people. Only 15 percent of the new entrants to the labor force will be native white males, compared to 47 percent in this category today.

4. The new jobs in service industries will demand much higher skill levels than today's jobs do. Few jobs will be created for those who cannot read, follow directions, and use mathematics. This will lead to both higher and lower unemployment: more joblessness among the least skilled, and less among the most educationally advantaged.

These trends suggest that the old approaches to managing people may no longer be appropriate responses to economic or social reality. The willingness of American managers to experiment with new approaches to managing people is healthy. To the extent that the newer approaches do enhance productivity and QWL, everybody wins. The problems facing us cannot simply be willed away, and because of this we may see even more radical experiments in organizations. The traditional role of the manager may be blurred further as workers take a greater and greater part in planning work, doing it, and controlling it. This change suggests that human resource management, an essential part of the job of all managers, will play an ever more crucial role in determining overall organizational effectiveness.

every major issue that labor has fought for in the last 10 years or so. In fact, more than one-fifth of national labor agreements now include clauses committing management and labor to plans for bettering the quality of work life. Joint labor-management cooperation is the very essence of QWL efforts, but participation can take several forms. The most effective of these seem to be those which combine (1) financial rewards to workers for productivity improvements, (2) job changes that involve substantial increases in worker responsibility and autonomy, and (3) substantial training of workers and managers in order to support greater worker involvement. Although there are many pitfalls associated with instituting a productivity improvement or QWL program, the potential financial gains may well justify the effort.

Discussion Questions

1-1 What are some of the pitfalls associated with pure self-fulfillment? How do they affect productivity and QWL?

1-2 Discuss alternative strategies for harnessing the energies of the "new breed" of workers concerned with QWL issues.

1-3 What common characteristics do the following organizations share: a hospital, a school, an auto repair shop, and a baseball team?

1-4 Just how appropriate is Japanese management style for American businesses?

1-5 In your opinion, what are three major causes of the decline in productivity? How would you remedy each one?

References

1. Argyris, C., & Schon, D. A. (1978). *Organizational learning: A theory of action perspective*. Reading, MA: Addison-Wesley.
2. Brody, M. (1987, June 8). Helping workers to work smarter. *Fortune*, pp. 86–88.
3. Burck, C. B. (1981). What's in it for the unions? *Fortune*, **104**, 88–92.
4. Can America compete? (1987, Apr. 20). *Business Week*, pp. 45–47.
5. Drosie, T. (1987, June 5). Gainsharing: The newest way to up productivity. *Hospitals*, p. 71.
6. Drucker, P. F. (1985, Nov. 26). How to measure white-collar productivity. *Wall Street Journal*, p. 30.
7. Fallows, J. (1980, September). American industry: What ails it, how to save it. *The Atlantic*, pp. 35–49.
8. Fein, M. (1982, August). Improved productivity through worker involvement. Paper presented at the annual meeting of the Academy of Management, New York.
9. French, J. L. (1987). Employee perspectives on stock ownership: Financial investment or mechanism of control? *Academy of Management Review*, **12**, 427–435.
10. General Accounting Office (1981, March). *Productivity sharing programs: Can they contribute to productivity improvement?* Gaithersburg, MD: USGAO, AFMD-81-22.

11. Giese, W. (1987, June 15). 4 of 5 of us say we enjoy going to work. *USA Today*, pp. 1A, 2A.

12. Goodman, P. S. (1979). *Assessing organizational change: The Rushton quality of work life experiment.* New York: Wiley.

13. Help wanted (1987, Aug. 10). *Business Week*, pp. 48–53.

14. Holley, W. H., Feild, H. S., & Crowley, J. C. (1981). Negotiating quality of work life, productivity, and traditional issues: Union members' preferred roles of their union. *Personnel Psychology*, **34**, 309–328.

15. Jacoby, S. M. (1982). Union-management cooperation in the U.S.: 1915–1945. Working paper, Graduate School of Management, UCLA.

16. Johnston, W. B. (1987). *Workforce 2000: Work and workers for the 21st century.* Indianapolis, IN: Hudson Institute.

17. Kendrick, J. W. (1984, Aug. 29). Productivity gains will continue. *Wall Street Journal*, p. 22.

18. Koten, J. (1987, Mar. 11). Steady progress disrupted by turbulence in economy. *Wall Street Journal*, p. 35.

19. Koten, J. (1987, Mar. 9). A once tightly knit middle class finds itself divided and uncertain. *Wall Street Journal*, p. 25.

20. Labor Letter (1986, Dec. 9) *Wall Street Journal*, p. 1.

21. Labor Letter (1987, Sep. 8). *Wall Street Journal*, p. 1.

22. Lawler, E. C., & Ledford, G. E. (1982). Productivity and the quality of work life. *National Productivity Review*, **2**, 2.

23. Lawler, E. E., & Mohrman, S. A. (1985, January–February). Quality circles: After the fad. *Harvard Business Review*, pp. 65–71.

24. Lawler, E. E. (1973). *Motivation in work organizations.* Monterey, CA: Brooks/Cole.

25. Lawler, E. E. (1982). Strategies for improving the quality of work life. *American Psychologist*, **37**, 486–493.

26. Lewin, D. (1981). Collective bargaining and the quality of work life. *Organizational Dynamics*. **10**, 37–53.

27. Macy, B., & Peterson, M. (1981, August). Evaluating attitudinal change in a longitudinal quality of work life intervention. Paper presented at the annual meeting of the Academy of Management, San Diego.

28. Marks, M. L., Mirvis, P. H., Hackett, E. J., & Grady, J. F., Jr. (1986). Employee participation in a quality circle program: Impact on quality of work life, productivity, and absenteeism. *Journal of Applied Psychology*, **71**, 61–69.

29. Mohrman, S. A. (1982, May). The impact of quality circles: A conceptual view. Paper presented at Bureau of National Affairs conference, "Current directions in productivity—Evolving Japanese and American practices." Houston.

30. Moore, B. E., & Ross, T. L. (1978). *The Scanlon way to improved productivity: A practical guide.* New York: Wiley.

31. Nurick, A. J. (1982). Participation in organizational change: A longitudinal field study. *Human relations*, **35**, 413–430.

32. O'Toole, J. (1981). *Making America work: Productivity and responsibility.* New York: Continuum.

33. Ouchi, W. G. (1981). *Theory Z: How American business can meet the Japanese challenge.* Reading, MA: Addison-Wesley.

34. Pascale, R. T., & Athos, A. G. (1981). *The art of Japanese management: Applications for American executives.* New York: Simon & Schuster.

35. Preaching the gospel of productivity (1982, Mar. 21). *The Washington Post*, pp. F3–F5.
36. Productivity: Why it's the no. 1 underachiever (1987, April 20). *Business Week*, pp. 54–55.
37. Quality circles can raise productivity, execs told (1982, March 21). *Atlanta Consitution*, pp. 4C–5C.
38. Rosen, C., Klein, K. J., & Young, K. M. (1986). When employees share the profits. *Psychology Today*, **20**, 30–36.
39. Rosow, J. M. (1981), QWL issues for the 1980s. *Training and Development Journal*, **35**, 33–52.
40. Sanger, D. E. (1987, Apr. 5). Americans search for ways to improve competitiveness. *Atlanta Constitution*, p. 17S.
41. Saporito, B. (1986, July 21). The revolt against "working smarter." *Fortune*, pp. 58–65.
42. Schlesinger, J. M. (1987, June 8). GM, UAW plan union participation in "quality network" at corporate level. *Wall Street Journal*, p. 6.
43. Schlesinger, J. M. (1987, Aug. 25). Costly friendship: Auto firms and UAW find that cooperation can get complicated. *Wall Street Journal*, pp. 1, 20.
44. Sethi, S. P., Namiki, N., & Swanson, C. L. (1984). *The false promise of the Japanese miracle*. Boston: Pitman.
45. Shetty, Y. K. (1982, March–April). Key elements of productivity improvement programs. *Business Horizons*, pp. 15–22.
46. Silk, L. (1987, Feb. 8). Women gain, but at a cost. *New York Times*, p. D2.
47. Thacker, J. W., & Fields, M. W. (1987). Union involvement in quality of work life efforts: a longitudinal investigation. *Personnel Psychology*, **40**, 97–111.
48. Tornatzky, L. G., & Solomon, T. (1982). Contributions of social science to innovation and productivity. *American Psychologist*, **37**, 737–746.
49. Walker, C. R., & Guest, R. H. (1952). *The man on the assembly line*. Cambridge, MA: Harvard University Press.
50. Weingarten, P. (1982, Oct. 10). The not-me generation. *The Denver Post*, Contemporary Magazine, pp. 32–35.
51. Working Smarter (1984, June 4). *Time*, p. 53.
52. Yankelovich, D. (1981, April). New rules in American life: Searching for self-fulfillment in a world turned upside down. *Psychology Today*, 35–91.

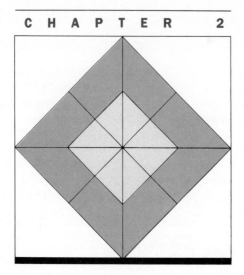

Human Resource Management: A Field in Transition

In 1951 Charles Bischoff, Jr., entered the job market armed with a degree in industrial psychology from Rutgers and a graduate degree in human relations from Seton Hall. He started out as a personnel interviewer at P. Ballantine & Sons (the Brewery), moved on to the American Sugar Refining Company, then to American Standard, Inc., and finally joined the Allied Corporation in 1963. Today at Allied, the fibers, plastics, and energy giant, Bischoff is director of management resources.

When asked recently how a personnel manager spent his time years ago, a broad smile crinkled Bischoff's face. "Making sure everybody got a birthday card on their birthday and a turkey on Thanksgiving," he replied, only half facetiously. The Personnel Department, he added, was "quite clearly the dumping ground for people who couldn't hack it in Operations."

Years ago, going way back, the personnel function was basically an employment function (according to the American Society for Personnel Administration). This probably stemmed from the behavior of the line supervisor. The supervisor used to walk out of the plant to find a long line of people, none of

*Adapted from: A human resource at Allied Corp., *The New York Times*, June 6, 1982, p. 5C.

whom even had a résumé, and he would say, "You, you, and you." Eventually, the supervisor didn't really have time for this activity, and so someone was made head of Personnel. Unforunately, this person was usually a dropout from somewhere else.

Apart from hiring new hands and making sure the paychecks got out on time, the personnel manager's job dealt with such minutiae as rounding up the best arms for the bowling league and doling out parking spots in the company lot. Indeed, over 25 years ago Peter Drucker, the famed management theorist, wrote, "The constant worry of all personnel administrators is their inability to prove that they are making a contribution to the enterprise.

Today the time cards and turkeys that Bischoff spoke of have given way to bigger considerations, "That phone could ring any minute," he says, jerking his hand toward his report-strewn desk, "and it's the chairman calling me up to his office."

The once-unobtrusive personnel manager has had a facelift. The days when management depended on the personnel chief to cart the watermelon to the company picnic are comic memories. In fact, the term "personnel" has been almost entirely jettisoned from the corporate vocabulary. Now there is the "manager of human resources," an increasingly influential figure.

QUESTIONS
1. Why has the work of the Personnel Department, or Human Resources Department, led to its growth in responsibility and prestige?
2. How do you think Mr. Bischoff's job has changed?

What's Ahead

Whereas Chapter 1 took a "macro" view in emphasizing the importance of effective "people management" in today's competitive environment, Chapter 2 takes a more "micro" view of what effective "people management" encompasses. Case 2-1 reveals the central theme of this chapter: changes in the role and scope of human resource management (HRM) activities. The chapter presents a general management perspective on the HRM function rather than a human resource (HR) director's perspective on the specialized activities of his or her department. We begin with a brief overview of the historical and intellectual roots of the field, together with an examination of the forces that have shaped modern HRM. Then we will consider top management's view of the role, objectives, and responsibilities of the HR department, the strategic use of this department, and the kinds of questions that general managers should consider in evaluating the HRM function. Finally, we will examine the productivity, quality of work life (QWL), and profit impacts of effective HRM in a number of key areas.

The Evolution of Human Resource Management

To appreciate where the HRM field is going, let's consider where it has come from. Modern HRM has emerged from nine interrelated sources:

1. Rapid technological change that increased the specialization of labor associated with the industrial revolution
2. The emergence of free collective bargaining, with constraints established for both unions and employers
3. The scientific management movement
4. Early industrial psychology
5. Governmental personnel practices growing out of the establishment of the Civil Service Commission
6. The emergence of personnel specialists and the grouping of these specialists into personnel departments
7. The human relations movement
8. The behavioral sciences
9. The social legislation and court decision of the 1960s and 1970s[13]

Let us now consider the first eight of these; the ninth is the subject of Chapter 3.

The industrial revolution

Three characteristics of the industrial revolution were the development of machinery, the linking of human power to the machines, and the establishment of factories in which a large number of people were employed. The result was a tremendous increase in job specialization as well as in the amount of goods that workers could produce. "Division of labor" became the rallying cry of this revolution. Listen as Adam Smith, writing in his *Wealth of Nations*, described the division of labor in a pin factory:

> One man draws out the wire, another straightens it, a third cuts it, a fourth points it, a fifth grinds it at the top for receiving the head; to make the head requires two or three distinct operations; to put it on is a peculiar business, to whiten the pins is another; it is even a trade by itself to put them into the paper; the important business of making a pin is, in this manner, divided into about eighteen distinct operations, which in some manufactories ["factories" in today's terminology] are performed by distinct hands, though in others the same man will sometimes perform two or three of them . . . (ref. 38, p. 5)

Charles Babbage, writing in his *On the Economy of Machinery and Manufactures*, noted the principal advantages of this division of labor:[2]

> Training time for new workers was reduced considerably since only a single task needed to be learned.
>
> Raw materials wastage was reduced.

Money was saved through more effective placement of workers, the result of which was a differential wage scale based upon skill level.

Time was saved by not requiring workers to switch from task to task, the result being that workers developed familiarity with special tools. And this greater familiarity stimulated workers' inventiveness in the use of these tools.

Nevertheless, Adam Smith also noted the disadvantages of this division of labor. He wrote, "The man whose whole life is spent performing a few simple operations . . . becomes as stupid and ignorant as it is possible for a human creature to become" (ref. 38, p. 772). Likewise, Karl Marx stressed the psychological consequences of capitalism and the division of labor:

> They [the capitalists] mutilate the worker into a fragment of a man, degrade him to the level of an appendage to a machine, destroy every remnant of charm in his work, and turn it into a hated toil. They estrange him from the intellectual potentialities of the labor process. (ref. 37)

To a significant extent, these problems are still with us today. An early reformer who tried to alleviate problems stemming from the division of labor was Robert Owen, successful entrepreneur and manager. About 1799 he established a partnership in the cotton-weaving mill at New Lanark, Scotland. He genuinely believed that people were creatures of their environment and that their behavior was a function of their treatment. Employers and communities, he believed, should work much harder to develop human talents and should eliminate practices that led to poor health and stifled the ability of that talent to produce its fullest.

Singled out for special attack by Owen were practices in the employment of children, such as beating seeming laggards and 7 A.M. to 8 P.M. working days. He saw these leading eventually to serious problems, such as empty minds and alcoholism.[9] Owen's special concern for employees resulted in his promotion of restrictions on child discipline, shorter working hours, safer working conditions, and better housing for the apprentices in his employ. He even attempted to reform the village of New Lanark, including rebuilding houses, improving sanitation, and cleaning the village streets at company expense.

Along with these improvements in the management of people, Owen also instituted what was perhaps the earliest *performance appraisal system*. He did this as a check on "inferior conduct." A block of wood, with four different sides painted white, yellow, blue, and black, was mounted on each machine. Each day the appropriate color was turned to the aisle to reflect each employee's previous day's production. Black meant bad, blue meant indifferent (average), yellow meant good, and white meant excellent. This practice was highly successful, but some of Owen's other efforts were not. For example, the promise of a special holiday in summer was not adequate inducement to all employees to come to work on New Year's Day and to give up the day's libations.[35]

These experiments by Owen at New Lanark contributed to the profitability of his mills and made him rich and famous. About 1813, in his *Address to the*

In the early 1900s, before the enactment of child labor laws, the employment and exploitation of children under the age of 16 was quite common. Here a young girl collects and delivers garments for tailors and cleaners.

Superintendents of Manufactories, he stated, "The time and money so spent, even while such improvements are in progress only, and but half their beneficial results attained, are now producing a return exceeding 50 percent."[9] In view of his efforts to improve the management of people at work, Owen has been recognized as "the pioneer of personnel management."[39]

Thus far we can see that the industrial revolution greatly accelerated the development of business and commerce. Owners and entrepreneurs generally did quite well for themselves, but the average citizen fared poorly in comparison to today's workers in terms of purchasing power and working conditions. Labor was considered a commodity to be bought and sold, and the prevailing political philosophy of laissez-faire resulted in little action by governments to protect the lot of workers.[13]

The emergence of free collective bargaining

Because of the way they were abused, it was inevitable that workers would organize to protect themselves and to improve their lot in life. From the perspective of workers, the industrial revolution fostered specialization and fostered the need for workers within each specialization to organize themselves against its abuses. Trade unions, also called "labor unions," spread rapidly, and so did the incidence of strikes (e.g., by New York bakers in 1741 in response to a municipal regulation governing the price of bread). In 1799 the Philadelphia Journeymen cordwainers (workers in cordovan leather, or shoemakers) attempted to bargain collectively with their employers. This attempt resulted in a management lockout of the workers, but ultimately it led to a negotiated settlement between the union and the employer association.[8]

Adversarial relations between labor and management persist to this very day, although the adversity is for the most part civilized compared to the violence that characterized many confrontations between management and labor 100 years ago. In 1886 four persons were killed by police while striking for an 8-hour day at the McCormick Reaper Works in Chicago. This incident was followed by a protest meeting in Haymarket Square in Chicago, where a bomb was thrown into the ranks of the police. In the ensuing melee, seven police officers and four workers were killed.[11]

Although the legislative history of labor relations in the United States will be covered thoroughly in Chapter 13, at this point you should keep in mind that the courts adopted an antiunion stance until 1935. In that year the Wagner Act, technically called the National Labor Relations Act, was passed. The act focused largely on labor's right to organize, and it provided that a majority of employees in an appropriate "bargaining unit" (as determined and certified by the National Labor Relations Board that the act created) could obtain exclusive collective bargaining rights for all the employees in that unit. It became an unfair labor practice for an employer to coerce or restrain employees in the exercise of their rights, to dominate or interfere with a labor organization, or to refuse to bargain collectively with a legal representative of the employees. Administration of the act was the responsibility of the National Labor Relations Board. Subsequent legislation refined, broadened, and set legal limits on the scope of management and union activities.

Viewed through the perspective of labor, the development of free collective bargaining and the American labor movement created the need for what we are now coming to recognize as effective human resource management.

Scientific management

Viewed through the perspective of management, the scientific management movement also created a need for effective human resource management. Frederick Winslow Taylor was the prophet of scientific management, and his "bible" was the stopwatch.[3] Taylor began his experiments in the steel industry, at the Midvale and Bethlehem plants in 1885. His most famous experiment involved a pig-iron shoveler named Schmidt. Using a stopwatch, Taylor studied Schmidt's labor in precise detail. As a result of technological improvements and the elimination of extraneous movements, Schmidt increased his productivity from 12.5 long tons (a long ton equals 2240 pounds) per day to 47.5 long tons per day! Every detail of Schmidt's job was specified: the size of the shovel,

Federick Winslow Taylor—engineer, inventor, efficiency expert.

the weight of the shovel's scoop, the bite into the pile, the weight scooped, the distance to walk, the arc of the swing, and the rest periods that Schmidt should take. This, in essence, is what scientific management is all about: It is the systematic analysis and breakdown of work into its smallest mechanical elements, and then their rearrangement into their most efficient combination.[3]

In addition to the scientific study of the task itself ("time-and-motion" study), Taylor argued that individuals selected to do the work should be as perfectly matched, physically and mentally, to the demands of the job as possible and that *overqualified* individuals should be excluded.

Employees should be trained carefully by supervisors (whose own work was also divided into specialties) to ensure that they performed the work exactly as specified by prior scientific analysis. In no case, however, should employees ever be called upon to work at a pace that would be detrimental to their health.

Finally, to provide an incentive for the employee to follow the detailed procedures specified (which were closely supervised by line supervisors on the shop floor), Taylor felt that the employee should receive an addition of from 30 to 100 percent of his or her ordinary wages whenever the task was done right and within the time limits specified—labor's first piecework incentive systems. Taylor was also interested in the social aspects of work, although he saw little good emerging from the social interaction within work groups. He felt that work groups fostered a level of individual efficiency equal to the level of the least productive worker in the group. In other words, he believed that the efficiency of the group would not be any greater than the efficiency of the least productive member.

Overall, there is little doubt that application of the principles of scientific management has resulted in much higher productivity than would otherwise have been possible. What is remarkable is not that Taylor was "correct in the context of his time," but that many of his insights are still valid today.[25]

Early industrial psychology

In 1913 Hugo Munsterberg's book, *Psychology and Industrial Efficiency*, described experiments in selecting streetcar operators, ship's officers, and telephone switchboard operators. His contributions to personnel management are noteworthy for his emphasis on the analysis of jobs in terms of (1) the abilities required to do them and (2) the development of testing devices. In the telephone industry, for example, many switchboard operators were susceptible to fatigue and nervous breakdown. Munsterberg's application of various kinds of tests, such as those for space perception, intelligence, and manual dexterity, indicated that the better performers on the tests also tended to be the better performers in actual work as rated by the company. Thus the tests proved valuable as aids in the selection of the telephone operators.[32]

Munsterberg's 1917 book, *Business Psychology*, included the results of questionnaires sent to hundreds of laborers, requesting anonymous data on attitudes toward their work, their involvement in the labor movement, and their leisure activities. This survey had the support of the first president of the American Federation of Labor, Samuel Gompers, and other labor leaders.[31]

Both Munsterberg and Taylor were concerned with how workers were selected for jobs as well as with the individual worker's feelings and aspirations. Although they differed on several issues (notably on how social structure affected productivity), Munsterberg's writings clearly suggest that he felt that the two emerging fields of personnel selection and social psychology (the study of how people affect and are affected by one another) were complementary.[31]

Paralleling these developments were advances in checking references given by workers, in the use of rating sheets for interviewers, and in statistical methods for estimating validity (the extent to which selection devices accurately forecast job performance). World War I accelerated the development of intelligence tests (the Army Alpha and the Army Beta) so that each individual could be matched more effectively with job requirements. Other kinds of psychological measures also appeared during and after World War I, such as measures of aptitude, interest, and personality.

The U.S. Civil Service Commission

The Pendelton Act of 1883 established the U.S. Civil Service Commission (today known as the U.S. Office of Personnel Management). A forerunner in progressive personnel policies, the act provided that competitive examinations be administered as a basis for employment in the public service. It also provided a measure of employment security for those selected, prohibited discharge for refusing to engage in political activity, encouraged a nonpartisan approach to appointments, and mandated that a commissioner administer the act.[40] Perhaps the major impact of this act was to foster employment promotion policies in the federal government on the basis of merit. Over the years, however, the progressive personnel policies of the Civil Service (e.g., by 1900 entrance criteria were developed for the majority of federal positions) have influenced personnel practices in state and local governments as well as in private industry.

Private industry's approach to personnel management

Historians consider 1912 the approximate date of the emergence of the modern personnel department.[12] The term "personnel," with its modern connotation of managing people in organizations, began to appear about 1909. It was used as a major item in the index of the Civil Service Commission report of that year, and in 1910 the secretary of commerce and labor used the term in a major heading in his annual report. Between 1900 and 1920, while advances were being made in scientific management, industrial psychology, and the federal civil service, a number of *personnel specialists* emerged in companies such as B. F. Goodrich, National Cash Register, and Standard Oil of California. The specialists managed such areas as employment, employee welfare (financial, housing, medical, and educational), wage setting, safety, training, and health. This kind of specialization formed the basis for the organization of the modern human resource department.

The human relations movement

In Chicago in 1923 the Hawthorne Works of the Western Electric Company provided the setting for one of the most famous behavioral research efforts of all time. The purpose of the research was to study the effects of illumination on worker productivity. In one experiment, production went up when the illumination increased. In another experiment, production went up when the illumination decreased. After 3 years of continually inconsistent results, the researchers concluded that in a situation involving people, it was impossible to change one condition (the lighting) without at the same time affecting other variables. Employee motiviation and work-group morale seemed to be the really crucial factors.

Subsequently Professors Elton Mayo, Fritz Roethlisberger, and T. North Whitehead of the Harvard Business School became associated with the project and continued to do research at the Hawthorne works until the early 1930s. The results of their experiments indicated that productivity was directly related to the degree of group teamwork and cooperation. The level of teamwork and cooperation, in turn, seemed to be related to the interest of the supervisor and the researchers in the work group, the lack of coercive approaches to productivity improvement, and the participation afforded the workers in changes affecting them.[34, 36] These relationships are shown in Figure 2-1. In short, the researchers came to view the organization of workers as a *social system*, in contrast to Taylor's view of that organization as a technical-economic system.

FIGURE 2-1

Conclusion of the Hawthorne experiments regarding the antecedents of high worker productivity.

One of the most useful techniques in modern HRM is *nondirective interviewing*, which was used extensively during the Hawthorne experiments. Nondirective interviewing is really nothing more than effective listening by the interviewer. Listening effectiveness is promoted by an interviewer who reflects the feelings expressed by the interviewee, by avoiding arguments, by refusing to take sides, and by being nonjudgmental. The researchers learned two lessons from the nondirective interviewing: (1) It seemed to enhance morale as a result of giving employees a chance to "vent," and (2) surface complaints and grievances were rarely the real problems. The conviction that group behavior and workers' feelings were associated with morale and productivity characterized much of the research and theorizing in the human relations movement for the next two decades. Unfortunately, these new concepts, popularized as the "Pet Milk theory," were widely misunderstood and misapplied. The Pet Milk Company advertised that it had better milk because Pet Milk came from contented cows. A similar idea, that happy workers are productive workers, provided the rationale for trying to improve the workers' social environment with company picnics, newly created status symbols, employee coffee rooms, and other gimmicks.

Argyris pointed out that the symptoms were still being treated rather than the disease itself:

> Research suggests that telling a worker he is an important part of the company, when through *actual experience* he sees he is a very minor part (thanks to task specialization) with little responsibility (thanks to chain of command, directive leadership, and management controls) may only *increase* the employee's dissatisfaction with management. These "fads" assume it is possible to make human relations better, *not* by attacking the causes (formal organization, directive leadership, and management controls) but in effect by making the activities outside the actual work situation more pleasant for the worker (e.g., new toilets, new cafeterias, sports, picnics, newspapers), or by sugar-coating the work situation. (ref. 1, pp. 154, 155)

The "Pet Milk" approach was widely discredited during the late 1950s. The 1957 recession led to a severe curtailment of human relations training programs. Failure to find evidence that these programs made a difference in workers' satisfaction or that happy workers were productive workers helped kill this approach to human resource management.[5] Many managers seemed to use human relations for the short-term purpose of manipulating workers to increase output rather than for the long-term goal of satisfying worker needs *while* meeting organizational needs. By 1960 the "happy worker" fad had largely ended.

The behavioral sciences

The behavioral science approach to managing people is an outgrowth of the human relations studies, although it embraces a wider base of academic and applied disciplines and is concerned with a wider range of problems.[13] *Behavioral sciences* refers to the social and biological sciences concerned with the study of human behavior (see Figure 2-2).

Much of the knowledge about HRM and many of its practical applications have come from such behavioral science disciplines as the following:

Industrial/organizational psychology. The study of the behavior of people at work

Social psychology. The study of how people affect and are affected by one another

Organization theory. Basic philosophies about why organizations exist, how they function, how they should be designed, and how they can be effective

Organizational behavior. The study of the causes of individual and group behavior and of how this knowledge can be used to make people more productive and satisfied in organizational settings

Sociology. The study of society, social institutions, and social relationships

Needless to say, much behavioral science research cuts across these disciplines. For example, a popular behavioral science research theme in the 1960s and 1970s was a matching of alternative leadership styles (e.g., democratic, autocratic, consultative) to the kinds of situations in which each style is most appropriate. For example, if a manager has high power because of his or her position but low expertise in a particular technical area, what leadership style is most appropriate? Leadership style is at once a research question for industrial-organizational psychologists, social psychologists, and organizational behaviorists. The specification of organizational and managerial situations is a focus of organization theory. As a result of behavioral science findings, a new understanding has emerged that universal practices that are effective in all situations are not to be found.

We now know that the ways people behave in organizations cannot be explained simply by human relationships. The organization itself, through its unique "culture," molds, constrains, and modifies human performance. The way the organization is structured, the authority attached to different positions, and job and technology requirements clearly affect behavior. Even though our present understanding of the determinants and effects of behavior in organizations is incomplete, we do have a better sense of the ways in which separate influences interact with each other to affect individuals.

FIGURE 2-2

Academic and applied disciplines that contribute to the behavioral science approach to managing people at work.

APPLIED

ACADEMIC

RESULTS OF
STUDIES OF
HUMAN RELATIONS
AT WORK

INDUSTRIAL/ORGANIZATIONAL
PSYCHOLOGY
SOCIAL PSYCHOLOGY
ORGANIZATION THEORY
ORGANIZATIONAL BEHAVIOR
SOCIOLOGY

THE BEHAVIORAL SCIENCE
APPROACH TO HUMAN
RESOURCE MANAGEMENT

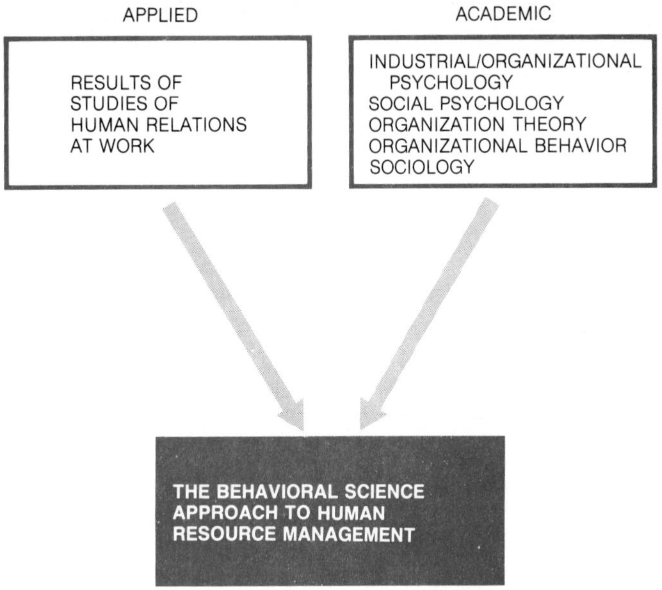

Another area that has exerted a considerable influence on HRM theory and practice is *general systems theory*. Systems theory has developed from such fields as biology, physics, and cybernetics (the study of mechnanical-electrical communications systems and devices). It has been applied and elaborated in every behavioral science field.

Research from the disciplines comprising the behavioral science approach and the systems approach will be applied to HRM throughout this book. The research spans a wide spectrum of settings and methods. Some researchers are interested in two-person or small-group dynamics, while others are interested in macro or total organizational processes (that is, organizational processes taken as a whole); some test their hypotheses in the laboratory, while others rely on field settings in actual organizations; some researchers are conceptualizers and model builders, while others are applications-oriented consultants and change agents. All play a vital role in the development and dissemination of knowledge that will help organizations do a better job of managing people at work. Subsequent chapters will draw extensively on this body of knowledge.

Three Growth Stages of Human Resource Management

The foundation for modern HRM rests on the nine factors listed earlier. Beyond that, HRM developed in three stages.

The first stage may be called the "file maintenance" stage, for it typified

HRM activities up through the mid-1960s and the degree of emphasis placed on employee concerns. The first part of Case 2-1 illustrates some typical HRM responsibilities at this stage of the field's development. "Personnel" was the responsibility of a special department. These responsibilities included screening applicants, orientation for new employees, collecting and storing personal data on each employee (date of birth, years of company service, education), planning the company picnic, and circulating memos "whose impertinence was exceeded only by their irrelevance."[9]

The second growth stage of HRM began soon after the Civil Rights Act of 1964 was passed. This is considered the "government accountability" stage. Discrimination laws, pension laws, health and safety laws, federal regulatory agencies and their interpretive guidelines, and court rulings affecting virtually every aspect of employment—all of these accelerated the rise in importance of the HRM function. Class action suits and the large financial settlements of the winning suits illustrated the costs of *personnel mismanagement*. Thus at American Telephone & Telegraph, a 1973 consent agreement with the federal government to bring the starting pay of women promoted to managerial positions up to the starting pay of men who were so promoted cost the company over $30 million.

Managers outside the HRM function began to take notice because top management let it be known that ineptitude in this area simply would not be tolerated. Staying out of federal court became a top organizational priority. These trends also signaled the need for particular competence in each aspect of the HRM field.

Within HRM there began to appear specialties in compensation and benefits, affirmative action (the promotion of minority concerns in all aspects of employment), labor relations, and training and development. Considerable resources were devoted to compliance activities, for example: filing government-required reports on the numbers of minorities and nonminorities recruited, selected, and promoted by job class. Many top executives viewed these activities as nonproductive drains on overall organizational performance.

In the late 1970s and early 1980s, when many firms were struggling simply to survive, a combination of economic and political factors (high interest rates, growing international competition, shrinking U.S. productivity) led to the demand for greater accountability in dollar terms of all the functional areas of business. Human resource management activities were not exempted from this emphasis on accountability. Although methods for assessing the costs and benefits of personnel programs are available, they are not widely known.[7] In addition, social trends (more women in the workforce, as well as more minorities, older workers, and more highly educated workers) have accelerated demands for improved quality of work life and for social responsibility.

Thus in the 1980s HRM has evolved to a third growth stage, "gaining and sustaining a competitive advantage." Top management looks to the HR department, as it does to line managers, to control costs, to enhance competitiveness, and to add value to the firm in everything it does. Consider a recent appraisal of the strategic importance of HRM by *Business Week:*

It is the most dramatic change in a managerial function since financial executives rose to power in the 1960s conglomerate era . . . . At a time when companies are constantly acquiring, merging, and spinning off divisions, entering new businesses and getting out of old ones, management must base strategic decisions more than ever on HR considerations—matching skills with jobs, keeping key personnel after a merger, and solving the human problems that arise from introducing new technology or closing a plant. (ref. 16, p. 58)

The responsibility for effective management of people, along with the effective management of physical and financial resources, is squarely on the shoulders of line managers—those directly responsible for the operations of the business (Figure 2-3). In terms of the discussion in Chapter 1 about changes in the technical and social environments, we now know that productivity improves most when all three factors of production—equipment, capital, and labor—are used most wisely; we cannot emphasize any one factor (e.g., computer equipment) to the exclusion of the rest (since, for example, it takes people who are properly selected, trained, and motivated to operate and maintain the computers). In many instances, HR departments only develop the tools and procedures to be used (eg., performance appraisal systems); line managers actually carry out these vital HRM activities. In the contemporary view, therefore, all managers, no matter what their line of responsibility (production, marketing, sales, or finance), are accountable to their organizations in terms of the financial impact of HRM operations and are accountable to their fellow employees in terms of the quality of work life they are providing. This suggests that the most effective approach to HRM may result from close interaction between the department charged with the administration of HRM and line managers charged with the responsibility for optimizing *all their resources.* To be sure, the HR department is still responsible for file maintenance and government accountability, but HRM in general is now viewed as a joint responsibility.

FIGURE 2-3

Line managers are responsible for optimizing the use of all three kinds of resources—physical, financial, and human—in order to generate useful output.

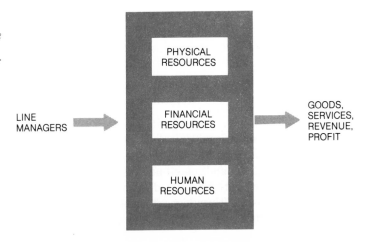

TABLE 2-1 *HRM activities and the responsibilities of line managers and the HR department*

Activity	Line management responsibility	HR department responsibility
Attraction	Providing data for job analyses, descriptions, and minimum qualifications; integrating strategic plans with HR plans at the unit level (e.g., department, division)	Job analysis, human-resource planning, recruitment, and affirmative action
Selection	Interviewing candidates, integrating information collected by HR department and making final decisions	Compliance with civil rights laws and regulations; application blanks, written tests, performance tests, interviews, background investigations, reference checks, and physical examinations
Retention	Fair treatment of employees, open communication, face-to-face resolution of conflict, promotion of teamwork, respect for the dignity of each individual, and pay increases based on merit	Compensation and benefits, labor relations, health and safety, and employee services
Development	On-the-job training, job enrichment, coaching, applied motivational strategies, and feedback to subordinates	Technical training, management and organization development, career planning, and counseling
Assessment	Performance appraisals and morale surveys	Development of performance appraisal systems and morale surveys; personnel research and audits
Adjustment	Discipline, discharge, promotions, and transfers	Layoffs, retirement counseling, and outplacement services

in any single part of the system have a reverberating effect on all other parts of the system. Simply knowing that this will occur is healthy, because then we will not make the mistake of confining our problems only to the part where they occur. We will recognize and expect that whether we are dealing with problems in selection, training, compensation, or labor relations, they are interrelated. In short the *systems approach* provides a conceptual framework for integrating the various components within the system and for linking the HRM system with larger organizational needs. As the scenario at the Hand Corporation illustrates, a major advantage of the systems approach to HRM is that consequences for all parts of the system can be identified when there is a proposed intervention into the system at any point. Attention is focused more sharply on the interrelationships between the various subsystems (that is, the aforementioned activities and responsibilities) and between the HRM system and the organization as a whole. These relationships have serious consequences for such vital statistics as labor turnover, absenteeism, waste and breakage, and production levels. Ultimately they affect employee productivity and job satisfaction.[16]

Other equally important interrelationships addressed by the systems approach include those between the HR department and the long-term business objectives of the organization (discussed below) and between the HR department and the external labor force (that is, available workers outside the firm). These relationships have serious consequences for the competitive status of the organization and thus for its continued viability.

As noted above, the activities of attraction, selection, retention, development, assessment, and adjustment are the special responsiblities of the HR department. But these responsibilities also lie within the core of every manager's job throughout any organization—and because line managers have authority (the organizationally granted right to influence the actions and behavior of the workers they manage), they have considerable impact on the ways that workers are actually utilized. This implies two things: A *broad objective* of HRM is to optimize the usefulness (i.e., the productivity) of all workers in an organization, and a *special objective* of the HR department is to help line managers manage those workers more effectively. The HR department accomplishes this special objective through policy initiation and formulation, advice, service, and control in resonance (close communication, understanding, and aims) with line managers when it comes to managing people. To be sure, each of the responsibilities of HRM is shared both by the HR department and by the line managers, as shown in Table 2-1.

The role and mission of the HR department: a top-management view

There is a perception among some people that this small department, with no revenue or profit-and-loss responsibility, somehow manages the human resources of the corporation. As noted earlier, this is not true, for *all managers*, regardless of their functional specialty, are responsible not only for managing capital and equipment but also for managing people. Another common perception is, in effect, that "Employees should be viewed as costs, not as assets." This also is not true, for as Bruce Ellig, Pfizer's top HR executive, noted: "You cut costs; you develop assets. The renaming of the personnel function to Human Resources in most organizations is at least an outward indication of that" (ref. 15, p. 41).

Recent in-depth interviews of 71 chief executive officers (CEOs) of major corporations indicated that in general, they subscribe to neither of these views. The HR department does not have the sole responsibility for managing people, and people are seen as assets, not just as costs. CEOs see HRM as one of the most important corporate functions—one to which they look for help in forging a competitive edge for the business. They cite quality of talent, flexibility and innovation, superior performance or productivity, and customer service as key factors in accomplishing this.[41] However, the CEOs also say that they expect more of the HRM function than they are getting. Despite such advances as HR planning, improved information systems, and new approaches to compensation, the function is often viewed as following, rather than leading, change. Often it is "responsive" rather than "proactive" (that is, anticipating events, not just reacting to them).

Using the HRM function strategically

In order to use the HRM function most effectively as a corporate resource, top management should consider doing the following things:

1. Define the HR department's responsibility as the maximization of corporate profits through the better management and utilization of people. The key issues are time and money. Concentrate the HRM function on ways to make people more productive—especially on ways to improve the employees' job skills, to improve their motivation by improving their quality of work life (QWL), and to improve the professional skills of managers.

2. The senior HR executive should report directly to the CEO. At present this occurs in about 70 percent of companies nationwide. Consider whether any corporate resource is more important than its people: Suppose that a fire destroyed all the plant and equipment of a 1000-employee firm; how long would it take to rebuild the plant and replace the equipment? One year? Now suppose that the same firm lost all its employees; how long would it take to replace the same level of competence and commitment? Considerably longer. Indeed, is any management function more important than managing the people who comprise the organization? HR policy cannot have any real meaning unless the CEO is intimately involved in its development.

3. Do not dilute the HRM function by saddling the HR department with unrelated responsibilities, such as the mail room and public relations. Do consider moving productivity functions, such as industrial engineering, into the HR department.

4. Require that HR executives be experienced businesspeople, for unless these executives are perceived as equals by their corporate peers, their ability to make significant contributions to the firm will be diminished. In today's climate of increased competition and cost control, there is simply no room for people who cannot have a significant impact on the firm's productivity and profitability.

HR initiatives: consider the possibilities

Study after study has shown that top management wants the HRM function to concentrate on people-related business issues involving productivity and cost containment. Here are some typical initiatives:[41, 20]

- Containing the costs of employee health care and other benefits
- Redesigning compensation programs, tying them closer to performance
- Improving productivity through employee involvement and meaningful performance appraisal

HR staff should help plan and implement changes in organizational structure or management practices, such as:

- Staffing changes resulting from downsizing, restructuring, mergers, or acquisitions.
- Increasing the innovation, creativity, and flexibility necessary to enhance competitiveness. Proactive HR departments are doing this by designing and facilitating the application of new approaches for job design (e.g., to promote entrepreneurship), succession planning, career development, and intraorganizational mobility.
- Managing the implementation of technological changes through improved staffing, training, and communications with employees.
- Promoting changes in relations with unions, particularly those changes which will enhance cooperation, productivity, and flexibility.
- Anticipating and influencing the management impact of new legislation and court decisions.

Key management questions to ask in evaluating the HRM function

Just as when evaluating any other function, a company's management should ask tough questions, such as:

- How many HR managers, professionals, and support staff does the company employ this year? How much does this cost the company? (Considering the total cost per person of salaries and benefits, equipment, supplies, computer time, heat, light, water, depreciation, and rent, employees cost about 3 times their annual salaries.[4])
- How do these numbers (people and dollars) relate to company revenues and to the employee population?
- How do these ratios compare with those of competitors and/or with national figures?
- What trends can be identified in the HR department over the past 5 years? What ratios would it be desirable to maintain in the future?

Evaluation from the HR perspective

It has been said many times that if HR people are to make meaningful contributions to an enterprise, they must think and act like businesspeople. To promote this sort of outlook, it is useful to ask, "How much profit must a profit center make to keep an HR department going"?

Suppose you run an HR department for a firm that makes bicycles. Last year the total cost to the company for your department's services was $1 million. How many bikes does the company have to sell to pay your way? Let's say that on a $200 bicycle, your company makes a profit of $20. Dividing this $20 into $1 million shows that 50,000 bikes must be sold to keep the HR department in business!

The point of this exercise is not to argue for the abolition of HR departments in order to save profits or to save selling more bikes. Certainly, if the HR department was not doing its work, somebody else would be doing much of it. Rather, the point is that there is an important connection between human resource management and profits. It is seldom discussed, but it should be, to promote increased awareness of how time and money are spent. Imagine an HR director asking how many bikes will have to be sold to support a new orientation program!

A second important question which management should ask and which HR people should be prepared to answer is "How much more product can be sold because of your services?" While many HR contributions are not related directly to the bottom line, it is important to promote increased awareness of how HR activities relate to the purposes of the organization. Here are some possible HR department responses in six key areas:[4]

- "Here's what we did for you (in recruiting, say), here's what it cost, and here's what you would have done without us and what it would have cost you."
- "Here's how much money we saved you by changing insurers in our benefits package."
- "Here's an idea that workers developed in a training program we were leading. It's now working and saving you $50,000 per year."
- "If you had not asked us to do this executive search, you would have had to go outside, at a cost of $30,000. We did it for $5000."
- "You used to have an unhappy person doing this job for $40,000 per year. As a result of our job redesign, you now have a motivated person doing the same work for $20,000."
- "In working with the union on a new contract, we found a new way to reduce grievances by 30 percent, saving the company 6429 hours per year in management time."

Even though precise bottom-line numbers might be hard to come by for many HR activities, it it important to encourage HR people to think in these terms.

Current status of HRM activities

Progressive organizations are rotating their best managers through the various specialized HRM functions as a required part of their development and as a way of bringing line experience to HRM problems. Higher levels of education and experience are required for individuals who are given such HRM assignments. In fact, the vice president of human resources frequently reports directly to the chief executive officer and sits on the board of directors and the planning committee. Salaries for top HR executives also reflect this increased stature. Among companies with more than $3 billion in revenue, HR chiefs earn, on average, $217,000 per year. In contrast, the top marketing executive averages $181,000.[23]

Impact of Effective HRM on Productivity, Quality of Work Life, and the Bottom Line

Even a seemingly simple issue such as the quality of the work environment for office workers can affect their productivity and QWL. In a study of 1047 office workers and 209 executives commissioned by Steelcase, Inc., 74 percent gave their employers high marks for providing good working conditions. Over 70 percent felt that their QWL had improved, as compared with only 58 percent who saw improvement in the quality of life generally. Negative responses were most common from workers in "pool offices," rows of adjacent desks with no space or partitions between them. Many executives seemed unaware of how highly workers rate conversational privacy as a part of their work environment. Over 99 percent of those surveyed saw a connection between satisfaction with their work area and their productivity.[28]

HRM's status also has increased in response to the high cost and importance of training and development; the constantly increasing costs of wages, salaries, and benefits; emphasis on improving productivity and the quality of work life; and attempts to tie human resource planning systems into corporate strategies specifically aimed at resolving the shortage of competent management and professional personnel. As the director of HR planning at Bank of America noted, "The perception used to be that human resources thought about the happiness of employees, and line managers thought about costs. Now both realize that the overriding concern is the yield from employees."[19]

Impacts of Effective Human Resource Management

For all its increased status, what impact does effective HRM have on productivity, QWL, and the bottom line? The following examples give a range of answers to this question.

Goal setting and feedback

Effective management of employees' goals and plans, together with constructive feedback telling them of their progress toward their goals, can produce impressive results. This was demonstrated in a study of sewing machine operators in a southwestern garment factory.[21] The 150 workers in the study assembled pairs of pants using an "assembly line" on which 34 separate operations (each requiring an average time of 18 seconds) were performed.

The quality of the work done was inspected at the end of the line by full-time inspectors. Each garment was inspected. Sewing errors were called to the attention of the operators only if the number of errors for a particular operator's segment of the total job was excessive in a 60-unit bundle of pants. Errors were mended by "menders," not by the operator who caused the error.

The plant where the study was conducted was experiencing more than twice the employee turnover normal for the garment industry at the time. When the study began, annual turnover was 216 percent, and daily absenteeism was 9.4 percent.

One purpose of the study was to determine the effects of goal setting and feedback on the operators' work. Challenging individual goals were set. The overall group goal was to reach the quality level of the best plants owned by the manufacturer. Feedback was accomplished by erecting 4- by 6-foot Plexiglas display boards on which the daily results for the workers were posted by management. Within a month after the goal setting and feedback were established, sewing errors decreased 66 percent; 1 year later, although the turnover was still unacceptably high, it had dropped from 216 to 136 percent.

Job redesign

Typists are a favorite target for job redesign because theirs is one of the few jobs in which so critical a function is performed by people so bored. In fact, one study found that 60 percent of all typists who quit their jobs do so because of boredom and lack of work, not because of overwork.[27]

The study's authors reported that in one division of Bankers Trust, typically bored typists were engaged in processing work that was more than typically critical—stock transfers. The problems were severe because of the consequences. In addition to the problems of high employee turnover and absenteeism, both the quality and the quantity of work were low. To deal with this situation, the following changes were introduced gradually over 6 months, and supervisors received formal training on how to cope with employee responses to the new changes:

1. Groups of customers were assigned to specific typists.
2. Individuals whose work was accurate and reliable were not required to have their work verified by checkers.
3. Other typists and checkers became teams, with each team responsible for the work done for a particular group of customers.
4. Typists corrected their own mistakes, and feedback from checkers was immediate for those whose work still required verification.

Redesigning the jobs resulted in work yielding considerably fewer errors. For the group of typists as a whole, the processing time was decreased. The speed of typists who worked without checkers and verified their own work was a bit slower, but not so slow as to take longer than if others had checked their work.

Rewards-based suggestion systems

Suggestion systems designed to improve the quality or speed of goods and services have gotten quite a bad reputation of late. Most managers are convinced that they simply do not work. Perhaps they do not because of faulty suggestion-system design and implementation.

One exception is Honeywell's Defense Systems and Avionics Division, based in Minneapolis.[42] One year this company division received over 18,000 suggestions (3.66 per employee) that resulted in a savings of over $1 million. The Honeywell Suggestion System rewards employees who offer cost-saving suggestions by recognizing them and paying them an amount based on their suggestions.

Cash is awarded to employees based on one-sixth of the total first year's anticipated savings. The more valuable the suggestion, the greater the reward: a clear application of "pay for performance."

The trend in this area is for companies to provide more top prizes with higher cash awards. For example, Pitney Bowes Business Systems raised its top prize from $30,000 paid over 3 years to $50,000 paid over 2 years. Ford Motor Company now allows *groups* of hourly workers, instead of just an *individual*, to win its top award of $6000. Recently, Eastman Kodak paid $3.6 million in awards, up to 8.7 percent from the previous year, and figures that it saved $16 million from the suggestions.[24]

Unique contributions of the HR department to profits

As noted earlier, a staff department such as HR must be able to demonstrate that what it does is important to the success of the organization and that the procedures it suggests provide positive results; otherwise, the HR department is perceived as nothing more than one of "happiness vendors." The HR staff must be able to demonstrate the impact of their programs on that indicator of corporate health—the bottom line. They must also be able to demonstrate the efficiency of their own departments. Only with such evidence will the HR staff be able to justify the priority setting and resource allocation that favors HRM and moves it toward parity with the other functional areas of business.[6]

Contrary to common belief, *all* aspects of HRM (including morale) can be measured and quantified in the same manner as any other function in an organization. Some of the major areas in which HRM can demonstrate measurable cost savings, productivity increases, and turnover reductions are as follows (all discussed more fully in later chapters).

Compensation policies and procedures Organizations that do not fully understand what a position is worth will most likely either overpay or underpay their employees. The result, of course, is incompetent overpaid employees, who do not leave and who are hard to get rid of, and competent underpaid employees, who do not stay. The key to avoiding this situation is a structured compensation plan that provides ranges accurately reflecting market worth in each job and in the firm's geographic area. The compensation structure need not be complicated or costly to develop, but it does require periodic attention if it is to be kept current.

Administration of employee benefits   HR managers usually try to get the greatest benefits coverage possible for employees at a given level of costs, but they do not always monitor the administration of benefit programs on an on-going basis. This policy can prove to be quite costly, especially when dividends, refunds, or increased benefits are not obtained because the premiums exceed the costs of the benefits paid out. When the benefits paid out to employees exceed the premiums contributed to pay for the benefits coverage, insurance carriers are quick to notify an organization of the need for increased premiums the following year. However, they will usually *not* inform an organization that there will be a dividend available for overpayment of premium contributions relative to benefit payments; the organization must ask for it.

Personnel tax management   Every firm pays personnel taxes, such as federal and state unemployment taxes, which are usually based on workforce turnover. These taxes are controllable to the same degree as insurance costs. The taxes are usually levied on the first $7000 of each employee's salary, and the rates vary from zero (in some states for employers who have had no recent experience with former employees collecting chargeable unemployment insurance) to over 6 percent of the payroll.[30] Thus a 2000-employee firm may be required to pay a 4 percent unemployment tax on the first $7000 of each employee's earnings ($280 per employee), for a total tax bill of $560,000. Suppose that as a result of a 10 percent drop in employee turnover, the firm is required to pay only a 3 percent unemployment tax on the first $7000 of each employee's earnings ($210 per employee). This represents a total tax bill of $420,000 and thus a savings of $140,000 over the old tax bill. It is the responsibility of the HR director to ensure that the organization is not paying a higher rate than necessary, for as turnover is controlled, these rates can often be reduced.

Recruiting, training, and management development   Recruiting requires considerable expertise, yet it is often assigned to an HR staff trainee. If a recruiter does not understand the compensation structure of the business, the job requirements, and the political conditions existing in the department for which he or she is recruiting, how can the right person be hired for the right job?

Potential losses from poor selection and training programs are subtle. Potential gains from valid selection and training programs are far larger than most of us realize. Consider that in 1986 the U.S. Navy estimated that it costs $1 million to train one new fighter pilot.[33] For the sake of illustration, assume an annual quota of 100 new fighter pilots, and assume that each unsuccessful candidate costs the Navy $250,000. If 80 percent of the candidates are successful, then 20 percent (or 20 additional candidates) must be selected and trained. At $250,000 per failure, 20 failures per year cost the Navy $5 million. If more valid selection procedures were used, so that only 15 percent failed (or 15 instead of 20 candidates in our example), the Navy would save $5 \times \$250,000$, or $1.25 million *each year*.

Affirmative action control   To most organizations, equal employment opportunity makes good business sense. However, HR staff have the financial responsiblity to ensure that affirmative action does not result in declining productivity or become an expensive social exercise. There is simply no good reason to lower bona fide occupational qualifications to accept unqualified minorities and women, when with more effort and a wider search, qualified women and minorities can be recruited.

Age discrimination may be more damaging and costly. With society's emphasis on youth, it is often the older manager who is furloughed or fired in a corporate reorganization. Sometimes firms do this as a pretext to avoid paying pensions. The odds are 5 to 1 that a recent college graduate will leave within the first 3 years of employment. The odds of a 50-year-old recruit staying with an organization for 15 productive years are far greater.[10]

Turnover and outplacement   Using proper accounting procedures to compute the real cost of turnover in terms of separation, replacement, and training costs reveals that six- or seven-figure annual turnover costs are common for large firms.[7] The control of these costs is the joint responsibility of line managers and HR staff. Once the cause of the turnover is identified and corrective action taken (e.g., job redesign, retraining, changes in compensation), even a modest reduction in the percentage of annual turnover can represent considerable savings.

Layoffs or involuntary turnovers are never a pleasant part of HRM, but even here money can be saved through sensible outplacement policies. *Outplacement* refers to a set of activities authorized and paid for by the present employer that will help laid-off employees find new jobs as soon as possible. Outplacement activities for lower-level workers can be handled by the HR staff, but for terminated executives a consulting firm that specializes in outplacement may be a wise investment. Terminated executives may find work more quickly and at a higher salary after being taught how to construct a résumé, how to market their professional expertise most effectively, how to negotiate salary, and how to develop the "hidden market" of available management positions that are never formally advertised. More important, the terminated executive maintains a good rapport with the old company and often becomes a supplier or customer. Finally, "bridging pay" (i.e., regular salary payments rather than a lump-sum severance payment) allows the executive to seek new employment while maintaining self-confidence. When new employment is secured, the bridging pay stops. Often the difference between bridging pay and severance pay, which is usually quite large for terminated executives, saves more than the fees charged by the outplacement consultant.

This has been just a brief glimpse into several areas where effective HRM can make a substantial contribution to the improvement of productivity, the quality of work life, and the bottom line. Although each area has been discussed separately, the overall objective is to develop a uniform financial reporting system for the entire HRM subsystem. Significant and timely information can be produced, both line managers and HR staff can see how their work is interconnected, and over time such a measurement system can become a very powerful tool.

CASE 2-1
Conclusion

Managing people at Allied-Signal Corporation

Government regulations affecting all aspects of employment really shook up top management and caused a reappraisal of organizational personnel policies in the 1970s. Such programs as the Equal Employment Opportunity Act, the Occupational Health and Safety Act, and the Employee Retirement Income Security Act were rife with formal requirements telling companies how to manage their employees. Top management, fearful of running afoul of Uncle Sam, was compelled to pay more attention to HRM.

Until 1979, HRM didn't count for much at Allied. Then a new CEO took over and began to stress such things as management development; succession planning; surveys of employee attitudes regarding such things as pay, promotions, coworkers, supervision, and opportunities for advancement; and retirement counseling. He also mandated that pink slips go out to 842 workers, thereby carving $30 million off the payroll. It is sad news to break to one person, but Bischoff had to break the news to 842 people. He remembers the layoff period as "the most difficult and the most emotionally charged [task] that I've ever been involved with."

The anguish of that period behind him, Bischoff described his other responsibilities—the design of complex compensation and benefits packages, executive searches, organizational planning, college relations, management training, and the computerized system that keeps track of Allied's salaried workers.

An air of trouble comes over any HR head when the subject of worker productivity is raised. "Productivity is an issue that is fast emerging as the issue of the 1980s" Bischoff said. Among other things, Allied has attacked impediments to productivity in labor contracts, such as rigid work rules, with considerable zeal and some success. The firm has started quality circles in some plants; it has instituted a retirement counseling program; and, to mollify the QWL demands of the increasingly independent workers of today, it is actively considering such things as flexible benefits. To the extent that both QWL and productivity can be improved through more effective HR management, everybody wins.

Bischoff's job still involves the same mundane matters that used to be the core of a personnel manager's job. The people in his department still dispense shirts or uniforms for company softball, golf, and bowling teams.

They arrange service award dinners, coax workers to donate some of their blood, and run a vanpool program to ferry employees to work.

There is also the human, often tragicomic side of personnel work. For instance, Bischoff is regularly approached by solace seekers. While he is walking through the halls or munching lunch in the company cafeteria, some employee will trot over and relate some tale of personal misery. The employee feels that he simply isn't paid what he's worth. Or he can't keep off the bottle. Or his kids are running amok. "People are borrowing your ears all the time," Bischoff admitted (probably because he radiates empathy).

Yes, personnel work has gotten much more complicated, but Bischoff still relishes the human touch. "I get great satisfaction every time I match up the right candidate with the right job," he said. "When I'm able to assist a person in his individual career, I get something out of that."

Summary

Modern HRM has evolved from nine interrelated sources: (1) the industrial revolution, (2) the emergence of free collective bargaining, (3) the scientific management movement, (4) early industrial psychology, (5) governmental personnel practices resulting from the establishment of the U.S. Civil Service Commission, (6) the emergence of personnel specialists and their grouping into personnel departments, (7) the human relations movement, (8) the behavioral sciences, and (9) the social legislation and court decisions of the 1960s and 1970s.

HRM today involves six major areas: attraction, selection, retention, development, assessment, and adjustment. Together they comprise the HRM system, for they describe a network of interrelated components. Top management views the HRM function as an important tool to enhance competitiveness. To accomplish this purpose, the HRM function must be used strategically. Its responsibility is the maximization of productivity, quality of work life, and profits through better management of people. To fulfill this responsibility, the senior HR executive should report directly to the CEO, the HRM function should focus on productivity-related activities, and the HR people should above all be businesspeople, accountable, just as any other function, in terms of their overall contributions to enhancing productivity and controlling costs.

Finally, contributions to improved productivity, QWL, and the bottom line can come from more effective management of a number of areas. These include but certainly are not limited to: improved work environments; goal setting and feedback; job redesign; rewards-based suggestion systems; compensation policies and procedures; benefits administration; personnel tax management; recruiting, training, and management development; affirmative action control; and turnover and outplacement.

TOMORROW'S FORECAST

A CEO expressed his views on people management in the late 1980s as follows:[18]

The human resource professional in the coming decade must become a more highly motivated, bottom-line manager completely in tune with the needs of the organization's top management. The thrust is to be proactive [anticipating events, not just reacting to them], scanning the internal and external horizons of the organization, alerting management to the issues and problems likely to affect the corporation significantly, and suggesting the ways and means of addressing them.

If this is the role for HR professionals, what will be the role of line managers in the HRM area? Predominantly it will be a set of activities that indicate an increased awareness of the implications of the phrase "human resources." Organizations and line managers will truly consider their employees as important resources "to be invested in prudently, to be used productively, and from whom a return can be expected—a return that should be monitored as carefully as is the return on any other business investment."[6] Human resource management is not only planning and controlling, manipulating numbers, and reporting to higher management. It is also relating on a daily basis to the employees of the company. All managers must emphasize the human side of the workforce and give more than lip service to honoring and understanding that side. This is the real challenge of managing people effectively.

Discussion Questions

2-1 Discuss the contributions of the industrial revolution, scientific management, and early industrial psychology to the development of modern HRM.

2-2 What were some of the strengths and weaknesses of the human relations movement?

2-3 How do the responsibilities and objectives of HRM contribute to employee productivity and employee job satisfaction?

2-4 In what ways can effective HRM contribute to profits?

2-5 What changes do you see in HRM over the next 5 years?

References

1. Argyris, C. (1957). *Personality and organization.* New York: Harper & Row.
2. Babbage, C. (1835). *On the economy of machinery and manufacturers* (4th ed.). London: Charles Knight.

3. Bell, D. (1972). Three technologies: Size, measurement, hierarchy. In L. E. Davis and J. C. Taylor (eds.), *Design of jobs*. London: Penguin.

4. Bellman, G. M. (1986). Doing more with less. *Personnel Administrator*, **31**, 46–52.

5. Brayfield, A. H., & Crockett, W. H. (1955). Employee attitudes and employee performance. *Psychological Bulletin*, **52**, 396–424.

6. Briscoe, D. R. (1982, November). Human resource management has come of age. *The Personnel Administrator*, **26**, 75–83.

7. Cascio, W. F. (1987). *Costing human resources: The financial impact of behavior in organizations* (2d ed.). Boston: PWS-Kent.

8. Cohen, S. (1960). *Labor in the United States*. Columbus, Oh: Charles E. Merrill.

9. Cole, M. (1953). *Robert Owen of New Lanark*. New York: Oxford University Press.

10. Driessnack C. H. (1979). Financial impact of effective human resources management. *The Personnel Administrator*, **23**, 62-66

11. Dulles, F. R. (1960). *Labor in America: A history* (2d rev. ed.). New York: Thomas Y. Crowell.

12. Eilbert, H. (1959). The development of personnel management in the United States. *Business History Review*, **33**, 345–364.

13. French, W. L. (1986). *The personnel management process* (6th ed.). Boston: Houghton Mifflin.

14. Harvey, L. J. (1986). Nine major trends in HRM. *Personnel Administrator*, **31**, 102–109.

15. Holder, J. (1986). Regaining the competitive edge. *Personnel Administrator*, **31**, 35–41, 122, 124.

16. Human resources managers aren't corporate nobodies anymore (1985, December 2). *Business Week*, pp. 58, 59.

17. Hutton, T. J. (1987). Human resources or management resources? *Personnel Administrator*, **32**, 66–74.

18. Janger, A. (1980). Personnel functions in modern management: Trends, problems, and practices. In W. B. Wolf (ed.), *Top management of the personnel function: Current issues and practices*. Ithaca, NY: New York State School of Industrial and Labor Relations, Cornell University.

19. Kiechel, W. III. (1987, Aug. 18). Living with human resources. *Fortune*, pp. 99, 100.

20. Klingner, D. E. (1979, September). Changing role of personnel management in the 1980s. *The Personnel Administrator*, **23**, 41–47.

21. Koch, J. L. (1979). Effects of goal specificity and performance feedback to work groups on peer leadership, performance, and attitudes. *Human Relations*, **32**, 819–840.

22. Labor Letter (1986, Aug. 26). *Wall Street Journal*, p. 1.

23. Labor Letter (1987, Sep. 8). *Wall Street Journal*, p. 1.

24. Labor Letter (1984, May 15). *Wall Street Journal*, p. 1.

25. Locke E. A. (1982). The ideas of Frederick W. Taylor: An evaluation. *Academy of Management Review*, **7**, 14–24.

26. Mayo, E. (1945). *The social problems of an industrial civilization*. Boston: Harvard University Press.

27. McAfee, R. B., & Poffenberger, W. (1982). *Productivity Strategies: Enhancing employee job performance*. Englewood Cliffs, NJ: Prentice-Hall.

28. Merry, R. W. (1979, Feb. 6). Office workers feel work environments have improved greatly in 10 years. *Wall Street Journal*, p. 1.

The particular laws we shall discuss within each category are:

Absolute prohibition	Conditional on federal funding
Thirteenth and Fourteenth Amendments to the U.S. Constitution	Executive Orders 11246, 11375, and 11478
Civil Rights Acts of 1866 and 1871	Rehabilitation Act (1973)
Equal Pay Act (1963)	Vietnam Era Veterans Readjustment Act (1974)
Title VII of the 1964 Civil Rights Act	
Age Discrimination in Employment Act (1967), as amended in 1986	
Immigration Reform and Control Act (1986)	

Involuntary servitude

The Thirteenth Amendment to the U.S. Constitution became effective on December 18, 1865; its main purpose was the abolition of slavery. In part, it states: "Neither slavery nor involuntary servitude, except as punishment for crime whereof the party shall have been duly convicted, shall exist within the United States, or any place subject to their jurisdiction." Traditionally the Thirteenth Amendment has been applied only in cases involving racial discrimination as a basis for the elimination of slavery and the "badges" (symbols) and "incidents" of slavery. However, any form of discrimination can be considered a badge or incident of slavery and is therefore liable to legal action under the Thirteenth Amendment.[32]

Equal protection

In 1868 the Constitution was amended to require all state and local governments to provide for all people "equal protection of the laws." Discrimination against any particular person or class is therefore prohibited not only in employment but also in the provision of public services (e.g., education, zoning, police protection).

The Fourteenth Amendment was used as the legal basis for suit in the landmark Supreme Court case, *Bakke v. Regents of the University of California*.[5] The central issue in the case was the legality of the admissions policy of the University of California at Davis medical school. The Davis system set aside 16 of 100 places in its entering classes for "disadvantaged" applicants who were members of racial minority groups. Since this admissions policy was a formal, numerically based racial quota system, whites could compete for only 84 of the 100 places, while minorities could compete for all 100. The Court ruled that the Fourteenth Amendment had been violated since all individuals

June 5, 1982. Alan Bakke graduates from the University of California at Davis medical school.

were not treated equally; the admissions program had disregarded the white individual's right to equal protection of the laws. Moreover, there was no previous history of racial discrimination at the school that might have justified a program of preferential selection in order to make up for past unlawful discrimination.

The Court also addressed the legality of "affirmative action" programs—*those actions appropriate to overcome the effects of past or present policies, practices, or other barriers to equal employment opportunity.*[52] The Court said that such programs are permissible as long as they consider applicants on an individual basis and do not set aside a rigid number of places for which whites cannot compete. Thus personnel selection decisions must be made on an individual, case-by-case basis. Race can be taken into account along with grades and extracurricular activities, for example, as one factor in an applicant's favor, but the overall decision to select or reject must be made on the basis of a combination of factors and not on the basis of race alone.

The Civil Rights Acts of 1866 and 1871

The Thirteenth and Fourteenth Amendments both grant Congress the power to enforce their provisions by enacting appropriate legislation. The Civil Rights Act of 1866 grants all citizens the right to make and enforce contracts for employment, and the Civil Rights Act of 1871 grants all citizens the right to sue in federal court if they feel they have been deprived of any rights or privileges guaranteed by the Constitution and laws.

Until recently, both of these laws were viewed narrowly as tools for Reconstruction era racial problems. This is no longer so. In *Johnson v. Railway Express Agency*, the Supreme Court held that while the Civil Rights Act of 1866 on its face relates primarily to racial discrimination in the making and enforcement of contracts, it also provides a federal remedy against racial discrimination in private employment as well.[50] It is a powerful remedy. Under this act, individuals are entitled to both equitable and legal relief, including compensatory and, under certain circumstances, punitive damages. And unlike Title VII (which will be discussed shortly), back-pay awards are not limited to 2 years.

The 1866 law also has been used recently to broaden the definition of racial discrimination originally applied to blacks. In a unanimous decision, the Supreme Court ruled in 1987 that race was equated with ethnicity during the legislative debate after the Civil War, and therefore Arabs, Jews, and other ethnic groups thought of as "white" are not barred from suing under the 1866 act. The Court held that Congress intended to protect identifiable classes of persons who are subjected to intentional discrimination solely because of their ancestry or ethnic characteristics. Under the law, therefore, race involves more than just skin pigment.[19]

The Equal Pay Act of 1963

This act was passed as an amendment to an earlier compensation-related law, the Fair Labor Standards Act of 1938. For those employers subject to the Fair Labor Standards Act (i.e., those engaged in interstate or foreign commerce or in the production of goods for such commerce), the Equal Pay Act requires that men and women working for the same establishment be paid the same rate of pay for work that is substantially equal in skill, effort, responsibility, and working conditions. Pay differentials are legal and appropriate if they are based upon seniority, merit, piece-rate payment systems, or any factor other than sex. Moreover, in correcting any inequity under the Equal Pay Act, employers must raise the rate of lower-paid employees, not lower the rate of higher-paid employees.

Hundreds of equal-pay suits were filed (predominantly by women) during the 1970s and early 1980s. The results of these suits have been extremely costly to some firms. American Telephone and Telegraph signed a consent decree with the government in 1973 to wipe out equal-pay problems permanently. By 1979 over 72,000 employees received pay increases at an annual cost of $53 million.[62]

Comparable worth   This issue has been billed as the "civil rights issue of the 1980s." The issue relates primarily to the fact that when women dominate an occupational field (such as nursing or secretarial work), the rate of pay for jobs within those occupations appears to be depressed unfairly when compared to the pay that men receive when working in jobs where they are the dominant incumbents within the occupational field (e.g., construction, house painting).[11] Comparable worth thus involves the knotty problem of how to make valid and accurate comparisons of the relative worth of unlike jobs. The key difference between the Equal Pay Act and comparable worth is this: The act requires equal pay for men and women who do work that is *substantially equal*. Comparable worth would require equal pay for work of *equal value* to an employer. For example, if an employer determined that the jobs of librarian (predominantly female) and electrician (predominantly male) were approximately of equal value, then their worth to that employer would be comparable, and the pay for the two jobs should be equivalent.

In the late 1970s women's groups who felt that women were the victims of discriminatory practices began taking their concerns to court. They sued employers under the Equal Pay Act of 1963 and the Civil Rights Act of 1964 (which follows this section). Comparable worth cases are proliferating, spurred on by facts such as the following:

- Eighty percent of the women in the workforce are crowded into only 20 of the Labor Department's 427 job categories.[60]
- A typical full-time working woman earns only 68 percent of a man's wage, a figure that has increased very slowly over the past 20 years.
- The more a job category is dominated by women, the less it pays—with the compensation going down about $42 per year for each additional percentage point of women employed in the category.

The wage gap between men and women is not caused simply by the undervaluing of women's work. Other reasons why women earn less money than men may be that they stay in the workforce less consistently, that they choose jobs of less intrinsic (monetary) value, and that they have less seniority. According to a National Academy of Sciences report, however, at least half of the wage gap cannot be explained by anything *but* sex discrimination.

Critics regard comparable worth as nothing short of a revolutionary threat to the free-market process of setting wages by supply and demand. By some estimates it could cost employers as much as $150 billion per year to raise female workers to the same levels as men who do jobs requiring comparable skill, effort, responsibility, and working conditions. Higher labor costs will lead inevitably to higher prices, thus fueling inflation.

On the other hand, supporters of comparable worth argue that the cost of ending sex discrimination should not be an excuse for illegal pay practices. They say that reliance on the marketplace merely institutionalizes the bias against women and that job evaluation schemes that give points for the skills, responsibility, and physical and mental effort to do a particular job—and the hazards and risks that job involves—are a better guide.[60] Although there are a number of alternative job evaluation methods, they all share the same objective: to rank-order jobs in terms of their relative worth or value to the firm. The focus is on the characteristics of jobs, not on the characteristics of the people who perform them.

The use of job evaluation as a safeguard against gender bias was under-scored by a review of over 150 court cases on this topic.[21] In the majority of cases, individual testimony, not the results of a job evaluation study, was submitted to the courts as evidence of job worth. Although there are many critics of job evaluation, the courts do accept it as a measure of job worth, and they have required its use as a remedy where illegal pay discrimination has been found. Currently 24 states have completed job evaluation studies, or are working on them, and have found that jobs dominated by women pay 20 percent less than equally demanding jobs usually held by men. So far, 13 states have moved to make up the difference, at a cost ranging from 2 to 5 percent of state payroll budgets.[55] The State of Washington is typical. After a 12-year legal battle, the state agreed to implement a job evaluation plan and to provide supplementary pay increases from 1986 to 1992 to affected employees. The total tab by 1992: $482 million.[75]

Yet there are limits to the extent to which comparisons between unlike jobs can be made. There is a difference between (1) a single business or gov-ernment entity using a unified classification system and (2) the practice of imposing categories broadly across business and professional lines, regardless of the labor markets in which organizations compete. Comparable worth as a legal theory can be applied only to a single employer, a single organization.[85] This is because the pay that one receives reflects a combination of inputs: "market" wages, the relative worth of the employee's job to the firm, and the individual characteristics of the employee (training, experience, and job per-formance). Despite heated arguments on both sides of the issue, the courts have yet to provide definite answers to this difficult question.

Title VII of the Civil Rights Act of 1964

The Civil Rights Act of 1964 is divided into several sections, or titles, each dealing with a particular facet of discrimination (e.g., voting rights, public accommodations, public education). Title VII is most relevant to the employ-ment context, for it prohibits discrimination on the basis of race, color, religion, sex, or national origin in all aspects of employment (including apprenticeship programs). Title VII is the most important federal EEO law because it contains the broadest coverage, prohibitions, and remedies. Through it, the Equal Em-ployment Opportunity Commission (EEOC) was created to ensure that em-ployers, employment agencies, and labor organizations comply with Title VII.

Some may ask why we need such a law. As an expression of social policy, the law was passed to guarantee that people would be considered for jobs not on the basis of the color of their skin, or their religion, or their gender, or their national origin, but rather on the basis of individual abilities and talents that are necessary to perform a job.

In 1972 the coverage of Title VII was expanded. It now includes (1) both public and private employers (including state and local governments and public and private educational institutions) with 15 or more employees, (2) labor organizations with 15 or more members, and (3) both public and private employment agencies. The 1972 amendments also prohibited the denial, termination, or suspension of government contracts (without a special hearing) if an employer has and is following an affirmative action plan accepted by the federal government for the same facility within the past 12 months. Finally, back-pay awards in Title VII cases are limited to 2 years.

Elected officials and their appointees are excluded from Title VII coverage, but they are still subject to the Fourteenth Amendment and the Civil Rights Acts of 1866 and 1871. The following are also specifically exempted from Title VII coverage:

1. *Bona fide occupational qualifications (BFOQs).* Discrimination on the basis of race, religion, sex, or national origin is permissible when any of these factors are bona fide occupational qualifications for employment, that is, when any of them is considered "reasonably necessary to the operation of that particular business or enterprise." The burden of proof rests with the employer to demonstrate BFOQs. (According to one personnel director, the only legitimate BFOQs that she could think of are sperm donor and wet nurse!) Both the EEOC and the courts interpret BFOQs quite narrowly.[5] Preferences of the employer, coworkers, or clients are irrelevant and do not constitute BFOQs.

2. *Seniority systems.* As we shall see shortly, the legal status of seniority has been hotly contested in the courts. Title VII explicitly permits bona fide seniority, merit, or incentive systems "provided that such differences are not the result of an intention to discriminate."

3. *Preemployment inquiries.* Inquiries regarding such matters as race, sex, or ethnic group are permissible as long as they can be shown to be job-related. Even if not job-related, some inquiries (e.g., regarding race or sex) are often necessary to meet the reporting requirements of federal regulatory agencies. Applicants provide this information on a voluntary basis.

4. *Testing.* An employer may give or act upon any professionally developed ability test provided the test is not used as a vehicle to discriminate unfairly on the basis of race, color, religion, sex, or national origin.

5. *Preferential treatment.* The Supreme Court has ruled that Title VII does not *require* the granting of preferential treatment to individuals or groups because of their race, sex, religion, or national origin on account of existing imbalances:

> The burden which shifts to the employer is merely that of proving that he based his employment decision on a legitimate consideration, and not an illegitimate one such as race. . . . Title VII forbids him from having as a goal a work force selected by any proscribed discriminatory practice, but it does not impose a duty to adopt a hiring procedure that maximizes hiring of minority employees. (ref. 33)

6. *Veterans' preference rights.* These are not repealed or modified in any way by Title VII. In *Personnel Administrator of Massachusetts v. Feeney,* the Supreme Court held that while veterans' preference does have an adverse impact on women's job opportunities, this was not caused by an *intent* to discriminate against women.[69] Both men and women veterans receive the same

FIGURE 3-3

The six exemptions to Title VII coverage.

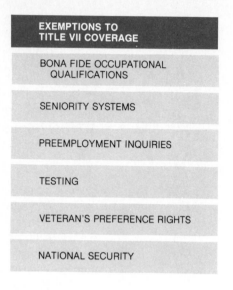

EXEMPTIONS TO TITLE VII COVERAGE
BONA FIDE OCCUPATIONAL QUALIFICATIONS
SENIORITY SYSTEMS
PREEMPLOYMENT INQUIRIES
TESTING
VETERAN'S PREFERENCE RIGHTS
NATIONAL SECURITY

preferential treatment, and male nonveterans are at the same disadvantage as female nonveterans.

7. *National security.* Discrimination is permitted under Title VII when it is deemed necessary to protect the national security (e.g., against members of the Communist party).

Initially it appeared that these exemptions (summarized in Figure 3-3) would blunt the overall impact of the law significantly. However, it soon became clear that they would be interpreted very narrowly both by the EEOC and by the courts.

The Age Discrimination in Employment Act of 1967

As amended in 1986, this act prohibits discrimination in pay, benefits, or continued employment for employees over the age of 40, unless an employer can demonstrate that age is a BFOQ for the job in question. Like Title VII, this law is administered by the EEOC. A key objective of the law is to prevent financially troubled companies from singling out older employees when there are cutbacks. However, the EEOC has ruled that when there are cutbacks, older workers can waive their rights to sue under this law (e.g., in return for sweetened benefits for early retirement) as long as the waiver is voluntary and written simply.[58]

The Immigration Reform and Control Act of 1986

This law applies to *every* employer in the United States, even to those with only one employee. It also applies to every employee—whether full-time, part-time, temporary, or seasonal. The act makes the enforcement of national immigration policy the job of every employer. While its provisions are complex, the basic features of the law fall into four broad categories:[13]

1. Employers may not hire or continue to employ "unauthorized aliens" (that is, those not legally authorized to work in this country).
2. Employers must verify the identity and work authorization of every new employee. Employers must examine documents provided by job applicants (e.g., U.S. passports for U.S. citizens; "green cards" for resident aliens, showing identity and work authorization). Both employer and employee then sign a form (I-9), attesting under penalty of perjury that the employee is lawfully eligible to work in the United States.
3. Employers with 4 to 14 employees may not discriminate on the basis of citizenship or national origin. Those with 15 or more employees are already prohibited from national origin discrimination by Title VII. However, this prohibition is tempered by an exception that allows employers to select an applicant who is a U.S. citizen over an alien when the two applicants are equally qualified.
4. "Amnesty" rights of certain illegal aliens. Those who can prove that they have resided in the United States continuously from January 1982 to November 6, 1986 (the date of the law's enactment) are eligible for temporary, and ultimately for permanent, resident status.

Penalties for noncompliance are severe. For example, for failure to comply with the verification rules, fines range from $100 to $1000 for *each* employee whose identity and work authorization have not been verified. The act also

Naturalization ensures Erica and Samantha Maiorano of their claim to the American dream. The Immigration Reform and Control Act allows employers to select an applicant who is a U.S. citizen over an alien when two applicants are equally qualified. (Source: D. S. Bradshaw (1987), Immigration reform: This one's for you, *Personnel Administrator*, 32(4), p. 37.)

With reasonable accommodation, disabled people can perform many different jobs.

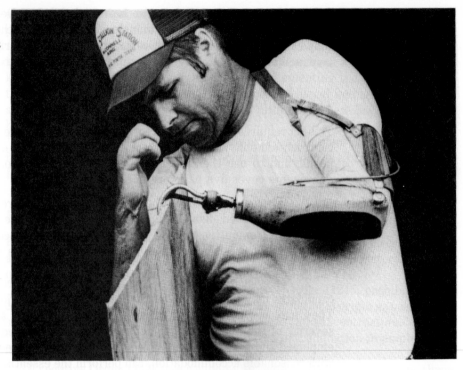

The purpose of this act is to eliminate *systemic discrimination.* i.e., any business practice that results in the denial of equal employment opportunity.[49] The act emphasizes "screening in" applicants, not screening them out. The act is enforced only through disabled applicants' complaints of unfair treatment to the Employment Standards Administration of the Department of Labor.

The Vietnam Era Veterans Readjustment Act of 1974

Federal contractors and subcontractors are required under this act to take affirmative action to ensure equal employment opportunity for Vietnam era veterans (August 5, 1964, to May 7, 1975). This act is enforced by the OFCCP.

Federal Enforcement Agencies: EEOC and OFCCP

The Equal Employment Opportunity Commission is an independent regulatory agency whose five commissioners (one of whom is chairperson) are appointed by the President and confirmed by the Senate for terms of 5 years. No more than three of the commissioners may be from the same political party. Like the OFCCP, the EEOC sets policy and in individual cases determines whether

FIGURE 3-4

Discrimination complaints: the formal process.

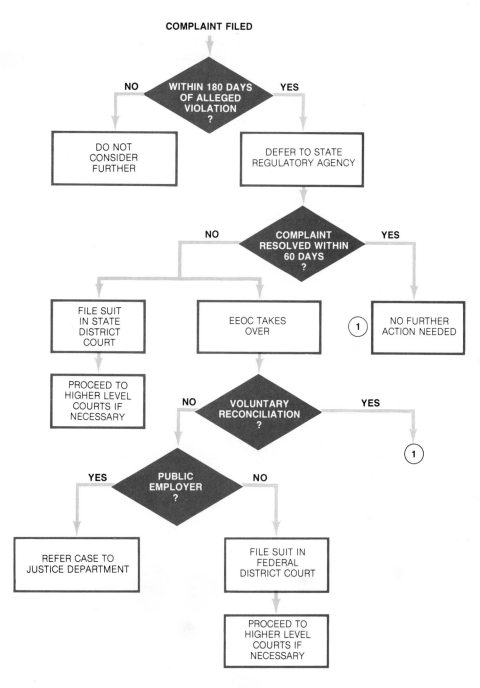

there is "reasonable cause" to believe that unlawful discrimination has occurred. If reasonable cause is found, then the EEOC can sue either on its own behalf or on behalf of a claimant. As far as the employer is concerned, the simplest and least costly procedure is to establish a system of internally resolving complaints that arise. However, if this system fails or if the employer does not make available an avenue for such complaints, an aggrieved individual (or group) can file a formal complaint with the EEOC. The process is shown graphically in Figure 3-4.

As Figure 3-4 indicates, complaints must be filed within 180 days of an alleged violation. If that requirement is satisfied, the EEOC immediately defers to a state agency charged with enforcement of fair employment laws (if one exists) for 60 days. If the complaint cannot be resolved within that time, the state agency can file suit in a state district court and appeal any decision to a state appellate court, the state supreme court, or to the U.S. Supreme Court. Alternatively to filing suit, the state agency may redefer to the EEOC. Again voluntary reconciliation is sought, but if this fails, the EEOC may refer the case to the Justice Department (if the defendant is a public employer) or file suit in federal district court (if the defendant is a private employer). Like state court decisions, federal court decisions may be appealed to one of 12 U.S. Courts of Appeal (corresponding to the geographical region or "circuit" in which the case arose). In turn, these decisions may be appealed to the U.S. Supreme Court, although very few cases are actually heard by the Supreme Court. Generally the Court will grant *certiorari* (review) when two or more circuit courts have reached different conclusions on the same point of law or when a major question of constitutional interpretation is involved. If certiorari is denied, then the lower court's decision is binding.

EEOC guidelines

The EEOC has issued a number of guidelines for Title VII compliance. Among these are guidelines on discrimination because of religion, national origin, sex, and pregnancy; guidelines on affirmative action programs; guidelines on employee selection procedures; and a policy statement on preemployment inquiries. These guidelines are not laws, although the Supreme Court indicated in *Albemarle v. Moody* that they are entitled to "great deference."[1] Violators may incur EEOC sanctions and possible court action.

Information gathering This is another major EEOC function, for each organization in the United States with 100 or more employees must file an annual report (EEO-1) detailing the number of women and minorities employed in nine different job categories ranging from laborers to managers and professionals. Over 300,000 organizations file these forms annually with the EEOC. Through computerized analysis of the forms, the EEOC is able to identify broad patterns of discrimination (systemic discrimination) and to attack them through class action suits. In any given year the EEOC typically has about

500 class action suits in progress, receives 70,000 complaints, and wins monetary awards that total over $36 million.[83]

The Office of Federal Contract Compliance Programs (OFCCP)

Contract compliance means that in addition to quality, timeliness, and other requirements of federal contract work, contractors and subcontractors must also meet equal employment opportunity and affirmative action requirements. These cover all aspects of employment, including recruitment, hiring, training, pay, seniority, promotion, and even benefits.

Companies are willing to go to considerable lengths to avoid loss of government contracts. Over a quarter of a million companies, employing 27 million workers and providing the government with over $100 billion in construction, supplies, equipment, and services, are subject to contract compliance enforcement by the OFCCP.[63] Contractors and subcontractors with more than $50,000 in government business and with 50 or more employees must prepare and implement written affirmative action programs.

In jobs where women and minorities are *underrepresented* in the workforce relative to their availability in the labor force, employers must establish goals and timetables for hiring and promotion. Theoretically, goals and timetables are distinguishable from rigid quotas in that they are flexible objectives that can be met in a realistic amount of time (Figure 3-5). Goals and timetables are not required under the handicapped workers and Vietnam veterans laws.

In its 1986 ruling in *Local 28 Sheet Metal Workers v. EEOC*, the Supreme Court found that Congress specifically endorsed the concept of non-victim-specific racial hiring goals to achieve compliance.[86] Further, the court noted the benefits of flexible affirmative action rather than rigid application of a color-blind policy that would deprive employers of flexibility in administering human resources. How do employers do in practice? One 7-year study of companies that set annual goals for increasing black male employment found that only

FIGURE 3-5

The distinction between rigid quotas and goals and timetables.

QUOTAS	DONE BY SPECIFIC DATE
START	

QUOTAS: INFLEXIBLE; *MUST* BE MET IN A SPECIFIED AMOUNT OF TIME

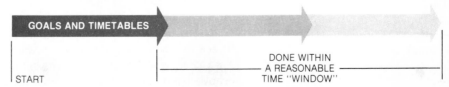

GOALS AND TIMETABLES

START

DONE WITHIN
A REASONABLE
TIME "WINDOW"

GOALS AND TIMETABLES: FLEXIBLE; *CAN* BE MET IN A REALISTIC AMOUNT OF TIME

one-tenth of the goals were achieved. Some may see this as a sign of failure, but it also reflects the fact that the goals were not rigid quotas. "Companies promise more than they can deliver, . . . but the ones that promise more do deliver more" (ref. 68, p. E5).

When a compliance review by the Office of Federal Contract Compliance Programs indicates problems that cannot easily be resolved, it tries to reach a conciliation agreement with the employer. Such an agreement might include back pay, seniority credit, special recruitment efforts, promotion, or other forms of relief for the victims of unlawful discrimination. In fiscal 1980, for example, the OFCCP collected over $9 million in back pay.[59]

The conciliation agreement is the OFCCP's preferred route, but if such efforts are unsuccessful, formal enforcement action is necessary. Contractors and subcontractors are entitled to a hearing before a judge. If conciliation is not reached before or after the hearing, employers may lose their government contracts, their payments may be withheld by the government, or they may be debarred from any government contract work. Debarment is the OFCCP's ultimate weapon, for it indicates in the most direct way possible that the U.S. government is serious about equal employment opportunity programs. Between 1965 and 1980, 24 companies were debarred from government work.[30]

Employment Case Law: Some General Principles

Although Congress enacts laws, the courts interpret the laws and determine how they shall be enforced. Such interpretations define what is called *case law*, which serves as a precedent to guide future legal decisions. And, of course, precedents are regularly subject to reinterpretation.

In the area of employment, a considerable body of case law has accumulated since 1964. Figure 3-6 illustrates areas where case law is developed most extensively. Lawsuits affecting virtually every aspect of employment have been filed, and in the following sections we shall consider some of the most significant decisions to date. It should be pointed out that in bringing suit under Title VII, the first step is to establish a *prima facie* case of discrimination (i.e., a body of facts presumed to be true until proven otherwise). However, the nature of prima facie evidence differs depending on the type of case brought before the court. If an individual is alleging that a particular employment practice had a *disparate impact* on all members of a class that he or she represents, then prima facie evidence is presented when adverse impact is shown to exist. Adverse impact is usually demonstrated by showing that the selection rate for the group in question is less than 80 percent of the rate of the dominant group (e.g., white males). If the individual alleges that he or she was *treated* differently from others in the context of some employment practice, then a prima facie case is usually presented by satisfying a four-part test first

FIGURE 3-6

*Areas comprising
the main body of
employment case
law.*

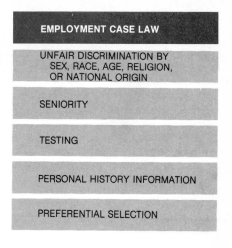

specified in the *McDonnell-Douglas v. Green* case,[64] wherein a plaintiff must be able to demonstrate that:

1. She or he is a member of a class of persons protected by Title VII.
2. She or he applied for and qualified for a job for which the employer was seeking applicants.
3. Despite having the qualifications, the applicant was rejected.
4. After rejection, the position remained open, and the employer continued to seek applications from persons with the plaintiff's qualifications.

Sex discrimination

Title VII explicitly states that the *individual*, not the group, is the appropriate unit to consider in discrimination proceedings. However, sex role stereotypes are deeply rooted in our society, with some jobs deemed absolutely inappropriate for members of a particular sex. Consider firefighting, for example.

> Firefighting, appropriately referred to as "combat" by those who practice it, places the issue of equal rights for women in a harsh light since lives are at stake. In the police force, the significance of an officer's sex is diminished by his or her right to carry a gun. In the armed forces, combat is not an issue; all women are simply channeled into noncombat jobs. Nowhere is there a greater potential for conflict between the ideal of affirmative action and the real need for competent service than in firefighting. (ref. 79, p. 37)

In the wake of a protracted legal battle, New York City swore a group of women into its firefighter training program for the first time in its 117-year history. By itself, that action did little to influence the attitudes of the nearly 12,000 male firefighters in the city, especially since the city itself adopted only a passive nondiscriminatory stance. The extent of its outreach was to open its exam to women in 1978, but 4 years (and almost $2 million) later, the city lost a class action suit by the 410 women who failed the physical ability test. The court ruled that the test discriminated unfairly against women (e.g., the dynamometer used to evaluate grip strength was adjustable for different hand sizes, but it was never actually adjusted for the women during the test) and that it did not evaluate job-related skills.[8] In 1986 the women were granted 2 years' back pay and retroactive seniority rights, that is, the seniority they would have had in 1977 when they first applied, compared to 1982, when they were hired.[4] However, a 1987 federal appeals court ruled that speed, rather than stamina, should be emphasized in the preemployment physical ability test. This standard, according to expert testimony, will make it more difficult for women to join the force.[76]

Suppose you run an organization that has 238 skilled crafts positions—all filled by men. Suppose that only a 2-point difference in test scores separates the best-qualified man from the best-qualified woman. Only one promotional opportunity is available. What do you do? Until a landmark Supreme Court decision in 1987 (*Johnson v. Santa Clara Transportation Agency*[51]), if you promoted the woman you opened yourself to being sued by the man. If you promoted the woman to correct past discrimination (thereby acknowledging past bias), you would open yourself to discrimination suits by women. No longer. The Supreme Court ruled unambiguously that in traditionally sex-segregated jobs, a qualified woman can be promoted over a marginally better-qualified man to promote more balanced representation. The Court stressed the need for affirmative action plans to be flexible, gradual, and limited in their effect on whites and men. The Court also expressed disapproval of strict numerical quotas except where necessary (on a temporary basis) to remedy severe past discrimination.

Many employers are in similar positions. That is, they have not been proven guilty of past discrimination, but they have a significant underrepresentation of women or minorities in various job categories. This decision clearly put pressure on employers to institute voluntary affirmative action programs, but at the same time it also provided some welcome guidance on what they were permitted to do.

Pregnancy   The Equal Employment Opportunity Commission's guidelines on the Pregnancy Discrimination Act of 1979 state:

> The basic principle of the Act is that women affected by pregnancy and related conditions must be treated the same as other applicants and employees on the basis of their ability or inability to work. A woman is therefore protected against such practices as being fired, or refused a job or promotion, merely because she is pregnant or has had an abortion. She usually cannot be forced to go on leave as long as she can still work. If other employees who take disability leave are entitled to get their jobs back when they are able to work again, so are women who have been unable to work because of pregnancy. (ref. 26)

It is important to note that an employer is never *required* to give pregnant employees special treatment. If an organization provides no disability benefits or sick leave to other employees, it is not required to provide them for pregnant employees.[80] While the actual length of maternity leave is now an issue to be determined by the women's and/or the company's physician, a 1987 Supreme Court decision in *California Federal Savings and Loan v. Guerra* upheld a California law that provides for up to 4 months of unpaid leave for pregnancy disability.[17] One large survey of company practices found that new mothers typically spend 1 to 3 months at home following childbirth, that job guarantees for returning mothers were provided by 35 percent of the companies, and that employers of 501 to 1000 employees are most likely to provide full pay.[70]

What percentage of women use disability benefits fully and then decide not to return to work? At Corning Glass Works, First Bank of Minneapolis, and Levi Strauss & Co., over 80 percent *do* return to work. Moreover, the provision of maternity leave benefits has helped to establish good rapport with employees.[70]

How much do these extra benefits cost? The Health Insurance Association of America estimated that the extension of health insurance coverage to pregnancy-related conditions of women employees and employees' spouses would increase premiums by an average of 13 percent.[80]

Reproductive hazards   Another way that sex discrimination may be perpetuated is by barring women from competing for jobs that pose occupational health hazards to their reproductive systems. In 1980 the EEOC and the Department of Labor issued interpretive guidelines on employment discrimination and reproductive hazards. The guidelines state:

> An employer's policy of protecting female employees from reproductive hazards by depriving them of employment opportunities without any scientific data is a per-se violation of Title VII. (ref. 28)

In separate cases, three federal appeals courts have ruled that the exclusion of fertile or pregnant women because of potential reproductive hazards constitutes illegal sex discrimination unless it is scientifically justifiable, or if there are no less discriminatory alternatives.[70] Mere exclusion of workers, both unions and managers agree, does not address chemicals remaining in the workplace where other workers may be exposed. Nor are women more sensitive to reproductive hazards than men. Changing the workplace, rather than the workforce, is a more enlightened policy.

Sexual harassment   In the vast majority of cases on this issue, females rather than males have suffered from sexual abuse at work. Such abuse may constitute illegal sex discrimination. It seems like only yesterday that sexual harassment was not a subject for legal concern. In 1936 one legal commentator expressed the typical (male) supervisor's attitude toward exploiting sexual consideration from female employees when he said, "There's no harm in asking!" At that time the courts found that a woman had no legal remedy unless she was actually assaulted or battered.[61] Today there is a broader view of what constitutes unacceptable behavior, but it is still surprisingly difficult to define sexual harassment. Perhaps the best definition to date is that proposed by the Michigan Task Force on Sexual Harassment in the Workplace:

> Sexual harassment includes . . . continual or repeated abuse of a sexual nature including, but not limited to, graphic commentaries on the victim's body, sexually suggestive objects or pictures in the workplace, sexually degrading words used to describe the victim, or propositions of a sexual nature. Sexual harassment also includes the threat or insinuation that lack of sexual submission will adversely affect the victim's employment, wages, advancement, assigned duties or shifts, academic standing, or other conditions that affect the victim's "livelihood."

This definition specifies examples of unacceptable conduct in the workplace; it does not rely on the victim's perception of objectionable actions. Also, it limits the bringing of sexual harassment suits based on isolated incidents that are not part of a continual or repeated pattern of behavior.[61]

While there are few well-controlled studies of the incidence of sexual harassment, available data indicate that its incidence among working women ranges from 42 to 70 percent.[3] These data indicate that about half the women in the workforce experience sexual harassment at one time or another. It is perilous self-deception for a manager to believe that sexual harassment does not exist in his or her own organization.

The Equal Employment Opportunity Commission has issued guidelines on sexual harassment, indicating that it is a form of sex discrimination under Title VII of the 1964 Civil Rights Act. Courts generally have agreed with this position. However, this is true only when the harassment is a *condition of employment*. For example, consider the case of *Barnes v. Costle:* The plaintiff rebuffed her director's repeated sexual overtures. She ignored his advice that sexual intimacy was the path she should take to improve her career opportunities. Subsequently the director abolished her job. The court of appeals found that sexual cooperation was a condition of her employment, a condition the director did not impose upon males. Therefore, sex discrimination occurred and the employer was liable.[6]

The courts have gone even further, holding employers responsible even if they knew nothing about a supervisor's conduct. For example, a federal appeals court held Avco Corporation of Nashville, Tennessee, liable for the sexually harassing actions of one of its supervisors against two female secretaries working under his supervision. The court found that the employer had a policy against sexual harassment but failed to enforce it effectively. Both the company *and* the supervisor were held liable. Regarding the company's liability, the court noted: "Although Avco took remedial action once the plaintiffs registered complaints, its duty to remedy the problem, or at a minimum, inquire, was created earlier when the initial allegations of harassment were reported" (ref. 22, p. A1).

Such suits can be expensive. In November, 1982, eight women miners won a settlement from Consolidated Coal Co. in a landmark $5.5 million sexual harassment suit. Charging that their privacy had been invaded, the women claimed that male coal miners spied on them as they showered and dressed. A peephole was bored into the women's locker-room wall from a supervisor's office, and although managers knew about the hole for a year, they failed to fill it in. The company settled just before the summation of the case in federal district court.[84]

Preventive actions by employers What can an employer do to escape liability for the sexually harassing acts of its managers or workers? An effective policy should have the following features: (1) a statement from the chief executive that states firmly that sexual harassment will not be tolerated, (2) a workable definition of sexual harassment, (3) a clear statement of possible sanctions for violators and protection for those who make charges, and (4) a clear statement that retaliatory action against an employee who makes charges will not be tolerated.[3, 52] Training and grievance procedures should complement such a policy, for the courts have made it clear that employers are expected to take remedial action as soon as they become aware of sexual harassment (heterosexual by either sex or homosexual by either sex). Such action is not limited to supervisor-subordinate relationships. The EEOC's guidelines hold an employer liable even for harassment of an employee by a nonemployee, such as a customer. The grievance procedure should assist the employee in informing management of any problems. Management must then take immediate and firm action in order to avoid the legal liability possible under the EEOC's guidelines.[38]

Age discrimination

The Equal Employment Opportunity Commission's guidelines on age discrimination emphasize that in order to discriminate fairly against employees over 40 years old, an employer must be able to demonstrate a "business necessity" for doing so. That is, it must be shown that age is a factor directly related to the safe and efficient operation of a business. To establish a prima facie case of age discrimination, an individual must show that:[74]

1. She or he is within the protected age group (over 40 years of age).
2. She or he is doing satisfactory work.
3. She or he was discharged despite satisfactory work performance.
4. The position was filled by a person younger than the person replaced.

For example, an employee named Schwager had worked for Sun Oil Ltd. for 18 years, and his retirement benefits were to be vested (i.e., not contingent on future service) at 20 years. When the company reorganized and had to reduce the size of its workforce, the average age of those retained was 35 years, while the average age of those terminated was 45.7 years. The company was able to demonstrate, however, that economic considerations prompted the reorganization and that factors other than age were considered in Schwager's termination. The local manager had to let one person go, and he chose Schwager because he ranked lowest in overall job performance among salespeople in his district and did not measure up to their standards. Job performance, not age, was the reason for Schwager's termination.

In another case, *Hodgson v. Greyhound Lines*, the Supreme Court upheld a lower court's ruling that the employer was able to show that age was related to the safe conduct of the business.[43] Greyhound contended that age was a bona fide occupational qualification and refused to hire applicants over 40. In the words of the court:

> We find . . . compelling . . . the statistical evidence reflecting, among other things, that Greyhound's safest driver is one who has 16 to 20 years of driving experience with Greyhound and is between 50 and 55 years of age, an optimum blend of age and experience with Greyhound which could never be attained in hiring an applicant 40 years of age or over.

To some, lifting the cap off mandatory retirements at age 70 signals a flood of age-related lawsuits. In many ways, however, it is much ado about nothing. Independent of federal law, 16 states, including Florida and California (the states with the largest concentrations of older people), already prohibit mandatory retirement at any age. There has been no appreciable increase in the number of age-related lawsuits in these states since 1978, the last time the Age Discrimination in Employment Act was amended. Second, the average retirement age in the United States is now 63; it has been falling gradually for the last 25 years despite age protections.[15] Many workers are eager to retire well before the traditional (and arbitrary) age of 65.

Employers can still fire unproductive workers, but the key is to base personnel decisions on ability, not on age. By offering truly voluntary early retirement programs (not "either accept this or you're fired"), firms can still plan for the future. For example, a federal judge recently dismissed a suit brought by four employees of the National Geographic Society challenging the company's early retirement program. The judge reasoned that since the workers had more than 2 months to decide about the plan, and that it really was a benefit, the company could not be sued.[54]

Seniority

Title VII explicitly permits bona fide seniority systems as long as they were not devised with the intent to discriminate unfairly. There has been considerable litigation over seniority (the term has been in vogue since the nineteenth century), but it was not until the Supreme Court's ruling in *California Brewers Assoc. v. Bryant* that a legal definition of the concept was issued.[16] The Court stated:

> "Seniority" is a term that connotes length of employment. A "seniority system" is a scheme that, alone or in tandem with "non-seniority" criteria, allots to employees ever-improving employment rights and benefits as their relative lengths of pertinent employment increase. (ref. 16, pp. 605, 606)

Although the prevalence of seniority clauses varies by type of industry, about 85 percent of union contracts contain such provisions.[66] They are major sources of legal and quasi-legal problems for both unions and management.[35] Legal disputes are subject to resolution by state or federal courts. Quasi-legal disputes are subject to resolution by joint union-management committees.

In the realm of quasi-legal affairs, seniority is the subject of many grievances. Collective bargaining contracts frequently require that personnel decisions regarding, for example, layoff or promotion be based upon a combination of seniority plus ability or qualifications. Grievances over such seniority provisions often are filed because the provisions are seldom precise about the manner of assessing worker ability.[20] In addition, seniority accounts for a substantial number of grievances in declining industries as workers strive to protect their rights to shrinking numbers of jobs.[65]

Unions and management have also encountered legal problems stemming from the impact of established seniority systems on programs designed to ensure equal employment opportunity. Three major seniority issues have been decided by the courts:

1. *Rightful place.* In *Franks v. Bowman Transportation Co.*, the Supreme Court ruled that Title VII does not bar relief in the form of retroactive seniority for minorities who were improperly denied employment opportunities after the effective date of the 1964 Civil Rights Act.[31] The Court concluded that without an award of seniority dating from the time of the company's refusal to hire each properly qualified minority applicant, an employee who applied for and attained such a position would never obtain his or her rightful place in the seniority hierarchy. For example, suppose a candidate applied for work and was unlawfully discriminated against in 1966, but, as a result of the time required to try the case, he or she was not authorized to reapply until 1976. Without an award of retroactive seniority, the candidate would lose 10 years' worth of seniority credit. This "rightful-place" approach has been adopted by the majority of courts evaluating seniority systems in Title VII cases.[35]

2. *Legality of facially neutral seniority systems that perpetuate minorities' employment disadvantage.* In 1977 the Supreme Court ruled in *International Brotherhood of Teamsters v. U.S.* that a bona fide seniority system initiated *prior* to the 1964 Civil Rights Act may apply different terms of employment if it operates in a neutral fashion and is not designed intentionally to discriminate because of race, color, religion, or national origin.[48]

A 1982 Supreme Court decision, *American Tobacco Co. v. Patterson*, extended the *Teamsters* decision to seniority systems implemented *after* 1965 (the effective date of the 1964 Civil Rights Act).[2] Unlike other measures used as a basis for staffing decisions (e.g., tests), the legality of seniority systems will not be judged in terms of adverse impact on women or minorities. The result of this ruling is to make it more difficult for civil rights groups and the EEOC to challenge seniority systems as biased.

3. *Last-hired–first-fired layoffs.* The courts have been quite clear in their rulings on the legitimacy of last-hired–first-fired layoffs (often referred to as

LIFO, or last-in–first-out, layoffs) when such decisions cause a disproportionate reduction in the number of minority and female employees. In two landmark decisions, *Firefighters Local Union No. 1784 v. Stotts*[29] (decided under Title VII) and *Wygant v. Jackson Board of Education*[36] (decided under the equal protection clause of the Fourteenth Amendment), the Supreme Court ruled that an employer may not protect the jobs of recently hired black employees at the expense of whites who have more seniority.[37] Voluntary modifications of seniority policies for affirmative action purposes remain proper, but where a collective bargaining agreement exists, consent of the union is required. Moreover, in the unionized setting, courts have made it clear that the union must be a party to any decree that modifies a bona fide seniority system.[14] Actions to date are encouraging. For example, unions and employers have voluntarily negotiated inverse seniority systems that allow senior workers to choose temporary layoff, thus enabling minority workers with less company service to retain their jobs.

Testing

Title VII clearly sanctions the use of "professionally developed" ability tests. Nevertheless, it took several landmark Supreme Court cases to clarify the proper role and use of tests. The first of these was *Griggs v. Duke Power Co.*, decided in favor of Griggs.[40] The employer was prohibited from requiring a high school education or the passing of an intelligence test as a condition of employment or job transfer where neither standard was shown to be significantly related to job performance:

> What Congress has forbidden is giving these devices and mechanisms controlling force unless they are demonstrably a reasonable measure of job performance. . . . What Congress has commanded is that any tests used must measure the person for the job and not the person in the abstract. (ref. 40, p. 428)

The ruling also included three other general principles:

1. The law prohibits not only open and deliberate discrimination but also practices that are fair in form but discriminatory in operation. For example, suppose an organization wants to use prior arrests as a basis for selection. In theory, arrests are a "neutral" practice since all persons are equally subject to arrest if they violate the law. However, if arrests cannot be shown to be job-related, and, in addition, if a significantly higher proportion of blacks than whites are arrested, then the use of arrests as a basis for selection is discriminatory in operation.
2. It is not necessary for the plaintiff to prove that the discrimination was intentional; intent is irrelevant. If the standards result in discrimination, they are unlawful.
3. Job-related tests and other personnel selection procedures are legal and useful.

Four years later, in *Albemarle Paper Co. v. Moody*, the Court again found for the plaintiff.[1] Albemarle's testing program failed to relate to its jobs in three ways:

1. Tests used to screen applicants for entry-level positions were validated (i.e., demonstrated to be predictive of later job performance) only for positions near the top of the various lines of progression and not at the job levels for which the tests were intended to be used.
2. The company conducted no job analyses to identify specific knowledges, skills, and abilities needed for effective job performance. Instead, it was simply *assumed* that tests validated for several jobs were fully appropriate for all jobs.
3. No specific criteria on which to evaluate individual job performance were developed through job analysis. Instead, supervisors were asked to compare each employee to every other employee and to judge which one of each pair was "better." The Court found such an approach inadequate since "there is no way of knowing precisely what criteria of job performance the supervisors were considering."

Sometimes the problem is not with the tests per se but rather with how the test results are *used*. This point was illustrated in *Guardians Assn. of N.Y. City Police Dept. v. Civil Service Comm. of N.Y.*[41] The city carefully developed its test and validated it using a content validity (nonstatistical) procedure. The city then rank-ordered all applicants in terms of their test scores and selected applicants on the basis of strict numerical scores. This procedure resulted in few minorities being selected, but when challenged, the city could not demonstrate that 1- or 2-point differences in test scores reflected genuine differences in job performance. Without a valid (e.g., statistical) basis for rank-ordering, such a procedure cannot be used.

The confidentiality of individual test scores has also been addressed. In 1979 the Supreme Court affirmed the right of the Detroit Edison Co. to refuse to hand over to a labor union copies of aptitude tests taken by job applicants and to refuse to disclose individual test scores without the written consent of employees.[53]

Personal history

Frequently job qualification requirements involve personal background information. If the requirements have the effect of denying or restricting equal employment opportunity, they may violate Title VII. For example, in the *Griggs v. Duke Power Co.* case, a purportedly neutral practice (the high school education requirement that excluded from employment a higher proportion of blacks than whites) was ruled unlawful because it had not been shown to be related to job performance.[40] Other allegedly neutral practices that have been struck down by the courts on the basis of non-job relevance include:

- Recruitment practices based upon present employee referrals, where the workforce is nearly all white to begin with.[25]
- Height and weight requirements.[24]
- Arrest records, because they show only that a person has been accused of a crime, not that she or he was guilty of it. Thus arrests may not be used as a basis for selection decisions,[39] except in certain sensitive and responsible positions (e.g., police officer, school principal).[82]
- Conviction records, unless the conviction is directly related to the work to be performed—for example, a person convicted of embezzlement applying for a job as a bank teller.[45]

Despite such decisions, it should be emphasized that personal-history items are not unlawfully discriminatory per se, but their use in each instance requires that job relevance be demonstrated. In short, the employer should be collecting information on a "need-to-know," not on a "nice-to-know," basis.

Preferential selection

In an ideal world, selection and promotion decisions would be "color-blind." That is, social policy as embodied in Title VII emphasizes that so-called reverse discrimination (discrimination against whites and in favor of minorities) is just as unacceptable as is discrimination by whites against minorities. As we saw earlier, this was decidedly not the situation in the *Regents of the University of California v. Bakke* case. However, since that case involved the legality of an affirmative action plan at a public educational institution, it did not affect private employers directly. The case of *United Steelworkers of America v. Weber* clearly did: Brian Weber, a white lab analyst at Kaiser Aluminum & Chemical Company's Grammercy, Louisiana, plant, brought suit under Title VII after he was bypassed for a crafts-retraining program in which the company and the union jointly agreed to reserve 50 percent of the available places for blacks.[81] As in *Regents of the University of California*, there was no proven record of bias at the plant on which to justify a quota. Thus the company and the union were caught in a dilemma. To eliminate the affirmative action plan was to run the risk of suits by minority employees and the loss of government contracts. To retain the plan when there was no previous history of proven discrimination was to run the risk of reverse discrimination suits by white employees. And to admit previous discrimination at the plant in order to justify the affirmative action plan was to *invite* suits by minority applicants and employees.

The Supreme Court ruled that employers can give preference to minorities and women in hiring for "traditionally segregated job categories" (i.e., where there has been a societal history of purposeful exclusion of blacks from the job category). Employers need not admit past discrimination in order to establish voluntary affirmative action programs. The Court also noted that the Kaiser plan was a "temporary measure" designed simply to eliminate a manifest racial imbalance.[9]

Subsequent cases have clarified a number of issues left unresolved by *Weber*. Five major affirmative action cases decided by the Supreme Court in 1986 and 1987 resolved several thorny issues for employers:[29, 51, 86]

1. Courts may order, and employers voluntarily may establish, affirmative action plans, including numerical standards, to address problems of underutilization of women and minorities.
2. The plans need not be directed solely to identified victims of discrimination, but may include general, classwide relief.
3. While the courts will almost never approve a plan that would result in whites *losing* their jobs through layoffs, the Court has apparently sanctioned plans that impose limited burdens on whites in hiring and promotions (i.e., postpones them).
4. Numerically based preferential programs should not be used in every instance, and they need not be based on an actual finding of discrimination.[23, 71]

The Supreme Court has not approved no-holds-barred affirmative action. If anything, its decisions suggest a careful balance between the rights of women and minorities and the rights of others competing for the same jobs. As Eleanor Holmes Norton, former chair of the EEOC, noted:

> Affirmative action alone cannot cure age-old disparities based on race or sex. But if Title VII is allowed to do its work, it will speed the time when it has outlived its usefulness and our country has lived up to its promises. (ref. 67, p. A27)

The Social Context of Personnel Decisions

In a broad sense, everything discussed up to this point is relevant to the social context of personnel decisions, even though the emphasis has been primarily on the legal context of personnel decisions. However, the special problems associated with two large, and growing, segments of the working population, women workers and older workers, deserve special mention.

Women in the workforce

Feminism was the last focus of the civil rights movement and of the more general social activism of the late 1960s. Potentially its constituency was the broadest and deepest, and so were the problems it addressed. In 1972 women questioned the possibility of having a family and holding a job at the same time. By the mid-1980s more women—including some of the daughters of the past generation—took it for granted that they should be able to manage both. Five forces account for the changed attitudes:

1. *Changes in the family.* Legalized abortion, contraception, divorce, and a declining birthrate have all contributed to a decrease in the proportion of most women's lives devoted to rearing children. Women are now important providers of family income.

2. *Changes in education.* Ever since World War II, increasing numbers of women have been attending college. By the mid-1980s, about a third of law school, medical school, and MBA students were female.[7]

3. *Changes in self-perception.* Many women experience considerable conflict over the relative importance of their work and family roles and over the social costs associated with upward mobility in the organizations they work for. Thus *a major goal of affirmative action for women is to raise the consciousness level of both women and men so that women can be given a fair chance to think about their interests and potential, to investigate other possibilities, to make an intelligent choice, and then to be considered for openings or promotions on an equal basis with men.*[12]

4. *Changes in technology.* Both in the home (e.g., frozen foods, microwave ovens) and in the workplace (e.g., robotics), advances in technology have reduced substantially the physical effort and time required to accomplish tasks. Thus more women can now qualify for formerly all-male jobs.

5. *Changes in the economy.* Ever since World War II there has been a shift away from goods production and toward service-related industries (e.g., health care, banking, law enforcement). Between now and 1995, almost 9 out of 10 of the 16 million new jobs projected will be in a service-producing industry.[77] Increasing numbers of employees in all types of industry are female.

This social revolution is characterized by these statistics:

- Of families having annual incomes that reach $40,000 to $50,000, 70 percent have working wives.
- Women are expected to hold about a third of the top jobs in major concerns by the year 2001 and to head 10 percent of all companies.[57]
- The percentage of married women in the workforce is now over 55 percent.
- The number of children with mothers who work is now larger than the number of children with mothers at home.
- An affluent, consumer-oriented society has developed that depends on two wage earners to support such a standard of living.

Now for the bad news:

- Of all female workers, 80 percent hold "pink-collar" jobs (i.e., jobs dominated by women) and are paid about 68 cents for every dollar that men earn.
- About 70 percent of all classroom teachers are women, yet for the same job they make an average of $3000 less than their male colleagues.[34]
- The situation is not much brighter on the management level: Despite a 20-year boom in the number of women in the workplace, female managers are mired mostly in the middle ranks. Only 2 percent of top executives are women, even though companies with more than 100 employees average 44 percent women.[10]
- Women in paid jobs still bear most of the responsibility for housework and family care.

In many instances, however, discrimination may not be the primary reason for the earnings gap. It may be that (1) women do not commit themselves to a career as early as men; that (2) most workers remain in sexually segregated jobs, many by choice; and that (3) American culture reinforces traditional roles for women.[73]

Perhaps the major need is for imaginative, creative organizational responses to accommodate the needs of the new workforce and the flexible family. For example, there are not many executives who can appreciate or allow that the skill of time management at home might be applied to office management. Adjustments to work schedules (flextime), extended maternity *and* paternity leaves, and quality day care based near the job come a little closer to workable solutions. Wang Laboratories, Inc., and Stride Rite Corp. have begun model day-care projects that might well become blueprints for other firms to follow.

The aging workforce

It was not too long ago that we used to hear predictions about the "greening" of America. Today organizations are more concerned about the "graying" of America and the composite effects of demographic trends, improvements in life expectancy, and changes in social legislation. Consider some demographic trends forecast by the Bureau of the Census: A middle-aged bulge is forming in the United States as a consequence of the 43 million babies born in the years immediately following World War II. Eventually the 35- to 45-year-old age group will increase by 80 percent, and by the year 2020 this group will be reaching age 65, increasing the relative size of that population from 12 to 17 percent of all Americans, a jump from 31 to 52 million people.[18]

Based on the rate of this change, the population between the ages of 62 and 64 will not be affected dramatically until the year 2000. Between 2000 and 2010 it will grow at a 48 percent rate. However, to assume that there is no cause for concern until 1999 would be an error, for this group will be moving through several critical career phases before reaching the preretirement years.

On top of all this, the 1986 amendments to the Age Discrimination in Employment Act further heighten the concern about job performance in the later years. The actual impact of the legislation depends, of course, on how older workers respond to the opportunity to remain on the job. Labor force participation rates are dropping for workers over age 55. In view of this trend, some companies are concluding that early retirements will offset the effects of extended tenure possibilities.

Research suggests that such a trend reflects worker income, education, job conditions, and retirement security. Dissatisfied workers and those with better pension plans seem more likely to opt out earlier.

What can managers do? Here are six priorities to consider in preparing for the changes in internal organizational environments that will inevitably occur:[78]

1. *Age profile.* Executives should look at the age distribution across jobs, as compared with performance measures, to see what career paths might conceivably open in the future and what past performance measures have indicated about those holding these positions.

2. *Job performance requirements.* Companies should then define more precisely the types of abilities and skills needed for various posts. Clear job specifications must serve as the basis for improved personnel selection, job design, and performance appraisal systems. For example, jobs may be designed for self-pacing, may require periodic updating, or may require staffing by people with certain physical abilities.

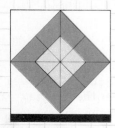

Impact of Legal and Social Factors on Productivity, Quality of Work Life, and the Bottom Line

There are both direct and indirect costs associated with unlawful discrimination. For example, sexual harassment can create high levels of stress and anxiety for both the victim and the perpetrator. These psychological reactions can lead to outcomes that increase labor costs for employers. Job performance may suffer, and absenteeism, sick leave, and turnover may increase. Unlawful discrimination that affects applicants rather than employees (e.g., sex, race, or age discrimination) may lead to recruitment difficulties because such organizations are less attractive to potential applicants. Both internal discrimination against present employees and external discrimination against job applicants can lead to costly lawsuits. Litigation is a time-consuming, expensive luxury that few organizations can afford. Lawsuits affecting virtually every aspect of the employment relationship have been litigated, and many well-publicized awards to victims have reached millions of dollars.

The legal and social aspects of the personnel management process should not be viewed in negative terms exclusively. Most of the present civil rights laws and regulations were enacted as a result of gross violations of individual rights. In most instances, the flip side of unlawful discrimination is good personnel practice. For example, it is good personnel practice to use a variety of recruitment media, not just present employee referrals; it is good practice to use properly developed and validated personnel selection procedures and performance appraisal systems. Similarly, it is good personnel practice to treat people as individuals, and not to rely on stereotyped group membership characteristics (e.g., stereotypes about women, ethnic groups, older workers, disabled workers). Finally, it just makes good sense to pay people equally, regardless of sex, if they are doing the same work. These kinds of personnel practices can enhance productivity, provide a richer quality of work life, and contribute directly to the overall profitability of any enterprise.

3. *Performance appraisal.* Along with improved analyses of jobs, companies must improve their analyses of individual performance. Age biases may be reflected in the format of the appraisal instrument as well as in the attitudes of managers; this is known as *age grading:* subconscious expectations about what people ought to be doing at particular times in their lives.[56] Management training programs should be developed to address and correct both of these biases. Both Banker's Life and Casualty Co. and Polaroid have teams that audit the appraisals of older workers to check for unfair evaluations. These units have also been used to redress general age prejudice in the workplace. Finally, a realistic understanding of current workforce capabilities is essential for effective human resource planning. A company simply cannot adjust its recruitment, selection, and development strategies appropriately without knowing the current strengths and weaknesses of its workers.

4. *Workforce interest surveys.* Once management acquires a better understanding of the basic abilities that workers have, and a clear vision of the company's human resource needs, it must then determine what current workers want. Interest surveys make this possible. Such understanding is essential in reducing the harmful personal and organizational consequences of midcareer plateauing. Moreover, if management decides that it wants to encourage selectively certain types of workers to continue with the organization while encouraging turnover of other types, it must next determine what effects different incentives will have on each group.

5. *Education and counseling.* Workers are understandably concerned about the direction of their lives after terminating current employment. Not surprisingly, therefore, counseling on retirement and second-career development are becoming increasingly common. IBM now offers tuition rebates for courses on *any* topic of interest within 3 years of retirement and continuing into retirement. To meet the needs of the workforce remaining on the job, career planning to avoid midcareer plateauing and training programs to reduce obsolescence should be developed. The educational programs must reflect the special needs of older workers (e.g., self-paced programs), for older workers can learn new tricks, but they need to be taught differently.

6. *Job structure.* Management may have more flexibility than anticipated in changing such conditions as work pace, the length or timing of the workday, leaves of absence, and challenges on the job. Nevertheless, any alternatives to traditional work patterns should be explored jointly with the workforce. Some union leaders, for example, have expressed reservations about part-time workers, whom they fear may threaten the power of organized labor.

A summary of these activities is presented in Figure 3-7.

Yes, America's workforce is aging, but America's organizations are not doomed to senility. Older workers still have much to offer, but organizations must examine their personnel policies carefully to ensure that their people are being used most effectively.

To Prepare for Coming Changes in Internal Organizational Environments

Develop an age profile of the present work force

Carefully assess job performance requirements

Check for possible unfairness in performance appraisals

Use interest surveys to determine what current workers want

Provide opportunities for employee training and career counseling

Explore with workers alternatives to traditional work patterns

---

CASE 3-1 Conclusion

2002: a personnel odyssey

"This is an evaluation of the performance of 927431 interviewing 928563. The legal questions and responses were as follows:

Question: Hello.

Applicant response: Hello.

Question: Are you a human being?

Applicant response: Yes I am.

Question: Are you alive?

Applicant response: Yes.

Statement: You're hired.

Applicant response: OK.

"While 927431 did propose some illegal inquiries, it is clear from the preceding transcript that the applicant was thoroughly interviewed and that virtually every legal line of questioning was pursued. The rating is highly satisfactory."

"Wait a minute. I never told the applicant that he or she was hired." I looked at my performance monitor. He smiled and said, "When it was clear to the computer that there was no justifiable reason for not employing the applicant, the computer added those words in your voice pattern. You've hired your first applicant."

Summary

The following laws were enacted to promote fair employment. They provide the basis for discrimination suits and subsequent judicial rulings:

- U.S. Constitution, Thirteenth and Fourteenth Amendments
- Civil Rights Acts of 1866 and 1871
- Equal Pay Act of 1963
- Title VII of the 1964 Civil Rights Act
- Age Discrimination in Employment Act of 1967 (as amended in 1986)
- Immigration Reform and Control Act of 1986
- Rehabilitation Act of 1973
- Vietnam Era Veterans Readjustment Act of 1974
- Executive Orders 11246, 11375, and 11478

The Equal Employment Opportunity Commission (EEOC) and the Office of Federal Contract Compliance Programs (OFCCP) are the two major federal regulatory agencies charged with enforcing these nondiscrimination laws. The EEOC is responsible for both private and public nonfederal employers, unions, and employment agencies. The OFCCP is responsible for ensuring compliance from government contractors.

TOMORROW'S FORECAST

Many organizations feel "swamped" by the gauntlet of laws, court rulings, and regulatory agency pronouncements that they must navigate through continually. Take heart, for as noted earlier, many of these requirements were established as a result of gross personnel mismanagement. Consider testing, for example. In the wake of the *Griggs v. Duke Power Company* and *Albemarle Paper Company v. Moody* Supreme Court cases, a number of firms abandoned tests. Years later, many of those same firms reinstituted tests but did so on the basis of careful research and conformity to professional standards. This is beneficial for organizations as well as applicants. In tomorrow's world of work, equitable, well-developed personnel policies and practices in virtually all areas can be expected, for a positive side effect of all these laws, rulings, and guidelines is *organizational enlightenment* regarding acceptable and unacceptable practices.

A considerable body of case law has developed, affecting almost all aspects of the employment relationship. Case law is most extensive in the following areas:

- Sex discrimination, sexual harassment, and pregnancy
- Age discrimination in employment
- Seniority
- Testing
- Personal history (specifically, preemployment inquiries)
- Preferential selection

Finally, it is vital that organizations devote special attention to the concerns of two large and growing segments of the working population—women and older workers. The bottom line in both cases is that, as managers, we need to be very clear about job requirements and performance standards, we need to treat people as individuals, and then we must evaluate each individual fairly relative to job requirements and performance standards.

Discussion Questions

3-1 If you were asked to advise a private employer (with no government contracts) of her equal employment opportunity responsibilities, what would you say?

3-2 Putting all the laws, court rulings, and interpretive guidelines into perspective, describe to the employer the downside risks of noncompliance as well as the benefits to be gained from full compliance.

3-3 Prepare a brief outline of an organizational personnel policy on sexual harassment. Be sure to include grievance, counseling, and enforcement procedures.

3-4 What steps would you take as a manager to ensure fair treatment for older employees?

3-5 In your opinion, what rights and privileges does seniority carry with it? What limitations should be placed on these rights and privileges?

References

1. *Albemarle Paper Company v. Moody*, 422 U.S. 407 (1975).
2. *American Tobacco Company v. Patterson*, 535 F2d 257 (CA-4, 1982).
3. Anderson-Davis, S. (1984). Sexual harassment: Facts vs. myths. Aurora, CO: Author.
4. Back pay is awarded to female firefighters (1986, May 15). *New York Times*, p. B11.
5. *Bakke v. Regents of the University of California*, 17 FEPC 1000 (1978).
6. *Barnes v. Costle*, 561 F2d 983 (D.C. Circuit 1977).
7. Bennett, A. (1986, Mar. 24). Following the leaders. *Wall Street Journal*, pp. 10D, 11D.

8. *Berkman et al. v. New York City et al.*, U.S. District Court, Eastern District of New York, 79 C 1813 (1982).

9. Beyond Bakke: High court approves affirmative action in hiring, promotion (1979, June 28). *Wall Street Journal*, pp. 1, 30.

10. Blumenthal, K. (1986, Mar. 24). Room at the top. *Wall Street Journal*, pp. 7D, 9D.

11. Blumrosen, R. (1980). Wage discrimination, job segregation, and women workers. *Employee Relations Law Journal*, **6**, 77–136.

12. Boyle, M. B. (1975). Equal opportunity for women is smart business. *Harvard Business Review*, **51**, 85–95.

13. Bradshaw, D. S. (1987). Immigration reform: This one's for you. *Personnel Administrator*, **32**(4), 37–40.

14. Britt, L. P. III. (1984). Affirmative action: Is there life after *Stotts? Personnel Administrator*, **29**(9), 96–100.

15. Cabot, S. J. (1987). Living with the new amendments to the Age Discrimination in Employment Act. *Personnel Administrator*, **32**(1), 53, 54.

16. *California Brewers Association v. Bryant*, 444 U.S. 598 (1982).

17. *California Federal Savings & Loan Association v. Guerra*, 42 FEP Cases 1073 (1987).

18. U.S. Bureau of the Census (1984, May). Projections of the population of the United States, by age, sex, and race: 1983–2080. *Current Population Reports*, Series P-25, No. 952.

19. Civil rights statutes extended to Arabs, Jews (1987, May 19). *Daily Labor Report*, pp. 1, 2, A-6.

20. Cohen, S. (1979). *Labor in the United States* (4th ed.). Columbus, OH: Charles E. Merrill.

21. Cooper, E. A., & Barrett, G. V. (1984). Equal pay and gender: Implications of court cases for personnel practices. *Academy of Management Review*, **9**, 84–94.

22. Court holds employer liable for harassment by supervisor (1987, June 1). *Daily Labor Report*, pp. A1, D1–D5.

23. Direction shifts with bias ruling (1986, August). *Resource*, pp. 1, 9.

24. *Dothard v. Rawlinson*, 433 U.S. 321 (1977).

25. *EEOC v. Radiator Specialty Company*, 610 F2d 178 (4th Cir. 1979).

26. Equal Employment Opportunity Commission (1979, Mar. 9). Pregnancy Discrimination Act: Adoption of interim interpretive guidelines, questions, and answers. *Federal Register*, **44**, 13,277–13,281.

27. Even though they hate the paperwork, most firms obey the new immigration law (1987, Aug. 28). *Wall Street Journal*, p. 19.

28. Finneran, H. M. (1980). Title VII and restrictions on employment of fertile women. *Labor Law Journal*, **30**, 224.

29. *Firefighters Local Union No. 1784 v. Stotts*, 104 S. Ct. 2576 (1984).

30. Firestone Tire is barred from U.S. jobs as a result of job discrimination case (1980, July 16). *Wall Street Journal*, p. 6.

31. *Franks v. Bowman Transportation Co.*, 424 U.S. 747 (1976).

32. Friedman, A. (1972). Attacking discrimination through the Thirteenth Amendment. *Cleveland State Law Review*, **21**, 161–178.

33. *Furnco Construction Corp. v. Waters*, 438 U.S. 567 (1978).

34. Gamarekian, B. (1987, July 22). Status of women rises, but pay lags, study finds. *New York Times*, p. A23.

35. Gordon, M. E., & Johnson, W. A. (1982). Seniority: A review of its legal and scientific standing. *Personnel Psychology, 35,* 255–280.

36. Grazulis, C. (1978). Understanding Section 503: What does it really say? *Personnel Administrator, 23,* 22–23.

37. Greenhouse, L. (1984, June 13). Seniority is held to outweigh race as a layoff guide. *New York Times,* pp. 1A, B12.

38. Greenlaw, P. S., & Kohl, J. P. (1981). Sexual harassment: Homosexuality, bisexuality, and blackmail. *Personnel Administrator, 26,* 59–62.

39. *Gregory v. Litton Systems, Inc.,* 472 F2d 631 (9th Cir. 1972).

40. *Griggs v. Duke Power Company,* 401 U.S. 424 (1971).

41. *Guardians Assn. of N. Y. City Police Dept. v. Civil Service Comm. of City of N. Y.* (1980, November). *The Industrial-Organizational Psychologist,* pp. 44–49.

42. High-tech advances revolutionize working environments for disabled (1985, December). *Resource,* pp. 1, 9.

43. *Hodgson v. Greyhound Lines, Inc.,* 419 U.S. 1122 (1975).

44. Hurley, E., CPA (1983, Feb. 5). Personal communication.

45. *Hyland v. Fukada,* 580 F2d 977 (9th Cir. 1978).

46. Immigration law creates a subclass of illegals bound to their bosses and vulnerable to abuses (1987, Sep. 2). *Wall Street Journal,* p. 44.

47. Implementation of Executive Order 11914 (1978). *Federal Register, 43,* 2137.

48. *International Brotherhood of Teamsters v. United States,* 432 U.S. 324 (1977).

49. Jackson, D. J. (1978). Update on handicapped discrimination. *Personnel Journal, 57,* 488–491.

50. *Johnson v. Railway Express Agency, Inc.,* 95 S. Ct. 1716 (1975).

51. *Johnson v. Santa Clara Transportation Agency* (1987, Mar. 26). *Daily Labor Report,* pp. A1, D1–D19.

52. Jones, J. E. Jr., Murphy, W. P., & Belton, R. (1987). *Discrimination in employment* (5th ed.). St. Paul, MN: West.

53. Justices uphold utility's stand on job testing (1979, Mar. 6). *Wall Street Journal,* p. 4.

54. Labaton, S. (1987, Aug. 3). Retirements are challenged. *New York Times,* p. D2.

55. Labor Letter (1986, July 15). *Wall Street Journal,* p. 1.

56. Labor Letter (1986, Dec. 2). *Wall Street Journal,* p. 1.

57. Labor Letter (1987, June 16). *Wall Street Journal,* p. 1.

58. Labor Letter (1987, Aug. 25). *Wall Street Journal,* p. 1.

59. Labor Letter (1980, Dec. 16). *Wall Street Journal,* p. 1.

60. Lewin, T. A. (1984, Jan. 1). A new push to raise women's pay. *New York Times,* pp. B–1, B–15.

61. Linenberger, P., & Keaveny, T. J. (1981). Sexual harassment: The employer's legal obligations. *Personnel, 58,* 60–68.

62. Loomis, C. F. (1979, Jan. 15). AT&T in the throes of "equal employment." *Fortune,* pp. 45–57.

63. Lublin, J. S., & Pasztor, A. (1985, Dec. 11). Tentative affirmative action accord is reached by top Reagan officials. *Wall Street Journal,* p. 4.

64. *McDonnell-Douglas v. Green,* 411 U.S. 972 (1973).

65. Miernyk, W. H. (1980). Coal. In G. C. Somers (ed.), *Collective bargaining: Contemporary American experience.* Madison, WI: Industrial Relations Research Organization, pp. 1–48.

66. Miller, R. U. (1980). Hospitals. In G. C. Somers (ed.), *Collective bargaining: Contemporary American experience*. Madison, WI: Industrial Relations Research Organization, pp. 373–433.
67. Norton, E. H. (1987, May 13). Step by step, the court helps affirmative action. *New York Times*, p. A27.
68. Pear, R. (1985, Oct. 27). The cabinet searches for consensus on affirmative action. *New York Times*, p. E5.
69. *Personnel Administrator of Massachusetts v. Feeney*, 19 FEP cases, 1377 (June 5, 1979).
70. *Pregnancy and employment: The complete handbook on discrimination, maternity leave, and health and safety*. (1987). Washington, DC: Bureau of National Affairs.
71. Replying in the affirmative (1987, Mar. 9). *Time*, p. 66.
72. Rogers, J. (1983, Jan. 28). Chairman of the board, RNL architects, Denver. Personal communication.
73. Rosenberg, R. (1986, Feb. 27). What harms women in the workplace. *New York Times*, p. A23.
74. *Schwager v. Sun Oil Company of PA*, 591 F2d 58 (10th Cir. 1979).
75. Settlement a victory for comparable worth (1986, Apr. 12). *Denver Post*, p. 1A.
76. Shipp, E. R. (1987, Apr. 14). Ruling could curtail hiring new women in fire department. *New York Times*, pp. A1, B4.
77. Silvassy, K. (1987, Apr. 4). Jobs on horizon for 1990s. *Atlanta Constitution*, pp. 1S, 4S.
78. Sonnenfeld, J. (1980). Dealing with the aging workforce. In E. L. Miller, E. H. Burack, & M. H. Albrecht (eds.), *Management of human resources*. Englewood Cliffs, NJ: Prentice-Hall.
79. Stabiner, K. (1982, July 11). The storm over women firefighters. *New York Times Magazine*, pp. 23ff.
80. Trotter, R., Zacur, S. R., & Greenwood, W. (1982). The pregnancy disability amendment: What the law provides, Part II. *Personnel Administrator*, **27**, 55–58.
81. *United Steelworkers of America v. Weber*, 99 S. Ct. 2721 (1979).
82. *Webster v. Redmond*, 599 F2d 793 (7th Cir. 1979).
83. Williams, L. (1987, Feb. 8). Harnessing the horses on job discrimination. *New York Times*, p. 54.
84. Women miners win Peeping Tom suit (1982, November). *Coal Age*, pp. 11, 13.
85. What's women's work worth? (1984, Feb. 17). *New York Times*, p. A-30.
86. *Wygant v. Jackson Board of Education*, 106 S. Ct. 1842 (1986); *Local 28 Sheet Metal Workers v. E.E.O.C.*, 106 S. Ct. 3019 (1986); *Local 93 Firefighters v. Cleveland*, 106 S. Ct. 3063 (1986).

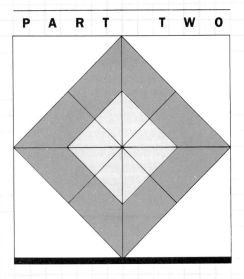

Employment

Now that you understand the environmental context within which human resource management activities take place, it is time to address three major aspects of the employment process: analyzing and designing jobs, determining their human resource requirements, and hiring employees. Logically, before an organization can select employees, it needs to be able to specify *what* work needs to be done, *how* it should be done, the *number* of people needed, and the *knowledge, skills, abilities, and other characteristics* required to do the work. Chapter 4 addresses the twin issues of job analysis and job design. Chapter 5 considers the emerging area of human resource planning, with special emphasis on the development of integrated human resource planning systems. Finally, Chapter 6 examines recruitment, screening, and personnel selection—why they are done, how they are done, and how they can be evaluated.

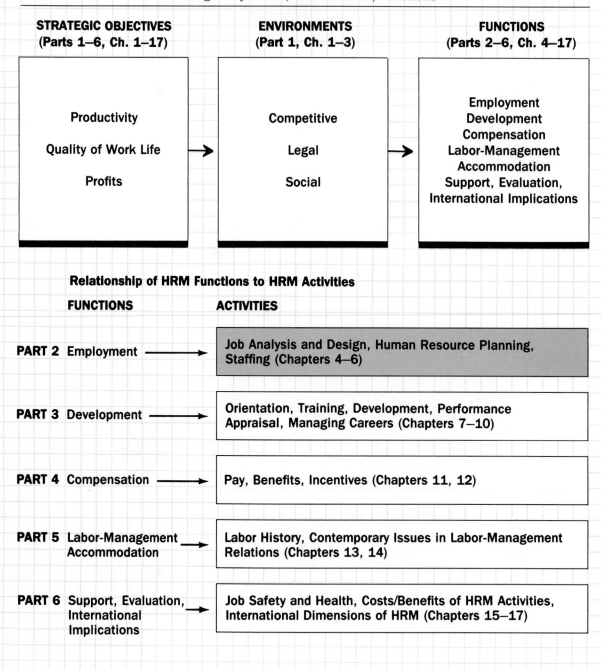

A Conceptual View of Human Resource Management:
Strategic Objectives, Environments, Functions

STRATEGIC OBJECTIVES (Parts 1–6, Ch. 1–17)	ENVIRONMENTS (Part 1, Ch. 1–3)	FUNCTIONS (Parts 2–6, Ch. 4–17)
Productivity Quality of Work Life Profits	Competitive Legal Social	Employment Development Compensation Labor-Management Accommodation Support, Evaluation, International Implications

Relationship of HRM Functions to HRM Activities

FUNCTIONS	ACTIVITIES
PART 2 Employment	Job Analysis and Design, Human Resource Planning, Staffing (Chapters 4–6)
PART 3 Development	Orientation, Training, Development, Performance Appraisal, Managing Careers (Chapters 7–10)
PART 4 Compensation	Pay, Benefits, Incentives (Chapters 11, 12)
PART 5 Labor-Management Accommodation	Labor History, Contemporary Issues in Labor-Management Relations (Chapters 13, 14)
PART 6 Support, Evaluation, International Implications	Job Safety and Health, Costs/Benefits of HRM Activities, International Dimensions of HRM (Chapters 15–17)

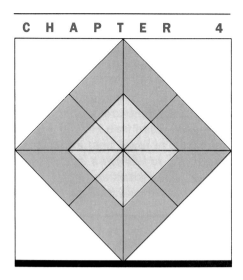

Analyzing and Designing Jobs

When it opened in 1948, Western Electric Co.'s Allentown, Pennsylvania, plant represented what the industrial future would be for all similar firms. Peering through microscopes, 700 women manually assembled the nation's first commercially produced transistors, creating an electronic revolution whose consequences are still burgeoning. Today the Allentown plant remains in the vanguard, producing the most sophisticated computer memory chips available. But the nature of the work has changed. The old airy rooms have given way to "clean cells" that filter out dust and humidity. Workers monitor computer consoles while numerically controlled machines make minute etchings on the silicon wafers. One observer of all this commented that Allentown is a symbol of what will happen all across American industry—skilled workers have become intelligent caretakers, and someday those workers, too, will disappear. This trend suggests that Americans are in for a decade of sweeping demographic, economic, and geographical realignment, and many will be wounded along the way.[29]

The American job market is undergoing the most fundamental change in more than four decades. High labor costs, outdated equipment, and global economic competition have forced smokestack industries to shrink; the United States may never regain its competitive advantage in autos, rubber, and steel.

Meanwhile, the service and high-tech industries in the United States are spawning new jobs—jobs that require skills that many workers simply do not possess.

On the other hand, the development of the microprocessor makes possible computers and automated equipment that can be operated by workers having very few or no technical skills. Indeed, after the installation of automated equipment in one firm, researchers found that the skills required went down, but the pay went up. Monitoring automated machines is not very difficult, but neither is it very interesting. This created the personnel management problem of identifying workers who would perform the job "responsibly." The company upgraded the job classification and the level of pay as a way of attracting these workers. But pay alone may not solve the problem of boredom in such jobs, as the following incident illustrates:

> The problem with the closed-circuit television system is that while it may perfectly well show someone sneaking up the back stairs, . . . the system is really only as alert as the guard in the back room monitoring the television screens where the cameras report what they see. And guards, although their payroll constitutes a substantial portion of museum budgets, simply aren't as attentive as one might guess. In fact a Federal agency . . . completed an 18-month long test . . . [that resulted in a disturbing conclusion]. Several thousand covert intrusions were conducted within view of closed-circuit television cameras monitored by professional guards, and only 5 percent were detected. (ref. 27)

The preceding example indicates that the new technology does not succeed in what it can do for two reasons: (1) It still needs human monitoring, and (2) no one has determined how to get the human to do the monitoring without becoming bored.

Nevertheless, there is plenty of technology now and more developing that will provide unprecedented opportunity for a stimulating sense of contribution for workers. The explosion of new technology will vastly increase the nation's ability to produce. Increased productivity produces economic activity and hence greater employment and wages.[29] Yet not all workers will enjoy opportunities resulting from this explosion. The new technological and economic order will involve a tremendous amount of individual displacement that will continue for a long time. In many basic industries the American worker has simply been priced out of world markets; in others his or her employer must automate rapidly in order to meet emerging competitive threats from abroad. As the head of Arthur D. Little's computer-integrated manufacturing group noted, "The question from manufacturers is whether they are going to reduce their workers by 25 percent by putting in robots, or by 100 percent by going out of business."[29]

In short, we are witnessing changes in the nature of work itself, as well as in the types of jobs available. This is altering how people regard their jobs. As already noted, new technology has reduced many skilled workers to the status of "intelligent caretakers." If organizations are to be maximally efficient, therefore, in the use of scarce (high-priced?) talent, the behavioral requirements of jobs must be understood carefully so that jobs can be designed to produce efficient and satisfying work. The obvious payoff is in higher productivity and a healthier bottom line for the firm and a more satisfying, rewarding quality of work life for employees.

QUESTIONS
1. What are some reasons why changes in the fundamental nature of work are occurring?
2. What steps should a worker take to be a beneficiary, not a victim, of these changes?
3. From a broad, macro perspective, develop an "action agenda" to help smooth the difficult transition that so many present and future workers face. Include specific strategies to be taken by the government, private industry, and educational institutions.

What's Ahead

Case 4-1 describes an all-too-common situation today: Fundamental changes are occurring in the nature of work. In order to manage these changes and the people who are affected by them, it is necessary to describe job requirements (this is the process of job analysis) and to design jobs that encourage improvements in productivity and in the quality of work life (this is the process of job design). This chapter begins by examining why and how we analyze job requirements. It then explores both classical and modern approaches to designing jobs. We will consider job design from three perspectives: individuals, groups, and self-managing work teams. We will also consider what is known about modified work schedules: condensed workweeks, flexible hours, and telecommuting. The chapter concludes with a review of company practices that illustrate new approaches to work design.

Alternative Perspectives on Jobs

Jobs are frequently the subject of conversation: "I'm trying to get a job"; "I'm being promoted to a new job"; "I'd sure like to have my boss's job." Or, as Samuel Gompers, first president of the American Federation of Labor, once said, "A job's a job; if it doesn't pay enough, it's a lousy job."

Jobs are important to individuals: They help determine standards of living, places of residence, status (value ascribed to individuals because of their position), and even one's sense of self-worth. Jobs are important to organizations because they are the vehicles through which work (and thus organizational objectives) are accomplished. The way to manage people to work efficiently is through answers to such questions as:

Who specifies the content of each job?

Who decides how many jobs are necessary?

Samuel Gompers, fiery ex-president of the American Federation of Labor. One of his most famous lines occurred in response to the question "What makes a good job?" His response: "A job's a job; if it doesn't pay enough, it's a lousy job."

How are the interrelationships among jobs determined and communicated?

Has anyone looked at the number, design, and content of jobs from the perspective of the entire organization, the "big picture"?

What are the minimum qualifications for each job?

What should training programs stress?

How should performance be measured on each job?

How much is each job worth?

Unfortunately, there is often a tendency, even an urgency, to get on with work itself ("Get the job done!") rather than to take the time to think through these basic questions. But this tendency is changing as firms struggle to cope with such problems as stagnant productivity, deregulation, and global economic competition. American firms are rethinking the fundamental principles that underlie the design of jobs. Experiments in job design that we consider "common" today, such as product assembly in steps by small groups of workers headed by a team leader, were considered radical departures from tried-and-true formulas only a few years ago. There is now a very practical, pressing reason for reexamining job design: The ability of our industries to compete—and, in some cases, to survive—is at stake.

Terminology of the study of work

Although terms like *task*, *duty*, and *job*, among others, are often used interchangeably in common conversation, technically there are distinct differences between them. Since these terms will be used throughout the book, let's be

FIGURE 4-1

The terms occupation, job family, job, position, duty, *and* task *in the context of a professional baseball team.*

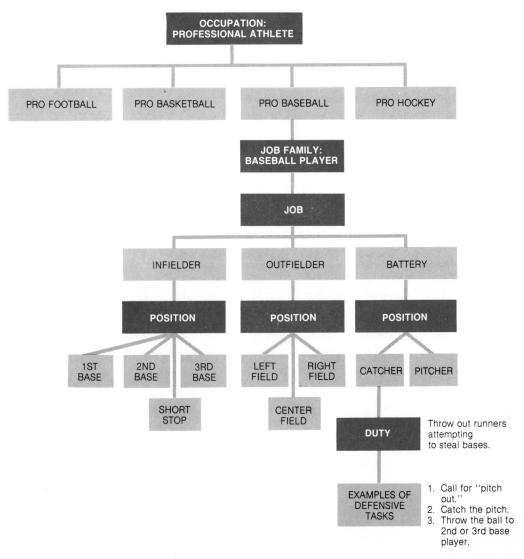

FIGURE 4-2

A hypothetical career in professional baseball.

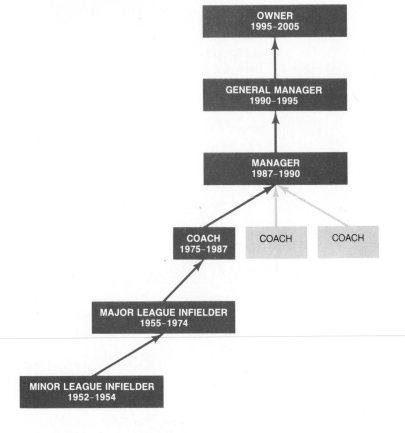

clear about the distinct meaning of each. The definitions that follow are generally consistent with those used by the U.S. Department of Labor:[44]

- A *task* is a distinct work activity carried out for a distinct purpose. Posting a ledger, typing a letter, and running a computer program are examples of tasks.
- A *duty* includes a large segment of the work comprising any number of tasks performed by an individual. An example of a duty of a personnel officer is "conducting a pay survey." This duty comprises the following tasks: (1) designing the survey questions, (2) distributing the survey to respondents, (3) tabulating and interpreting the results, and (4) distributing the results to the survey respondents. In the context of job analysis, the term *duty* does not imply a sense of "obligation" to perform.
- A *position* consists of one or more duties performed by a given individual in a given firm at a given time, such as director of marketing. There are as many positions in a firm as there are workers.
- A *job* is a group of positions that are similar in their significant duties, such as two or more computer programmers—level I. It is possible, however,

for a job to involve only one position, depending on the size of the organization, such as the director of marketing or vice president of research.

- A *job family* is a group of two or more jobs that either require similar worker characteristics or contain parallel work tasks: for example, sales jobs and production jobs.
- An *occupation* is a group of similar jobs found in different organizations at different times: for example, accountants, engineers, and purchasing agents. The distinction between a job and an occupation is chiefly one of scope. The term *job* is used more narrowly and implies a within-organization reference. The term *occupation* implies an across-organization reference.
- A *career* covers a sequence of positions, jobs, or occupations that one person engages in during his or her working life.

Figures 4-1 and 4-2 illustrate each of the concepts behind and the relationships between the terms used in the study of work.

The term *job analysis* describes the process of obtaining information about jobs. As we shall soon see, this information is useful for a number of business purposes. Regardless of how it is collected, it usually includes information about the tasks to be done on the job, and the personal characteristics (education, experience, specialized training) necessary to do the tasks.

An overall written summary of task requirements is called a *job description*. An overall written summary of worker requirements is called a *job specification*.

Together, a job description and a job specification comprise a job analysis. An abbreviated example of a job description is shown in Figure 4-3, and an abbreviated example of a job specification is shown in Figure 4-4.

Why study job requirements?

Sound personnel management practice dictates that thorough, competent job analyses always be done, for they provide a deeper understanding of the behavioral requirements of jobs. This in turn creates a solid basis on which to make job-related personnel decisions. Unfortunately, job analyses are often done for a specific purpose (e.g., training design) without consideration of the many other uses of this information. Some of these other uses, along with a brief description of each, are listed below. Many of them have been incorporated into Figure 4-5.

Organizational structure and design. By clarifying job requirements and the interrelationships among jobs, responsibilities at all levels can be specified, promoting efficiency and minimizing overlap or duplication.

Human resource planning. Job analysis is the foundation for forecasting the need for human resources as well as for plans for such activities as training, transfer, or promotion. Frequently job analysis information is incorporated into a human resource information system (HRIS).

Job evaluation and compensation. Before jobs can be ranked in terms of their overall worth to an organization or compared to jobs in other firms

FIGURE 4-3

*A portion of a job
description.*

Position Title: Labor Relations Specialist

Reports To: Manager, Labor Relations

ACCOUNTABILITY OBJECTIVE:

Serves as an assistant to the Manager of the Labor Relations section of
the Personnel Department by providing effective and efficient support
in organizational maintenance of the labor-management relations
function.

SPECIFIC ACCOUNTABILITIES:

1. Provides expert opinion on the interpretation of company policies
   and procedures, collective bargaining contracts, and local, state,
   and federal laws.

2. Assists supervisors in composing documentation when disciplinary
   action is pending to ensure inclusion of all pertinent facts leading to
   the violation of company policy and procedures.

3. Resolves grievance cases filed by the union, as well as grievance
   cases filed by non-bargaining-unit employees.

4. Provides monthly statistics on the number of disciplinary actions and
   issues.

5. Assembles data for contract negotiations by assisting in the preparation of analyses of job classifications, statistics relative to bargaining unit's turnover, pay recommendations, and benefits.

6. Assists in supervisory training through individual and group discussions of the role of the supervisor in counseling, disciplinary actions,
   and grievance procedures.

FIGURE 4-4

*A portion of a job
specification.*

Position Title: Labor Relations Specialist

Required Knowledges, Abilities, and Skills

1. Knowledge of fundamental personnel management/utilization
   principles.

2. Knowledge of basic statistical methods.

3. Knowledge of basic principles of compensation administration.

4. Knowledge of principles and laws pertaining to labor relations and
   collective bargaining.

5. Ability to interpret and explain company personnel policies, rules,
   and regulations.

6. Ability to communicate effectively, both verbally and in writing.

7. Ability to assess a situation, draw valid conclusions, and make
   sound recommendations.

FIGURE 4-5

Job analysis is the foundation for many human resource management programs. (Source: R. C. Page and D. M. Van De Voort (1988), Human resource planning and job analysis. In W. F. Cascio (ed.), Planning, employment, and placement, vol. 2 of the ASPA/BNA Human resource management series. Washington, DC: Bureau of National Affairs.)

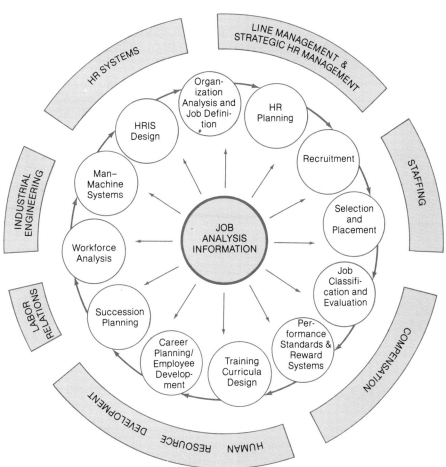

for purposes of pay surveys, their requirements must be understood thoroughly. Job descriptions and specifications provide such understanding to those who must make job evaluation and compensation decisions.

Recruitment. The most important information an executive ("headhunter") or company recruiter needs is full knowledge of the job(s) in question.

Selection. Any method used to select or promote applicants must be based on a keen, meaningful forecast of job performance. An understanding of just what a worker is expected to do on the job, as reflected in job-related interviews or test questions, is necessary for such a meaningful forecast.

Placement. In many cases, applicants are first selected and then placed on one of many possible jobs. When there is a clear picture of the needs of a job and the abilities of the workers to fulfill those needs, then personnel selection decisions will be accurate, and workers will be placed in the specific jobs where they will be the most productive. That is, selection and placement tend to go hand in hand. On the other side of the selection-placement coin, when there is a blurred picture of the needs of a job, personnel selection decisions will not be accurate, and placement will probably be worse.

Orientation, training, and development. Training a worker can be very costly, as we shall see later. Up-to-date job descriptions and specifications help ensure that training programs reflect actual job requirements. In other words, "What you learn in training today you'll use on the job tomorrow."

Performance appraisal. If employees are to be judged in terms of how well they do those parts of their jobs which really matter, those which distinguish effective from ineffective performers, then critical and non-critical job requirements must be specified. Job analysis does this.

Career path planning. If the organization (as well as the individual) does not have a thorough understanding of the requirements of available jobs and how jobs at succeeding levels all relate to one another, then effective career path planning is impossible.

Labor relations. The information provided by job analysis is helpful to both management and unions for contract negotiations, as well as for resolving grievances and jurisdictional disputes.

Engineering design and methods improvement. To design equipment to perform a specific task reliably and efficiently, engineers must understand exactly the capabilities of the operator and what he or she is expected to do. Similarly, any improvements or proposed new working methods must be evaluated relative to their impact on the overall job objectives.

Job design. As with methods improvement, changes in the way work is accomplished must be evaluated through a job analysis, focusing on the tasks to be done and on the behaviors required of the people doing the tasks.

Safety. Frequently, in the course of doing a job analysis, unsafe conditions (environmental conditions or personal habits) are discovered and thus may lead to safety improvements.

Vocational guidance and rehabilitation counseling. Informed decisions regarding career choices may be derived meaningfully from comprehensive job descriptions and specifications.

Job classification systems. Selection, training, and pay systems are often keyed to job classification systems, also referred to as "job families." Without job analysis information, it is impossible to determine reliably the structure of the relationships between jobs in an organization.

Dynamic characteristics of jobs

There are two basic things to keep in mind when thinking about what job analysis is and what it should accomplish:

One, as time goes on, everything changes, and so do jobs. This has been recognized only recently; the popular view of a job was that what it required did not change; a job was a static thing, designed to be consistent although the workers who passed through it were different. Now we know that for a job to produce efficient output, it must change according to the workers who do it. In fact, the nature of jobs might change for three reasons:[3]

- *Time.* For example, lifeguards, ski instructors, and accountants do different things at different times of the year.
- *People.* Particularly in management jobs but also in teaching or coaching, the job is what the incumbent makes of it.
- *Environment.* Such changes may be technological—for example, word processing has drastically changed the nature of many secretarial jobs. Or the changes may be situational, as in a recent collective bargaining agreement between Gulf Oil Corp. and the Oil, Chemical, and Atomic Workers union, in which the company has "total flexibility" in assigning work across traditional craft lines; thus welders may be assigned as helpers to pipe fitters, boilermakers, and forklift operators.

Two, job analysis comprises job specifications and people requirements that should reflect *minimally* acceptable qualifications for job holders. Frequently they do not, reflecting instead a profile of the *ideal* job holder. For example, in evaluating positions for government and industry, the EEOC found that more than 65 percent of the jobs requiring a college degree could easily be handled by workers who are not college graduates.[13]

How are job specifications set? Typically by consensus among experts—immediate supervisors, job incumbents, and job analysts. Such a procedure is professionally acceptable, but care must be taken to distinguish between required and desirable qualifications. The term *required* denotes inflexibility; that is, it is assumed that without this qualification, an individual absolutely would be unable to do the job. *Desirable* implies flexibility; it is "nice to have" this ability, but it is not a "need to have." To be sure, required qualifications will exist in almost all jobs, but care must be exercised in establishing them, for they must meet a higher standard.

How do we study job requirements?

There are a number of methods used to study jobs. At the outset it is important to note that no one of them is sufficient. Some combination of methods must be used to obtain a total picture of the task and the physical, mental, social, and environmental demands of the job. Here are five common methods of job analysis:

1. *Job performance.* With this approach, an analyst actually does the job under study to get firsthand exposure to what it demands. (In the 1980 Florida

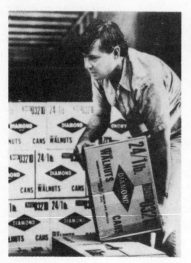

To identify with workers' concerns, ex-Florida governor Bob Graham worked 100 different jobs in 100 days during his election campaign. Here he is shown unloading a truckload of walnuts into a warehouse, covered with mud as he works a drilling rig, and in his official capacity as governor.

governor's race, one of the candidates actually performed 100 different jobs so that he could better identify with the workers' concerns.)

2. *Observation.* The analyst simply observes a worker or group of workers doing a job. Without interfering, the analyst records the what, why, and how of the various parts of the job. Usually this information is recorded in a standard format.

3. *Interview.* In many jobs where it is not possible for the analyst actually to perform the jobs (e.g., airline pilot) or where observation is impractical (e.g., architect), it is necessary to rely on workers' own descriptions of what is done, why it is done, and how it is done. Like recordings of observations, a standard format should be used to collect input from all workers to survey the requirements of a particular job. In this way all questions and responses can be restricted to job-related topics. But more important, standardization makes it possible to compare what different people are saying within the overall survey.

4. *Critical incidents.* These are vignettes comprising brief actual reports that illustrate particularly effective or ineffective worker behaviors. For example:

> On January 14, Mr. Vin, the restaurant's wine steward, was asked about an obscure bottle of wine. Without hesitation, he described the place of vintage and bottling, the meaning of the symbols on the label, and the characteristics of the grapes in the year of vintage.

When a large number of these little incidents are collected from knowledgeable individuals, they are abstracted and categorized according to the general job area they describe. The end result draws a fairly clear picture of actual job requirements.

5. *Structured questionnaires.* With this approach, the worker is presented with a list of tasks or a list of behaviors (e.g., negotiating, coordinating, using both hands), or both. Each task or behavior is rated in terms of whether or not it is performed, and, if so, it is further described in terms of characteristics such as frequency, importance, difficulty, and relationship to overall performance. The ratings provide a basis for scoring the questionnaires and for developing a profile of actual job requirements.[7] One of the most popular structured questionnaires is the Position Analysis Questionnaire (PAQ).

The PAQ is a behavior-oriented job analysis questionnaire.[33] It consists of 194 items that fall into the following categories:

Information input. Where and how the worker gets the information to do her or his job

Mental processes. The reasoning, planning, and decision making involved in a job

Work output. Physical activities as well as the tools or devices used

Relationships with other persons.

Job context. Physical and social

The items provide either for checking a job element if it applies or for rating it on a scale, such as in terms of importance, time, or difficulty. An example of some PAQ items is shown in Figure 4-6. While structured job

FIGURE 4-6
Sample PAQ items.

5.3 Personal and Social Aspects	

Code	Importance to This Job (I)
DNA	Does not apply
1	Very minor
2	Low
3	Average
4	High
5	Extreme

This section includes various personal and social aspects of jobs. Indicate by code the *importance* of these aspects as part of the job.

148　I　Civic obligations (because of the job the worker assumes, or is expected to assume, certain civic obligations or responsibilities)

149　I　Frustrating situations (job situations in which attempts to deal with problems or to achieve job objectives are obstructed or hindered, and may thus contribute to frustration on the part of the worker)

150　I　Strained personal contacts (dealing with individuals or groups in "unpleasant" or "strained" situations, for example, certain aspects of police work, certain types of negotiations, handling certain mental patients, etc.)

analysis questionnaires are growing in popularity, the newest applications use computer-generated graphics to help illustrate similarities and differences across jobs and organizational units.[37]

The preceding five methods of job analysis represent the popular ones in use today. Table 4-1 considers the pros and cons of each method. Regardless of the method used, the workers providing job information to the analyst must be knowledgeable about the jobs in question[11, 17]; however, there seem to be

TABLE 4-1 *Advantages and disadvantages of five popular job analysis methods*

Job Performance

Advantages   With this method there is exposure to actual job tasks; to the physical, environmental, and social demands of the job. It is appropriate for jobs that can be learned in a relatively short period of time.

Disadvantages   This method is inappropriate for jobs that require extensive training or are hazardous to perform.

Observation

Advantages   Direct exposure to jobs can provide a richer, deeper understanding of job requirements than workers' descriptions of what they do.

Disadvantages   If the work in question is primarily mental, observations alone may reveal little useful information. Critical yet rare job requirements (e.g., "copes with emergencies") simply may not be observed.

Interviews

Advantages   This method can provide information about standard as well as nonstandard activities and about physical as well as mental work. Since the worker is also his or her own observer, he or she can report on activities that would not be observed often. In short, the worker can provide the analyst with information that might not be available from any other source.

Disadvantages   Workers may be suspicious of interviewers and their motives; interviewers may ask ambiguous questions. Thus distortion of information (either as a result of honest misunderstanding or as a result of purposeful misrepresentation) is a real possibility. For this reason, the interview should never be used as the sole job analysis method.

Critical Incidents

Advantages   This method focuses directly on what people do in their jobs, and thus it provides insight into job dynamics. Since the behaviors in question are observable and measurable, information derived from this method can be used for most possible applications of job analysis.

Disadvantages   It takes considerable time to gather, abstract, and categorize the incidents. Also, since by definition the incidents describe particularly effective or ineffective behavior, it may be difficult to develop a profile of average job behavior—our main objective in job analysis.

Structured Questionnaires

Advantages   This method is generally cheaper and quicker to administer than other methods. Questionnaires can be completed off the job, thus avoiding lost productive time. Also, where there are large numbers of job incumbents, this method allows an analyst to survey all of them, thus providing a breadth of coverage that is impossible to obtain otherwise. Furthermore, such survey data often can be quantified and processed by computer, which opens up vast analytical possibilities.

Disadvantages   Questionnaires are often time-consuming and expensive to develop. Rapport between analyst and respondent is not possible unless the analyst is present to explain items and clarify misunderstandings. Such an impersonal approach may have adverse effects on respondent cooperation and motivation.

no differences in the quality of information provided by high as opposed to low performers.[9] In terms of the types of data actually collected, the most popular methods today are observation, interviews, and structured questionnaires.

Analyzing managerial jobs

There are a number of special considerations in analyzing managerial jobs. One is that managers tend to adjust the content of their jobs to fit their own styles rather than to fit the needs of the managerial tasks to be done. The result of this is that when it comes to querying them about their work, they will describe what they actually do, having lost sight of what they should be doing. Another consideration is that it is difficult to identify what a manager does over time because her or his activity differs from time to time, whether it be one activity one month or week or day, and then some other activity the following day or week or month. Indeed, managers' activities change throughout the day. As immediate situations or general environments change, so will the content of a manager's job, and each such change will affect managers differently in different functional areas, different geographical areas, and different organizational levels (i.e., first-line supervisors versus divisional vice presidents). To analyze them, we must identify and measure the fundamental dimensions along which they differ and change. That is, we must identify what managers actually do on their jobs, and then we must specify behavioral differences due to time, person, and environmental changes.

Two methods of analyzing managerial jobs are based on questionnaires. They are the Management Position Description Questionnaire (MPDQ) and the Supervisor Task Description Questionnaire (STDQ).

The MPDQ is a 197-item behaviorally based instrument for describing, comparing, classifying, and evaluating executive positions in terms of their content.[42] An example of one portion of the MPDQ is shown in Figure 4-7.

The STDQ describes 100 work activities of first-line supervisors in seven areas:[12]

- Working with subordinates
- Organizing work of subordinates
- Work planning and scheduling
- Maintaining efficient quality and production
- Maintaining safe and clean work areas
- Maintaining equipment and machinery
- Compiling records and reports

Responses from 251 first-line supervisors from 40 plants yielded few differences in the supervisors' jobs regardless of technology or function. These results imply that with the exception of the technical knowledge that may be required in a first-line supervisory job, organizations should be able to develop selection, training, and performance appraisal systems for first-line supervisors that can be applied generally throughout the organization.

FIGURE 4-7

*Sample
Management
Position Description
Questionnaire items.*

Part 8
Contacts

To achieve organizational goals, managers and consultants may be required to communicate with employees at many levels within the company and with influential people outside of the company. This part of the questionnaire addresses the nature and level of these contacts.

Directions:

Step 1 — Significance

For each contact and purpose of contact noted on the opposite page, indicate how significant a part of your position each represents by assigning a number between 0 to 4 to each block. Remember to consider both the importance and the frequency of the contact.

0—Definitely not a part of the position.

1—Minor significance to the position.

2—Moderate significance to the position.

3—Substantial significance to the position

4—Crucial significance to the   position.

Step 2 — Other Contacts

If you have any other contacts, please elaborate on their nature and purpose below.

_____
_____
_____
_____
_____
_____
_____
_____
_____
_____
_____

Purpose of Contact

Internal Contacts	Share information regarding past, present, or anticipated activities or decisions.	Influence others to act or decide in a manner consistent with your objectives.	Direct the plans, activities, or decisions of others.
1. Executives.	10	11	12
2. Group Managers (managers report to position).	13	14	15
3. Managers (supervisors report to position).	16	17	18
4. Supervisors (no supervisors report to position).	19	20	21
5. Professional/Administrative Exempt.	22	23	24
6. Clerical or Support staff (Nonexempt).	25	26	27
7. Other Nonexempt employees.	28	29	30

External Contacts	Provide/gather information or promote the organization or its products/services.	Resolve problems.	Sell products/ services.	Negotiate contracts/ settlements, etc.
8. Customers of the company's products or services.	31	32	33	34
9. Representatives of vendors/subcontractors.	35	36	37	38
10. Representatives of other companies or professional organizations and institutions.	39	40	41	42
11. Representatives of labor unions.	43	44	45	46
12. Representatives of influential community organizations.	47	48	49	50
13. Individuals such as applicants or shareholders.	51	52	53	54
14. Representatives of the media, including the press, radio, television, etc.	55	56	57	58
15. National, state, or regional elected government representatives and/or lobbyists.	59	60	61	62
16. Local government officials and/or representatives of departments such as: customs, tax, revenue, traffic, procurement, law enforcement, and environment.	63	64	65	66

Job analysis: relating method to purpose

Given such a wide choice among available job analysis methods, the combination of methods to use is the one that best fits the purpose of the job analysis research (e.g., employee selection, training design, performance appraisal). Table 4-2 is a matrix that suggests some possible match-ups between job analysis methods and various human resource management purposes. The table simply illustrates the *relative* strengths of each method when used for each purpose. For example, the job performance method of job analysis is most appropriate for the development of tests and interviews, training design, and performance appraisal system design.

Costs and Benefits of Alternative Job Analysis Methods

Key considerations in the choice of job analysis methods are the method-purpose fit, cost, practicality, and an overall judgment of their appropriateness for the situation in question. Comparative research based on the purposes and practicality of these seven job analysis methods has yielded a pattern of results similar to that shown in Table 4-2.[31, 32] In terms of costs, the PAQ (a behavior checklist) was the least costly method to use, while critical incidents was the most costly. However, cost is not the only consideration in choosing a job analysis method. Appropriateness for the situation is another. While the PAQ is used widely, it may be most appropriate for analyzing higher-level jobs since a college-graduate reading level is required to comprehend the items.[2] Related to the issue of appropriateness is an awareness that *behavioral* similarities in jobs may mask genuine *task* differences between them. For example, the jobs performed by typists, belly dancers, and male disco dancers may appear quite similar—all three require fine motor movements!

A thorough job analysis may require a considerable investment of time, effort, and money. Choices among methods must be made. If the choices are based on a rational consideration of the trade-offs involved, they will result in the wisest use of time *and* effort *and* money.

Occupational information

Ever since its initial publication in 1939, and continuing through the present fourth edition, the *Dictionary of Occupational Titles* (*DOT*) has been the standard source of occupational information in the United States.[34] The purpose of the *DOT* is to help the U.S. Employment Service match workers with jobs and to provide counseling and vocational guidance to job seekers. For each of thousands of distinct occupations, four broad characteristics are listed: measures of the complexity of each occupation's tasks; each occupation's training requirements; the interests, aptitudes, and temperaments that characterize an occupation; and its physical demands and working conditions.

33. McCormick, E. J., Jeanneret, P. R., & Mecham, R. C. (1972). A study of job characteristics and job dimensions as based on the Position Analysis Questionnaire (PAQ). *Journal of Applied Psychology, 56,* 347–368.

34. Miller, A. R., Treiman, D. J., Cain, P. S., & Roos, P. A. (eds.) (1980). *Work, jobs, and occupations: A critical review of the Dictionary of Occupational Titles.* Washington, DC: National Academy Press.

35. Morgenthaler, E. (1986, Oct. 7). Although the scarcities are fewer, some job skills are in short supply. *Wall Street Journal,* p. 37.

36. Needle, D. (1986, May 19). Telecommuting: Off to a slow start. *InfoWorld,* pp. 43–46.

37. Page, R. C., & Van De Voort, D. M. (1988). Human resource planning and job analysis. In W. F. Cascio (ed.), *Planning, employment, and placement,* vol. 2 of the ASPA/BNA *Human resource management series.* Washington, DC: Bureau of National Affairs.

38. Saporito, B. (1986, July 21). The revolt against "working smarter." *Fortune,* pp. 58–64.

39. Smith, A. (1976). *An inquiry into the nature and causes of the wealth of nations* (1776). R. H. Campbell, A. S. Skinner, & W. B. Todd (eds.). London: Oxford University Press.

40. *Stress in the workplace: Costs, liability, and prevention* (1987). Washington, DC: Bureau of National Affairs.

41. Taylor, F. W. (1911). *The principles of scientific management.* New York: Harper & Row.

42. Tornow, W. W., & Pinto, P. R. (1976). The development of a managerial taxonomy: A system for describing, classifying, and evaluating executive positions. *Journal of Applied Psychology,* **61,** 410–418.

43. U.S. Department of Commerce (1986). *Statistical abstract of the United States: 1987.* Washington, DC: USGPO.

44. U.S. Department of Labor (1972). *Handbook for analyzing jobs.* Washington, DC: USGPO.

45. Wall, T. D., Kemp, N. J., Jackson, P. R., & Clegg, C. W. (1986). Outcomes of autonomous workgroups: A long-term field experiment. *Academy of Management Journal,* **29,** 280–304.

46. Walton, R. E. (1972). How to counter alienation in the plant. *Harvard Business Review,* **50,** 70–81.

47. Walton, R. E. (1978, Spring). The Topeka story: Teaching an old dog food new tricks. *The Wharton Magazine,* pp. 38–46.

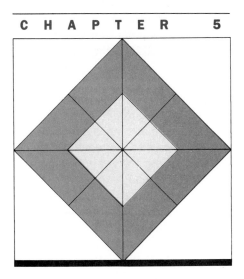

Determining Human Resource Requirements

CASE 5-1

*Forecasting terminations at a Canadian aluminum smelter**

A large Canadian aluminum smelting plant was located in a community that was small and remote—40 miles from the nearest small town, 200 miles from the nearest medium-size city, over 500 miles from the nearest metropolitan area. Because of its location, the smelter was dependent on a limited local supply of labor.

During a 2-year period (1972 to 1973) employees voluntarily terminated—they quit their jobs in higher numbers than ever before in the history of the company. The reasons for the increased turnover will be explained shortly, but at this point it is important to consider the effects on the organization of the increased turnover.

The Personnel Department found itself scrambling to meet the staffing demands of the plant supervisors. One consequence of this scramble for new hires was that selection standards were loosened. An increasing number of young, single, highly mobile workers was hired, many of whom quit after only a few months in the plant. The result: Personnel had to find replacements for employees just hired as replacements.

Smelting is a continuous-process technology, one of whose main characteristics is a stable production level. Any organization having stable pro-

*Adapted from: L. T. Pinfield, A case study of the application of a terminations forecast model, *Human Resource Planning*, **4**, 1982, 18–32.

duction levels plans a stable workforce level—that is, employee recruitment results in a flow of new hires that matches the flow of employees expected to terminate. One of the things that caused a woeful mismatch at the smelter was the procedure by which plant supervisors estimated the number of new hires needed.

Approximately 10 days in advance of a particular week's schedule, supervisors prepared their staffing charts, making allowance for planned leaves and also for unplanned absences. From these charts they identified the extent of their staffing deficit and requested that a certain number of new employees be assigned to their section the following week.

Unfortunately, the lead time needed for recruitment of certain trade skills was at least 2 weeks, more often 3, for local hires, and as long as 3 months for journeyworkers relocating from distant areas. But Personnel was expected to find and hire replacements in less than 2 weeks. This timing became a major factor in the deteriorating relations between the operating departments and Personnel. As a result, an investigation was undertaken to identify what caused the increase in labor turnover and to recommend ways to alleviate it or its effects on the organization. More on this later.

Background

The plant was built in the early 1950s. During that time huge technical problems had to be surmounted to get the plant started and operating smoothly. As the plant developed, so also did a technical mentality pervade management at all levels, and it persisted long after the main technical problems were resolved. One of the effects of that mentality was that Personnel was seen as merely staff support to operations. Personnel issues were seen as not nearly so important as issues arising from production and operations. The only time personnel issues were considered more important was during the two labor strikes the company had to deal with.

In the spring of 1973, when escalating turnover was recognized as a major problem, several events were identified as contributing factors.

First, the previous director of Personnel had been ill and incapacitated for some time. Until the appointment of a new director in the fall of 1972, Personnel had been underrepresented in senior management levels.

Second, in the fall of 1972, a new local union had won certification to represent the bulk of the workers. It is possible that the election of a new union fostered a more militant set of worker attitudes, which contributed to increased dissatisfaction and turnover.

Third, a new provincial government had been elected in the fall of 1972. Some thought that the new government's policy of encouraging unionization of employees had reduced the traditional pay differential between northern industrial jobs and metropolitan service jobs. Also, the new government's liberalization of requirements for unemployment insurance payments seemed to make it easier for workers to quit their jobs and search for better jobs elsewhere.

Fourth, jobs elsewhere were more plentiful than in the recent past.

Further investigation

The jobs were performed in a hot, dirty work setting. Nevertheless, unskilled workers readily accepted these jobs because of the high wages offered. Immediately following the training period, the new hires felt the brunt of the unpleasant working conditions. Further, the community provided no amenities that might help workers enjoy where they lived and keep them in jobs they did not enjoy. Consequently, when jobs appeared plentiful elsewhere, the particularly mobile members of the workforce simply left; the less mobile soon left as well. The result—high turnover.

Further investigation indicated that many of the forces contributing to this high turnover were outside the control of the company in general and beyond the influence of the Personnel Department in particular.

To provide job satisfaction through upgrading the social attractiveness of the community, there was little that company officials could do. Nor was there much they could change within the company toward upgrading the environment of the job: Working conditions were considered fixed in the short run; they could be changed only through expensive, technical innovations, and only in the long run. The company did make an effort to clean and paint rest and hygienic facilities, to subsidize recreational opportunities, and to improve transportation between the community and the plant. These changes reduced job dissatisfaction, but they did not increase job satisfaction. Although there was a slight reduction in turnover, it remained high enough so that the company decided the thing to do was to explore ways to live with high turnover. That is, high turnover became part of the company's general business strategy. One example of the impact that high turnover has on the firm is in terms of job design. That is, jobs need to be "simplified" so that workers can be trained to perform them in as little time as possible.

Development of a terminations forecast model

With the help of an outside consultant, the company developed a model to forecast plantwide terminations. The model looked at the number of terminations throughout the past and extrapolated, or projected, from that information the number of terminations that could occur in the near future. The model then refined that projection based on a comparison between the actual terminations in the most recent month and the terminations previously forecast for that month. In other words, the model adjusted its forecast based on how well it had only recently forecast.

The terminations forecast model, with data from the 2 most recent years,

1972 and 1973, was used to prepare a preliminary forecast for terminations in 1974. Based on this forecast, recruitment plans were made through the first 4 months of 1974. The forecast and actual experience proved remarkably close. As a result, Personnel and operations management were able to agree on and deal with the levels of terminations likely to be encountered during the remainder of the year. Moreover, plant managers began to have confidence in the ability of Personnel to handle staffing problems. This confidence improved to the point where Personnel proposed an experiment which might reduce labor turnover but which would also increase the direct labor costs of production: the proposal was accepted. The experiment was called a "stability bonus," and, in the conclusion to this case, we shall see what it was and how it worked.

QUESTIONS
1. Do you think plant management made the right decision in attempting to live with the high labor turnover?
2. What alternative solutions might you propose?

What's Ahead

Case 5-1 shows how a model of a process—in this case, terminations—helped managers plan for and resolve a chronic problem, staffing shortages. This chapter is concerned with planning, but planning of a special kind: human resource planning (HRP). The chapter first describes the interaction between general business plans and human resource plans, with special emphasis on the roles of labor markets and information systems in the HRP process. It then describes how companies forecast the supply of and demand for labor. Lots of real-life examples are included along the way so that you can see how the techniques described are actually used in practice. Let's begin by answering the question "Why plan?"

Why Plan?

Successful football coaches do it; history shows that great generals have done it; leading organizations routinely do it.

Do what?

Plan.

Planning helps reduce the uncertainty of the future and thereby enables us to do a better job of coping with it. General Patton is said to have known his enemy's strategy and tactics almost better than the enemy itself! Football coaches plan their strategies after spending hours reviewing their opponents' game films. Corporate planners, through their knowledge of legal, economic, political, and social trends and events, are able to direct their firms to do a better job of responding to current and future demands of the marketplace.

In short, *planning leads to success*—not all the time, but studies consistently show that planners outperform nonplanners. Another way of looking at it is that *planning helps organizations do a better job of coping with change.* If there were no change, there would be no need to plan. But change—technological, social, political, and environmental—is a bald fact of organizational life.

One of the benefits of planning is that simply by doing it, managers *define their objectives.* When managers define their objectives, their organizations can do a better job of focusing resources toward those products and/or services that are most consistent with their objectives. By providing such clear direction (as Chrysler and Lee Iacocca did in the early 1980s), the context and meaning of each manager's and each employee's job is defined clearly. Research indicates that managers who define their objectives perform better and are more satisfied with their jobs than those who do not.[20]

Types of plans: strategic, tactical, and human resources

Strategic planning is the process of setting objectives and deciding on the actions to achieve them.[36, 38] Strategic planning for an organization includes:

- *Defining philosophy.* Why does the organization exist? What unique contribution does it make?
- *Formulating statements of identity, purpose, and objectives.* What is the overall mission of the organization? Are the missions of divisions and departments consistent with the mission of the organization?
- *Evaluating strengths and weaknesses.* Identify factors that may enhance or inhibit any future courses of action aimed at achieving objectives.
- *Determining design.* What are the components of the organization, what should they do, and how should they relate to each other, toward achieving objectives and fulfilling the organization's mission?
- *Developing strategies.* How will the objectives, at every level, be achieved? How will they be measured, not only in quantitative terms of what is to be achieved, but also in terms of time?
- *Devising programs.* What will be the components of each program, and how will the effectiveness of each program be measured?

Strategic planning differs considerably from short-range tactical (or operational) planning. It involves fundamental decisions about the very nature of the business. Strategic planning may result in new business acquisitions, divestitures of current (profitable or unprofitable) product lines, new capital investments, or new management approaches.[21]

For example, a key theme for many U.S. firms in the 1980s has been "back to basics." Often this includes downsizing or restructuring in response to unprecedented global competition and financial turbulence. In addition to traditional rivals in Europe and Japan, American companies face an ever-expanding roster of competitors in developing countries, from South Korea to Brazil. On top of that, there were over 4000 mergers and acquisitions, worth a record $190 billion, in 1986 alone! This is why over half of the Fortune 1000 largest U.S. corporations underwent some form of significant reorganization by 1987.[29]

Consider an example at the level of the individual firm. Between 1981 and 1987 General Electric (GE) spent $11.1 billion to buy 338 businesses, including RCA, a $6.3 billion acquisition. During the same period, GE shed 232 businesses worth $5.9 billion and closed 73 plants and offices. As GE's chairman said, "The managers in the 1980s who hang onto losing business ventures, for whatever reason, won't be around in the 1990s" (ref. 29, p. 45).

Strategic planning is therefore long-range in scope, and it may involve substantial commitments of resources. Almost always it involves considerable data collection, analysis, and repeated review and reevaluation by top management.

Tactical, or operational, planning deals with the normal growth of current operations, as well as with any specific problems that might disrupt the pace of planned, normal growth. Purchasing new or additional office equipment to enhance production efficiency (e.g., word processors), coping with the recall of a defective product (e.g., defective brakes in cars), or dealing with the need to design tamper-proof bottle caps (e.g., in the pharmaceutical industry) are examples of tactical planning problems. Beyond the obvious difference in time frames distinguishing strategic planning and tactical planning, the other difference between the two is the degree of change resulting from the planning—and hence the degree of impact on human resource planning.

Human resource planning (HRP) parallels the plans for the business as a whole. HRP focuses on questions such as: What do the proposed business strategies imply with respect to human resources? What kinds of internal and external constraints will (or do) we face? For example, restrictive work rules in a collective bargaining contract are an internal constraint, while a projected shortfall in the supply of college graduate electrical engineers (relative to the demand for them by employers) is an external constraint. What are the implications for staffing, compensation practices, training and development, and management succession? What can be done in the short run (tactically) to prepare for long-term (strategic) needs?

COMPANY EXAMPLE

Philips, the Dutch multinational corporation

In Holland, the Philips Company recently decided to open a new plant to capitalize on its competitive advantages. One important advantage was that existing production facilities were already located in Holland. Another was that the Dutch workforce viewed Philips as an attractive place to work. Before building the new plant, elaborate strategic studies were made. Of course, one of the factors under study was the availability of qualified human resources.

But the study especially focused on how to build in changes in the manufacturing technology to match the characteristics of the labor force 20 years ahead. Machines and methods used to produce the products efficiently by today's labor force may not be used efficiently as the labor force grows older. This is an important consideration because one of the cultural characteristics of Dutch workers is that they tend not to move from one location to another during their working careers. Hence it is difficult to transfer employees and almost impossible to replace them. So to maintain its competitive advantage, Philips attempted to incorporate into the production planning process the characteristics of the future labor force. Since the planners anticipated that the future workforce will be better educated and more independent, they tried to design the manufacturing process in a way that might permit improved opportunities for job rotation, job sharing, and job enrichment. This represents a true integration of planning—strategic and human resource—to optimize overall company performance.[2]

More on human resource planning

Although HRP means different things to different people, general agreement exists on its ultimate objective—namely, the most effective use of scarce talent in the interest of the worker and the organization. Thus we may define HRP broadly as *an effort to anticipate future business and environmental demands on an organization, and to provide the personnel to fulfill that business and*

FIGURE 5-1

Hypothetical control and evaluation process applied to a human resource planning system.

OBJECTIVE: INCREASE REPRESENTATION OF WOMEN BY 15% IN ENTRY–LEVEL MANAGEMENT JOBS OVER THE NEXT TWO YEARS.

STRATEGY: PROVIDE INCREASED OPPORTUNITIES FOR TRAINING IN BASIC MANAGEMENT SKILLS.

PROGRAM: BY THE END OF THE FIRST QUARTER OF THE FISCAL YEAR, PROVIDE A "CAREER ASSESSMENT" DAY FOCUSING ON INDIVIDUAL APTITUDES AND INTERESTS FOR ALL WOMEN INTERESTED IN MANAGEMENT JOBS. FOR THOSE WITH THE REQUIRED APTITUDES, PROVIDE SPECIAL COURSES IN DECISION MAKING (2ND QUARTER OF THE FISCAL YEAR), SUPERVISORY SKILLS (3RD QUARTER), AND FINANCIAL ANALYSIS (4TH QUARTER).

EVALUATION OF THE PROGRAM—TWO YEARS LATER

KEY QUESTIONS TO ASK:

1. WAS OUR INITIAL OBJECTIVE (15%) TOO AMBITIOUS?

2. WERE WOMEN IN NON–MANAGEMENT JOBS REALLY ENCOURAGED AND PERMITTED TO ATTEND TRAINING CLASSES?

3. WAS THE CAREER ASSESSMENT THOROUGH? DID IT PROVIDE USEFUL PLANNING INFORMATION?

4. WHAT PERCENTAGE OF THE WOMEN COMPLETED THE TRAINING COURSES SATISFACTORILY?

5. SHOULD WE CHANGE OUR EFFORTS TO RECRUIT WOMEN INTO MANAGEMENT JOBS? IF SO, HOW, IN LIGHT OF THE ANSWERS TO THESE QUESTIONS?

satisfy those demands.[6] This general view suggests several specific, interrelated activities that together comprise an HRP system. They include:

- *A personnel inventory* to assess current human resources (skills, abilities, and potential) and to analyze how they are currently being used
- *A human resource forecast* to predict future personnel requirements (the number of workers needed, the number expected to be available, the skills mix required, internal versus external labor supply)
- *Action plans* to enlarge the pool of people qualified to fill the projected vacancies through such actions as recruitment, selection, training, placement, transfer, promotion, development, and compensation
- *Control and evaluation* to provide feedback on the overall effectiveness of the human resource planning system by monitoring the degree of attainment of human resource objectives (an example of a hypothetical control and evaluation procedure is shown in Figure 5-1)

Relationship of Human Resource Planning to Strategic and Tactical Planning

A variety of HRP applications exists.[13] For example, HRP itself can be strategic (long-term and general) or tactical (short-term and specific). It may be done organizationwide, or it may be restricted to divisions, departments, or any common employee groups. Or it may be carried out on a recurring basis (e.g., annually) or only sporadically (e.g., when launching a new product line or at the outset of a capital expansion project). Regardless of its specific application, almost all experts agree that if HRP is to be genuinely effective, it must be linked with the different levels of general business planning, not as an end or *goal* in and of itself, but rather as a *means* to the end of building more competitive organizations. The overall process is directed by line managers. When line managers perceive that human resource practices help them achieve their goals, they are more likely to initiate and support HRP efforts. Furthermore, the process raises important human resource questions.[39] How business planning affects HRP is depicted in Figure 5-2.

The long-range perspective (2 to 5 years or longer) of strategic planning flows naturally into the middle-range perspective (1 to 2 years) of operational planning. Annual budgeting decisions provide specific timetables, allocations of resources, and standards for implementing strategic and operational plans. As the time frame shortens, planning details become increasingly specific.

At the level of strategic planning, HRP is concerned with such issues as assessing the management implications of future business needs, assessing factors external to the firm (e.g., demographic trends, social trends), and gauging the internal supply of employees over the long run. The focus here is to analyze issues, not to make detailed projections.

At the level of operational, or tactical, planning, HRP is concerned with

FIGURE 5-2

Impact of three levels of business planning on human resource planning.

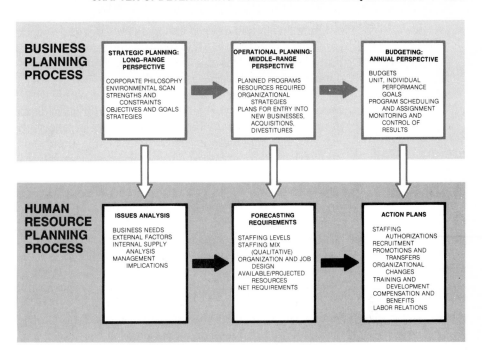

detailed forecasts of employee supply (internal and external to the organization) and employee demand (numbers needed at some future time period). Based on the forecasts, as Case 5-1 noted, specific action plans can be undertaken. These may involve recruitment, decruitment (easing some workers out), promotions, training, or transfers. Procedures must be established to control and evaluate progress toward targeted objectives.

Unfortunately, it appears that in practice, general business planning does not include HRP as an integral partner.[27] Few firms have established planning and control staffs whose purpose specifically is to evaluate the impact of external issues on human resources and thus on the contingency planning of the firm.[35] Although the theory of vertical planning integration (general business and HRP) is well-developed, it is not put into practice.

Labor Markets: The Foundation of Human Resource Objectives

Human resource objectives cannot be developed in a vacuum. First, they must be consistent with the planned future direction of the organization; that is, they must be consistent with long-range strategic plans. Second, they must be consistent with tactical business objectives (Figure 5-2). The staffing mix, staffing levels, job design, and available and/or projected resources ultimately depend on the structure and functioning of internal and external labor markets. Let us therefore discuss labor market issues first and then say more about human resource objectives.

A *labor market* is a geographical area within which the forces of supply (people looking for work) interact with the forces of demand (employers looking for people) and thereby determine the price of labor.[30] In a *tight labor market*, demand by employers exceeds the available supply of workers, which tends to exert upward pressure on wages. In a *loose labor market*, the reverse is true; the supply of workers exceeds employer demand, exerting downward pressure on wages. In recent years the labor market for electrical engineers, nurses, and bus mechanics has been fairly tight; wages for these jobs have been increasing steadily. On the other hand, the labor market for lawyers, steelworkers, and unskilled labor has been fairly loose in recent years, reducing pressure for wage increases for these workers.

Unfortunately, it is not possible to define the geographical boundaries of a labor market in any clear-cut manner.[30] Employers needing key employees will recruit far and wide if necessary. From the perspective of job applicants, movement from a labor market in one geographical area to another is also quite restricted. There are exceptions: During 1982, in the depths of the recession, hundreds of unemployed auto workers left Detroit for Houston in the hope of finding work. In 1986, as oil prices plummeted, workers moved from Houston to other cities. Such movements reflect an underlying turbulence in the environment. In short, employers do not face a single, homogeneous market for labor but rather a series of discontinuous, segmented labor markets over which supply and demand conditions vary substantially. Economists focus on this fact as the major explanation for wage differences between occupations and between geographical areas.

Of practical concern to managers, however, is a reasonably accurate definition of labor markets for planning purposes. Here are some factors that are important for defining the limits of a labor market:[30, 42]

- Geography
- Education and/or technical background required to perform the job
- Industry
- Licensing or certification requirements
- Union membership

Companies may use one or more of these factors to help define their labor markets. Thus an agricultural research firm that needs to hire four veterinarians cannot restrict its search to a local area since the market is national or international in scope. Union membership is not a concern in this market, but licensing and/or certification is. Typically a doctor of veterinary medicine degree is required along with state licensure to practice. Applicants are likely to be less concerned with where the job is located and more concerned with job design and career opportunities. On the other hand, suppose a hospital is trying to hire a journeyworker plumber. The hospital will be looking at a labor market defined primarily by its geographic proximity and secondarily by people whose experience, technical background, and (possibly) willingness to join a union after employment qualify them for the job.

Internal versus external labor markets

The discussion thus far has concerned the structure and function of external labor markets. Internal labor markets also affect HRP, in many cases more directly, because firms often give preference to present employees in promotions, transfers, and other career-enhancing opportunities. Each employing unit is a separate market. At Delta Airlines, for example, virtually all jobs above the entry level are filled by internal promotion rather than by outside recruitment. Delta looks to its present employees as its source of labor supply, and workers look to this "internal labor market" to advance their careers. In the internal labor markets of most organizations, employees peddle their talents to available "buyers."[1] Three elements comprise the internal labor market:

- Formal and informal practices that determine how jobs are organized and described
- Methods for choosing among candidates
- Procedures and authorities through which potential candidates are generated by those responsible for filling open jobs

In an open internal labor market, every available job is advertised throughout the organization, and anyone can apply. Preference is given to internal candidates by withholding outside advertising until the job has been on the internal market for several days. Finally, each candidate for a job receives an interview.

When looking at internal labor markets for HRP purposes, it is critical to anticipate the aging of the workforce, along with terminations (unavoidable or controllable), and normal employee flows through various jobs over time. The more keenly this is done, the more useful will be the estimates of the supply of workers at some future time period.

More on establishing human resource objectives

Objectives can be expressed either in behavioral terms ("By the third week of training, you should be able to do these things . . . ") or in end-result terms ("By the end of the next fiscal year five new retail stores should be open, and each should be staffed by a manager, an assistant manager, and three clerks"). In the context of cost control in compensation, for example, the following questions should prove useful in setting human resource objectives:[42]

- What level will the wage rate be for an occupation?
- How many people will be employed?

- How much more will our firm have to pay to attract more employees?
- How would the number of people our company would employ change if the wage were lower? If it were higher?

HRP objectives vary according to such things as the type of environment a company operates in, its strategic and tactical plans, and the current design of jobs and employee work behaviors. As examples, consider some of McDonald's human resource objectives: Define jobs narrowly so that they are easy to learn in a short period of time; pay minimum wages to most nonmanagement employees so that the cost of turnover is low; design jobs to minimize decision making by the human operator (e.g., computer-controlled cooking operations, item labeling on cash registers).[37]

The remote Canadian aluminum smelter described at the start of this chapter decided to operate under a very different set of human resource objectives. Pay high wages to compensate for the dirty, routine jobs to be done, recognize that the local community has low entertainment value (so provide company transportation to other areas on weekends), and finally, given these harsh conditions, live with high turnover by forecasting it accurately and taking steps to ensure adequate staffing at all times.

As another example of HRP objectives, the Philips Company decided to build a futuristic plant in an area where the workforce is quite stable. The company focused its human resource objectives on minimizing turnover (since workers are so hard to replace), paying competitive wages, and designing jobs to challenge the workforce anticipated 20 years hence.

Setting human resource objectives is art as much as it is science. It requires conscious forethought based on the kind of future the firm wants to create for itself. It requires teamwork; it cannot be left to serendipity.

The Role of Information Systems in HRP

"Managers of the future are likely to be information managers." Statements like this appear a lot these days. But have things really changed? Over 15 years ago it was estimated that in any white-collar job up to 90 percent of the work involved seeking and obtaining information.[25] It's not that the basic managerial job has changed; the technology available to do the work has changed—by leaps and bounds. What is an information system? What is it with respect to HRP?

> A human resource information system (HRIS) is the method by which an organization collects, maintains, analyzes, and reports information on people and jobs. The "system" refers simply to the process of integrating a variety of disparate activities into a logical, meaningful whole to accomplish a given objective. (ref. 43)

While it is true that managers need accurate, relevant, and timely data for decision making, computers may not help if record keeping and data collection were incomplete and inaccurate to begin with. Computers also may not help if careful attention is not paid to exactly what kind of information is needed, particularly at top management levels. A survey by Dennison National Corp. of 60 administrative and data processing executives of 52 of the largest U.S. corporations seemed to confirm this. The survey concluded:

> The inefficient use of computers actually can have a negative effect on productivity. They produce, on a daily basis, volumes of wasted data—data that is too detailed, irrelevant, or obsolete; of little use to management at any level. (ref. 8)

This may be one reason why nearly 80 percent of major corporations now have a manager of their human resource information systems, double the number 5 years ago. These managers need both a technical and a human resources management background. They are responsible for entering personnel data into the computer, analyzing it, extracting it, and presenting it in a form usable to corporate decision makers. Syntex Corp., for example, recently used its system to correlate employee ages and activities to help the company decide whether to build an employee exercise center.[17]

The configuration of an HRIS should be based on sound prior planning, including a clear specification of objectives, thorough analysis of system requirements, and careful attention to detail, for a wide variety of data will be required. Particular attention should be devoted to helping management *and* operative employees understand what an HRIS is, what its uses are, and how it will help the firm. One painful lesson learned from unsuccessful attempts to implement any kind of HRIS or decision support system is that without the full support and cooperation of those who will be affected by the new system, its chances for success are minimal.[4, 26]

Microcomputer-based human resource information systems

Until recently, only mainframe computers or minicomputers had the computational power and storage capacity to support an HRIS. Now, however, microcomputers are driving full-function HR information systems. Some provide only basic record-keeping functions for 50-employee organizations. Others meet all the personnel information needs of firms with thousands of employees, sending information back and forth to a mainframe-based system. In cases where there are several users wanting to gain access to the data at the same time, a local-area network (LAN) may help. With the addition of special circuit boards, wiring, and software, it is possible to set up the personnel database on one computer (the "file server") and have other computers access it simultaneously, while still using the microcomputer's operating system.

Indeed, the microcomputer-based HRIS gives the HR professional instant access to all kinds of employee information, thereby making it possible to answer a wide variety of personnel research questions. Such information might include demographics (age, sex, address, and so forth), position, compensation and benefits, performance, education, and information on training skills—from 100 to 500 or more pieces of individual data per employee.

Today there are at least 300 microcomputer-based programs for personnel applications.[16] Generally they provide the following features:

1. Preformatted computer screens for inputting or displaying this information
2. From a dozen to 50 or more standard reports
3. A report writer for making customized reports
4. Utilities for performing such functions as backing up the data and making mass updates[15]

Scores of programs can enhance the productivity of individuals and departments. Here are some common applications:

- Computer-based training (e.g., orientation, benefits communication), complete with color graphics.
- Attendance and timekeeping.
- Payroll.
- Word processing and high-quality graphics (graphs and charts, including computerized animation).
- Organizational development (programs that can analyze an organization's culture, identify organizational strengths and weaknesses, or help build work groups by identifying people who have complementary skills).
- Safety and health (programs that track exposure to toxic chemicals, record accidents, log training, and store employee medical histories).
- Database management (programs that help build customized databases for job posting, employee assistance monitoring, distribution lists, or other applications that would otherwise be housed in file cabinets).
- Spreadsheets for salary planning, survey analysis, departmental budgeting, affirmative action planning, and labor contract costing.
- Statistical analyses, from simple descriptive statistics to regression and linear programming.
- Telecommunications. With communications software and a modem, computers can "talk" to each other via phone lines. It then becomes possible to send and receive electronic mail, to use electronic bulletin boards, and to access vast databases of articles, statistics, and legal decisions.

These are just some of the ways that the microcomputer can facilitate the operation of an integrated HR system. As one commentator noted, "The candy store is open; how do you want to spend your nickel?"[15]

Personal privacy

Two crucial issues that must be considered in setting up and maintaining an HRIS are data security and personal privacy. Data security is a technical problem that can be dealt with in several ways, including the use of passwords and elaborate codes. Personal privacy in the information age is an ethical and moral issue. Here are some general recommendations provided by one expert:

1. Set up guidelines and policies to protect information in the organization: on types of data to be sought, on methods of obtaining the data, on retention and dissemination of information, on employee or third-party access to information, and on mishandling of information.
2. Inform employees of these information-handling policies.
3. Become thoroughly familiar with state and federal laws regarding privacy.

Here are some specific recommendations:[9]

1. Avoid fraudulent, secretive, or unfair means of collecting data. When possible, collect data directly from the individual concerned.
2. Do not maintain secret files on individuals. Inform them of what information is stored on them, the purpose for which it was collected, how it will be used, and how long it will be kept.
3. Collect only job-related information that is relevant for specific decisions.
4. Maintain records of individuals or organizations who have regular access or who request information on a need-to-know basis.
5. Periodically allow employees the right to inspect and update information stored on them.
6. Gain assurance that any information released to outside parties will be used only for the purposes set forth prior to its release.

The Federal Privacy Act of 1974 provides limits for federal agencies when collecting, using, and disseminating information about individuals. Under this act, individuals have three specific rights: (1) the right to access any personal records about them and to review, copy, and amend erroneous portions of the records; (2) the right to prevent information in their files from being used for any purpose other than the purpose for which it was collected; and (3) the right to sue for damages that occur as a result of intentional action that violates the act. At present, the act does not affect private industry, but it does suggest the direction that any future legislation might take.

Personnel inventories

One use of the HRIS is in the development of a personnel inventory for human resource planning. An integrated HRP system requires two kinds of information before any specific action plans can be undertaken:

1. A *personnel inventory* that provides an assessment of the knowledges, skills, abilities, experience, and career aspirations of the present workforce
2. A *forecast* of future human resource needs

These two kinds of information must complement each other; an inventory of present talent is not particularly useful for planning purposes unless it can be analyzed in terms of future human resource requirements. On the other

FIGURE 5-3

*An integrated
human resource
planning system.*

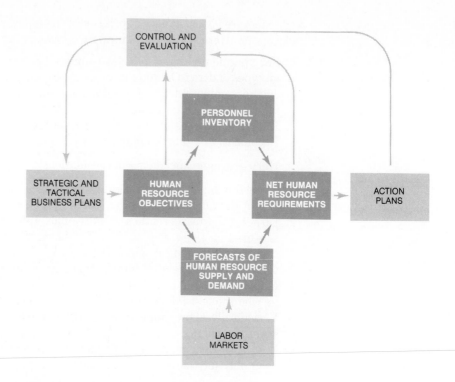

hand, a forecast of human resource requirements is useless unless it can be evaluated relative to the current and projected future supply of workers available internally. Only at that time, when we have a clear understanding of the projected surpluses or deficits of employees in terms of their numbers, their skills, or their experience, does it make sense to initiate action plans to rectify projected problems. Such an integrated HRP system is shown in Figure 5-3.

At the outset, some managerial issues need to be addressed. For example, what does management see as the major uses of this database comprising the personnel inventory? Who should be included in the inventory (just managerial, professional, and technical employees or everyone above a certain level)? How can the information best be obtained and updated? What kinds of reports should be produced?

Projected uses   Although secondary uses of the personnel inventory data may emerge, the primary uses must be specified at the concept development stage. This will provide direction and scope regarding who and what kinds of data should be included.

Some common uses of a personnel inventory are: identification of candidates for promotion, management succession planning, assignment to special projects, transfer, training, affirmative action planning and reporting, compensation planning, career planning, and organizational analysis.

Who should be included? Some organizations, particularly those which require their employees to move frequently (only half facetiously, a manager once quipped that the letters "IBM" really mean "I've been moved!") or those which frequently reconfigure temporary task forces or project teams, routinely include all their employees in the skills inventory. Others use the inventory primarily for management succession planning and therefore include only managers.

Obtaining and updating information As noted earlier, before any data are collected for inclusion in the personnel inventory, employees should be provided with a clear statement about their privacy safeguards and the potential impact on their privacy of all such in-house systems.

Employees should not be asked to provide information about themselves that has already been recorded elsewhere (e.g., hire date, date of birth, education). As much information as possible should be retrieved from personnel files or from the payroll-benefits system. Employees should be asked to provide only nonredundant, new information (e.g., skills, career aspirations). Information that changes frequently (e.g., salary information, job classifications) may be updated automatically on a regular basis by merging with a payroll program. Information that changes less frequently (e.g., educational level or licensure and/or certification) can be generated by having each employee complete a standardized update form at periodic intervals, such as annually.

Reports Perhaps the best approach to take in considering how to generate new reports containing employee information is to examine present reports: Which items are superfluous? What new items or data summaries should be included? In general, only need-to-know information should be included. It's easy to overwhelm reports (so-called information overload) by including "nice-to-know" information as well.

Reports fall into three broad categories: operational reports, regulatory reports, and analytical reports:

Operational reports are used in day-to-day management. Examples include total job vacancies, new hires, quits, retirements, promotions, and wages (subdivided by seniority, pay grade, and step within pay grade).

Regulatory reports are those required by federal, state, and local agencies, such as the Equal Employment Opportunity Commission and the Occupational Safety and Health Administration (see p. 555).

Analytical reports are used within the company for research purposes, but they are generated less frequently. Examples might include sex, race, or age distributions of the workforce by department, division, or management level, or an employee benefits usage report categorized by level of payout, or a validity study that indicates statistically the relationship between selection test scores and job performance ratings.

This personnel inventory program is intended to facilitate the transfer of managers among the company's various operating units. Initially, a test group of 30 managers was selected for a system trial. Members of this group provided information on a preliminary form and then commented on the design of the form. The form was revised and reviewed by functional heads and general managers in the operating companies, as well as by personnel managers. Ultimately many kinds of information were incorporated into a computerized personnel inventory that fit the mix of businesses in which Dun & Bradstreet is engaged.

Once a user accesses the personnel inventory, a single computer program will lead her or him through any one or more procedures (e.g., searching employee files, adding new information, generating different types of reports on employees) by asking a series of questions requiring only "yes" or "no" or "choose-one" responses. For example, to use the personnel inventory to identify candidates for promotion to a specific job, the user first must specify the selection criteria to be used (e.g., education, experience, foreign language competency). Then the computer will identify appropriate candidates by name, and, according to instructions from the user, it will generate long or short résumés either on a screen or in hard copy. Multiple selection criteria may be used in the candidate identification process, and they may be changed during the search.[11]

Human Resource Forecasts

The purpose of human resource forecasting is to estimate labor requirements at some future time period. Such forecasts are of two types: (1) the external and internal supply of labor, and (2) the external and internal demand for labor. The two types of forecasts should be considered separately because each rests on a different set of assumptions and depends on a different set of variables.[41]

Internal supply forecasts relate to conditions *inside* the organization, such as the age distribution of the workforce, terminations, retirements, and new hires within job classes. Both internal and external demand forecasts, on the other hand, depend primarily on the behavior of some business factor (e.g., student enrollments, projected sales, product volume) to which personnel needs can be related. Unlike internal and external supply forecasts, internal and external demand forecasts are subject to many uncertainties—in domestic or worldwide economic conditions, in technology, and in consumer behavior, just to name a few. In the following sections we will consider briefly the human resource forecasting techniques that have proven to be practical and useful.

Forecasting external human resource supply

Recruiting and hiring new employees is essential for virtually all firms, at least over the long run. Whether this is due to projected expansion of operations or to normal workforce attrition, forays into the labor market are necessary.

Several agencies regularly make projections of external labor market conditions and estimates of the supply of labor to be available in general categories. Included among these agencies are: the Bureau of Labor Statistics of the U.S. Department of Labor, the Engineering Manpower Commission, and the Public Health Service of the Department of Health and Human Services. For new college and university graduates, the Northwestern Endicott-Lindquist Report is one of the most respected barometers of future hiring decisions. An example of one set of forecasts made at the end of 1986 to predict 1987 hires is shown in Table 5-1.

It is important to consider both the future supply of workers in a particular field and the future demand for them. To focus only on supply could be a grave mistake. For example, let's look at Table 5-1. Suppose we want to hire 16 MBAs with nontechnical BA degrees. In 1986, 60 companies hired 1717 such graduates. But in 1987, *69* companies were predicted to hire 925 such graduates. Competition will be stiffer than in 1986, and sophisticated recruiting may be necessary. Organizations in both the public and private sectors are finding

TABLE 5-1 *Projected employment of inexperienced college graduates in 1987, as reported by 230 companies*

Bachelor's level	Forecast 1987		Historical data 1986	
	No. companies	**No. grads.**	**No. companies**	**No. grads.**
Engineering	130	8,490	126	11,895
Accounting	121	7,783	101	6,493
Sales-marketing	84	1,950	85	2,578
Business administration	82	3,021	76	2,241
Liberal arts	52	1,304	52	605
Computer	104	3,280	93	3,606
Chemistry	40	396	29	239
Mathematics or statistics	32	257	26	331
Economics or finance	51	411	41	591
Other fields	42	1,094	41	1,010
Totals: bachelor's level		27,986		29,589
Master's level				
Engineering	57	1,012	55	1,809
Other technical fields	37	411	34	797
M.B.A. with technical B.S.	37	302	24	584
M.B.A. with nontechnical B.A.	69	923	60	1,717
Accounting	20	1,064	21	1,038
Other nontechnical fields	13	468	23	340
Total: master's level		4,182		6,285

Source: Adapted from Victor R. Lindquist, "The Northwestern Endicott-Lindquist Report," Published by the Northwestern University Placement Center, Evanston, Illinois.

that they require projections of the external labor market to prevent personnel surpluses or deficits.

Forecasting internal human resource supply

A reasonable starting point for projecting a firm's future supply of labor is its current supply of labor. In the case of management employees, perhaps the simplest type of internal supply forecast is the *management succession plan*, a concept that has been discussed in the planning literature for over 20 years.[19, 28] The process for developing such a plan includes setting a planning horizon, identifying replacement candidates for each key position, assessing current performance and readiness for promotion, identifying career development needs, and integrating the career goals of individuals with company goals. The overall objective, of course, is to assure the availability of competent executive talent in the future.

COMPANY EXAMPLE

Succession planning in the Ministry of Transportation and Communications (MTC), Province of Ontario

MTC, one of the leading transportation authorities in North America, is responsible for the management of a highway network comprising approximately 13,000 miles of provincial roads. It also manages the subsidy allocation for an additional 62,500 miles of municipal roads and is involved in the planning for provincial commuter rail and air services. Major operational activities include planning, design, construction, maintenance, and research related to transportation systems and facilities.

The full-time workforce consists of approximately 2600 management and 7700 bargaining-unit employees, although for practical reasons, succession planning has been limited to middle and senior management (about 1300 positions). Succession planning is one of the responsibilities of every manager.

Current and future business plans and the assessed skills and potential of the management workforce provide the main inputs to the planning system.

FIGURE 5-4

Corporate human resource demand forecasting model used at the Ontario Ministry of Transportation and Communications. See text for explanations of the data that go into each column.

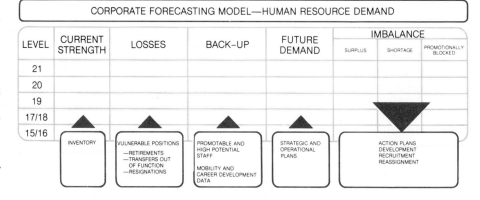

Meaningful forecasts can be done only for large job families. Hence, MTC's operations have been divided into five primary and eight secondary functions, and separate analyses are done for each of these functions. Figure 5-4 illustrates the various data that are used in the forecast to determine potential shortages, surpluses, the numbers of promotable staff blocked from promotion (e.g., because there is no higher-level job to progress to in a particular job family), and the annual training and development effort required to maintain backup strength.

- Current strength is determined from a personnel inventory maintained by the corporate planning group.
- Losses are made up of resignations, dismissals, transfers, and retirements. Resignations, dismissals, and transfers are assessed from historical data, modified by current and future trends. Retirement figures are based on a review of individual retirement ranges.

FIGURE 5-5

Management succession forecasting model used at the Ontario Ministry of Transportation and Communications. An explanation of the numbers in each box is contained in the lower right corner of the figure. For example, at job level 17/18 in 1988, staff strength is 120 persons, of whom 24 are promotable. Four persons were promoted "out," 8 were promoted "in," 1 was recruited externally, 3 retired, 2 were projected to resign, and 20 were promotionally blocked.

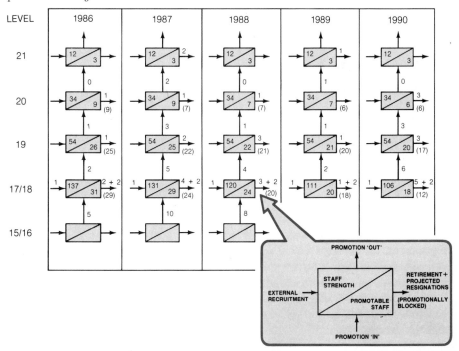

- Backup is determined from two sources: (1) As part of the annual appraisal process, managers identify those employees who are considered promotable within the next 1-year planning cycle; and (2) in a separate annual process, managers identify those high-potential individuals who have the ability to progress to two responsibility levels higher—in more than one function—during a 5-year forecast period.
- Future demand is forecast on the basis of current as well as future business plans. These are determined by MTC's strategic policy committee (comprised of the CEO and senior executives) with input from six planning groups.

Finally, the data for management succession planning for each function are manipulated by means of a computerized forecasting model (Figure 5-5). The model was chosen because it is simple to use and because it is flexible enough to be able to analyze situations that vary according to staffing levels, turnover rates, and replacement strategies.[31]

Markov analysis   Another approach that can be used to develop a forecast of the internal supply of human resources is called *Markov analysis*.[32, 40] Although it is conceptually complex,[3] it can be used without understanding the underlying theory. It tracks past patterns of personnel movements (transitions) and uses them to project future patterns. As a simple example, let us use hypothetical personnel movements in a public accounting firm (Figure 5-6). The analysis begins with the development of a transition matrix in which each cell represents the historical average percentage (in decimal-equivalent form) of employees who move between job categories (states) from one period to

FIGURE 5-6

Hypothetical Markov analysis of human resource supply in a public accounting firm.

(A)

JOB LEVEL	PROBABILITIES OF MOVEMENT				
	P	M	S	J	EXIT
PARTNER (P)	.80				.20
MANAGER (M)	.10	.70			.20
SENIOR (S)		.05	.80	.05	.10
JUNIOR (J)			.15	.65	.20

(B)

JOB LEVEL	BEGINNING STAFFING LEVELS	P	M	S	J	EXIT
PARTNER	40	32				8
MANAGER	80	8	56			16
SENIOR	120		6	96	6	12
JUNIOR	160			24	104	32
NET FORECASTED AVAILABILITIES		40	62	120	110	68

another (e.g., one year to the next). Typically a 5- to 10-year base period is used to estimate these annual average percentages—the longer the base period, the more meaningfully will each past movement represent a probability of future movement.

Figure 5-6A indicates, for example, that in any given year an average of 80 percent (0.80 in decimal-equivalent form) of the partners remain with the firm, while an average of 20 percent leave. For junior accountants, in any given year about 65 percent stay in that job category, 15 percent are promoted to senior accountants, and 20 percent leave the firm. Using these historical data as representative of the probability of transition in each category, future personnel movements (supply) can be projected. Multiplying the staffing level in each category at the beginning of a planning period by the transition probabilities within each and summing the columns yields net future supply of labor within the organization.

A one-period projection for the accounting firm is shown as Figure 5-6B. If the next year is like the past, the firm can expect to have the same number of partners, 40, and the same number of senior accountants, 120, next year. But there will be 18 fewer managers and 50 fewer junior accountants. These data, reflecting personnel movements, together with plans for expansion, contraction, or maintenance of steady state staffing levels, can be used to determine how to match projected labor supplies with needs. This may involve increased outside recruitment for junior and senior accountants, coupled with increased promotions of senior accountants to managers, or some other strategy that is consistent with the general business plans of the firm.

Despite its assumed popularity, research into the accuracy and applicability of Markov analysis is not extensive.[7, 45] Results so far are mixed. Both Weyerhaeuser and the Eaton Corporation found that the model provided accurate, useful information that was accepted by decision makers.[5, 18] But Markov analysis failed in two attempts to use it at Corning Glass Works.[13] Clearly, research is needed to identify the variables that determine the success or failure of Markov analysis as a technique for forecasting human resource supply.

Forecasting human resource demand

In contrast to supply forecasting, demand forecasting is beset with multiple uncertainties—changes in technology; consumer attitudes and patterns of buying behavior; local, national, and international economies; number, size, and types of contracts won or lost; and government regulations that might open new markets or close off old ones, just to name a few. Consequently, forecasts of human resource demand are often more subjective than quantitative, although in practice a combination of the two is typically used.

This section presents one subjective approach—the Delphi technique—and one quantitative approach—trend analysis—for forecasting demand. The techniques are basically easy to describe and understand, but applying them may be complex, for they require a variety of data.

The Delphi technique   Delphi is a structured approach for reaching a consensus judgment among experts about future developments in any area that might affect a business (e.g., the level of a firm's future demand for labor). Originally developed as a method to facilitate group decision making, it has also been used in human resource forecasting. Experts are chosen on the basis of their knowledge of internal factors that might affect a business (e.g., projected retirements), their knowledge of the general business plans of the organization, or their knowledge of external factors that might affect demand for the firm's product or service and hence its internal demand for labor. Experts may range from first-line supervisors to top-level managers. Sometimes experts internal to the firm are used, but if the required expertise is not available internally, then one or more outside experts may be brought in to contribute their opinions. To estimate the level of future demand for labor, an organization might select as experts, for example, managers from corporate planning, personnel, marketing, production, and sales.

The Delphi technique was developed during the late 1940s at the Rand Corporation's "think tank" in Santa Monica, California. Its objective is to predict future developments in a particular area by integrating the *independent* opinions of experts.[10] Face-to-face group discussion among the experts is avoided since differences in job status among group members may lead some individuals to avoid criticizing others and to compromise on their good ideas. To avoid these problems, an intermediary is used. The intermediary's job is to pool, summarize, and then feed back to the experts the information generated independently by all the other experts during the first round of forecasting. The cycle is then repeated, so that the experts are given the opportunity to revise their forecasts and the reasons behind their revised forecasts. Successive rounds usually lead to a convergence of expert opinion within three to five rounds.

In one application, Delphi did provide an accurate 1-year demand forecast for the number of buyers needed for a retailing firm.[22] To be most useful, the following guidelines should be followed:

- Give the expert enough information to make an informed judgment. That is, give him or her the historical data that have been collected, as well as the results of any relevant statistical analysis that has been conducted, such as staffing patterns and productivity trends.
- Ask the kinds of questions that a unit manager can answer. For example, instead of asking for total staffing requirements, ask by what percentage staffing is likely to increase or only ask about anticipated increases in key employee groups, such as marketing managers or engineers.
- Do not require precision. Allow the experts to round off figures, and give them the opportunity to indicate how sure they are of the forecasted figures.
- Keep the exercise as simple as possible, and especially avoid questions that are not absolutely necessary.
- Be sure that classifications of employees and other definitions are understood in the same way by all experts.

▪ Enlist top management's and the experts' support for the Delphi process by showing how good forecasts will benefit the organization and small-unit operations and how they will affect profitability and workforce productivity.[14]

Trend analysis

There are many factors affecting what goes on in any particular business organization. The basic idea behind this method of forecasting human resource demand is to determine which factor of a business most significantly relates to its workforce in terms of size and makeup. Then we measure the past trends of this business factor in relation to the numbers of people employed, and we project from that what the future trend will be and, hence, the future demand in terms of the workforce.

There are six steps in this quantitative method:[44]

1. Find an appropriate business factor that relates to the number of people employed.
2. Plot the historical record of that factor in relation to workforce size.
3. Compute the average output per individual worker per year. This is known as labor productivity.
4. Determine the trend in labor productivity.
5. Make necessary adjustments in the trend, past and future.
6. Project to the target year.

Now let's discuss each of these six factors.

The business factor   As noted earlier, general business plans provide the foundation for all human resource forecasting. This is nowhere more obvious than in demand forecasting, for the critical first step in this process is to select a business factor to which workforce size can be related.

For a university, the appropriate factor might be student enrollments, for a hospital it might be patient-days, for a retail shoe operation it might be inventory-adjusted sales revenue, and for a steel company it might be tons of steel output.

To be useful, the business factor must satisfy at least two requirements. First, *it should relate directly to the essential nature of the business* so that business planning is done in terms of that factor. Thus it makes little sense for the retail shoe operation to project human resource needs against units sold if all other business planning is done in relation to dollar volume of sales and if frequent price changes make conversion from dollars to units difficult.

Second, *changes in the selected factor must be proportional to the number of employees required*. For example, after a $15 million automation of Arrow Company's domestic plants, the shirtmaker boosted worker productivity by 25 percent and was able to make far more dress shirts with far fewer people. Now, for example, one worker controlling two machines can attach plackets (slits in a garment that form a closure) to 95 dozen shirts in 1 hour. Using older machines, it would have taken more than $4^{1}/_{2}$ hours to do the same amount of work.[23] Plackets per hour might therefore be used as the business factor against which to project human resource requirements.

Selecting the proper business factor can be a major problem in some industries, particularly where workforce size is not proportional to product volume. In the airline industry, for example, it takes just as many air traffic controllers and ground personnel to handle airplane landings when the planes are full as when they are almost empty. Moreover, the same organization may produce many products, some of which require high labor input while others do not. Under these circumstances, human resource forecasts for the entire organization may be misleading, and separate forecasts must be made for different product groups or segments of the workforce (e.g., research, production, maintenance).

The historical relationship between the business factor and workforce size Once a business factor is selected, the task of the forecaster is to develop a quantitative relationship between past staffing levels and past levels of the business factor. This may be difficult to determine, especially if HRP is new to the firm and if such historical data do not exist or are burdensome to retrieve. A hospital needs to know, for example, that last year it took 1050 nurses to provide care over 1400 patient-days, or approximately three nurses for every four patients per 24-hour day.

Labor productivity This ratio—output per individual worker—is known as *labor productivity*. Figure 5-7 presents hypothetical figures showing the av-

FIGURE 5-7

Hypothetical human resource demand for registered nurses in a hospital. To determine the number of nurses employed in any given year, multiply column 2, patient-days per year, by column 3, the nurse/patient ratio. In 1976, for example, the hospital recorded 3,000 patient-days × 3/15 (nurse/ patient ratio) = 600 nurses employed. Assume that these are actual, not projected, *employment levels.*

	BUSINESS FACTOR	LABOR PRODUCTIVITY	HUMAN RESOURCE REQUIREMENTS
CALENDAR YEAR	PATIENT–DAYS PER YEAR	NURSE/PATIENT RATIO	NUMBER OF REGISTERED NURSES EMPLOYED
1976	3,000	3/15	600
1980	2,880	3/12	720
1984	2,800	3/10	840
1988	1,920	3/6	960

erage daily number of patients cared for per three shifts of registered nurses from 1976 to 1988. In this figure, the total number of patient-days per year is multiplied by the labor productivity figure for that year to yield the total number of nurses employed. Thus in calendar year 1988, let's say St. Elsewhere hospital recorded 1920 patient-days $\times$ $^3/_6$ (nurse/patient ratio) = 960 nurses employed to care for these patients. To forecast staffing requirements accurately, it is necessary to know the *rate* at which labor productivity and the business factor are changing. These rates of change are critical because projections of the demand for labor for the target year must reflect the labor productivity and the demand for goods or services anticipated at that time.

Determining the trend in labor productivity and adjustments to the trend   To determine the average annual rate of productivity change during the past 5 or, preferably, 10 years, data representing output and the size of the labor force during that period must be collected. With those data we can calculate the average annual productivity change and, along with projected changes in the business factor, use it as a forecast of what the change will be for the forthcoming year(s).

Unless, of course, there are reasons for considering why the change will be different from average for the forthcoming year. That is why we should be especially keen about analyzing the data from the past and evaluating the causes of any past changes deviating from the average annual change in productivity.

To continue on with our earlier hospital example, many hospitals have had to hire increasing numbers of nurses over the past 10 years. One reason for this is that hospitals are hiring fewer nurse's aides, and registered nurses are taking over many tasks formerly reserved for physicians only. Also, most hospitals have moved away from the concept of "team nursing," whereby registered nurses and nurse's aides shared different aspects of the care for each patient (e.g., medications, personal hygiene). Most hospitals now subscribe to the "total-patient-care" concept, whereby one nurse handles all the nursing tasks involved in caring for a patient. The result, of course, is a drop in the nurse/patient ratio. In 1976, for example, that ratio was 3 registered nurses per 15 patients per 24-hour day. By 1988, the ratio dropped to 3 registered nurses per 6 patients per 24-hour day. Counterbalancing these changes, however, have been two others, namely, the rapid growth in outpatient clinics and changes in federal and private-sector funding (insurance) for health care. These changes mean fewer inpatients and shorter hospital stays for those who are admitted. Now look back at Figure 5-7, at the column labeled "Patient-days per year." In 1976, St. Elsewhere recorded 3000 patient-days. By 1988 that figure had dropped to 1920 as a result of the changes just noted.

Such changes must be tempered with the judgment of experienced line managers, who interpret the reasons for past changes, anticipate the impact of future changes, and estimate how much both past and future changes will affect forecasts of human resource needs.

Projecting future staffing needs to the target year Once the data have been collected, the projection of staffing needs to the target year is straight-forward (Figure 5-8). In part *A* of this figure, actual and projected levels of the business factor (that is, patient-days per year) and actual and projected labor productivity are shown through the year 2000. Just as in Figure 5-7, when labor productivity is multiplied by the number of patient-days projected, the number of registered nurses needed in any given year can be determined. In Figure 5-8*B*, required staffing levels are plotted by calendar year. Notice also how adjustments to the projection (e.g., to account for the slower rate of increase in patient-days, plus the constant nurse/patient ratio anticipated from 1992 through 2000) yield a net figure for human resource demand at that time.

FIGURE 5-8

Hypothetical human resource demand forecast for registered nurses in a hospital. To determine the number needed in any given year, multiply patient-days per year (the business factor) by the nurse/patient ratio (labor productivity). These figures are shown in part A of the figure. Part B shows the number of nurses actually employed through 1988 and projected to be employed through 2000, based on adjustments to the long-term employment trend.

(A)

CALENDAR YEAR	BUSINESS FACTOR PATIENT–DAYS PER YEAR	LABOR PRODUCTIVITY NURSE/PATIENT RATIO	HUMAN RESOURCE REQUIREMENTS NUMBER OF REGISTERED NURSES EMPLOYED	
1976	3,000	3/15	600	⎤
1980	2,880	3/12	720	⎬ ACTUAL
1984	2,800	3/10	840	⎪
1988	1,920	3/6	960	⎦
1992	1,400	3/4	1,050	⎤
1996	1,520	3/4	1,140	⎬ PROJECTED
2000	1,660	3/4	1,245	⎦

(B)

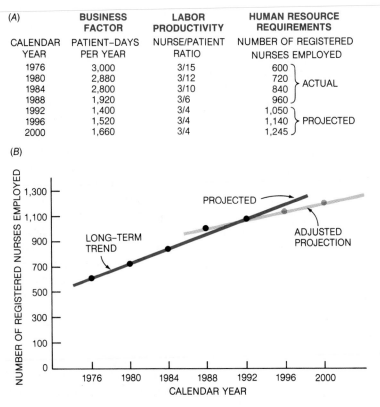

In the year 2000, therefore, St. Elsewhere expects 1660 patient-days $\times$ $^3/_4$ (nurse/patient ratio) = 1245 registered nurses needed at that time.

Finally, a forecast of *net* human resource demand (shortages or surpluses) is determined simply by subtracting the supply forecast from the demand forecast. For example, suppose that in 2000 St. Elsewhere forecasts an internal *supply* of 1100 nurses, but, as Figure 5-8 shows, the *demand* for nurses is projected to be 1245. The net demand for nurses in 2000, therefore, is +145.

How accurate is accurate?

Accuracy in forecasting the demand for labor varies considerably by firm and by industry type (e.g., utilities versus women's fashions): roughly from 2 to 20 percent error.[44] Certainly factors such as the duration of the planning period, the quality of the data on which forecasts are based (e.g., expected changes in the business factor and labor productivity), and the degree of integration of HRP with strategic business planning all affect accuracy. How accurate a labor demand forecast should be depends on the degree of flexibility in staffing the workforce. That is, to the extent that people are geographically mobile, multiskilled, and easily hired, there is no need for precise forecasts.[14] How accurate a labor demand must be depends on each case for each firm.

Matching forecast results to action plans

Labor demand forecasts affect a firm's programs in many different areas, including recruitment, selection, performance appraisal, training, transfer, and many other types of career enhancement activities. These activities all comprise "action programs." Action programs help organizations adapt to changes in the environment of business. In the past decade or so, one of the most obvious changes in the business environment has been the large influx of women and minorities into the workforce. To adapt to these changes, organizations have provided extensive training programs designed to develop management skills in the women and minorities. Also, they have provided training programs for supervisors and coworkers in human relations skills to deal effectively with the women and minorities.[24]

Assuming a firm has a choice, however, is it better to *select* workers who already have developed the skills necessary to perform competently or to select workers who do not have the skills immediately but who can be *trained* to perform competently? This is the same type of "make-or-buy" decision that managers often face in so many other areas of business. In contexts as different as a decision regarding whether or not to subcontract outside the firm for a certain part of a larger product, or a decision regarding whether or not to subcontract out for a service such as outplacement counseling, managers have found that it is often more cost effective to buy, rather than to make. This is also true in the context of personnel selection versus personnel training.[34] Put your money and resources into selection. Always strive *first* to develop the most accurate, the most valid personnel selection process that you can; *then* apply those action programs which are most appropriate in further increasing the performance of your employees.

Good selection programs are characterized first by high validity. Highly valid selection programs are backed up by research showing that people who are most likely to succeed on the job do well on selection measures administered prior to hire, while those who are not likely to succeed do poorly on the selection measures. A second characteristic of good selection programs is that few people are selected relative to the number who apply. If only the "cream of the crop" are selected, then those who are selected will tend to be employees with high ability. With high-ability employees, the productivity gain from a training program in, say, Fortran IV might be greater than the gain from the same program with lower-ability employees. Further, even if the training is about equally effective with well-selected, higher-ability employees and poorly selected, lower-ability employees, the required training *time* may be reduced for higher-ability employees. Thus training costs will be reduced, and the *net*

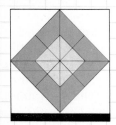

Impact of HRP on Productivity, Quality of Work Life, and the Bottom Line

An in-depth field study of six medium to large midwestern companies found management succession planning to be the one HRP activity that was both pervasive and well accepted in all six firms.[33] In fact, management succession planning was considered by many to be the sum and substance of HRP; it was the only activity that had a proven record of success in integrating HRP with strategic business planning. Human resource forecasting had been tried and discarded at several of the six firms. And while five of the six firms had a human resource information system, use of the computer to assist in matching people to positions (either at the level of management or nonmanagement) was rare.

Another view of the practical impact of HRP was provided at Corning Glass Works. Summing up the results of all their work, the researchers concluded that, as a result of HRP, the staffing process has been improved (search time for internal job candidates was reduced by as much as 50 percent with no loss of quality and with much less chance of overlooking qualified candidates), and so have, to a lesser extent, recruiting, career planning and development, and equal employment opportunity and affirmative action.[12] On the other hand, HRP has had no observable effect on education and training, compensation, and communications or on the relationships between these. With respect to HRP's impact on profits or return on investment, a number of managers described the money-saving implications of particular forecasts and action plans, but none claimed that HRP had increased profits substantially.

effectiveness of training will be greater when applied along with a highly valid personnel selection process. One of the most popular action plans, one that includes many of the strategies just noted, is career path planning (discussed in Chapter 10).

Control and evaluation of HRP systems

The purpose of control and evaluation is to guide HRP activities, identifying deviations from the plan and their causes. For this reason, we need yardsticks to measure performance. Qualitative and quantitative objectives can both play useful roles in HRP. Quantitative objectives make the control and evaluation process more objective and measure deviations from desired performance more precisely. Nevertheless, the nature of evaluation and control should always match the degree of development of the rest of the HRP process.[41] In newly instituted HRP systems, for example, evaluation is likely to be more qualitative than quantitative, with little emphasis placed on control. This is because supply and demand forecasts are likely to be based more on "hunches" and subjective opinions than on hard data. There is also considerable uncertainty about the reasonableness of HRP objectives. For example, if we set as an objective to recruit 15 percent more females into entry-level management positions within 2 years, is that wildly overambitious? About right? Or too low? The first time around, most human resource planners will answer, "We just don't know." Under these circumstances, human resource planners should attempt to assess the following:[41]

- The extent to which human resource planners are tuned into personnel problems and opportunities and the extent to which their priorities are sound
- The quality of their working relationships with personnel and financial specialists and line managers who supply data and use HRP results (How closely do the human resource planners work with these specialists and line managers on a day-to-day basis?)
- The quality of communications among the parties involved (Does the human resource planner feel comfortable just picking up the phone to call a financial specialist or a line manager for information?)
- The extent to which decision makers, from line managers who hire employees to top managers who develop long-term business strategy, are making use of HRP forecasts, plans, and recommendations
- The perceived value of HRP among decision makers (Do they view the information provided by human resource planners as useful to them in their own jobs?)[41]

In more established HRP systems where objectives and action plans are both underpinned by measured performance standards, key comparisons might include the following:[13]

- Actual staffing levels against forecast staffing requirements (In Figure 5-8, for example, St. Elsewhere forecast that 1050 registered nurses will be needed in 1992. In 1993, as a basis for evaluating future projections, it is important that the hospital compare the *actual* number employed in 1992, say 1075, to the *forecasted* number.)
- Actual levels of labor productivity against anticipated levels of labor productivity (In Figure 5-8, for example, the hospital anticipated a $^3/_4$ nurse/patient ratio in 1992. In 1993 it is important to know whether or not this level actually occurred.)
- Actual personnel flow rates against desired rates
- Action programs implemented against action programs planned (Were there more or fewer? Why?)
- The *actual* results of the action programs implemented against the *expected* results (e.g., improved applicant flows, lower quit rates, improved replacement ratios)
- Labor and action program costs against budgets
- Ratios of action program benefits to action program costs

The advantage of quantitative information is that it highlights potential problem areas and it can provide the basis for constructive discussion of the issues. Let us see how this is done in one company.

COMPANY EXAMPLE

Control and evaluation of HRP at Corning Glass Works (CGW)

An in-depth study provided considerable insight into each phase of the HRP process.[12] With regard to control and evaluation, the broad process is as follows: Four personnel development managers are responsible for assembling and analyzing corporate demand and supply of managers and professionals in four functional areas: manufacturing and engineering; sales and marketing; finance, data processing, and planning; and personnel. These managers estimate the number of likely vacancies that will occur in key positions in their functional areas during the forecast year.

These results are used to stimulate discussion and action planning by appropriate line managers. Action planning (e.g., decisions to provide skill training, job rotation) in the four functional areas can be highly complex since solutions often cut across divisional lines and may require sacrifices by various units. Thus a job rotation program may require that a manager spend time in all four functional areas. Although beneficial results have not come easily, successes have been experienced, particularly with plant manager positions. Since HRP was instituted, vacancies at this level have been reduced by roughly 50 percent, and geographic transfers have been curtailed sharply.

Ongoing evaluation and control takes place during the quarterly reviews held with each personnel development manager by the director of management and professional personnel. These reviews follow a standard format. Each personnel development manager reports on 14 areas: staffing levels; equal employment opportunity and affirmative action; key vacancies and candidates;

other vacancies and candidate pools; surpluses; losses of employees; transfers in; transfers out; internal movement rates; recruiting; other additions to the workforce; performance problems; organizational issues; and other (e.g., audit completions, career path reviews, policy communications). Within each area, the personnel development manager indicates major variances from forecasts or plans and discusses possible corrective action. The sessions typically produce agreement about action to be taken in the division during the upcoming quarter.

After the review sessions, the personnel development managers carry the quarterly reviews to their divisions. In these meetings, priorities are reexamined by the line managers, and action plans are established as needed. The occasional disagreements that arise between line managers and the staff are usually worked through at the division level. The resolution is carried back to the director of management and professional personnel, who typically accepts the line managers' decisions but who may try to influence them directly.[12]

**CASE 5-1
Conclusion**

Forecasting terminations at a Canadian aluminum smelter

A 2-year collective bargaining agreement negotiated in October 1973 called for a 12 percent pay increase in the first year and a 9 percent pay increase in the second year. However, as a result of high inflation during the winter of 1973–1974 and as other collective bargaining agreements were announced, the union asked for an early reopening of negotiations. After careful consideration of the cost of terminations projected for the remainder of the year, company officials offered to implement the second-year increase in May of 1974 instead of as originally scheduled for October of 1974, *but only to those employees who were still on the payroll as of October 24, 1974.* The union accepted the terms of this "stability bonus." Terminations during the summer of 1974, though high, were lower than those forecast before the stability bonus scheme was implemented.

The bonuses for not quitting were paid in November 1974; the total amount was approximately $650,000. Clearly, senior management was most interested in determining if the stability bonus had been successful in reducing terminations and if its consequences had justified its cost. Since the forecast of terminations for the first 4 months of 1974 had been very accurate, it was assumed that, had the stability bonus not been implemented, the level of terminations would have been as predicted by the forecast model. The difference between the forecasted and actual terminations indicated that approximately 170 employees had remained on the payroll who otherwise would have quit. To determine the total cost of turnover, the estimated average cost per terminating employee was multiplied by the number of employees who quit. This result suggested that nonincurred termination costs were approximately 50 percent of the stability bonus paid out. The terminations forecasting model and the bonus were both successful.

Summary

Strategic business planning is the long-range process of setting organizational objectives and deciding on action programs to achieve the objectives. Operational, or tactical, planning deals with the normal, ongoing growth of current operations or with specific problems that temporarily disrupt the pace of normal growth. Annual budgeting decisions provide specific timetables, allocations of resources, and implementation standards. The shorter the planning time frame, the more specific must be the planning details.

Strategic and operational business objectives dictate what human resource objectives must be. So also do internal and external labor markets. Human resource planning (HRP) parallels general business planning. Broadly speaking, HRP is an effort to anticipate future business and environmental demands on an organization and to meet the personnel requirements dictated by those conditions. This general view suggests several interrelated activities that together comprise an integrated HRP system. These include (1) an inventory of personnel currently on hand, (2) forecasts of human resource supply and human resource demand at some future time period, (3) action plans such as training or job transfer to meet forecasted human resource needs, and (4) control and evaluation procedures.

An integrated HRP system requires two kinds of information before specific action plans can be undertaken: (1) an assessment of the knowledge, skills, abilities, experience, and career aspirations of the current workforce, and (2) a forecast of human resource needs. The two kinds of information must complement each other, for an inventory of present talent is not really useful for

---

TOMORROW'S FORECAST

There is no shortage of conceptual models of the HRP process; what is sorely lacking are evaluations of how accurately they represent the process. Much of the HRP literature is still prescriptive ("This is how it should be done") and exhortatory ("It simply *must* be done"), although a number of case studies are beginning to appear. In addition to developing forecasts of human resource supply and demand, researchers are also developing forecasts of terminations (as in Case 5-1) and retirements. Given the aging of the population and shifting demographic trends, more models can be expected to be implemented in organizations in the future. Research is needed to test the usefulness of the various HRP methods and techniques, both statistical and judgmental. Political issues involved in getting various forecasting methods and action plans adopted need to be addressed (e.g., the quality of relations between human resource planners and line managers), as well as various strategies that might help overcome problems when the forecasts and action plans are actually implemented.

planning purposes unless it can be analyzed in terms of future requirements. On the other hand, a human resource forecast is not really useful unless it can be evaluated relative to the current and future supply of workers available internally. Only at that point does it make sense to initiate action plans to allay projected problems. Forecasting may be done on a judgmental basis (e.g., management succession charts or the Delphi technique) or on a statistical basis (e.g., Markov analysis or trend analysis). The precision required of the forecasts varies according to the degree of flexibility in the workforce (how easy it is to hire, train, or transfer).

Control and evaluation procedures are necessary to guide HRP activities, identifying deviations from the plan and their causes. Certainly the nature of control and evaluation should match the degree of sophistication of the rest of the HRP process.

Discussion Questions

5-1 What does it mean to establish an "integrated" HRP system? Is it integrated vertically, horizontally, or both ways?

5-2 For purposes of management succession planning, what information would you want in order to evaluate "potential"?

5-3 What do you see as the key uses of a personnel inventory? What kinds of personnel information do you need to provide these uses?

5-4 Discuss the pros and cons of alternative safeguards for personnel information privacy.

5-5 In your opinion, is it more cost-effective to "buy" or to "make" competent employees?

5-6 Why should the output from forecasting models be tempered with the judgment of experienced line managers?

References

1. Alfred, T. M. (1967). Checkers or choice in manpower management. *Harvard Business Review*, **45**, 157–167.
2. Alpander, G. C., & Botter, C. H. (1981). An integrated model of strategic human resource planning and utilization. *Human Resource Planning*, **4**, 189–208.
3. Bartholomew, D. J., & Forbes, A. F. (1979). *Statistical techniques for manpower planning*. Chichester, England: Wiley.
4. Bloom, E. P. (1982). Creating an employee information system. *The Personnel Administrator*, **27**, 67–70.
5. Buller, P. F., & Maki, W. R. (1981). A case history of a manpower planning model. *Human Resource Planning*, **4**, 129–138.
6. Cascio, W. F. (1987). *Applied psychology in personnel management* (3d ed.). Englewood Cliffs, NJ: Prentice-Hall.

FIGURE 6-1

*The employee
recruitment/selection
process.*

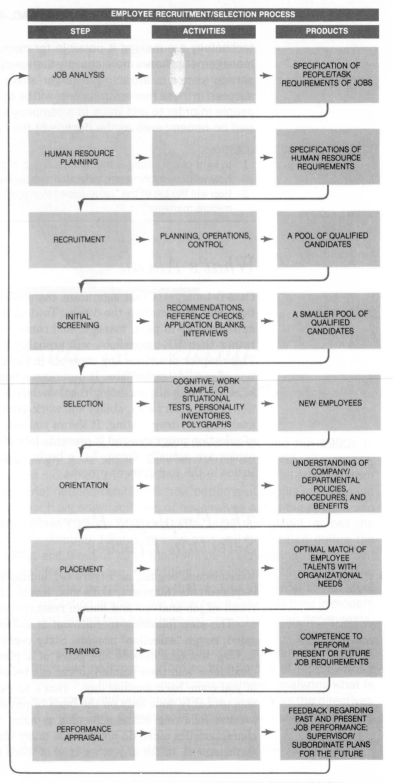

EMPLOYEE RECRUITMENT/SELECTION PROCESS		
STEP	**ACTIVITIES**	**PRODUCTS**
JOB ANALYSIS		SPECIFICATION OF PEOPLE/TASK REQUIREMENTS OF JOBS
HUMAN RESOURCE PLANNING		SPECIFICATIONS OF HUMAN RESOURCE REQUIREMENTS
RECRUITMENT	PLANNING, OPERATIONS, CONTROL	A POOL OF QUALIFIED CANDIDATES
INITIAL SCREENING	RECOMMENDATIONS, REFERENCE CHECKS, APPLICATION BLANKS, INTERVIEWS	A SMALLER POOL OF QUALIFIED CANDIDATES
SELECTION	COGNITIVE, WORK SAMPLE, OR SITUATIONAL TESTS, PERSONALITY INVENTORIES, POLYGRAPHS	NEW EMPLOYEES
ORIENTATION		UNDERSTANDING OF COMPANY/ DEPARTMENTAL POLICIES, PROCEDURES, AND BENEFITS
PLACEMENT		OPTIMAL MATCH OF EMPLOYEE TALENTS WITH ORGANIZATIONAL NEEDS
TRAINING		COMPETENCE TO PERFORM PRESENT OR FUTURE JOB REQUIREMENTS
PERFORMANCE APPRAISAL		FEEDBACK REGARDING PAST AND PRESENT JOB PERFORMANCE; SUPERVISOR/ SUBORDINATE PLANS FOR THE FUTURE

*FOR PURPOSES OF CLARITY AND SIMPLICITY IN THE TABLE, RELEVANT ACTIVITIES ARE SHOWN ONLY FOR RECRUITMENT, INITIAL SCREENING. AND SELECTION–THE TOPICS OF THIS CHAPTER.

of course, are samples of behavior, either through tests and personal interviews or through the testimony of others about a candidate, as with reference checks.

Past the selection stage, we are no longer dealing with job candidates, we are dealing with new employees. Typically the first step in their introduction to company policies, practices, and benefits (technically, this is called "socialization") is an *orientation program.* Orientation may take up several hours or several weeks; it may be formal, informal, or some combination of the two. As we shall see in the next chapter, orientation has more significant and lasting effects than most people might expect.

Placement occurs after orientation; placement is the assignment of individuals to jobs. In large firms, for example, individuals may be selected initially on the basis of their potential to succeed in general management. After they have been observed and assessed during an intensive management training program, however, the organization is in a much better position to assign them to specific jobs within broader job families, such as marketing, production, or sales. (There are instances in which employees are selected specifically to fill certain positions; these are so-called one-shot selection-placement programs.) The technical expertise and the resources necessary to implement optimal placement programs (select, orient, then place) are found mostly in very large organizations, such as the military.

Once new employees are selected, oriented, and placed, they can then be *trained* to achieve a competent level of job performance. As we shall see in the next chapter, training is big business.

Finally, *performance appraisal* provides feedback to employees regarding their past and present job performance proficiency, and it provides a basis for improving performance in the future.

The first time a new employee's performance is appraised, it is like pushing the button that starts a continuous loop, more precisely a continuous feedback loop comprising the employee's performance, the manager's appraisal of it, and the communication between the two about performance and appraisal.

Of course, all the phases of recruiting and selecting employees are interrelated. But the final test of all phases comes with the appraisal of job performance. There is no point in reporting that, say, 150 possible candidates were recruited and screened, that 90 offers were extended, and that 65 candidates were hired and trained if the first appraisal of their performance indicates that most were inept. You must always remember that when you evaluate the performance of new hires, you are doing so within the context of a system, a network of human resource activities, and you are really appraising recruitment, selection, and training, among other HRM activities.

Developing recruitment policies: legal and environmental issues

As a framework for setting recruitment policies, let us consider four different possible company postures:[67]

1. *Passive nondiscrimination* is a commitment to treat all races and both sexes equally in all decisions about hiring, promotion, and pay. No attempt is made to recruit actively among prospective minority applicants. This posture fails to recognize that discriminatory practices in the past may block prospective applicants from seeking present job opportunities.
2. *Pure affirmative action* is a concerted effort by the organization actively to expand the pool of applicants so that no one is excluded because of past or present discrimination. However, the decision to hire or to promote is based on the best-qualified individual, regardless of race or sex.
3. *Affirmative action with preferential hiring* goes further than pure affirmative action; it systematically favors women and minorities in hiring and promotion decisions. This is a "soft-quota" system.
4. *Hard quotas* represent a mandate to hire or promote specific numbers or proportions of women or minority-group members.

Both private and government employers find hard quotas an unsavory strategy for rectifying the effects of past or present unfair discrimination. Nevertheless, the courts have ordered "temporary" quotas in instances where unfair discrimination has obviously taken place and where no other remedy is feasible.[60] Temporary quotas have bounds placed on them. For example, a judge might order an employer to hire two black employees for every white employee until the percentage of black employees reaches x percent.

Passive nondiscrimination misses the mark. This became obvious as far back as 1968, when the secretary of labor publicly cited the Allen-Bradley Company of Milwaukee for failure to comply with Executive Order 11246 by not actively recruiting blacks. The company was so well known in Milwaukee as a good place to work that it usually had a long waiting list of friends and relatives of current employees. As a matter of established business practice, the company preferred to hire referrals from current employees; almost no public recruiting was done for entry-level job openings. As a result, because almost all present employees were white, so were almost all referrals.

As noted in Chapter 3's discussion of legal issues in employment, preferential selection is a sticky issue. However, in several landmark cases the Supreme Court established the following principle:[1] *Personnel selection decisions must be made on a case-by-case basis; race or sex can be taken into account as one factor in an applicant's favor, but the overall decision to select or reject must be made on the basis of a combination of factors*, such as entrance test scores and previous performance. That leaves us with pure affirmative action as a recruitment and selection strategy. Indeed, in a free and open competitive labor market, that's the way it ought to be.

Workforce utilization

Workforce utilization is simply a way of identifying whether or not the composition of the workforce—measured by race and sex—employed in a particular job category in a particular firm is representative of the composition of the entire labor market available to perform that job. To see what considerations this implies, let's consider this situation: There is a town where the workforce comprises 100 workers; half are white, and half are black; among the black workers there are 10 qualified arc welders, and among the whites there are 5 qualified arc welders. Now let's say that the firm in this town needs and has on staff 12 arc welders, 6 white and 6 black. What's going on here? For one thing, all 5 white welders are employed. And where did that sixth white welder come from? He commutes from a town 60 miles away, while 4 local black welders remain unemployed! Now can you begin to see what workforce utilization is all about?

One of the main things that must be considered in workforce utilization is the available labor market, which the courts seem to prefer to refer to as the "relevant labor market." As you might detect from the example, the relevant labor market for a particular job comprises the workers who have the skills needed to perform that job and who are within reasonable commuting distance to that job.

In computing workforce utilization statistics, a table such as Table 6-1 is prepared, where the job group "managers" is examined. (Similar analyses must also be done for eight other categories of employees specified by the EEOC.) This table shows that of 90 managers, 20 are black and 15 are female. However, labor market data indicate that 30 percent and 10 percent of the available labor market for managers are black and female, respectively. Hence, for workforce representation to reach parity with labor market representation, 0.30×90, or 27, of the managers should be black and 0.10×90, or 9, should be female. The recruitment goal, therefore, is to hire 7 more blacks to reach parity with the available labor force. What about the 6 excess female managers? The utilization analysis serves simply as a "red flag," calling attention to recruitment needs. The extra female managers will not be furloughed or fired. However, they may be given additional training, or they may be transferred to other jobs that might provide them with greater breadth of experience, particularly if utilization analyses for those other jobs indicate a need to recruit additional females.

At this point, a logical question is, how large a disparity between the composition of the workforce employed and the composition of the available

TABLE 6-1 *Black and female utilization analysis for managerial jobs*

Managers employed by the firm			Percent available in relevant labor market		Utilization*		Goal	
Total	Blacks	Females	Blacks	Females	Blacks	Females	Blacks	Females
90	20	15	30	10	−7 (22%)	+6 (17%)	27	9

*Under the "utilization" column, the −7 for blacks means that according to the relevant labor market, the blacks are underrepresented by 7 managers, and the +6 for females means that not only are the females adequately represented, but there are 6 more female managers than needed to meet parity according to the relevant labor market.

labor market constitutes a prima facie case of unfair discrimination by the employer? Fortunately the Supreme Court has provided some guidance on this question in its ruling in *Hazelwood v. United States.*[28] To appreciate the Court's ruling, it is necessary to describe the reasoning behind it. In examining disparities between workforce representation and labor force representation, the first step is to compute the difference between the *actual* number of employees in a particular job category (e.g., the 20 black managers in Table 6-1) and the number *expected* if the workforce were truly representative of the labor force (27 black managers). The Court ruled that if the difference between the actual number and the expected number is so large that the difference would have only 1 chance in 20 of occurring by chance alone, then it is reasonable to conclude that race was a factor in the hiring decisions made. If the odds of the difference occurring by chance alone are greater than 1 in 20 (e.g., 1 in 10), then it is reasonable to conclude that race was not a factor in the hiring decisions. Statistical tests can be used to compute the probability that the differences occurred by chance.

Recruitment Planning

Recruitment begins with a clear specification of (1) human resources needed (e.g., through human resource forecasts and workforce utilization analyses) and (2) when they are needed. Implicit in the latter specification is a time frame—the duration between the receipt of a résumé and the time a new hire starts work. This time frame is sometimes referred to as "the recruitment pipeline." The "flow" of events through the pipeline is represented in Table 6-2. The table shows that if an operating manager sends a requisition for a new hire to the Human Resources Department today, it will take almost a month and a half, 43 days on average, before the employee fulfilling that requisition actually starts work. The HR department must make sure that operating and staff managers realize and understand information such as is represented by this pipeline.

One of the ways that operating and staff managers can be sure that their recruitment needs will fit the length of the recruitment pipeline is by examining

TABLE 6-2 *Events and their duration comprising a hypothetical recruitment pipeline*

Average number of days from	
Résumé to invitation	5
Invitation to interview	6
Interview to offer	4
Offer to acceptance	7
Acceptance to report for work	21
Total length of the pipeline	43

the segments of the overall workforce by job group (e.g., clerical, sales, production, engineering, or managers). For each of these job groups, the HR department, with the cooperation of operating managers who represent each job group, should examine what has occurred over the past several years in terms of new hires, promotions, transfers, and turnover. This will help provide an index of what to expect in the coming year, other things remaining equal.

Managing Recruitment Operations

Administratively, recruitment is one of the easiest activities to foul up—with potentially long-term publicity for the firm. The following guidelines can help to avoid such snafus:

- Incoming applications and résumés must be logged in at some central point (they have a way of getting lost in a hurry).
- Activities at important points in the recruitment pipeline must be recorded for each candidate at the same central point. It is truly embarrasing when a candidate appears for a company visit but no one at the company has been notified in advance.
- Acknowledgments and "no interest" letters must be entered against the candidates' central records. Failure to respond to an inquiry or formal application connotes one of two things: incompetence or snobbishness.
- Offers, acceptances, and the terms of employment (e.g., salary) must be recorded and evaluated relative to open personnel requisitions. Drastically different salary offers to the same candidate by managers in different departments also signal confusion.
- Records of individuals who do not receive offers should be kept for a reasonable period of time (e.g., 1 year).

Companies frequently decide to retain a search firm to fill certain positions. Consider the following facts: Only 55 to 60 percent of all contracts to search for qualified personnel are fulfilled; of those fulfilled, only 40 percent are fulfilled within the promised time estimate. Some 50 percent of the fulfilled searches take 2 or 3 times longer than originally estimated.[20] In short, many employers are being sold recruitment services that will never be provided. Employers evaluating a search firm should carefully consider the following indications that the firms can do competent work:[20, 45]

- The firm has defined its market position by industries rather than by disciplines or sells itself as a jack-of-all-trades.
- The firm understands how your organization functions within the industries served.
- The firm is performance-oriented and compensates the search salesperson substantially on the basis of assignment completion.
- The firm combines the research and recruiting responsibilities into one function. Doing so allows the researcher-recruiter to make a more

comprehensive and knowledgeable presentation to targeted candidates on behalf of the client.

- The firm uses primary research techiques for locating sources. Secondary research techniques in the form of computerized databases, résumé files, and directories will not locate the real performers in any industry or discipline. In fact, only one in 300 unsolicited résumés is likely to be shown to a client. Only one in 3000 may get a job.[37]

- The firm is organized to function as a task force in the search for candidates, particularly where they are being recruited for multiple assignments or when speed of placement is essential.

Affirmative action recruiting

Special measures are called for in affirmative action recruiting: employers should use women and minority-group members (1) in their personnel offices as interviewers; (2) on recruiting trips to high schools, colleges, and job fairs; and (3) in employement opportunity advertisements.[6]

Employers need to establish contacts in the minority community based on credibility between the employer and the contact and credibility between the contact and the minority community. Various community organizations might be contacted, and minority-group leaders should be encouraged to visit the employer and to talk with employees. For example, the current edition of *The Black Resource Guide* lists over 3000 church leaders, political figures, educators, newspapers, radio stations, and national associations.[11] Allow plenty of lead time for the minority-group contacts to notify prospective applicants and for the applicants to apply for available positions.

Frequent use of the phrase "an equal opportunity employer" is an affirmative action "must."

Recognize two things: (1) that it will take time to establish a credible, workable affirmative action recruitment program and (2) that there is no payoff from passive nondiscrimination.

Evaluation and control of recruitment operations

The reason for evaluating past and current recruitment operations is simple: to improve the efficiency of future recruitment efforts. To do this, it is necessary to analyze systematically the performance of the various recruitment sources. The following kinds of information should be considered:

- *Cost of operations*, that is, labor costs of company recruitment personnel, operational costs (e.g., recruiting staff's travel and living expenses, agency fees, advertising expenses, brochures, supplies, and postage), and overhead expenses (e.,g., rental of temporary facilities and equipment)
- *Cost per hire, by source*
- *Number and quality of résumés by source*
- *Acceptance/offer ratio*

- *Analysis of postvisit and rejection questionnaires*
- *Salary offered—acceptances versus rejections*

Evidence indicates, unfortunately, that the evaluation of recruitment activities by large organizations is honored more in the breach than in the observance. Few firms link their recruitment practices to posthire effectiveness, and evaluation is more subjective than quantitative. In one study, for example, just over half the firms even bothered to calculate the average cost per hire in their college recruitment operations (over $2100 in 1987 dollars).[62] The cost per hire for inexperienced people making under $30,000 averaged $2593 in 1987. For those making over $100,000 it averaged $44,750.[22] Given the rapid proliferation of human resource information systems, with at least a dozen that provide applicant-tracking features at a cost ranging from $500 to $10,000, there is no excuse for not evaluating this costly activity.[26]

Organizations may benefit greatly from such analyses. In terms of turnover, differences by recruitment source have been observed in a variety of samples (e.g., bank tellers, clerical employees, insurance agents, and trade workers).[19, 27] In one study, for example, seven sources regularly used by a New York bank yielded quit rates within a year after hire that varied from 21 to 40 percent.[27] This pattern was sustained over a 4-year period. If the bank had limited its recruiting to the best four sources (former workers, candidates referred by their high schools, present employee referrals, and walk-ins) and neglected the worst three sources (newspaper ads, the bank's hiring agency, and other hiring agencies), it would have reduced its quit rate by 9 percent. In 1987 dollars, this would have saved the bank $438,000 over the 4 years. (In Chapter 16 we will examine in detail the elements involved in calculating the cost of employee turnover.)

It appears that the performance, absenteeism, and attitudes of employees recruited by one type of source will differ from those characteristics of employees recruited from other sources. In a sample of 112 research scientists, Breaugh found that those recruited through college placement offices or newspaper ads were inferior in performance, higher in absenteeism, and lower in job satisfaction and job involvement than the research scientists recruited through professional journal and/or convention advertisements or who made contact on their own initiative.[13]

A study of the recruitment process from the perspective of applicants examined how applicants regarded the various sources of information (on-campus interviewer-recruiter, friend, job incumbent, professor) about a job opportunity.[25] The researchers investigated whether applicants regarded the information source as credible or not, which sources provided favorable or unfavorable job information, and which sources led to greater acceptances of job offers. The study indicated that the on-campus interviewer-recruiter, the first and often the only representative of a company seen by applicants, was not liked, not trusted, and not perceived as knowing much about the job. The study also indicated that applicants were more inclined to believe unfavorable information than favorable information. Furthermore, applicants were more

Recruiters and Computers

A new computer-based requisition tracking system is giving recruiters at New England Medical Center more time for the professional aspects of their jobs and cutting the time needed for the purely clerical aspects of the operation by about 20 hours per week. The old system was built on three sets of logs. One was kept by the receptionist who took in job requisitions, the second was kept by the secretary who distributed the requisitions to the various recruiters, and the third was kept by the recruiters, who used the logs to keep track of their individual positions.

Every other week, the recruiters brought up to date a *jobs posting list* consisting of over 300 positions. These lists, often with illegible corrections, were given to the secretary for preparing an update. Another weekly report, *number of days to fill positions*, was prepared from the same information. *Offer letters* were typewritten forms with fill-in blanks, done by hand, for information such as name, salary, position, and title.

The new system involves a "master" station and three "slaves" networked together, one for each of the recruiters. The system tracks all position requisitions, logs the resulting hire information, and feeds back the information in various forms. It serves as an *automated log book,* and it produces a series of reports, including the biweekly job postings, open requisition reports, new-hire orientation reports, and other management data. It also produces the offer letters.

The system provides a series of menus backed up with "Help" screens for each one so that people do not need a lot of technical knowledge to use it. With new network software becoming available, management expects the unit to be able to upload the data from this system directly into the mainframe computer, thereby saving another keypunch entry.[23]

likely to accept jobs when the source of information about the job was not the interviewer. Later research has shown that job attributes (supervision, job challenge, location, salary, title) are more important to applicants' reactions than are recruitment activities (e.g., demographic characteristics of recruiter, behavior during the interview); in short, the recruitment message predominates over its media.[70]

A conceptual framework that might help explain these findings is that of the "realistic job preview" (RJP).[56] An RJP requires that, in addition to telling applicants about the nice things a job has to offer (e.g., pay, benefits, opportunities for advancement), recruiters must also tell applicants about the unpleasant aspects of the job. For example "It's hot, dirty, and sometimes you'll have to work on weekends." Research in actual company settings has indicated consistent results.[57] That is, when the unrealistically positive expectations of job applicants are lowered to match the reality of the actual work setting *prior to hire*, job acceptance rates may be lower and job performance is unaffected, but job satisfaction and survival are higher for those who receive an RJP. These conclusions have held up in different organizational settings (e.g., manufacturing versus service jobs) and when different RJP techniques are used (e.g., plant tours versus slide presentations versus written descriptions of the work). In fact, RJPs improve retention rates, on average, by 9 percent.[50]

Nevertheless, RJPs are not appropriate for all types of jobs. They seem to work best (1) when few applicants are actually hired (that is, the *selection ratio* is low), (2) when used with *entry-level positions* (since those coming from outside to inside the organization tend to have more inflated expectations than those who make changes internally), and (3) when *unemployment is low* (since job candidates are more likely to have alternative jobs to choose from).[73]

Screening and Selection Methods

Now, before considering some of the more popular preemployment screening and selection methods, we need to focus on the fundamental technical requirements of all assessment methods—reliability and validity.

Reliablity of measurement

The goal of an evaluation and selection program is to identify applicants who score high on selection measures that purport to assess knowledge, skills, abilities, or other characteristics that are critical for job performance. Yet we always run the risk of making errors in personnel selection decisions. Selection errors are of two types: selecting anyone who should be rejected (erroneous acceptances) and rejecting anyone who should be accepted (erroneous rejections). These kinds of errors can be avoided by measurement procedures that are reliable and valid.

A measurement is considered to be reliable if it is free of errors or if it is consistent under conditions that might introduce error.[33] By *errors* we mean any factors that cause a person's *obtained* score to deviate from his or her *true* score. Examples of errors are *the time period when a measure was taken*, e.g., blood pressure readings taken at 8 A.M. and at 4 P.M. may differ significantly; *the particular sample of items chosen*, e.g., form A and form B of a test of mathematical aptitude; or *scorer variance*, i.e., different interpretations of the same individual's score on some measure by two raters working independently. As you might suspect, errors are present to some degree in all measurement situations.

By *consistency* we mean the stability or dependability of a person's scores over time. Examples of consistent measurements under conditions that might introduce errors are identical scores on a hearing test administered first on Monday morning and then again on Friday night, or nearly identical scores on a measure of vocational interests administered at the beginning of a student's sophomore year in college and then again at the end of her or his senior year.

In employment settings, people are generally assessed only once. That is, they are given, for example, one test of their knowledge of a job or one application form or one medical exam or one interview. The procedures through which these assessments are made must be standardized in terms of content, administration, and scoring. Standardization will assure that the results of each such assessment will produce the "truest," most accurate picture of each person's abilities.

Those who desire more specific information about how reliability is actually estimated in quantitative terms should consult the technical appendix at the end of this chapter.

Validity of measurement

Reliability is certainly an important characteristic of any measurement procedure, but it is simply a means to an end, a step along the way to a goal. Unless a measure is reliable, it cannot be valid. This is so because unless a measure produces consistent, dependable, stable scores, we cannot begin to understand what implications high versus low scores have for later job performance and economic returns to the organization. Such understanding is the goal of the validation process. In fact, the various validation strategies all focus on two broad issues: (1) *what* a test or other assessment procedure measures, and (2) *how well* it measures (i.e., the relationship between scores from the procedure and some measure or rating of actual job performance).

Scientific standards for validation are described in greater detail in *Principles for the Validation and Use of Personnel Selection Procedures*,[58] and legal standards for validation are contained in the *Uniform Guidelines on Employee Selection Procedures*.[72] For those who desire an overview of the various strategies used to validate personnel selection procedures, see the technical appendix at the end of the chapter.

How prevalent is validation? What measures of job performance effectiveness are typically used? Which strategy is more popular: concurrent or predictive validity? Both concurrent and predictive validity rely on statistical techniques to measure the strength of relationship between selection test scores and actual job performance levels. They differ in that selection measures are administered to current employees when a concurrent strategy is used, and selection measures are administered to job applicants when a predictive validity strategy is used. Partial answers to the questions just posed above are contained in Table 6-3.

As the table indicates, only 16 percent of the 437 companies surveyed have validated one or more of their selection procedures in accordance with the *Uniform Guidelines*. (When the same survey was repeated in 1988, this figure had risen to almost 50 percent.) In addition, while formal performance evaluation records or supervisors' evaluations prepared specifically for validation

TABLE 6-3 *Company validation practices*

	Percentage of companies					
	All companies (437)	**By industry**			**By size**	
		Mfg. (194)	**Nonmfg. (158)**	**Nonbus. (85)**	**Large (101)**	**Small (336)**
Procedures have been validated according to the federal *Uniform Guidelines*	16%	13%	16%	20%	29%	12%
Criteria used to measure "success on the job"	(68)	(25)	(26)	(17)	(29)	(39)
• Formal performance evaluation records	37%	40%	35%	35%	45%	31%
• Statement of supervisor specifically for validation process	31	28	31	35	45	21
• Length of service	21	24	19	18	21	21
• Production rate	18	20	23	6	21	15
• Absence-tardiness record	16	24	12	12	14	18
• Success in training programs	16	16	12	24	21	13
• Pay increases and/or promotions earned	9	12	8	6	10	8
• Work samples	9	12	4	12	7	10
• Other	4	4	—	12	7	3
• No answer	47	48	42	53	28	62
Relationship of validation test scores and criteria data*						
• Concurrent (same time period)	29	32	23	35	38	23
• Predictive (criteria data collected at a later time)	18	20	19	12	24	13
• No answer	53	48	58	53	38	64

*Percentages are based on the number of companies that have validated any of their selection procedures according to the federal *Uniform Guidelines*.

Source: Bulletin to Management, ASPA-BNA Survey 45, Employee Selection Procedures, Washington, DC: Bureau of National Affairs, May 5, 1983, p. 8.

research are the most popular measures of job success, at least six other types of success criteria are also used. Finally, concurrent validation is used roughly 50 percent more frequently than predictive validation by those firms in the survey. The same survey also indicated that since the issuance of the *Uniform Guidelines* in 1978, selection procedures have been litigated or challenged by a government agency in 5 percent or less of the firms surveyed.[14] Does this mean that validation need not be done since the chances of being caught are slim? Hardly, for, as we shall see later in this chapter, the dollar benefits to the firm from using valid selection procedures are far larger than most of us would have believed.

Now let's consider some of the most common screening and selection methods used as bases for employment decisions.

Recommendations and reference checks

The most common techniques used to screen outside job applicants are recommendations and reference checks.[14] They can provide four kinds of information about a job applicant: (1) education and employment history, (2) character and interpersonal competence, (3) ability to perform the job, and (4) the willingness of the past or current employer to rehire the applicant.

A recommendation or reference check will be meaningful only if the person providing it (1) has had an adequate opportunity to observe the applicant in job-relevant situations, (2) is competent to evaluate the applicant's job performance, (3) can express such an evaluation in a way that is meaningful to the prospective employer, and (4) is completely candid.[49]

Unfortunately, evidence is beginning to show that there is little candor, and thus little value, in written recommendations and referrals, especially those which the law requires must be revealed to applicants if they petition to see them. Specifically, the Family Educational Rights and Privacy Act of 1974 (the Buckley Amendment) gives students the legal right to see all letters of recommendation written about them.

Recent research suggests that if letters of recommendation are to be meaningful, they should contain the following information:[35]

- Degree of writer familiarity with the candidate—time known, and time observed per week.
- Degree of writer familiarity with the job in question. To help the writer make this judgment, the reader should supply to the writer a description of the job in question.
- Reader expectations about how negative information and the letter's confidentiality influence the reader's evaluation of the candidate.
- Specific examples of performance—goals, task difficulty, work environment, and extent of cooperation from coworkers.
- Individuals or groups to whom the candidate is compared.

When seeking information about a candidate from references, consider the following guidelines:[46, 61]

- Request job-related information only; put it in written form to prove that your hire or no-hire decision was based on relevant information.
- Obtain from job candidates their written permission to check references prior to doing so.
- Stay away from subjective areas, such as the candidate's *personality*.
- Evaluate the credibility of the source of the reference material. Under most circumstances, an evaluation by a past immediate supervisor will be more credible than an evaluation by a personnel officer.
- Wherever possible, use public records to evaluate on-the-job behavior or personal conduct—e.g., court records, bankruptcy, workers' compensation records.
- Remember that the courts have ruled that a reference check of an applicant's prior employment record does not violate his or her civil rights as long as the information provided relates solely to work behavior and to reasons for leaving a previous job.[46, 61]

What should you do if you are asked to *provide* reference information? Here are some useful guidelines:[61]

- Obtain written consent from the employee prior to providing reference data.
- Do not blacklist former employees.
- Keep a written record of all released information.
- Make no subjective statements, such as "He's got a bad attitude." Be specific, such as "He was formally disciplined three times last year for fighting at work."
- So long as you know the facts and have records to back you up, you can feel free to challenge an ex-employee's ability or integrity. But official records are not always candid. A file might show that an executive "resigned," but not that the company avoided a scandal by letting him quit instead of firing him for dishonesty. When there is no supporting data, never even whisper about the man's sticky fingers.[32]
- If you are contacted by phone, use a telephone "call back" procedure to verify information provided on a job application by a former employee. Ask the caller to give her or his name, title, company name, and the nature and purpose of the request. Next, obtain the written consent of the employee to release the information. Finally, call back the company by phone. Do not provide any information; only say whether or not the information the caller already has is correct.
- Release only the following general types of information (subject to written consent of the employee): dates of employment, job titles during employment and time in each position, promotion, demotions, attendance record and salary, and reason for termination (no details, just the reason). Sweetening of résumés and previous work history is common.[48] Key aspects of previous history should always be verified.[52] How common? It has been reported that 20 to 25 percent of all résumés and job applications include at least one major fabrication.[46]

Reference checking is not an infringement on privacy when fair reference checking practices are used. It is a sound evaluative tool that can provide objectivity for employers and fairness for job applicants.

Employment application forms

Employment application forms are indiscriminate and unrestrictive. That is the way they must be. Thus the screening process does not begin with the application form; it begins after the HR department receives it. As a result, organizations frequently find themselves deluged with applications for employment for only a trickle of jobs to be filled. As an example, consider that a typical public utility company *receives* about 75 applications a day (each of which must be screened), *interviews* about 4 of the 75 applicants, and *selects* maybe 1 of the 4. Considerable staff-hours are required just for screening these applications. Alaska Airlines attempted to cause applicants to screen themselves before applying for 40 jobs as flight attendants. How did they do that? By charging applicants a $10 fee for filing an application for employment. More than 5000 people applied and paid the filing fee![2] It is not clear whether or not the filling fee discouraged any applicants. But at least the company recovered some of the costs associated with screening the applicants.

An important requirement of all employment application forms is that they ask only for information that is valid and fair with respect to the nature of the job. Recent studies of application blanks used by 200 organizations indicated that, for the most part, the questions required information that was job-related and necessary for the employment decision.[47, 51] On the other hand, over 95 percent of the forms included one or more legally indefensible questions. Employment application forms should be reviewed regularly to be sure that the information they require complies with equal employment opportunity guidelines and case law. Here are some guidelines that will suggest what questions should be deleted:[51]

- Any question that might lead to an adverse impact on the employment of women, minorities, the disabled, or people over 40 years old
- Any question that does not appear to be job-related or that does not concern a bona fide occupational qualification
- Any question that could possibly constitute an invasion of privacy

Some organizations have sought to identify statistically significant relationships between responses to questions on application forms and later measures of job performance (e.g,. tenure, absenteeism, theft).[9] Such "weighted application blanks" (WABs) are often highly predictive.[30] In one study, for example, 28 objective questions were examined for a random sample of the employment applications representing 243 current and former circulation route managers at a metropolitan daily newspaper.[42] A statistical procedure (multiple regression analysis) was used to identify which people were most likely to stay on the job for more than 1 year (the breakeven point for employee orientation and training costs). Several interesting findings resulted from the study: (1) questions on the WAB that best predicted time on the job at the beginning of the study did not predict time on the job several years later. Hence, WAB questions need to be rechecked periodically. (2) The statistical analysis showed that those items which "conventional wisdom" might suggest or those used by interviewers did not predict employee turnover accurately. (3) An independent check in a new sample of job candidates showed that the WAB was able to identify employees who would stay on the job longer than 1 year in 83 percent of the cases. (4) The length of the time employees stayed on previous jobs was unrelated to their length of stay on their current jobs. (5) The best predictors were "experience as a sales representative," "business school education," and "never previously worked for this company."

Executives balk at spending the time and money on personnel research. Nevertheless, poor hires are expensive. SmithKline Beckman Corporation spends

Video Résumés?

Yes, they're here—but maybe not to stay. With the popularity of video-cassette recorders at home and at work, the video résumé may seem like an inevitable development. Candidates can look their best, rehearse answers to questions, and, in general, present themselves in the "best possible light."

These efforts get mixed reviews from employers and recruiters, many of whom consider video résumés to be costly gimmicks that fail to provide as much useful information as an ordinary résumé. Here are some of their objections: Answers are shallow rather than in-depth, the videos take considerable time to review, and they could cause legal problems for employers who reject candidates from protected groups. As the director of human resources for Apple Computer noted: "We get 9000 résumés a month; we don't have time to watch videos when we're going through our screening process."[36] Stay tuned for future developments.

an average of $10,000 to recruit and train each worker.[39] That's $1 million for every 100 workers hired. Those kinds of numbers often tend to cast new light on this neglected area.

Employment interviews

Researchers have been studying the employment interview for more than 60 years for two purposes: (1) to determine the reliability (consistency) and validity (accuracy) of the employment decisions based on assessments derived from the interview and (2) to discover the various psychological factors that influence interviewer judgments. Hundreds of research articles on these issues have been published, along with periodic reviews of the "state of the art" of interviewing research and practice.[4] Until recently, the employment interview was considered an unreliable basis for employment decisions. However, research is beginning to indicate that the interview works well when:

1. The interview is limited to information that a prior job analysis indicates is important for successful job performance.
2. Interviewers are trained to evaluate behavior objectively.
3. The interview is conducted along a specific set of guidelines.[5]

The interview was originally considered a poor basis for employment decisions because interviewers' decisions were influenced by such factors as first impressions, personal feelings about the kinds of characteristics that lead to success on the job, and contrast effects, among other nonobjective factors. *Contrast effects* describe a tendency among interviewers to evaluate a current candidate's interview performance relative to those which immediately preceded it. If a first candidate received a very positive evaluation and a second candidate is just "average," interviewers tend to evaluate the second candidate more negatively than is deserved. The second candidate's performance is "contrasted" to that of the first. Finally, research indicates that when interviewers' evaluations of job candidates are in the form of specific predictions of job behavior rather than in terms of general impressions about each candidate, less distortion between actual and perceived interview behavior is found. Employers are therefore likely to achieve nonbiased hiring decisions if they concentrate on shaping interviewer behavior.[21, 54]

One way to shape interviewer behavior is to establish a specific system for conducting the employment interview. Here are some things to consider to set up such a system:[24]

- Determine the requirements of the job through a job analysis that considers the input of the incumbent along with the inputs of the supervisor and the HR representative.
- To know what to look for in applicants, focus only on those knowledges, skills, abilities, and other characteristics (KSAOs) necessary for the job. Be sure to distinguish between entry-level and full-performance KSAOs.
- Screen résumés and application forms by focusing on (1) key words that match job requirements, (2) quantifiers and qualifiers that show whether applicants have these requirements, and (3) skills that might transfer from previous jobs to the new job.
- Develop interview questions that are strictly based on the job analysis results; use "open-ended" questions (those which cannot be answered with a simple yes or no response); and use questions relevant to the individual's ability to perform, motivation to do a good job, and overall "fit" with the firm. Also consider asking "what would you do if . . . ?" questions. Such questions comprise the "situational" interview, which is based on the assumption that a person's expressed behavioral intentions are related to subsequent behavior. In the situational interview, candidates are asked to describe how they think they would respond in certain job-related situations. Their answers tend to be remarkably consistent with their actual (subsequent) job behavior.[41, 74]
- Conduct the interview in a relaxed physical setting. Begin by putting the applicant at ease with simple questions and general informaton about the organization and the position being filled. Throughout, note all nonverbal cues, such as lack of eye contact and facial expressions, as possible indicators of the candidate's interest in and ability to do the job.
- To evaluate applicants, develop a form containing a list of KSAOs weighted for overall importance to the job, and evaluate each applicant relative to each KSAO.

A systematic interview developed along these lines will minimize the uncertainty so inherent in decision making that is based predominantly on "gut feeling."

<table>
<tr><td>

COMPANY EXAMPLE

ROI from structured interviewing at J. C. Penney

</td></tr>
</table>

For most organizations, return-on-investment (ROI) analyses are an integral part of the decision process of any purchase, marketing strategy, new product development, etc. And, although they commonly are not, ROI analyses should be part of any assessment of human resources programs. The J. C. Penney Company tried to determine ROI from a structured interviewing program and began by developing a standard interview for identifying, evaluating, and selecting employees to fit each of a number of different, specific jobs in the company. Each standard interview was based on an intensive training program that taught interviewers how to evaluate their own behavior as well as that of job candidates.

The first step toward developing a standard interview was an analysis of each job that focused on present as well as anticipated future job-related KSAOs required from the first day on the job. Extensive involvement of upper-level management throughout the design helped to assure continued support and commitment to the program.

The aim of each job analysis was to identify the skills, experience, and personal characteristics that workers needed to perform each job successfully. From those qualifications for each job category, the best methods of screening and selecting applicants were determined. These methods turned out to be structured interviews, work simulations, written tests, or some combination of the three. No matter which screening-selection method was used, they were all called "Certified Interview" programs because the structured interview was at the core of all the programs. Interviewers were trained in intensive 4-day workshops; they were reviewed annually to determine that they were maintaining established company standards in the screening-selection process. Those falling below company standards were required to attend 1-day refresher training sessions.

The actual selection process differs slightly for external and internal candidates. External candidates undergo a screening interview, during which they receive basic information about the company and the job they are applying for, including a Supplemental Information Form detailing exactly what the job entails. The external candidates who survive this screening stage are joined by internal candidates; each is interviewed by at least one certified interviewer. Interviewers record examples of behavior elicited in an interviewing booklet specially designed for each job category. If additional data are required to assess applicants for a particular job, then simulations, written tests, or other selection instruments are administered after the interview by other trained individuals. Hence, candidates may see several different company people during the selection-promotion process. All evaluators then meet to integrate their data and to select the most suitable candidates.

Evaluating the system

To evaluate the system, J. C. Penney conducted a study of several hundred hired candidates comprising two groups. One group represented candidates selected through traditional methods; the other represented candidates selected through the certified interviewing (CI) program. The objective was to compare each group's attrition and performance over a 2 $\frac{1}{2}$-year period. Except for the fact that more minority-group members had been hired through the CI program than through traditional methods, no other statistically significant difference occurred on any demographic variable at the beginning of the study. The members of both groups had been selected and placed in their positions at approximately the same time and into the same type of company units throughout the United States. Hence all company policies as well as U.S. economy changes impacted on both groups identically. Finally, there were no significant differences found on any of the component test scores between candidates from minority groups and any others.

Results

After 2 $\frac{1}{2}$ years, the CI group hirees had 45 percent less turnover than hirees in the traditional group. Moreover, minorities hired through the CI program showed 54.4 percent less turnover than minorities hired traditionally. To gauge the program's impact on performance all employees were rated on the same performance appraisal system. Without knowing which employees were hired under which system, supervisors consistently rated the CI employees higher in performance and more readily promotable than those in the traditional group.

To evaluate these results, two types of ROI analyses were done. One focused on the savings generated by CI in terms of turnover percentages. To retain 1000 people in a position after 2 years, the company would have to hire either 1733 through the traditional method or 1304 through the CI program. Hiring 429 fewer individuals through the CI program at an average annual salary of $19,000 yields a savings (in 1987 dollars) of $8.1 million *in salary alone*, not counting additional recruiting and training costs.

Another, more comprehensive, ROI analysis was based on a utility analysis of the total personnel system under the traditional and CI approaches. Utility analysis is basically a method that allows a manager to compare all the costs associated with selecting, training, and paying workers against the dollar benefits resulting from their work. The utility analysis indicated a net payoff for the CI program of over $9 million (in 1987 dollars) over 2 $\frac{1}{2}$ years.[18]

What do these figures mean? Currently most organizations implement programs with little, if any, means of evaluating their long-range impact. However, it may make more sense simply to get basic comparative measures in place. Any model that shows a resonable ROI (i.e., any return that covers program costs plus some surplus) may well change the attitude of the organization toward funding personnel programs based on their positive impact on the bottom line.

As the J. C. Penney case illustrates, the first step in developing a program for evaluating and selecting new employees is to do a comprehensive job analysis. The results of that process—the specification of critical job dimensions and employee KSAOs—provide *clues* regarding what types of selection measures to use to assess critical job requirements.

Ability tests

The major types of mental ability tests used in business today include measures of general intelligence; verbal, nonverbal, and numerical skills; spatial relations ability (the ability to visualize the effects of manipulating or changing the position of objects); motor functions (speed, coordination); mechanical information, reasoning, and comprehension; clerical aptitudes (perceptual speed tests); and inductive reasoning (the ability to draw general conclusions on the basis of specific facts presented). When job analysis shows that the abilities or aptitudes measured by such tests are important for successful job performance, the tests are among the most valid predictors currently available (see Table 6-4).

Work-sample tests

Work-sample, or performance, tests are standardized measures of behavior whose primary objective is to assess the ability to do rather than the ability

TABLE 6-4 *Average validities of alternative predictors of job performance*

Entry-level + training		Current performance used to predict future performance	
Cognitive ability tests	.53	Work-sample tests	.54
Job tryout	.44	Cognitive ability tests	.53
Biographical inventories	.37	Peer ratings	.49
Reference checks	.26	Ratings of the *quality* of performance in past work experience (behavioral consistency ratings)	.49
Experience	.18	Job knowledge tests	.48
Interview	.14	Assessment centers	.43
Ratings of training and experience	.13		
Academic achievement	.11		
Amount of education	.10		
Interest	.10		
Age	−.01		

Source: J. E. Hunter & R. E. Hunter, Validity and utility of alternative predictors of job performance, *Psychological Bulletin, 96,* 1984, 72–98.

to know. They may be *motor*, involving physical manipulation of things (e.g., trade tests for carpenters, plumbers, electricians) or *verbal*, involving problem situations that are primarily language-oriented or people-oriented (e.g., situational tests for supervisory jobs).[7] Since work samples are miniature replicas of actual job requirements, they are difficult to fake, and they are unlikely to lead to charges of discrimination or invasion of privacy. Their use in one study of 263 applicants for city government jobs led to a reduction of turnover from 40 percent to less than 3 percent in the 9 to 26 months following their introduction. The reduction in turnover saved the city over $500,000 in 1987 dollars.[15] Nevertheless, since each candidate must be tested individually, work-sample tests are probably not cost-effective when large numbers of people must be evaluated.

Chapter 8 will have more to say about predictors used primarily in managerial selection (e.g., assessment centers, situational tests, personality and interest inventories). For the present, let us briefly examine two other types of predictors currently used in employment decisions: polygraphs and handwriting analysis.

Polygraph examinations

Polygraph (literally, "many pens") examinations are quick and inexpensive ($25 to $50 per person) in comparison to reference checks or background investigations ($100 to $500 and up, depending on the degree of detail required). Professional polygraphers claim their tests are accurate in more than 90 percent of criminal and employment cases *if* interpreted by a competent examiner. Critics claim that the tests are accurate only two-thirds of the time and are far more likely to be unreliable for a subject who is telling the truth.[34, 64] In the employment context they are used primarily with employees who handle cash and goods. For example, Caesars World uses polygraphs extensively at its Las Vegas club, and according to Prudential-Bache Securities, the tests are common on Wall Street. But most use is limited to tests for theft, and often as a last resort.[75]

Prior to 1988, some 2 million polygraph tests were administered each year, 98 percent in private industry.[55] However, a federal law passed in 1988 severely restricts the use of polygraphs in the employment context. Indeed, arbitrators had long held that the refusal of an employee to submit to a polygraph exam does not consitute "just cause" for discharge, *even* when the employee has agreed in advance (e.g., on a job application) to do so on request.[69] Finally, when a polygrapher working for Mesmer Dairy Stores was convicted of sexually harassing female job applicants and employees, the company was also found liable by a New York State appeals court.[40] In view of these results, one implication seems clear: If firms are going to use polygraph exams for any purpose, careful attention needs to be paid to the training and experience of the examiners who administer them.

Handwriting analysis

Handwriting analysis (graphology) is reportedly used as a hiring tool by 85 percent of all European companies.[43] In Israel, graphology is more widespread than any other personality measurement. Its use is clearly not as widespread in America, although sources estimate that over 3000 American firms retain handwriting analysts as personnel consultants. Such firms generally require job applicants to provide a one-page writing sample. Experts then examine it (at a cost of $50 to $250) from 3 to 10 hours. More than 300 personality traits, including enthusiasm, imagination, and ambition are assessed.[71] Are the analysts' predictions valid? In one study involving the prediction of sales success, 103 writers supplied two samples of their handwriting—one "neutral" in content, the second autobiographical. The data were then analyzed by 20 professional graphologists to predict supervisors' ratings of each salesperson's job performance, each salesperson's *own* ratings of his or her job performance, and sales productivity. The results indicated that the type of script sample did not make any difference. There was some evidence of interrater agreement, but there was no evidence for the validity of the graphologists' predictions.[59] Similar findings have been reported in other well-controlled studies.[10] In short, there is little to recommend the use of handwriting analysis as a predictor of job performance.

Drug testing

Drug screening tests that began in the military and spread to the sports world are now becoming more common in employment. Nearly 30 percent of employers of new college graduates now screen job applicants for drug use, and another 20 percent plan to do so within the next 2 years. Most test for both marijuana and hard drugs, citing safety as the reason.[38]

Critics charge that such screening violates an individual's right to privacy and that frequently the tests are inaccurate.[12] Employers counter that the widespread abuse of drugs is reason enough for wider testing. The "man in the street" tends to agree, for in a recent poll, nearly 70 percent of the respondents said they would favor a drug-testing program in their company.[53]

At present there is no legal prohibition against drug testing, but to avoid legal challenge, consider instituting the following common-sense procedures:[3, 68]

1. Inform all employees and job applicants, in writing, of the company's policy regarding drug use.
2. Include the policy, and the possibility of testing, in all employment contracts.
3. Present the program in a medical and safety context. That is, drug screening will help improve the health of employees and will also help ensure a safer workplace.
4. Check the testing laboratory's experience, its analytical methods, and the way it protects the security and identity of each sample.
5. If drug testing will be used with employees as well as job applicants, tell employees in advance that it will be a routine part of their employment.

Honesty tests

It is estimated that white-collar crime costs businesses $67 billion per year, and according to a congressional study, crime increases retail prices by 15 percent.[31] With statistics like these, it should come as no surprise that written honesty tests are being used more frequently by employers. Yet the validity of the tests is suspect.[44, 63] If an employer does decide to use the tests, the best advice is to use the results simply as one additional piece of information, in addition to other screening devices. Do not base an employment decision *solely* on the outcome of an honesty test.

Choosing the right predictor

Determining the right predictor depends on the following:

- *The nature of the job*
- An estimate of the *validity of the predictor* in terms of the size of the correlation coefficient that summarizes the strength of the relationship between applicants' scores on the predictor and their corresponding scores on some measure of performance [the correlation coefficient can range from -1 to $+1$, with higher values indicating stronger relationships and therefore more valid (accurate) prediction]
- *The selection ratio*, or percentage of applicants selected
- *The cost of the predictor*

To the extent that job performance is multidimensional (as indicated in job analysis results), multiple predictors, each focused on critical knowledge, skills, abilities, or other characteristics, might be used. Other things being equal, predictors with the highest estimated validities should be used; they will tend to minimize the number of erroneous acceptances and rejections, and they will tend to maximize workforce productivity. Table 6-4 summarizes the accumulated validity evidence on a number of potential predictors. The predictors fall into two categories: those which can be used for entry-level hiring into jobs that require subsequent training and those which depend on the use of current job performance or job knowledge to predict future job performance.

It is important to take into account the selection ratio in evaluating the overall usefulness of any predictor, regardless of its validity. On the one hand, low selection ratios mean that more applicants must be evaluated; on the other hand, low selection ratios also mean that only the "cream" of the applicant crop will be selected. Hence predictors with lower validity may be used when the selection ratio is low since we need distinguish only the very best qualified from everyone else.

Finally, the cost of selection is a consideration, but not a major one. Of course, if two predictors are roughly equal in estimated validity, then the less costly procedure should be used. However, the trade-off between cost and validity should almost always be resolved in favor of validity. Go for the more valid procedure, because the major concern is not the cost of the procedure, but rather the cost of a mistake if the wrong candidate is selected or promoted. In management jobs, such mistakes are likely to be particularly costly.[16]

Estimating the Economic Benefits of Selection Programs

If we assume that n workers are hired during a given year and that the average job tenure of those workers is t years, the dollar increase in productivity can be determined from Equation 6-1. Admittedly, this is a "cookbook recipe," but the formula was derived over 40 years ago and is well established in applied psychology (cf. refs. 17 and 65):

$$\Delta U = ntr_{xy}\, \mathrm{SD}_y\, \overline{Z} \qquad\qquad (6\text{-}1)$$

where ΔU = increase in productivity in dollars
n = number of persons hired
t = average job tenure in years of those hired
r_{xy} = the validity coefficient representing the correlation between the predictor and job performance in the applicant population
SD_y = the standard deviation of job performance in dollars (roughly 40 percent of annual wage)[29]
$\overline{Z}$ = the average predictor score of those selected in the applicant population, expressed in terms of standard scores

When Equation 6-1 was used to estimate the dollar gains in productivity associated with use of the Programmer Aptitude Test (PAT) to select computer programmers for federal government jobs, given that an average of 618 programmers per year are selected, each with an average job tenure of 9.69 years, the payoff per selectee was $64,725 over his or her tenure on the job. This represents a per-year productivity gain of $6679 for each new programmer.[65] Clearly the dollar gains in increased productivity associated with the use of valid selection procedures (the estimated true validity of the PAT is .76) are not trivial. Indeed, in a globally competitive environment, businesses need to take advantage of every possible strategy for improving productivity. The widespread use of valid selection and promotion procedures should be a priority consideration in this effort.

Valid selection and promotion procedures also benefit applicants in several ways. One, a more accurate matching of applicant knowledge, skills, ability, and other characteristics and job requirements helps enhance the likelihood of successful performance. This, in turn, helps workers feel better about their jobs and adjust to changes in their jobs, as they are doing the kinds of things they do best. Moreover, since we know that there is a positive spillover effect between job satisfaction and life satisfaction, the accurate matching of people and jobs will also foster an improved quality of life, not just an improved quality of work life, for all concerned.

**CASE 6-1
Conclusion**

*Recruiting and
selecting in the
1990s*

To cope with the rapid-fire pace of change that will continue on into the 1990s, recruitment and selection strategies will change drastically. Instead of recruiting and selecting workers to perform a single, well-defined job, the challenge will be to find and to select those people who have the intellectual ability and personal flexibility to be retrained for many different jobs throughout their (sometimes temporary) tenure in a firm. It will be "back to basics." That is, workers will need fundamental literacy, number and communication skills, the ability to learn and the ability to reason, to draw conclusions, to express ideas, and to exercise judgment. These are, and will continue to be, key predictors of success on the kinds of jobs that will be created as the service sector continues to expand.

As their numbers dwindle, middle managers will act more as coaches to the troops below and as coordinators who exchange information horizontally with other middle managers rather than relaying it between upper and lower ranks. For example, let's say that it is 1992 and you have just been named product manager at a company that makes telephone answering machines. Your job is to negotiate separately with specialists in design, engineering, production, marketing, and distribution, coordinating all the functions involved in making and selling your product. You are operating on a matrix basis.

It's a fast-track assignment for people with good interpersonal skills. Indeed, the shift from top-down hierarchies to horizontal management helps explain why courses in negotiation and human resource management are popular offerings at many business schools.

Summary

Recruitment begins with a clear statement of objectives, based on the types of knowledge, skills, abilities, and other characteristics that an organization needs. Objectives are also based on a consideration of the sex and ethnic-group representation of the workforce, relative to that of the surrounding labor force. Finally, a recruitment policy must spell out clearly the organization's intention to evaluate and screen candidates without regard to factors such as race, sex, age, or disability, where these characteristics are unrelated to a person's ability to do a job successfully. The actual process of recruitment begins with a specification of human resource requirements—numbers, skills mix, levels, and the

| TOMORROW'S FORECAST | It is disturbing to see in Table 6-3 that so few companies have actually validated their selection procedures in accordance with the Uniform Guidelines. |

It is disturbing to see in Table 6-3 that so few companies have actually validated their selection procedures in accordance with the Uniform Guidelines. On the other hand, since only about 5 percent of firms have been involved in litigation over their selection procedures since 1978, this is not surprising. Apparently many employers felt that the task of validating tests was more trouble than it was worth.[8] In short, scare tactics ("Validate, or else lose in court") have not led to widespread efforts by employers to validate their selection and promotion procedures. However, recent research has shown that separate validity studies are not necessary when similar jobs are performed in different organizations (e.g., clerical jobs, computer programmers). Research has also shown that the dollar gains in productivity associated with the use of valid selection and promotion procedures far outweigh the costs of the procedures. These research findings provide strong *positive* inducements for employers to use the most valid procedures available. As these findings become more widely publicized, we fully expect that employers will do so.

time frame within which such needs must be met. In managing and controlling recruitment operations, consideration should be given to the cost of operations and to an analysis of the performance of each recruitment source since recruitment success is determined by the number of persons who actually perform their jobs successfully.

Applicants may be screened through recommendations and reference checks, the information on application forms, or employment interviews. In addition, some firms use written ability or honesty tests, work-sample tests, drug tests, polygraph examinations, or handwriting analysis. In each case, careful attention must be paid to the reliability and validity of the information obtained. *Reliability* refers to the consistency or stability of scores over time or over different situations that might introduce error into the scores. The process of *validation* is an attempt to learn two things: (1) what a test or other selection procedure measures, and (2) how well it measures. Recent research indicates, at least for ability tests, that a test that accurately forecasts performance on a particular job in one situation will also forecast performance on the same job in other situations. Hence it may not be necessary to conduct a new validity study each time a predictor is used. Recent research has also demonstrated that the dollar benefits to the organization that uses valid selection procedures may be substantial. In choosing the right predictors for a given situation, careful attention must be paid to four factors: the nature of the job, the estimated validity of the predictor(s), the selection ratio, and the cost of the predictor(s). Doing so can pay handsome dividends to organizations and to employees alike.

Discussion Questions

6-1 Discuss some of the key considerations involved in selecting an executive search firm.

6-2 What special measures might be necessary for a successful affirmative action recruitment effort?

6-3 Discuss the conditions under which realistic job previews are and are not appropriate.

6-4 How can the accuracy of preemployment interviews be improved?

6-5 Why are reliability and validity key considerations for all assessment methods?

6-6 Discuss the pros and cons of using polygraph examinations in employment decisions.

Technical Appendix

The estimation of reliability

A quantitative estimate of the reliability of each measure used as a basis for personnel decisions is important for two reasons: (1) If any measure is challenged legally, reliability estimates are important in establishing a defense, and (2) a measurement procedure cannot be any more valid (accurate) than it is reliable (consistent and stable). To estimate reliability, a *coefficient of correlation* (a measure of the degree of relationship between two variables) is computed between two sets of scores obtained independently. As an example, consider the set of scores shown in Table 6-5.

In Table 6-5, two sets of scores were obtained from two forms of the same test. The resulting correlation coefficient is called a *parallel forms reliability estimate*. By the way, the correlation coefficient for the two sets of scores shown in Table 6-5 is .93, a very strong relationship. (The word "test" is used in the broad sense here to include any physical or psychological measurement instrument, technique, or procedure.) However, the scores in Table 6-5 could just as easily have been obtained from two administrations of the same test at two different times (*test-retest reliability*) or from independent ratings of the same test by two different scorers (*interrater reliability*). Finally, in situations where it is not practical to use any of the preceding procedures and where a test can be administered only once, a procedure known as *split-half reliability* is used. With this procedure, a test is split statistically into two halves (e.g., odd items and even items) after it has been given, thus yielding two scores for each individual. In effect, therefore, two sets of scores (so-called parallel forms) from the same test are created for each individual. Scores on the two "half tests" are then correlated. However, since reliability increases as we sample larger and larger portions of a particular area of knowledge, skill, or ability, and since we have cut the length of the original test in half,

TABLE 6-5 *Two sets of hypothetical scores for the same individuals on form A and Form B of a mathematical aptitude test*

Person no.	Form A	Form B
1	75	82
2	85	84
3	72	77
4	96	90
5	65	68
6	81	82
7	93	95
8	59	52
9	67	60
10	87	89

The coefficient of correlation between these sets of scores is .93. It is computed from the following formula:

$$r = \frac{\Sigma\, Z_x Z_y}{N}$$

where r = the correlation coefficient

Σ = sum of

Z_x = the standard score on form A, where $Z = x$, each person's raw score on form A, minus $\bar{x}$, the mean score on form A, divided by the standard deviation of form A scores

Z_y = the standard score on form B

N = the number of persons in the sample (10 in this case)

the correlation between the two half tests *underestimates* the true reliability of the total test. Fortunately, formulas are available to correct such underestimates.

Validation strategies

Although a number of procedures are available for evaluating validity, three of the best known strategies are *construct validity, content validity,* and *criterion-related validity.* The three differ in terms of the conclusions and inferences that may be drawn, but they are interrelated logically and also in terms of the operations used to measure them.

Evaluation of the *construct validity* of a psychological measurement procedure begins by formulating hypotheses about the characteristics of those with high scores on a particular measurement procedure, in contrast to those with low scores. For example, we might hypothesize that sales managers will score significantly higher on the managerial interests scale of the California Psychological Inventory (CPI) than will pharmacy students (in fact, they do), and that they will also be more decisive and apt to take risks as well. The hypotheses form a tentative theory about the nature of the psychological construct, or trait, that the CPI is believed to be measuring. These hypotheses may then be used to predict how people at different score levels on the CPI will behave on other tests or in other situations during their careers. Construct validation is not accomplished in a single study. It requires that evidence be accumulated from different sources to determine the meaning of the test scores in terms of how people actually behave. It is a logical as well as an empirical process.

The *content validity* of a measurement procedure is also a judgmental, rational process. It requires an answer to the following question: *Is the content of the measurement procedure a fair, representative sample of the content of the job it is supposed to represent?* Such judgments can be made rather easily by job incumbents, supervisors, or other job experts when job-knowledge or work-sample tests are used (e.g., typing tests and tests for electricians, plumbers, and computer programmers). However, content validity becomes less appropriate as the behaviors in question become less observable and more abstract (e.g., the ability to draw conclusions from a written sample of material). In addition, since judgments of content validity are not expressed in quantitative terms, it is difficult to justify *ranking* applicants in terms of predicted job performance, and it is difficult to estimate directly the dollar benefits to the firm from using such a procedure. To overcome these problems, we need a criterion-related validity strategy.

The term *criterion-related validity* calls attention to the fact that the chief concern is with the relationship between predictor [the selection procedure(s) used] and criterion (job performance) scores, not with predictor scores per se. Indeed, the content of the predictor measure is relatively unimportant, for it serves only as a vehicle to predict actual job performance.

There are two strategies of criterion-related validation: *concurrent* and *predictive*. A *concurrent strategy* is used to measure job incumbents. Job performance (criterion) measures for this group are already available; so immediately after a selection measure is administered to this group, a correlation coefficient between predictor scores and criterion scores (over all individuals in the group) can be computed. A procedure identical to that shown in Table 6-5 is used. If the selection measure is valid, then those employees with the highest (or lowest) job performance scores should also score highest (or lowest) on the selection measure. In short, if the selection measure is valid, then there should exist a systematic relationship between scores on that measure and job performance. The higher the test score, the better the job performance (and vice versa).

When *predictive validity* is used, the procedure is identical, except that job candidates are measured. Methods currently used to select employees are used, and the new selection procedure is simply added to the overall process. However, candidates are selected *without using* the results of the new procedure. At a later date (e.g., 6 months to a year) when a meaningful measure of job performance can be developed for each new hire, scores on the new selection procedure can be correlated with job performance scores. At that point, the strength of the predictor-criterion relationship can be assessed in terms of the size of the correlation coefficient.

Validity generalization

A traditional belief of testing experts is that validity is situation-specific. That is, a test with a demonstrated validity in one setting (e.g., to select bus drivers in St. Louis) might not be valid in another, similar setting (e.g., bus drivers in Atlanta), possibly as a result of differences in specific job tasks, duties, and behaviors. Thus it would seem that the same test used to predict bus driver success in St. Louis and in Atlanta would have to be validated separately in each city.

Recent research has cast serious doubt on this assumption (see refs. 29 and 66 for reviews). In fact, it has been shown that the major reason for the variation in validity coefficients across settings is the size of the samples— they were too small. When the effect of sampling error is removed, the validities observed for similar test-job combinations across settings do not differ significantly. In short, the results of a validity study conducted in one situation can be generalized to other situations as long as it can be shown that jobs in the two situations are similar.

Since thousands of studies have been done on the prediction of job performance, validity generalization allows us to use this database to establish definite values for the average validity of most predictors. The average validities for predictors commonly in use are shown in Table 6-4.

References

1. Affirmative action upheld by high court as a remedy for past job discrimination (1986, July 3). *New York Times*, pp. A1, B9.
2. Alaska Airlines sets job application handling fee (1983, Jan. 19). *Aviation Daily*, p. 1.
3. Angarola, R. T. (1985). Drug testing in the workplace: Is it legal? *Personnel Administrator*, 30(9), 79–89.
4. Arvey, R. D. & Campion, J. E. (1982). The employment interview: A summary and review of recent research. *Personnel Psychology*, **35**, 281–322.
5. Arvey, R. D., Miller, H. E., Gould, R., & Burch, P. (1987). Interview validity for selecting sales clerks. *Personnel Psychology*, **40**, 1–12.
6. Ash, P. (1974). *Meeting civil rights requirements in your selection programs.* Chicago: International Personnel Management Association, Personnel Report 742.
7. Asher, J. J., & Sciarrino, J. A. (1974). Realistic work sample tests: A review. *Personnel Psychology*, **27**, 519–533.
8. Baker, D. D., & Terpstra, D. E. (1982, August). Employee selection: Must every test be validated? *Personnel Journal*, pp. 602–605.

9. Barge, B. N. (1987, August). Characteristics of biodata items and their relationship to validity. Paper presented at the 95th annual meeting of the American Psychological Association, New York.

10. Ben-Shakhar, G., Bar-Hillel, M., Bilu, Y., Ben-Abba, E., & Flug, A. (1986). Can graphology predict occupational success? Two empirical studies and some methodological ruminations. *Journal of Applied Psychology, 71*, 645–653.

11. *Black resource guide* (7th ed., 1987). 501 Oneida Place NW, Washington, DC 20011.

12. Bogdanich, W. (1987, Feb. 2). False negative: Medical labs, trusted as largely error-free, are far from infallible. *Wall Street Journal*, pp. 1, 14.

13. Breaugh, J. A. (1981). Relationships between recruiting sources and employee performance, absenteeism, and work attitudes. *Academy of Management Journal, 24*, 142–147.

14. *Bulletin to Management* (1983, May 5). ASPA-BNA survey No. 45: Employee selection procedures. Washington, DC: Bureau of National Affairs.

15. Cascio, W. F., & Phillips, N. (1979). Performance testing: A rose among thorns? *Personnel Psychology, 32*, 751–766.

16. Cascio, W. F., & Ramos, R. A. (1986). Development and application of a new method for assessing job performance in behavioral/economic terms. *Journal of Applied Psychology, 71*, 20–28.

17. Cascio, W. F. (1987). *Costing human resources: The financial impact of behavior in organizations* (2d ed.). Boston: PWS-Kent.

18. Daum, J. W. (1983, August). Two measures of R.O.I. on intervention—Fact or fantasy? Paper presented at the annual convention of the American Psychological Association, Anaheim, CA.

19. Decker, P. J., & Cornelius, E. T. (1979). A note on recruiting sources and job survival rates. *Journal of Applied Psychology, 64*, 463–464.

20. Dee, W. (1983). Evaluating a search firm. *Personnel Administrator, 28*(3), 41-43, 99–100.

21. Dipboye, R. L. (1982). Self-fulfilling prophecies in the recruitment-selection interview. *Academy of Management Review, 7*, 579–586.

22. Farish, P. (ed.) (1987, October). *Recruiting Trends*, p. 1.

23. Farish, P. (ed.) (1987, September). *Recruiting Trends*, p. 1.

24. Felton, B., & Lamb, S. R. (1982). A model for systematic selection interviewing. *Personnel, 59*(1), 40–49.

25. Fisher, C. D., Ilgen, D. R., & Hoyer, W. D. (1979). Source credibility, information favorability, and job offer acceptance. *Academy of Management Journal, 22*, 94–103.

26. Frantzreb, R. B. (1987). Microcomputer software: What's new in HRM. *Personnel Administrator, 32*(7), 67–100.

27. Gannon, M. J. (1971). Source of referral and employee turnover. *Journal of Applied Psychology, 55*, 226–228.

28. Hazelwood School District v. U.S., 433 U.S. 299 (1977).

29. Hunter, J. E., & Schmidt, F. L. (1983). Quantifying the effects of psychological interventions on employee job performance and work-force productivity. *American Psychologist, 38*, 473–478.

30. Hunter, J. E., & Hunter, R. E. (1984). Validity and utility of alternative predictors of job performance. *Psychological Bulletin, 96*, 72–98.

31. Jacobs, S. L. (1985, Mar. 11). Owners who ignore security make worker dishonesty easy. *Wall Street Journal*, p. 25.

32. Job references: Handle with care (1987, Mar. 9). *Business Week*, p. 124.

33. Kerlinger, F. N. (1986). *Foundations of behavioral research* (3d ed.). New York: Holt, Rinehart, and Winston.

34. Kleinmutz, B. (1985, July–August). Lie detectors fail the truth test. *Harvard Business Review*, **63**, 36–42.

35. Knouse, S. B. (1987). An attribution theory approach to the letter of recommendation. *International Journal of Management*, 4(1), 5–13.

36. Knowlton, J. (1987, June 22). Smile for the camera: Job seekers make more use of video résumés. *Wall Street Journal*, p. 29.

37. Labor Letter (1988, May 10). *Wall Street Journal*, p. 1.

38. Labor Letter (1986, Dec. 2). *Wall Street Journal*, p. 1.

39. Labor Letter (1987, June 30). *Wall Street Journal*, p. 1.

40. Labor Letter (1987, Apr. 28). *Wall Street Journal*, p. 1.

41. Latham, G. P., & Saari, L. M. (1984). Do people do what they say? Further studies of the situational interview. *Journal of Applied Psychology*, **69**, 569–573.

42. Lawrence, D. G., Salsburg, B. L., Dawson, J. G., & Fasman, Z. D. (1982). Design and use of weighted application blanks. *Personnel Administrator*, **27**(3), 47–53, 101.

43. Levy, L. (1979). Handwriting and hiring. *Dun's Review*, **113**, 72–79.

44. Lohmann, B. (1986, June 29). "Honesty test" is lying in wait for jobseekers. *Honolulu Star Bulletin*, p. B4.

45. LoPresto, R. (1986). Ethical recruiting. *Personnel Administrator*, **31**(11), 90–91.

46. LoPresto, R. L., Mitcham, D. E., & Ripley, D. E. (1986). *Reference checking handbook*. Alexandria, VA: American Society for Personnel Administration.

47. Lowell, R. S., & DeLoach, J. A. (1982). Equal employment opportunity: Are you overlooking the application form? *Personnel*, **59**(4), 49–55.

48. Mansfield, S. (1982, Apr. 5). Job fraud rampant in the U.S. *The Denver Post*, pp. 1c–2c.

49. McCormick, E. J., & Ilgen, D. R. (1985). *Industrial psychology* (8th ed.). Englewood Cliffs, NJ: Prentice-Hall.

50. McEvoy, G. M., & Cascio, W. F. (1985). Strategies for reducing employee turnover: A meta-analysis. *Journal of Applied Psychology*, **70**, 342–353.

51. Miller, E. C. (1980). An EEO examination of employment applications. *Personnel Administrator*, **25**(3), 63–69, 81.

52. Morris, J. (1982, July 26). Craft can checkmate the "creative" résumé. *The Miami Herald*, p. 16b.

53. Most in survey favor drug tests (1986, Sep. 15). *Denver Post*, p. 9A.

54. Mullins, T. W. (1982). Interviewer decisions as a function of applicant race, applicant quality, and interviewer prejudice. *Personnel Psychology*, **35**, 163–174.

55. Polygraph testing hit (1986, October). *Resource*, p. 13.

56. Popovich, P., & Wanous, J. P. (1982). The realistic job preview as a persuasive communication. *Academy of Management Review*, **7**, 570–578.

57. Premack S. L., & Wanous, J. P. (1985). A meta-analysis of realistic job preview experiments. *Journal of Applied Psychology*, **70**, 706–719.

58. Principles for the validation and use of personnel selection procedures (3d ed., 1987). College Park, MD: Society of Industrial-Organizational Psychology.

59. Rafaeli, A., & Klimoski, R. J. (1983). Predicting sales success through handwriting analysis: An evaluation of the effects of training and handwriting sample content. *Journal of Applied Psychology*, **68**, 212–217.

60. Replying in the affirmative (1987, Mar. 9). *Time*, p. 66.

61. Rice, J. D. (1978). Privacy legislation: Its effect on pre-employment reference checking. *Personnel Administrator*, **23**, 46–51.

62. Rynes, S. L., & Boudreau, J. W. (1986). College recruiting in large organizations: Practice, evaluation, and research implications. *Personnel Psychology*, **39**, 729–757.

63. Sackett, P. R. (1985). Honesty testing for personnel selection. *Personnel Administrator*, 30(9), 67–76.

64. Saxe, L., Dougherty, D., & Cross, T. (1985). The validity of polygraph testing. *American Psychologist*, **40**, 355–356.

65. Schmidt, F. L., Hunter, J. E., McKenzie, R., & Muldrow, T. (1979). The impact of valid selection procedures on workforce productivity. *Journal of Applied Psychology*, **64**, 609–626.

66. Schmidt, F. L., Pearlman, K., Hunter, J. E., & Hirsch, H. R. (1985). Forty questions about validity generalization and meta-analysis. *Personnel Psychology*, **38**, 697–798.

67. Seligman, D. (1973, March). How "equal opportunity" turned into employment quotas. *Fortune*, pp. 160–168.

68. Shults, T. F. (1986, June 3). If a company tests for drugs. *New York Times*, p. A27.

69. Susser, P. A. (1986). Update on polygraphs and employment. *Personnel Administrator*, 31(2), pp. 28, 32.

70. Taylor, M. S., & Bergmann, T. J. (1987). Organizational recruitment activities and applicants' reactions at different stages of the recruitment process. *Personnel Psychology*, **40**, 261–285.

71. The write stuff (1983, July 4). *Time*, p. 46.

72. Uniform guidelines on employee selection procedures (1978). *Federal Register*, **43**, 38, 290–38, 315.

73. Wanous, J. P. (1980). *Organizational entry: Recruitment, selection and socialization of newcomers*. Reading, MA: Addison-Wesley.

74. Weekley, J. A., & Gier, J. A. (1987). Reliability and validity of the situational interview for a sales position. *Journal of Applied Psychology*, **72**, 484–487.

75. Wired up (1983, Aug. 29). *Time*, p. 17.

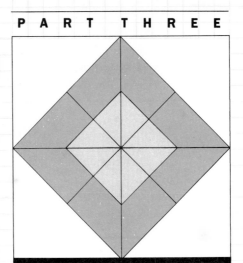

Development

Once employees are "on board," their personal growth and development over time become a major concern. Change is a fact of organizational life, and to cope with it effectively, planned programs of employee orientation, development, and career management are essential. These issues are addressed in Chapters 7 through 10. Chapter 7 examines what is known about orienting and training employees. However, because the identification and development of management talent is a topic that deserves special treatment, this is examined in Chapter 8. Chapter 9 is concerned with performance appraisal—particularly with the design, implementation, and evaluation of appraisal systems. Finally, Chapter 10 considers the many issues involved in managing careers—those of men, of women, and of dual-career couples. The overall objective of Part Three is to establish a framework for managing the development process of employees as their careers unfold in organizations.

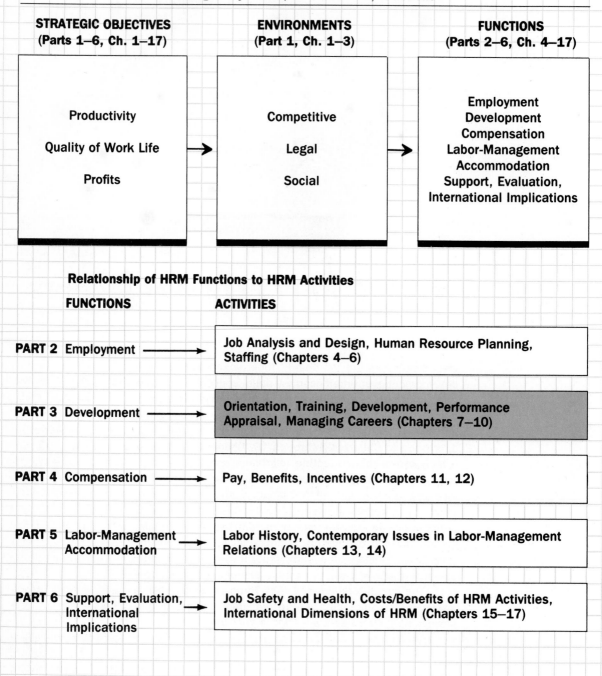

A Conceptual View of Human Resource Management: Strategic Objectives, Environments, Functions

STRATEGIC OBJECTIVES (Parts 1–6, Ch. 1–17)	ENVIRONMENTS (Part 1, Ch. 1–3)	FUNCTIONS (Parts 2–6, Ch. 4–17)
Productivity Quality of Work Life Profits	Competitive Legal Social	Employment Development Compensation Labor-Management Accommodation Support, Evaluation, International Implications

Relationship of HRM Functions to HRM Activities

FUNCTIONS	ACTIVITIES
PART 2 Employment	Job Analysis and Design, Human Resource Planning, Staffing (Chapters 4–6)
PART 3 Development	Orientation, Training, Development, Performance Appraisal, Managing Careers (Chapters 7–10)
PART 4 Compensation	Pay, Benefits, Incentives (Chapters 11, 12)
PART 5 Labor-Management Accommodation	Labor History, Contemporary Issues in Labor-Management Relations (Chapters 13, 14)
PART 6 Support, Evaluation, International Implications	Job Safety and Health, Costs/Benefits of HRM Activities, International Dimensions of HRM (Chapters 15–17)

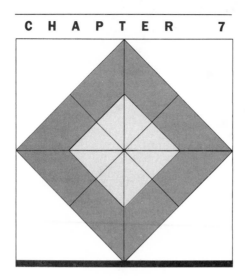

Orienting and Training Employees

Dan M. is a 29-year-old unemployed steelworker with a wife and three young children. He's been laid off from U.S. Steel's Aliquippa, Pennsylvania, plant for almost a year. Dan is standing in front of a hotel in Pittsburgh, outside the National Alliance of Business (NAB) conference on dislocated workers. (When jobs are lost permanently, the workers who held those jobs are said to be "dislocated.") Rain is pouring down, but Dan has stood outside for more than 4 hours, chanting and carrying signs along with 3500 others, arguing about the President's economic policies.

"I ain't mad at the President," Dan says, "I just wanna go back to work." Sadly, Dan's job is probably never going to come back, nor are the jobs of many of the other 80,000 dislocated steelworkers in the Pittsburgh area who are exhausting their unemployment benefits.

Says the head of a private-industry council in Allegheny County, Pennsylvania, "All those angry people out there don't have [the President] to blame for their troubles: there is no one to blame but us in business and in the unions. We have never been honest enough with the unemployed to tell them the plain truth—'Your job ain't coming back.' We have to do that and get on with retraining these people for jobs with a future." That was the whole point

*Adapted from: Dislocated workers: Put the past behind, *Resource*, April 1983, pp. 1–2.

of the NAB conference: put the past behind with its mistakes, and move on—quickly—to retrain employees for jobs that promise long-term growth and employment.

The Jobs Training Partnership Act (JTPA), effective October 1, 1983, is the key to the federal government's pursuit of putting people back to work. The JTPA makes available $85 million in training for dislocated workers.

John Dunlop, former secretary of labor, said: "A society ought not to be hostile to all dislocation, because it's the price of progress, and there is no progress without change. If change is to result for the good of the whole public, the costs of dislocation should not fall solely on those who are unemployed. Business must think of giving local communities advance notice of plant shutdowns to give the area time to plan and administer programs to shift employees to other industries." Along with this, governments must acknowledge the political realities facing the labor force, including our national shift in age, occupations, and lifestyles.

There is also another perspective on this issue: the human costs to displaced workers. People, not machines, are displaced. The people have preferences for different kinds of work, and while being trained for new jobs, which they may not like as well as their old jobs, they are losing income. Further, the new jobs may pay less than the old ones, with consequent harm to the standard of living of the displaced workers' families. This may be the price of progress, but it is important to recognize that it is a very high price indeed.

What does the future hold? We can be reasonably confident that the number of jobs will increase in the United States, but all of us should expect that there will continue to be worker displacement as the world economy responds to rapid changes in technology. To respond effectively to these changes and achieve greater competitiveness in world markets, labor, management, and government must work together as a partnership, with the recognition that cooperation, not adversarial one-upmanship, is the real key to long-term success.

Cooperative ventures that worked

The city of Des Moines, Iowa, established the Mayor's Task Force on Plant Closings and Job Retraining to effect a strong labor-management-government coalition. This team approach to retraining brought together 55 local leaders to help find ways of reemploying over 4000 people who were about to be laid off from several industries in the surrounding eight-county area. The committee set the following goals:

- Project occupations where there will be a growing need for workers.
- Identify funding and other resources to aid displaced workers.
- Provide centers where workers can get counseling, job search and placement assistance, and referral to other services.
- Assess the skills of displaced workers.
- Develop and implement job training programs.

The task force determined that less than 10 percent of Des Moines' employment base was manufacturing in nature, though all layoffs were occurring in that sector. Most of the affected workers had worked in one factory all their lives; they knew little about other kinds of jobs, and they had little or no experience looking for a job.

QUESTIONS
1. What do you think makes programs such as this one successful?
2. Are there any other goals you would add to those identified by the Des Moines task force?
3. What do you see as the respective roles of labor, management, and government in such cooperative ventures?
4. For companies in declining industries, what do you think are the responsibilities of company management to its dislocated workers?

What's Ahead

Change, growth, and sometimes displacement (as Case 7-1 illustrates) are facts of modern organizational life. The stock market crash of October 19, 1987, vividly illustrated this fact. In the wave of layoffs following the crash, over 15,000 professionals in the financial services industry lost their jobs. As they found new jobs, they found out what all new employees do: It is necessary to "relearn the ropes" in the new job setting. Orientation, the subject of the first part of this chapter, can ease that process considerably, with positive results both for the new employee and for the company. Like orientation, training also helps deal with change—technological and social. Training is big business in the United States, and the second half of this chapter examines some current issues in the design, conduct, and evaluation of training programs.

New Employee Orientation: An Overview

One definition of *orientation* is "familiarization with and adaptation to a situation or environment." Eight out of every 10 organizations in the United States that have more than 50 employees provide orientation.[13] However, the time and effort devoted to its design, conduct, and evaluation are woefully inadequate. In practice, orientation is often just a superficial indoctrination into company philosophy, policies, and rules; sometimes it includes the presentation of an employee handbook and a quick tour of the office or plant. This can be a very costly mistake. Here is why.

In one way, a displaced worker from the factory who is hired into another environment is similar to a new college graduate. Upon starting a new job, both will face a kind of "culture shock." As they are exposed for the first time to a new organizational culture, they find that the new job is not quite what they imagined it to be. In fact, coming to work at a new company is not unlike visiting a foreign country. Either you are told about the local customs or else you learn them on your own by a process of trial and error. An effective orientation program can help lessen the impact of this shock. But there must be more, such as a period of "socialization," or learning to function as a contributing member of the corporate "family."

The cost of hiring, training, and orienting a new person is far higher than most of us realize. In the insurance industry, for example, the 1987 replacement cost for a field examiner was approximately $55,000, and for a competent salesperson it was $72,000.[7] As another example, consider that in 1986 the U.S. Navy estimated that it would lose 550 fighter pilots as a result of attrition. At a cost of $1 million to train one new fighter pilot, that adds up to an annual training cost of over half a billion dollars![36]

Moreover, since the turnover rate among new college hires can be as great as 40 percent during the first 12 months, such costs can be quite painful. In the case of stockbroker trainees, it takes approximately 2 years for the average broker trainee to become fully productive.[4] Yet during this period, depending on the level of wage and how it is determined, the trainee is drawing 100 percent of his or her wage before the organization can recoup its investment.

The experiences during the initial period with an organization can have a major impact on a new employee's career. A new hire stands on the "boundary" of the organization—certainly no longer an outsider, but not yet embraced by those within. There is great stress. The new hire wants to reduce this stress by becoming incorporated into the "interior" as quickly as possible. Consequently, it is during this period that an employee is more receptive to cues from the organizational environment than she or he is ever again likely to be. Such cues to proper behavior may come from a variety of sources; for example:

- Official literature of the organization
- Examples set by senior people
- Formal instructions given by senior people
- Examples given by peers
- Rewards and punishments that flow from his or her efforts
- Response to her or his ideas
- Degree of challenge in the assignments that he or she receives

Special problems may arise for a new employee whose young life has been spent mainly in an educational setting. As he approaches his first job, the recent graduate may feel motivated entirely through personal creativity. He is information-rich but experience-poor, eager to apply his knowledge to new processes and problems. Unfortunately, there are conditions that may stifle this creative urge. During his undergraduate days, the new employee exercised direct control over his work. But now he faces regular hours, greater restrictions, possibly a less pleasant environment, and a need to work *through* other people—often finding that most of the work is mundane and unchallenging. In short, three typical problems face the new employee:

1. *Problems in entering a group.* The new employee asks herself whether she will (a) be acceptable to the other group members, (b) be liked, and (c) be safe—that is, free from physical or psychological harm. These issues must be resolved before she can feel comfortable and productive in the new situation.

2. *Naive expectations.* Organizations find it much easier to communicate factual information about pay and benefits, vacations, and company policies than they do about employee norms (rules or guides to acceptable behavior), company attitudes, or "what it really takes to get ahead around here." Simple fairness suggests that employees ought to be told about these intangibles. The bonus is that being up-front and honest with job candidates produces positive results. As we saw in Chapter 6, the research on realistic job previews (RJPs) indicates that job acceptance rates will likely be lower for those who receive an RJP, but job survival rates will be far higher.

3. *First-job environment.* Does the new environment help or hinder the new employee trying to climb aboard? Can peers be counted on to socialize the new employee to desired job standards? How and why was the first job assignment chosen? Is it clear to the new employee what she or he can expect to get out of it?

The first year with an organization is the critical period during which an employee will or will not learn to become a high performer. The careful matching of company and employee expectations during this period can result in positive job attitudes and high standards, which then can be reinforced in new and more demanding jobs.

*Planning, Packaging, and Evaluating an Orientation Program**

New employees need specific information in three major areas:

- Company standards, expectations, norms, traditions, and policies
- Social behavior, such as approved conduct, the work climate, and getting to know fellow workers and supervisors
- Technical aspects of the job

These needs suggest two levels of orientation: company and departmental. There will be some matters of general interest and importance to all new employees, regardless of department, and there will also be matters relevant only to each department. The HR department should have overall responsibility for program planning and follow-up (subject to top-management review and approval), but specific responsibilities of the HR department and the im-

---

*Much of the material in this section is drawn from two sources: Lubliner[28] and St. John[48].

mediate supervisor should be made very clear to avoid duplication or omission of important information.

Some key considerations at the orientation planning stage are:

- Program goals
- Range of topics to be considered
- Timing and duration of orientation sessions
- Company topics versus departmental and job topics
- Specific training to be conducted by the HR department and by supervisors
- Technical versus social aspects of orientation
- Methods for encouraging employee discussion sessions and feedback afterward
- Training HR representatives and supervisors prior to conducting orientation sessions
- Checklist of topics to ensure follow-up by HR representatives and supervisors
- Employee handbook: i.e., the topics it covers, its organization, and provisions for keeping it current
- Program flexibility to accommodate employee differences in education, intelligence, and work experience

In organizations that assign many (e.g., more than 15) subordinates to each supervisor, the supervisor may delegate the informal orientation activities to a subordinate.

Approaches to orientation that should be avoided are:[48]

Emphasis on paperwork. The new employee is given a cursory welcome, after completing forms required by the HR department. Then the employee is directed to his or her immediate supervisor. The likely result: The employee does not feel like part of the company.

Sketchy overview of the basics. A quick, superficial orientation, and the new employee is immediately put to work—sink or swim.

Mickey Mouse assignments. The new employee's first tasks are insignificant duties, supposedly intended to teach the job "from the ground up."

Suffocation. Giving too much information too fast is a well-intentioned but disastrous approach, causing the new employee to feel overwhelmed and "suffocated."

We know from other companies' mistakes what works and what does not. For example, at the outset of orientation, each new employee should be given an information kit or packet prepared by the HR department to supplement the verbal and/or audiovisual orientation. Such a kit might include the materials and information shown in Table 7-1.

At the outset of a group orientation session, one or more representatives of top management should talk about company philosophy and expectations—describing exactly what employees can expect from management and vice versa. These statements can also be reinforced and made official policy when

TABLE 7-1 *Sample items to be included in an employee orientation kit*

- A current company organization chart
- A projected company organization chart
- Map of the facility
- Key terms unique to the industry, company, and/or job
- Copy of policy handbook
- Copy of union contract
- Copy of specific job goals and descriptions
- List of company holidays
- List of fringe benefits
- Copies of performance evaluation forms, dates, and procedures
- Copies of other required forms (e.g., supply requisition and expense reimbursement)
- List of on-the-job training opportunities
- Sources of information
- Detailed outline of emergency and accident-prevention procedures
- Sample copy of each important company publication
- Telephone numbers and locations of key personnel and operations
- Copies of insurance plans

Source: W. D. St. John, The complete employee orientation program, *Personnel Journal*, May 1980, p. 375.

included in a prominent place in the employee handbook or orientation kit. Following this, HR department representatives should discuss issues that are of general importance to all departments. These issues might include an overview of the company (its history, traditions, and products and services), a review of key policies and procedures, a summary of the fringe benefits, an outline of safety and accident-prevention procedures, a discussion of employee-management and union-management relations, and a description of the physical facilities.

Obviously not all of these topics will apply in every situation in every organization. The list should be tailored to fit the particular needs of the firm— be it a hospital, a manufacturing facility, a bank, or a service organization. The departmental or job orientation provided by supervisors will likely be even more variable, for it must describe the organization of the department, how it interfaces with other departments, the departmental policies and procedures, and the job duties, standards of performance, and responsibilities, and it must include a tour of the department and introduce the new employees to their coworkers.

Orientation follow-up

The worst mistake a company can make is to ignore the new employee after orientation. Almost as bad is an informal open-door policy: "Come see me sometime if you have any questions." Many new employees are simply not assertive enough to seek out the supervisor or HR representative—more than likely they fear looking "dumb." What is needed is formal and systematic orientation follow-up: for example, by the immediate supervisor after the new employee has been on the job 1 day and again after 1 week, and by the HR representative after the new employee has been on the job 1 month. Many of the topics covered during orientation will need to be explained briefly again, once the employee has had the opportunity to experience them firsthand. This is natural and understandable in view of the blizzard of information that needs to be communicated during orientation. In completing the orientation follow-up, a checklist of items covered should be reviewed with each new employee or small group of employees to ensure that all items were in fact covered. The completed checklist should then be signed by the supervisor, the HR representative, and the new employee prior to being filed in the new employee's personnel file.

Evaluation of the orientation program

At least once a year, the orientation program should be reviewed to determine if it is meeting its objectives and to suggest future improvements. To improve orientation, candid, comprehensive feedback is needed from everyone involved in the program. This feedback can be provided in several ways: through round-table discussions with new employees after their first year on the job, through in-depth interviews with randomly selected employees and supervisors, and through questionnaires for mass coverage of all recent hires. Issues such as the following should guide the evaluation of an orientation program:[28]

1. *Is the program appropriate?* Do all the elements—the physical setting, the literature, the means of presentation—convey an accurate impression of the company's character?

2. *Is the program easy to understand?* Since employees representing diverse jobs and backgrounds are often oriented during the same session, do the content and style of the program apply to all of them? Is the written and visual information well organized, not condescending, and easily understood?

3. *Is the program interesting?* Will it capture and hold the new employees' attention? A 1-minute slide presentation with prerecorded narration is often more effective than a 15-minute reading by an HR representative. When interest wavers, listener resistance rises, and minimal information is communicated.

4. *Is the program flexible?* Since much of a good orientation presentation deals with a company's scope of business, is it possible that this segment of orientation might also be used as part of other employee and nonemployee communication? In this way management can get extra mileage out of the dollars invested in the orientation program. Finally, can changes in the program be made easily if the company diversifies or drops an operation?

5. *Is the program personally involving?* Does it stress the importance of people to the company? Many firms have impressive-looking plants, machinery,

and facilities. The differences, for the most part, lie with the people who make up the organization. Employees, especially the newly hired, should come away from orientation with a sense that management cares about them, their families, and their communities.

6. *Is the program economical?* From a management perspective, is the cost of the entire orientation process reasonable? An effective orientation program including visuals, literature, and collateral material can be written, designed, and produced at less cost than the annual salary paid to one medium-level employee. In one study, for example, 18 of 20 Hewlett-Packard executives interviewed spontaneously claimed that the success of their company depends on the company's people-oriented philosophy. It's called "the HP Way." Here is how founder Bill Hewlett describes it:

> I feel that, in general terms, it is the policies and actions that flow from the belief that men and women want to do a good job, a creative job—and that if they are provided with the proper environment, they will do so. It is the tradition of treating every individual with consideration and respect and recognizing personal achievements. This sounds almost trite, but Dave (co-founder Packard) and I honestly believe in this philosophy. (ref. 41, p. 6F)

COMPANY EXAMPLE

New employee orientation at Corning Glass Works

In the early 1980s Corning faced a problem similar to that found in many other firms: New people were getting the red-carpet treatment while being recruited, but once they started work, it was often a different story—a letdown. Often their first day on the job was disorganized and confusing, and sometimes this continued for weeks. One new employee said, "You're planting the seeds of turnover right at the beginning."

It became clear to managers at Corning that a better way was needed to help new employees make the transition to their new company and community. Corning needed a better way to help these new people get off on the right foot—to learn the how-tos, the wheres, and the whys, and to learn about the company's culture and its philosophies. And the company had to ensure the same support for newly hired secretaries in a district office, sales representatives working out of their homes, or engineers in a plant.

The Corning orientation system and how it works

Three features distinguish the Corning approach from others:

1. It is an *orientation* process, not a program.
2. It is based on guided self-learning. New people have responsibility for their own learning.
3. It is long-term (15 to 18 months), and it is in-depth.

Material distribution. As soon as possible after a hiring decision is made, orientation material is distributed:

- The new person's supervisor gets a pamphlet entitled *A Guide for Supervisors.*

- The new person gets an orientation plan.

The prearrival period. During this period the supervisor maintains contact with the new person, helps with housing problems, designs the job, and makes a preliminary MBO (management by objectives) list after discussing this with the new person, gets the office ready, notifies the organization that this has been done, and sets the interview schedule.

The first day. On this important day, new employees have breakfast with their supervisors, go through processing in the personnel department, attend a *Corning and You* seminar, have lunch with the seminar leader, read the workbook for new employees, are given a tour of the building, and are introduced to coworkers.

The first week. During this week, the new employee (1) has one-to-one interviews with the supervisor, coworkers, and specialists; (2) learns the how-tos, wheres, and whys connected with the job; (3) answers questions in the workbook; (4) gets settled in the community; and (5) participates with the supervisor in firming up the MBO plan.

The second week. The new person begins regular assignments.

The third and fourth weeks. The new person attends a community seminar and an employee benefits seminar (a spouse or guest may be invited).

The second through the fifth month. During this period, assignments are intensified and new people have biweekly progress reviews with their supervisors, attend six two-hour seminars at intervals (on quality and productivity, technology, performance management and salaried compensation plans, financial and strategic management, employee relations and EEO, and social change), answer workbook questions about each seminar, and review answers with their supervisor.

The sixth month. The new employee completes the workbook questions, reviews the MBO list with the supervisor, participates in a performance review with the supervisor, receives a certification of completion for Phase I orientation, and makes plans for Phase II orientation.

The seventh through the 15th months. This period features Phase II orientation: division orientation, function orientation, education programs, MBO reviews, performance reviews, and salary reviews.

The new person learns with help and information from:

- The immediate supervisor, who has guidelines and checklists
- Colleagues, whom the new person interviews before starting regular assignments
- Attendance at nine 2-hour seminars at intervals during the first 6 months
- Answers to questions in a workbook for new employees

Figure 7-1 provides an overview of how the system works.

Objectives of the program

Corning set four objectives, each aimed at improving productivity. The first was to reduce voluntary turnover in the first 3 years of employment by 17 percent. The second was to shorten by 17 percent the time it takes a new person to learn the job. The third was to foster a uniform understanding among employees about the company: its objectives, its principles, its strategies, and what the company expects of its people. The fourth was to build a positive attitude toward the company and its surrounding communities.

FIGURE 7-2

Calculation of benefits and costs in the Corning Glass Works orientation program. Note: The term M denotes thousands.

A. Benefit Estimate:

A 17 percent decrease in the number of voluntary separations among those with three years or less of service:

$ 852M

A decrease in the time required to learn the job—from six months to five months:

489M

TOTAL $1,341M

B. Cost Estimate:

	First Year Only	Ongoing Annual
Materials and salaries of developers, instructors, administrators	$171M	$95M

C. Benefit/Cost Ratio:

First year: $1,341M : 171M = 8 : 1
Ongoing annual: $1,341M : 95M = 14 : 1

The following formula was used to estimate productivity gains per year.

Improved Retention Rate:

| Number of voluntary separations (3 or less years' service), 1980 | × | 17% expected decrease with orientation | × | $30M investment in new hire | = | Annual productivity gain |

Shorten Learning Curve from Six Months to Five Months:

| One month average base salary × 65% | × | Number of new hires per year | = | Annual productivity gain |

Measuring the results

After 2 years, voluntary turnover among new hires was reduced by 69 percent—far greater than the 17 percent expected after 3 years. Corning also anticipates a major payback on its investment in the orientation system: an 8:1 benefit/cost ratio in the first year and a 14:1 ratio annually thereafter. These computations are shown in Figure 7-2.

Lessons learned

As a result of the 2 years it took to develop the system and Corning's 2 years of experience with it, the company offers the following considerations to guide the process of orienting new employees. They apply to any type of organization, large or small, and to any function or level of job:[31]

1. The impressions formed by new employees within their first 60 to 90 days on a job are lasting.
2. Day 1 is crucial—new employees remember it for years. It must be managed well.
3. New employees are interested in learning about the *total* organization—and how they and their unit fit into the "big picture." This is just as important as is specific information about the new employee's own job and department.
4. Give new employees major responsibility for their own orientation, through guided self-learning, but with direction and support.
5. Avoid information overload—provide it in reasonable amounts.
6. Recognize that community, social, and family adjustment is a critical aspect of orientation for new employees.
7. Make the immediate supervisor ultimately responsible for the success of the orientation process.
8. Thorough orientation is a "must" for productivity improvement. It is a vital part of the total management system—and therefore the foundation of any effort to improve employee productivity.

In summary, the results of Corning's research are exciting and provocative. They suggest that we should be at least as concerned with preparing the new employee for the social context of his or her job and for coping with the insecurities and frustrations of a new learning situation as with the development of the technical skills necessary for job performance. The question of how best to teach those technical skills is also critically important. The design, conduct, and evaluation of employee training programs is a strategic issue that simply cannot be ignored.

Employee Training

As the demands of the second industrial revolution spread, companies are coming to regard training expenses as no less a part of their capital costs than plants and equipment. Total training outlays by U.S. firms are now $30 billion—and rising.[44] At the level of the individual firm, Motorola is typical. It budgets about 1 percent of annual sales (2.6 percent of payroll) for training. It even trains workers for its key suppliers, many of them small- to medium-size firms without the resources to train their own people in such advanced specialties as computer-aided design and defect control. Taking into account training expenses, wages, and benefits, the total cost amounts to about $90 million. The results have been dramatic, according to a company spokesperson: "We've documented the savings from the statistical process control methods and problem-solving methods we've trained our people in. We're running a rate of return of about 30 times the dollars invested—which is why we've gotten pretty good support from senior management" (ref. 3, p. 87).

Retraining, too, can pay off. A study by the Work in America Institute found that retraining current workers for new jobs is more cost-effective than firing them and hiring new ones—not to mention the difference that retraining makes to employee morale.[3] And in "downsizing" industries where there are no alternatives to furloughs, unions are working with management to retrain displaced workers. The Milpitas, California, assembly plant of Ford Motor Company is a case in point.

| **COMPANY EXAMPLE** *Labor-management cooperation in employee retraining* | A year before Ford Motor Company closed its Milpitas, California, plant, management, together with United Auto Workers officials, began to assess the 2100 hourly workers' training needs. Idle portions of the plant and the cafeteria were used to teach remedial English and math skills, and Ford also offered "vocational exploration" classes for up to 2 weeks so that employees could try new skills in areas such as auto upholstery and forklift operations. Even though the plant is now closed, the company still runs a center there for other training and placement services. About 375 workers |

landed new jobs within 4 months after the plant closed. Others who were not so lucky disliked being unemployed, but they felt that Ford treated them in a "humane" way.[27]

While the potential returns from well-conducted training programs are hefty, considerable planning and evaluation are necessary in order to realize these returns. The remainder of this chapter examines some key issues that managers need to consider. Let us begin by defining our terms.

What is training?

Traditionally, lower-level employees were "trained," while higher-level employees were "developed." This distinction, focusing on the learning of hands-on skills versus interpersonal and decision-making skills, has become too blurry in practice to be useful. Throughout the remainder of this chapter and the next, therefore, the terms *training* and *development* will be used interchangeably.

Training consists of planned programs designed to improve performance at the individual, group, and/or organizational levels. Improved performance, in turn, implies that there have been measurable changes in knowledge, skills, attitudes, and/or social behavior.

Unfortunately, too much emphasis is often placed on the techniques and methods of training to be used and not enough on first defining what the employee should learn in relation to desired job behaviors. Furthermore, very few organizations place much emphasis on assessing the outcomes of training activities. That is, they overlook the need to determine whether the training objectives were met.

One way to keep in mind the phases of a training program is to portray them graphically, in the form of a model that illustrates the interaction among the phases of the program. One such model is shown in Figure 7-3.

The *assessment* (or planning) *phase* serves as a foundation for the entire training effort. As Figure 7-3 shows, both the *training phase* and the *evaluation phase* depend on inputs from assessment. If the assessment phase is not carefully done, then the training program as a whole will have little chance of achieving what it is intended to do.

Assuming that the objectives of the training program are carefully specified, the next task is to design the environment in which to achieve those objectives. This is the purpose of the training phase, "a delicate process that requires a blend of learning principles and media selection, based on the tasks that the trainee is eventually expected to perform" (ref. 12, p. 21).

Finally, if both the assessment phase and the training phase have been done competently, then evaluation should present few problems. Evaluation is a twofold process that involves (1) establishing indicators of success in training, as well as on the job, and (2) determining exactly what job-related changes have occurred as a result of the training. Evaluation must provide a continuous stream of feedback that can be used to reassess training needs, thereby creating input for the next stage of employee development.

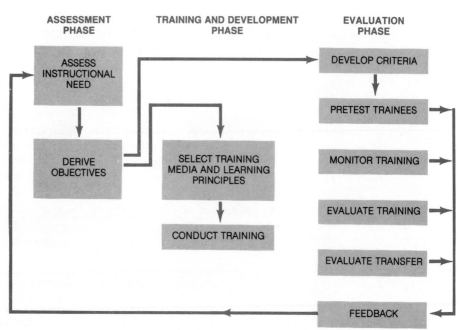

FIGURE 7-3

A general systems model of the training and development process. Note how information developed during the evaluation phase provides feedback, and therefore new input, to the assessment phase. This initiates a new cycle of assessment, training and development, and evaluation.

Now that we have a broad overview of the training process, let us consider the elements of Figure 7-3 in greater detail.

Assessing training needs

There are three levels of analysis for determining the needs that training can fulfill:[32]

Organization analysis focuses on identifying where within the organization training is needed.

Operations analysis attempts to identify the content of training—what an employee must do in order to perform competently.

Individual analysis determines how well each employee is performing the tasks that make up his or her job.

Training needs might surface in any one of these three broad areas. But to ask productive questions regarding training needs, an "integrative model" such as shown in Figure 7-4 is needed.

At a general level, training needs must be analyzed against the backdrop of organizational objectives and strategies. Unless this is done, time and money may well be wasted on training programs that do not advance the cause of the company.[35] People may be trained in skills they already possess (as happened

FIGURE 7-4

Training needs assessment model.

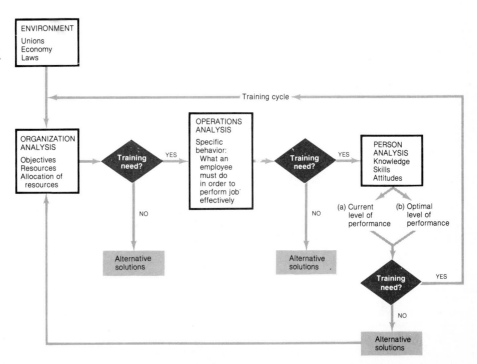

to members of a machinists' union of a major airline not long ago); the training budget may be squandered on "rest and recuperation" sessions, where employees are entertained but learn little in the way of required job skills or job knowledge; or the budget may be spent on glittering hardware that meets the training director's needs but not the organization's.

Analysis of the organization's external environment and internal climate is also essential. Trends in union activity, governmental intervention, productivity, accidents, illnesses, turnover, absenteeism, and on-the-job employee behavior all provide relevant information at this level. The important question then becomes "Will training produce changes in employee behavior that will contribute to our organization's goals?"

In short, the critical first step is to relate the assessment of training needs to the achievement of organizational goals. If that connection cannot be made, the training is probably unnecessary. However, if a training need is identified at this organizational level, then an operations analysis is the next step.

Operations analysis requires a careful examination of the job to be performed *after* training. It involves: (1) a systematic collection of information that describes exactly *how* jobs are done, so that (2) standards of performance for those jobs can be determined; (3) how tasks are to be performed to meet the standards; and (4) the knowledge, skills, abilities, and other characteristics necessary for effective task performance. Job analyses, performance appraisals, interviews (with jobholders, supervisors, and higher management), and analyses of operating problems (quality control, downtime reports, and customer complaints) all provide important inputs to the analysis of training needs.

Finally there is *individual analysis*. At this level, training needs may be defined in terms of the following general idea: The difference between desired performance and actual performance is the individual's training need. Performance standards, identified in the operations analysis phase, constitute desired performance. Individual performance data, diagnostic ratings of employees by their supervisors, records of performance kept by workers in diary form, attitude surveys, interviews, or tests (job knowledge, work sample, or situational) can provide information on *actual* performance against which each employee can be compared to *desired* job performance standards. A gap between actual and desired performance may be filled by training.

However, assessing the needs for training does not end here. To evaluate the results of training and to assess what training is needed in the future, needs must be analyzed regularly *and* at all three levels.

- At the organizational level, needs must be analyzed by the managers who set the organization's goals.
- At the operations level, needs must be analyzed by the managers who specify how the organization's goals are going to be achieved.
- At the individual level, needs must be analyzed by the managers and workers who do the work to achieve those goals.

COMPANY EXAMPLE

From needs analysis, to training, to results!

At Pacific Northwest Bell, installers were uncertain about whether and how much they could charge for work on noncompany equipment and wiring, so they were billing very little. The company, in turn, seeing little revenue generated by the labor hours spent, had stopped marketing the technicians' services.

A team of internal consultants—a company manager, a representative of the International Brotherhood of Electrical Workers, and a representative of the Communications Workers of America—recognized this problem and tried to solve it by involving a cross section of interested parties. The new task force agreed on two goals: to increase revenues and to increase job security.

A subcommittee of two task developers and two technicians developed a training program designed to teach installers *how* and *what* to charge, and also *why* they should keep accurate records: to increase their job security. The committee agreed to measure the revenues generated by time and materials charging so that these revenues could be weighed against labor costs in layoff decisions.

The training consisted of two 6-hour days and was presented by technicians to about 400 installers throughout Washington State and Oregon. In addition to the course, the task force identified the need for a hot line that technicians could call when bidding for a job. The line was set up, and one of the course instructors was promoted to a management position for answering calls.

Results

The results of the training and hot line were phenomenal, as shown by the pattern of revenues from work on noncompany equipment. In January, prior to the training course, the installers had billed $589. In April, when half the workers had completed the training, they billed $21,000 in outside work. By the following February, billings for customized work and charges reached $180,000. Total revenues over the 14-month period were about $1.4 million, or nearly twice the task force's projection of $831,000.

In light of these results, the company now markets the installers' services aggressively. For example, if an installation crew drives by a construction site on their way from another job, they stop and bid on the work. The hot line receives about 50 calls per day from systems technicians, installers, the business office, and customers.

The efforts of the task force increased company revenues, and also the job security of the installers. Demand for their services grew with increased bidding on jobs, and more installers were added, providing union members in other job titles with opportunities for promotions or transfers into this work group. Future layoffs are unlikely, since the savings in labor costs must be weighed against the revenues generated by the installers.[18] Careful assessment of the need for training, coupled with the delivery of a training program that met targeted needs, produced results that startled management, the union, and the installation technicians. Everybody won.

Issues in the Design and Conduct of Training Programs

Equal employment opportunity

The federal "Uniform Guidelines on Employee Selection Procedures" affect five areas of training:[49] job entry, training program admission, the training process itself, career decisions, and affirmative action plans.

Job entry training may be necessary before a person can be considered for entry to a job: for example, passing a pole-climbing course prior to being considered for a job as a telephone installer or repairer. Legal problems may arise in instances where women or minorities are less likely to pass the training course than white men (that is, "adverse impact" exists) *and* the company has no proof that the training requirements are related to job proficiency. To avoid such difficulties, all trainees must be given an equal chance to complete the training successfully. And, of course, the validity of the training requirements must be demonstrated. The company must be able to show that people with the training perform their jobs better than those without the training.

Another area affected by the guidelines is *admission into the training program.* Legally, Title VII of the 1964 Civil Rights Act prohibits discrimination against individuals on the basis of their race, sex, age, religion, or national origin in admission to apprenticeship or other training programs. When discriminatory practices have been uncovered and brought to court, the courts have made decisions effecting far-reaching changes.[39]

The training process itself may have an adverse impact on women and minorities. For example, physical equipment for training may be designed primarily for men, thereby making it difficult for some women to use because of their generally shorter legs and arm reach. (Redesign of the equipment might eliminate this problem.) The vocabulary level in training manuals may require a reading ability far higher than is necessary to perform the job itself, thus eliminating those with less education. In short, if the training process itself consistently results in inferior performance by women and minorities, the program may have to be redesigned *unless* such inferior training performance is reflected in corresponding inferior job performance.

Career decisions, such as retention in the training program or preferential job assignment, are sometimes made on the basis of measures collected during training. Again, if women and minorities consistently perform poorly in training, the performance measures themselves must be validated to show that performance in training reflects later performance on the job. Sound personnel practice dictates that this be done anyway to assess whether training dollars are being spent well.

Affirmative action plans commonly specify goals for the recruitment, selection, and training of women and minorities. In the biggest consent decree ever, General Motors agreed (with the EEOC) to spend $42.5 million over 6 years to hire, train, and promote more women and minorities. GM agreed to establish companywide hiring goals for women and minorities in eight job categories, including apprentices, supervisors, security officers, and sales managers. The company also agreed to spend over $21 million on training this target group for higher-level positions and to provide an additional $15 million educational package of endowments and scholarships for more than 100,000 employed and laid-off women and minorities and their families.[25] Clearly the legal aspects of training programs should not be underestimated. However, neither should they preoccupy us to the point of not considering other, equally critical, aspects of training design and implementation, such as maximizing trainees' learning.

Trainability

Organizations provide training to those who are most likely to profit from it; individuals prefer to be trained in the things that interest them and in which they can improve. To provide instruction for trainees in areas in which they have no aptitude or interest will not benefit them and will certainly not benefit the organization.

From a cost-benefit perspective, the largest cost component of training is the cost of paying the trainees during the training period. Hence, cost savings are possible if training time can be reduced. Perhaps the easiest way to do this is by identifying and training only those employees who clearly are "trainable." *Trainability* refers to how well a person can acquire the skills, knowledge, and behavior necessary to perform a job, achieving its specified outcome within a given time.[42] It is a combination of an individual's ability and motivation.

Can a person's ability to learn a job be predicted? Recent research suggests that the answer is a cautious yes. For example, one study showed that current methods for assigning enlisted Navy personnel to specific jobs could be improved by using a concept called "miniature training and evaluation testing."[45] Using this approach, a recruit is trained (and then subsequently tested) on a sample of the tasks that he or she will be expected to perform on the job. The approach is based on the premise that a recruit who demonstrates that he or she can learn to perform a *sample* of the tasks of a Navy job will be able to learn and to perform satisfactorily *all* the tasks of that job, given appropriate on-the-job training. In fact, a battery of nine training-evaluation situations derived from a job analysis of typical entry-level tasks for various naval occupations, such as sailor, firefighter, and air crew member, was able to improve substantially the accuracy of prediction of job performance over that obtained with standard written tests.

Although "can-do" (ability) factors are necessary, it is important to recognize that "will-do" (motivational) factors also play a vital role in the prediction of trainability. For example, the Navy School for Divers found that a seven-item trainee confidence measure significantly predicted graduation from its 10-week training program in Scuba and Deep Sea Air procedures.[43] Each of the following items is answered on a 6-point scale from "disagree strongly" (score of 1) to "agree strongly" (score of 6):

1. I have a better chance of passing this training than most others do.
2. I volunteered for this training program as soon as I could.
3. The knowledge and experience that I gain in this training may advance my career.
4. Even if I fail, this training will be a valuable experience.
5. I will get more from this training than most people.
6. If I have trouble during training, I will try harder.
7. I am more physically fit for this training than most people.

Trainees most likely to profit from training can be identified reasonably accurately when measures such as these are combined with two other kinds of information: (1) the extent of each potential trainee's job involvement and career planning[37, 38] and (2) each employee's choice to select the training in question.[16] Once these trainees have been identified, it becomes important to structure the training environment for maximum learning. Attention to the fundamental principles of learning is essential.

Principles of learning

To promote efficient learning, long-term retention, and application of the skills or factual information learned in training back to the job situation, training programs should incorporate principles of learning developed over the past century. Which principles should be considered? It depends on whether the trainees are learning skills (e.g., drafting) or factual material (e.g., principles of life insurance).[50]

To be most effective, *skill learning* should include four essential ingredients: (1) goal setting, (2) behavior modeling, (3) practice, and (4) feedback.

However, when the focus is on *learning facts*, the sequence should change only slightly: namely, (1) goal setting, (2) meaningfulness of material, (3) practice, and (4) feedback. Let's consider each of these in greater detail.

Motivating the trainee: goal setting   A person who wants to develop herself or himself will do so; a person who wants to be developed rarely is. This statement illustrates the role that motivation plays in training—to learn, you must *want* to learn. And it appears from evidence that the most effective way to raise a trainee's motivation is by setting goals. Goal setting has a proven track record of success in improving employee performance in a variety of settings and cultures.[30, 33] On average, goal setting leads to a 10 percent improvement in productivity, and it works best with tasks of low complexity.[52]

✗ Goal theory is founded on the premise that an individual's conscious goals or intentions regulate her or his behavior.[26] Research indicates that once a goal is accepted, difficult but attainable goals result in higher levels of performance than do easy goals or even a generalized goal such as "do your best." These findings have three important implications for motivating trainees:

1. The objectives of the training program should be made clear at the outset. Each objective should describe the desired behavior, the conditions under which it should occur, and the success criteria by which the behavior will be judged.[29] For example:

   In a 4-hour performance test at the end of 1 month of training [conditions], you will be able to reupholster an armchair, a couch, and a hassock, demonstrating the correct procedures at each step in the process [desired behavior]. All steps must be executed in the correct order and must meet standards of fit and trim specified in the textbook [success criteria].

2. Goals should be challenging and difficult enough that the trainees can derive personal satisfaction from achieving them, but not so difficult that they are perceived as impossible to reach.

3. The ultimate goal of "finishing the program" should be supplemented with subgoals during training, such as trainer evaluations, work-sample tests, and periodic quizzes. As each hurdle is cleared successfully, trainee confidence about attaining the ultimate goal increases.

While goal setting clearly affects the trainees' motivation, so also do the *expectations* of the trainer. In fact, expectations have a way of becoming self-fulfilling prophecies so that the higher the expectations, the better the trainees perform. Conversely, the lower the expectations, the worse the trainees perform. This phenomenon of the self-fulfilling prophecy is known as the *Pygmalion effect*. Legend has it that Pygmalion, a king of Cyprus, sculptured an ivory statue of a maiden named Galatea. Pygmalion fell in love with the statue, and, at his prayer, Aphrodite, the goddess of love and beauty, gave it life. Pygmalion's fondest wish, his expectation, came true.

Behavior modeling　Much of what we learn is acquired by observing others. We will imitate other peoples' actions when they lead to desirable outcomes for those involved (e.g., promotions, increased sales, or more accurate tennis serves). The models' actions serve as a cue as to what constitutes appropriate behavior.[2] A *model* is someone who is seen as competent, powerful, and friendly and has high status within an organization. We try to identify with this model because her or his behavior is seen as desirable and appropriate. Modeling tends to increase when the model is rewarded for behavior and when the rewards (e.g., influence, pay) are things the imitator would like to have. In

Pygmalion in Action: Managers Get the Kind of Performance They Expect

To test the Pygmalion effect and to examine the impact of instructors' prior expectations about trainees on the instructors' subsequent style of leadership toward the trainees, a field experiment was conducted at a military training base.[7] A total of 105 trainees in a 15-week combat command course were matched on aptitude and assigned randomly to one of three experimental groups. Each group corresponded to a particular level of expectation that was communicated to the instructors: high, average, or no prespecified level of expectation (due to insufficient information). Four days before the trainees arrived at the base, and prior to any acquaintance between instructors and trainees, the instructors were assembled and given a score (known as command potential, or CP) for each trainee that represented the trainee's potential to command others. The instructors were told that the CP score was developed on the basis of psychological test scores, data from a previous course on leadership, and ratings by previous commanders. The instructors were also told that course grades predict CP in 95 percent of the cases. The instructors were then given a list of the trainees assigned to them, along with their CPs, and asked to copy each trainee's CP into his or her personal record. The instructors were also requested to learn their trainees' names and their CPs before the beginning of the course.

The Pygmalion hypothesis that the instructor's prior expectation influences the trainee's performance was confirmed. Trainees of whom instructors expected better performance scored significantly higher on objective achievement tests, exhibited more positive attitudes, and were perceived as better leaders. In fact, the prior expectations of the instructors explained 73 percent of the variability in the trainees' performance, 66 percent in their attitudes, and 28 percent in leadership. The lesson to be learned from these results is unmistakable: Trainers (and managers) get the kind of performance they expect.

the context of training (or coaching or teaching), we attempt to maximize the trainees' identification with a model. For us to do this well, research suggests that we do the following:

1. The model should be similar to the observer in age, sex, and race. If the observer sees little similarity between himself or herself and the model, it is unlikely that the model's behaviors will be imitated.
2. Portray the behaviors to be modeled clearly and in detail. To focus the trainees' attention on specific behaviors to be imitated, provide them with a list of key behaviors to attend to when observing the model, and allow them to express the behaviors in language that is most comfortable for them. For example, when one group of supervisors was being taught how

to "coach" employees, the supervisors received a list of the following key behaviors:[19] (1) focus on the problem, not on the person; (2) ask for the employees' suggestions, and get their ideas on how to solve the problem; (3) listen openly; (4) agree on the steps that each of you will take to solve the problem; and (5) plan a specific follow-up date.

3. Rank the behaviors to be modeled in a sequence from least to most difficult; be sure the trainees observe lots of repetitions of the behaviors being modeled.

4. Finally, have the behaviors portrayed by several models, not just one. [11, 24]

Behavior modeling overcomes one of the shortcomings of earlier approaches to training: telling instead of showing. For example, trainees used to be told to be "good communicators"—a behavior which most people agree is useful and which most trainees were already familiar with prior to the program—but the trainees were never shown *how* to be good communicators. Behavior modeling teaches a desired behavior effectively by:

> providing the trainee with numerous, vivid, detailed displays (on film, videotape, or live) of a manager-actor (the model) performing the specific behaviors and skills we wish the viewer to learn (i.e., modeling); giving the trainee considerable guidance in and opportunity and encouragement for behaviorally rehearsing or practicing the behaviors he/she has seen the model perform (i.e., role playing); [and] providing him/her with positive feedback, approval, or reward as the role playing enactments increasingly approximate the behavior of the model (i.e., social reinforcement). . . . (ref. 11, p. 37)

Meaningfulness of the material   Factual material is learned more easily and remembered better when it is meaningful.[32] *Meaningfulness* refers to material that is rich in associations for the trainees and is therefore easily understood by them. To structure material to maximize its meaningfulness:

1. Provide trainees with an overview of the material to be presented during the training. Seeing the overall picture helps trainees understand how each unit of the program fits together and how it contributes to the overall training objectives.[50]

2. Present the material by using examples, terms, and concepts that are familiar to the trainees in order to clarify and reinforce key learning points. Such a strategy is *essential* when training the hard-core unemployed.[14]

3. Complex intellectual skills are invariably composed of simpler skills, and it is necessary to master these simpler skills before the complex skills can be learned.[10] This is true whether one is learning accounting, computer programming, or x-ray technology.

Thus the basic principles of training design consist of (a) identifying the component tasks of a final performance, (b) ensuring that each of these component tasks is fully achieved, and (c) arranging the total learning situation in a sequence that will ensure a logical connection from one component to another.[9]

Practice (makes perfect) For anyone learning a new skill or acquiring factual knowledge, there must be the opportunity to practice what is being learned. Practice has three aspects: active practice, overlearning, and the length of the practice session. Let's consider each of these.

Active Practice. During the early stages of learning, the trainer should be available to oversee directly the trainee's practice; if the trainee begins to "get off the track," the inappropriate behaviors can be corrected immediately, before they become ingrained in the trainee's behavior. This is why low instructor-trainee (or teacher-pupil) ratios are so desirable. It also explains why so many people opt for private lessons when trying to learn or master a sport such as tennis, golf, skiing, or horseback riding. Particularly during skills learning, it is simply not enough for a trainee to verbalize (or to read out of an instruction book) what she or he is expected to do. Only active practice provides the internal cues that regulate motor performance. As practice continues over time, inefficient motions are discarded and internal cues associated with smooth, precise performance are retained. To develop a deeper appreciation of these principles, watch almost any professional athlete performing his or her specialty. Then you will see why "practice makes perfect."

Overlearning. When trainees are given the opportunity to practice far beyond the point where the task has been performed correctly several times, the task becomes "second nature" and is said to be "overlearned." For some tasks, overlearning is critical. This is true of any task that must be performed infrequently and under great stress: for example, attempting to kick a winning field goal with only seconds left in a football game. It is less important in types of work where an individual practices his or her skills on a daily basis (e.g., auto mechanics, electronics technicians, assemblers). Overlearning has several advantages:

- It increases the length of time that the training material will be retained.
- It makes the learning more "reflexive" so that tasks become "automatic" with continued practice.
- The quality of performance is more likely to be retained during periods of emergency or added stress.
- It facilitates the transfer of training to the job situation.

Length of the Practice Session. Consider these two situations: (1) You have only 1 week to memorize the lines of a play, and (2) you have only 1 week to learn how to pole-vault. In both cases you have only 12 hours available to practice. What practice schedule will produce the greatest improvement? Should you practice 2 hours a day for 6 days, should you practice for 6 hours each of the final 2 days before the deadline, or should you adopt some other schedule? The two extremes represent *distributed* practice (which implies rest intervals between sessions) and *massed* practice (in which the practice sessions are crowded together). Although there are exceptions, most of the research evidence on this question indicates that for the same amount of practice, learning is better when practice is distributed rather than massed.[12] Here are two reasons why:

- Continuous practice is fatiguing, so that individuals cannot show all that they have learned. Their performance is therefore lower than it would be if they were rested.
- During a practice session, people usually learn both the correct performance and also some irrelevant performances that interfere with it. But the irrelevant performances are likely to be less well practiced and so may be forgotten more rapidly between practice sessions. Performance should therefore improve if there are rest intervals between practice sessions.

One exception to this rule is when difficult material, such as hard puzzles or other "thought" problems, must be learned. There seems to be an advantage in staying with the problem for a few massed practice sessions at first, rather than spending a day or more between sessions.

Feedback   *Feedback* is a form of information about one's attempts to improve. Feedback is essential for learning and for trainee motivation. The emphasis should be on *when* and *how* the trainee has done something correctly: for example, "You did a good job on that report you turned in yesterday—it was brief and to the heart of the issues." Feedback promotes learning and motivation in three ways:

1. It provides direct information to trainees about the correctness of their responses, thereby allowing them to make adjustments in their subsequent behavior.
2. When somebody who cares about your success is paying close attention to you, be it trainer, coach, or teacher, it makes the learning process more interesting and hence maximizes your willingness to learn.
3. Feedback leads to the setting of specific goals for maintaining performance.[8, 30]

To have the greatest impact, feedback should be provided as soon as possible after the trainee's behavior. It need not be instantaneous, but there should be no confusion regarding exactly what the trainee did and the trainer's reaction to it. Feedback need not always be positive either.

To be acquired, modified, and sustained, behavior must be rewarded, or reinforced.[46] The principle of reinforcement also states that punishment leads only to a temporary suppression of behavior and is a relatively ineffective influence on learning. Reward says to the learner, "Good, repeat what you have done." Punishment says, "Stop it, you made the wrong response." Mild punishment may serve as a warning for the learner that he or she is getting off the track, but unless the learner is told immediately what he or she needs to do to get back on the track (corrective feedback), punishment can be intensely frustrating.

Both rewards and mild punishment can and should be used in a training situation, but keep in mind that the most powerful rewards are likely to be those provided by the trainee's immediate supervisor. In fact, if the supervisor does not reinforce what is learned in training, then the training will be transferred ineffectively to the job, if at all.

COMPANY EXAMPLE

The effect of training and feedback on a behavioral safety program

This study was conducted in the vehicle maintenance division of a large western city's department of public works. The department had one of the highest accident rates in the city, averaging three lost-time accidents per month prior to the study.[22] Desired safety practices were behaviorally defined for 55 vehicle maintenance workers, and follow-up data were collected three to four times a week for almost a year.

There were four general categories of items: proper use of equipment and tools, use of safety equipment, housekeeping, and general safety procedures. An example of a safety item under "use of safety equipment" is: "When using the brake machine, wear full face shield or goggles. When arcing brake shoes, wear a respirator."

Five experimental conditions were introduced: (a) baseline measurement of the accident rate at the beginning of the study; (b) Training Only 1 (desired practices were discussed, illustrated, and posted); (c) Training and Feedback 1 (supervisors observed daily and provided feedback about the section's safety level on graphs); (d) Training Only 2 (after the twenty-sixth week); and (e) Training and Feedback 2 (after the thirty-sixth week).

During the Training Only 1 phase, employees showed only *slight* improvements; however, their performance increased *substantially* during the Training and Feedback 1 phase. At this point the authors concluded that training *alone* is not sufficient to improve and maintain performance. This conclusion was confirmed during the Training Only 2 phase when performance declined. Performance improved once again during the Training and Feedback 2 phase. The overall program appeared to have a beneficial effect on accident reduction since the lost-time accident rate declined to 0.4 per month during the 8-month period of the program. In the year following the program it rose to 1.8 per month, but this was still substantially below the 3.0 per month recorded in the year prior to the program. The lesson to be learned from the study is that training alone is a necessary but not a sufficient condition for learning and long-term behavior change. Feedback, a readily accepted and effective motivational strategy, must also be provided.

Individual differences

Individual differences are glaringly obvious in the training environment. Some trainees are fast learners, some are slow learners, some begin at higher initial states than others, some are capable of higher terminal states than others, and some improve very little despite continued practice. These variations in

FIGURE 7-5

A typical S-shaped learning curve with a plateau.

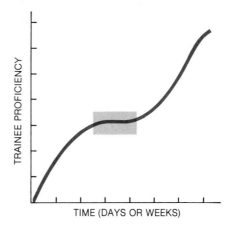

learning patterns are the result of differences in ability and motivation among trainees. Trainers need to be flexible enough to modify their training strategies to accommodate these differences (e.g., through optional additional practice sessions or more detailed explanations and demonstrations). However, research on human learning indicates that there are remarkable similarities in the overall learning pattern of trainees: It follows the S-shaped pattern shown in Figure 7-5.[17]

During the early practice trials, rapid improvement occurs (in common parlance this is sometimes called beginner's luck). Eventually, however, there is a period of no improvement in the learning curve, described as a *plateau* because it has been preceded by improvement and will be followed by improvement. There are several possible reasons for the plateau: There may be a temporary decrease in motivation related to discouragement with the decreasing gains in the typical learning curve; the trainee may be in the process of integrating different skills (e.g., moving from a letter habit to a word habit in learning to type); or the trainee may need a different method of instruction. In any case, it is important to recognize that this leveling process is normal; to maintain motivation and continued improvement, it is essential that trainees be given continued support and encouragement at this time.

Transfer of training

Transfer refers to the extent to which knowledge, skills, abilities, or other characteristics learned in training can be applied on the job. Transfer may be *positive* (i.e., it enhances job performance), *negative* (i.e., it hampers job performance), or *neutral*. Long-term training or retraining probably includes segments that contain all three of these conditions. Training that results in negative transfer is costly in two ways—the cost of the training (which proved to be useless) and the cost of hampered performance.

To facilitate the transfer from learning to doing, designers of training programs should consider the following:[12, 50]

- Maximize the similarity between the training situation and the job situation.
- Provide as much experience as possible with the task being taught (so that the trainees can deal with situations that do not exactly fit textbook examples).
- When teaching concepts or skills, provide a variety of examples (for the same reason as above).
- Ensure that principles are well understood (particularly in jobs that require the *application* of principles to solve problems, such as engineering, investment analysis, or computer programming).
- Design the training so that the trainees can see its applicability to their jobs ("What you learn in training today, you'll use on the job tomorrow").
- Either assign or allow the trainees to generate their own behavioral goals for applying what was learned in training. Have the trainees discuss their intentions and activities for attaining these goals with other trainees, rate their progress subsequently (e.g., in 1 month), return their ratings to the trainer, and attend a later group session.[51]
- Ensure that what is learned in training is rewarded on the job. If immediate supervisors or top management, by their example or words, do not support what was learned in training, do not expect the training to have much impact on job behavior.

Selecting training methods

New training methods appear every year. While some are well-founded in learning theory or models of behavior change (e.g., behavior modeling), others result more from technological than from theoretical developments (e.g., videotape, computer-based business games).

Training methods can be classified in three ways: information presentation, simulation methods, or on-the-job training.[5]

Information presentation techniques include lectures, conference methods, correspondence courses, motion pictures, reading lists, closed-circuit TV and videotapes, behavior modeling and systematic observation, programmed instruction, computer-assisted instruction, sensitivity training, and organization development (see Chapter 8).

Simulation methods include the case method, role playing, programmed group exercises, the in-basket technique, and business games (see Chapter 8).

On-the-job training methods include orientation training, apprenticeships, on-the-job training, near-the-job training (using identical equipment but away from the job itself), job rotation, committee assignments (or junior executive boards), on-the-job coaching, and performance appraisal.

To choose the training method (or combination of methods) that best fits a given situation, *what is to be taught* must first be defined carefully. That is the purpose of the needs assessment phase. *Only then* can the method be chosen that best fits these requirements. To be useful, the chosen method should meet the minimal conditions needed for effective learning to take place; that is, the training method should:

- Motivate the trainee to improve his or her performance.
- Clearly illustrate desired skills.
- Provide for active participation by the trainee.
- Provide an opportunity to practice.
- Provide timely feedback on the trainee's performance.
- Provide some means for reinforcement while the trainee learns.
- Be structured from simple to complex tasks.
- Be adaptable to specific problems.
- Encourage positive transfer from the training to the job.

Evaluating Training Programs

Training must be evaluated by systematically documenting the outcomes of the training in terms of how trainees actually behave back on their jobs and the relevance of the trainees' behavior to the objectives of the organization.[47] To assess the utility or value of training, we seek answers to four questions:

1. Did change occur?
2. Is the change due to training?
3. Is the change positively related to the achievement of organizational goals?
4. Will similar changes occur with new participants in the same training program?[12]

In evaluating training programs, we measure change in terms of four categories:[21]

Reaction. How do the participants feel about the training program?

Learning. To what extent have the trainees learned what was taught?

Behavior. What on-the-job changes in behavior have occurred because of attendance at the training program?

Results. To what extent have cost-related behavioral outcomes (e.g., productivity or quality improvements, turnover or accident reductions) resulted from the training?[20]

Since measures of reaction and learning are concerned with out⸱ the training program per se, they are referred to as *internal cr⸱⸱* of behavior and results indicate the impact of training on⸳ they are referred to as *external criteria.*

Measures of reaction typically focus on participants'

subject and the speaker, suggested improvements in the program, and the extent to which the training will help them do their jobs better. Trainee learning can be assessed by giving a paper-and-pencil test (especially when factual information has been presented) or through performance testing following skill training.

Assessing changes in on-the-job behavior is more difficult than measuring reaction or learning because factors other than the training program may also effect improved performance (e.g., lengthened job experience, outside economic events, and changes in supervision or performance incentives). To rule out these rival hypotheses, it is essential to design a plan for evaluation that includes *before* and *after* measurement of the trained group's performance relative to that of one or more untrained control groups. However, the post-training appraisal of performance should not be done sooner than 3 months (or more) following the training so that the trainees have an opportunity to put into practice what they have learned.

Finally, the impact of training on organizational results is the most significant but most difficult measure to make. *Measures of results are the bottom line of training success.* Exciting developments in this area have come from recent research showing how the general utility equation (Equation 6-1 in Chapter 6) can be modified to reflect the dollar value of improved job performance resulting from training.[6] Utility formulas are now available for evaluating the dollar value of a single training program compared to a control group, a training program readministered periodically (e.g., annually), and a comparison among two or more different training programs.

COMPANY EXAMPLE

Evaluating the business impact of management training at CIGNA Corporation

CIGNA (the insurance company) set out to demonstrate the impact on productivity and performance of a 7-day training program in basic management skills.[40] The evaluations were based on repeated measures of work-unit performance both *before* and *after* training. Some specific features of the program were:

- Productivity was a central focus of the program.
- As part of their training, the participants were taught how to create productivity measures.
- The participants were taught how to use productivity data as performance feedback and as support for performance goal setting.
- The participants wrote a productivity action plan as part of the training, and they agreed to bring back measurable results to a follow-up session.
- Individualized productivity measures were put in place as part of the action plan. These plans were tailored to measure results in specific, objective terms.

The results of the training in basic management skills were evaluated, of necessity, in individual work units. Let us consider one such unit—that of a premium collections manager. Collecting premiums on time is important in the insurance business, because late premiums represent lost investment opportunities. Through survey feedback from her subordinates, the manager of this unit found that her problems (only 75 percent of the premiums were collected on time) stemmed from poor human resource management skills, coupled with a failure to set clear performance goals.

After being trained, this manager dramatically altered many of her management behaviors. One year later her unit was collecting 96 percent of the premiums on time. This improvement yielded extra investment income of $150,000 per year. What was the return on the fully loaded cost of training her? The training costs included the costs of facilities, program development amortized over 25 programs, trainer preparation time, general administration, corporate overhead, and the salaries plus benefits of the participants over the 7-day program. These came to $1600 per participant. It looks like the returns generated by the collections manager as a result of the action plan ($150,000) relative to the training's cost ($1600) were phenomenal. But were *all* these gains due to her training? Probably not.

What would have happened had training not occurred? Extrapolating from the rate of improvement prior to training, the researchers concluded that the collections rate would have been up to about 84 percent, from 75 percent. The additional 12-point improvement that was provided—in part—by the program (which generated about $85,000 in extra investment income) represents the upper bound of the effects of the training program. (Other economic factors, such as lower unemployment, may also have contributed to the gain). Nevertheless, it represents about a 50-to-1 return on the dollars invested.

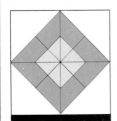

Impact of Current Training Costs and Practices on Productivity, Quality of Work Life, and the Bottom Line

In an exhaustive study of training activities in U.S. organizations, Gordon collected data from CEOs, personnel directors, and training directors from 991 organizations (ranging in size from 50 to over 10,000 employees) in 12 industries.[13] The types of training most frequently provided are shown in Table 7-2. What is perhaps most striking about the data in Table 7-2 is the breadth and depth of training provided in U.S. industry. The important thing for us to keep in mind, however, is that while the programs shown in Table 7-2 *can* contribute to improved productivity, quality of work life, and bottom line performance, they can do so only by adhering to the basic principles of training design, as presented in this chapter. In terms of costs, aggregate 1987 budgeted training expenditures in U.S. firms were approximately $40 billion.[34] These costs included hardware budgets (e.g., VCRs, computers), off-shelf budgets (expenditures for prepackaged programs), custom-design budgets, and outside services budgets. These costs do not include salary costs of trainers and trainees. If included, the total cost to business to provide job training is approximately $180 billion per year.[44] As we have seen earlier, however, training programs that are properly designed and evaluated can yield benefits that are far greater.

TABLE 7-2 *Types of training most frequently provided*

Type of training	Percent providing
New employee orientation	80.8
Performance appraisals	66.2
New equipment operation	57.2
Leadership	54.2
Time management	52.8
Train the trainer	47.1
Word processing	46.0
Hiring and selection process	45.8
Goal setting	45.6
Interpersonal skills	45.3
Product knowledge	42.9
Public speaking and/or presentation	41.6
Team building	39.4
Problem solving	38.5
Stress management	38.5
Computer programming	38.3
Motivation	38.1
Planning	37.3
Safety	36.8
Personal computer use	35.4
Data processing	33.1
Listening skills	33.0
Writing skills	32.1
Conducting meetings	31.7
Delegation skills	31.4
Decision making	30.3
Strategic planning	28.6
Management information systems	26.1
Negotiating skills	20.9
Manufacturing (production planning, cost estimating)	17.2
Outplacement and/or retirement planning	16.9
Creativity and/or creative thinking	16.3
Purchasing	14.8
Finance	14.5
Other (subjects not listed)	13.2
Nutrition	12.4
Reading skills	9.5
Foreign language	5.5

**CASE 7-1
Conclusion**

The dislocated worker

To help dislocated workers in Des Moines, two transition centers were set up to retrain people for banking and insurance careers—the two main professional service industries in the area. The two centers recruit participants and place them in programs offered by local educational institutions. Area employers have provided funding to these programs and hire many of the displaced workers once their training is completed. The efforts of this task force have been successful—80 percent of the retrained workers found new jobs within a year of their termination from the factories.

Dislocated workers are not all unskilled or semiskilled. Even highly skilled workers are feeling the effects of a changing labor market. Labor Department grants are being used to teach new skills *and* to relocate geologists, petroleum engineers, and other professionals in Oklahoma and Texas. Officials say that oil and gas geologists who wish to change careers can be retrained in 2 months to fill a need for hydrologists; engineers are becoming science teachers. Other workers in Texas and Oklahoma are being given the opportunity to learn new computer skills, and then, if they wish, they are sent to cities with high-tech jobs.[23]

An innovative California program funded by the state has encouraged such experiments as the $1.4 million mobile classroom operated by the Los Angeles City College system. The trailer, filled with computer-controlled lathes and other modern equipment, is trucked out to aerospace plants to retrain assembly workers as skilled machinists. The costs: $2600 per worker for 410 hours of training; the benefits: shorter periods of unemployment for trainees, and a 55 percent average increase in their wages. What is the bottom line on all of this? Even executives who have trouble believing that any government program could turn a profit are finding in their own plants and offices that investments in human capital have a high payback.[3]

Business can help organizations that are coordinating retraining efforts in three ways:

1. Provide feedback on proposed and existing programs.
2. Identify occupations for the development of retraining programs.
3. Serve on review boards that assess the effectiveness of retraining efforts.

Summary

Clearly, a new employee's initial experience with a firm can have a major effect on his or her later career. To maximize the impact of orientation, it is important to recognize that new employees need specific information in three major areas: (1) *company standards, traditions, and policies;* (2) *social behavior;* and (3) *technical aspects of the job.* This suggests two levels of orientation: company, conducted by an HR representative, and departmental, conducted by the immediate supervisor. To ensure proper quality control plus continual improvement, an *orientation follow-up* is essential (e.g., after 1 week by the supervisor and after 1 month by an HR representative).

The pace of change in our society is forcing both employed and displaced workers continually to acquire new knowledge and skills. In most organizations, therefore, lifelong training is essential. To be maximally effective, training programs should follow a three-phase sequence: *needs assessment, implementation,* and *evaluation. What is to be learned* must first be defined clearly before a particular method or technique is chosen. To define what is to be

TOMORROW'S FORECAST	Economic and technological trends provide clear signals that training is a growth industry. The pace of innovation, change, and development is faster, faster, year by year. Obsolescence bedevils all of us. Perhaps the Paul Principle expresses this phenomenon most aptly: *Over time, people become uneducated, and therefore incompetent, to perform at a level they once performed at adequately.*[1] Training is an important antidote to obsolescence. In addition to the many productivity-enhancing training programs provided (see Table 7-2), many firms are also offering the kinds of training that will enhance quality of work life as well (e.g., personal growth, career planning, and safety). This trend is likely to continue. What is also likely, however, is continued research that will provide stable and accurate estimates of the percentage improvements in job performance and productivity expected from various kinds of training interventions.[15] Such estimates are crucial to the widespread application of utility analysis in training evaluation. This type of research will enable us someday to provide managers with accurate estimates of dollar gains in productivity of alternative training strategies, and it can also guide training specialists in adjusting their programs so as to make them more attractive from a cost-benefit viewpoint.

learned, a continuous cycle of organization analysis, operations analysis, and analysis of the training needs of employees is necessary.

Training needs must then be related to the achievement of broader organizational goals and be consistent with management's perceptions of strategy and tactics.

Beyond these fundamental concerns, issues of equal employment opportunity, trainability, and principles of learning—goal setting, behavior modeling, meaningfulness of material, practice, feedback, and transfer of training—are essential considerations in the design of any training program. The choice of a particular technique should be guided by the degree to which it fits identified needs and incorporates the learning principles.

In evaluating training programs, we measure change in terms of four categories: *reaction, learning, behavior,* and *results.* Measures of the impact of training on organizational results are the bottom line of training success. Fortunately, advances in utility analysis now make evaluations possible in terms of dollar benefits and dollar costs.

Discussion Questions

7-1 Discuss the impact of office automation on workforce training.

7-2 Why is orientation so often overlooked by organizations?

7-3 Think back to your first day on the latest job you have held. What could have been done to hasten your socialization to the organization and your adjustment to the job?

7-4 Training has been described by some as intensely "faddish." As an advisor to management, describe how the firm can avoid succumbing to training fads.

7-5 How does goal setting affect trainee learning and motivation?

7-6 Outline an evaluation procedure for a training program designed to teach sales principles and strategies.

References

1. Armer, P. (1970). The individual: His privacy, self-image, and obsolescence. *Proceedings of the meeting of the panel on science and technology, 11th "Science and Astronautics."* Washington, DC: USGPO.
2. Bandura, A. (1986). *Social foundations of thought and action: A social cognitive theory.* Englewood Cliffs, NJ: Prentice-Hall.
3. Brody, M. (1987, June 8). Helping workers to work smarter. *Fortune*, pp. 86–88.
4. Brownlee, D. (1983, June). Personal communication.
5. Campbell, J. P., Dunnette, M. D., Lawler, E. E., & Weick, K. E. (1970). *Managerial behavior, performance, and effectiveness.* New York: McGraw-Hill.
6. Cascio, W. F. (1987). *Costing human resources: The financial impact of behavior in organizations* (2d ed.). Boston: PWS-Kent.
7. Eden, D., & Shani, A. B. (1982). Pygmalion goes to boot camp: Expectancy, leadership, and trainee performance. *Journal of Applied Psychology,* **67,** 194–199.
8. Erez, M. (1977). Feedback: A necessary condition for the goal-setting–performance relationship. *Journal of Applied Psychology,* **62,** 624–627.
9. Gagné, R. M. (1962). Military training and the principles of learning. *American Psychologist,* **18,** 83–91.
10. Gagné, R. M. (1977). *The conditions of learning.* New York: Holt, Rinehart, & Winston.
11. Goldstein, A. P., & Sorcher, M. (1974). *Changing supervisor behavior.* New York: Pergamon Press.
12. Goldstein, I. L. (1986). *Training in organizations: Needs assessment, development, and evaluation* (2d ed.). Monterey, CA: Brooks/Cole.
13. Gordon, J. (1986). Training magazine's industry report, 1986. *Training,* **23**(10), 26–66.
14. Gray, I., & Borecki, T. B. (1970). Training programs for the hard-core: What the trainer has to learn. *Personnel,* **47,** 23–29.
15. Guzzo, R. A., Jette, R. D., & Katzell, R. A. (1985). The effects of psychologically based intervention programs on worker productivity: A meta-analysis. *Personnel Psychology,* 38, 275–291.
16. Hicks, W. D., & Klimoski, R. J. (1987). Entry into training programs and its effects on training outcomes: A field experiment. *Academy of Management Journal,* **30,** 542–552.
17. Hilgard, E. R., & Atkinson, R. C. (1967). *Introduction to psychology* (4th ed.). New York: Harcourt, Brace, & World.

18. Hilton, M. (1987). Union and management: A strong case for cooperation. *Training and Development Journal*, **41**(1), 54–55.

19. Hogan, P. M., Hakel, M. D., & Decker, P. J. (1986). Effects of trainee-generated versus trainer-provided rule codes on generalization in behavior-modeling training. *Journal of Applied Psychology*, **71**, 469–473.

20. Kirkpatrick, D. L. (1977). Evaluating training programs: Evidence vs. proof. *Training and Development Journal*, **31**, 9–12.

21. Kirkpatrick, D. L. (1983). Four steps to measuring training effectiveness. *Personnel Administrator*, **28**(11), 19–25.

22. Komaki, J., Heinzmann, A. T., & Lawson, L. (1980). Effect of training and feedback: Component analysis of a behavioral safety program. *Journal of Applied Psychology*, **65**, 261–270.

23. Labor Letter (1987, Apr. 28). *Wall Street Journal*, p. 1.

24. Latham, G. P., & Saari, L. M. (1979). The application of social learning theory to training supervisors through behavior modeling. *Journal of Applied Psychology*, **64**, 239–246.

25. Lienert, P. (1983, Oct. 19). Discrimination settlement will cost GM $42.5 million. *Denver Post*, p. 3A.

26. Locke, E. A. (1968). Toward a theory of task motivation and incentives. *Organizational Behavior and Human Performance*, **3**, 157–189.

27. Lublin, J. S. (1983, Oct. 11). Labor letter. *Wall Street Journal*, p. 1.

28. Lubliner, M. (1978, April). Employee orientation. *Personnel Journal*, pp. 207–208.

29. Mager, R. F. (1962). *Preparing instructional objectives*. Palo Alto, CA: Fearon.

30. Matsui, T., Kakuyama, T., & Onglatco, M. L. U. (1987). Effects of goals and feedback on performance in groups. *Journal of Applied Psychology*, **72**, 407–415.

31. McGarrell, E. J., Jr. (1984). An orientation system that builds productivity. *Personnel Administrator*, **29**(10), 75–85.

32. McGehee, W., & Thayer, P. W. (1961). *Training in business and industry*. New York: Wiley.

33. Mento, A. J., Steel, R. P., & Karren, R. J. (1987). A meta-analytic study of the effects of goal setting on performance: 1966–1984. *Organizational Behavior and Human Decision Processes*, **39**, 52–83.

34. Mitchell, C. (1987, Sep. 28). Corporate classes: Firms broaden scope of their education programs. *Wall Street Journal*, p. 35.

35. Moore, M. L., & Dutton, P. (1978). Training needs analysis: Review and critique. *Academy of Management Review*, **3**, 532–454.

36. Navy worried about growing jet losses (1986, Mar. 23). *Honolulu Star Bulletin*, pp. A1–A4.

37. Noe, R. A., & Schmitt, N. (1986). The influence of trainee attitudes on training effectiveness: Test of a model. *Personnel Psychology*, **39**, 497–523.

38. Noe, R. A. (1986). Trainees' attributes and attitudes: Neglected influences on training effectiveness. *Academy of Management Review*, **11**, 736–749.

39. Norton, E. H. (1987, May 13). Step by step, the court helps affirmative action. *New York Times*, p. A27.

40. Paquet, B., Kasl, E., Weinstein, L., & Waite, W. (1987). The bottom line. *Training and Development Journal*, **41**(6), 27–33.

41. Peters, T. J., & Waterman, R. H., Jr. (1983, Apr. 28). In search of excellence. *The Denver Post*, p. 6F.

42. Robertson, I., & Downs, S. (1979). Learning and the prediction of performance: Development of trainability testing in the United Kingdom. *Journal of Applied Psychology*, **64**, 42–50.

43. Ryman, D. H., & Biersner, R. J. (1975). Attitudes predictive of diving training success. *Personnel Psychology*, **28**, 181–188.

44. *Serving the new corporation* (1986). Alexandria, VA: American Society for Training and Development.

45. Siegel, A. I. (1983). The miniature job training and evaluation approach: Additional findings. *Personnel Psychology*, **36**, 41–56.

46. Skinner, B. F. (1969). *Contingencies of reinforcement: A theoretical analysis*. East Norwalk, CT: Appleton-Century-Crofts.

47. Snyder, R. A., Raben, C. S., & Farr, J. L. (1980). A model for the systematic evaluation of human resource development programs. *Academy of Management Review*, **5**, 431–444.

48. St. John, W. D. (1980, May). The complete employee orientation program. *Personnel Journal*, pp. 373–378.

49. Uniform guidelines on employee selection procedures (1978). *Federal Register*, **43**, 38, 290–38, 315.

50. Wexley, K. N., & Latham, G. P. (1981). *Developing and training human resources in organizations*. Glenview, IL: Scott, Foresman.

51. Wexley, K. N., & Baldwin, T. T. (1986). Posttraining strategies for facilitating positive transfer: An empirical exploration. *Academy of Management Journal*, **29**, 503–520.

52. Wood, R. E., Mento, A. J., & Locke, E. A. (1987). Task complexity as a moderator of goal effects: A meta-analysis. *Journal of Applied Psychology*, **72**, 416–425.

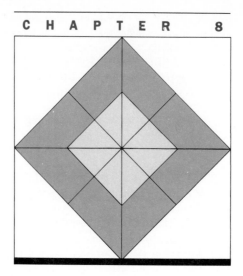

C H A P T E R   8

Identifying and Developing Management Talent

Between 1975 and 1983, Radio Corporation of America (RCA) became a revolving door for chairpersons and presidents, eight of them whirling through the top doors during that 8-year period. Successors did not succeed. The selection process just broke down. By 1981 profits were down by 83 percent, and the company had become "the laughingstock of Wall Street" as Chairperson Thornton Bradshaw put it. The board of directors finally took control by firing its chairperson and installing in his place Bradshaw, who had been president of Atlantic Richfield and an RCA director for the previous 9 years.

The board gave Bradshaw a 5-year contract and three goals to accomplish: (1) Find a way to stabilize the dissension-torn company, (2) find out what kind of a company it should be, and (3) by the end of 5 years, find a replacement for himself as chairperson. To achieve the third goal, Bradshaw retained Gerard Roche, chairperson of the Heidrick & Struggles search firm, to mount an exhaustive hunt. As Bradshaw explained, "The problem was how to conduct a wide external search and still keep it quiet. We didn't want people at RCA to get upset, though it was apparent that there was no suitable successor within the organization." Bradshaw had used Roche once before to find a director for

---

*Adapted from: Braking the revolving door at RCA, *Fortune*, May 2, 1983, p. 59; and Fine Tuning, *Wall Street Journal*, Mar. 6, 1985, pp. 1, 33.

RCA. "I knew he had a tremendous file," Bradshaw said. "More important, I knew he could keep a secret."

Roche produced an initial list of 75 names. "Mature, experienced, low-key, nonflamboyant, but with a high energy level: those were the characteristics we were looking for," said Roche. "We didn't want some star-fire executive with a big ego who would knock down the structure Brad was trying to build." But few executives possessing those traits also had the desired "mirror image," which is the way Roche referred to the experience in broadcasting, electronics, aerospace, international sales, and finance that the candidate needed to run RCA.

Bradshaw and Roche met frequently, while the chairperson kept the board apprised of progress. Very quickly they cut the list to a dozen. "All of them were gainfully employed," recalls Bradshaw, "and, we assumed, happy with what they were doing." Roche contacted each. Some said they did not want to be considered, but would talk. Others sounded interested. Bradshaw invited each to lunch—most often at his New York apartment. "If they showed up at RCA," he says, "somebody would have surely asked, 'What in hell's he doing here?'"

One by one the list of names shrank. "There were only three or four who were really outstanding," said Bradshaw. By then the finalists were being subjected to "intensive reviews" by the board's executive committee. Members of the committee (e.g., the chairperson of Lehman Brothers Kuhn Loeb; the president of Marine Midland bank; the president of Cooper Industries; the former chairperson of R. H. Macy & Co.) were asked to use their references to check out each candidate as discreetly as possible. Said one board member, "When the board brought Brad in, we said we wanted quality and we got it. The same went for his heir apparent. We couldn't afford a mistake." Another board member put it more bluntly, "I don't think Brad could have picked somebody we didn't want." Last September, Bradshaw and the members of the executive committee made their choice.

QUESTIONS
1. Critique the process used by RCA to evaluate and screen a new president for the company.
2. Identify some of the key reasons possible for the near-immediate failure of new company presidents or chief executive officers (CEOs).
3. If you were a new CEO promoted from within RCA, outline an action plan for your first 6 months in office.

What's Ahead

Case 8-1 describes the sometimes wrenching process of selecting a top manager. In fact, management selection decisions are some of the most important and most difficult personnel decisions that organizations face. Compounding these difficulties are the constant needs to align management selection with business strategy and to provide ongoing opportunities for managers to develop professionally. These two themes, management selection and management development, are the topics discussed in this chapter. We will see that there is a wide range of selection and development methods to choose from and that much is known about each one. We also will examine evidence of the relative effectiveness of the methods, so that managers can choose those methods which best fit their long- and short-range objectives.

Identifying Management Talent

"Chief executives can fail or succeed depending on whether they attract the trust of their colleagues," says the editor of *Harvard Business Review*, himself a director of Xerox. "It's a rather slippery thought, but it's important, especially with all the hoopla about the failure of the American manager because he's too short-term oriented and not concerned about the development of people" (ref. 81, p. 61).

To develop insight into the process that companies use to identify executive talent, *Fortune* interviewed 25 current and former chief executives.[81] The discussion that follows is drawn primarily from this source. CEOs identify the most sought-after qualities as integrity, self-confidence, physical and mental fitness, the ability to think strategically, and a facility for communicating ideas. They also expect their successors to be homegrown—either at headquarters or at a major division.

In the best of times, selecting a top executive is a process of evaluating impressions, much of it unspoken and intuitive. Says Irving Shapiro, former CEO of Du Pont, "It's a close call. You're looking for that indefinable extra quality—wisdom in all its aspects. Besides, I think that fellow has fire in his belly" (ref. 81, p. 61).

Headhunters believe that search committees frequently feel frustrated because they are searching for a composite—a mythical executive who combines all the best traits of the candidates being considered. This is an impossible dream. Another problem for search committees, often largely composed of outside directors, is that they do not have enough contact with the candidates. Says a former CEO, "They meet them on a legal deal or on a financial deal, but they don't know who can stand up at a stockholders' meeting and take the kind of pounding you get there, or if a candidate is going to blow up every time he talks to the press" (ref. 81, p. 64).

While success in choosing a top executive may be elusive, failure is not. J. Peter Grace, the chairperson of W. R. Grace & Co. since 1945, describes the process this way: "Even when I'm not a director of a company in the process of picking a new chief executive, I think I know when they've picked a lemon. If the chief executive is imaginative and has good ideas, but isn't too well organized, his No. 2 man may be able to put the pieces together. But when No. 2 gets promoted, they discover he hasn't got the innovation or the drive, and his entire capability hinged on working alongside his old boss. I've seen this happen a number of times" (ref. 81, p. 62).

What does it take to succeed at the top? Professor Eugene Jennings, a frequent consultant to top managers, calls that the "biggest guessing game in the business." "It's always been a gamble and it always will be, because there's no rung on the way up the corporate ladder that prepares you for the last one" (ref. 81, p. 64). Fortunately, as we shall see, the identification, selection, and development of managers at lower levels is easier and more scientific since we can specify in more detail the knowledge, skills, abilities, and other characteristics necessary for success.

COMPANY EXAMPLE

The new breed of chief executive officers

Until recently, the most obvious trait of the corporate boss was his dullness. There was the gray flannel suit, the obsession with crunching numbers, the belief that the best way to run a company was to build up a bureaucracy. The boss was unapproachable. Today, he or she is a flag-bearer, not only to employees but also to Wall Street, Washington, and the press.[52]

Faced with foreign competition, the takeover phenomenon, the switch from a manufacturing to a service economy, today's CEOs— people like Lee Iacocca of Chrysler, Hicks Waldron of Avon, John Akers of IBM, and John Welch of General Electric—shun the old ways of managing and have brought new excitement to rusty companies.

These bosses detest bureaucracy and revere decentralization. "Intrapreneurship" (encouraging an independent entrepreneurial spirit within large corporations) is a buzzword. These CEOs hop into their corporate jets and confront the troops—"management by walking around"—slapping backs and inspiring through the force of their own charisma and ability to deliver a speech. As one top executive recruiter noted, "To reach the top rungs, they must be media stars" (ref. 52, p. 77).

The Special Problems of Selecting Managers

Results from a number of research studies suggest that *different abilities* are necessary for success at different levels of management. Practicing managers would be the first to admit that success in a nonmanagement job reveals little about an individual's potential for success in a management job. The requirements in the two jobs are just too different. Nevertheless, what usually happens is that individuals are promoted into management jobs *because* they are top performers in nonmanagement jobs. This may be one reason why the current rate of turnover among managers is 25 percent.[46]

A less well known fact is that success as a first-level manager may reveal little about potential as a third- or fourth-level manager, again because different abilities are necessary for success at these levels. For example, Control Data Corporation found long-range planning, monitoring business indicators, coordinating, customer relations and marketing, and consulting to be the most important dimensions of top-level management. At lower management levels, these dimensions were much less important than supervising subordinates to ensure that they complete the work assigned to them;[76] however, tomorrow's first-line supervisors will have to be capable of doing more than simply "getting the work out." In addition to heightened pressures to be technically proficient, they will interact with more people *outside* the immediate work group, and they will spend more time counseling, mentoring, and facilitating the operations of autonomous work groups.[50]

A further problem with research on the selection of managers is that since the number of executive positions decreases as the organizational level increases, the number of managers required for statistically valid research is almost impossible to obtain at higher management levels.

A final problem is that the full range of abilities is not represented among managers, for by the time candidates are considered for managerial positions, they have already been screened. Since they therefore comprise a rather homogeneous group, it is difficult to identify predictors that will accurately forecast *differences* in performance.

On top of these potential problems, companies sometimes make matters worse by giving short shrift to management selection. Here are seven of the most common mistakes:[44]

1. Failure to define job specifications clearly and objectively often results in a failure to select a person with the right characteristics for the job. This is the most common mistake, and a very expensive one.
2. Specifications (as we have seen) are frequently made in terms of "fog-bound" generalities—e.g., "dynamic," "creative."
3. In some cases, job specifications are unnecessarily couched in excessively narrow terms—for example, 10 years' experience in the design of microchips for navigational systems.
4. Companies frequently miss an excellent candidate for a position because of their failure to allow for exceptions—for example, in dress or in personal habits.
5. Failure to consider the realities of the marketplace can result in unrealistic expectations on the part of management recruiters—for example, failing to recognize that the "ideal" candidate probably does not exist or that a qualified candidate might not be willing to take a job at your company for reasons such as promotion opportunities, pay, location, or dual-career considerations.
6. Many companies make costly mistakes in timing, either by beginning the search too soon or by beginning it too late.
7. Competent evaluation and interviewing skills are absolutely vital to executive selection, yet this area is neglected by most executives.

With these warnings as a guide, let us begin our treatment by considering just what it is that managers actually do.

What do managers actually do?

The classical management theorists, beginning with Henri Fayol, the father of modern management theory, sought to identify the core functions of management.[20] These were given the acronym *POSDCORB—planning, organizing, staffing, directing, coordinating, reporting, and budgeting.* The classical functions still represent the most useful way of classifying the manager's job, but they tell us little about what managers actually *do* on their jobs. Reality is far messier, for organizations are constantly changing. To identify and develop effective managers, we must have a clear understanding of the nature of managerial work. Despite thousands of studies in the leadership-management literature, this domain remains elusive. We know that effective managers are *optimizers* of technical, capital, and human resources,[19] but the types of problems they face, in what mix, and what environments they cope with remain largely unknown.

However, there are some things about managers that we do know. Observations and interviews with first-line supervisors, middle managers, and CEOs indicate that modern managers do not have sufficient time for POSDCORB either for themselves or for their subordinates.[72, 73] They must perform a large quantity of work at an unrelenting pace, work that is characterized by brevity, variety, and discontinuity. Hence the job of managing is not most appropriate for reflective, systematic planners. Rather, the modern manager must be ever prepared to respond to stimuli; he or she must prefer "live" rather than delayed action. Field studies also indicate that higher-level managers spend less time on paperwork and more time in meetings,[55] that managers typically begin their days with administration and become more interactive later in the day,[23] and that managers in organizations facing fast-changing environments spend more time talking with each other than do managers in stable environments.[58] In one study, researchers extracted over 200 managerial events and problems in over 40 hours of "typical day" interviews with managers at all levels.[65] Subsequent sorting of the 200 events and problems by five independent raters yielded 12 clusters of problems and/or activities that seem to comprise managerial work. These are presented in Table 8-1.

These results yield three implications about identifying and developing managerial talent.

First, we need to select individuals who prefer live action rather than delayed action. To the extent that we can show people what managing is really like (and therefore provide a realistic job preview of the job), selection errors and training costs may be reduced.

Second, managerial activities are highly variable and unrelated. Hence training programs are needed that will help managers reorient their mental processes quickly (e.g., from "routine administration" to "hip shots") as they encounter different problems that need resolution.[91]

And third, a primary objective of management development should be to provide trainees with opportunities to recognize the *actual nature* of their managerial work. This can be done in two ways: either by providing answers to a set of diagnostic questions about one's managerial work or by a simulation of the manager's job.[73]

The diagnostic questions might include ones such as these:[73]

- Where do I get my information? And how do I get it?
- What information do I disseminate in my organization?
- Do I balance information collecting with action taking?
- Is there any system to my time scheduling, or am I just reacting to time pressures of the moment?
- How do my subordinates react to my managerial style?

Simulation involves the construction of a model that synthesizes the essential variables of the real system being studied. Although the results of

TABLE 8-1 *Problems and/or activities that comprise managerial work*

Activity	Definition	Examples
1. Symbolic	Activities in which the manager represents symbolically or ceremonially the unit or organization	Going to anniversary dinners; attending retirement parties; making speeches; joining civic organizations
2. Staff development and education	Deciding on and arranging for educational and developmental activities for oneself, one's staff, or the organization; also, performing mentor roles	Requesting organization development help; picking university courses; detecting lack of financial education in the organization; meeting with consultants or taking personal time to help staff
3. Monitor	Gathering information on the progress of work; looking for deviations	Visiting production sites; reviewing engineering strategies, subordinate performance, and financial and production statements
4. Disseminator	Informing others of unit or organizational activities; basic information sharing	Budget reports; informing other divisions of activities; distributing statistical summaries on department issues; explaining sensitive issues to those concerned
5. Entrepreneur	Finding or creating opportunities to improve work activities	Examine requests for new products, proposals to diversify product lines, new advertising campaigns; prepare competitive bids; invest in land or other corporations; take greater advantage of tax credits

TABLE 8-1 *(continued)*

6. Resource allocation	Using available resources (human, technical, mechanical, physical, financial) for work accomplishment	Project planning; arranging interview job candidates; staffing arrangements after transfer or promotions; subcontracting
7. Hip shots	Taking immediate action in response to a serious problem	Cost overruns; change in sales or production forecast; pollution or affirmative action problems; emergencies (strikes, fires, etc.)
8. Persuasion	Using influence to gain some control over forces that are not directly controllable	Choosing board nominees; testifying at trade assocations; selling new products internally; negotiating contracts; requesting major expenditures; negotiating with government officials; finding adequate housing for employees; getting community improvements
9. Structuring and design	Changing organizational structure to improve work processes	Reorganize divisions; set up depreciation or budgeting procedures; set up reporting relationships, staff meetings, etc.
10. Routine administration	Taking care of formal requirements	Reviewing applications; in-basket materials; MBO reviews; coordination of paperwork; estimate costs and issue purchase orders on routine matters
11. Network construction	Joining or participating in activities to create potentially useful contacts	Serving on external boards and in community groups
12. Nuisances	Time-consuming events not directly related to organizational goals	Customer complaints; phones out of order; interruptions

Source: M. W. McCall, Jr., & M. M. Lombardo, *Looking Glass, Inc.: The first three years*, Greensboro, NC: Center for Creative Leadership, Technical Report 13, 1979, pp. 22, 23.

simulation may not reproduce the same results as from the actual system, they are useful as a basis for predicting behavior in the actual system. Moreover, they can be achieved at less cost and in a shorter time than is possible by constructing and operating the real system.[80] An example of a simulation of a manager's job is Looking Glass, Inc.[65] Exhibit 8-1 is a brief description of it. Looking Glass was designed to simulate upper-level management work. Unlike a psychological test, or even an assessment center (discussed later in this chapter), it was not designed to measure a particular trait, aspect of behavior, or performance criterion. It was designed solely to generate relatively typical managerial behavior. Evidence thus far accumulated indicates that the content of Looking Glass is a realistic representation of an upper-level manager's work.

...ically observing how managers in the simulation spent their time,
...ne memos they wrote, and logging their use of the telephone, it was
...to find out how closely their activities coincided with those of managers
...field. The results of about 40 studies of ongoing managerial work that
...used observation or diary keeping compared quite favorably with activity
...terns generated through Looking Glass, Inc.[65]

Business strategy and management selection

Clearly there should be a fit between the intended strategy of an enterprise
and the managers who are expected to implement it. Unfortunately, very few
firms actually link strategy and manager selection in a structured, logical way.
Nevertheless, we can learn how to effect such a fit by considering a two-
dimensional model that relates an organization's strategy during the stages of
its development to the style of its managers during each stage.[87]

For strategic reasons, it is important to consider the stage of development
of a business because many characteristics of a business—such as its growth
rate, product lines, market share, entry opportunity, and technology—change
as the organization changes. One possible set of relationships between the
development stage and the management selection strategies is shown in Figure
8-1. While a model such as this is useful conceptually, in practice the stages
might not be as clearly defined, and there are many exceptions.

EXHIBIT 8-1	**An Overview of Looking Glass, Inc.**

Looking Glass is a 6-hour simulation of a moderate-size manufacturing corporation. In each standardized run, 20 participants are
assigned to 20 top-management roles ranging from president to plant manager and spanning three divisions. Their task: to run the company for a day
in any way they want.

The simulation begins the evening before the run with a series of events
designed to familiarize participants with the company, their roles, and each
other. During this session, participants and staff are introduced, a slide
show explaining the company is shown, participants are assigned roles and
spend some time at their desks, and job descriptions and annual reports
are distributed. This is followed by some time for the participants to socialize.

The following morning Looking Glass opens for business. Each participant spends the first 45 minutes at his or her desk reviewing an in-basket
containing today's mail. Each in-basket contains 28 to 50 items ranging
from the trivial (e.g., wine sale prices) to the significant (e.g., cost figures
on plant expansion).

After the first 45 minutes, the telephone system is turned on and the
managers are free to call meetings, send memos, place phone calls, etc.
Using memo or phone, participants can contact anyone inside or outside

the company. Trained staff play these "ghost" roles using standardized responses to the most commonly asked questions.

The simulation concludes with a brief address by the president and a lengthy session of filling out questionnaires. This is followed by 1 to 3 days of training conducted by the staff of the participating organization.

The development of Looking Glass ensured that a range of management problems and issues exists in the company. They cover many areas, including finance, personnel, legal, production, sales, R&D, safety, etc. Examples of the issues include:

- An opportunity to acquire a new plant
- Deciding what to do with a plant that has lost money the last few years
- Pollution and discrimination problems
- Supply shortages
- Production capacity limits
- A lawsuit with a major customer
- Competition with foreign manufacturers

There are three divisions in Looking Glass, each of which faces a different kind of external environment. The Advanced Products Division (APD) manufactures products for the electronics and communications industries and exists in an unstable, highly volatile business environment. The Commercial Glass Division (CGD) makes light bulb casings and flat glass, and it faces a reasonably stable, predictable environment characterized by high-volume, low-margin products and well-established customer relations. The Industrial Glass Division (IGD) faces an environment containing both unstable and stable components because it makes products varying from auto glass (relatively stable) to spacecraft windows (highly unstable).

Source: M. W. McCall, Jr., & M. M. Lombardo, *Looking Glass, Inc.: The first three years,* Greensboro, NC: Center for Creative Leadership, Technical Report 13, 1979, Appendix A.

Organizations that are just starting out are in the *embryonic* stage. They are characterized by high growth rates, basic product lines, heavy emphasis on product engineering, and little or no customer loyalty.

Organizations in the *high-growth* stage are concerned with two things: fighting for market share and building excellence in their management teams. Product lines are refined and extended, and customer loyalty begins to build.

Mature organizations emphasize the maintenance of market share, cost reductions through economies of scale, more rigid management controls over workers' actions, and the generation of cash to develop new product lines. In contrast to the "freewheeling" style of an embryonic organization, there is much less flexibility and variability in the mature organization.

Finally, an *aging* organization struggles to hold market share in a declining market, and it demands extreme cost control obtained through consistency

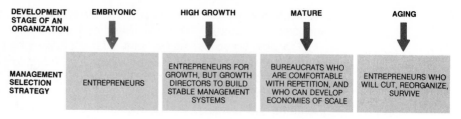

FIGURE 8-1

The relationship between the development stage of an organization and the management selection strategy that best "fits" each stage.

and centralized procedures. Economic survival becomes the primary motivation.

Different management styles seem to "fit" each of these development stages best. At the embryonic stage there is a need for enterprising managers who can thrive in high-risk environments. These are known as entrepreneurs (Figure 8-1). They are decisive individuals who can respond rapidly to changing conditions.

During the high-growth stage there is still a need for entrepreneurs, but it is also important to select the kinds of managers who can develop stable management systems to preserve the gains achieved during the embryonic stage. We might call these managers "growth directors."

As an organization matures, there is a need to select the kind of manager who does not need lots of variety in her or his work, who can oversee repetitive daily operations, and who can search continually for economies of scale. Individuals who fit best in mature organizations have a "bureaucratic" style of management.

Finally, an aging organization needs "movers and shakers" to reinvigorate it. Strategically it becomes important to select (again) entrepreneurs capable of doing whatever is necessary to ensure the economic survival of the firm. This may involve divesting unprofitable operations, firing unproductive workers, or eliminating practices that are considered extravagant.

Admittedly, these characterizations are coarse, but at least they provide a starting point in the construction of an important link between the development stage of an organization and the management selection strategy. Such strategic concerns may be used to recast management job analyses from static descriptions of how management jobs *are* done to dynamic prescriptions of how they *should* be done. The prescriptions of how jobs should be done will then guide the selections of the managers to do them.

Management Selection Methods

Managers can be evaluated and selected on the basis of the results of psychological measurements. The term *measurements* is used here in the broad sense, implying tests and inventories. *Tests* are standardized measures of behavior (e.g., math, vocabulary) that have right and wrong answers. And *inventories* are standardized measures of behavior (e.g., interests, attitudes, opinions) that do not have right and wrong answers. Inventories can be falsified to present an image that a candidate *thinks* a prospective employer is looking for. Tests cannot be falsified. In the context of personnel selection, tests are preferable, for obvious reasons. Inventories are probably best used for purposes of placement or development because in those contexts there is less motivation for a manager to present an image other than what he or she really is. Nevertheless, as we shall see, inventories have been used (with modest success) to select managers. What follows is a brief description of available methods and techniques, together with an assessment of their track records to date.

Tests of mental abilities

Reviews of research conducted between 1919 and 1972 indicated that successful managers were most accurately forecast by tests of their intellectual ability, their ability to draw conclusions from verbal or numerical information, and by their interests.[33, 53, 63] Further research has found two other types of mental abilities that are related to successful performance as a manager: fluency with words and space visualization (the ability to visualize the effects of changes in the position of objects in space).[36, 54, 56]

Objective personality and interest inventories

Objective personality and interest inventories provide a clear stimulus, such as statements about preferences for various ways of behaving, and a clear set of responses from which to choose. Here is an example of an objective measure of personality; the examinee's task is to select the alternatives that are most (M) and least (L) descriptive of herself or himself:

Prefers to get up early in the morning	M	L
Does not get enough exercise	M	L
Follows a well-balanced diet	M	L
Does not care for popular music	M	L

Ever since 1944, Sears has used objective personality and interest inventories as part of a larger "executive battery" of measures to predict management success. It has done so very successfully.[7, 8] Measures of "general activity" have proven especially accurate. This is consistent with the finding that successful managers prefer immediate rather than delayed action.[72, 73]

Projective measures

Projective measures present an individual with ambiguous stimuli (primarily visual) and allow him or her to respond in an open-ended fashion (Figure 8-2): for example, by telling a story regarding what is happening in the picture. Based on how the individual structures the situation through the story he or she tells, an examiner (usually a clinical psychologist) makes inferences concerning the individual's personality structure.

Basically, the difference between an objective and a projective test is this: In an objective test, the test taker tries to guess what the examiner is thinking. In a projective test, the examiner tries to guess what the test taker is thinking![47]

Although early research showed projective measures *not* to be accurate predictors of management success,[51] they can provide useful results when the examinee's responses are related to motivations to manage (e.g., achievement motivation, willingness to accept a leadership role).[9, 35, 68] Moreover, measures

FIGURE 8-2

Sample projective stimulus. Candidates are told to look at the picture briefly and then to write the story it suggests. Stories are scored in terms of the key themes expressed.

of intelligence are unrelated to scores on projective tests. So a combination of both types of instruments can provide a fuller picture of individual "can-do" (intelligence) and "will-do" (motivational) factors than can either one used alone.

Measures of leadership ability

At first glance, one might suspect that measures of leadership ability are highly predictive of managerial success since they appear to tap directly a critical management job requirement. Scales designed to measure two key aspects of leadership behavior, *consideration* and *initiating structure*, have been developed and used in many situations. Consideration reflects management actions oriented toward developing mutual trust, respect for subordinates' ideas, and consideration of their feelings. Initiating structure, on the other hand, reflects the extent to which an individual defines and structures her or his role and those of her or his subordinates toward task accomplishment.

Unfortunately, questionnaires designed to measure consideration and initiating structure have been inaccurate predictors of success in management.[49, 83] This is not to imply that leadership is unimportant in managerial jobs. Rather, it may be that the majority of such jobs are designed to encourage and reward managing (doing things right) rather than leading (doing the right things).

Personal-history data

Based on the assumption that one of the best predictors of future behavior is past behavior, biographical information has been used widely and successfully in managerial selection. As with any other method, careful, competent research is necessary if "biodata" are to prove genuinely useful as predictors of managerial success. Here is one example of this kind of effort.

During the development of its management selection process, Standard Oil of New Jersey (SONJ) asked prospective managers to complete a background survey of the following areas: home and family, education, vocational planning, finances, hobbies and leisure-time activities, health history, and social relations. SONJ then identified items in the background survey that were related statistically to overall success as a manager. These items comprise a "success index."[59] They can be used legally because the company showed that they were job-related. The success index considers an individual's entire career—the many judgments and decisions that many managers have made about him or her—and not the favorable or unfavorable biases of one or a few supervisors. Successful executives in SONJ tend to show a total life pattern of successful endeavors. They were high performers in college, they actively pursue leadership opportunities, and they see themselves as forceful, dominant, assertive, and confident.

Peer assessment

Peers evaluate managerial behavior from a different perspective than do the managers themselves. Actually the term *peer assessment* is a general term denoting three basic methods that members of a well-defined group use in judging each others' performance: *Peer nomination* requires each group member to designate a certain number of group members as highest or lowest on a performance dimension. *Peer rating* requires each group member to rate the performance of every group member. *Peer ranking* requires each group member to rank the performance of all other members from best to worst.

Reviews of over 50 studies found all three methods of peer assessment to be reliable, valid, and free from bias.[82] Peer assessments implicitly require people to consider privileged information about their coworkers. Hence it is essential that peers be thoroughly involved in the planning and design of the peer assessment method to be used.

Situational tests

The objective of a situational test or work sample is to assess "the ability to do" (that is, the ability to apply theory) rather than "the ability to know" (knowledge of theory for theory's sake). There are two types of situational tests to evaluate and select managers: *group exercises*, in which participants are placed in a situation where the successful completion of a task requires interaction among the participants, and *individual exercises*, in which participants complete a task independently. The following sections consider three of the most popular situational tests: the leaderless group discussion, the in-basket test, and the business game.

Leaderless group discussion (LGD)   The LGD is simple and has been used for decades. A group of participants is given a job-related topic and is asked simply to carry on a discussion about it for a period of time. No one is appointed leader, nor is anyone told where to sit. Instead of using a rectangular table (with a "head" at each end), a circular table is often used so that each position carries equal weight. Observers rate the performance of each participant.

For example, IBM uses an LGD in which each participant is required to make a 5-minute oral presentation of a candidate for promotion and then subsequently defend her or his candidate in a group discussion with five other participants. All roles are well-defined and structured. Seven characteristics are rated, each on a 5-point scale of effectiveness: aggressiveness, persuasiveness or selling ability, oral communications, self-confidence, resistance to stress, energy level, and interpersonal contact.[92]

LGD ratings have forecast managerial performance accurately in virtually all the functional areas of business.[6, 89] Previous LGD experience appears to have little effect on present LGD performance, although prior training clearly does.[57, 77] Individuals in one study who received a 15-minute briefing on the history, development, rating instruments, and research relative to the LGD were rated significantly higher than untrained individuals. To control for this, all those with prior training in the LGD should be put into the same groups.

The in-basket test   A situational test designed to simulate important aspects of a position, the in-basket tests an individual working independently. In general, it takes the following form:

> It consists of the letters, memoranda, notes of incoming telephone calls, and other materials which have supposedly collected in the in-basket of an administrative officer. The subject who takes the test is given appropriate background information concerning the school, business, military unit, or whatever institution is involved. He is told that he is the new incumbent of the administrative position and that he is to deal with the material in the in-basket. The background information is sufficiently detailed that the subject can reasonably be expected to take action on many of the problems presented by the in-basket documents. The subject is instructed that he is not to play a role, he is not to pretend to be someone else. He is to bring to the new job his own background of knowledge and experience, his own personality, and he is to deal with the problems as though he were really the incumbent of the administrative position. He is not to say what he would do; he is actually to write letters and memoranda, prepare agenda for meetings, make notes and reminders for himself, as though he were actually on the job. (ref. 30, p. 1).

Some sample in-basket items are shown in Figure 8-3.

Although the situation is relatively unstructured for the candidate, each candidate faces the same complex set of materials. At the conclusion of the in-basket test, each candidate leaves behind a packet full of notes, memos, letters, etc., that provide a record of his or her behavior. The test is then scored by describing (if the purpose is development) or evaluating (if the purpose is selection for promotion) what the candidate did in terms of such dimensions as self-confidence, organizational and planning abilities, written communications, decision making, risk taking, and administrative abilities. The dimensions to be evaluated are identified through job analysis prior to designing or selecting the exercise. The major advantages of the in-basket, therefore, are its flexibility (it can be designed to fit many different types of situations) and the fact that it permits *direct* observation of individual behavior within the context of a job-relevant, standardized problem situation.

More than two decades of research on the in-basket indicate that it validly forecasts subsequent job behavior and promotion.[12, 14, 89] Moreover, since performance on the LGD is not strongly related to performance on the in-basket,[89] in combination they are potentially powerful predictors of managerial success.

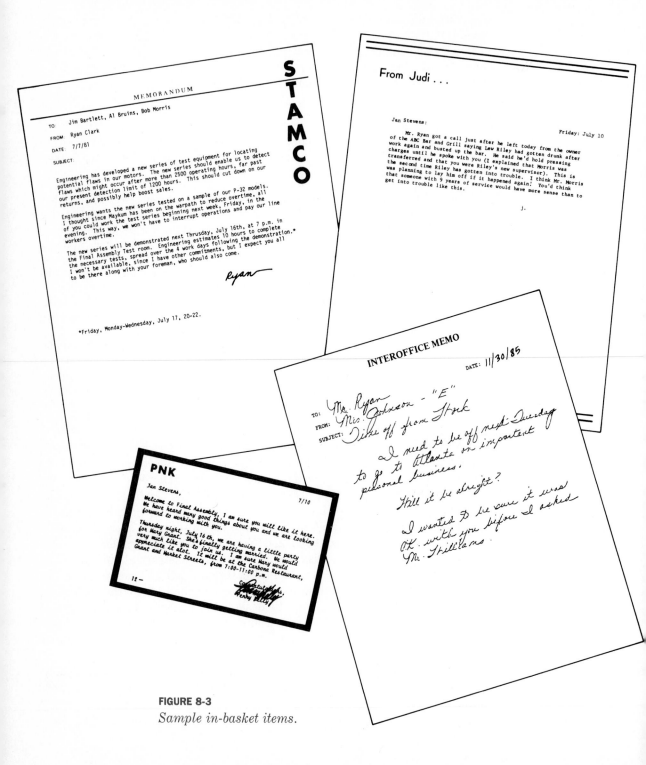

FIGURE 8-3

Sample in-basket items.

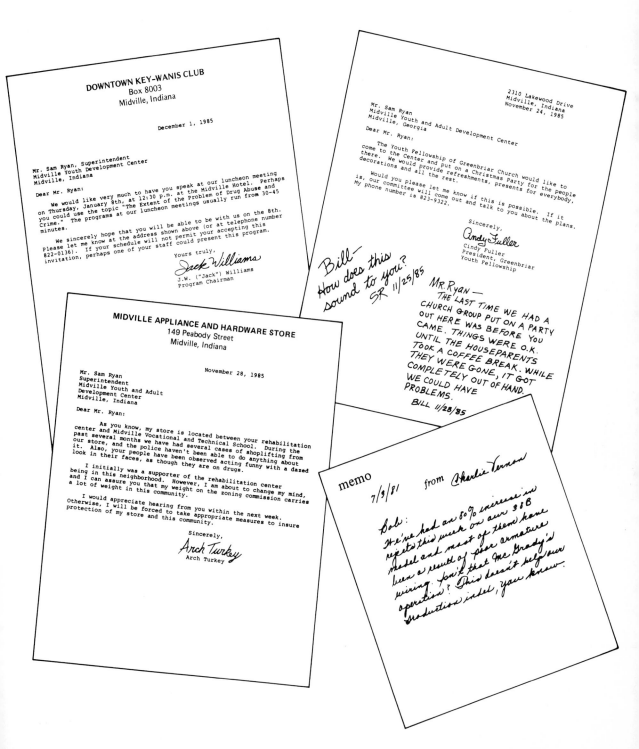

DOWNTOWN KEY-WANIS CLUB
Box 8003
Midville, Indiana

December 1, 1985

Mr. Sam Ryan, Superintendent
Midville Youth Development Center
Midville, Indiana

Dear Mr. Ryan:

We would like very much to have you speak at our luncheon meeting
on Thursday, January 8th, at 12:30 p.m. at the Midville Hotel. Perhaps
you could use the topic "The Extent of the Problem of Drug Abuse and
Crime." The programs at our luncheon meetings usually run from 30-45
minutes.

We sincerely hope that you will be able to be with us on the 8th.
Please let me know at the address shown above (or at telephone number
822-0136). If your schedule will not permit your accepting this
invitation, perhaps one of your staff could present this program.

Yours truly,

Jack Williams

J.W. ("Jack") Williams
Program Chairman

2310 Lakewood Drive
Midville, Indiana
November 24, 1985

Mr. Sam Ryan
Midville Youth and Adult Development Center
Midville, Georgia

Dear Mr. Ryan:

The Youth Fellowship of Greenbriar Church would like to
come to the Center and put on a Christmas Party for the people
there. We would provide refreshments, presents for everybody,
decorations and all the rest.

Would you please let me know if this is possible. If it
is, our committee will come out and talk to you about the plans.
My phone number is 823-9322.

Sincerely,

Andy Fuller

Cindy Fuller
President, Greenbriar
Youth Fellowship

---

*Bill—
How does this
sound to you?
SR 11/25/85*

*MR. RYAN—
THE LAST TIME WE HAD A
CHURCH GROUP PUT ON A PARTY
OUT HERE WAS BEFORE YOU
CAME. THINGS WERE O.K.
UNTIL THE HOUSEPARENTS
TOOK A COFFEE BREAK. WHILE
THEY WERE GONE, IT GOT
COMPLETELY OUT OF HAND.
WE COULD HAVE
PROBLEMS.
BILL 11/28/85*

MIDVILLE APPLIANCE AND HARDWARE STORE
149 Peabody Street
Midville, Indiana

November 28, 1985

Mr. Sam Ryan
Superintendent
Midville Youth and Adult
Development Center
Midville, Indiana

Dear Mr. Ryan:

As you know, my store is located between your rehabilitation
center and Midville Vocational and Technical School. During the
past several months we have had several cases of shoplifting from
our store, and the police haven't been able to do anything about
it. Also, your people have been observed acting funny with a dazed
look in their faces, as though they are on drugs.

I initially was a supporter of the rehabilitation center
being in this neighborhood. However, I am about to change my mind,
and I can assure you that my weight on the zoning commission carries
a lot of weight in this community.

I would appreciate hearing from you within the next week.
Otherwise, I will be forced to take appropriate measures to insure
protection of my store and this community.

Sincerely,

Arch Turkey

Arch Turkey

---

memo   7/9/81   from Charlie Vernon

*Bob:
We've had an 80% increase in
rejects this week on our 38B
model and most of them have
been a result of poor armature
wiring. Isn't that McGrady's
operation? This doesn't help our
production intol, you know.*

Business games   The business game is a situational test, a living case in which candidates play themselves, not an assigned role, and are evaluated within a group. Like the in-basket, business games are available for a wide variety of executive activities, from marketing to capital asset management. They may be simple (focusing on very specific activities) or complex models of complete organizational systems. They may be computer-based or manually operated, rigidly programmed or flexible.[24, 26, 34] They will probably be used more frequently for training purposes, given the continued development and availability of personal computers and simulation software—for example, stock market simulations, and battle simulations for the military academies.

COMPANY EXAMPLE

IBM's manufacturing problem

In this exercise, six participants must work together as a group to operate a manufacturing company. They must purchase raw materials, manufacture a product, and sell it back to the market. Included in the exercise are a product forecast and specific prices (that fluctuate during the exercise) for raw materials and completed products. No preassigned roles are given to the participants, but each one is rated in terms of aggressiveness, persuasiveness or selling ability, resistance to stress, energy level, interpersonal contact, administrative ability, and risk taking. In one IBM study, performance on the manufacturing problem accurately forecast changes in position level for 94 middle managers 3 years later.[92] When the in-basket score was added as an additional predictor, the forecast was even more accurate.

Business games have several advantages. One, they compress time; events that might not actually occur for months or years are made to occur in a matter of hours. Two, the games are interesting because of their realism, competitive nature, and the immediacy and objectivity of feedback. And three, such games promote increased understanding of complex interrelationships among organizational units.

Business games also have several drawbacks. One, in the context of training, some participants may become so engrossed in "beating the system" that they fail to grasp the underlying management principles being taught. And two, creative approaches to solving problems presented by the game may be stifled, particularly if the highly innovative manager is penalized financially during the game for her or his unorthodox strategies.[91]

Based on available research, a rough "scorecard" indicating the overall effectiveness of each of the predictors discussed above is shown in Table 8-2.

Assessment centers

The assessment center approach was first used by German military psychologists during World War II to select officers. They felt that paper-and-pencil

TABLE 8-2 *Accuracy of various procedures used to assess potential for management*

Procedure	Accuracy
Mental ability tests	5
Objective personality and interest inventories	4
Projective techniques	3
Measures of leadership ability	1
Interviews	2
Personal history data	4
Peer assessment	4
Situational tests (when used in combination, as in an assessment center)	5

Procedures are rated on a 1-to-5 scale, where 1 = poor prediction and 5 = accurate prediction. It is important to stress, however, that no single procedure or combination of procedures is perfectly accurate. Even the most accurate procedures available account for only about 25 percent of the variability in actual job performance among managers. The following rating scheme was therefore used for each procedure, based on the average correlation between scores on the procedure and measures of actual job performance:

Average correlation	Accuracy score
.00 to .10	1
.10 to .20	2
.20 to .30	3
.30 to .40	4
.40 to .50	5

tests took too narrow a view of human nature; therefore, they chose to observe each candidate's behavior in a complex situation to develop a broader appraisal of his or her reactions. Borrowing from this work and that of the War Office Selection Board of the British Army during the early 1940s, the U.S. Office of Strategic Services used the method to select spies during World War II. Each candidate had to develop a cover story that would hide her or his identity during the assessment. Testing for the ability to maintain cover was crucial, and ingenious situational tests were designed to seduce candidates into breaking cover.[69, 75]

After World War II many military psychologists and officers joined private companies, where they started small-scale assessment centers. In 1956, AT&T was the first to use the method as the basis for a large-scale study of managerial progress and career development. As a result of extensive research conducted over 25 years, AT&T found that managerial skills and abilities are best measured by the following procedures:[15]

1. *Administrative skills.* Performance on the in-basket test
2. *Interpersonal skills.* LGD, manufacturing problem
3. *Intellectual ability.* Paper-and-pencil ability tests
4. *Stability of performance.* In-basket, LGD, manufacturing problem
5. *Work-oriented motivation.* Projective tests, interviews, simulations
6. *Career orientation.* Projective tests, interviews, personality inventories
7. *Dependency on others.* Projective tests

But assessment centers do more than just *test* people. The assessment center method is a process that evaluates a candidate's potential for management from three sources: (1) multiple assessment techniques, such as situational tests, tests of mental abilities, and interest inventories; (2) standardized methods of making inferences from such techniques, because assessors are trained to distinguish between effective and ineffective behaviors of the candidates; and (3) pooled judgments from multiple assessors to rate each candidate's behavior.

Today assessment centers take many different forms, for they are used in a wide variety of settings and for a variety of purposes. Over 2000 organizations are now using the assessment center method, and more are doing so every year.[32] In addition to evaluating and selecting managers, the method is being used to train and upgrade management skills, to encourage creativity among research and engineering personnel, to resolve interpersonal and interdepartmental conflicts, to assist individuals in career planning, to train managers in performance appraisal, and to provide information for human resource planning and organization design.[32]

The assessment center method offers great flexibility. The specific content and design of a center can be tailored to the characteristics of the job in question. For example, when used for management selection, the assessment center method should be designed to predict how a person would behave in that next-higher-level management job. By relating each candidate's performance on the assessment center exercises to such indicators as the management level subsequently achieved 2 (or more) years later or current salary, researchers have shown that the predictions for each candidate are very accurate. An accurate reading of each candidate's behavior *before* the promotion decision is made can help avoid potentially costly selection errors (erroneous acceptances as well as erroneous rejections).

As a specific example of the flexibility of the assessment center method in using multiple assessment techniques, consider the following six types of exercises used to help select U.S. Army recruiters:[12]

- *Structured interview.* Assessors ask a series of questions targeted at the subject's level of achievement motivation, potential for being a "self-starter," and commitment to the Army.
- *Cold calls.* The subject has an opportunity to learn a little about three prospects and must phone each of them for the purpose of getting them

to come into the office. Assessor role players have well-defined characters (prospects) to portray.

■ *Interviews.* Two of the three cold-call prospects agree to come in for an interview. The subject's job is to follow up on what was learned in the cold-call conversations and to begin promoting Army enlistment to these people. A third walk-in prospect also appears for an interview with the subject.

■ *Interview with concerned parent.* The subject is asked to prepare for and conduct an interview with the father of one of the prospects that he or she interviewed previously.

■ *Five-minute speech about the Army.* The subject prepares a short talk about an Army career that she or he delivers to the rest of the group and to the assessors.

■ *In-basket.* The subject is given an in-basket filled with notes, phone messages, and letters on which he or she must take some action.

A third feature of the assessment center method is assessor training. Assessors are typically line managers two or more levels above the candidates, trained (from 2 days to several weeks depending on the complexity of the center) in interviewing techniques, behavior observation, and in-basket performance. In addition, assessors usually go through the exercises as participants before rating others. This experience, plus the development of a consensus by assessors on effective versus ineffective responses by candidates to the situations presented, enables the assessors to standardize their interpretations of each candidate's behavior. Standardization ensures that each candidate will be assessed fairly, that is, in terms of the same "yardstick."

Instead of professional psychologists, line managers are often used as assessors for several reasons:

1. They are thoroughly familiar with the jobs for which candidates are being assessed.
2. Their involvement in the assessment process contributes to its acceptance by participants as well as by line managers.
3. Participation by line managers is a developmental experience for them and may contribute to the identification of areas where they need improvement themselves.[64]
4. Assessors can be more objective in evaluating candidate performance since they usually do not know the candidates personally.[18]

Despite these potential advantages, cumulative evidence across assessment center studies indicates that professional psychologists provide more valid assessment center ratings than do managers.[32]

With the assessment center method, the judgments of multiple assessors are pooled in rating each candidate's behavior. The advantage of pooling is that no candidate is subject to ratings from only one assessor. Since judgments from more than one source tend to be more reliable and valid, pooling enhances the overall accuracy of the judgments made. Each candidate is usually evaluated by a different assessor on each exercise. Although assessor judgments are made independently, the judgments must be combined into an overall rating on each dimension of interest. A summary report is then prepared and shared with each candidate.

These features of the assessment center method—flexibility of form and content, the use of multiple assessment techniques, standardized methods for interpreting behavior, and pooled assessor judgments—account for the successful track record of this approach over the past three decades. It has consistently demonstrated high validity, with correlations between assessment center performance and later job performance as a manager sometimes reaching the .50s and .60s.[32, 42, 53] Both minorities and nonminorities, and men and women, acknowledge that the method provides them a fair opportunity to demonstrate what they are capable of doing in a management job.[43]

In terms of its bottom-line impact, two studies have shown that assessment centers *are* cost-effective, even though the per-candidate cost may vary from as little as $50 to over $2000. Using the general utility equation (Equation 6-1), both studies have demonstrated that the assessment center method should not be measured against the cost of implementing it, but rather against the cost (in lost sales and declining productivity) of promoting the wrong person into a management job.[21, 22] In a first-level management job, the gain in improved job performance as a result of promoting people via the assessment center method is about $2700 per year. However, if the average tenure of first-level managers is, say, 5 years, the gain per person is about $13,500.

Despite its advantages, the method is not without potential problems. These include:[1, 53, 93]

- Adoption of the assessment center method without carefully analyzing the need for it, and without adequate preparations to use it wisely
- Blind acceptance of assessment data without considering other information on candidates, such as past and current performance
- The tendency to rate only general "exercise effectiveness," rather than performance relative to individual behavioral dimensions, as the number of dimensions exceeds the ability of assessors to evaluate each dimension individually.
- Lack of control over the information generated during assessment: for example, "leaking" assessment ratings to operating managers
- Failure to evaluate the utility of the program in terms of dollar benefits relative to costs
- Inadequate feedback to participants

Here is an interesting finding: Ratings of management potential made after a review of personnel files correlated significantly (.46) with assessment ratings, suggesting that assessment to some extent might duplicate a much simpler and less costly process.[39] This conclusion held true for predictions made regarding each candidate's progress in management 1 and 8 years after assessment.[41] However, when the rating of management potential was added to the assessment center prediction, the validity of the two together (.58) was higher than either one alone. What does the assessment center prediction add? Not much if we are simply trying to predict each candidate's rate and level of *advancement*. But if we are trying to predict *performance* in management— that is, to clarify and evaluate the promotion system in an organization—then assessment centers can be of considerable help, even if they serve only to capture the promotion policy of the organization.[41]

The view from participants   In another study, researchers interviewed 37 recent candidates (19 were high scorers and 18 were low scorers) to determine their reactions to being evaluated by the assessment center process.[88] The researchers did not know which subjects were high or low scorers until after the interview. Both groups agreed by large margins that the method measures important managerial traits and that they would be glad to attend again. By a somewhat smaller margin, they also agreed that they understood what the center was all about before they attended, that their performance was not impaired by stress or tension, and that they understood clearly the feedback given on their performance. High and low scorers disagreed, however, on the accuracy of the assessors' evaluations, on the value of developmental recommendations received, and on the benefits to their careers from their attendance. Not surprisingly, most low scorers were negative on all three points.

With respect to feedback, the researchers recommended that feedback interviews be held within 2 weeks after assessment, that assessors explain fully the bases for their evaluations, and that a follow-up interview be held by the immediate supervisor to review the candidates' strengths and weaknesses identified at the center. Both should agree on future actions to capitalize on candidates' strengths and to overcome their weaknesses. Such an approach makes good sense, for much of the organization's investment in diagnosing strengths and weaknesses would be wasted if the information were not used for developmental purposes. Since one purpose of development is to improve present job performance, significant benefits could accrue to the organization long before the candidate is again considered for promotion. Let us now examine this topic in greater detail.

Developing Management Talent

In general terms, the goals of management development include:

- To increase the job performance effectiveness of managers
- To enhance job satisfaction

- To meet equal employment opportunity commitments
- To prevent the knowledge, skills, or abilities of managers from becoming obsolete
- To help individuals learn about their personal strengths, weaknesses, and interests so that they can make better decisions about job opportunities along various career paths

Although these goals have changed somewhat over the past 20 years, the types of development activities designed to achieve them, at least at the middle-management level, have not. The subject areas deemed most important and covered most often in middle-management training programs over the past 20 years are principles of management, communications, and interpersonal skills. The number 1 industrial training problem continues to be the lack of a systematic approach to management development efforts.[70] Here's how one firm deals with this problem.

COMPANY EXAMPLE

TRW's strategic management seminar

At TRW, *systems learning* helps focus attention on the important concept of "transfer of training."[28] All training activities are designed with a built-in compatibility between what managers are expected to learn and what they are expected to do on their jobs. Here is an example.

Following instruction in the concepts of competitive strategy, a three-phase strategic management seminar was presented to natural business teams within TRW: for example, a division vice president and his or her staff. In phase I, each team receives two things: (1) more instruction in the concepts of competitive strategy and (2) a detailed assignment. The teams must apply the concepts to their business and develop an action strategy. Each team must plan a maximum of six actions that it will take over the next 18 months, and it must designate responsibility to particular team members for each action. The teams then "go home" to work on their strategies for about 8 weeks.

Phase II of the seminar is called the "midterm review." A seminar faculty member visits each team to review its progress on the assignment and provides detailed feedback on how well the team is applying the concepts. Sometimes major changes are made at this point as teams recognize, for example, that their competitive analysis is not thorough enough.

Over the following 8 weeks, Phase III of the program, each team prepares its final strategic presentation—to be delivered in the presence of two or three other teams. After each team presents its strategy, the audience provides constructive comments and criticisms. Next, the audience votes on whether to accept or reject the strategy, indicating on their ballots what they like and dislike about the strategy. The votes and comments are collected and offered to the presenting team, along with comments and concerns from the faculty member. What's happening here? A powerful peer review process.

To encourage a tight "fit" between training and application, some changes in TRW's organizational practices were necessary—such as changing the process of developing strategic plans, modifying the compensation system so that long-term management is rewarded, and changing the performance appraisal process to emphasize long-term thinking, planning, and action. However, the biggest change of all was senior management's willingness to encourage the kind of risk taking required to implement some of the strategies. This is the essence of systems learning.

TRW's approach to "systems learning" suggests that transfer of training (that is, the adoption of concepts and practices learned in training to practice on the job) will be greatest when the following steps are taken:

1. Define the content of the program(s) in terms of the strategic needs of the organization. Failure to do this will result in training that will have no impact on organizational outcomes.
2. Identify and assign individuals to training based on careful selection standards. To do this, survey employee interests, obtain input from immediate supervisors, and review career development plans and performance appraisals. Always ask, "Does this person really need the training?"
3. Ensure that classroom content is directly relevant to the work setting (i.e., that the training is content valid). Specific behaviors, activities, and goals that are required on the job should be reflected in the content of the training.
4. Ensure the practical application of the training to the work setting by means of systematic follow-up. Close the training program with an "application plan" session that reiterates the most important and relevant learning points, reduces them to specific goals, reduces the goals to specific activities, identifies appropriate coworkers to assess progress toward the goals, and establishes a time frame for self-monitoring. At the end of the self-monitoring period, a "coach" (perhaps the original trainer) then meets with each participant to review progress and use of the applications plan. The ultimate objective is to ensure that participants have a reason for using what they have learned and actually adopt the new behaviors in the work setting.[2]

This approach to management development requires a serious commitment by the organization. A number of management development methods are available. Any one of them *can* contribute to the objectives of management development, but only if the technique is prudently selected, diligently applied, and rigorously evaluated. Table 8-3 presents 23 approaches to management development, categorized according to their broad objectives. Often the techniques are used in combination in long-term development programs. The following sections give a brief description of each technique; references are provided for more in-depth information.

TABLE 8-3 *Common management development techniques categorized by objectives*

Self-insight and environmental awareness	Decision-making and behavioral skills	Motivation to manage
Managerial role theory	Vroom-Yetton model	Coaching
Double-loop learning	Grid seminars	Role motivation theory
Sensitivity training	Case study	Need for achievement
Transactional analysis	The incident process	Survey feedback
Self-directed management development	Rational manager training	Behavior modeling
Interactive skills training	Conference	Behavior modification
Leader match	Assessment centers	
	Role playing	
	Junior board	
	Understudy assignments	

Note: Descriptions of the techniques are drawn primarily from K. N. Wexley & G. P. Latham, *Developing and training human resources in organizations*, Glenview, IL: Scott, Foresman, 1981.

Self-insight and environmental awareness

The left column of Table 8-3 indicates seven approaches to development that foster self-insight and environmental awareness, which refer to an understanding of how one's actions affect others and how one is viewed by others. Techniques that foster this understanding include the following.

Managerial role theory   This theory requires that the trainee become aware of a "contingency theory of managerial work." At any time the work of a manager is contingent on four basic variables—the *organizational environment, functional specialty, leadership style, and the situation at hand.* Managerial effectiveness is influenced when managers examine their own work, what they do, and why they do it. To stimulate this kind of thinking, Mintzberg offers 14 self-study questions.[73] In addition, a neutral third party should be asked to observe and record the manager's behavior on the job, analyze the results, and feed the results back to the manager.

Double-loop learning   This approach focuses on training leaders to move from one set of behavioral strategies (termed Model I) to a presumably "better" set of behaviors (Model II) by becoming aware of *the difference between what they do and what they think they should do in managing others.*[3] Model I people strive to attain four primary values: (a) achieve self-defined purposes, (b) win rather than lose, (c) suppress negative feelings, and (d) maximize rationality and minimize emotionality. To satisfy these values, people learn a set of action strategies ("single-loop learning") that result in other people's becoming defensive and secretive about their activities. Model II strategies encourage the sharing of information, free and informed choice, and internal commitment among people. Those who understand Model II become skilled at inviting "double-loop learning"—knowing how to articulate what they believe in and encouraging healthy inquiry and questioning of their beliefs. The difference between single- and double-loop learning is shown in Figure 8-4.

FIGURE 8-4

The contrast between single-loop learning and double-loop learning.

SINGLE-LOOP LEARNING—FEEDBACK ENABLES AN ORGANIZATION TO CARRY ON ITS PRESENT POLICIES OR TO ACHIEVE ITS PRESENT OBJECTIVES

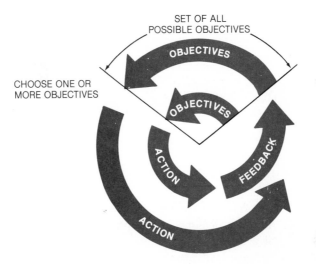

DOUBLE-LOOP LEARNING—BY AVOIDING A "WIN–LOSE" STRATEGY, FEEDBACK ENABLES AN ORGANIZATION TO QUESTION THE APPROPRIATENESS OR WISDOM OF PRESENT OBJECTIVES AND POLICIES, AND PERHAPS TO CHOOSE NEW ONES.

Sensitivity training Small groups of 8 to 14 persons who meet in unstructured learning situations, focus on the "here-and-now" behavior taking place in their own group, and attempt to enhance their awareness of their behavioral characteristics and/or group processes. Sometimes the leader's role is passive, while in other instances it is more prominent.[86] Goals of the process include: (a) improved understanding of how and why trainees act toward others and of how their actions affect others, (b) insight into why others act the way they do, (c) improved listening skills, (d) insight into how groups operate, (e) increased tolerance and understanding of others, and (f) experimentation with new ways of acting toward people and feedback about how these new ways affect people.[19]

Transactional analysis   This technique was developed in the 1950s by Eric Berne. He analyzed the daily transactions that take place among people and described them using simple, nontechnical language.[10] According to the book *I'm OK—You're OK* (T. A. Harris, 1969), what makes a person feel "OK" or "not OK" is the amount of "stroking" that she or he receives of each type: positive, negative, or plastic (artificial).[38] The kinds of strokes a person wants to receive from others, according to the theory, are the result of years of childhood conditioning. Further, all transactions entail two strokes, the stimulus and the response to that stimulus. The behavior observed during transactions falls into three categories, or ego states, that everyone possesses: parent, adult, and child. Through a process known as "structural analysis," transactional analysts describe the ego states that occur during a given transaction.

Self-directed management development   This technique assumes that the best way to help managers improve themselves is to encourage them to become involved in thinking about and setting goals for their own development and career growth. The process begins with a self-assessment of managerial capabilities to help individuals gain insight into the skills they must acquire to become effective managers. Individuals then decide for themselves whether they possess the motivation and potential to manage others. Individuals are taught that they must assume primary responsibility for their own development. To do so, they prepare personal development plans to acquire the knowledge, skills, abilities, and other characteristics to enhance their managerial talents or to pursue another career of their choice.

Interactive skills training   This 5-day course for managers at all organizational levels is designed to increase trainee self-awareness.[79] The course consists of a series of 30-minute to 2½-hour exercises, each dealing with a particular interactive situation that is important for managers to handle effectively—e.g., persuading, briefing, participating in meetings, handling discipline and grievances, and fact-finding for problem solving or decision making. A detailed review session follows each module. The trainer maximizes the meaningfulness of this feedback by helping the trainee to compare this information to his or her self-perceptions, to other trainees' behaviors, and to the behaviors of effective performers. At the end of the 5-day course, participants must describe how they intend to apply the lessons learned during training to change their managerial behavior on the job.

Leader match   Based on the "contingency model" of leader behavior, it was developed over the past 25 years by Fiedler and his associates.[29] According to the theory, the effectiveness of a leader depends on a proper match between her or his style of motivating subordinates and the degree to which the situation in which the leader works enables her or him to have control and influence over subordinates as well as the task itself. A leader's control over a situation is determined by three things: (a) leader-member relations (good versus poor), (b) the degree to which a task is structured or ambiguous, and (c) the power inherent in the leader's position. The training program is designed to teach people how to become aware of their primary motivational style through a self-study workbook, to diagnose the situation in which they are working, and to *change the situation* to fit their personality rather than the converse.

Decision making and behavioral skills

The middle column of Table 8-3 shows 10 approaches to management development, each having the objective to improve the manager's ability to make decisions and to solve job-related problems in a constructive fashion. These approaches are described below.

The Vroom-Yetton model   One aspect of leadership behavior, namely, the extent to which managers should involve subordinates in decision making, is focused on.[90] Managers should not always be autocratic or participative. Rather, they should be taught to diagnose a problem and to determine the best decision-making style. The training program teaches managers to assess situations correctly (via a seven-question, decision-tree format) in order to choose the appropriate level of subordinate participation that will improve the chances of making more effective decisions. Flexibility in leadership behavior is essential because people and situations are constantly changing.

Grid seminars   These comprise a six-phase program that lasts anywhere from 3 to 5 years. The program begins by examining managerial behavior and style and then systematically widens its focus to team and intergroup development, and then to the total organization. It is designed around the concept of leadership known as the "managerial grid," a two-dimensional depiction of managerial behavior (Figure 8-5).[11] The 9-point horizontal axis of the grid is called "concern for production," and the 9-point vertical axis is called "concern for people." For any manager, the intersection of one of the 9×9 possible combinations represents his or her management style. According to the model, the 9,9 position (team management) is the ideal management style and the key to corporate excellence. The seminars are designed to teach managers how to behave in this fashion.

The case study approach   This approach to management development was pioneered at the Harvard Business School. Based on a written description of an organizational problem, each trainee diagnoses the underlying issues and decides what should be done in the situation described. Then the individual meets with other trainees, and, as a small group, they discuss the various diagnoses and proposed solutions. The role of the trainer is to facilitate the group's learning by providing a climate for group discussion. No attempt is made to lecture to the participants; the trainer merely helps them discover

FIGURE 8-5

The managerial grid.

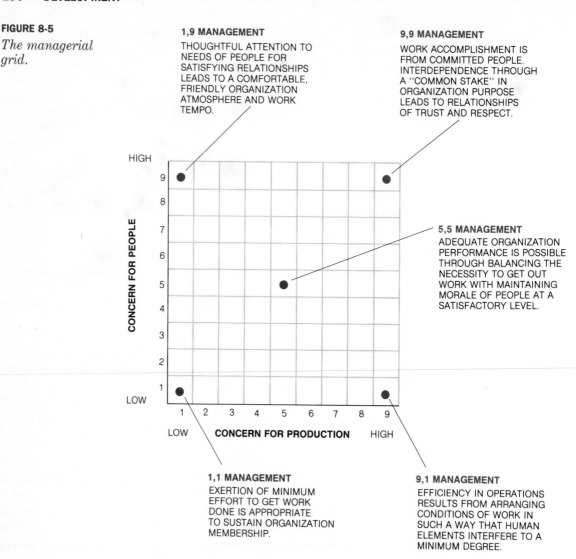

1,9 MANAGEMENT
THOUGHTFUL ATTENTION TO NEEDS OF PEOPLE FOR SATISFYING RELATIONSHIPS LEADS TO A COMFORTABLE, FRIENDLY ORGANIZATION ATMOSPHERE AND WORK TEMPO.

9,9 MANAGEMENT
WORK ACCOMPLISHMENT IS FROM COMMITTED PEOPLE. INTERDEPENDENCE THROUGH A "COMMON STAKE" IN ORGANIZATION PURPOSE LEADS TO RELATIONSHIPS OF TRUST AND RESPECT.

5,5 MANAGEMENT
ADEQUATE ORGANIZATION PERFORMANCE IS POSSIBLE THROUGH BALANCING THE NECESSITY TO GET OUT WORK WITH MAINTAINING MORALE OF PEOPLE AT A SATISFACTORY LEVEL.

1,1 MANAGEMENT
EXERTION OF MINIMUM EFFORT TO GET WORK DONE IS APPROPRIATE TO SUSTAIN ORGANIZATION MEMBERSHIP.

9,1 MANAGEMENT
EFFICIENCY IN OPERATIONS RESULTS FROM ARRANGING CONDITIONS OF WORK IN SUCH A WAY THAT HUMAN ELEMENTS INTERFERE TO A MINIMUM DEGREE.

CONCERN FOR PEOPLE (vertical axis: LOW 1 to HIGH 9)

CONCERN FOR PRODUCTION (horizontal axis: LOW 1 to HIGH 9)

for themselves the managerial concepts and principles underlying the case, how the problem might have been avoided, and what can be done to prevent the problem from recurring.[4]

The incident process   Trainees are required to read individually a briefly sketched incident and then, as a group, to assume the role of a specific person in the situation.[78] They must identify the issue requiring decisive action and obtain the facts necessary to arrive at a solution. Individuals make independent decisions, debate the various decisions within the group, and then hear what was actually done in the particular situation and what the consequences were of those decisions. The team leader supplies only that information which is requested specifically. Unlike the case study, where trainees are given all the facts concerning a situation, the incident process attempts to move the training closer to reality by simulating the way managers actually make decisions. No one gives them all the facts; the management trainees must determine the facts for themselves.

Rational manager training   This approach has the following objectives: (a) to make managers aware of aids to effective decision making and problem solving, (b) to give them practice in applying those aids, and (c) to provide feedback on the results of their performance.[48] The program lasts from 2 to 5 days, depending on the target population. During this time a group of about 15 managers grapples with the problems and decisions of a simulated organization. These trainees have their own offices, talk to each other on the telephone, and hold group meetings to solve the problems at hand. In a follow-up feedback session, the trainees examine the assumptions they made and how they used the information available to them. The trainer identifies inadequate methods of problem analysis and decision making and shows the trainees where they could have improved had they followed the systematic procedures prescribed in the course.

The conference method   Such topics as human relations, safety education, effective customer communications, and sales training are taught.[40] The conference is structured around a small-group meeting in which a leader trained in group decision methods helps the group identify and define a problem, guides the discussion so that it is constantly directed toward the problem, and summarizes the principles or explanations that reflect the consensus of the group in dealing with the problem.[60]

Assessment centers   Such centers are often used for training purposes.[32] However, their impact on each manager's development depends on the amount and quality of *feedback* provided to candidates. Consider, for example, how an in-basket exercise was used to train middle-management candidates.[62] AT&T compared the responses of management candidates to those of experienced managers. The candidates were wordier, less likely to take action on the basis of the importance of the problem, saw fewer implications for the organization as a whole, tended to make final (as opposed to investigatory) decisions more frequently, and tended to resort to complete delegation instead of retaining some element of control. The experienced managers' approaches to dealing with the in-basket materials served as the basis for discussing the "appropriate" ways of dealing with the problems.

Role playing   This technique is frequently used to teach skills such as interviewing, grievance handling, performance reviews, leadership styles, and effective communication. It incorporates four key principles of learning: active participation, modeling, feedback (e.g., through videotape replays), and practice.[84] Participants are told to imagine themselves in situations presented by the trainer. Typically not all members of a group role play at the same time. Instead, part of the group acts as observers, but, before a session ends, all participants role-play at least once. Discussion follows immediately after each role-play. Issues and problems that emerged during the enactment are examined, so that both the role players and the observers understand the underlying principles that were demonstrated and their organizational implications.

Junior boards   Promising young middle-level managers can experience problems and responsibilities faced by high-level executives in their company using this method. Junior managers are exposed to critical aspects of their organization's business, thus enabling them to develop the capacity to identify and explore broad issues. Approximately a dozen young executives from diverse functions within the organization serve on the board for a term of 6 months or longer. The board is ordinarily allowed to study any problems faced by the organization (e.g., personnel policies, organization design, interdepartmental conflicts, executive compensation) and make recommendations to the senior board of directors (i.e., the official board elected by the stockholders).

Understudy assignments   These are designed to ensure that the organization will have trained personnel to assume key high-level positions as necessary. This approach also promotes the long-range development of homegrown top executives. An understudy to a senior executive relieves the executive of certain responsibilities, thereby giving the understudy an opportunity to learn certain aspects of the job and the executive's style of handling it. The benefits that the trainee derives from this experience depend greatly on the executive's ability to teach effectively via oral communication and behavior modeling. Indeed, much of the executive's motivation to train the managerial "apprentice" depends upon the quality of their relationship.[27]

Motivation to manage

The right column of Table 8-3 indicates six approaches to management development, each having the objective to maximize the manager's desire to perform well. These approaches are described below.

Coaching   This is one of the most popular management development techniques. Managers who coach employees well "model" the correct behaviors being taught, assign specific and challenging goals, and provide employees with frequent and immediate feedback concerning their job performance. The training of managers to conduct effective coaching sessions with their employees usually incorporates a series of modeling films, role-playing activities, and/or workbook exercises focused on the modeling films and the role-playing activities. The broad objective of such training is to increase employee motivation by giving employees more open lines of communication with their bosses, concrete feedback on areas needing improvement, positive reinforcement for what they do well, and specific goals for change.

Role motivation theory   This theory is based on the assumption that key attitudes and motives affect an individual's choice of a managerial career, success achieved, and speed of advancement.[71] Attitudes are measured by a "fill-in-the-blanks" inventory called the Miner Sentence Completion Scale. They are: favorable attitude toward authority, desire to compete, assertive motivation, desire to exercise power, desire for a distinctive position, and a sense of responsibility. Training is oriented toward positive changes in all six areas— i.e., the "motivation to manage." In 1-hour, once-a-week training sessions using lecture-discussion teaching methods, trainees learn why subordinates perform ineffectively and what a manager can do in such situations. Trainees think of themselves as being in the managerial role, experience the emotions associated with it, and focus on the implications for managerial effectiveness.

Achievement motivation theory   This approach seeks to stimulate each individual's "need for achievement."[67] The training program is designed primarily for entrepreneurs in small-business settings. It teaches people to think and act in high-achievement terms through their responses to projective tests and through their behavior in a business game. Through self-study, trainees develop a clear understanding of the role that high-need-for-achievement people must play in a business setting. Trainees then decide for themselves whether they want to be that kind of person and whether being an entrepreneur is really part of their career plan. Toward the end of the course, each trainee sets specific performance goals for the next 2 years. Every 6 months trainees report on their progress. The high interpersonal support of the group seems to enhance the overall success of the program.

While a high need for achievement is strongly related to success as an entrepreneur,[68] it seems not to be related to managerial success in a bureaucracy. In bureaucratic situations where technical expertise is not critical, the need for power, and the willingness to exert it, are more important than a high need for achievement.[25]

Survey feedback   To begin with, a rigorous measurement of the way the organization is presently functioning is taken.[61] This measurement is made by administering anonymous questionnaires to all employees. The responses are then tabulated for every work group in the organization and for the organization as a whole. Each manager receives a summary of this information, based on the responses of his or her own immediate subordinates. A change agent (i.e., a person skilled in applied behavioral science methods) meets privately with the manager-recipient for the purpose of maximizing his or her understanding of the survey information. Subsequently the change agent attends a meeting between the manager and the subordinates for the purpose of examining survey

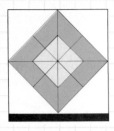

Impact of Management Selection and Development on Productivity, Quality of Work Life, and the Bottom Line

Sufficient evidence has now accumulated in the research literature to erase any doubt about the potential dollar gains in productivity resulting from valid personnel selection programs. These gains are far larger than most of us would have predicted, and they have clear implications for organizational policymakers: *Select* the highest-caliber managers, for they are most likely to profit from development programs. Do not assume that a large investment in *training* can transform marginally competent managers into innovative and motivated top performers.

However, this maxim should not imply that training is an ineffective strategy. One of the greatest fears of employees and managers is obsolescence of their skills. Given the pace of change in modern society and technology, retraining is imperative in order to enable managers to compete for available jobs and to enable organizations to compete in the marketplace. Continual investment in training and learning is therefore essential, as it has such a direct impact on the productivity of organizations and the quality of work life of those who work in them.

findings and discussing implications for corrective action. The change agent's role is to help group members better understand the feedback information, set goals, and formulate action plans for the change effort.[13]

Behavior modeling　The assumption here is that most human behavior is learned by observing models.[5] As a result of observing others, an individual forms an idea of how behaviors are performed and of the effects they produce. This coded information serves as a guide for action. Because people can learn from example before actually performing themselves, they are spared needless trial and error. According to this theory, therefore, people do not merely react to external influences as if they were unthinking organisms. Rather, they select, organize, and transform the stimuli that impinge upon them.

Behavior modification　The assumption here is that "behavior is a function of its consequences."[85] That is, if a behavior is followed by positive outcomes, it will tend to be repeated; if a behavior is followed by negative outcomes, it will tend not to be repeated. Hence behavior can be strengthened, maintained, or weakened by making specific consequences contingent on specific behaviors. Strategies for doing this include positive reinforcement, escape and avoidance learning, punishment, and extinction (i.e., ignoring an undesired behavior, thereby decreasing the likelihood that it will be repeated). These strategies can be used singly or in various combinations. With regard to positive reinforcement, its effectiveness depends primarily upon its scheduling. In a training situation, trainers should initially provide trainees with *continuous* reinforcement. However, once the desired behavior has been learned, an intermittent schedule should be used because it leads to higher performance and heightened resistance to extinction. Behavior modification programs have been successful in improving such areas as attendance, safety, and production.[37]

Summary and conclusions about management development

The techniques in Table 8-3 have been presented separately for purposes of exposition; in practice, however, organizations frequently use several techniques in combination to enhance their impact. Moreover, most of the techniques presented have been aimed at the individual manager, although many jobs in modern organizations are highly interdependent.

Success in a project or mission often depends on the ability of managers to work well with one another on task forces or problem-solving committees. Consequently, team-building programs and other related organization development methods are being used more widely: (1) to clarify role expectations and obligations of team members; (2) to improve problem-solving, decision-making, and planning activities; and (3) to reduce interpersonal conflict.*

The published and unpublished literature on the effectiveness of managerial training has often produced conflicting results and left more unanswered questions than definitive statements. Recently, quantitative procedures were used to cumulate results across 70 studies that had the following characteristics: (1) Each study involved managers, (2) each evaluated the effectiveness of one or more training programs, and (3) each included at least one control or comparison group.[17] In all, six training content areas, seven training methods, and four types of criteria were investigated. The content areas were (1) general management, (2) human relations and leadership, (3) self-awareness, (4) problem solving and decision making, (5) rater training, and (6) motivation and values. The training methods were (1) lecture, (2) lecture and group discussion, (3) leader match, (4) sensitivity training, (5) behavioral modeling, (6) lecture and group discussion with role playing or practice, and (7) multiple techniques (three or more methods, such as lecture, group discussion, and case study). The criteria included (1) subjective measures of learning, (2) objective measures of learning, (3) subjective measures of on-the-job behavior, and (4) objective measures of on-the-job behavior.

The results indicated that management training and development efforts are, in general, moderately effective. In terms of objective measures of training results, over all the content areas the training improved job performance by almost 20 percent, although there was considerable variability around this estimate. In terms of content, general management programs and self-aware-

---

*Space constraints do not permit a detailed discussion of these approaches here, but French and Bell (ref. 31) devote their entire book to this topic.

ness programs were more effective than human relations programs or problem-solving and decision-making programs. In terms of subjective measures of changes in on-the-job behavior, the most effective training methods were behavior modeling, leader match, lecture, and lecture and discussion plus role playing or practice, in that order. The effects of sensitivity training and multiple techniques were highly variable and depended on the trainer's level of experience.[17]

CASE 8-1
Conclusion

Selecting a
president
for RCA

The new president of RCA was Robert Frederick, executive vice president of General Electric. The combination of training and experience that Roche was so anxious to obtain seemed almost perfect. Formerly chief of corporate planning and development at GE, Frederick had also headed GE's international operations, GE Credit Corporation—a subsidiary similar to RCA's CIT Financial—and the consumer products group, which included appliances and GE's television and radio stations.

Frederick did not accept immediately. "I knew GE wasn't going to promote me. . . . That was my top-out job. But the issue was: Do I leave a company that had been good to me for 34 years for a company that had, you might say, an uneven performance record and a reputation for chewing up management?" The decision was made even harder because the security blackout imposed by Bradshaw meant Frederick could not talk it over with pals and business associates. But he liked Brad. "He seemed open, supportive, and looking for leadership," says Frederick. "It was not a situation where he'd want to hang on."

Bradshaw remained chairperson for 3 more years. By the time Frederick assumed command, one senior manager described him as having "a great capacity to absorb information and to work with diverse personalities; he has been a very stabilizing influence on the company." Paradoxically, Frederick provided stability by shaking up management. By the time Frederick took command, 70 percent of RCA's 60 top managers either were new or held jobs that they had not held 3 years previously. But he provided a vision—and a sense of urgency to bring that vision to life. Said Frederick, "There's no one here who doesn't have a sense of urgency. It isn't a question of wanting to be on the leading edge—we have no choice."

What is this vision? Recently an internal task force concluded that the top priority is to link such diverse businesses as satellite systems and TV-set manufacturing, so as to develop home-entertainment services and so-called transaction-oriented services—home shopping, banking, and information retrieval. To do this, RCA must invent what amounts to the next generation of home electronics. To ensure the continuity of leadership that will bring his vision to life, Frederick is already grooming the next generation of RCA managers and seeking a new president and chief executive officer from within RCA's ranks.

TOMORROW'S FORECAST

On the one hand, it is discouraging to note that firms make management selection decisions primarily on the basis of background investigations and interviews and that relatively few supplement this information with valid test or assessment center results.[16] On the other hand, this practice is understandable since relatively few firms have estimated statistically the validity of their selection procedures or estimated the bottom-line impact of the selection procedures. As utility analysis procedures (Equation 6-1) are applied more widely and as more firms become aware of the potential dollar gains from valid selection procedures, more of them will be used.

In the area of management development, public and private employers spend approximately $30 to $40 billion a year in direct and indirect costs, excluding the salary costs of the trainees.[74] Aluminum Co. of America (Alcoa) is typical of firms investing large amounts of time and money on development efforts, and getting lots of top-management support for doing so.

> Unable to count on ever-rising demand for aluminum, the company is diversifying into new product areas and altering the way it does business. The company's human-resources department spent an entire year developing training programs that challenge the company's old management structure. Workshops for male and female employees warn men that Alcoa's all-boy network must begin to include more women and minorities. A new managers' seminar teaches first-line supervisors how to motivate employees and also how to confront their own bosses. Such programs have been offered for years at many service and consumer products companies, but they are still unusual among heavy manufacturers. Alcoa's chairperson, Charles Parry, says the goal is a "more participatory style of management." He believes that more participation by managers and workers can only improve productivity. "It isn't a matter of being altruistic . . . but of staying competitive." Parry regularly attends the training workshops to talk with participants. He also chairs the company's equal employment opportunity committee, which sets guidelines for hiring and promoting women and minorities. "You make time for what you consider important," he says. (ref. 45, p. 33)

Improved productivity, concern for the quality of work life, and "staying competitive" (i.e., bottom-line profitability) are the major reasons why increasing attention will be paid to management selection and development in tomorrow's world of work.

Summary

To select a CEO, current CEOs look for integrity, self-confidence, physical and mental fitness, the ability to think strategically, and a facility for communicating ideas. However, the selection process is largely based on impressions, and much of the process is unspoken and intuitive. At lower management

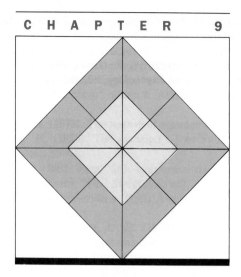

Appraising Employee Performance

CASE 9-1

A performance management system for Corning Glass Works*

The Performance Management System at Corning was designed explicitly to deal with two major conflicts in performance appraisal: (1) employee development versus administrative decisions, and (2) measurement precision versus organization development. The first conflict occurs when supervisors use the appraisal system for employee development while their employees' promotions, salary increases, or other personnel actions are tied closely to it. The second conflict occurs when reliability and validity considerations are overemphasized to the exclusion of similar efforts that focus on the *implementation* of the appraisal system. What happens is that managers may overtly reject it because of a lack of understanding of the technique or because of its lack of practical utility. The Corning system attempts to manage these conflicts constructively.

Until 10 years ago there was no formal performance appraisal system at Corning Glass Works. The primary method of appraisal was to talk directly to other managers who knew the person rather than to search out performance-related information from the Personnel Department. In other words, informal exchanges on the telephone or in a bar determined the fate of many careers.

*Adapted from: M. Beer, et al., A performance management system: Research, design, introduction, and evaluation, *Personnel Psychology*, **31**, 1978, 505–535.

Discontent with such a system led to the Performance Management System project.

Corning has a tradition of transferring salaried employees across functions and divisions as part of their management development. Thus an important requirement for the appraisal system was to cover a broad range of performance dimensions and provide performance information relevant for decisions about cross-functional and cross-divisional transfers or promotions. The objective, therefore, was to develop a system that would be sound from a measurement perspective but that would also provide a *common language* for describing the performance of professional and managerial employees.

The system that was finally developed over several years of research has three basic components: Management by objectives (MBO) focuses on tasks, or *what* gets done; performance development and review focuses on methods, or *how* the job gets done; finally, salary and placement review focuses on administrative decision making.

Management by objectives

Like many other companies, Corning originally adopted the MBO approach because it was the "thing to do," although the program was never pushed systematically throughout the corporation. Yet MBO, which is based on setting goals and tracking progress toward them, is popular for several reasons. One, it directs the supervisor's attention exclusively toward task results and away from making judgments about the personal attributes of subordinates. Two, since managers in general have a rather low level of analytical skill regarding individual behavior, they are far more comfortable and skillful in analyzing numbers and tasks.[41] Three, some managers are so results-oriented that they feel they do not have time for any of that "personal stuff." In sum, MBO is acceptable to managers because it makes the performance review process, the feedback of performance results, a little less threatening and less emotionally difficult for managers. However, MBO was also used because of research showing that the goal-setting process itself is motivating and because MBO seems to enhance the quality of supervisor-subordinate relationships.

Performance development and review

Unfortunately, the strength of MBO is also its weakness. Although it enhances accountability and responsibility by focusing attention on what needs to be done and on quantifiable measures of accomplishment, it is not especially useful when it comes to improving subordinates' ability to perform effectively. This is so because MBO does not provide diagnostic information about why an individual is *not* performing. Further, it cannot be used exclusively in making personnel decisions because, although a person may be successful in his or her current job, the next-level job may require behaviors and skills that the current job does not demand. Unless the performance appraisal system allows management to determine whether he or she has these attributes, mistakes in promotion decisions are inevitable.

The performance development and review system that emerged was geared mainly to helping supervisors develop their subordinates. It is based on ratings by supervisors of their subordinates on a 76-item questionnaire that taps 19 key areas of behavior. These are:

Openness to influence	Constructive initiative
Priority setting	Work accomplishment
Thoroughness and accuracy	Credibility
Organizational perspective	Formal communications
Collaboration	Decisiveness
Subordinate participation	Flexibility
Support for company	Team building
Unit improvement	Control
Unit's productivity	Supportiveness
Conflict resolution	

Results from the questionnaires are helpful to managers in two ways. One, they force managers to observe the actual performance of their subordinates. Two, they help managers analyze the performance of their subordinates through the "performance profile." This profile is a computer-generated pictorial display of subordinates' strengths and shortcomings as deviations from a centerline that represents the subordinate's *own mean*. The scores are meaningless for comparing individuals to each other, but they are very useful for promoting individual development. Since every profile includes strengths as well as short-comings, about the only way managers can avoid talking to a subordinate about his or her shortcomings is to "lose" the profile! The combination of MBO and performance development and review thus provides a complete performance appraisal process.

Salary and placement review

The results of MBO and performance development and review are intended to flow into salary and placement decisions. Although there is no prescribed way to do this, a form used for these recommendations is included in the total Performance Management System package. The manager is asked to note the subordinate's overall performance and potential after she or he has conducted a performance development and review session and has consolidated her or his impressions in this session and in MBO sessions conducted throughout the previous year. These ratings are reviewed by the manager's supervisor and forwarded to the Personnel Department. Salary decisions and career discussions with subordinates are expected to reflect the ratings and be consistent with them. In theory, this discussion should be conducted at a time different from the MBO or performance development and review discussions because its emphasis on evaluation would not mix well with the emphasis on development of MBO and performance development and review. In actual practice, however, subordinates are told about their performance and potential ratings immediately following the performance development and review session. As we shall see, this has led to some predictable problems.

Implementation of the performance management system

Introducing the system was as important a task as *developing* it. To be effective, the Performance Management System had to be accepted and used properly. To encourage this, managers attended a 2-day educational program that described the performance development and review system, the rationale for the different components, and the process of splitting MBO, performance development and review, and salary review into three separate interviews with a subordinate. Lecture, discussion, and experience-based training techniques were used in the program.

Considerable time was spent training managers in appraisal feedback interviews. Because the objective of performance development and review was employee development, managers were trained to conduct effective interviews. Certainly the elaborate research that led to the performance development and review rating system would be wasted if managers failed to conduct competent, constructive interviews with their subordinates! To develop such skills, films of effective and ineffective interviews (role-played by Corning managers) were developed for critique and discussion. In addition, participants were asked to role-play a development interview using a performance development and review profile. Finally, they were asked to complete the 76-item questionnaire on one of their subordinates, they were given a profile of the results, and they were asked to prepare for an actual performance development and review session.

There were some other important aspects of the introduction of the performance management system. First, since Corning has a divisional structure and the divisions are fairly heterogeneous, each division was approached separately about the introduction of the system. A division is a homogeneous product group with profit responsibility, headed by a vice president and general manager who has reporting to him or her a staff of functional managers. There are eight divisions within the company. The 2-day educational program was held in the most receptive division first. Education started at the top and ultimately included all salaried employees. As a result of an enthusiastic response to the Performance Management System by the top managers in the division, the system was introduced to the rest of the company, division by division.

As new divisions introduced the system and showed enthusiasm, support grew across the company. In addition, an important strategy for gaining acceptance was to include *both* superior and subordinate managers in the same educational sessions. This made it very clear to everyone involved that they were expected to use this program together, especially the development interview. It communicated to the manager that she or he was expected to behave in accordance with program guidelines, even if this was not consistent with her or his current style of operation. Such a strategy helped both the manager and the subordinate understand the system, and it seemed to encourage participation and enthusiasm. Finally, the presence of both manager and subordinate in the same session made it possible for a subordinate to raise questions later if the Performance Management System was not applied properly. How has the system actually worked in practice? We will find out at the end of the chapter.

QUESTIONS

1. Do you agree or disagree with the three-pronged approach of the Performance Management System? Why?
2. Almost any approach to human resource management has advantages as well as disadvantages associated with it. What do you see as the pros and cons of the Performance Management System?
3. You have just read about the strategy used to *introduce* the Performance Management System. Can you suggest a strategy to keep it going?

What's Ahead

Case 9-1 reveals just how complex performance management can be, for it includes both developmental (feedback) and administrative (pay, promotions) issues, and it includes technical aspects (design of an appraisal system) and interpersonal aspects (appraisal interviews). This chapter's objective is to present a balanced view of the appraisal process, considering both its technical and its interpersonal aspects. The chapter thus considers legal and technical concerns (such as the design of performance standards, appraisal formats, and rater training), explores the interpersonal issues involved in appraisal interviews, and provides a set of guidelines for competent management practice. Let's begin by examining the nature of the performance appraisal process.

Performance Appraisal: A Complex and Often Misunderstood Process

As the Corning system indicates, performance appraisal has many facets. It is an exercise in observation and judgment, it is a feedback process, and it is an organizational intervention. It is a measurement process as well as an intensely emotional process. Above all, it is an inexact, human process. While it is fairly easy to prescribe how the process *should* work, descriptions of how it *actually* works in practice are rather discouraging. In a recent survey of

4000 employees at 190 companies, 70 percent believed that review sessions had not given them a clear picture of what was expected of them on the job or of where they could advance in the company. Only half said that their bosses helped them set job objectives, and only one in five said that reviews were followed up during the ensuing year.[33] Some managers give short shrift to appraisals—and their subordinates know it.

This chapter examines some of the reasons for common problems in the appraisal process and considers how the application of research findings in the area of performance appraisal can improve the process. Let us begin by defining our terms:

- *Performance* refers to an employee's accomplishment of assigned tasks.
- *Performance appraisal* is the systematic description of an employee's job-relevant strengths and weaknesses.
- *Appraisal period* is the length of time during which an employee's job performance is observed in order to make a formal report of it.
- *Performance management* is the total process of observing an employee's performance in relation to job requirements over a period of time and then of making an appraisal of it. Information gained from the process may be used to determine the relevance of individual and work-group performance to organizational purposes, to improve the effectiveness of the unit, and to improve the work performance of employees.[49]

Before addressing some common problems in performance appraisal, let us first consider the major organizational purposes served by appraisal systems. In general, appraisal serves a twofold purpose: (1) to improve the work performance of employees by helping them realize and use their full potential in carrying out their firms' missions, and (2) to provide information to employees and managers for use in making work-related decisions. More specifically, appraisals serve the following purposes:

1. Appraisals support personnel decisions to promote outstanding performers; to weed out marginal or low performers; to train, transfer, or discipline others; and to justify merit increases (or no increases). In short, appraisal serves as a key input for administering a formal organizational reward and punishment system.[24]
2. Appraisals are used as criteria in test validation. That is, test results are correlated with appraisal results to evaluate the hypothesis that test scores predict job performance.[21] However, if appraisals are not done carefully, or if considerations other than performance influence appraisal results, then the appraisals cannot be used legitimately for any purpose.
3. Appraisals provide feedback to employees and thereby serve as vehicles for personal and career development.
4. Once the development needs of employees are identified, appraisals can help establish objectives for training programs.
5. As a result of the proper specifications of performance levels, appraisals can help diagnose organizational problems. They do so by identifying training

needs and the knowledge, abilities, skills, and other characteristics to consider in hiring, and they also provide a basis for distinguishing between effective and ineffective performers. Appraisal therefore represents the beginning of a process, rather than an end product.[36]

The organizational and human contexts of performance appraisal

Having seen the multiple purposes for which appraisal systems can be used to manage human resources wisely, let us now consider some enlightening findings from actual practice:

1. Surveys show that up to 93 percent of performance appraisal programs ask the immediate supervisor to take the *sole* responsibility for doing the appraisal.[25]
2. A typical manager has limited contact with his or her employees. Studies indicate that managers spend only 5 to 10 percent of their workweek with any one subordinate. These contacts are in a limited range of settings, such as formal meetings.[25] Managers therefore have access only to a small (and perhaps unrepresentative) sample of their subordinates' work.
3. Accuracy in appraisal is less important to managers than motivating and rewarding their subordinates. Many managers will not allow excessively accurate ratings to cause problems for themselves, and they attempt to use the appraisal process to their own advantage.[50]
4. Standards and ratings tend to vary widely and, often, unfairly. Some raters are tough, others are lenient. Some departments have highly competent people, others have less competent people. Consequently, employees subject to less competition or to lenient ratings can receive higher appraisals than do equally competent or superior associates.
5. Personal values and bias can replace organizational standards. Thus unfairly low ratings may be given to valued subordinates so that they will not be promoted out of the rater's department, or outright bias may lead to favored treatment for some employees.
6. Sometimes the validity of performance appraisals is reduced by the resistance of supervisors to making them. Rather than confront their less effective subordinates with negative ratings, negative feedback in appraisal interviews, and below-average salary increases, some supervisors take the easy way out and give average or above-average ratings to inferior performers. Alternatively, a supervisor might award average ratings to inferior performers in a misguided attempt to "encourage them to do better." The result is that the average ratings reinforce inferior performance.
7. Some supervisors complain that performance appraisal is pointless paperwork. This author's surveys of over 1000 supervisors in a county hospital over a 3-year period indicated that fewer than 20 percent could cite *any* use of appraisals in personnel management. Is their "pointless paperwork" reaction really a surprise?

*The appraisal
interview can be as
stressful for the boss
as it is for the
subordinate.*

8. Performance appraisals interfere with more constructive supervisor-subordinate coaching relationships. Appraisal interviews tend to emphasize the superior position of the supervisor by placing her or him in the role of judge, thus countering her or his equally important roles of teacher and coach. In organizations that are attempting to promote supervisor-subordinate participation in decisions, such situations can be downright destructive. As we saw in Case 9-1, however, Corning Glass Works handles this problem by separating discussions aimed at employee development (performance development and review and MBO) from those aimed at administrative decisions (salary and placement review).

It is easy to understand how the foregoing list could engender a sense of hopelessness in any manager or organization thinking about appraisal. However, despite their shortcomings, appraisals continue to be used widely, especially as a basis for tying pay to performance.[14] To attempt to avoid these shortcomings by doing away with appraisals is no solution, for whenever people interact in organized settings, appraisals will be made—formally or informally. The real challenge, then, is to identify appraisal techniques and practices that (1) are most likely to achieve a particular objective and (2) are least vulnerable to the obstacles listed above. Let us begin by considering some of the fundamental requirements that determine whether a performance appraisal system will succeed or fail.

Requirements of effective appraisal systems

Legally and scientifically, the key requirements of any appraisal system are relevance, sensitivity, and reliability. In the context of ongoing operations, the key requirements are acceptability and practicality.[20] Let's consider each of these.

Relevance   This implies that there are (1) clear links between the performance standards for a particular job and an organization's goals and (2) clear links between the critical job elements identified through a job analysis and the dimensions to be rated on an appraisal form. In short, relevance is determined by answering the question "What really makes the difference between success and failure on a particular job?"

Performance standards translate job requirements into *levels* of acceptable or unacceptable employee behavior. They play a critical role in the job analysis–performance appraisal linkage, as Figure 9-1 indicates. More will be said about performance standards later in this chapter.

Relevance also implies the periodic maintenance and updating of job analyses, of performance standards, and of appraisal systems. Should the system be challenged in court, relevance will be a fundamental consideration in the arguments presented by both sides.

Sensitivity   This implies that a performance appraisal system is capable of distinguishing effective from ineffective performers. If it is not, and the best employees are rated no differently from the worst employees, then the appraisal system cannot be used for any administrative purpose, it certainly will not help employees to develop, and it will undermine the motivation of supervisors ("pointless paperwork") and of subordinates.

A major concern here is the purpose of the rating. One study found that raters process identical sets of performance appraisal information differently, depending on whether a merit pay raise, a recommendation for further development, or the retention of a probationary employee is involved.[65] These results highlight the conflict between appraisals made for administrative pur-

FIGURE 9-1

Relationship of performance standards to job analysis and performance appraisal.

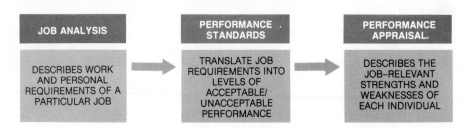

JOB ANALYSIS	PERFORMANCE STANDARDS	PERFORMANCE APPRAISAL
DESCRIBES WORK AND PERSONAL REQUIREMENTS OF A PARTICULAR JOB	TRANSLATE JOB REQUIREMENTS INTO LEVELS OF ACCEPTABLE/ UNACCEPTABLE PERFORMANCE	DESCRIBES THE JOB-RELEVANT STRENGTHS AND WEAKNESSES OF EACH INDIVIDUAL

poses and those made for employee development. Appraisal systems designed for administrative purposes demand performance information about differences *between* individuals, while systems designed to promote employee growth demand information about differences *within* individuals. The two different types of information are not interchangeable in terms of purposes, and that is why performance management systems designed to meet both purposes (such as the Corning system) are more complex and costly. In practice, only one type of information is usually collected, and it is used for some administrative purpose.[37] As we have seen, performance appraisal need not be a zero-sum game, but unfortunately it usually is.

Reliability   A third requirement of sound appraisal systems is reliability. In this context it refers to consistency of judgment. For any given employee, appraisals made by raters working independently of one another should agree closely. But raters with different perspectives (e.g., supervisors, peers, subordinates) may see the same individual's job performance very differently.[12] To provide reliable data, each rater must have an adequate opportunity to observe what the employee has done and the conditions under which he or she has done it; otherwise, unreliability may be confused with unfamiliarity.

Note that throughout this discussion there has been no mention of the validity or accuracy of appraisal judgments. This is because we really do not know what "truth" is in performance appraisal. However, by making appraisal systems relevant, sensitive, and reliable—by satisfying the scientific and legal requirements for workable appraisal systems—we assume that the resulting judgments are valid as well.

Acceptability   In practice, acceptability is the most important requirement of all, for it is true that human resource programs must have the support of those who will use them, or else human ingenuity will be used to thwart them. Unfortunately, many organizations have not put much effort into garnering the front-end support and participation of those who will use the appraisal system. The emphasis has been more on technical soundness than on the attitudinal and interpersonal components of performance appraisal programs.

Ultimately it is management's responsibility to define as clearly as possible the type and level of job behavior desired of employees. While this might seem obvious, consider three kinds of behavior that managers might exhibit:

1. Managers may not know what they want, and they may find it extremely painful even to discuss the issue.
2. Managers might fear that when employees find out what they want, the employees may not like it.
3. Some managers feel that they lose flexibility by stating their objectives in advance. "If I tell them what I want, then they will do only those things." This is management and appraisal by reaction: "I'll see what they do and then tell them whether I like it or not."

Clearly these attitudes run counter to research findings in performance appraisal. Under these circumstances we are playing power games with people and undermining the credibility and acceptability of the entire appraisal system. How much simpler it is to enlist the active support and cooperation of subordinates by making explicit exactly what aspects of job performance they will be evaluated on! Instead of promoting secrecy, we should be promoting more openness in human resource management, so that we can say, "This is what you must be able to do in order to perform competently." Only then can we expect to find the kind of acceptability and commitment that is so sorely needed in performance appraisal.

Practicality   This implies that appraisal instruments are easy for managers and employees to understand and to use. The importance of this was brought home forcefully to me in the course of mediating a conflict between a county's Metropolitan Transit Authority (MTA) and its Central Personnel unit. Here's what happened:

Practical Performance Appraisal for Bus Drivers. The conflict developed over Central Personnel's *imposition* of a new appraisal system on all county departments regardless of each department's need for the new system. MTA had developed an appraisal system jointly with its union 5 years earlier, and it was working fine. In brief, each MTA supervisor (high school–educated) was responsible for about 30 subordinates (a total of 890 bus drivers who were also high school–educated or less). The "old" appraisal system was based on a checklist of infractions (e.g., reporting late for work, being charged with a preventable traffic accident), each of which carried a specified number of points. Appraisals were done quarterly, with each driver assigned 100 points at the beginning of each quarter. A driver's quarterly appraisal was simply the number of points remaining after all penalty points had been deducted during the quarter. Her or his annual appraisal (used as a basis for decisions regarding merit pay, promotions, and special assignments) was simply the average of the four quarterly ratings. Both supervisors and subordinates liked the old system because it was understandable and practical and also because it had been shown to be workable over a 5-year period.

The new appraisal system required MTA supervisors to write quarterly narrative reports on each of their 30-odd subordinates. Central Personnel had made no effort to determine the ratio of supervisors to subordinates in the various departments. Not surprisingly, therefore, objections to the new system surfaced almost immediately. MTA supervisors had neither the time nor the inclination to write quarterly narratives on each of their subordinates. The new system was highly impractical. Furthermore, the old appraisal system was working fine and was endorsed by MTA management, employees, and their union. MTA managers therefore refused to adopt the new system. To dramatize their point, they developed a single, long, detailed narrative on an outstanding bus driver. Then they made 890 copies of the narrative (one for each driver), placed a different driver's name at the top of each "appraisal," and sent the 2-foot-high stack of "appraisals" to Central Personnel. MTA made its point. After considerable haggling by both sides, Central Personnel backed down and allowed MTA to continue to use its old (but acceptable and eminently practical) appraisal system.

In a broader context, we are concerned with developing decision systems. From this perspective, *relevance*, *sensitivity*, and *reliability* are simply technical components of a performance appraisal system designed to make decisions about employees. As we have seen, just as much attention needs to be paid to ensuring the *acceptability* and *practicality* of appraisal systems. These are the five basic requirements of performance appraisal systems, and none of them can be ignored. However, since some degree of error is inevitable in all personnel decisions, the crucial question to be answered in regard to each appraisal system is whether its use results in less human, social, and organizational cost than is currently paid for these errors. Answers to that question can result only in a wiser, fuller utilization of our human resources.

Legal Issues in Performance Appraisal

The triggering mechanism for legal action in this area, as in other personnel management areas, is adverse impact. That is, if the selection or promotion or layoff rate for one group is less than 80 percent of the highest rate for any group, then adverse impact is shown. Thus if 80 percent of males who apply for a job are selected but only 60 percent of the females who apply are selected, there is an adverse impact against females because their selection rate (60 percent) is less than 0.80 × 0.80, or 64 percent. Although this is the most common method used to determine adverse impact, there are a number of cases in which other types of information were considered by the courts.[39] Sometimes comparisons are made between the percentages of minorities employed in high- and low-level positions within a company. In other instances labor market comparisons are made, such as between the percentage of upper-level minority employees and the percentage of that minority in the relevant labor market. Finally, average performance appraisal scores of minority and nonminority groups may be compared. Adverse impact is established if, for example, a court finds statistically significant differences between the average scores of blacks and whites. Such wide discrepancies in the types of data considered by the courts in assessing adverse impact place a heavy burden on employers who are trying to defend their appraisal systems. What can be done?

One thing we can do is to learn from case law in this area, for there is a rich body of case law on performance appraisal. Three reviews found similar results.[4, 19, 27] To avoid legal difficulties, consider taking the following steps:

1. Conduct a job analysis to determine the characteristics necessary for successful job performance.

2. Incorporate these characteristics into a rating instrument. This may be done by tying rating instruments to specific job behaviors (e.g., BARS, see page 327), but the courts routinely accept less sophisticated approaches, such as simple graphic rating scales. Regardless of the method used, provide written standards to all raters.

3. Train supervisors to use the rating instrument properly, including how to apply performance standards when making judgments. The uniform application of standards is very important. The vast majority of cases *lost* by organizations involved evidence that subjective standards were applied unevenly to minority and nonminority employees.

   As we saw earlier, performance appraisal results are used in the selection process to establish the validity of selection instruments. Steps 1, 2, and 3 are identical in that process.

4. Formal appeal mechanisms, coupled with higher-level review of appraisals, are desirable.

5. Document the appraisals and the reason for any termination decisions. This information may prove decisive in court. Credibility is enhanced with documented appraisal ratings that describe instances of poor performance.

6. Provide some form of performance counseling or corrective guidance to assist poor performers.

Here is a good example of step 6. In *Stone v. Xerox* the organization had a fairly elaborate procedure for assisting poor performers.[59] Stone was employed as a sales representative and in less than 6 months had been given several written reprimands concerning customer complaints about his selling methods and failure to develop adequate written selling proposals. As a result, he was placed on a 1-month performance improvement program designed to correct these deficiencies. This program was extended 30 days at Stone's request. When his performance still did not improve, he was placed on probation and told that failure to improve substantially would result in termination. Stone's performance continued to be substandard, and he was discharged at the end of the probationary period. When he sued Xerox, he lost.

Certainly, the type of evidence required to defend performance ratings is linked to the *purposes* for which the ratings are made. For example, if appraisal of past performance is to be used as a predictor of future performance (i.e., promotions), evidence must be presented to show (1) that the ratings of past performance are, in fact, valid, and (2) that the ratings of past performance are statistically related to *future* performance in another job.[61] At the very least, this latter step should include job analysis results indicating the extent to which requirements of the lower- and higher-level jobs overlap. Finally, to assess adverse impact, organizations should keep accurate records of who is eligible for and interested in promotion. These two factors, *eligibility* and *interest*, define the "applicant group."

In summary, it is not difficult to offer prescriptions for scientifically sound, court-proof appraisal systems, but as we have seen, implementing them requires diligent attention by organizations, plus a commitment to make them work. In developing a performance appraisal system, the most basic requirement is for specific performance standards. Let us consider how to develop them.

Developing Performance Standards

Common sense dictates that fair performance appraisal requires a standard against which to compare employee performance. The clearer the performance standard is, the more accurate the appraisal can be. Thus the first step in effectively managing employee performance is to review existing standards, and to develop new ones if needed. Unfortunately, many supervisors simply *assume* that employees know what they are supposed to do on their jobs. Nothing could be further from the truth. At a recent Business Roundtable breakfast, a human resources executive from an insurance company described a study in which his company learned from field interviews with employees that as many as two-thirds could not describe clearly the requirements of their jobs and the performance standards on which they were evaluated!

Performance standards should contain two basic kinds of information for the benefit both of employee and of supervisor: *what* is to be done and *how well* it is to be done. The identification of job tasks, duties, and critical elements (see Chapter 4) describes *what* is to be done. This is crucial, for sound human resource management dictates that the content of the appraisal should reflect the nontrivial content of the job; such information provides content-related evidence of the validity of the appraisal system. Performance standards focus on *how well* the tasks are to be done. To be most useful, each standard should be stated clearly enough so that manager and subordinate both know what is expected and whether it has been met. Standards should be written to describe *fully satisfactory* performance for critical as well as noncritical tasks.[18]

Since job tasks and performance standards are interrelated, it is common practice to develop them at the same time. Whatever method of job analysis is used should take into account both quantitative and qualitative aspects of performance.[49] Further, each standard should refer to a specific aspect of the job. Examples are:

Quantitative	Qualitative
Number of forms processed	Accuracy, quality of work
Amount of time used	Ability to coordinate (e.g., staff, activities)
Number of errors	Ability to analyze (e.g., data, machine malfunctions)
Number of pages typed	Ability to evaluate (e.g., customer complaints, market research)

TABLE 9-1 *Performance standards for an electric meter reader*

Critical (C) or noncritical (NC) tasks	Performance standard (fully satisfactory)
Records readings from residential and commercial meters (C)	Two legibility errors per 480 character entries; one transposition error per 400 meters read as shown by computer and manual checks
Inspects meters for damage or tap-ins (C)	Reports 80 percent of damaged meters found on routes as confirmed by spot checks made by service inspectors
Indicates extremes in usage (NC)	Indicates extremely high or low readings 90 percent of the time as shown by spot computer checks
Complies with safety standards (C)	Complies with safety standards 100 percent of the time
Interacts with customers (C)	No more than two customer complaints per month

Almost all jobs involve both aspects of performance but in varying proportions, depending on the nature of the job. Obviously, it is easier to measure performance against standards that can be described in quantitative terms. However, managerial jobs have an added component. That is, in addition to results that reflect the manager's own performance, other results reflect the performance of the organizational unit for which the manager is responsible. For managerial jobs, therefore, initial performance standards still should be determined by job analysis, even though they may be modified later (as a result of joint agreement by manager and subordinate) to incorporate goals to be achieved. Goals that meet minimum standards are documented in quantitative terms, if possible; for example, a specified kind and amount of work will be done within a certain time limit. Doing so allows managers to assess their progress even before any formal appraisal takes place. An example of a set of performance standards for an electric meter reader is shown in Table 9-1.

Who Should Evaluate Performance?

The most fundamental requirement for any rater is that he or she has an adequate opportunity to observe the ratee's job performance over a reasonable period of time (e.g., 6 months). This suggests several possible raters.

The immediate supervisor If appraisal is done at all, it will probably be done by this person. She or he is probably most familiar with the individual's performance and, in most jobs, has had the best opportunity to observe actual job performance. Furthermore, the immediate supervisor is probably best able to relate the individual's performance to departmental and organizational objectives. Since she or he also is responsible for reward (and punishment) decisions, it seems only logical to make the immediate supervisor responsible for performance appraisal as well.

Peers   In some jobs, such as outside sales, law enforcement, and teaching, the immediate supervisor may observe a subordinate's actual job performance only rarely (and indirectly, through written reports). Sometimes objective indicators, such as number of units sold, can provide useful performance-related information, but in other circumstances the judgment of peers is even better. Peers can provide a perspective on performance that is different from that of immediate supervisors. Thus a police officer's partner is in a far better position to rate day-to-day performance than is a desk-bound sergeant or lieutenant. However, to reduce potential friendship bias while simultaneously increasing the feedback value of the information provided, it is important to specify exactly what the peers are to evaluate[22]—for example, "The quality of her help on technical problems." In fact, peer assessments are probably best considered as only part of a performance appraisal system that includes input from all sources that have unique information or perspectives to offer.

Subordinates   Appraisal by subordinates can be a useful input to the immediate supervisor's development. Subordinates know firsthand the extent to which the supervisor *actually* delegates, how well he or she communicates, the type of leadership style he or she is most comfortable with, and the extent to which he or she plans and organizes. Appraisal by subordinates is used regularly by universities (students rate faculty) and by some large firms where managers have many subordinates. In the small firm or in situations where managers have few subordinates, however, it is easy to identify who said what. Thus considerable trust and openness are necessary before subordinate appraisals can pay off. Like peer assessments, they provide only one piece of the appraisal puzzle.

Self-appraisal   There are several arguments to recommend wider use of self-appraisals. The opportunity to participate in the performance appraisal process, particularly if appraisal is combined with goal setting, improves the ratee's motivation and reduces her or his defensiveness during the appraisal interview.[42] On the other hand, self-appraisals tend to be more lenient, less variable, and more biased and to show less agreement with the judgments of others.[55] Since employees tend to give themselves higher marks than their supervisors do, self-appraisals are probably more appropriate for counseling and development than for personnel decisions.

Clients served   In some situations the "consumers" of the individual's or organization's services can provide a unique perspective on job performance. Examples abound: subscribers to a cable television service, bank customers, clients of a brokerage house, and citizens of a local police or fire-protection district. Although the clients' objectives cannot be expected to correspond completely with the organization's objectives, the information that clients provide can provide useful input for personnel decisions, such as regarding promotion, transfer, and need for training. It can also be used to assess the impact of training or as a basis for self-development.

Computers   As noted earlier, employees spend a lot of time unsupervised by their bosses. Now technology has made continuous supervision possible—and very real to millions of workers. What sort of technology? Computer software that monitors employee performance.

In summary, several different sources of appraisal information can be used, although they are more useful for some purposes than for others. The various sources and their uses are shown in Table 9-2.

Using Computers to Monitor Job Performance

To proponents, it is a great new application of technology to improve productivity. To critics, it represents the ultimate intrusion of Big Brother in the workplace. For several million workers today, being monitored on the job by a computer is a fact of life.[15]

Computers measure quantifiable tasks performed by secretaries, factory and postal workers, and grocery and airline clerks. For example, several airlines regularly monitor the time that reservation agents spend on each call. Until now, lower-level jobs have been affected most directly by computer monitoring. But as software becomes more sophisticated, even engineers, accountants, and doctors are expected to face electronic scrutiny.

Critics feel that overzealous employers will get carried away with information gathering and overstep the boundary between work performance and privacy. Moreover, being watched every second can be stressful, thereby stifling worker creativity, initiative, and morale.

Not everyone views monitoring as a modern-day version of *Modern Times*, the Charlie Chaplin movie where the hapless hero was tyrannized by automation. At the Third National Bank of Nashville, for example, encoding clerks can earn up to 25 percent more than their base pay if their output is high—and they like that system.

To be sure, monitoring itself is neither good nor bad; how managers use it determines its acceptance in the workplace. Practices such as giving employees access to data collected on them and establishing procedures for challenging erroneous records can alleviate the fears of employees. At American Express, for example, monitored employees are given feedback about their performance every 2 weeks.

Managers who impose monitoring standards *without* asking employees what is reasonable may be surprised at the responses of employees. Tactics can include VDT operators who pound the space bar or hold down the underlining bar while chatting, and telephone operators who hang up on customers with complicated problems. The lesson, perhaps, is that even the most sophisticated technology can be thwarted by human beings who feel they are being pushed beyond acceptable limits.[15]

TABLE 9-2 *Sources and uses of appraisal data*

	Source				
Use	Supervisor	Peers	Subordinates	Self	Clients
Personnel decisions	X	X			X
Self-development	X	X	X	X	X
Personnel research	X	X			X

One of the primary sources of information about issues relevant to appraisal is the *attitudes* of those who will be affected by the system. A survey of employees in one federal agency indicated a strong preference for appraisal by immediate supervisors and, to a lesser extent, by the people for whom they provided service. The majority of respondents favored more than one rater, and some felt that peers and subordinates were potentially valid sources of information.[10] Another important consideration is the timing and frequency of performance appraisal.

When and How Often Should Appraisal Be Done?

Traditionally, formal appraisal is done once, or at best, twice a year. Research over the past 20 years has indicated that once or twice a year is far too infrequent.[52] Considerable difficulties face a rater who is asked to remember what several employees did over the previous 6 or 12 months. Research on this issue indicates that biased ratings may result under these circumstances, especially if information has been stored in the rater's memory according to irrelevant, oversimplistic, or otherwise faulty categories.[53] Unfortunately, faulty categorization seems to be the rule more often than the exception. In a well-known study, students were asked to recall some pictures showing a white man brandishing a razor and a black man with a hat.[2] A short while after viewing the pictures, a large percentage of the students described the black man as holding the razor and the white man as having the hat. The lesson to be learned is that people often forget the details of what they have observed and that they reconstruct the details on the basis of their existing mental categories.

In the survey of federal employees noted earlier, a majority of the employees were dissatisfied with the use of performance data collected once or twice a year for any important personnel decision. A common recommendation was to do appraisals upon the completion of projects or upon the achievement of important milestones in large-scale projects.[10] Such an approach has merit because the appraisals are likely to provide more accurate inputs to personnel decisions, and they have the additional advantage of sending clear messages

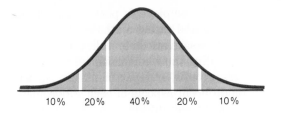

10% 20% 40% 20% 10%

FIGURE 9-2

Example of a forced distribution. Forty percent of the ratees must be rated "average," 20 percent "above average," 20 percent "below average," 10 percent "outstanding," and 10 percent "unsatisfactory."

that a relatively small portion of employees is truly outstanding, a relatively small portion is unsatisfactory, and everybody else falls in between. Figure 9-2 illustrates this method, assuming that five rating categories are used.

Forced distribution does eliminate clustering almost all employees at the top of the distribution (rater *leniency*), at the bottom of the distribution (rater *severity*), or in the middle (*central tendency*). However, it can foster a great deal of employee resentment if an entire group of employees *as a group* is either superior or substandard. It is most useful when a large number of employees must be rated and there is more than one rater.

Behavioral checklist This is one of the most popular rating formats. The rater is provided with a series of statements that describe job-related behavior. His or her task is simply to "check" which of the statements, or the extent to which each statement, describes the employee. In this approach raters are not so much evaluators as reporters or describers of job behavior. And descriptive ratings are likely to be more reliable than evaluative (good-bad) ratings.[58] In one such method, the Likert method of *summated ratings*, a declarative statement (e.g., "She or he follows up on customer complaints") is followed by several response categories, such as "always," "very often," "fairly often," "occasionally," and "never." The rater checks the response category that he or she thinks best describes the employee. Each category is weighted, for example, from 5 ("always") to 1 ("never") if the statement describes desirable behavior. An overall numerical rating (or score) for each employee is then derived by *summing* the weights of the responses that were checked for each item. A portion of a summated rating scale for appraising teacher performance is shown in Figure 9-3.

A special type of behavioral checklist is known as the *forced-choice* system. This technique was developed specifically to reduce rater leniency and to establish objective standards for comparing individuals.[56] To do this, checklist items are arranged in groups from which the rater chooses statements that are most or least descriptive of each employee. An overall rating for each employee is then derived by applying a special scoring key to the rater's descriptions. For example, here are four items used to rate Air Force instructors:[7]

	STRONGLY AGREE	AGREE	NEUTRAL	DISAGREE	STRONGLY DISAGREE
THE TEACHER WAS WELL PREPARED.					
THE TEACHER USED UNDERSTANDABLE LANGUAGE.					
THE TEACHER MADE ME THINK.					
THE TEACHER'S FEEDBACK ON STUDENTS' WORK AIDED LEARNING.					
THE TEACHER KNEW HIS OR HER FIELD WELL.					

FIGURE 9-3

A portion of a summated rating scale. The rater simply checks the response category that best describes the teacher's behavior. Response categories vary in scale value from 5 points (Strongly Agree) to 1 point (Strongly Disagree). A total score is computed by summing the points associated with each item.

1. Patient with slow learners.
2. Lectures with confidence.
3. Keeps the interest and attention of the class.
4. Acquaints classes with the objective of each lesson in advance.

All four statements are favorable, and all are equally socially desirable, but only 1 and 3 were found to be characteristic of effective instructors. Since the rater does not know what the scoring weights for each statement are, in theory (at least) she or he cannot play favorites. In practice, raters often become irritated with forced-choice scales. They want to say openly how they rate someone and not be second-guessed or tricked into making "honest" appraisals. An additional drawback is the difficulty and cost of developing the forms; in one study, for example, researchers evaluated 1200 one-page essays of effective state trooper performance in order to develop a forced-choice instrument comprised of four dimensions.[38] Finally, forced-choice forms are of little use (and may even have a negative effect) in appraisal interviews, for the rater is unaware of the level of performance represented by the items he or she chooses. To overcome these difficulties, some form of critical-incident scale may be used.

Critical incidents   These are brief anecdotal reports by supervisors of things employees did that were particularly effective or ineffective in accomplishing parts of their jobs. They focus on behaviors, not traits. For example, a store manager in a retail computer store observed Mr. Wang, the word processing salesperson, do the following:

> Mr. Wang encouraged the customer to try our new word processing package by having the customer sit down at the computer and write a letter. The finished product was full of typographical and spelling errors, each of which was highlighted for the customer when Mr. Wang applied a "spelling checker" to the written material. As a result, Mr. Wang sold the customer the word processing program plus a typing tutor and a spelling checker program.

These little anecdotes force attention on the ways that situations determine job behavior and also on ways of doing the job successfully that may be unique to the person described. Hence they can provide the basis for training programs. Critical incidents also lend themselves nicely to appraisal interviews because supervisors can focus on actual job behaviors rather than on vaguely defined traits. Performance, not personality, is judged.

Like other rating methods, critical incidents also have their drawbacks. One, supervisors may find that recording incidents for their subordinates on a daily or even a weekly basis is burdensome. Two, the *rater* sets the standards by which subordinates are judged; yet motivation is likely to be enhanced if *subordinates* have some say in setting the standards by which they will be judged. And three, in their narrative form, incidents do not permit comparisons across individuals or departments. To overcome this problem, graphic rating scales may be used.

Graphic rating scale   This is probably the most widely used rating method.[46] A portion of one such scale is shown in Figure 9-4.

Many different forms of graphic rating scales exist. In terms of the amount of structure provided, the scales differ in three ways:

1. The degree to which the meaning of the response categories is defined (in Figure 9-4, what does "conditional" mean?)
2. The degree to which the individual who is interpreting the ratings (e.g., a higher-level reviewing official) can tell clearly what response was intended
3. The degree to which the performance dimensions are defined for the rater (in Figure 9-4, for example, what does "dependability" mean?)

Graphic rating scales may not yield the depth of essays or critical incidents, but they are less time-consuming to develop and administer, the results can be expressed in quantitative terms, more than one performance dimension is considered, and since the scales are standardized, comparisons across employees can be made. Graphic rating scales have come under frequent attack, but when compared to more sophisticated forced-choice scales, the graphic scales have proven just as reliable and valid[38] and they are more acceptable to raters.[7]

FIGURE 9-4

A portion of a graphic rating scale.

RATING FACTORS	LEVEL OF PERFORMANCE				
	UNSATISFACTORY	CONDITIONAL	SATISFACTORY	ABOVE SATISFACTORY	OUTSTANDING
ATTENDANCE					
APPEARANCE					
DEPENDABILITY					
QUALITY OF WORK					
QUANTITY OF WORK					
RELATIONSHIP WITH PEOPLE					
JOB KNOWLEDGE					

FIGURE 9-5

*A behaviorally
anchored rating
scale to assess the
job knowledge of
police patrol
officers.*

JOB KNOWLEDGE—AWARENESS OF PROCEDURES, LAWS, AND
COURT RULINGS AND CHANGES IN THEM.

**HIGH
(7,8, or 9)**

ALWAYS FOLLOWS CORRECT PROCEDURES FOR
EVIDENCE PRESERVATION AT THE SCENE OF
A CRIME.

IS FULLY AWARE OF RECENT
COURT RULINGS, AND CONDUCTS
HIMSELF OR HERSELF ACCORDINGLY.

SEARCHES A CITIZEN'S VEHICLE WITH
PROBABLE CAUSE, THEREBY DISCOVERING
SMUGGLED NARCOTICS.

**AVERAGE
(4,5, or 6)**

ARRESTS A SUSPECT AT 11:00 P.M. ON A
WARRANT ONLY AFTER INSURING THAT THE
WARRANT HAD BEEN CLEARED FOR NIGHT
SERVICE.

DISTINGUISHES BETWEEN CIVIL MATTERS
AND POLICE MATTERS.

SELDOM HAS TO ASK OTHERS ABOUT POINTS
OF LAW.

EXAMPLES OF THE
BEHAVIOR OF PATROL
OFFICERS WHO ARE
USUALLY RATED HIGH,
AVERAGE, AND LOW
ON JOB KNOWLEDGE
BY SUPERVISORS.

**LOW
(1,2, or 3)**

IS CONSISTENTLY UNAWARE OF GENERAL
ORDERS AND/OR DEPARTMENTAL POLICY.

ARRESTS A SUSPECT FOR A MISDEMEANOR
NOT COMMITTED IN HIS OR HER PRESENCE.

MISINFORMS THE PUBLIC ON LEGAL MATTERS
THROUGH LACK OF KNOWLEDGE.

Behaviorally anchored rating scales (BARS)   These are a variation of
the simple graphic rating scale. Their major advantage is that they define the
dimensions to be rated in behavioral terms and use critical incidents to describe
various levels of performance. BARS therefore provide a common frame of
reference for raters. An example of the job knowledge portion of a BARS for
police patrol officers is shown in Figure 9-5. BARS require considerable effort
to develop,[9] yet there is little research evidence to support the superiority of
BARS over other types of rating systems.[19, 36] However, the participative
process required to develop them provides information that is useful for other
organizational purposes, such as communicating clearly to employees exactly
what "good performance" means in the context of their jobs.

Results-oriented rating methods

Management by objectives (MBO)   This is a well-known process of managing that relies on goal setting to establish objectives for the organization as
a whole, for each department, for each manager within each department, and

for each employee. MBO is not a measure of employee behavior; rather, it is a measure of each employee's contribution to the success of the organization.[17]

In theory, objectives are established by having the key people affected do three things: (1) meet to *agree on the major objectives* for a given period of time (e.g., 1 year, 6 months, or quarterly); (2) *develop plans* for how and when the objectives will be accomplished; and (3) *agree on the "yardsticks"* for determining whether the objectives have been met. Progress reviews are held regularly until the end of the period for which the objectives were established. At that time, those who established objectives at each level in the organization meet to evaluate the results and to agree on the objectives for the next period.[51]

To some, MBO is a complete system of planning and control and a complete philosophy of management.[1, 54] In theory, MBO promotes success in each employee because, as each employee succeeds, so do that employee's manager, the department, and the organization. But this is true *only* to the extent that individual, departmental, and organizational goals are compatible.[5] Very few applications of MBO have actually adopted a formal "cascading process" to ensure such a linkage. An effective MBO system takes from 3 to 5 years to implement, and since relatively few firms are willing to make that kind of commitment, it is not surprising that MBO systems often fail.[40] Here is a further problem:

> MBO neither proposes nor provides a measurement system that permits a comparison of ratees' scores. Thus, any time [that appraisal] data are to be used for the purpose of comparing ratees' performances, the management strategy of MBO has little (or nothing) to contribute. Furthermore, to date, no research has assessed the ability of MBO to serve other purposes for performance appraisal beyond that of improvement in performance. Thus, we have no way of knowing whether the goal-setting framework might serve as the basis for an ongoing [appraisal] system that dictates important personnel decisions (e.g., regarding merit pay or promotion). (ref 8, pp. 123, 124)

Work planning and review This is similar to MBO; however, it places greater emphasis on the periodic review of work plans by the supervisor and the subordinate in order to identify goals attained, problems encountered, and the need for training.[52] This was the approach used by Corning Glass Works, as described in Case 9-1. Work planning and review is based primarily on each supervisor's judgment about whether a goal has or has not been attained, while MBO relies more on objective, countable evidence. In practice, the two approaches are often indistinguishable. For example, as Table 9-1 illustrates, performance standards are often written with specific percentages to indicate different levels of effectiveness. Even though the standards might be incorporated into an MBO system, if the percentages can be derived *only* on the basis of judgment, then the supposedly results-oriented MBO method quickly becomes a more process-oriented work planning and review system.

When should each technique be used?

You have just read about a number of alternative appraisal formats, each with its own advantages and disadvantages. At this point you are probably asking yourself, "What's the bottom line? I know that no method is perfect, but what should I do?" First, remember that the rating format is not as important as the relevance and acceptability of the rating system. Second, here is some advice based on systematic comparisons among the various methods.

An extensive review of the research literature that relates the various rating methods to indicators of performance appraisal effectiveness found no clear "winner."[8] However, the researchers were able to provide several "if . . . then" propositions and general statements based on their study. Among these are:

- If employees must be compared across raters for important personnel decisions (e.g., promotion, merit pay), then MBO and work planning and review should not be used. They are not based on a standardized rating scheme for all employees.
- If there is low trust in the appraisal system and if the ratings are linked to important personnel decisions, then the forced-choice method should be used since it is more resistant to deliberate rating inflation than other methods. However, no rating method is foolproof.
- If a BARS is used, then diary keeping should also be made a part of the process. This will improve the accuracy of the ratings, and it also will help supervisors distinguish between effective and ineffective employees.
- If objective performance data are available, then MBO is the best strategy to use. Research indicates that work planning and review is not as effective as MBO under these circumstances.
- In general, the best methods of appraisal are the most difficult to use and maintain: BARS, MBO, and forced-choice systems.
- Methods that focus on describing, rather than evaluating, behavior (e.g., BARS, summated rating scales) produce results that are the most interpretable across raters.
- No rating method has been an unqualified success when used as a basis for merit pay or promotional decisions.
- When certain statistical corrections are made, the correlations between scores on alternative rating formats are very high. Hence all the formats measure essentially the same thing.

Appraisal Errors and Rater Training Strategies

The use of ratings assumes that the human observer is reasonably objective and accurate. As we have seen, raters' memories are quite fallible, and raters

TABLE 9-3 *Supervisory activities before, during, and after appraisal*

Before
Communicate frequently with subordinates about their performance.
Get training in performance appraisal interviewing.
Plan to use a problem-solving approach rather than "tell-and-sell."
Encourage subordinates to prepare for PA interviews.

During
Encourage subordinate participation.
Judge performance, not personality and mannerisms.
Be specific.
Be an active listener.
Set mutually agreeable goals for future improvements.

After
Communicate frequently with subordinates about their performance.
Periodically assess progress toward goals.
Make organizational rewards contingent on performance.

problem-solving approach, subordinates express stronger motivation to improve performance than when other approaches are used.[64] Yet evidence indicates that most organizations still use a "tell-and-sell" approach in which a manager completes an appraisal independently, shows it to the subordinate, justifies the rating, discusses what must be done to improve performance, and then asks for the subordinate's reaction.[63] Are the negative reactions of subordinates really that surprising?

If organizations are really serious about fostering improved job performance as a result of appraisal interviews, then the kinds of activities shown in Table 9-3 are essential *before, during,* and *after* appraisals. Let's briefly examine each of these important activities.

Frequent communication   Research on the appraisal interview at General Electric indicated clearly that once-a-year performance appraisals are of questionable value and that coaching should be a day-to-day activity.[52] Recent research strongly supports this view. Thus one study found that communication of the appraisal in an interview is most effective when the subordinate already has relatively accurate perceptions of her or his performance *before* the session.[34]

Managers often focus their efforts on managing problem employees—ineffective performers. But what about problem bosses? The typical problem boss avoids confrontation with employees and rarely gives them face-to-face feedback.[43] Conversely, individuals are most likely to seek feedback (1) on important issues, (2) in new or uncertain situations, and (3) when they feel they are failing to attain goals.[3] Performance improves most when employees are encouraged to seek feedback and are then given the freedom to choose feedback on those aspects of performance they need to improve most. This approach is efficient, for it minimizes the time needed to receive and evaluate feedback.[35]

Training in appraisal interviewing   Consider this approach. Researchers working with the Army Research Institute developed seven BARS for the appraisal interview.[11] The dimensions are: structuring and controlling the interview, establishing and maintaining rapport, reacting to stress, obtaining information, resolving conflict, developing the subordinate, and motivating the subordinate. The researchers also developed a series of eight videotapes of fictitious interviews between eight different managers and one subordinate. The eight managers differ significantly in the extent to which they are effective on the seven BARS dimensions, and expert ratings are available on their performances.[13] The scales and the videotapes are excellent training devices for illustrating effective and ineffective behaviors during the appraisal interview.

Use a problem-solving, rather than a "tell-and-sell," approach, as noted earlier.

Encourage subordinate preparation   Research conducted in a large midwestern hospital indicated that subordinates who spent more time prior to appraisal interviews analyzing their job responsibilities and duties, the problems being encountered on the job, and the quality of their performance were more likely to be satisfied with the appraisal process, more likely to be motivated to improve their performance, and more likely actually to improve.[16]

Encourage participation   A perception of ownership, a feeling by the subordinate that his or her ideas are genuinely welcomed by the manager, is related strongly to subordinates' satisfaction with the appraisal interview. Participation encourages the belief that the interview was a constructive activity, that some current job problems were cleared up, and that future goals were set.[29, 63]

Judge performance, not personality   In addition to the potential legal liability of dwelling on personality rather than on job performance, supervisors are far less likely to change a subordinate's personality than they are his or her job performance. Maintain the problem-solving, job-related focus established earlier, for evidence indicates that supervisory support enhances employees' motivation to improve.[26]

Be specific, and be an active listener   By being candid and specific, the supervisor offers very clear feedback to the subordinate concerning past actions. She or he also demonstrates knowledge of the subordinate's level of performance and job duties. By being an active listener, the supervisor demonstrates genuine interest in the subordinate's ideas. Active listening requires that you do the following things well: (1) Take the time to listen—hold all phone

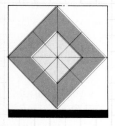

Impact of Performance Appraisal on Productivity, Quality of Work Life, and the Bottom Line

Performance appraisal is fundamentally a *feedback* process. And research indicates that feedback may result in increases in performance varying from 10 to 30 percent.[45] That is a fairly inexpensive way to improve productivity; but, to work effectively, feedback programs require sustained commitment. The challenge for managers, then, is to provide feedback regularly to all their employees.

The cost of failure to provide such feedback may result in the loss of key professional employees, the continued poor performance of employees who are not meeting performance standards, and a loss of commitment by *all* employees. In sum, the myth that employees know how they are doing without adequate feedback from management can be an expensive fantasy.[62]

calls and do not allow interruptions; (2) communicate verbally and nonverbally (e.g., by maintaining eye contact) that you genuinely want to help; (3) as the subordinate begins to tell his or her side of the story, do not interrupt and do not argue; (4) watch for verbal as well as nonverbal cues regarding the subordinate's agreement or disagreement with your message; and (5) summarize what was said and what was agreed to. Specific feedback and active listening are essential to subordinates' perceptions of the fairness and accuracy of appraisals.[44]

Set mutually agreeable goals   How does goal setting work to improve performance? Studies demonstrate that goals direct attention to the specific performance in question, that they mobilize effort to accomplish higher levels of performance, and that they foster persistence for higher levels of performance.[60] The practical implications of this work are clear: set specific, challenging goals, for this clarifies for the subordinate precisely what is expected and leads to high levels of performance. We cannot change the past, but appraisal interviews that include goal setting and feedback can affect future job performance.

Continue to communicate, and assess progress toward goals regularly   Periodic tracking of progress toward goals (e.g., through work planning and review) has three advantages: (1) It helps keep behavior on target, (2) it provides a better understanding of the reasons behind a given level of performance, and (3) it enhances the subordinate's commitment to perform effectively.

Make organizational rewards contingent on performance   Research results are clear-cut on this point. If subordinates see a link between appraisal results and personnel decisions regarding issues like merit pay and promotion, they are more likely to *prepare* for appraisal interviews, to *participate* actively in them, and to be *satisfied* with the overall performance appraisal system.[16] Furthermore, managers who base personnel decisions on the results of appraisals are likely to overcome their subordinates' negative perceptions of the appraisal process.

**CASE 9-1
Conclusion**

*A performance
management
system for Corning
Glass Works*

Five years after the implementation of the Performance Management System, it was still being used, with some minor changes.[6] Four conclusions seem warranted now:

1. The MBO portion of the system needs strengthening through the training of managers. Apparently MBO is not used consistently throughout the organization. This is not surprising in view of the emphasis on performance development and review (PD&R) in the initial introduction of the Performance Management System.

2. PD&R is the strongest and most widely used and accepted portion of the system. Managers perceive it to be very helpful in conducting employee development interviews because the behavioral statements serve as an agenda and as a tool that aids communication. The following steps were taken in the last 2 years to achieve these results:

   a. Corporate policy now requires all managers of salaried employees to conduct a PD&R *prior to* submitting any recommendations regarding salary actions.

   b. Just as personnel specialists talk with supervisors about the performance of their subordinates, they also ask subordinates about the PD&R interview. Constructive comments about the interview are communicated to the manager, and help is provided where necessary. This amounts to continuous feedback about PD&R.

   c. The computer-generated profile of each employee's strengths and weaknesses has been made optional. A common procedure now used is to have subordinates rate themselves on the behavioral statements *prior to* their PD&R interviews. During the interview itself, the supervisor and subordinate go through each behavioral statement, compare ratings, and discuss discrepancies.

3. Plans are being made to link PD&R more closely with career planning by developing lists of behaviors particularly important for various jobs. In this way, the review of each employee's strengths and weaknesses will be more meaningful because it can be assessed in relation to potential success in a different job and in relation to decisions about career directions.

4. Top management is using the system, but there seems to be some doubt within top management about the applicability of PD&R's behavioral

statements to their level of management. Their acceptance of the system will probably determine its long-term fate.

Flexibility in design and implementation is the most consistent theme underlying the success of the Performance Management System. At a number of junctures changes were made based on information about problems. The deemphasis of the computer-generated employee profile is a good example, as is the recognition of the need for strengthening MBO. This is a useful way to introduce innovations within organizations.

Summary

Performance appraisal is the systematic description of an employee's job-relevant strengths and weaknesses. It serves two major purposes in organizations: (1) to improve the job performance of employees and (2) to provide information to employees and managers for use in making decisions. In practice, many PA systems fail because they do not satisfy one or more of the following requirements: relevance, sensitivity, reliability, acceptability, and practicality. The failure is frequently accompanied by legal challenge to the system based on its adverse impact against a protected group.

Many of the problems of performance appraisal can be alleviated through participative development of performance standards that specify, for each job, *what* needs to be done and *how well* it is being done. Appraisals are usually done by immediate supervisors, although other individuals may also have unique perspectives or information to offer. These include peers, subordinates, the clients served, and the employees themselves.

Performance appraisal is done once or twice a year in most organizations, but research indicates that this is far too infrequent. It should be done upon the *completion* of projects or upon the achievement of important milestones. The rating method used depends on the purpose for which the appraisal is

---

TOMORROW'S FORECAST

For years, personnel specialists have searched for the "perfect" appraisal method as if it were some kind of miraculous cure for the many pitfalls that plague performance appraisal in organizations. Such a method does not exist. In tomorrow's world of work, far more emphasis needs to be placed on *process issues* in appraisal, such as rater-ratee acceptability of the system, participation in the process for setting standards, and rater training in behavior observation and feedback. Factors such as appraisal purpose, timing, and frequency are no less important. In sum, performance appraisal is a dialogue involving people and data; both technical and human issues are involved. As the Corning case illustrates, neither can be overemphasized at the expense of the other.

intended. Thus comparisons among employees are most appropriate for generating rankings for salary administration purposes, while MBO, work planning and review, and narrative essays are least appropriate for this purpose. For purposes of employee development, critical incidents or behaviorally anchored rating scales are most appropriate. Finally, rating methods that focus on *describing* rather than *evaluating* behavior (e.g., BARS, summated rating scales) are the most interpretable across raters.

Rater judgments are subject to various types of biases: leniency, severity, central tendency, and halo, contrast, and recency errors. To improve the reliability and validity of ratings, however, emphasis must be placed on training raters to observe behavior more accurately rather than on showing them "how to" or "how not to" rate. To improve the value of appraisal interviews, systematic training for supervisors is essential.

Discussion Questions

9-1 How do you recognize an effective performance appraisal system?

9-2 What are the major human issues involved in appraisal?

9-3 The chief counsel for a large corporation comes to you for advice. She wants to know under what circumstances the firm's appraisal system is legally most vulnerable. How would you advise her?

9-4 Working in small groups, develop a set of performance standards for a supermarket checker.

9-5 Discuss alternative strategies for controlling rater leniency.

9-6 How can we overcome employee defensiveness in performance appraisal interviews?

9-7 Can discussions of employee job performance be separated from salary considerations? Yes or no? If yes, how?

References

1. Albrecht, K. (1978). *Successful management by objectives: An action manual.* Englewood Cliffs, NJ: Prentice-Hall.
2. Allport, G. W. (1954). *The nature of prejudice.* Reading, MA: Addison-Wesley.
3. Ashford, S. J. (1986). Feedback-seeking in individual adaptation: A resource perspective. *Academy of Management Journal,* **29,** 465–487.
4. Barrett, G. V., & Kernan, M. C. (1987). Performance appraisal and terminations: A review of court decisions since *Brito v. Zia* with implications for personnel practices. *Personnel Psychology,* **40,** 489–503.
5. Barton, R. F. (1981). An MCDM approach for resolving goal conflict in MBO. *Academy of Management Review,* **6,** 231–241.
6. Beer, M., et al., (1978). A performance management system: Research design, introduction, and evaluation. *Personnel Psychology,* **31,** 505–535.

7. Berkshire, J. R., & Highland, R. W. (1953). Forced-choice performance rating: A methodological study. *Personnel Psychology*, **6**, 355–378.
8. Bernardin, H. J., & Beatty, R. W. (1984). *Performance appraisal: Assessing human behavior at work*. Boston: PWS-Kent.
9. Bernardin, H. J., & Smith, P. C. (1981). A clarification of some issues regarding the development and use of behaviorally anchored rating scales. *Journal of Applied Psychology*, **66**, 458–463.
10. Bernardin, H. J. (1986). A performance appraisal system. In R. A. Berk (ed.), *Performance assessment*. Baltimore: Johns Hopkins University Press, pp. 277–304.
11. Borman, W. C., Hough, L. M., & Dunnette, M. D. (1978). *Performance ratings: An investigation of reliability, accuracy, and relationships between individual differences and rater error*. Alexandria, VA: Final Report to the Army Research Institute for the Behavioral and Social Sciences.
12. Borman, W. C. (1974). The rating of individuals in organizations: An alternate approach. *Organizational Behavior and Human Performance*, **12**, 105–124.
13. Borman, W. C. (1979). Format and training effects on rating accuracy and rater errors. *Journal of Applied Psychology*, **64**, 410–421.
14. Brophy, B. (1985, June 26). Appraisals widely used. *USA Today*, p. 6B.
15. Brophy, B. (1986, Sep. 29). New technology, high anxiety. *U.S. News & World Report*, pp. 54, 55.
16. Burke, R. S., Weitzel, W., & Weir, T. (1978). Characteristics of effective employee performance review and development interviews: Replication and extension. *Personnel Psychology*, **31**, 903–919.
17. Campbell, J. P., Dunnette, M. D., Lawler, E. E., & Weick, K. E. (1970). *Managerial behavior, performance, and effectiveness*. New York: McGraw-Hill.
18. Carlyle, J. J., & Ellison, T. F. (1984). Developing performance standards. Appendix B in H. J. Bernardin and R. W. Beatty, *Performance appraisal: Assessing human behavior at work*. Boston: PWS-Kent.
19. Cascio, W. F., & Bernardin, H. J. (1981). Implications of performance appraisal litigation for personnel decisions. *Personnel Psychology*, **34**, 211–226.
20. Cascio, W. F. (1982). Scientific, legal, and operational imperatives of workable performance appraisal systems. *Public Personnel Management*, **11**, 367–375.
21. Cascio, W. F. (1987). *Applied psychology in personnel management* (3d ed.). Englewood Cliffs, NJ: Prentice-Hall.
22. Cederblom, D., & Lounsbury, J. W. (1980). An investigation of user acceptance of peer evaluations. *Personnel Psychology*, **33**, 567–579.
23. Cederblom, D. (1982). The performance appraisal interview: A review, implications, and suggestions. *Academy of Management Review*, **7**, 219–227.
24. Cummings, L. L. (1973). A field experimental study of the effects of two performance appraisal systems. *Personnel Psychology*, **6**, 489–502.
25. DeVries, D. L., Morrison, A. M., Shullman, S. L., & Gerlach, M. L. (1981). *Performance appraisal on the line*. New York: Wiley.
26. Dorfman, P. W., Stephan, W. G., & Loveland, J. (1986). Performance appraisal behaviors: Supervisor perceptions and subordinate reactions. *Personnel Psychology*, **39**, 579–597.
27. Feild, H. S., & Holley, W. H. (1982). The relationship of performance appraisal system characteristics to verdicts in selected employment discrimination cases. *Academy of Management Journal*, **25**, 392–406.

28. Feldman, J. (1986). A note on the statistical correction of halo error. *Journal of Applied Psychology*, **71**, 173–176.

29. Greller, M. M. (1978). The nature of subordinate participation in the appraisal interview. *Academy of Management Journal*, **22**, 646–658.

30. Guion, R. M. (1986). Personnel evaluation. In R. A. Berk (ed.), *Performance assessment*. Baltimore: Johns Hopkins University Press, pp. 345–360.

31. Heneman, R. L. (1986). The relationship between supervisory ratings and results-oriented measures of performance: A meta-analysis. *Personnel Psychology*, **39**, 811–826.

32. Hogan, E. A. (1987). Effects of prior expectations on performance ratings: A longitudinal study. *Academy of Management Journal*, **30**, 354–368.

33. Hymowitz, C. (1985, Jan. 17). Bosses: Don't be nasty (and other tips for reviewing a worker's performance). *Wall Street Journal*, p. 28.

34. Ilgen, D. R., Mitchell, T. R., & Frederickson, J. W. (1981). Poor performers: Supervisors' and subordinates' responses. *Organizational Behavior and Human Performance*, **27**, 386–410.

35. Ilgen, D. R., & Moore, C. F. (1987). Types and choices of performance feedback. *Journal of Applied Psychology*, **72**, 401–406.

36. Jacobs, R., Kafry, D., & Zedeck, S. (1980). Expectations of behaviorally anchored rating scales. *Personnel Psychology*, **33**, 595–640.

37. Kavanagh, M. J. (1982). Evaluating performance. In K. M. Rowland & G. R. Ferris (eds.), *Personnel management*. Boston: Allyn & Bacon, pp. 187–226.

38. King, L. M., Hunter, J. E., & Schmidt, F. L. (1980). Halo in a multidimensional forced-choice performance evaluation scale. *Journal of Applied Psychology*, **65**, 507–516.

39. Kleiman, L. S., & Durham, R. L. (1981). Performance appraisal, promotion, and the courts: A critical review. *Personnel Psychology*, **34**, 103–121.

40. Kondrasuk, J. N. (1981). Studies in MBO effectiveness. *Academy of Management Review*, **6**, 419–430.

41. Labor letter (1984, Aug. 28). *Wall Street Journal*, p. 1.

42. Labor letter (1985, June 25). *Wall Street Journal*, p. 1.

43. Labor letter (1987, Feb. 24). *Wall Street Journal*, p. 1.

44. Landy, F. J., Barnes-Farrell, J., & Cleveland, J. N. (1980). Perceived fairness and accuracy of performance evaluation: A follow-up. *Journal of Applied Psychology*, **65**, 355–356.

45. Landy, F. J., Farr, J. L., & Jacobs, R. R. (1982). Utility concepts in performance measurement. *Organizational Behavior and Human Performance*, **30**, 15–40.

46. Landy, F. J., & Rastegary, H. (1988). Criteria for selection. In M. Smith & I. Robertson (eds.), *Advances in personnel selection and assessment*. New York: Wiley.

47. Latham, G. P., Wexley, K. N., & Pursell, E. D. (1975). Training managers to minimize rating errors in the observation of behavior. *Journal of Applied Psychology*, **60**, 550–555.

48. Lazer, R. I., & Wikstrom, W. S. (1977). *Appraising managerial performance: Current practices and future directions*. New York: The Conference Board, Report 723.

49. Levinson, P. (1979). *A guide for improving performance appraisal*. Washington, DC: Office of Personnel Management, USGPO, Stock No. 006-000-01121-7.

50. Longenecker, C. O., Sims, H. P., Jr., & Gioia, D. A. (1987). Behind the mask: The politics of employee appraisal. *Academy of Management Executive*, **1**, 183–193.

51. McConkie, M. L. (1979). A clarification of the goal-setting and appraisal process in MBO. *Academy of Management Review*, **4**, 29–40.

52. Meyer, H. H., Kay, E., & French, J. R. P. (1965). Split roles in performance appraisal. *Harvard Business Review*, **43**, 123–129.

53. Mount, M. K., & Thompson, D. E. (1987). Cognitive categorization and quality of performance ratings. *Journal of Applied Psychology*, **72**, 240–246.

54. Odiorne, G. S. (1965). *Management by objectives: A system of managerial leadership*. Belmont, CA: Fearon.

55. Shore, L. M., & Thornton, G. C., III. (1986). Effects of gender on self- and supervisory ratings. *Academy of Management Journal*, **29**, 115–129.

56. Sisson, D. E. (1948). Forced-choice, the new Army rating. *Personnel Psychology*, **1**, 365–381.

57. Smith, D. E. (1986). Training programs for performance appraisal: A review. *Academy of Management Review*, **11**, 22–40.

58. Stockford, L., & Bissell, H. W. (1949). Factors involved in establishing a merit rating scale. *Personnel*, **26**, 94–116.

59. *Stone v. Xerox* (1982). 685 F. 2d 1387 (11th Cir.).

60. Tubbs, M. E. (1986). Goal setting: A meta-analytic examination of the empirical evidence. *Journal of Applied Psychology*, **71**, 474–483.

61. *United States v. City of Chicago* (1978). 573 F. 2d 416 (7th Cir.).

62. Walther, F., & Taylor, S. (1983). An active feedback program can spark performance. *Personnel Administrator*, **28**(6), 107–111, 147–149.

63. Wexley, K. N. (1986). Appraisal interview. In R. A. Berk (ed.), *Performance assessment*. Baltimore: Johns Hopkins University Press, pp. 167–185.

64. Wexley, K. N., Singh, V. P., & Yukl, G. A. (1973). Subordinate participation in three types of appraisal interviews. *Journal of Applied Psychology*, **58**, 54–57.

65. Zedeck, S., & Cascio, W. F. (1982). Performance appraisal decisions as a function of rater training and purpose of the appraisal. *Journal of Applied Psychology*, **67**, 752–758.

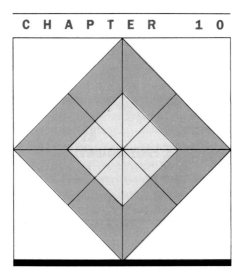

Managing Careers

CASE 10-1

Corporate career management comes of age*

In the past several years companies have begun to take a more active, systematic approach to the career development of their employees. This new approach is based on an underlying assumption that would have been considered heresy 10 or 20 years ago—that each employee is responsible for his or her own career development.

In the past, many companies assumed responsibility for the career pathing and growth of their employees. The company determined to what position, and at what speed, people would advance. That approach worked reasonably well in the corporate climate of the 1950s and 1960s. However, the corporate disruptions of the recent past have rendered this approach to employee career development largely unworkable. Acquisitions, divestitures, rapid growth, and downsizing have left many companies unable to deliver on the implicit career promises made to their employees. Organizations find themselves in the painful position of having to renege on career mobility opportunities their employees had come to expect. In extreme cases, employees who expected career growth no longer even had jobs!

*Source: Human Resource Consulting Group, Inc. Newsletter, January, 1987, pp. 1, 2.

Increasingly, corporations have come to realize that they cannot win if they take total responsibility for the career development of their employees. The old strategy of controlling the career growth of employees from "hire" to "retire" does not work anymore. In today's turbulent times, companies have found that at best they cannot develop the full potential of their employees; at worst, they cannot even continue to provide jobs for them. No matter what happens, employees often blame top management or "the company" for their own suboptimal career growth.

One company changed its approach to career growth as a result of pressure from its professional workforce. Employees felt suffocated by 20+ years of management determining people's career progress for them. Task teams worked with top management to develop career self-management training for employees, and career counseling skills for managers. As a result, increases in employee productivity, enhanced morale, and decreased turnover of key employees has more than justified the new approach to employee career management.

Characteristics of the new approach

A key feature of the new career management concept is that the company and the employee are *partners* in career development. Employees are responsible for knowing what their skills and capabilities are, what assistance they need from their employers, asking for that assistance, and preparing themselves to assume new responsibilities.

Although primary and final responsibility for career development rests with each employee, the company has complementary responsibilities. The company is responsible for communicating to employees where it wants to go and how it plans to get there (the corporate strategy), providing employees with as much information about the business as possible, and responding to the career initiatives of employees with candid, complete information. One of the most important contributions a company can make to each employee's development is to provide him or her with *honest* performance feedback about current job performance.

This approach to career management can be summed up as follows: Assign employees the responsibility for managing their own careers, then provide the support that they need to do it. This support takes different forms in different companies, but usually contains several core components.

QUESTIONS
1. Should employees be responsible for their own career development?
2. Is the new approach to corporate career management likely to be a passing fad, or is it here to stay?
3. What kinds of support mechanisms are necessary to make career self-management work?

What's Ahead

As Case 10-1 demonstrates, corporate career management has come a long way in the last several decades. This chapter presents a number of topics that have sparked this reevaluation. We will consider the impact of mergers, acquisitions, and downsizing on corporate loyalty, the impact of dual-career couples on the career management process, and the major issues that workers and managers must deal with during the early, middle, and late career stages of the adult life cycle. Finally we will examine alternative patterns of career change: promotions, demotions, lateral transfers, relocations, layoffs, and retirements. Career management has many facets, both for the individual and for the organization. Case 10-1 emphasized that in the new concept of career management the company and the employee are partners in career development. This theme is emphasized throughout the chapter. Let's begin by attempting to define what is meant by the word "career."

Toward a Definition of "Career"

In everyday parlance, the word "career" is used in a number of different ways. People speak of "pursuing a career"; "career planning" workshops are common; colleges and universities hold "career days," during which they publicize jobs in different fields and assist individuals through "career counseling." A person may be characterized as a "career" woman or man who shops in a store that specializes in "career clothing." Likewise, a person may be characterized as a "career military officer." We may overhear a person say, "That movie 'made' his career" (i.e., it enhanced his reputation), or in a derogatory tone, after a subordinate has insulted the CEO, "She can kiss her career goodbye" (i.e., she has tarnished her reputation). Finally, an angry supervisor may remark to her dawdling subordinate, "Watney, are you going to make a career out of changing that light bulb?"

As these examples illustrate, the word "career" can be viewed from a number of different perspectives. From one perspective *a career is a sequence of positions occupied by a person during the course of a lifetime.* This is the *objective* career. From another perspective, though, *a career consists of the changes in values, attitudes, and motivation that occur as a person grows older.*[28] This is the *subjective* career. Both of these perspectives, objective and subjective, focus on the individual. Both assume that people have some degree of control over their destinies, that they can manipulate opportunities in order to maximize the success and satisfaction derived from their careers.[26] They assume further that HR activities should recognize career stages and assist employees with the development tasks they face at each stage. Career planning is important because *the consequences of career success or failure are linked closely with each individual's self-concept, identity, and satisfaction with career and life.*

Adult life-cycle stages

For years, researchers have attempted to identify the major developmental tasks that employees face during their working lives and to organize these tasks into broader career stages. Although a number of models have been proposed, very little research has tested their accuracy. One review of the research in this area concluded that there is little evidence for the existence of the career stages hypothesized in *any* of the models. Moreover, there is little, if any, agreement about whether career stages are linked to age or not. Most theorists give age ranges for each stage, but these vary widely. Consequently, it may make more sense to think in terms of career stages linked to time. This would allow a "career clock" to begin at different points for different individuals, based on their backgrounds and experiences.[48] Table 10-1 represents a model of adult life-cycle stages that has been synthesized from the work of a number of researchers in the field. It is not necessarily more valid than any alternative model, and, as with all such models, it should be viewed as a broad guideline rather than as an exact representation of reality.

Career Management: Individuals Focusing on Themselves

In thinking about the implications of Table 10-1, it is important to emphasize the increasingly *temporary* relationships between individuals and organizations. If, as a consequence, organizations are less powerful in providing traditional career guidance, then ultimate responsibility for career development reverts to the individual. Unfortunately, few individuals are technically prepared (and willing) to handle this assignment. This is not surprising, for very few college programs address specifically the problems of managing one's own career. However, as long as it remains difficult for organizations to match the career expectations of their employees (a following section shows actual corporate examples of this), one option for employees will be to switch organizations. Guidelines for doing this fall into the following three major categories:[67]

Select a field of employment and an employer

1. You cannot manage your career unless you have a macro, long-range objective. The first step, therefore, is to think in terms of where you ultimately want to be, recognizing, of course, that your career goals will change over time.
2. View every potential employer and position in terms of your long-range career goal. That is, how well does this job serve to position me in terms of my ultimate objective?
3. Accept short-term trade-offs for long-term benefits. Some low-paying jobs can provide extremely valuable training opportunities or career contacts.

TABLE 10-1 *A brief characterization of adult life-cycle stages*

Life phase	Major psychic tasks	Marker events	Characteristic stance
Leaving the family (16 or 18 to 20–24)	Separate self from family; reduce dependence on familial support and authority; develop new home base; regard self as adult.	Leave home; new roles and more autonomous living arrangements; college, travel, army, job. Initial decisions about what to study, career, love affairs.	A balance between "being in" and "moving out" of the family.
Getting into the adult world (early twenties to 27–29)	Explore available possibilities of adult world to arrive at initial vision of oneself as an adult. Fashion an initial life structure; develop the capacity for intimacy; create a Dream; find a mentor.	Provisional commitment to occupation and first stages of a career; being hired; first job; adjusting to work world; quitting, being fired; unemployment; moving; marriage; decision to have a child; child goes to school; purchase a home; community activities; organizational roles.	"Doing what one should." Living and building for the future; transiency is an alternative track.
Age 30 transition (late twenties to early thirties)	Reexamine life structure and present commitments; make desired changes, particularly to incorporate deeper strivings put aside in the twenties.	Change occupation or directions within an occupation; go back to school; love affair; separation; divorce, first marriage; remarriage.	"What is life all about now that I'm doing what I should? What do I want out of life?"
Settling down (early thirties)	Make deeper commitments; invest more of self in work, family, and valued interests; become a junior member of one's occupational tribe; set a timetable for shaping one's life vision into concrete long-term goals; parenting.	Death of parents; pursue work, family activities, and interests; children old enough for mother to return to school.	Concern to establish order and stability in life, and "making it," with setting long-range goals and meeting them.
Becoming one's own person (35–39 to 39–42)	Become serious member of occupational group; prune dependent ties to boss, critics, colleagues, spouse, mentor. Seek independence and affirmation by society in most valued role. For a woman whose first career is in the home, a growing comfort with family responsibilities and independence to seek valued interests and activities.	Crucial promotion, recognition; break with mentor.	Suspended animation; waiting for the confirmatory event; time becomes finite and worrisome.

(continued)

TABLE 10-1 (*Continued*)

Life phase	Major psychic tasks	Marker events	Characteristic stance
Midlife transition (early forties)	Create a better fit between life structure and self; resolve experience of disparity between inner sense of the benefits of living within a particular structure and what else one wants in life.	Change in activities from realization that life ambitions might not develop; change of career; remarriage; empty nest; a second career for women whose first career was in the home; loss of fertility; death of friend, sibling, or child.	Awareness of bodily decline, aging, own mortality; emergence of feminine aspects of self for men, masculine aspects for women.
Restabilization (a 3-year period around 45)	Enjoy one's choices and life style.	Become a mentor; share knowledge and skills with younger friends and associates; contribute to the next generation; develop new interests or hobbies; occupational die is cast for men.	
Transition into the fifties (late forties to mid-fifties)	Another reexamination of the fit between life structure and self; need for redirection, a whole new beginning for some.	Last chance for women to have a career, or vigorously pursue a deferred life goal or interests—family crises, home duties diminished, change in husband's job status.	An imperative to change so that deferred goals can be accomplished—"It is perhaps late, but there are things I would like to do in the last half of my life."
Restabilization, mellowing and flowering (late fifties, early sixties)	Accomplishing important goals in the time left to live.	New opportunities related to career and valued interests; personally defined accomplishments.	A mellowing of feelings and relationships; spouse is increasingly important; greater comfort with self,.
Life review, finishing up (sixties and beyond)	Accepting what has transpired in life as having worth and meaning; valuing oneself and one's choices.	Retirement of self and spouse; aging; death of friends, spouse, and self.	Review of accomplishments; eagerness to share everyday human joys and sorrows; family is important; death is a new presence.

Source: R. P. Weathersby & J. M. Tarule, *Adult development: Implications for higher education*, Washington, DC: American Association for Higher Education, Research Report 4, 1980.

4. Consider carefully whether to accept highly specialized jobs or isolated job assignments that might restrict or impede your career development.

Know where you are

1. Always be aware of opportunities available to you in your current position— e.g., training programs that might further your career development.
2. Carefully and honestly assess your current performance. How do you see yourself, and how do you think higher management sees your performance?

3. Try to recognize when you and your organization have outlived your utility for one another. This is not an admission of failure but rather an honest reflection of the fact that there is little more the organization can do for you, and, in turn, that your contribution to the organization has reached a point of diminishing returns.

Plan your exit

1. Try to leave at *your* convenience, not the organization's. To do this you must do two things well: (a) know when it is time to leave (as before), and (b) be aware of career opportunities that fit into your long-range career plan.
2. Leave your current organization on good terms and not under questionable circumstances.

Up to this point it may sound like managing your career is all one-sided. This is not true; the organization should be a proactive force in this process. To do so, organizations must think and plan in terms of shorter employment relationships. This can be done, as it often is in professional sports, through fixed-term employment contracts, with options for renegotiation and extension.

A second strategy for organizations is to invest adequate time and energy in job design and equipment. Given that mobility among workers is expected to increase, careful attention to these elements will make it easier to make replacements fully productive as soon as possible. How does the self-management of careers work in practice? If Hewlett-Packard's experience is any indication, we can expect to see more of it in the future.

COMPANY EXAMPLE
Helping employees self-manage their careers at Hewlett-Packard

A 3-month course in personal career management was developed at Hewlett-Packard's Colorado Springs Division based on two methods: self-assessment and subsequent application of findings to the workplace to chart a career path for each employee.[74]

The idea of self-assessment as the first step toward career planning is certainly not new. Self-help books have flooded the market for years. However, books alone lack a critical ingredient for success: *the emotional support of a group setting* where momentum and motivation can be shared and maintained. Make no mistake about it, self-assessment can be a grueling process.

Hewlett-Packard uses six devices to generate data for self-assessment (based on earlier work for a second-year Harvard M.B.A. course in career development). These include:

- *A written self-interview.* Participants are given 11 questions about themselves, they are asked to provide facts about their lives (people, places, events), and they are asked to discuss the future and the transitions they have made. This autobiographical sketch provides core data for the subsequent analysis.

- *Strong-Campbell Interest Inventory.* Participants complete this 325-item instrument to determine their preferences about occupations, academic subjects, types of people, and so forth. An interest profile is developed for each individual by comparing her or his responses to those of successful people in a wide range of occupations.
- *Allport-Vernon-Lindzey Study of Values.* Each participant makes 45 choices among competing values in order to measure the relative strength of theoretical, economic, aesthetic, social, political, and religious values.
- *24-hour diaries.* Participants log their activities during one workday and also during one nonworkday. This information is used to confirm, or occasionally to contradict, information from the other sources.
- *Interviews with two "significant others."* Each participant asks a friend, spouse, relative, coworker, or someone else of importance questions about himself or herself. The two interviews are tape-recorded.
- *Lifestyle representations.* Participants depict their lifestyles using words, photos, drawings, or whatever else they choose.

A key ingredient in this program is its emphasis on an *inductive* approach. That is, the program begins by generating new data about each participant, rather than by starting with generalizations and deducing from them more specific information about each person. The process proceeds from the specific to the general (inductive), rather than from the general to the specific (deductive). Participants slowly recognize generalizations or themes within the large amounts of information they have produced. They come to tentative conclusions about these themes, first in each device individually and then in all the workshop's instruments as a whole, by analyzing the data they have collected.[74]

Following the self-assessment, department managers interview subordinates to learn about their career objectives. They record these objectives and describe the people and positions currently in their departments. This information is then available for senior management to use in devising an overall human resource plan, defining skills required, and including a timetable. When data on the company's future needs are matched against each employee's career objectives, department managers can help employees chart a career course in the company (e.g., through training or additional job experience). Career development objectives for each employee are incorporated into performance objectives for future performance appraisals. The department head monitors the employee's career progress as part of the review process, and she or he is responsible for offering all possible support.

Results of the career self-management program

Senior managers at Hewlett-Packard found that after the workshops they had far more flexibility in moving employees than previously. The company was able either to give employees reasons to stay where they were, to develop a new path for them in the company, or to help them move out. Significantly, the Colorado Springs Division's overall turnover rate was unchanged in the year following the workshops. At an estimated $40,000 replacement cost for a departing middle manager, this was a welcome finding.

Within 6 months after the course, 37 percent of the participants had advanced to new jobs within the company, while 40 percent planned moves within the following 6 months. Of those who advanced, 74 percent credited the program for playing a significant part in their job change. The workshops also helped the company meet its affirmative action targets since the sessions were open to all employees who expressed an interest in career development.

Perhaps the most persuasive reason for helping employees to manage their own careers is the need to remain competitive. Although it might seem like a contradiction, such efforts can enhance a company's stability by developing more purposeful, self-assured employees. As noted earlier, today's employees are more difficult to manage. Companies that recognize the need to provide employees with satisfying opportunities will have the decided advantage of a loyal and industrious workforce.

One of the most challenging career management problems that organizations face today is that of the dual-career couple. Let's examine this issue in detail.

Dual-career couples: problems and opportunities

Dual-career couples face the problems of managing work and family responsibilities. Furthermore, it appears that there may be an interaction effect that compounds the problems and stresses of each separate career.[26] This implies that, by itself, career planning and development may be meaningless unless an employee's role as a family member also is considered, particularly when this role conflicts with work activities.[44] What can be done?

Research indicates that if dual-career couples are to manage their family responsibilities successfully, they must be flexible; they must be mutually committed to both careers; they must adopt coping mechanisms (e.g., separating work and nonwork roles clearly, accepting all role demands as given and finding ways to meet them); and they must develop the competencies to manage their careers through career information and planning, goal setting, and problem solving.[29, 66]

From an organizational perspective, successful management of the dual-career couple requires (1) flexible work schedules, (2) special counseling, (3) training for supervisors in career counseling skills, and (4) the establishment of support structures for transfers and relocations. What have organizations actually done? Two national surveys found the following results.[14, 35]

As part of a package deal, many companies provide assistance to the "trailing" spouse in finding a suitable job consistent with the spouse's career plans. Alternatively, companies that have eliminated the nepotism taboo might hire the trailing spouse themselves. Roughly four-fifths of the organizations surveyed reported *no* restrictions against hiring both husband and wife. This may be a strategy for attracting and retaining top talent, particularly in technical occupations, which more women are entering. Thus a national survey done for General Electric found that 50 percent of all female technologists were married to technologists. However, another reason for the elimination of no-spouse rules is that they have come under attack in the courts on the grounds that they amount to illegal discrimination on the basis of gender. Women are usually the ones who are forced to leave a company or are not hired in the first place.[40] The hiring of couples seems to work best at large concerns, where more jobs are available and it is easier physically to separate spouses from each other in different offices or buildings. This makes it easier to conform to most firms' policies on this issue: *An employee cannot be placed under the direct or indirect supervision of a spouse.* The advantages of hiring both spouses are:

- It helps lure prospective employees to remote communities where suitable jobs for a spouse might be hard to find.
- It cuts recruiting and relocation costs.
- It encourages executives already on board to accept transfers.
- It makes employees less susceptible to offers from rival firms.

However, like any other HR policy, the advantages of spouse hiring need to be weighed against the following disadvantages:[17, 22]

- There is considerable risk that disciplining or firing one spouse will cause the other to leave as well.
- Outplacement assistance for one spouse as a result of a layoff may in reality become outplacement assistance for both spouses, if the other voluntarily quits.
- Couples employed by the same firm may encounter tremendous strains when one of them encounters problems at work. The partner cannot just say, "This is between you and your boss; I don't want to get into the middle of it."
- Couples worry that in matters of promotion, transfer, and compensation they will be seen by the company as a team, instead of as individuals.

As reported by firms in the national surveys mentioned earlier, 53 percent provided flexible work hours for dual-career couples, 30 percent provided assistance in finding employment for working spouses of relocated employees, and 27 percent provided relocation counseling. Evidence is mounting that more and more large corporations are adopting these practices.[12, 18] Finally, 22 percent of the companies surveyed offered special counseling for dual-career couples.

There are also several things that organizations have *not* done. Few firms provide training for supervisors on how to deal with employees who are partners in dual-career couples. Such training is important, for research indicates that when a wife works, the husband often develops lower levels of job and life satisfaction.[69] Wives' employment boosts the mental health of wives but often depresses the mental health of husbands. Why? Some husbands may not yet be ready to abandon the "good provider" role: that is, the traditional role of being sufficiently resourceful as a provider for one's family that one's wife does not *have* to enter the labor force.

In addition to supervisory training, relatively few firms provide job sharing or child care. With regard to child care, demand for the service has never been greater. In response, the number of day-care centers increased about 77 percent between 1977 and 1987, to 235,000.[64] Nevertheless, only 3300 companies out of an estimated 46,000 mid- to large-size concerns in the United States currently provide any child-care assistance.[52] Here are some reasons why employer-supported child care will continue to grow:

- By 1990, an estimated 75 percent of all families will have two incomes.[15]
- There has been a significant rise in the number of single parents, over half of whom use child-care facilities.
- More and more, career-oriented women are arranging their lives to include motherhood *and* professional goals.

For firms considering child care, here are three options:[24]

1. Set up a clearinghouse for information about child care available in the local community.
2. Refer employees to existing day-care facilities in the community at a reduced rate. The rate can be reduced by negotiating with one or more local providers, by paying a company subsidy of 10 to 50 percent to the providers, or by giving the employees vouchers that reimburse any local center 100 percent of the child-care expenses.
3. The employer may provide a child-care center on or near the worksite.

To assess the quality of child care provided, parents should actually see the facility to be used. Safety, healthy food, child curriculum and activities, parent involvement, and space and equipment are key areas to probe.[1]

Employers who presently provide some form of child-care assistance report the following *advantages:*

- Tax savings (the Economic Recovery Tax Act of 1981 allows employers to deduct the cost of child-care benefits, both for on-site and for referral subsidies)
- Reduced turnover
- Improved morale and employer-employee relations
- Effective recruitment tool
- Positive community image

However, there are also *disadvantages* to providing child care. These include:[1]

- The equity of benefits (not all employees can take advantage of employer-assisted child care)

- The company expense of voucher and vendor plans
- The substantial expense of the on-site option
- Considerable liability exposure for employers providing on-site child care
- Lack of evidence in well-controlled studies that child care increases employee productivity or reduces absenteeism or lateness[49]

Managing dual-career couples, from an individual as well as from an organizational perspective, is difficult. But if current conditions are any indication of long-term trends, then we can be quite sure of one thing: This "problem" is not going to go away.

Career Management: Organizations Focusing on Individuals

In this section we will examine current organizational practices used to manage workers at various stages of their careers. Let's begin by considering organizational entry.

Organizational entry

Once a person has entered the workforce, the next stage is to enter a specific organization, to settle down, and to begin establishing a career there.[72] *Entry* refers to the process of "moving inside," or becoming more involved in a particular organization.[65] To do this well, a process known as socialization is essential. *Socialization* refers to the mutual adaptation of the new employee and the new employer to one another. Learning organizational policies, norms, traditions, and values is an important part of the process. Getting to know one's peers, supervisor, and subordinates is, too. Over time, organizations adapt to new employees—e.g., the younger generation, the older employee, the hard-core unemployed. Since most turnover occurs *early* in a person's tenure with an organization, programs that accelerate socialization will tend also to reduce early turnover (i.e., at entry) and therefore reduce a company's overall turnover rate.

Two of the most effective methods for doing this are realistic job previews (see Chapter 6) and new-employee orientation (see Chapter 7). A third is "mentoring." A mentor is a teacher, advisor, sponsor, and confidante.[43] He or she should be bright and well-seasoned enough to understand the dynamics of power and politics in the organization and also be willing to share this knowledge with a new hire. Organizations should actively promote mentor relationships and provide sufficient time for the mentor and the new hire to meet on a regularly scheduled basis, at least initially. The mentor's role is to teach the new hire "the ropes," to provide candid feedback on how he or she is being perceived by others, and to serve as a confidential "sounding board" for dealing with work-related problems. If successful, mentor relationships can help reduce the inflated expectations that newcomers often have about organizations, can relieve the stress experienced by all new hires, and, best of all, can improve the newcomer's chances for survival in the organization.

Unfortunately, women and blacks often find themselves excluded from mentoring relationships. Part of the difficulty is that mentoring is frequently based on friendship, admiration, and nurturing developed outside a 9-to-5 schedule. As one minority recruitment firm noted, "Whites usually don't see blacks at the beach, sailing, or on weekends, because they lead separate lives away from the job."[19] Moreover, some men hesitate to take on female protégés because of the sexual innuendoes that often accompany such relationships.

This may be changing, as firms like Bank of America try to overcome the barriers by assigning mentors to three or four promising young executives for a year at a time. While such company intervention may turn out to be fruitless, just being picked as a mentor, according to one 35-year-old female branch bank manager, boosted her self-esteem. This is a central goal of any mentoring effort.

Early career: the impact of the first job

Many studies of early careers focus on the first jobs to which new employees were assigned. The positive impact of initial job challenge upon later career success and retention has been found many times in a wide variety of settings. Among engineers, challenging early work assignments were related to strong initial performance as well as to the maintenance of competence and performance throughout the engineer's career.[53] In other words, challenging initial job assignments are an antidote to career obsolescence.

The characteristics of the first supervisor are also critical. He or she must be personally secure, unthreatened by the new subordinate's training, ambition, and energy, and able to communicate company norms and values.[65] Beyond that, the supervisor ideally should be able to play the roles of coach, feedback provider, trainer, role model, and protector in an accepting, esteem-building manner.[26]

One other variable affects the likelihood of obtaining a high-level job later in one's career: *initial aspirations.*[60] Employees should be encouraged to "aim high" because, in general, higher aspirations lead to higher performance. Parents, teachers, employers, and friends should therefore avoid discouraging so-called impractical aspirations.

COMPANY EXAMPLE

Impact of the first job on later career success

For over 20 years researchers generally accepted the view that unless an individual has a challenging first job and receives quick, early promotions, the entire career will suffer. This is a "tournament" model of upward mobility. It assumes that everyone has an equal chance in the early contests but that the losers are not eligible for later contests, at least not those of the major tournament. An alternative model is called "signaling" theory. It suggests three cues ("signals") that those responsible for promotion may use: (1) prior history of promotions (a signal of ability), (2) functional-area background, and (3) number of different jobs held.

A recent study examined the patterns of early upward mobility for 180 employees of an oil company over an 11-year period.[21] The company's very detailed job classification systems and actual salary grades served as measures of career attainment. The results generally did not support the tournament model of career mobility, because the losers—those passed over in the early periods—were later able to move up quickly. Rather, the results were more analogous to a horse race: position out of the gate had relatively little effect in comparison to position entering the home stretch.

Different mobility patterns for administrative and technical personnel helped to explain why the pattern of the early years did not always persist. Those who started early in administrative positions began to move up early, but also plateaued early. A technical background meant a longer wait before upward movement, followed by relatively rapid promotion. The number of different positions held also predicted higher attainment.

In summary, one's past position, functional background, and number of different jobs all seem to act as signals to those making decisions about promotions. All were related strongly to career attainment. Together they accounted for over 60 percent of the variability in promotions.

Managing men and women in midcareer

Most of the findings to be reported in this section are based on research with males. Since the entry of large numbers of females into the workforce is fairly recent, it is too soon to know for sure whether and to what extent the research findings generalize to both sexes. Nevertheless, the theory that a crisis occurs in the lives of American workers between the ages of 35 and 50 is well supported by research. The crisis is variously known as "middlescence," "middle-age crisis," and "midlife transition." The following issues may arise at this stage:[6, 72]

- Awareness of advancing age and awareness of death
- Awareness of bodily changes related to aging
- Knowing how many career goals have been or will be attained
- Search for new life goals
- Marked change in family relationships
- Change in work relationships (one is now more of a "coach" than a novice or "rookie")
- Growing sense of obsolescence at work (as Satchel Paige once said, "Never look back; someone may be gaining on you")
- Feeling of decreased job mobility and increased concern for job security[68]

One's career is a major consideration during this period. If a person has been in the same job for 10 years or more (sometimes less), he or she must face the facts of corporate politics, changing job requirements, possibilities of promotion, demotion, or job loss altogether.[6] The fact of the matter is, promotions will slow down markedly over the next decade as middle-level managers are put into "holding patterns."

At General Electric, for example, employees are remaining in job assignments longer in some divisions and are not having the same chance to move upward that employees once had. Lower-level managers are staying longer in the same jobs. At Southern California Gas Company, a larger group is competing for fewer management opportunities, according to the company's vice president for industrial relations. "We told people, 'Go to school, study hard, work hard on your job and the sky's the limit.' That's not the case anymore. The truly superior performer is always in short supply. But the large group that's not quite that outstanding will have it tough."[25]

The rapid growth of technology and the accelerating development of new knowledge require that a person in midlife make some sort of *change* for her or his own survival. A 30-year-old might make the statement, "I can afford to change jobs or careers a couple of more times before I have to settle down." But a 40-year-old faces the possibility that there is only one chance left for change, and now may be the time to take it.[6]

Not everyone who goes through this period in life is destined to experience problems, but everyone does go through the transition, and some are better equipped to cope than are others. Why is this so? And how can we cope? Although midcareer might sound as though it is all "gloom and doom," one bright spot is the knowledge that *having realistic expectations about impending crises and transitions can actually ease the stress and pain.*[27] Life planning and career planning exercises are available that encourage employees to face up to feelings of restlessness and insecurity, to reexamine their values and life goals, and to set new ones or to recommit themselves to old ones.

One strategy is to *train midcareer employees to develop younger employees* (i.e., to serve as coaches or mentors). Both parties can win under such an arrangement. The midcareer employee keeps himself or herself fresh, energetic, and up to date, while the younger employee learns to see the "big picture" and to profit from the experience of the older employee. An important psychological need at midcareer is to build something lasting, something that will be a permanent contribution to one's organization or profession. The development of a future generation of leaders could be a significant, lasting, and highly satisfying contribution.[27]

Another strategy for coping with midcareer problems is to *deal with or prevent obsolescence.* To deal with the problem, some firms send their employees to seminars, workshops, university courses, and other forms of "retooling." But a better solution is to prevent obsolescence from occurring in the first place. Research with engineers indicated that this can be done through challenging initial jobs; periodic changes in assignments, projects, or jobs; work climates that contain frequent, relevant communications; rewards that are tied closely to performance; and participative styles of leadership.[53] Furthermore,

may become bitter and angry. Family problems may also occur because of the added emotional and financial strain. For those who remain, it is important that they retain the highest level of loyalty, trust, teamwork, motivation, and productivity possible. This doesn't just happen—and unless there is a good deal of face-to-face, candid, open communication between senior management and "survivors," it probably won't. Within the community, layoff policies should consider the company's reputation and image, in addition to the impact of the layoff on the local economy and social services agencies. Although layoffs are intended to *reduce* costs, some costs may in fact *increase*.[57] These include:

Direct costs	Indirect costs
Severance pay, pay in lieu of notice	Recruiting and employment cost of new hires
Accrued vacation and sick pay	Training and retraining
Supplemental unemployment benefits	Increase in unemployment tax rate
Outplacement	Potential charges of unfair discrimination
Pension and benefit payoffs	Low morale among remaining employees
Administrative processing costs	Heightened insecurity and reduced productivity

What are the options? One approach is to initiate a program of *job sharing* to perform the reduced workload. While no one is laid off, everyone's workweek and pay are reduced. This helps the company to reduce labor costs. In an area experiencing high unemployment, it may be better to have all employees share the "misery" rather than to lay off selected ones. Some of the benefits of job sharing are:

- Twice as much talent and creativity is available.
- Employees tend to work harder since they are working for a shorter period of time.
- Benefits continue.
- Overtime is reduced.
- Training is easier.

Job sharing is not without its drawbacks:

- There is a lack of job continuity.
- Supervision is inconsistent.
- Accountability is not centered in one person.
- Expenses increase because many benefits are a function of the employee, not the amount of pay.[23]

However, when Motorola reviewed job sharing at its facilities in Arizona, it found that avoiding layoffs saved an average of $1868 per employee—and $975,000 in total.[37]

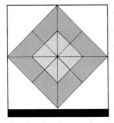

Impact of Career Management on Productivity, Quality of Work Life, and the Bottom Line

From first-job effects through midcareer transition to preretirement counseling, career management has a direct bearing on productivity, quality of work life, and the bottom line. It is precisely because organizations are sensitive to these concerns that career management activities have become as popular as they are. The saying "Organizations have many jobs, but individuals have only one career" is as true today as it ever was. While organizations find themselves in worldwide competition, most individuals are striving for achievement, recognition, personal growth, and "the good life." Unless careers are managed effectively by both individuals and organizations, neither can achieve their goals.

Retirements. For selected employees, *early retirement* is a possible alternative to being laid off. Early retirement programs take many forms, but typically they involve partial pay stretched over several years along with extended benefits. Early retirement programs are intended to provide incentives to terminate; they are not intended to replace regular retirement benefits. Any losses in pension resulting from early retirement are usually offset with attractive incentive payments. Many combinations of incentives have been offered with varying degrees of success. More than 900 employees retired under a Sears plan that included profit sharing, a medical plan, life insurance, and a lifetime employee discount on merchandise. Chicago-based Blue Cross and Blue Shield had 41 percent of its eligible employees leave under a plan offering health and dental coverage, life and accident insurance, and vision benefits. The key to success, according to these firms, is *to understand, before the incentives are offered, the needs of the employees targeted to leave.*[3]

Since mandatory retirement at a specified age can no longer be required legally, most employees will choose their own times to retire. More of them are choosing to retire earlier than age 65. In 1940, for example, 40 percent of workers continued to work after the age of 65. By 1978, that number had decreased to 17 percent, and by 1987 it was 15 percent.[13] Research indicates that both personal and situational factors affect retirement decisions. Personally, individuals with Type A behavior patterns (hard-driving, aggressive, impatient) are less likely to prefer to retire, while those with obsolete job skills, chronic health problems, and sufficient financial resources are more likely to retire. Situationally, employees are more likely to retire to the extent that they have reached their occupational goals, that their jobs have undesirable characteristics, that home life is seen as preferable to work life, and that there are attractive alternative (leisure) activities.[5]

As we have seen, however, work is becoming more and more common among retirees. In fact, fully one-third of a surveyed group of retired senior executives returned to a full-time job within 18 months of their retirement. Why? More than half did so for reasons of job satisfaction, enjoyment, or sense of accomplishment.[62] Old attitudes die hard. Proclamations like the following are heard less often:

> At last! Thirty long years of slugging it out in the old nine-to-five rodent regatta come to an end. Thirty years of stomach-perforating office politics and brain-blunting busywork brought to a halt. Retirement. Hooray! Free at last. I'm free at last. Clean out my desk, turn on my pension, ride that clanky train home one last time, and then I'll never work again. (ref. 30, p. 157)

Resignations. Resignation, or voluntary worker turnover, has been increasing steadily over the past 15 years, particularly among white-collar and professional workers.[67] Employees who resign should avoid "burning bridges" behind them, leaving anger and resentment in their wake; instead, they should leave gracefully and responsibly, stressing the value of company experience.[11]

**CASE 10-1
Conclusion**

Corporate career management comes of age

Programs of corporate career management often include one or more of the following support mechanisms.

Self-assessment The goal of self-assessment is to help employees focus on appropriate career goals. Training typically takes the form of workshops designed to help employees walk themselves through the difficult and sometimes emotional self-assessment process. It is a process of identifying and calibrating one's professional aptitudes and capabilities and of identifying improvements that will enhance one's career growth. As we saw in the Hewlett-Packard example, that company has pioneered in offering self-assessment training to its employees at all levels.

Career planning Workshop training is also used to teach employees how to plan their career growth once they have determined where they want to go. They learn skills for career self-management as well as how to "read" the corporate environment and to become "savvy" about how to get ahead in their own companies. General Electric and Citibank have been leaders in raising this kind of awareness in their employees.

Supervisory training Employees frequently turn first to their immediate supervisors for help with career management. At Sikorsky Aircraft, for example, supervisors are taught how to provide relevant information and to question the logic of each employee's career plans, but *not* to give specific career advice. Giving advice relieves the employee of responsibility for managing his or her own career.

Succession planning Simply designating replacements for key managers and executives is no guarantee that those replacements will be ready when needed. Enlightened companies are adopting an approach to succession planning that is consistent with the concept of career self-management. They develop their employees broadly, to prepare them for any of several positions that may become available. As business needs change, broadly developed people can be moved into positions that are critical to the success of the business.

The practice of making career self-management part of the corporate culture has spread rapidly over the past several years. Companies are using this approach to build a significant competitive advantage. Given today's turbulent, sometimes convulsive corporate environments, plus workers who seek greater control over their own destinies, it may be the only approach that can succeed over the long term.

Summary

A career is a sequence of positions occupied by a person during the course of a lifetime. Career planning is important because the consequences of career success or failure are closely linked with an individual's self-concept and identity, as well as with career and life satisfaction. This chapter has addressed career management from three perspectives. The first was that of *individuals focusing on themselves:* self-management of one's own career, establishment of career objectives, and dual-career couples. The second perspective was that of *organizations focusing on individuals:* that is, managing individuals during early career (organizational entry, impact of the first job); midcareer, including strategies for coping with midlife transitions and "plateaued" workers; and late career (age 50 and over) stages. We considered the implications of each of these stages for human resource management, both in large- and in small-business settings and also in the context of equal employment opportunity. Finally, a third perspective was that of *organizations focusing on their own maintenance and growth.* This requires the development of organizational

TOMORROW'S FORECAST Throughout the chapter we have highlighted emerging trends in this area. *Demographically* we can expect the labor force in the next two decades to contain more workers (male and female) competing for middle-management jobs, more older workers either delaying retirement or returning to work after retirement, and more dual-career couples. *Organizationally* we can expect to see larger numbers of career management programs that emphasize the special problems of early, middle, and late career stages. The pace of demographic, technological, and social change will not slacken. The real challenge, however, will be to manage change effectively, and not to allow change to manage us.

career management systems based on career paths defined in terms of employee behaviors. It involves the management of patterns of career movement up, down, over, and out.

Discussion Questions

10-1 Why is the design of one's first permanent job so important?

10-2 What practical steps can be taken to minimize midcareer crises?

10-3 What strategies can you suggest for avoiding the problems associated with older workers clogging the career paths of younger workers?

10-4 Discuss the special problems faced by dual-career couples.

10-5 You have just learned that you are being transferred to another location. Your supervisor asks what the company can do to smooth the process. What would you tell her?

10-6 What kinds of problems are associated with managing older and younger workers?

References

1. Adolph, B., & Rose, K. (1985). *The employer's guide to child care.* New York: Praeger.
2. Anderson, J. C., Milkovich, G. T., & Tsui, A. (1981). A model of intra-organizational mobility. *Academy of Management Review,* **6,** 529–538.
3. Baenen, L. B., & Ernest, R. C. (1982). An argument for early retirement incentive planning. *Personnel Administrator,* 27(8), 63–66.
4. Bass, B. M., Cascio, W. F., McPherson, J. W., & Tragash, H. J. (1976). Prosper—Training and research for increasing management awareness of affirmative action in race relations. *Academy of Management Journal,* **19,** 353–369.
5. Beehr, T. A. (1986). The process of retirement: A review and recommendations for future investigation. *Personnel Psychology,* **39,** 31–55.
6. Bell, J. E. (1982, August). Mid-life transition in career men. *AMA Management Digest,* pp. 8–10.
7. Better down than out (1978, May 15). *Time,* p. 61.
8. Beutell, N. J. (1983). Managing the older worker. *Personnel Administrator,* 28(8), 31–38, 64.
9. Bird, C. P., & Fisher, T. D. (1986). Thirty years later: Attitudes toward the employment of older workers. *Journal of Applied Psychology,* **71,** 315–317.
10. Brooke, J. (1986, Jan. 19). Retirees, many bored, try "un-retirement." *New York Times,* pp. A1, A26.
11. Brooks, A. (1985, Dec. 2). Quitting a job gracefully. *New York Times,* p. B12.
12. Brooks, A. (1987, June 1). Following a wife to a new job. *New York Times,* p. B8.
13. Bureau of National Affairs (1987). Older Americans in the workforce: Challenges and solutions. *Labor Relations Week,* 1(27), 1–237.
14. *Corporations and two-career families: Directions for the future* (1981). New York: Catalyst.

15. Collie, H. C. (1986). Corporate relocation: Changing with the times. *Personnel Administrator*, **31**(4), 101–106.
16. Copperman, L. F., & Keast, F. D. (1981, Summer). Older workers: A challenge for today and tomorrow. *Human Resource Management*, pp. 13–18.
17. Couples at same firm—An idea catches on (1983, Sep. 12). *U. S. News and World Report*, p. 71.
18. Driessnack, C. H. (1987). Spouse relocation: A moving experience. *Personnel Administrator*, **32**(8), 94–102.
19. Feinstein, S. (1987, Nov. 10). Women and minority workers in business find a mentor can be a rare commodity. *Wall Street Journal*, p. 39.
20. Ference, T. P., Stoner, J. A., & Warren, E. K. (1977). Managing the career plateau. *Academy of Management Review*, **2**, 602–612.
21. Forbes, J. B. (1987). Early intraorganizational mobility: Patterns and influences. *Academy of Management Journal*, **30**, 110–125.
22. Ford, R., & McLaughlin, F. (1986). Nepotism: Boon or bane? *Personnel Administrator*, **31**(11), 78–86.
23. Frease, M., & Zawacki, R. A. (1979). Job sharing: An answer to productivity problems. *Personnel Administrator*, **24**(10), 35–38.
24. Friedman, D. E. (1985). *Corporate financial assistance for child care*. New York: Conference Board.
25. Gottschalk, E. C., Jr. (1981, Oct. 22). Blocked paths: Promotions grow few as "baby boom" group eyes managers' jobs. *Wall Street Journal*, pp. 1, 16.
26. Greenhaus, J. H. (1987). *Career management*. Chicago: Dryden.
27. Hall, D. T. (1976). *Careers in organizations*. Pacific Palisades, CA: Goodyear.
28. Hall, D. T., & Associates (eds.) (1986). *Career development in organizations*. San Francisco: Jossey-Bass.
29. Hall, F. S., & Hall, D. T. (1979). *The two-career couple*. Reading, MA: Addison-Wesley.
30. Hedberg, G. (1983, December). Planning for your post-job job. *Money*, **12**(12), 157–167.
31. Howard, A., & Bray, D. W. (1982, Mar. 21). AT&T: The hopes of middle managers. *The New York Times*, p. 1F.
32. Hunsaker, J. S. (1983). Work and family life must be integrated. *Personnel Administrator*, **28**, 87–91.
33. Hymowitz, C., & Schellhardt, T. D. (1986, Oct. 20). After the ax. *Wall Street Journal*, p. 27.
34. Kennedy, J. L. (1983, Oct. 23). 55 is only a speed limit, not a sign-off to productivity. *Denver Post*, p. 2B.
35. Kopelman, R. E., Rosenzweig, L., & Lally, L. H. (1982). Dual-career couples: The organizational response. *Personnel Administrator*, **27**(9), 73–78.
36. Labor letter (1982, Oct. 26). *Wall Street Journal*, p. 1.
37. Labor letter (1986, Apr. 1). *Wall Street Journal*, p. 1.
38. Labor letter (1987, May 5). *Wall Street Journal*, p. 1.
39. Labor letter (1987, May 19). *Wall Street Journal*, p. 1.
40. Labor letter (1987, Sep. 8). *Wall Street Journal*, p. 1.
41. Latack, J. C., & Dozier, J. B. (1986). After the ax falls: Job loss as a career transition. *Academy of Management Review*, **11**, 375–392.
42. Ledvinka, J. (1975). Technical implications of equal employment law for manpower planning. *Personnel Psychology*, **28**, 299–323.
43. Levinson, D. J. (1978). *The seasons of a man's life*. New York: Knopf.

permanent: firing executives or offering them early retirement; asking employees to work longer hours, to take fewer days off, and to shorten their vacations; reducing the coverage of medical plans or asking employees to pay part of the costs; trimming expense accounts with bans on first-class travel and restrictions on phone calls and entertainment.[41]

> **COMPANY EXAMPLE**
>
> *Cutbacks at American Standard, Inc.*
>
> American Standard is a diversified manufacturer of building and transportation products. In 1982 it earned $2.20 per share, compared with $4.07 per share in 1981. To control labor costs, the company froze salaries, cut officers' pay 5 percent, and reduced the corporate staff by 17 percent through dismissals and early retirements. Says the company's executive vice president, "It's a terrible process, but it's not all bad. If once in a decade you are forced to think austerity, you probably face up to some situations you should have faced all along" (ref. 41, p. 51).

In good times managers did not have to get rid of poor performers. Bad times made that unpleasant task harder to avoid. Certainly any serious effort to cut management costs must focus on the payroll. This is because an executive costs a company roughly *double* his or her annual salary. Here's why. In 1987 benefits cost an average of 39 percent of base pay. Office, secretarial, and travel expenses make up the rest. Hence, getting rid of a $75,000-a-year executive and not replacing him or her saves about $150,000 per year.

Paying what the company can afford

To cover its labor costs and other expenses, a company must earn sufficient revenues through the sales of its products or services. It follows, then, that an employer's ability to pay is constrained by its ability to compete. The nature of the product or service market affects a firm's external competitiveness and the pay level it sets.[44]

Key factors in the product or service markets are the degree of competition among producers (e.g., fast-food outlets) and the level of demand for the products or services (e.g., the number of customers in a given area). Both of these affect the ability of a firm to change the prices of its products or services. If an employer cannot change prices without suffering a loss of revenues due to decreased sales, then the employer's ability to raise the level of pay is constrained. If the employer does pay more, it has two options: try to pass the increased costs on to consumers, or hold prices fixed and allocate a greater portion of revenues to cover labor costs.[44]

As is well known, the U.S. steel industry has been struggling with a host of problems in recent years. These range from the lofty, uncompetitive wages of unionized employees, to the antiquated state of many mills and fabricating plants, to the relentless pressure of foreign competitors who are themselves burdened with bulging capacity and weak domestic markets. Because of excessively generous wage settlements throughout the 1970s, steelworker employment costs in 1987 averaged over $22 per hour, after a 6-month strike at USX Corporation.[63] This is 58 percent higher than the $13.88 average for all U.S. manufacturing industries.[5] As a result, how can U.S. steel compete in world markets? Only if the cost per unit produced is lower than the competition's, for labor is only one part of overall production costs. If production costs other than labor cannot be reduced, then high labor costs will render a company uncompetitive.

Programs that encourage and reward performance

Firms are continuing to relocate to areas where organized labor is weak and pay rates are low. They are developing pay plans that channel more dollars into incentive awards and fewer into fixed salary. They are trying to get rid of automatic cost-of-living raises, and they are passing over more employees for raises so that they can award top performers meaningful pay increases. These programs all have a profit and productivity orientation and a commitment to share success with employees who produce.

On the other hand, employees will not *automatically* accept this orientation toward improved performance, for, in a sense, firms are "changing the rules" of the compensation game. The key to a genuine pay-for-performance system is for management to promote this kind of understanding in everything it says and does: *Better performance will increase productivity, and outstanding performers will see a share of that benefit in their paychecks.*[4] Chapter 12 will discuss more fully the pay-for-performance theme and how it can be put into effect.

INTERNATIONAL APPLICATION	**Tying Pay to Performance in the United States and Japan**

In an effort to hold down labor costs, thousands of U.S. companies are changing the way they increase workers' pay. Instead of the traditional annual increase, millions of workers in industries as diverse as supermarkets and aircraft manufacturing are receiving cash bonuses. For most workers, the plans mean less money. The bonuses take many names: "profit sharing" at Abbott Laboratories and Hewlett-Packard, "gain sharing" at Mack Trucks and Dana Corporation, and "lump-sum payments" at Boeing. All have two elements in common: (1) They can vary with the company's fortunes, and (2) they are not permanent. Because the bonuses are not folded into base pay, there is no compounding effect over time. This means that both wages and benefits rise more slowly. The result: a flattening of wages nationally.[71]

Today, 40 percent of all workers covered by major union agreements have bonus provisions in their contracts. How have unions reacted? In the view of the AFL-CIO, "Where there is justification for belt-tightening, then profit sharing is not an unreasonable means of passing on earnings when times improve" (ref. 71, p. D3).

In summary, "flexible pay"—tied mostly to profitability and promising better job security, but not guaranteeing it—is at the heart of the evolving bonus system. Employees are being asked to share the risks of the new global marketplace. How large must the rewards be? MIT economist Martin Weitzman estimates that over the long run the proper bonus level is 20 to 25 percent of total compensation, because it would give workers a pay increase equal to the rate of inflation plus productivity gains. But in the United States most bonus payments have been averaging about 10 percent of a worker's base pay annually. Conversely, the Japanese currently pay many workers a bonus system that represents about 25 percent of base pay. No other industrial nation bases pay on a bonus system.

Have such plans generated greater productivity in the U.S. manufacturing sector in recent years? Maybe, but an equally plausible explanation is that the gains were due to automation, to company efforts to give workers more of a say in how they do their jobs, and to the fear of workers that if they did not improve their productivity, their plants would become uncompetitive and would be closed.[71] In short, the jury is still out on the productivity impact of bonus systems as well as on their effect on worker motivation and organizational commitment.

Strategic Integration of Compensation Plans and Business Plans

Unfortunately, the rationale for many compensation programs is "Two-thirds of our competitors do it" or "That's corporate policy." Compensation plans need to be tied to the strategic mission of an organization and should take their direction from that strategic mission. They must support general business strategy.[19]

This approach to managing compensation and business strategies dictates that actual levels of compensation should *not* strictly be a matter of what is being paid in the marketplace. Instead, compensation levels derive from an assessment of what *must* be paid to attract and retain the right people, what the organization can *afford*, and what will be *required* to meet the strategic goals of the organization. Table 11-2 illustrates how different compensation strategies can be applied in firms that differ (a) in their business strategies and (b) in their market positions and maturity.

In firms that are growing rapidly, business strategy tends to be focused on one objective: Invest to grow. To be consistent with this business strategy, compensation strategy should stimulate an enterprising, entrepreneurial style

TABLE 11-2 *Linking compensation strategy to business strategy*

Business strategy	Market position and maturity	Compensation strategy	Blend of compensation
Invest to grow	Merging or growing rapidly	Stimulate entrepreneurialism	High cash with above-average incentives for individual performance
			Modest benefits
Manage earnings— protect markets	Normal growth to maturity	Reward management skills	Average cash with moderate incentives on individual, unit, or corporate performance
			Standard benefits
Harvest earnings— reinvest elsewhere	No real growth or decline	Stress cost control	Below-average cash with small incentive tied to cost control
			Standard benefits

Source: Adapted from R. J. Greene & R. G. Roberts, Strategic integration of compensation and benefits, *Personnel Administrator,* **28**(5), 1983, 82. Copyright, 1983, The American Society for Personnel Administration, Alexandria, VA.

of management (see Chapter 5). To do this, the firm should emphasize high cash payments with above-average incentives ("high risk, high reward"). In "mature" firms (see Chapter 5), business strategy is oriented primarily toward managing earnings and protecting markets. Compensation strategy should therefore reward management skills, and, to do this, there should be a blend of average cash payments, moderate incentives, and standard benefits. In the "aging" firm (see Chapter 5), the most appropriate strategy is to harvest earnings and reinvest them elsewhere. Compensation strategy emphasizes the control of costs. To implement such a strategy, standard benefits are combined with below-average cash, and modest incentives are tied directly to the control of costs.

Determinants of Pay Structure and Level

In simplest terms, marginal revenue product theory in labor economics holds that the value of a person's labor is what someone is willing to pay for it.[44] In practice, a number of factors *interact* to determine wage levels. Some of the most influential of these are labor market conditions, legislation, collective bargaining, management attitudes, and an organization's ability to pay. Let us examine each of these.

Labor market conditions

As noted in Chapter 5, "tight" versus "loose" labor markets have a major impact on wage structures and levels. Thus if the demand for certain skills is high while the supply is low (a "tight" market), there tends to be an *increase* in the price paid for these skills. Conversely, if the supply of labor is plentiful, relative to the demand for it, wages tend to *decrease*. As an example, consider the following starting salaries for 1987 college graduates with Bachelor's degrees:[13]

Area	Average starting salary
Engineering	$28,932
Chemistry	27,048
Computer Science	26,280
Mathematics, Statistics	25,548
Accounting	22,512
Business Administration	21,972
Liberal Arts	20,508
Sales-Marketing	20,232
Education	18,194

To a considerable extent, these differences in starting salaries reflect different labor market conditions in the various fields. Another impact of labor market supply and demand factors can be seen in the wages paid by companies in different geographic locations. In one survey, 97 percent of Fortune 500 companies reported using some kind of geographic adjustment. For example, an employee earning an annual salary of $41,700 could expect to receive the following salary by geographic area, adjusted to 1987 dollars:[68]

Anchorage	$53,664	Memphis	$36,180
Glendale, CA	49,589	Richmond, VA	37,971
Los Angeles	47,861	Boston	40,236
New York	47,094	Indianapolis	41,223
Detroit	49,109	Houston	46,418

Supply and demand are critical considerations, for at a salary of $41,700, Boston's cost of living is $52,270 while Houston's is $39,518, just the opposite of what might be expected. A final factor that can affect the supply of labor and hence tighten the market is the relative *hazard* level of the work. Consider the following example.

COMPANY EXAMPLE

"Jumpers" who make 12 hours' pay for 10 minutes' work

The catch—and there has to be one—is the job site. Every year the nuclear industry recruits hundreds of "jumpers" who fix the aging innards of the nation's nuclear generating stations. The atmosphere is so radioactive that jumpers can stay only about 10 minutes before, in industry parlance, they "burn out." As compensation for their 10 minutes' work, they receive 12 hours' pay. Typically, jumpers are people with few skills or job prospects elsewhere. They crawl into the power plants unsupported by any labor union, health insurance plan, or job security.[76] Repairs often have to do with corrosion or leakage of water pipes, a process that can be slowed but not stopped completely.

What are the risks? The Nuclear Regulatory Commission estimates that if each of 10,000 workers is exposed to 5000 millirems (roughly 250 chest x-rays) over the course of a year, three to eight of them will eventually die of cancer as a result of the exposure. If they are exposed to that level for 30 years, 5 percent of them will die of cancer.

The system pleases jumpers because it makes for lots of jobs. Said one, "Last year I think I got over 4000 millirems. I like to work till I get my limit. If you don't reach your limit, you're wasting your time" (ref. 76, p. 19).

Jumpers have a particular incentive to absorb the maximum radiation permitted on a given job. They get a bonus of several hundred dollars each time they "burn out" on an assignment. Between jobs they complete a battery of medical records, security checks, and psychological evaluations. "They don't want someone nutty in the reactor, messing things up," said one jumper. "You have to be a little weird to do this job. You just can't be *too* weird" (ref. 76, p. 19).

Highly hazardous work pays well; but then again it has to, in order to attract workers who are willing to take the risks. The forces discussed thus far affect pay levels to a considerable extent. So also does government legislation.

Legislation

As in other areas, legislation related to pay plays a vital role in determining internal organization practices. Although all the relevant laws cannot be analyzed here, a summary of the coverage, major provisions, and federal agencies charged with administering four major federal wage-hour laws is presented in Table 11-3, and a summary of four major income-maintenance laws is presented in Table 11-4. Wage-hour laws set limits on minimum wages to be paid and maximum hours to be worked. Income-maintenance laws were enacted to provide employees and their families with income security in case of death, disability, unemployment, or retirement.

TABLE 11-3 *Four major federal wage-hour laws*

	Scope of coverage	Major provisions	Administrative agency
Fair Labor Standards Act (FLSA) of 1938 (as amended)	Employers involved in interstate commerce with two or more employees and annual revenues greater than $362,500. Exemption from overtime provisions for managers, supervisors, executives, outside salespersons, and professional workers.	Minimum wage of $3.35 per hour for covered employees; time and one-half pay for over 40 hours per week; restrictions by occupation or industry on the employment of persons under 18; prohibits wage differentials based exclusively on sex—equal pay for equal work. No extra pay required for weekends, vacations, holidays, or severance.	Wage and Hour Division of the Employment Standards Administration, U.S. Department of Labor
Davis-Bacon Act (1931)	Federal conractors involved in the construction or repair of federal buildings and public works, with a contract value over $2000.	Employees on the project must be paid prevailing community wage rates for the type of employment used. Overtime at time and one-half for more than 40 hours per week. Three-year blacklisting of contractors who violate this act.	Comptroller General and Wage and Hour Division
Walsh-Healy Act (1936)	Federal contractors manufacturing or supplying materials, articles, or equipment to the federal government, with a value exceeding $10,000 annually.	Same as Davis-Bacon. Under the Defense Authorization Act of 1986, overtime is required only for hours worked in excess of 40 per week, not 8 per day, as previously.[26]	Same as FLSA
McNamara-O'Hara Service Contract Act (1965)	Federal contractors who provide services to the federal government with a value in excess of $2500.	Same as Davis-Bacon.	Same as Davis-Bacon

Of the four laws shown in Table 11-3, the Fair Labor Standards Act affects almost every organization in America. It is the source of the terms "exempt employees" (exempt from the overtime provisions of the law) and "nonexempt employees." It established the first national minimum wage (25 cents an hour) in 1938; subsequent changes in the minimum wage and in national policy on equal pay for equal work for both sexes (the Equal Pay Act of 1963) were passed as amendments to this law.

The remaining three laws shown in Table 11-3 apply only to organizations that do business with the federal government in the form of construction or by supplying goods and services. More will be said later in this chapter (in the section "Components of the Benefits Package") about each of the four income-maintenance laws shown in Table 11-4.

Collective bargaining

Another major influence on wages in unionized *as well as* nonunionized firms is collective bargaining. Nonunionized firms are affected by collective bargaining agreements made elsewhere since they must compete with unionized firms for the services and loyalties of workers. Collective bargaining affects two key factors: (1) the *level* of wages and (2) the *behavior of workers* in relevant labor markets. In an open, competitive market, workers tend to gravitate toward higher-paying jobs. To the extent that nonunionized firms fail to match the wages of unionized firms, they may have difficulty attracting and keeping workers. Furthermore, benefits negotiated under union agreements have had the effect of increasing the "package" of benefits in firms that have attempted to avoid unionization. In addition to wages and benefits, collective bargaining is also used to negotiate procedures for administering pay, procedures for resolving grievances regarding compensation decisions, and methods used to determine the relative worth of jobs.[45]

Managerial attitudes and an organization's ability to pay

These factors have a major impact on wage structures and levels. It was noted earlier how the labor costs of U.S. steelworkers had to be reduced in order to compete in global markets. This is an important principle. Regardless of an organization's espoused competitive position on wages, its ability to pay will ultimately be a key factor that limits actual wages.

This is not to downplay the role of management philosophy and attitudes on pay. On the contrary, management's desire to maintain or to improve morale, to attract high-caliber employees, to reduce turnover, and to improve employees' standards of living also affect wages, as does the relative importance of a given position to a firm.[54] A safety engineer is more important to a chemical company than to a bank. Wage structures tend to vary across firms to the extent that managers view any given position as more or less critical to their firms. Despite the appearance of scientific precision, compensation administration will always reflect management judgment to a considerable degree. Ultimately top management renders judgments regarding the overall competitive pay position of the firm (above-market, at-the-market, or below-market rates), factors to be considered in determining job worth, and the relative weight to be given seniority and performance in pay decisions. They are key determinants of the structure and level of wages.

TABLE 11-4 *Four major income-maintenance laws*

Law	Scope of coverage	Funding	Benefits	Administrative agency
Social Security Act (1935)	Full coverage for retirees, dependent survivors, and disabled persons insured by 40 quarters of payroll taxes on their past earnings or earnings of heads of households. Federal government employees hired prior to January 1, 1984, and railroad workers are excluded.	For 1988, payroll tax of 7.15% for employees and 7.15% for employers on the first $45,000 in earnings. Self-employed persons pay 12.3% of this wage base. Both the percentage rate and the maximum earnings base are scheduled to rise through 1990.	*Full retirement payments* after age 65, or at reduced rates after 62, to worker and spouse. Size of pension depends on past earnings. *Survivor benefits* for the family of a deceased worker or retiree. At age 65 a widow or widower receives the full age-65 pension granted to the deceased. A widow or widower of any age with dependent children under 16, and each unmarried child under 18, receives a 75% benefit check. *Disability benefits* to totally disabled workers, after a 5-month waiting period, as well as to their spouses and children. *Health insurance* for persons over 65 (Medicare). All benefits are adjusted upward whenever the consumer price index (CPI) increases more than 3% in a calendar year and trust funds are at a specified level.	Social Security Administration

Federal Unemployment Tax Act (1935)	All employees except some state and local government workers, domestic and farm workers, railroad workers, and some nonprofit employees.	Payroll tax of at least 3.4% of first $7000 of earnings paid by employer. (Employees also taxed in Alaska, Alabama, and New Jersey.) States may raise both the percentage and base earnings taxed through legislation. Employer contributions may be reduced if state experience ratings for them are low.	Otherwise, the adjustment is based on the lower of the CPI increase or the increase in average national wages (1983 amendments). Benefits average roughly 50% of average weekly earnings and are available for up to 26 weeks. Those eligible for benefits have been employed for some specified minimum period and have lost their jobs through no fault of their own. Most states exclude strikers. During periods of high unemployment, benefits may be extended for up to 52 weeks.	U.S. Bureau of Employment Security, U.S. Training and Employment Service, and the several state employment security commissions
Workers' compensation (state laws)	Generally, employees of nonagricultural, private-sector firms are entitled to benefits for work-related accidents and illnesses leading to temporary or permanent disabilities.	One of the following options, depending on state law: self-insurance, insurance through a private carrier, or payroll-based payments to a state insurance system. Premiums depend on the riskiness of the occupation and the experience rating of the insured.	Benefits average about two-thirds of an employee's weekly wage and continue for the term of the disability. Supplemental payments are made for medical care and rehabilitative services. In case of a fatal accident, survivor benefits are payable.	Various state commissions

(continued)

TABLE 11-4 (*Continued*)

Law	Scope of coverage	Funding	Benefits	Administrative agency
Employee Retirement Income Security Act (ERISA) (1974)	Private-sector employees over age 21 enrolled in noncontributory (i.e. 100% employer-paid) retirement plans who have 1 year's service.	Employer contributions.	The 1986 Tax Reform Act authorizes several formulas to provide vesting of retirement benefits after a certain length of service (5–7 years). Once an employee is "vested," receipt of the pension is not contingent on future service. Authorizes tax-free transfer of vested benefits to another employer or to an individual retirement account ("portability") if a vested employee changes jobs and if the present employer agrees. Employers must fund plans on an actuarially sound basis. Pension trustees ("fiduciaries") must make prudent investments. Employers may insure vested benefits through the federal Pension Benefit Guaranty Corporation.	Department of Labor, Internal Revenue Service, Pension Benefit Guaranty Corporation

An Overview of Pay System Mechanics

The procedures described below for developing pay systems help those involved in the development process to apply their judgments in a systematic manner. Hallmarks of success in compensation management, as in other areas, are understandability, workability, and acceptability. Our broad objective in developing pay systems is to assign a monetary value to each job in the organization (a base rate) and an orderly procedure for increasing the base rate (e.g., based on merit, seniority, or some combination of the two). To develop such a system, we need four basic tools:

1. Job analyses and job descriptions
2. A job evaluation plan
3. Pay surveys
4. A pay structure

Job analyses and descriptions were considered in Chapter 4. In the context of pay system design, they serve two purposes:

1. They identify important characteristics of each job so that the relative worth of jobs can be determined.
2. From them we can identify, define, and weight *compensable factors* (common characteristics of all jobs that an organization is willing to pay for, such as skill, effort, responsibility, and working conditions). Once job analyses and descriptions have been developed, the next step is to evaluate the jobs.

A number of job evaluation methods have been developed since the 1920s, and many, if not most, of them are still used. They all have the same final objective, and they all yield similar results.[18] The objective of all the methods is to rank jobs in terms of relative worth to the organization so that an equitable rate of pay can be determined for each job. A brief description of some common approaches to job evaluation, along with their relative advantages and disadvantages, is presented in Tables 11-5a and 11-5b.

Although firms such as General Foods, General Motors, Procter and Gamble, and Anheuser-Busch have been experimenting with knowledge-based pay,[70] the point-factor method remains the most popular approach. As an illustration (see page 398), let's consider a point-factor method developed and used by Hay and Associates.

TABLE 11-5a *Quantitative job evaluation methods*

Approach	Methodology	Advantages	Disadvantages
Point factor	Select compensable factors. Define the degrees within each factor on a numerical scale. Weight the compensable factors. Analyze and describe the jobs in terms of the compensable factors. Determine which degree definition for each factor best fits the job. Assign points for each factor based on the evaluation. Arrange a job-worth hierarchy based on the total points for each job.	Reliable Relatively objective Easy to evaluate new or revised jobs	Expensive to develop or purchase Difficult to control evaluator bias[3, 46]
Factor comparison	Select compensable factors. Analyze and describe the jobs in terms of the compensable factors. Vertically rank the jobs on each factor. Weight each factor in terms of its relative importance to the organization. Calculate the total points for each job. Develop a job-worth hierarchy based on total points.	Relatively reliable Scales are easy to use Compensable factors tailored to organization Easy to communicate	No degree definitions Difficult to evaluate new or revised jobs
Job component	In the job component approach, one or more independent variables are related to a "dependent" variable in a statistical equation. Choose a dependent variable and independent variables that are considered important in predicting and explaining pay relationships. Enter the data using a statistical software package. The resulting statistical model can be used for auditing current systems or for assigning pay rates in a new system.	Objective Comprehensive Statistically accurate Management-oriented	Expensive to develop or purchase Time-consuming Complex Difficult to communicate to employees

TABLE 11-5b *Nonquantitative, "whole-job" job content methods*

Approach	Methodology	Advantages	Disadvantages
Ranking	Identify the most "important" job in the job set. Identify the next most important job. Continue this process until all jobs are arranged in a hierarchy.	Simple to administer Inexpensive Quickly implemented Little training required	No specific standards No detail or documentation May be superficial Incumbent may unduly influence evaluation
Classification	Create job grades with generic definitions at each grade level. Compare the job descriptions with the grade descriptions. Assign each job to the grade most closely matching the level of work performed.	Simple to administer Inexpensive Quickly implemented Little training required	Jobs may be forced into classes they do not fit Descriptions can be rigged to fit a class
Slotting	Use the existing hierarchy. Compare the new or revised job with the jobs already assigned to existing job grades. Assign the job to the grade containing other jobs that appear similar in overall worth.	Simple to administer Inexpensive Quickly implemented Little training required	Cannot be used as stand-alone method because it is based on a preexisting structure No specific standards

Nonquantitative, whole-job evaluation methods require *each evaluator individually* (1) to determine which compensable factors he or she will use to compare the jobs, (2) to "weight" the compensable factors, and (3) to define and apply factors to jobs. These may produce inconsistent ratings across evaluators.

ILLUSTRATION

A Brief Look at the Hay Job Evaluation System

At the outset it is important to note two principles: (1) A job evaluation study often becomes an exercise in semantics—trying to express in words perceptible differences in jobs; and (2) jobs have to be explained in response to probing questions about what they require. Usually both tasks are accomplished by a committee comprised of employees who are familiar with company jobs, with guidance from an outside consultant.

The process of job evaluation is an enormously time-consuming, complex, and often frustrating task that is subject to all the political pressures and biases so "natural" among committee members who represent different functional areas. To establish the relationship among jobs in terms of relative worth to the firm, the job evaluation committee uses a systematic procedure that compares one job with another.

Experience has shown that this is easier to do if the committee compares *aspects* of jobs (that is, compensable factors) that are common to all jobs, to various degrees, rather than *whole* jobs. In the Hay system, three compensable factors are analyzed. They are *know-how, problem solving*, and *accountability*. Each is defined on a guide chart. An example of the Hay guide chart for the know-how factor is shown in Figure 11-1.

Each guide chart is composed of a point scale, similar to the one shown in Figure 11-1, in which adjacent terms differ by approximately 15 percent. The guide charts themselves reveal what is meant by "know-how," "problem solving," and "accountability." Each of these compensable factors is broken down in terms of more specific "building blocks." For example, know-how (see Figure 11-1) has three components:

1. Scientific disciplines, specialized techniques, and practical procedures
2. Managerial know-how
3. Human relations skills

Within component 1, A, B, C, and D are the degrees of trained skills where know-how is characterized by education plus work experience. The specialized technical and professional skills built on subjects not included in a secondary education are represented by E, F, G, and H.

Management know-how (component 2) deals exclusively with the management process independent of scientific disciplines (component 1) and human relations skills (component 3). The intersection of ratings on components 1, 2, and 3 falls into one of three "slots." Jobs in slot I primarily consist of specialized "on-the-spot" execution; coordination of people or activities is minimal. Jobs in slot II involve coordination and integration of activities (as distinct from merely supervising them). Jobs in slot III emphasize total departmental operations or administration of a strategic corporate function (e.g., the job "director of computer operations").

Human relations (component 3) has three degrees:

1. *Basic*. Ordinary courtesy is sufficient.
2. *Important*. Handling people in situations where repercussions are anticipated but are not critical considerations in the overall content of the position.
3. *Critical*. Motivating others to do something is a critical requirement of the job, and the job cannot be done without such emphasis on human relations skills.

Working with job analyses and the three guide charts, the task of the evaluation committee is to develop a point "profile" of each job on each compensable factor. The total number of points for each job is determined by adding the points assigned to each of the three factors. Note that points are assigned to jobs *independently* of market wage rates.

To provide a structure for evaluating all the jobs in an organization, the committee begins with a group of jobs called "benchmarks." Benchmark jobs:

■ Are well established, with clear job contents
■ Represent each functional area and vary from low to high job content
■ Represent a large number of in-house jobs

Job evaluation committee members make their judgments independently, through secret voting. Differences among members are resolved subsequently in an open discussion. Each member's task is to arrive at a point total for each job on each factor. In the case of know-how, for example, the total is found in the slot that represents the intersection of ratings on components 1, 2, and 3. As an illustration, let's consider the job of "administrative clerk." Here is what compensation specialists call a "thumbnail sketch" of the job:

Performs a variety of clerical tasks such as payroll, accounts receivable, accounts payable, or other specialized clerical work requiring knowledge of policies and procedures and a moderate degree of independent judgment.

In terms of Figure 11-1, the job evaluation committee might decide that the job of administrative clerk rates a C-I-1 on the compensable factor know-how. That is, the level of scientific disciplines is a C (vocational), the level of managerial know-how is a I, and the level of human relations skill involved also merits a 1. Note that within each cell there are three different point totals to choose from. This is done to allow the committee some flexibility in arriving at a point total. In the C-I-1 cell, let's assume that the committee assigned a total of 87 points to know-how.

As judgments accumulate within a slot, the slot assumes a pattern into which new jobs can reliably be fit. The pattern itself is established through the consensus of the committee members. Once set, it should not be tampered with as long as the jobs themselves do not change.

The next step is to translate point totals into a pay structure. Current

KNOW-HOW

© HAY ASSOCIATES 1984

DEFINITION: Know-How is the sum total of every kind of skill, however acquired, needed for acceptable job performance. Know-How has three dimensions — the requirements for:

- Practical procedures, specialized techniques, and scientific disciplines.
- • Know-How of integrating and harmonizing the diversified functions involved in managerial situations occurring in operating, supporting, and administrative fields. This Know-How may be exercised consultatively (about management) as well as executively, and involves in some combination the areas of organizing, planning, executing, controlling and evaluating.
- • • Active, practicing, person-to-person skills in the area of human relationships.

MEASURING KNOW - HOW: Know-How has both scope (variety) and depth (thoroughness). Thus, a job may require some knowledge about a lot of things, or a lot of knowledge about a few things. The total Know-How is the combination of scope and depth. This concept makes practical the comparison and weighing of the total Know-How content of different jobs in terms of: "HOW MUCH KNOWLEDGE ABOUT HOW MANY THINGS."

• • • HUMAN RELATIONS SKILLS

1. **BASIC:** Ordinary courtesy and effectiveness in dealing with others through normal contacts, and request for or providing information.

2. **IMPORTANT:** Understanding, influencing and/or serving people are important considerations in performing the job, causing action or understanding in others.

3. **CRITICAL:** Alternative or combined skills in understanding, selecting, developing and motivating people are important in the highest degree.

• • • Human Relations Skills ➝

PRACTICAL PROCEDURES

A. BASIC

Basic work routines plus work indoctrination.

B. ELEMENTARY VOCATIONAL

Familiarization in uninvolved, standardized work routines and/or use of simple equipment and machines.

C. VOCATIONAL

Procedural or systematic proficiency, which may involve a facility in the use of specialized equipment.

SPECIALIZED TECHNIQUES

D. ADVANCED VOCATIONAL

Some specialized (generally nontechnical) skill(s), however acquired, giving additional breadth or depth to a generally single functional element.

E. BASIC TECHNICAL - SPECIALIZED

Sufficiency in a technique which requires a grasp either of involved practices and precedents; or of scientific theory and principles; or both.

F. SEASONED TECHNICAL - SPECIALIZED

Proficiency, gained through wide exposure or experiences in a specialized or technical field, in a technique which combines a broad grasp either of involved practices and precedents or of scientific theory and principles; or both.

G. TECHNICAL - SPECIALIZED MASTERY

Determinative mastery of techniques, practices and theories gained through wide seasoning and/or special development.

SCIENTIFIC DISCIPLINES

H. PROFESSIONAL MASTERY

Exceptional and unique mastery in scientific or other learned disciplines.

FIGURE 11-1

Illustrative industrial Hay guide chart for the compensable factor "Know-How."

wages (so-called going rates) in the industry and within the relevant labor market are surveyed, and then a chart, as in Figure 11-2, is prepared, relating current wage rates to the total points assigned each job. For each point total, a trend line is fitted to indicate the *average* relationship between points assigned to the benchmark jobs and the hourly wages paid for those jobs.

●● BREADTH OF MANAGEMENT KNOW-HOW

I. NONE OR MINIMAL		II. RELATED			III. DIVERSE			IV. BROAD			V. TOTAL			
●rformance or supervision an activity (or activities) ▯hly specific as to objec▯ e and content, with ap▯ ▯priate awareness of re▯ ▯ed activities.		Operational or conceptual integration or coordination of activities which are relatively homogeneous in nature and objective.			Operational or conceptual integration or coordination of activities which are diverse in nature and objectives, in an important management area.			Integration of major functions in an operating complex, or Company-wide coordination of a strategic function which significantly affects corporate planning or operations.						
2	3	1	2	3	1	2	3	1	2	3	1	2	3	
57	66	66	76	87	87	100	115	115	132	152	152	175	200	
66	76	76	87	100	100	115	132	132	152	175	175	200	230	A
76	87	87	100	115	115	132	152	152	175	200	200	230	264	
76	87	87	100	115	115	132	152	152	175	200	200	230	264	
87	100	100	115	132	132	152	175	175	200	230	230	264	304	B
100	115	115	132	152	152	175	200	200	230	264	264	304	350	
100	115	115	132	152	152	175	200	200	230	264	264	304	350	
115	132	132	152	175	175	200	230	230	264	304	304	350	400	C
132	152	152	175	200	200	230	264	264	304	350	350	400	460	
132	152	152	175	200	200	230	264	264	304	350	350	400	460	
152	175	175	200	230	230	264	304	304	350	400	400	460	528	D
175	200	200	230	264	264	304	350	350	400	460	460	528	608	
175	200	200	230	264	264	304	350	350	400	460	460	528	608	
200	230	230	264	304	304	350	400	400	460	528	528	608	700	E
230	264	264	304	350	350	400	460	460	528	608	608	700	800	
230	264	264	304	350	350	400	460	460	528	608	608	700	800	
264	304	304	350	400	400	460	528	528	608	700	700	800	920	F
304	350	350	400	460	460	528	608	608	700	800	800	920	1056	
304	350	350	400	460	460	528	608	608	700	800	800	920	1056	
350	400	400	460	528	528	608	700	700	800	920	920	1056	1216	G
400	460	460	528	608	608	700	800	800	920	1056	1056	1216	1400	
400	460	460	528	608	608	700	800	800	920	1056	1056	1216	1400	
460	528	528	608	700	700	800	920	920	1056	1216	1216	1400	1600	H
528	608	608	700	800	800	920	1056	1056	1216	1400	1400	1600	1840	

Once a midpoint trend line is fitted, two others are also drawn: (1) a trend line that represents the *minimum* rate of pay for each point total and (2) a trend line that represents the *maximum* rate of pay for each point total.[73]

The final step in attaching dollar values to jobs using the point method is to establish *pay grades*, or ranges, characterized by a point spread from minimum to maximum for each grade. Starting wages are given by the trend

FIGURE 11-2

Chart relating hourly wage rates to the total points assigned to each job. Three trend lines are shown: minimum, midpoint, and maximum, as well as 11 pay grades. Within each pay grade there is a 30 percent spread from minimum to maximum and a 50 percent overlap from one pay grade to the next.

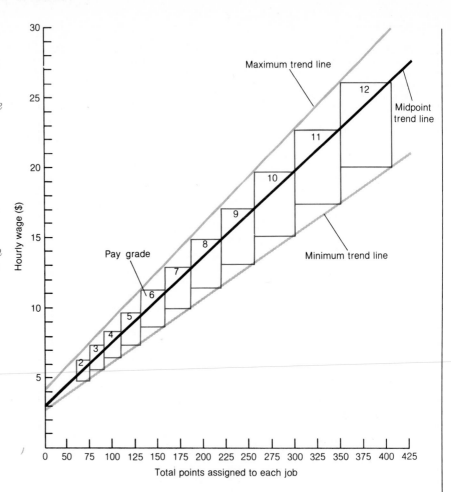

TABLE 11-6 *Illustrative pay structure showing pay grades, the spread of points within grades, the midpoint of each pay grade, and the minimum and maximum rates of pay per grade*

Grade	Point spread	Midpoint	Minimum rate of pay	Maximum rate of pay
2	62–75	68	$ 5.00	$ 6.50
3	76–91	83	5.75	7.47
4	92–110	101	6.61	8.60
5	111–132	121	7.60	9.89
6	133–157	145	8.75	11.37
7	158–186	172	10.06	13.07
8	187–219	203	11.57	15.03
9	220–257	238	13.30	17.29
10	258–300	279	15.30	19.88
11	301–350	325	17.59	22.87
12	351–407	379	20.23	26.30

ORG. UNIT _____

MGR. OR SUPV. _____

ANNUAL COMPENSATION PLANNING WORKSHEET

EMPLOYEE NAME	JOB TITLE	LAST SALARY ADJUSTMENT				CURRENT SALARY	RANGE MINIMUM	RANGE MIDPOINT	RANGE MAXIMUM	PERFORMANCE APPRAISAL	FORECAST SALARY ADJUSTMENT (If Any)				
		Amt.	%	Date	Type*						Amt.	%	Date	New Salary	Inter-val

*Code for "Type"
1—Promotion
2—Merit

PREPARED BY _____

FIGURE 11-3 *Annual compensation planning worksheet.*

line that represents the *minimum* rate of pay for each pay grade, while the highest wages that can be earned within a grade are given by the trend line that represents the *maximum* rate of pay. The pay structure is described numerically in Table 11-6.

For purposes of our "administrative clerk" example, let's assume that the job evaluation committee arrived at a total allocation of 142 points across all three compensable factors. The job therefore falls into pay grade 6. Starting pay is $8.75 per hour, with a maximum pay rate of $11.37 per hour.

The actual development of a pay structure is a complex process, but there are certain rules of thumb to follow:

- Jobs of the same general value should be clustered into the same pay grade.
- Jobs that clearly differ in value should be in different pay grades.
- There should be a smooth progression of point groupings.
- The new system should fit realistically into the existing allocation of pay within a company.

- The pay grades should conform reasonably well to pay patterns in the relevant labor markets.[60]

Once such a pay structure is in place, the determination of each individual's pay becomes a more systematic and orderly procedure. A compensation planning worksheet, such as that shown in Figure 11-3, can be very useful to managers confronted with these weighty decisions.

The pay structure described above relates only to *direct* cash payments. However, the total compensation package includes *indirect* payments as well. This is the important area of employee benefits and services, and we will consider it further in the sections that follow.

Employee Benefits and Services

Benefits currently account for over 39 percent of the total compensation costs for each employee. Yesterday's "fringes" have become today's (expected) benefits and services. Here are some reasons why benefits have grown:[22, 73]

- The imposition of wage ceilings during World War II forced organizations to offer more benefits in place of wage increases to attract, retain, and motivate employees.
- The interest by unions in bargaining over benefits has grown, particularly since wages have risen to the point where they now satisfy basic employee needs. Once granted, benefits are unlikely to be withdrawn.
- Internal Revenue Service Code treatment of benefits makes them preferable to wages. Even after the Tax Reform Act of 1986, many benefits remain nontaxable to the employee and are deductible by the employer. With other benefits, taxes are deferred. Hence employees' disposable income increases since they are receiving benefits and services that otherwise they would have to purchase with after-tax dollars.
- Granting benefits (in a nonunionized firm) or bargaining over them (in a unionized firm) confers an aura of social responsibility on employers; they are "taking care" of their employees.

Components of the Benefits Package

There are many ways to classify benefits, but we will follow the classification scheme used by the U.S. Chamber of Commerce. According to this system, benefits fall into three categories: security and health, payments for time not worked, and employee services. Within each of these categories there is a bewildering array of options. The following discussions consider only the most popular options and cover only those which have not been mentioned previously.

TABLE 11-7 *Employer benefit payments as a percentage of payroll*

Type of program	1955	1965	1975	1986
Legally required payments	3.6	4.9	8.0	11.1
Welfare and retirement plans	8.2	9.6	13.7	15.3
Paid time off	8.5	10.2	13.7	12.9
Total	20.3	24.7	35.4	39.3

Source: *Employee Benefits, 1986,* Washington, DC: U.S. Chamber of Commerce, 1987.

Table 11-7 illustrates changes in the costs of employer payments for benefits as a percentage of payroll from 1955 to 1986. As the saying goes, "You've come a long way, baby."

Security and health benefits

The following are included in the security and health category:

Life insurance

Workers' compensation

Accidental death and dismemberment coverage

Hospitalization, surgical, and maternity coverage

Health maintenance organizations (HMOs)

Other medical coverage

Sick leave

Pension plans

Social Security

Unemployment insurance

Supplemental unemployment insurance

Severance pay

Insurance is the basic building block of almost all benefits packages, for it protects employees against income loss caused by death, accident, or ill health. Most organizations provide *group* coverage for their employees. The plans may be contributory (in which employees share in the cost of the premiums) or noncontributory.

It used to be that when a worker switched jobs, he or she lost health insurance coverage. The worker had to "go naked" for months until coverage began at a new employer. No longer. Under the Consolidated Omnibus Budget Reconciliation Act (COBRA) of 1986, companies with at least 20 employees must make medical coverage available at group insurance rates for as long as 18 months after the employee leaves—whether the worker left voluntarily, retired, or was dismissed. The law also provides that, following a worker's death or divorce, the employee's family has the right to buy group-rate health insurance for as long as 3 years. Employers who do not comply can be sued and denied corporate tax deductions related to health benefits.[50] With this in mind, let us consider the major forms of security and health benefits commonly provided to employees.

Group life insurance   This type of insurance is usually yearly renewable term insurance; that is, each employee is insured 1 year at a time. Actual amounts of coverage vary, but one rule of thumb is to have it equal roughly 2 years' income. This amount provides a reasonable financial cushion to the surviving spouse during the difficult transition to a different way of life. Thus a manager making $40,000 per year may have a group term-life policy with a face value of $80,000 or $100,000.

Workers' compensation   These payments vary by state, as pointed out in Table 11-4. Disability benefits, which have been extended to cover stress and occupational disease, tend to be highest in states where organized labor is strong.[37] A state's industrial structure also plays a big part in setting disability insurance rates. Thus serious injuries are more common and costly among Oregon loggers and Michigan machinists than among assembly line workers in a Texas semiconductor plant. Sometimes the costs can get out of hand. In Maine, for example (which changed its disability law in 1983), employment in the Bass shoe division of Chesebrough-Pond's Inc. rose 40 percent from 1978 to 1983. However, during the same period workers' compensation premiums went from $150,000 to $3.6 million, a 2300 percent increase.[9] Trends such as these have prompted high-cost states, such as Minnesota, Florida, Michigan, and Maine, to lower workers' compensation premiums so that they can continue to attract and retain businesses in their states.

Accidental death and dismemberment coverage   Such coverage provides a supplemental one-time payment when death is accidental, and it provides a range of benefits for accidental loss of limbs or sight. Long-term disability (LTD) plans cover employees who are disabled 6 months or longer, usually at 50 to 75 percent of their base pay, until they begin receiving pension benefits. Fewer than 50 percent of medium and large businesses provide such coverage, but as one expert noted: "long-term disability is more important than life insurance. The person is still alive and may have no income at all without such coverage."[61]

LTD costs are extremely high. Based on seven case studies, *direct* nonmedical disability costs (hidden plus visible costs), given as a percentage of annual salary, for an executive earning $40,000 per year were as follows:[12]

Hidden direct costs	
Predisability productivity loss (prior 5 years)	28%
Postdisability productivity loss (until a replacement becomes fully productive)	39
Replacement cost	30
Retraining cost	32

Visible direct costs

Salary continuance until disability pay	48
Disability payments (percent of salary to age 65)	62
Increased pension payments	15
Increased life insurance	11

An executive earning $40,000 per year at age 40 who did not previously qualify for pension benefits will cost her or his employer, on average, over $848,000, excluding medical costs until retirement age. If payment is not required as a lump sum, the net present value of the payments reduces the liability to $511,000.[12] This expenditure is still very large for *one*, possibly preventable, medical event.

Hospitalization, surgical, and maternity coverage   These are essential benefits for most working Americans. Self-insurance is out of the question since the costs incurred by one serious, prolonged illness could easily wipe out a lifetime of savings and assets and place a family in debt for years to come. Major medical coverage (economic insulation against catastrophic illness) has grown in popularity, partly in response to runaway medical costs. In 1987, for example, 11.3 percent of the U.S. gross national product (the total value of retail prices of all goods and services produced in 1987) was spent on medical care, compared with only 5.4 percent in 1960.[23] That is over $1500 for every man, woman, and child in America! At the level of the individual company, General Motors estimates that its health-care bill adds about $370 to the cost of producing a car.[68] Why?

The major reason is that *the health-care industry has little incentive to hold costs down.* Most company-sponsored group insurance plans provide almost open-ended coverage. Doctors can provide the most advanced and expensive tests and treatment programs available. Afterward, the patient can count on receiving automatic reimbursement of up to 75 percent or more of the charges. All the incentives are to provide very high-quality service at a very high cost. Considering the amounts they spend, corporations are amazingly ignorant on the matter. Said one General Electric executive, "We know more about what goes into the cost of a 75-cent box of screws we use on the factory floor than we know about what goes into the cost of health care."[56]

As a result of widespread publicity of this problem, "cost containment" has become a watchword in the boardroom as well as in the health-care industry itself. Here are some measures that firms have taken to gain tighter management control over the cost of health care:

1. Raise deductibles and copayments by employees. Such steps are a belated adjustment for inflation. Plans with $50 deductibles were established in the 1950s, when that sum paid for 2 days in the hospital; now it does not cover room-and-board costs for a single day's stay. Furthermore, copayments by employees may encourage more responsible use of the health-care system. Employees are clearly bearing more of the economic load. A 1987 survey showed that only 38 percent of firms pay all hospital room-and-board charges incurred by employees or their dependents. Back in 1981, 84 percent of the same plans picked up the tab in full.[34]

2. Induce employees voluntarily to choose reduced medical coverage through flexible benefit plans (more on this shortly).

3. Remove the irrational incentives in plans that favor hospitalization over less costly outpatient care. For example, Sperry Corp. pays 100 percent for home health care but less if an employee checks into a hospital.[28]

4. Require a second surgical opinion prior to elective surgery. At Chrysler and at J. C. Penney, for example, if the employee fails to get a second opinion, the company will not pay the entire bill. One study of such programs estimates they could save $2.63 for every dollar spent on second opinions.

5. If employees must go to the hospital, set some rules. Refuse to let them enter on the weekend if treatment is not scheduled until Monday. Have large hospital bills audited (this could cut expenses by as much as 8 percent). Require preadmission certification, that is, doctor's clearance for the treatment desired for the employee before he or she enters the hospital. If additional treatment or tests are given, companies refuse to pay bills unless doctors can confirm that a deviation from the original plan was necessary.[56]

The federal government has begun to shift some costs to the private sector. Currently the federal government pays almost 50 percent of the nation's health-care bill, and 75 percent of hospital patients do not pay full price for their hospitalization (Medicare, Medicaid, and Blue Cross pay considerably less than the going rates).[21] The 25 percent who do pay full price not only pay their own charges but also pay inflated charges to make up for those who do not pay the normal rates. This is known as cost shifting. Because of Medicare's diagnosis-related grouping (DRG), which caps payments in 467 diagnostic categories, the dollar value of cost shifting is staggering: $8 billion in 1983, and $16 billion in 1985.

DRG-based reimbursement standardizes diagnoses and treatments. An average cost for each category is determined, and the hospital is reimbursed at this rate regardless of the number of days a patient stays or the number of tests that are done. Although this system applies only to Medicare patients, it will revolutionize the hospital industry. If history is any indication, hospitals will try to shift costs that are not met by Medicare to other customers. Those who do not have effective methods of managing medical costs (this includes most businesses) will have no other choice than to pick up the tab.[21]

HMOs A final proposed cost containment approach is the health maintenance organization (HMO). An *HMO* is an organized system of health care that assures the delivery of services to employees who enroll voluntarily under a prepayment plan. The emphasis is on preventive medicine, that is, maintaining the health of each employee. Legally, HMOs are authorized under the HMO Act of 1973 (as amended in 1976 and 1978). Major features of the law are: (1) invalidation of state laws prohibiting HMOs, (2) a program of federal loans and grants for HMO development, (3) management and service criteria that an HMO must meet for federal qualification, and (4) the "dual choice" provision, whereby employers which have 25 or more employees and which are covered by minimum-wage requirements must offer the HMO option if the area has a federally qualified HMO.[21]

The objective of HMOs is to control health-care costs by keeping people *out* of the hospital. Deere & Co., the agricultural equipment manufacturer, used to pay for a staggering 1400 hospital days each year for every 1000 workers. Then in 1980 Deere took the lead in helping local doctors to establish an HMO, and annual hospitalization has since dropped to 500 days per thousand workers. Yet there are drawbacks. Plan members give up the freedom to choose their doctors, and for companies with scattered employment sites, the location of the HMO may be inconvenient. As of 1987, there were 626 HMOs nationwide, enrolling almost 26 million people. Just over half of the HMOs were federally qualified.[43]

To overcome some employees' complaints about the lack of freedom to choose their doctors in an HMO, some firms have contracted with organizations of health-care professionals (including physicians, dentists, and hospitals), so-called preferred provider organizations (PPOs), to deliver health-care services at reduced rates and with close utilization review. As many as 300 PPOs now exist, with heavy concentrations in Florida and Washington, DC.[17, 21]

Other medical coverage Medical coverage for areas such as dental care, vision care, drug abuse, alcoholism, and mental illness is growing rapidly. In 1986, for example, the Bureau of Labor Statistics found these percentages of medium and large firms offering benefits: 40 percent offered vision care, 71 percent offered dental care, and 99 percent offered mental health care.[72]

Sick-leave programs These programs provide short-term insurance to workers against loss of wages due to short-term illness. However, in many firms such well-intended programs have often *added* to labor costs because of abuse by employees and because of the widespread perception that sick leave is a right and that if it is not used, it will be lost ("use it or lose it"). To overcome the negative effects of sick-pay programs, one firm instituted a "well-pay program" that rewards employees for *not* being absent or sick.[20] Over a 1-year period, the firm barely broke even after paying out well-pay bonuses.

Pensions A *pension* is a sum of money paid at regular intervals to an employee (or to his or her dependents) who has retired from a company and is eligible to receive such benefits. Before World War II, private pensions were rare. However, two developments in the late 1940s stimulated their growth: (1) clarification of the tax treatment of employer contributions and (2) the 1948 Inland Steel case, in which the National Labor Relations Board ruled that pensions were subject to compulsory collective bargaining.[75]

There were no standards and little regulation, which led to abuses in funding many pension plans and to the denial of pension benefits to employees who had worked many years. Perhaps the most notorious example of this occurred in 1963 when Studebaker closed its South Bend, Indiana, car factory and stopped payments to the seriously underfunded plan that covered the workers. Only those already retired or on the verge of retirement received the pension benefits they expected. Others got only a fraction—or nothing.[10]

Incidents like these led to the passage of the Employee Retirement Income Security Act (ERISA, see Table 11-4) in 1974. Despite increased regulation, ERISA has generally been beneficial. In 1970, 30 percent of couples aged 65 to 69 received a private pension. By 2004, 88 percent will.[75]

Money set aside by employers to cover pension obligations has become the nation's largest source of capital.[52] By 1987, the total was almost $2 trillion, more than double the total in 1980 and about 7 times the 1970 amount.[64] This is an enormous force in the nation's capital markets. At the end of 1983, for example, the $10.39 billion assets of the U.S. pension fund of IBM equaled 45 percent of total stockholders' equity.[62] And the 1984 divestiture of AT&T into eight operating companies posed an intriguing dilemma for its pension fund managers: how to divide $33 billion in stocks, $17 billion in bonds, and $4 billion in real estate eight ways!

In general, the financial health of most private pension plans is good. However, to ensure that covered workers will receive their accrued benefits even if their companies fail, ERISA created the Pension Benefit Guaranty Corporation (PBGC). This agency acts as an insurance company, collecting annual premiums from companies covered under ERISA. A company can still walk away from its obligation to pay pension benefits to employees entitled to receive them, but it must then hand over up to 30 percent of its net worth to the PBGC for distribution to the affected employees. The agency fully guarantees only benefit promises that have been in effect for at least 5 years, and the guarantee stops just short of $22,300 per year.

As of 1987, the PBGC has assumed the financial responsibility for 1345 pension plans. Since 1982, a fifth of the domestic steel industry has filed for bankruptcy-law protection, leaving the agency with a crushing $3.83 billion deficit (pension payments minus premiums collected), $2.32 billion of which belongs to LTV Steel. To shore up the PBGC, Congress tripled the employer insurance premium to $8.50 per worker in 1986.[6] While that step might seem extreme, consider that the PBGC insures the pensions of one out of every three U.S. workers. It is important that as retirees, most workers end up getting nearly all that is promised to them—and they do.

How pension plans work. Each year, pension funds are typically set aside and managed by trustees or outside financial institutions, frequently insurance companies. As an incentive for employers to begin and maintain such plans, the government defers taxes on the pension contributions and their earnings. Retirees pay taxes on the money as they receive it.

Traditionally, most big corporate plans have been *defined-benefit plans*— under which an employer promises to pay a retiree a stated pension, often expressed as a percentage of preretirement pay. The most common formula is 1.5 percent of average salary over the last 5 years prior to retirement ("final average pay") times the number of years employed. In determining final average pay, the company may use base pay alone or base pay plus bonuses and other compensation. Standard Oil of Ohio uses the former method, Standard Oil of California, the latter.[53] Examples of annual pensions as a function of years of service and final average pay are shown in Figure 11-4. When combined with Social Security benefits, that percentage is often about 50 percent of final average pay. The company then pays into the fund each year whatever is needed to cover expected benefit payments.

A second type of pension plan, now more popular than defined-benefit plans, is called a *defined-contribution plan*.[31] Examples include stock bonuses, savings plans, profit sharing, and various kinds of employee stock-ownership plans.[11, 24, 65] Defined-contribution plans fix a rate for employer *contributions* to the fund. Future *benefits* depend on how fast the fund grows. Such plans have great appeal for employers because the company will never owe more than what was contributed. However, since the amount of benefits received depends on the investment performance of the monies contributed, employees cannot be sure of the size of their retirement checks. In fact, regardless of whether a plan is a defined-benefit or defined-contribution plan, employees will

FIGURE 11-4

Relationship of annual retirement benefits to years of service and final average salary.

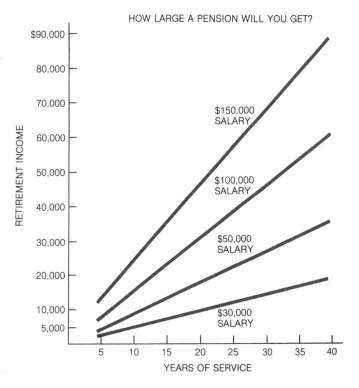

not know what the *purchasing power* of their pension checks will be, because the inflation rate is variable.

What appears to be evolving is a system that will make employees (instead of employers) more responsible for how much money they have for retirement. Individual Retirement Accounts (IRAs) are a good example of this. Created by the Economic Recovery Tax Act of 1981, IRAs allow individuals to contribute up to $2000 per year. The Tax Reform Act of 1986 eliminated the tax deduction for contributions to IRAs for those employees who (1) are active participants in a qualified retirement plan at work and (2) have an adjusted gross income of $50,000 or more on a joint return or $35,000 on a single return. However, the *interest* on all IRA contributions continues to compound tax-free until it is withdrawn.

The ideal pension plan is one that is adjusted (indexed) each year to maintain the purchasing power of the dollar according to changes in the cost of living. *ERISA does not require indexing.* Although Social Security benefits have been indexed to changes in the consumer price index since 1975, only about 5 percent of private pension plans have some form of indexation, and even that amount is limited. For example, Aetna and Grumman both use the consumer price index as a basis for adjusting pension payments, but they limit the maximum yearly increase to 3 percent. Pension managers strongly resist indexation for two reasons: (1) The amount of money paid out will increase for those already retired, and (2) larger reserves have to be set aside to fund future increases on a sound basis. Tying pensions to inflation could add 1 to 2 percent of payroll to an employer's retiree costs, atop the 4 to 7 percent of payroll that companies now set aside.[38]

Unisex pensions. Nathalie Norris, an employee of the state of Arizona, paid $199 per month into an annuity retirement plan offered by the state—the amount deducted from the paychecks of both male and female state employees earning the same salary. But Norris discovered that upon retirement she would get $34 per month *less* than male employees. This figure was based on actuarial tables showing that women, on average, live longer than men. Norris sued the state, and in a 1983 Supreme Court ruling, she won. The Court ruled that federal laws prohibiting sex discrimination in employment also bar employee-sponsored retirement plans that pay men higher benefits than women. Starting August 1, 1983, all contributions to such plans must be used to finance a system of *equal* payments to employees of both sexes. However, the Court denied retroactive relief to women, which could have cost insurance companies as much as $1.2 billion annually.[1] As a result of this ruling, many insurance companies have developed "merged-gender mortality tables" that show the combined number of persons living, the combined number of persons dying, and the merged-gender mortality rate for each age. The effect on benefits depends on the income option(s) elected at the time retirement income begins. For men aged 65, this could mean a monthly income decrease of up to 8 percent, while for women aged 65, it could mean a monthly income increase of up to 8 percent.[67]

Pension reforms that benefit women. These reforms were incorporated into the Retirement Equity Act of 1984. Corporate pension plans must now include younger workers and permit longer breaks in service. Women typically start work at younger ages than do men, and they are more likely to stop working for several years in order to have and care for children. However, since the new rules apply to both sexes, men also will accrue larger benefits. There are five major changes under the act:[51]

1. As of January 1, 1985, pension plans must include all employees 21 or older (down from 25). This will extend pension coverage to an additional 600,000 women and to 500,000 men.
2. Employers must use 18 rather than 22 as the starting age for counting years of service. Typically employees need 10 years of service to be fully "vested," or entitled to receive their pensions regardless of any future service. Thus a worker hired at age 19 can join a plan at 21 and can be fully vested by age 29.
3. Employees may have breaks in service of as long as 5 years before losing credit for prior years of work. In addition, a year of maternity or paternity leave cannot be considered a break in service.
4. Pension benefits may now be considered a joint asset in divorce settlements. State courts can award part of an individual's pension to the ex-spouse.
5. Employers must provide survivor benefits to spouses of fully vested employees who die before reaching the minimum retirement age.

These new rules are expected to boost pension costs by 3 percent.

Social Security   Provisions for this program were outlined in Table 11-4. Social Security is an income-maintenance program, not a pension program. It is the nation's best defense against poverty for the elderly, and it has worked well. Without it, according to a 1987 study, the poverty rate among the elderly would have jumped from 12.4 to 47.6 percent.[47] Although this national program of old-age, survivors', disability, and health insurance was strengthened considerably by the 1983 amendments to the law, many people are convinced that they could have invested their payroll taxes more wisely than the government has. Are they right? The Social Security Administration calculated what an individual, ignoring Medicare and some other insurance features, would have to spend at age 65 just to finance a monthly annuity similar to the one that she or he will get from Social Security.

A single male who retired at age 65 in 1980 would have had to invest $64,000 *immediately* at an interest rate exceeding inflation by 2.5 percent to generate an income stream of approximately $125,000—the amount he will get from Social Security if he lives another 14.3 years (average male life expectancy). This is a ratio of about $6 in benefits for every $1 paid in taxes. By any standard, that is a pretty good return on investment. Most individuals could not have done better by investing on their own.

However, future beneficiaries will receive, in general, relatively smaller benefits in relation to their payroll taxes. For example, a single male retiring at age 65 in 1990 can expect to receive a ratio of benefits to taxes paid of just slightly better than 3 to 1.[8]

The Congressional Budget Office projects that the system will be solvent through the year 2020. At that time, however, as the baby boomers retire, Social Security tax outlays will exceed tax revenues. To meet such long-term funding needs, the system will have to be reformed again. If not, economic pressures may force workers to contribute as much as 30 percent of their earnings to the system.[59]

Unemployment insurance   Although 97 percent of the workforce is covered by federal and state unemployment insurance laws, each worker must meet eligibility requirements in order to receive benefits. That is, an unemployed worker must: (1) be able and available to work and be actively seeking work; (2) not have refused suitable employment; (3) not be unemployed because of a labor dispute (except in Rhode Island and New York); (4) not have left a job voluntarily; (5) not have been terminated for gross misconduct; and (6) have been employed previously in a covered industry or occupation, earning a designated minimum amount for a specified minimum amount of time. Many claims are disallowed for failure to satisfy one or more of these requirements.

Every unemployed worker's benefits are "charged" against one or more companies. The more money paid out on behalf of a firm, the higher is the unemployment insurance rate for that firm. In 1987, however, average unemployment taxes paid by employers in two-thirds of the states were lower than those paid the previous year. This decline was due partly to the generally buoyant economy that saw fewer people filing claims. However, it also was due to a growing sensitivity by state governments that high unemployment insurance taxes can be a black eye on a state's business climate. In 1987, for example, unemployment taxes per worker varied from a high of $680 in Alaska to a low of $112 in New Hampshire.[15]

Supplemental unemployment insurance   This type of insurance is common in the auto, steel, rubber, flat glass, and farm equipment industries. Employers contribute to a special fund for this purpose (e.g., Chrysler contributes 23 cents per hour worked per employee). At General Motors, eligible workers receive almost 95 percent of their after-tax weekly pay. As long as unemployment is not severe, such plans are indeed beneficial.[39]

Severance pay   Such pay is not legally required, and, because of unemployment compensation, many firms do not offer it. However, some provide severance payments to employees when they leave instead of giving them advance notice of their dismissal. Length of service, organization level, and the cause of the termination are key factors that affect the size of severance agreements. The average terminated executive receives about $55,000 in benefits,[29] although chief executive officers with management contracts may receive 2 to 3 years of salary in the event of a takeover.[35]

Payments for time not worked

Included in this category are such benefits as the following:

Vacations	Personal excused absences
Holidays	Grievances and negotiations
Reporting time	Sabbatical leaves

COMPANY EXAMPLE

Paid public-service leaves at Xerox

Some employees work with the disabled, others do alcohol and drug counseling, and still others do preretirement counseling. All are Xerox employees on 1-year leaves with full pay. Social commitment is a driving force behind the Xerox program, begun in 1971, but it is not the only rationale for the leaves. Public-service leaves boost the morale and skills of employees, according to those responsible for the program, and they make Xerox a more desirable place to work. Former leave takers say their careers were not affected by the leaves, and many feel that their careers were advanced. Nevertheless, the program also has its problems. Of 131 leave takers surveyed, 40 percent reported major or moderate reentry difficulties on returning to work. More than one-third have quit, regarding their Xerox work as "not very rewarding or extremely unrewarding," in contrast with their high opinion of volunteer work. Many reported that their Xerox bosses acted as if they had been let down because the employees had left. Despite these problems, Xerox aims to continue the program, at a direct cost of about $500,000 per year. Employees want such a program, and society needs them.[66]

Employee services

A broad group of benefits falls into the employee services category. Employees qualify for them purely by virtue of their membership in the organization, and not because of merit. Some examples are:

Tuition aid	Thrift and short-term savings plans
Credit unions	Stock purchase plans
Auto insurance	Corporate exercise facilities
Food service	Moving and transfer allowances
Company car	Transportation and parking
Career clothing	Merchandise purchasing
Legal services	Christmas bonuses

Counseling	Service and seniority awards
Child adoption	Umbrella liability coverage
Child care	Social activities
Elder care	Referral awards
Gift matching	Purchase of used equipment
Charter flights	

At many companies these benefits go begging, largely as a result of employees' lack of knowledge that they exist. For example, although 1.6 million workers are eligible for tuition aid, only 4 percent of white-collar workers and about 1 percent of blue-collar workers use it.[27]

Special benefits for executives

Top executives are sometimes privy to three special perquisites. The first of these is the *"golden parachute,"* an employment contract provision that guarantees (typically) one to six top executives a cash severance equal to several years' salary if they are fired without cause after a takeover or if their status or responsibilities are downgraded by the new management. The Tax Reform Act of 1986 preserved "golden parachute" provisions for closely held firms; but for others, any payment to an executive that exceeds 3 times the annual salary and is made in connection with a change in control of a business becomes nondeductible to the paying corporation. On top of that, the recipient must pay an additional 20 percent tax on the payment.[48] In 1987 the directors of UAL, Inc., the holding company for United Airlines, took action consistent with the new law. Fearing a change in control of UAL, they made 37 executives eligible for severance payments of 1 to 3 times their base salaries until 1992, or retirement, if that is earlier.[25]

A second special benefit for top executives is the *supplemental retirement benefit plan*. Such plans are particularly desirable because of changes wrought by the Tax Reform Act of 1986. That law drastically cut guaranteed retirement benefits under qualified (by the IRS) pension plans. Such benefits are typically figured as a percentage of the retiring executive's average salary in the final 3 to 5 years, multiplied by years of service. But as of 1987, companies cannot consider annual salary that exceeds $120,000 in those years.[7] Supplemental retirement agreements are sometimes negotiated to make up for this shortfall in the pensions of highly paid executives. Of course, the agreements are not insured by the government, and they could become worthless should the company go bankrupt.

The *"key executive" life insurance policy* is a third special benefit. The company pays the premiums, and, when the executive retires, he or she gets the cash value of the policy, including appreciation, in a lump sum. If he or she dies before retiring, the company gets back what it has contributed in premiums, and the spouse receives the remainder of the settlement. Leveraged whole-life insurance programs purchased by companies to fund these benefits have become less attractive as a result of the Tax Reform Act of 1986, because the interest on premium loans over $50,000 per executive is no longer deductible. Such benefits will probably continue to be offered, but companies will need to find different methods to fund them.[42]

Benefits Administration

Benefits and equal employment opportunity

Equal employment opportunity requirements also affect the administration of benefits. Consider as examples health-care coverage and pensions. Effective in 1987, an amendment to the Age Discrimination in Employment Act eliminates mandatory retirement at any age. It also requires employers to continue the same group health insurance coverage offered to younger employees to employees over the age of 70. Medicare payments are limited to what Medicare would have paid for in the absence of a group health plan and to the actual charge for the services. This is another example of government "cost shifting" to the private sector.

With regard to pensions, the IRS considers a plan *discriminatory* unless the employer's contribution for the benefit of lower-paid employees covered by the plan is comparable to contributions for the benefit of higher-paid employees. An example of this is a salary reduction plan [known as 401(k)] authorized by the Tax Equity and Fiscal Responsibility Act. The plan permits significant savings out of pretax compensation, produces higher take-home pay, and results in lower Social Security taxes. The catch: *The plan has to be available to everyone in any company that implements it.* Although the Tax Reform Act of 1986 capped employee contributions at $7000 per year, indexed to changes in the cost of living, two-thirds of eligible employees—the same as prior to the act—are salting away part of their earnings in such plans as this.[32] For those firms which match employee contributions, the most popular match is 50 cents for every dollar of employee contribution.[33]

Costing benefits

Despite the high cost of benefits, many employees take them for granted. A major reason for this is that employers have failed to do in-depth cost analyses of their benefit programs and thus have not communicated the value of their benefit programs to employees. Four methods have been developed for costing employee benefits and services. Although each has value individually, a combination of all four often enhances their impact on employees. The four methods are:[22]

- *Annual cost of benefits for all employees.* Valuable for developing budgets and for describing the total cost of the benefits program
- *Cost per employee per year.* Calculated by dividing the total cost of each benefit program by the number of employees participating in it

TABLE 11-8 *Employee benefits: The forgotten extras*

Listed below are the benefits for the average full-time employee (annual salary $19,000).

Benefit	Who pays	SUN's annual cost	Percentage of base earnings	What you receive
Health, dental, and life insurance	SUN and You	$1521.90	8.01	Comprehensive health and dental plus life insurance equivalent to 1 times your annual salary
Holidays	SUN	950.00	5.00	13 paid holidays
Annual leave (vacation)	SUN	731.50	3.85	10 days vacation per year (additional days starting with sixth year of service)
Sick days	SUN	875.90	4.61	12 days annually
Company retirement	SUN	2076.70	10.93	Vested after 5 years of service
Social security	SUN and You	1273.00	6.70	Retirement and disability benefits
Workers' compensation and unemployment insurance	SUN	190.00	1.00	Compensation if injured on duty and if eligible; income while seeking employment
Total		$7619.00, or $3.66 per hour	40.10	

The dollar amount and percentages will differ slightly depending upon your salary. If your annual salary is less than $19,000, the percentage of your base pay will be greater. If your salary is greater than $19,000, the percentage will be less but the dollar amount will be greater. Benefit costs to SUN, Inc. on behalf of our 5480 employees represent over $41,700,000 per year.

- *Percentage of payroll.* Total annual cost divided by total annual payroll (this figure is valuable in comparing benefits costs across organizations)
- *Cents per hour.* Calculated by dividing the total annual cost of benefits by the total number of hours worked by all employees during the year

A company example of actual benefits costs (the name of the firm is fictitious) is presented in Table 11-8. All four methods of costing benefits have been incorporated into the table. Can you find an example of each?

Cafeteria, or flexible, benefits

The theory underlying this approach to benefits is simple: Instead of all workers at a company getting the same benefits, each worker can pick and choose among alternative options "cafeteria style." Thus the elderly bachelor might pass up maternity coverage for additional pension contributions. The mother whose children are covered under her husband's health insurance may choose legal and auto insurance instead. The typical plan works like this:

Workers are offered a package of benefits that includes "basic" and "optional" items. Basics might include modest medical coverage, life insurance equal to a year's salary, vacation time based on length of service, and some retirement pay. But then employees can use "flexible credits" to choose among such additional benefits as full medical coverage, dental and eye care, more vacation time, additional disability income, and higher company payments to the retirement fund. Nationwide, about 22 percent of firms have flexible benefit plans.[36] They were devised largely in response to the rise in the number of two-income families. When working spouses both have conventional plans, their basic benefits, such as health and life insurance, tend to overlap. Couples rarely can use both plans fully. But if at least one spouse is covered by a "flex" plan, the family can add benefits, such as child care, prepaid legal fees, and dental coverage, that otherwise they might have to buy on their own.

There are advantages for employers as well. Under conventional plans, employers risked alienating employees if they cut benefits, regardless of increases in the costs of coverage. Flexible plans allow them to pass some of the increases onto workers more easily. Instead of providing employees a set package of benefits, the employer says, "Based on your $27,000 annual salary, I promise you $5500 to spend any way you want." If health-care costs soar, the employee—not the employer—decides whether to pay more or to take less coverage.

This is what has happened at PepsiCo ever since "flex" was introduced in 1980. But company surveys show that fully 80 percent of the participants are satisfied with the plan.[55]

Two other potential obstacles have now been removed. One, the Tax Reform Act of 1986 has removed any doubt about the legality of flexible benefits plans. Two, personal-computer software programs have slashed the cost and the administrative complexity of flexible benefits plans. As a result, such plans are now being designed for companies with as few as 20 employees.[16]

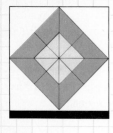

Impact of Pay and Benefits on Productivity, Quality of Work Life, and The Bottom Line

High salary levels alone do not ensure a productive and motivated workforce. This is evident in the auto industry where wages are among the highest in the country—yet quality problems and high absenteeism persist. A critical factor, then, is not *how much* a company pays its workers but, more important, *how the pay system is designed, communicated, and managed.* As we have seen repeatedly throughout this chapter, excessively high labor costs, coupled with benefits offered *only* because "everybody else is doing it," adversely affect productivity, work quality, and the bottom line. Although management's desire to improve the standard of living of all company employees is understandable, excessively high labor costs can bankrupt a company. This is especially likely if, to cover its labor costs, the company cannot price its products competitively. If that happens, productivity and profits both suffer directly, and the quality of work life suffers indirectly. A systematic pay structure helps ensure that each employee is paid equitably and competitively. Current data from a wage survey must then be used to maintain the company's relative position on pay. When sensible compensation policies are established using the principles discussed in this chapter, everybody wins. This is because competitive wages and benefits, fully costed out and communicated to employees, have direct payoffs to the company, to the employees' quality of work life, and to the lives of their families as well.

Despite these potential advantages, two disadvantages, neither insurmountable, remain. One, insurers fear that employees' adverse selection of benefits will drive up costs (e.g., the only employees who choose dental insurance coverage are those with bad teeth). But this fear has been eased by new methods of pooling small-business risks and by better ways of predicting (and thus pricing) the benefits that employees will choose.[16] Two, major communications efforts are needed to help employees understand their benefits fully. Since employees have more choices, they often experience anxiety about making the "right" choices. In addition, they need benefits information on a continuing basis to ensure that their choices continue to support their changing needs.[2] Careful attention to communication can enhance recruitment efforts, help cut turnover, and make employees more aware of their total package of benefits.

Communicating the benefits

Try to make a list of good reasons why any company should not make a deliberate effort to market its benefits package effectively. It will be a short list. Today, we are in what might be called the "third generation of employee benefits communication." Printed materials provided by insurance companies comprised the first generation. The booklets were written from the insurer's viewpoint, not from the reader's. Their technical language provided little real communication.

The second generation started when companies began to provide personalized, computer-generated statements of the dollar value of benefits to employees—in plain English (see Table 11-8). Today, with the rapid proliferation of office automation, we are in the third generation of benefits communication. Microcomputers and interactive videos have added a new dimension to this process. Here are some innovative applications:

- A food-processing corporation installed computers at work locations. Now employees can obtain quick answers to "coverage" situations.
- Computer-aided design methods are being used to show how all elements of a benefits program combine to produce an image consistent with a company's culture. This is typically a series of unrelated shapes that, when combined, produce the image of, say, an airplane (for an airline), a company's major product (e.g., a car), or a company symbol (e.g., a pyramid).
- Aetna has developed a microcomputer system that captures and records employee benefit choices, producing personalized confirmation letters.

Initiating communications technology can be time-consuming and expensive. But so is a benefits plan that no one understands or appreciates.[74]

| CASE 11-1 Conclusion *Pay for performance?* | If performance does not determine pay, then what does? For one thing, company size. Studies show that the correlation between company size and pay, although not perfect, is very high, and superior to any other pay-related variable tested. Is this logical? Many compensation experts argue that it is, on the ground that the CEO of an enlarged company is making decisions that affect more assets and more employees. While that argument is persuasive, |

it also suggests that the board of directors' tolerance of poor performance should be lower in a large company than in a small company. Yet this case has demonstrated that directors are unwilling to be hard-nosed about the pay of top executives, particularly those chaps who are fellow members of the board.

Stockholders who perceive that they are being fleeced by management are often more likely to sell than fight. That might be the simple solution, but it does little to cure the deficiencies of a system. Instead, at annual stockholder meetings, concerned stockholders might ask a few pointed questions of directors who are members of the board's compensation committee. A lot of directors are uneasy about their position, and some may even be looking for the kind of ammunition such a question could provide.[40]

Summary

Contemporary pay systems (outside the entertainment and professional sports fields) are characterized by cost containment, pay and benefit levels commensurate with what a company can afford, and programs that encourage and reward performance. Compensation plans need to be tied to the strategic mission of an organization, and they should take their direction from that strategic mission. However, actual wage levels depend on labor market conditions, legislation, collective bargaining, management attitudes, and an organization's ability to pay. Our broad objective in developing pay systems is to assign a monetary value to each job in the organization (a base rate) and an orderly procedure for increasing the base rate. To develop such a system, we need four basic tools: job analyses and job descriptions, a job evaluation plan, pay surveys, and a pay structure.

Direct payments are only one part of the total compensation package that each employee receives. Indirect payments in the form of benefits and services must also be considered. Presently these account for 39 percent of the total compensation cost for each employee. There are three major benefit components: security and health, payments for time not worked, and employee services. Despite the high cost of benefits, many employees take them for granted. A major reason for this is that employers have not done in-depth cost analyses or communicated the value of their benefits programs. This is a multimillion-dollar oversight. Certainly the counseling that must accompany the implementation of a flexible benefits program, or at least a personalized statement of annual benefits, can do much to alleviate this problem.

TOMORROW'S FORECAST For the foreseeable future, "efficiency" and "cost containment" will be the watchwords in the financing of benefit programs. Efficiency in the design of benefits will be increasingly emphasized in an effort to eliminate and to prevent overlap. Flexible compensation and benefits will expand as cost pressures close in and as the makeup of the workforce continues to change. Responding to changes in family relationships, there will be a trend toward improved benefits for spouses and toward the treatment of earned pension rights as property, subject to division in the event of divorce. Taken together, employee benefit programs provide a blanket of protection against the contingencies of life. They are an integral part of our social structure, and they will continue to be in the future.[58]

Discussion Questions

11-1 What steps can a company take to integrate its compensation system with its general business strategy?

11-2 Discuss the pitfalls to be avoided in analyzing pay survey results. (*Hint*: See ref. 57.)

11-3 How do the pay practices of unionized firms affect those of nonunionized firms?

11-4 How do management's attitudes and philosophy affect compensation and benefits?

11-5 What can firms do to control health-care costs?

11-6 Discuss the pros and cons of flexible benefits.

References

1. A bow to unisex pensions (1983, July 18). *Newsweek*, p. 66.
2. Anthony, R. J. (1986). A communication program model for flexible benefits. *Personnel Administrator*, **31**(6), 65–76.
3. Arvey, R. D. (1986). Sex bias in job evaluation procedures. *Personnel Psychology*, **39**, 315–335.
4. Bates, M. W. (1983, March). A look at cash compensation. *Personnel Journal*, pp. 198–200.
5. Beazley, J. E. (1986, June 11). U.S. Steel, union are at odds on eve of talks. *Wall Street Journal*, p. 6.
6. Beazley, J. E. (1987, May 21). Agency in crisis. *Wall Street Journal*, pp. 1, 12.
7. Bettner, J. (1986, Oct. 28). Executive dreams: What benefits to request under the new tax law. *Wall Street Journal*, p. 35.
8. Carlson, E. (1982, July–August). Social Security: Could you have done better? *Dynamic Years*, pp. 44–47.
9. Carlson, E. (1983, Oct. 11). States' widely varying laws on disability costs irk firms. *Wall Street Journal*, p. 35.
10. Colvin, G. (1982, Oct. 4). How sick companies are endangering the pension system. *Fortune*, pp. 72–78.
11. Donoghue, W. (1983, Aug. 7). Employee stock plan not always best deal. *Denver Post*, p. 16E.
12. Edwards, M. R. (1981). Permanent disability: What does it cost? *Human Resource Planning*, **4**, 209–220.
13. Endicott, F. S., & Lindquist, V. (1987). The 1987 Northwestern Endicott-Lindquist Report. *Personnel Administrator*, **32**, 74–76.
14. Executive pay: Who got what in '86 (1987, May 4). *Business Week*, p. 58.
15. Firms' unemployment taxes fell in most states this year. (1987, Dec. 29). *Wall Street Journal*, p. 17.
16. Galante, S. P. (1986, July 21). Employers acquiring a taste for providing benefit "menus." *Wall Street Journal*, p. 17.
17. Gannes, S. (1987, Apr. 13). Strong medicine for health bills. *Fortune*, pp. 70–74.
18. Gomez, L. R., Page, R. C., & Tornow, W. W. (1982). A comparison of the practical utility of traditional, statistical, and hybrid job evaluation approaches. *Academy of Management Journal*, **25**, 790–809.
19. Greene, R. J., & Roberts, R. G. (1983). Strategic integration of compensation and benefits. *Personnel Administrator*, **28**(5), 79–82.
20. Harvey, B. H., Schultze, J. A., & Rogers, J. F. (1983). Rewarding employees for not using sick leave. *Personnel Administrator*, **28**(5), 55–59.

21. Hayes, M. (1986). The crisis in health care costs. *Personnel Administrator*, **31**(7), 56–62, 126, 130.
22. Henderson, R. I. (1982). *Compensation management* (3d ed.). Reston, VA: Reston.
23. James, F. E. (1987, Sep. 29). Medical expenses resist control and keep going one way: Higher. *Wall Street Journal*, p. 29.
24. Jochim, T. C. (1979). Employee stock ownership programs: The next economic revolution? *Academy of Management Review*, **4**, 439–442.
25. Kilman, S., & Valente, J. (1987, Apr. 21). UAL officials get "golden parachute" employment pacts. *Wall Street Journal*, p. 2.
26. Labor Department publishes final rules on overtime for federal projects (1986, Apr. 10). *Daily Labor Report*, p. A2.
27. Labor Letter (1980, Aug. 12). *Wall Street Journal*, p. 1.
28. Labor Letter (1984, Sep. 18). *Wall Street Journal*, p. 1.
29. Labor Letter (1986, May 13). *Wall Street Journal*, p. 1.
30. Labor Letter (1986, July 29). *Wall Street Journal*, p. 1.
31. Labor Letter (1987, Apr. 14). *Wall Street Journal*, p. 1.
32. Labor Letter (1987, May 15). *Wall Street Journal*, p. 1.
33. Labor Letter (1987, July 1). *Wall Street Journal*, p. 1.
34. Labor Letter (1987, July 7). *Wall Street Journal*, p. 1.
35. Labor Letter (1987, Sep. 8). *Wall Street Journal*, p. 1.
36. Labor Letter (1987, Sep. 15). *Wall Street Journal*, p. 1.
37. Labor Letter (1987, Sep. 22). *Wall Street Journal*, p. 1.
38. Labor Letter (1987, Nov. 10). *Wall Street Journal*, p. 1.
39. Lifetime security (1977, Nov. 14). *Business Week*, p. 56.
40. Loomis, C. J. (1982, July 12). The madness of executive compensation. *Fortune*, pp. 42–46.
41. Main, J. (1982, Sep. 20). Hard times catch up with executives. *Fortune*, pp. 50–54.
42. McMillan, J. D. (1986). Tax reform: What it means (part one). *Personnel Administrator*, **31**(12), 95–100.
43. Medical benefits. (1987, June 15). *The Medical-Economic Digest*, pp. 6–7.
44. Milkovich, G. T., & Newman, J. M. (1987). *Compensation* (2d ed.). Plano, TX: Business Publications.
45. Mills, D. Q. (1986). *Labor-management relations* (3d ed.). New York: McGraw-Hill.
46. Mount, M. K., & Ellis, R. A. (1987). Investigation of bias in job evaluation ratings of comparable worth study participants. *Personnel Psychology*, **40**, 85–96.
47. Older Americans in the workforce: Challenges and solutions (1987). Washington, DC: Bureau of National Affairs.
48. Padwe, G. W. (1987, March). How golden are your parachutes? *Nation's Business*, p. 62.
49. Pay vs. performance in ten industries (1982, July 12). *Fortune*, pp. 47–52.
50. Peers, A. (1987, June 29). Firms now must offer health insurance to some ex-workers—but at what price? *Wall Street Journal*, p. 29.
51. Pension reform has something for everyone (1984, Aug. 27). *U. S. News & World Report*, p. 67.
52. Pension assets (1986, Mar. 6). *Wall Street Journal*, p. 23.
53. Personal affairs (1982, Nov. 22). *Forbes*, pp. 230–233.
54. Pfeffer, J., & Davis-Blake, A. (1987). Understanding organizational wage structures: A resource dependence approach. *Academy of Management Journal*, **30**, 437–455.

55. Reibstein, L. (1986, Sep. 16). To each according to his needs: Flexible benefits plans gain favor. *Wall Street Journal*, p. 33.

56. Richman, L. S. (1983, May 2). Health benefits come under the knife. *Fortune*, pp. 95–110.

57. Rynes, S. L., & Milkovich, G. T. (1986). Wage surveys: Dispelling some myths about the "market wage." *Personnel Psychology*, **39**, 71–90.

58. Salisbury, D. L. (1982, February). Benefits trends in the '80s. *Personnel Journal*, pp. 104, 105, 108.

59. Sen. Durenberger says Social Security reform needed to meet funding needs (1987, June 24). *Daily Labor Report*, pp. A9–A10.

60. Sibson, R. E. (1967). *Wages and salaries: A handbook for line managers* (rev. ed.). New York: American Management Association.

61. Slater, K. (1986, May 23). Medical and disability plans: How to tell if a firm's employee benefits measure up. *Wall Street Journal*, p. 21.

62. Smith, R. (1984, Feb. 27). Buying in. *Wall Street Journal*, pp. 1, 16.

63. Steel (1987, Feb. 4). *Labor Relations Week*, p. 97.

64. Stricharchuk, G. (1987, Aug. 26). Fading benefit. *Wall Street Journal*, pp. 1, 6.

65. Swad, R. (1981, June). Stock ownership plans: A new employee benefit. *Personnel Journal*, pp. 453–455.

66. Tannenbaum, J. A. (1981, May 6). Paid public service leaves buoy workers, but return to old jobs can be wrenching. *Wall Street Journal*, p. 29.

67. The *Norris* decision and merged-gender annuity rates (1983, August). TIAA-CREF, Notice to Annuity Owners.

68. Thomsen, D. J. (1980, March). Compensation and benefits. *Personnel Journal*, p. 177.

69. Those sky-high health costs (1982, July 12). *Time*, pp. 54–55.

70. Tosi, H., & Tosi, L. (1987). What managers need to know about knowledge-based pay. In D. A. Balkin & L. R. Gomez-Mejia (eds.), *New Perspectives on compensation*. Englewood Cliffs, NJ: Prentice-Hall, pp. 43–48.

71. Uchitelle, L. (1987, June 26). Bonuses replace wage rises and workers are the losers. *New York Times*, pp. A1, D3.

72. U.S. Department of Labor (1987, June). *Employee benefits in medium and large firms*. Washington, DC: USGPO, Bulletin 2281.

73. Wallace, M. J., Jr., & Fay, C. H. (1983). *Compensation theory and practice*. Boston: PWS-Kent.

74. Watters, D. A. (1986). New technologies for benefits communication. *Personnel Administrator*, 31(11), 110–114.

75. Widder, P. (1982, May 31). Individuals gain more control over their pensions. *Denver Post*, pp. 1C, 8C.

76. Williams, M. (1983, Oct. 12). Ten minutes' work for 12 hours' pay? What's the catch? *Wall Street Journal*, pp. 1, 19.

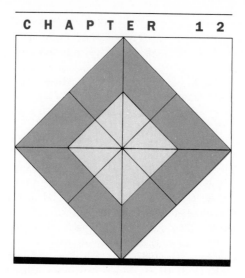

Motivational Strategies for Improving Performance and Productivity

CASE 12-1

The 100 Club: a million-dollar incentive plan*

In 1981 the 325 employees who manufactured paper egg cartons at a Diamond International plant in Palmer, Massachusetts, faced an uncertain future. Styrofoam containers were creating stiff competition, the recession was affecting profits adversely, and workers were worried about being laid off. Labor-management relations were strained at best. Over 65 percent of the plant's workforce felt that management did not treat them with respect, 56 percent approached their work pessimistically, and 79 percent thought they were not being rewarded for a job well done.

Then the director of human resources of the Diamond plant devised a system of productivity incentives called the "100 Club." It is disarmingly simple. Employees are allocated points in recognition of above-average performance. Any employee who works a full year without having an industrial accident is awarded 20 points; 100 percent attendance is worth 25 points. Every year on February 2 (the anniversary of the program's launching date), points are tallied and a record is sent to the individual's home. Upon reaching 100 points, the worker gets a light-blue nylon jacket emblazoned with the company

*Adapted from: Hot 100, *Time*, July 4, 1983, p. 46.

logo and a patch signifying membership in the "100 Club." Every one of the plant's employees has now earned a jacket.

Those who accumulate more than 100 points can receive additional gifts. With 500 points, employees can choose from such items as a blender, cooking accessories, a wall clock, or a cribbage board. Diamond's management is quick to point out that none of the prizes is beyond the purchasing power of the workers; the real value is this: *It's a sign of appreciation from the company.* "For too long, the people who have got the majority of attention have been those who cause problems," says Diamond's director of human resources. "[Our] program's primary focus is the recognition of good employees."

QUESTIONS
1. Do you think recognition alone is enough to motivate employees, or does it always have to be tied to pay?
2. How might Diamond's recognition program affect error rates, grievances, and time lost due to absences?
3. Can such a program be sustained over time? If so, how?

What's Ahead

Case 12-1 raises an issue that is compelling to many managers—how can we gain and sustain employee motivation for high quality and high productivity? The constant interplay between theory and practice is shown throughout this chapter. To begin, the chapter reviews and integrates theories of applied motivation, suggests a unified motivational framework for management practice, and then illustrates this framework with a company example. Next it examines what is known about incentives and merit pay—what is applied, and what works. It considers incentives both for executives and for lower-level employees and explains how the Tax Reform Act of 1986 affects these incentives. To show the impact of incentive systems applied at the individual, group, and organizationwide levels, many company examples are presented. The chapter concludes with an examination of three key policy issues in pay planning and administration: the impact of inflation on pay, pay compression, and pay raises.

Alternative Strategies for Building Employee Trust and Productivity

As pointed out in Chapter 1, there has been a decline in the rate of increase of U.S. industrial productivity relative to that of other industrialized nations. A number of reasons have been suggested for this decline, and among these reasons are changes in the motivation and work ethic of the American worker. Critics point to the declining role of work in American life coupled with rising demands for more leisure.

However, many management policies and practices are at least partly to blame for employees' attitudes. Many firms proudly point to their productivity increases and claim that the increases are due to employees' working smarter, not harder. But in many other firms, managements fail to reward employees for working either harder or smarter.

Many powerful tools lie within management's control, but the tools have to be applied consistently and within the framework of an overall *strategy* for performance improvement. Such a strategy must coordinate the various elements of human resource management into a unified program whose focus is to enhance employees' motivation to work; too often, managers have sacrificed *equitable* treatment for *equality* of treatment.[37] To see how such a strategy might be applied in practice, let's examine three popular categories of motivation theories.

Motivation theories

A close look at all theories of human motivation reveals a common driving principle: *People do what they are rewarded for doing.*[11] In general, the theories can be classified into one of three categories: need theories, reinforcement theories, and expectancy theories.

Need theories   These suggest that individuals have certain physical and psychological needs that they attempt to satisfy. *Motivation* is a force that results from an individual's desire to satisfy these needs (e.g., hunger, thirst, social approval). Conversely, a satisfied need is not a motivator. Thus, while a hungry man might well be susceptible to a "Big Mac Attack," after several Big Macs that same individual might find the prospect of yet another to be distinctly uninviting. The most popular need theories are:

- Maslow's hierarchy of needs, ranging from physiological needs to safety, belonging, esteem, and self-actualization needs.[35]
- Herzberg's two-factor theory, whereby the satisfaction of needs has one of two effects: It either causes employees to be *satisfied* with their jobs or it prevents employees from being *dissatisfied* with their jobs.[18]
- McClelland's classification of needs according to their intended effects: that is, they satisfy employee needs for achievement, affiliation, or power.[36]

Reinforcement theories   Also known as incentive theories or operant conditioning, reinforcement theories are based on a fundamental principle of learning—the Law of Effect.[52] Its statement is simple: *Behavior that is rewarded tends to be repeated; behavior that is not rewarded tends not to be repeated.* If management rewards behaviors such as high-quality work, high productivity, timely reports, or creative suggestions, these behaviors are likely to increase. However, the converse is also true: Managers should not expect sustained, high performance from employees if they consistently ignore employees' performance and contributions.

Expectancy theories While reinforcement theories focus on the *objective relationship* between performance and rewards, expectancy theories emphasize the *perceived relationships*—what does the person expect? According to expectancy theories, individual decision making is the product of three general concepts—*valence* (the value employees attach to the rewards), *instrumentality* (the belief that performance will be rewarded), and *expectancy* (a person's belief that if she exerts effort, she will perform well).[9, 20, 56] Employees who believe that their efforts will lead to effective performance and who anticipate important rewards for their accomplishments become productive and stay productive as the rewards meet their expectations.[11]

Rewards that motivate behavior

There are two types of rewards, or reinforcers, that motivate behavior—*primary rewards* and *secondary rewards*. Primary rewards directly satisfy basic physiological needs, such as hunger, thirst, activity, rest, and sex. Generally these are not relevant to work motivation.

Secondary rewards, such as money, do not satisfy needs directly, but through experience we learn that they can be used in exchange for things that do satisfy needs. Secondary rewards are clearly relevant to work motivation. The degree to which employees must learn about secondary rewards varies. For example, most people have a strong liking of and desire for *money* before they enter the workforce. But many new employees have not acquired a strong liking for *recognition* or the *self-satisfaction* that comes from doing a job well. Recognition and pride in craftsmanship are secondary rewards that must be learned. Good management practices make these lessons easier to understand.[10]

Unlike primary reinforcers (e.g., Big Macs), secondary rewards do not become satiated. Have you ever met a person who complained about getting *too much* recognition or social approval? Probably not. In fact, the more recognition a person gets, the more important recognition becomes as a secondary reward. *The desire to obtain additional recognition can become a powerful need that employees strive to fulfill.*

Successful marketing organizations have long recognized the impact that recognition can have on behavior. The adage "People work for money, but they live for recognition" is an example of this philosophy. When added to commissions and other financial incentives, recognition awards (such as "the million-dollar club") keep salespeople motivated even after they are financially secure.

Primary and secondary rewards are usually specific to an individual or group (e.g., recognition of an entire department). Managers have long known that individual rewards—such as piece-rate payments, sales commissions, and performance bonuses that tie individual rewards to individual performance—can be effective motivators if they "fit" the type of work performed. They are obviously inappropriate for assembly line jobs, where work is paced automatically. Nevertheless, research indicates that when incentives geared to reward *individuals* do fit the situation, performance increases an average of 30 percent, while incentives geared to reward *groups* increase performance an average of 18 percent.[32] However, as noted in Chapter 11, the total compensation package that each employee receives includes indirect as well as direct financial payments. Benefits, cafeteria privileges, and company-subsidized tuition are examples of indirect payments, or "system rewards," that employees receive for being members of the system.[23] They have little impact on the day-to-day performance of employees, but they do tie people to the system. They tend to reduce turnover and to increase loyalty to the company. As you can see, there are a number of alternative strategies available for building employee trust and productivity. However, at this point you are probably also asking yourself, "How do I proceed, and when should I use each strategy?"

Integration and application of motivation theories

The intent here is to develop meaningful prescriptions for managers to follow in motivating subordinates, based on the above brief review of motivation theories and types of rewards. Broadly speaking, managers need to focus on three key areas of responsibility in order to coordinate and integrate human resource policy:[37]

1. Performance definition
2. Performance facilitation
3. Performance encouragement

These key areas are shown graphically in Figure 12-1.

FIGURE 12-1

Steps that managers can take to motivate employees to improve their performance.

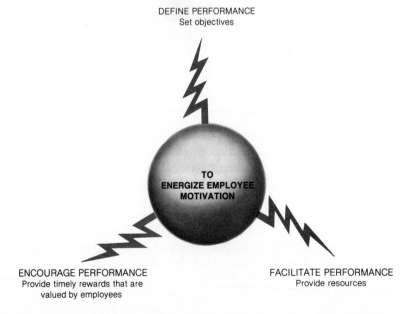

DEFINE PERFORMANCE
Set objectives

TO
ENERGIZE EMPLOYEE
MOTIVATION

ENCOURAGE PERFORMANCE
Provide timely rewards that are
valued by employees

FACILITATE PERFORMANCE
Provide resources

Performance definition   This is a description of what is expected of employees, plus the continuous orientation of employees toward effective job performance. The discussions of job analysis and performance standards in Chapters 4 and 9, respectively, are clearly relevant here. Performance description includes three elements: goals, measures, and assessment.

As discussed in Chapters 2 and 7, *goal setting* is an effective performance improvement strategy. It enhances accountability and clarifies the direction of employee effort. At Hewlett-Packard, for example, the president commented, "The corporate goals [concerning profit, customers, fields of interest, growth, people, management, and citizenship] provide the basic framework for the management-by-objectives system, which gives individual managers a lot of freedom to be entrepreneurial and innovative. They are a kind of glue—the basic philosophy, the basic sense of direction, sort of a value set—that draws everyone together" (ref. 42, p. 55).

The mere presence of goals, however, is not sufficient. Management must also be able to operationalize and therefore *measure* the accomplishment of goals. This is where performance standards play a vital role, for they specify what "fully successful" performance means. Goals such as "make the company successful" are too vague to be useful.

The third aspect of performance definition is *assessment*. Regular assessment of progress toward goals encourages a continuing orientation toward job performance. If management takes the time to identify measurable goals but then fails to do assessment, it is asking for trouble. This is so because if there is no assessment of performance on these goals, then the goals cannot motivate employees to improve their performance.[37] The goals only send negative messages to employees regarding management's commitment to the goals. Almost as damaging is vague, sloppy performance appraisal. This reflects poorly on management and also leads to misinformation about individual and organizational performance. Misinformation, in turn, makes it impossible to reward performance accurately. Hence it reduces the potential of the entire reward system to motivate employees. It should be obvious by now that performance definition (through goals, operational measures, and regular assessment) plays a pivotal role in employee motivation.

Performance facilitation   This area of responsibility involves the elimination of roadblocks to performance. Like performance definition, it also has three aspects: removing performance obstacles, providing the means and adequate resources for performance, and carefully selecting personnel.

Improperly maintained equipment, delays in receiving supplies, poor physical design of work spaces, and inefficient work methods are obstacles to performance that management must eliminate in order to create highly supportive task environments. Otherwise, motivation will decline as employees become convinced that management does not really care about getting the job done.

A similar problem can arise when management fails to provide adequate financial, material, or human resources to get a job done right. Such a strategy is self-defeating and excessively costly in the long run, for employees begin to doubt whether their assigned tasks *can* be done well.

Finally, careful selection of employees is essential to employee motivation to perform. Poor staffing procedures ("placing round pegs in square holes") guarantee reduced motivation by placing employees in jobs that either demand too little of them or require more of them than they are qualified to do. Such a strategy results in overstaffing, excessive labor costs, and reduced productivity.

Performance encouragement   This is the last key area of management responsibility in a coordinated approach to motivating employee performance. It has five aspects:

- Value of rewards
- Amount of rewards
- Timing of rewards
- Likelihood of rewards
- Fairness of rewards

The value and amount of the rewards relate to the choice of rewards to be used. Management must offer rewards to employees (e.g., job redesign, flexible benefits systems, alternative work schedules) that employees personally value. Then a sufficient *amount* of reward must be offered to motivate the employee to put forth effort to receive it. How much is enough?

When one manager was asked how much of a raise he gave his top performer, he replied proudly, "Why I gave him 8 percent." When asked what his worst performer got, the manager responded, "7 percent, but the difference really was based on merit."[37] Certainly the belief that a 1 percent differential is sufficient to reward high performance is wishful thinking.

The issues of the timing and likelihood of rewards relate to the link between performance and outcomes. Whether the rewards are in the form of raises, incentive pay, promotions, or recognition for a job well done, timing and likelihood are fundamental to an effective reward system. If there is an *excessive delay* between effective performance and the receipt of rewards, the rewards lose their potential to motivate subsequent high performance.

The final issue, fairness, can also encourage or discourage effective performance. Fairness is related to, but is not the same thing as, pay satisfaction. Satisfaction depends on the *amount* of reward received and on how much is still desired. Satisfaction is comprised of four aspects: the level of pay and benefits, the extent to which workers perceive their earnings as fair or deserved, comparisons with other people's pay, and noneconomic satisfactions, such as intrinsic satisfaction with the content of one's work.[5] Pay satisfaction certainly includes perceptions of fairness or unfairness, but the concepts of fairness and unfairness are distinctly different:

1. Fairness depends on a comparison between the rewards one receives and one's contributions to the organization, relative to some comparison standard. Such a standard might be:

Others. A comparison with other people either within or outside the organization

Self. A comparison with one's own rewards and contributions at a different time and/or with one's evolving views of self-worth

Systems. A comparison with what the organization has promised

These comparison standards are used in varying degrees, depending on the availability of information and on the relevance of the standard to the individual.[1, 21, 28] Fairness is also related to the employees' understanding of their company's pay system. Those who say that they understand the system also tend to perceive it as fair.[40] However, most experts would limit open discussion of salaries to the pay ranges that each employee could expect; in short, openness is the best policy, but only to a point.[26]

2. The practices most likely to produce feelings of unfairness are *adjustments* in pay. However, organizations with carefully designed policies need only ensure that actions match intentions. It probably makes much less difference to employees' perceptions of pay fairness what these policies are than seeing that they are followed consistently. But organizations that say one thing and do another find that pay injustice is one of their most important products.[1]

Thus, while pay satisfaction is important, from the organization's standpoint it is even more important that every employee consider her or his pay to be fair, with some room for improvement. The point is that employees should be encouraged to improve their salaries, presumably by improving their performance.

In summary, the complexities of employee motivation, combined with the problems of reduced productivity, make coordinated human resource policy essential in modern organizations. The impact of pay as a motivator cannot be viewed apart from the broader schema of personnel activities ranging from job analysis to selection and placement and to training and performance appraisal. All are part of a human resource management *system.* So, in formulating future human resource policies, management must:[37]

- Quit relying on employee *indebtedness* to encourage performance and instead consider what the organization *owes* to good performers.
- Consider the *context* of performance and productivity problems.
- Determine whether or not current human resource management policies and practices really do motivate employees to perform their jobs better.

Now, in an extended company example, let's see how these ideas were implemented in practice.

COMPANY EXAMPLE

Increasing performance and productivity at North American Tool & Die, Inc. (NATD)*

This example is recounted in the words of the president and chief executive officer of NATD, a computer components contract manufacturer in San Leandro, California. His is an old-fashioned philosophy, the belief that *people* make the difference between success and failure.

"My partner and I set three objectives when we bought NATD in June 1978: (1) to expand the company while raising profits, (2) to share whatever wealth was created, and (3) to create an atmosphere that would allow everyone to feel satisfaction and even to have fun on the job. The only way to do this, we decided, was to create an atmosphere of complete trust between us (the owners) and *all* our employees. However, when you say you want such an atmosphere you truly have to believe in it. Then you have to work at improving relations every day in every situation. Otherwise, your employees will sense the hypocrisy and all will be for naught."

Goal 1: Growth and profits

"We bought a job shop with a reputation for acceptable but not outstanding quality. The only way our quality would improve is if our employees improved it—every day, on every job, on every part. Ours is a highly technical business. We produce hundreds of different parts with a tolerance of 0.019 of an inch. That's about one-fourth the thickness of a human hair. NATD manufactures each of those different parts by the thousands each year. Thus the company's well-being depends entirely on employees caring a great deal about their performance.

"To encourage this feeling, we spread the gospel of quality and repeatedly recognize employee efforts to eliminate all rejects. Each month, there's a plantwide meeting—on company time—with a threefold purpose. First, we recognize one employee (no supervisors allowed) who has done a super job of producing good quality during that month. A check for $50 is just a token of what we give. Of much greater import is the 'Super Person of the Month' plaque. The employee's name is engraved on the plaque, and it is prominently and permanently displayed in the plant. Second, each employee is given a silver dollar for every year of service if his or her employment anniversary occurs during the month of the meeting. Finally, we share with our 'family' where we've been, where we are, and where we're going—in percentages when appropriate. In that way, each employee knows firsthand what's going on at his or her company."

Goal 2: Sharing the wealth

"We share ownership primarily through our employee stock ownership plan. We give each employee shares of NATD stock each year, according to three

*Adapted from: T. H. Melohn, How to build employee trust and productivity, *Harvard Business Review*, January–February 1983, pp. 56–59.

simple selection criteria. The employee must be at least 24 years old, work at least 1000 hours a year, and be on the payroll at year end. In our judgment, our people have earned the right to be given company stock without any cash outlay of their own. It's not a warrant, a reduced-price purchase plan, matching dollars, or an option. It's free.

"By the way, my partner and I waived our right to participate in this program. We wanted the number of shares allotted for our employees to be that much larger, that much more meaningful. The shares we grant annually are newly issued—we do not realize any gain by selling our own. NATD's employee stock ownership program has also been instrumental in lowering our rejection rates from customers and improving our productivity and delivery time.

"We also try to stress equitable compensation as a motivational tool. We hold compensation reviews twice annually. This is not a rubber-stamp operation. Each employee has a one-on-one performance review with his or her boss. Each is told, 'Here's where you're doing well, and here's where you need to improve, and here's what the company can do to help.'

"Finally, we use cash bonuses to reward innovative employees. In recent months several employees have taken action to help the company and win cash. In one instance, a young employee decided on his own to develop a means to rivet a very difficult part and also to automate the entire process. In another, a department foreman who saw that our labor cost for an important job was too high devised a new method of doing ten operations at one time. He challenged his young associate to 'top this' and soon found the entire production step completely automated! Our labor costs were reduced 80 percent."

Goal 3: Satisfaction and fun

"With our strong belief in the importance of our employees, we pay careful attention to the selection process. We hire a certain kind of person—one who cares about himself, his family, and his company. The person must be honest, willing to speak up, and curious, be it as a sweeper, machine operator, plant foreman, or office manager. That's why I interview each prospective employee myself. My purpose is to determine if the candidate will fit into the NATD family. Perhaps that concept seems old-fashioned, but to us it's pivotal. This process of lengthy evaluation and interviewing is a lot of work, but the results are well worth it.

"Let's face it, the traditional adversary role between management and employees is not productive. In encouraging employee satisfaction at NATD, we follow the tenet that our employees deserve the same treatment we expect from them. They want to know about their future compensation, their potential career paths, how they are contributing, and what they can do to grow. To keep people involved and caring, we work at giving out *real* compliments— not just the perfunctory 'Good job, Smith'—but statements of sincere appreciation for each person's special efforts and accomplishments.

"Compliments don't cost a company anything. We all need them and even crave them. Recognition—both personal and professional—is a major motivating factor. At least two or three times a week we go through the plant chatting with each employee and complimenting those who've worked well. Employees care deeply about their work. If you can tap this well of concern and mesh it with the goals of your corporation, the results will truly stun you.

"To summarize the last three years at NATD, our sales have gone from $1.8 million to over $6 million, our pretax earnings have increased well over 600 percent, our stock appreciated 36 percent in 1980 and again in 1981, our customer reject rate has declined from 5 percent to 0.3 percent, our productivity has doubled, our turnover rate has dropped from 27 percent to 6 percent, and we've all had a good time."

Effective implementation

"My job as CEO is to outline the company's objectives and the strategies to attain those goals. To achieve them, we place heavy emphasis on true delegation of responsibility.

"We believe that our managers really want to manage, but we realize that certain conditions must be met before they can become effective managers. First, we work *with* managers to be sure the goals are clear and in fact attainable. Second, we give our employees the tools to reach the goals. Third, we let our managers alone and allow them flexibility. The last thing any manager needs is a second-guessing or a preemptive superior.

"Each supervisor is responsible for on-time production with no rejects and at maximum efficiency. How the supervisor does it is totally up to him or her. We then make sure our managers and employees get credit for their successful accomplishments—from us, from their peers, and in their paychecks.

"Incidentally, we attach no blame to failure. If we have given a job 'our best shot,' there's no problem. If our people are inhibited by the fear of failure, they won't dare to try. If we don't try the unexplored and the untested, then our growth rate and profitability will suffer. And that's no fun."

Overall summary and integration

NATD has applied a logic and a framework to its management practice that has resulted in a coordinated human resource management policy. Such a policy clearly has impacted all three of the general themes of this book: productivity, quality of work life, and the bottom line. It also dovetails nicely with the motivation guidelines suggested earlier:

- *Performance definition*. NATD has established goals, measures, and assessments.
- *Performance facilitation*. NATD has removed obstacles to effective performance, it has provided the resources that its employees need to perform their jobs well, and it has emphasized careful personnel selection.

■ *Performance encouragement*. NATD has provided rewards that employees value (recognition, stock ownership, cash bonuses) in sufficient *amount* to encourage future performance, with a *high likelihood* of actually receiving the rewards, with appropriate *timing* (twice a year compensation reviews), and with a genuine concern for employees' perceptions of *fair* treatment.

Performance definition, facilitation, and encouragement "set the stage" for employees to become motivated. But there is nothing like an effective incentive system to really energize behavior.

Requirements of Effective Incentive Systems

At the outset it is important to distinguish merit systems from incentive systems. Both are designed to motivate employees to improve their job performance. Most commonly, merit systems are applied to exempt employees in the form of permanent increases to their base pay. The goal is to tie pay increases to each employee's level of job performance. Incentives (e.g., sales commissions, profit sharing) are one-time supplements to base pay. They are also awarded on the basis of job performance, and they are applied to broader segments of the labor force, including nonexempt and unionized employees.

Properly designed incentive programs work because they are based on two well-accepted psychological principles: (1) Increased motivation improves performance, and (2) recognition is a major factor in motivation.[47] Unfortunately, however, many incentive programs are improperly designed, and they do not work. They violate one or more of the following rules (shown graphically in Figure 12-2):

FIGURE 12-2

Requirements of effective incentive programs.

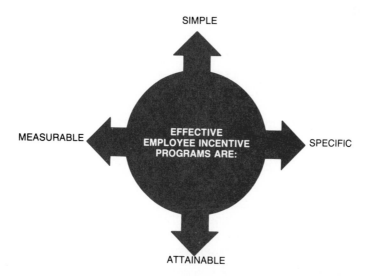

Be simple. The rules of the system should be brief, clear, and understandable.

Be specific. It is not sufficient to say, "Produce more," or "Stop accidents." Employees need to know precisely what they are expected to do.

Be attainable. Every employee should have a reasonable chance to gain something.

Be measurable. Measurable objectives are the foundation on which incentive plans are built. Program dollars will be wasted (and program evaluation hampered) if specific accomplishments cannot be related to dollars spent.

Now let us consider in more detail the development and administration of an incentive program.* The process begins with the statement of an operational *goal* that the plan intends to help workers achieve. The next step is to develop a budget.

Three elements make up the overall incentive budget: (1) administration, (2) promotional materials and services, and (3) awards. In general, most programs managed internally require *no more than 10 percent of the total budget for promotion and administration.* The remaining 90 percent can be allocated for awards.

The cost of awards can be either fixed or variable. In a *closed-ended* budget, management decides in advance what the maximum expenditure will be—either by an arbitrary allocation or by fixing a percentage of anticipated savings. However, in incentive programs that encourage unlimited performance improvements, an *open-ended* budget is appropriate since the awards will depend on the performance levels achieved.

When developing incentive-program budgets, *up to 50 percent of the anticipated savings can be applied to the cost of the program itself.* To motivate employees to put forth the extra effort necessary to receive incentive awards, they should be able to earn *between 1 and 7 percent of their quarterly or 6-month salaries.*[13] Now let's set up a hypothetical program using the guidelines described so far.

COMPANY EXAMPLE *An effective incentive-program budget at Skyline Contractors*	Skyline Contractors employs 350 workers at an average wage of $9.50 per hour, or $19,760 per year. The firm has a serious problem with employee absences, latenesses, and unexcused departures from work. The direct and indirect costs associated with absenteeism alone are almost $350,000 per year. Latenesses, extended breaks, and other unexcused departures from work areas result in another $75,000 per year. Management's goal is to cut these costs by 40 percent, which would yield a gross savings of $170,000 per year.

Following the guideline that a company can profitably apply up to 50 percent of the anticipated savings from an incentive program to the cost of the program itself, Skyline decides to allocate 40 percent of the anticipated

*Many of the ideas in this section are drawn from Dwortzan.[13]

TABLE 12-1 *An incentive budget for skyline contractors*

Participants	Minimum budget (1%)	Skyiine budget (2%)	Maximum budget (7%)
300 workers @ $9,880 = $2,964,000	$29,640	$59,280	$207,480
5 shop stewards @ $10,000 = $50,000	500	1,000	3,500
10 supervisors @ $12,500 = $125,000	1,250	2,500	8,750
Total	$31,390	$62,780	$219,730

savings to its incentive program. Forty percent of the anticipated savings of $170,000 yields $68,000. This is now the theoretical budget for Skyline's incentive program.

Some 300 employees are scheduled to participate, plus 5 shop stewards and 10 supervisors. The program is scheduled to run 6 months. During this period, the supervisors (average annual salaries of $25,000) will each earn $12,500. The 5 shop stewards will each earn $10,000 during this period, and the 300 employees will each earn $9880. By multiplying the average salaries by 1 percent and 7 percent (the guidelines for motivating employee effort), the minimum and maximum awards budgets can be determined. These figures, and others required to estimate the incentive program budget, are shown in Table 12-1.

Skyline decides to stay at the low end of the salary guidelines, allocating 2 percent (or $62,780) to awards. Since the program will run a full 6 months and involve over 300 employees, the theoretical budget must be increased to allow for promotion and administration expenses (an additional 10 percent of $62,780, or $6278). Thus the total budget is $69,058 ($62,780 + $6278). This is well within the minimum and maximum guidelines, and it is less than 50 percent of the anticipated savings (50 percent of $170,000 = $85,000). Remember, aside from administrative and promotional expenses, Skyline's incentive program costs *nothing* until its objectives have been achieved and awards have been won. The budget shown in Table 12-1 will not be spent unless Skyline reaches its goals. If the final budget winds up higher than anticipated, it is because Skyline's original 40 percent goal was exceeded.

Administering and promoting the incentive program

The results of an incentive program often correspond to the efforts exerted to promote the program. To maximize these efforts, consider the following:

- Get top executives involved at kick-off and awards ceremonies.
- Educate supervisors and department heads regarding rules and what is expected of them personally; their support is crucial to the success of the entire program.
- Use a dramatic kick-off.
- Provide interim promotions and reports.

- To provide variety and excitement, break up a long program by changing the emphasis and/or type of awards.
- Get families involved by offering prizes for children as well as adults. Send promotional materials and congratulatory letters to employees' homes.
- Follow through to ensure that employees actually receive the awards or prizes they earn. Sometimes (unfortunately) rules are changed to prevent employees from claiming their prizes—trips cannot be taken because of workloads or because the spouse cannot come along. Needless to say, this is very demoralizing for employees.
- End with a flair—banquets, award ceremonies, or in-house publicity. Then repeat the most productive parts of the original program.

Merchandise versus cash awards

Many firms prefer merchandise awards because they stand apart from wages and are permanent reminders of the program, its objectives, and the source of the gift—the company. Merchandise is recognizable, and it is a source of pride to the recipient. Cash awards tend to cost more to the company, since merchandise awards often can be purchased at prices far below retail. Cash also gets absorbed into regular wages, leaving nothing tangible and specifically identifiable with the program.

On the other hand, *nothing else can be used to satisfy as broad a range of needs as money.* Properly administered, money carries enormous motivational value. Besides, given the range of employee preferences for various types of awards, it may make more sense to adopt a "flexible awards" program that will allow employees to choose (similarly valued) awards that they want most. Since cash in the form of merit pay is probably the most popular award used to tie rewards to performance, let's examine the kinds of conditions that (1) impede and (2) facilitate such programs.

Barriers to Effective Implementation of Merit Pay

In some ways it is easier to assemble a list of reasons why merit pay *won't* work[58] than to describe the conditions under which it *will*. Often merit-pay systems fail for one or more of the following reasons:

1. *The incentive value of the reward offered is too low.* A person earning $2000 per month who gets a 5 percent merit increase subsequently earns $2100 per month. The "stakes," after taxes, are nominal.[43]
2. *The link between performance and rewards is weak.* If performance is measured annually on a one-dimensional scale, then employees will remain unclear about just what is being rewarded. In addition, the timing of a merit-pay award may have little or no relevance to the performance of desirable behaviors.[48]

FIGURE 12-3

Why merit-pay systems fail.

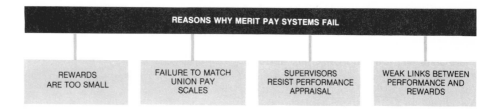

3. *Supervisors often resist performance appraisal.* Few supervisors are trained in the art of giving feedback accurately, comfortably, and with a minimum likelihood of creating other problems. (See Chapter 9.) If there is no appeal procedure for employees who are dissatisfied with their appraisals, feelings of unfairness are inevitable.
4. *Union contracts influence pay-for-performance decisions within and between organizations.* Multiyear contracts with cost-of-living provisions create pressures on pay at other levels and for nonunion employees. Failure to match union wages over a 3- or 4-year period (especially during periods of high inflation) invites dissension and turnover.

These reasons for the failure of merit-pay systems are shown graphically in Figure 12-3.

Barriers can be overcome

IBM increased labor productivity in the manufacturing of typewriters by nearly 200 percent over a 10-year period. At least half of this increase in productivity was due to two practices:

1. Pay employees for productivity, and only for productivity.
2. Promote employees for productivity, and only for productivity.[55]

Furthermore, research on the effect of merit-pay practices on performance in white-collar jobs indicates that all merit reward systems are not equal.[24] *Those which tie performance more closely to rewards are likely to generate higher levels of performance,* particularly after a year or two. In addition, *merit systems that incorporate a wide range of possible increases tend to generate higher levels of job performance after 1 year.* Some typical ranges used in successful merit systems are: Digital Equipment, 0 to 30 percent; Xerox, 0 to 13 percent; and Westinghouse, 0 to 19 percent.

Guidelines for Effective Merit-Pay Systems

Those affected by the merit-pay system must support it if it is to work as designed. This is in addition to the requirements for incentive programs shown in Figure 12-2. From the very inception of a merit-pay system, it is important that employees feel a sense of "ownership" of the system. To do this, consider

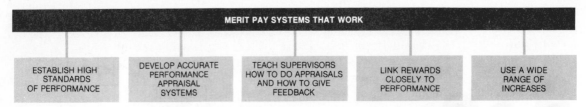

FIGURE 12-4 *Guidelines for effective merit-pay systems.*

implementing a merit-pay system on a step-by-step basis (for example, over a 2-year period), coupled with continued review and revision. Here are five steps to follow:

1. *Establish high standards of performance.* Low expectations tend to be self-fulfilling prophecies. In the world of sports, successful coaches such as Landry, Wooden, and Shula have demanded excellence. Excellence rarely results from expectations of mediocrity.
2. *Develop accurate performance appraisal systems.* Focus on job-specific, results-oriented criteria. Consider using multiple raters and appraisal formats that focus on the behavior of employees.
3. *Train supervisors in the mechanics of performance appraisal and in the art of giving feedback to subordinates.* Ineffective performance must be managed constructively.
4. *Tie rewards closely to performance.* Use semiannual performance appraisals to reward or to deny merit increases.
5. *Use a wide range of increases.* Make pay increases meaningful.

Merit-pay systems can work, but diligent application of these guidelines is essential if they are to work effectively. The guidelines are depicted in Figure 12-4.

Merit pay in the context of overall compensation

Within this framework, managers need to consider the following issues along with merit pay per se.

- Consult union contract provisions (if appropriate) concerning *who* must be involved in the design and implementation of merit-pay systems and grievance procedures.
- Do a thorough job analysis to capture the work behaviors and work outcomes used to appraise performance. Share these with job incumbents and reach consensus on job requirements before proceeding further.
- Establish a pay range for each class of jobs.
- The midpoint of a pay range (see Figure 11-2) is the basis for comparing employees in terms of their pay levels. It represents a proper rate of pay for an experienced worker performing satisfactorily.
- Inexperienced, newly hired employees are normally paid at the minimum of the range. However, market adjustments (based upon labor supply and

demand) may result in a starting rate above the minimum for certain jobs. Experienced people entering a job class are normally paid a rate consistent with their experience (e.g., at the midpoint of the pay range).

- Satisfactory performers may progress from their starting rates to the midpoints of their rate ranges on the basis of merit.
- Above-average performers may progress by above-average increments to the midpoint of the pay range (50th percentile) or even to a level midway between the midpoint and the maximum (75th percentile). Ordinarily no more than 30 percent of employees in a job category are in this group (Figure 12-5).
- Superior performers may progress to the maximum of the pay range. Ordinarily no more than 20 percent of employees in a job class will fall between the 75th percentile and the maximum (Figure 12-5).

FIGURE 12-5

Performance-based movements within rate ranges characterized by a 25 percent spread from minimum to midpoint and a 25 percent spread from midpoint to maximum.

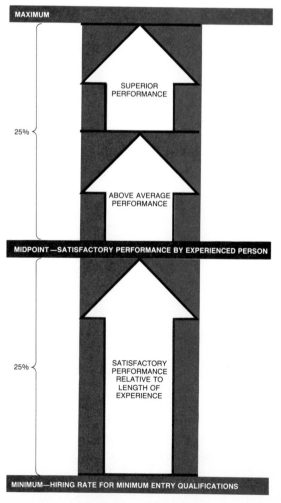

Once installed, merit-pay systems must be audited periodically to ensure that they are achieving the goals for which they were designed.[19] Questions like the following should be addressed:

- What is the percentage range of pay increases within high, average, and low performance levels?
- What is the increase *by supervisor* within each performance category? Is the same level of performance rewarded similarly across supervisors?
- What is the relationship between merit increases and turnover? Are leavers predominantly from the lower end of the performance scale?

Merit pay represents a significant cost outlay as well as a powerful motivational tool. It pays to check periodically whether it is working as designed.

Incentives for Executives

Companies with a history of outperforming their rivals, regardless of industry or economic climate, have two common characteristics: (1) a long-term, strategic view of their executives and (2) stability in their executive groups.[38] It makes sense, therefore, to develop integrated plans for total executive compensation so that rewards are based on achieving the company's long-term strategic goals. This may require a rebalancing of the elements of executive reward systems (Figure 12-6): base salary, annual (short-term) incentives, long-term incentives, regular employee benefits, and special benefits for executives (perquisites).

FIGURE 12-6

Elements of executive reward systems.

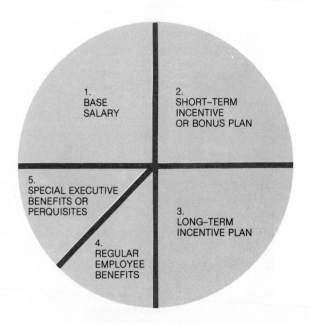

1. BASE SALARY
2. SHORT–TERM INCENTIVE OR BONUS PLAN
3. LONG–TERM INCENTIVE PLAN
4. REGULAR EMPLOYEE BENEFITS
5. SPECIAL EXECUTIVE BENEFITS OR PERQUISITES

Regardless of the exact form of rebalancing, base salaries will continue to be the center point of executive compensation.[7] This is because they generally serve as an index for benefit values. Objectives for short- and long-term incentives frequently are defined as a percentage of base salary. However, incentives are likely to become more long- than short-term-oriented. Here's why:

1. Annual, or short-term, incentive plans encourage the efficient use of existing assets. They are usually based on indicators of corporate performance, such as net income, total dividends paid, or some specific return on investment (i.e., net profit divided by net assets). Most such bonuses are paid immediately in cash, with CEOs receiving an average of 48 percent of their base pay, senior management 35 percent, and middle management 22 percent.[8]

2. Long-term plans encourage the development of new processes, plants, and products that open new markets and restore old ones. Hence long-term performance encompasses qualitative progress as well as quantitative accomplishments. Long-term incentive plans are designed to reward strategic gains rather than short-term contributions to profits. They are as common in owner-controlled firms (at least 5 percent of outstanding stock is held by an individual or organization not involved in the actual management of a company) as they are in management-controlled firms (no individual or organization controls more than 5 percent of the stock).[15] This is the kind of view that we should be encouraging among executives, for it relates consistently to company success.

Let's examine this topic in more detail.

Objectives of long-term incentives

There are a number of possible long-term incentive plans, but it becomes possible to choose one or more only after the strategic objectives of the program have been identified. Long-term incentives then allow a firm to execute its strategy. In general, two strategic objectives are to:

1. Motivate executives to maximize the future growth and profitability of the company.
2. Retain outstanding executives, and attract executives from the outside labor market.

Specific objectives of alternative long-term incentive plans might include the following.

1. Minimize the potential impact of the plan on earnings.
2. Provide favorable tax treatment for the company.
3. Minimize potential negative cash flow and dilution on earnings.
4. Minimize the cash outlay required by executives.
5. Provide executives with a means of accumulating capital at comparatively favorable tax rates.
6. Dissociate executives' rewards from dependence on the stock market (especially since the stock market crash of October 19, 1987).[45]

Since some of these objectives are incompatible with others, it is important (1) first to select objectives that are most relevant to the organization's overall compensation strategy and (2) then to decide which long-term incentive plan can best meet or fulfill the objectives. There is a long menu to choose from, and some of the most popular forms are described below.

Forms of long-term incentives

In general, long-term incentive plans fall into two broad categories. The first applies to firms that have decided *not* to dissociate executives' rewards from dependence on the stock market; that is, executive gain is tied to the growth in stock prices. Examples of incentives in this category are stock options, stock appreciation rights (SARs), and restricted stock. The second category ties the gain to predefined levels of company performance; examples include offering the executive performance units or performance shares.[12]

Long-term incentive plans in both categories are described in Table 12-2, and Figure 12-7 shows how these long-term incentives relate to one another in terms of what an executive can hope to gain from them.

TABLE 12-2 *A glossary of long-term incentive plans*

Plan	Description
Incentive stock option (ISO)	Executive receives right to purchase stock at stipulated price over specific period of time, in conformance with Internal Revenue Code.
Nonqualified stock option (NQSO)	Similar to incentive stock option, but without conformance with Internal Revenue Code.
Stock appreciation rights (SARs)	Company grants executive the right to appreciation in underlying stock over time.
Phantom stock plans	Executive receives units analogous to company shares and, at some point in the future, receives the value of the stock appreciation plus dividends.
Restricted stock awards	Executive receives outright grant of shares free or with discount, but is restricted from transferring stock until certain conditions are met; if conditions are not met, stock is forfeited.
Performance unit plan	Executive earns specially valued units at no cost, based on achievement of predetermined performance targets.
Performance share plan	Executive receives shares of stock, based on achievement of predetermined performance targets.
Formula value stock plan	Executive earns rights to special class of stock (not publicly traded) that is valued according to a formula, such as book value.

FIGURE 12-7

Potential gains to executives from alternative long-term incentives. (Reprinted, by permission of the publisher, from "Long-term Incentives for Management, Part I: An Overview," by F. W. Cook, from Compensation Review, *second quarter, p. 18, © 1980 American Management Association, New York. All rights reserved.*

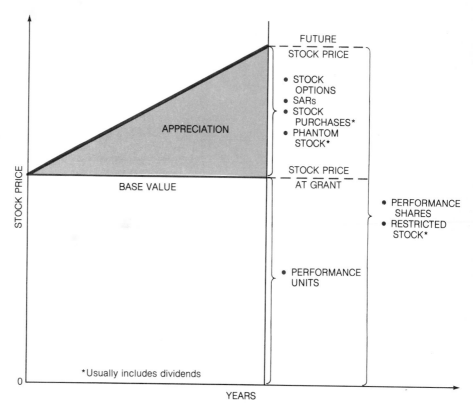

Impact of the Tax Reform Act of 1986 on incentives for executives

This act has had a major impact on executive benefits, principally on long-term incentives and on retirement benefits. Since the impact on retirement benefits was discussed in Chapter 11, the focus here will be on long-term incentives.

Diversification of incentives is more important than ever. Since no one knows how the tax law will ultimately affect markets and corporate balance sheets, ideally executives should receive compensation from several sources. Such a combination might include restricted stock, unfettered performance shares, and stock options. Since more than 90 percent of the largest U.S. companies offer some type of stock option to their executives, let's consider them in detail.[3]

There are two kinds of stock options: incentive options and nonqualified options. Only the former are affected by the Tax Reform Act of 1986. Here's how. In the past, executives could exercise an incentive option and—after holding the stock for 1 year—have the difference between the option and sale price taxed at low capital gains rates. As of 1988, however, capital gains are taxed like ordinary income, and so this break has disappeared. However, such options still retain an important advantage: They are not taxed when exercised, only when sold, assuming that the shares have appreciated in value. Non-qualified options are taxed twice: when the options are exercised and when the shares are sold.[6] When the options are exercised, executives pay taxes on the "bargain element," the difference between the exercise price and the stock's current trading price. *However, that same amount is a tax deduction that an employer gets when the options are exercised.* Employers stand to reap millions of dollars in tax savings, therefore, if they can persuade executives to give up the special tax status of their ISOs.[7] As an executive, what can you do?

The best way to receive nonqualified options under the new tax law is through a tandem plan that includes a cash offset for the taxes that are due when the option is exercised. Typically linked to company profitability goals, such plans often let executives accumulate performance units equal to the amount of taxes on the options they are granted.[6]

Stock appreciation rights (SARs) are also less attractive now, but for a different reason. SARs were embraced in the 1970s, but the bull market of the 1980s and the takeover craze have made them less attractive to companies. The problem is that gains in the value of the SARs must be charged against company earnings quarter by quarter because SARs can be exercised at any time and must be honored, usually in cash. For a company granting SARs, the better its stock performs, the bigger the drain on earnings. For example, suppose an executive gets 10,000 shares at $50 per share, a normal award for a big company. If the stock price increases to $100 per share, the executive has a profit of $500,000. In a typical big company, she or he will be one of about 40 SAR holders. So the company has a charge to earnings of $20 million. Because companies tend to award SARs every year, the cumulative effect on earnings can be staggering.[41]

So on the one hand SARs are terrific incentives: They can channel big dollars into the pockets of managers who have done well for shareholders. On the other hand, SARs frequently come back to haunt the same executives by cutting quarterly earnings, draining off cash, deflating stock prices, and angering shareholders. These problems are even worse when a company is targeted by corporate raiders. When its stock suddenly comes into play, the firm's earnings-deflating SAR obligations can double or triple within weeks—just when management needs as much shareholder goodwill as it can muster.[41]

To counter these effects, dozens of large companies (such as Walt Disney, Westinghouse, and United Technologies) are devising ingenious ways to lessen and even avoid the drain on earnings. These include interest-free loans to executives to exercise their stock options, "tax-offset bonuses" to compensate for taxes due, allowing executives to pay for options with company stock they already own, and substituting restricted stock for SARs. With restricted stock the company takes a known charge to earnings at the time of the grant and none thereafter.

Experts in executive compensation expect the current trend toward using long-term performance incentives to continue. However, plans that measure success only in terms of gains in stock prices have been criticized for not rewarding individual or corporate performance. As a result, some employers are now tying incentive awards to *unit* as well as to companywide performance. The following company examples show how two firms approach this issue differently.

COMPANY EXAMPLE
Long-term performance incentives at Champion International

Champion measures its managers by comparing the growth in earnings per share of Champion stock with that of 15 competitors in the forest products industry. It is an all-or-nothing program. If Champion International beats the industry average, 12 senior executives receive an award equal to one-fourth of their total regular bonuses over a 4-year term. If growth in earnings per share falls below the average, they get nothing.

Champion feels that basing long-term executive incentive compensation on how well the company does against its competitors helps reduce one of the main criticisms of performance plans: that external factors such as inflation, interest rates, and general economic activity are often more crucial to a company's prosperity than are the best efforts of its executives. These kinds of external factors affect all firms in an industry to the same extent.

COMPANY EXAMPLE
Combining incentives at Honeywell

Honeywell awards incentive pay to 70 of its division managers, based equally on the performance of their units and of the corporation. The managers receive stock for meeting certain return-on-investment goals for their units over a 3-year period. Says the director of corporate compensation: "We're sending two messages: One is you are a key player and you are responsible for total corporate results. But we also want you to be concerned about improving your own operating units. . . . If you want incentive pay to change [managerial] behavior, a manager has got to believe he has some control over what's being measured."[46]

The plan also reflects Honeywell's diverse and decentralized structure. Its units sell everything from computers to alarm systems, and decision making is pushed down to the various units. Combining corporate and unit incentives makes sense in light of the diverse nature of Honeywell's business. This is a good example of how one company ties its long-term incentives to its long-term business strategy.

Other companies have tried to refine such policies even further, using different measurements to correspond to the unit's strategy. The idea is that executives of a new, risky unit should be judged on, say, building market share, while executives of a stable, mature unit should be judged on generating cash or on cutting costs.[46] Given the number of mergers and acquisitions that have taken place throughout the 1980s, these kinds of arrangements are likely to be even more popular in the future.

Incentives for Lower-Level Employees

As noted earlier in this chapter, a common practice is to supplement employees' pay with increments related to performance. These are known variously as "incentives," "bonuses," "commissions," or "piecework plans." All are offered as rewards for improvements in job performance.

Most of these plans have a "baseline," or normal, work standard; performance above this standard is rewarded. The baseline should be high enough so that employees are not given extra rewards for what is really just a normal day's work. On the other hand, the baseline should not be so high that it is impossible to earn additional pay.

It is more difficult to specify work standards in some jobs than in others. At the level of top management, for instance, what constitutes a "normal" day's output? To overcome this barrier, top managers are provided with targets, such as:

- Growth in earnings per share of company stock.
- Penetration of new markets or the introduction of successful new products.
- Success of diversification or integration programs.
- When set realistically, targets are designed to motivate high performance and to provide a measure of executive worth.

As one moves down the organizational hierarchy, however, jobs can be defined more clearly and shorter-run goals and targets can be established.

Setting workload standards

Incentive systems are all dependent on workload standards. The standards provide a relatively objective definition of the job, they give employees targets to shoot for, and they make it easier for supervisors to assign work equitably. Once the workload standards are set, employees have an opportunity to earn more than their base salaries, often as much as 20 to 25 percent more. In short, they have an incentive to work harder *and* smarter.

In setting workload standards for production work, the ideal job (ideal only in terms of ability to measure performance, not in terms of improving work motivation or job satisfaction) should (1) be highly repetitive, (2) have a short job cycle, and (3) produce a clear, measurable output. However, before explicit workload standards can be set, management must do the following:

- Describe the job by means of job analysis.
- Decide *how* the job is to be done (motion study).
- Decide *how fast* the job should be done (time study).

The standards themselves will vary, of course, according to the *type* of product or service (e.g., a hospital, a factory, or a cable television company); the *method of service delivery;* the degree to which service can be *quantified;* and *organizational needs,* including legal and social pressures. In fact, the many different forms of incentive plans for lower-level employees really differ only along two dimensions:

1. How the premium rates are determined
2. How the extra payments are made

COMPANY EXAMPLE

Performance-linked pay plans for lower-level employees

Increasingly, companies are dangling incentive compensation down to lower-level managers and key workers, such as engineers, investment officials, and others who especially aid the company. For example, John Hancock Mutual Life Insurance Co. rewards lower managers with up to 10 percent of their salaries for "extraordinary work." Shawmut Co. has a similar plan for its bank lenders, giving as much as 25 percent of base pay. And Hewlett-Packard gives 200 to 300 special stock options a year to employees who show extra accomplishment.

Indeed, a 1987 survey of 747 firms found that 49 percent offer individual incentives to lower managers and that 48 percent offer them to key professional and technical employees. Both figures are more than double the previous year.[27]

Among companies that provide incentive awards, these are the most popular: lump-sum individual awards (65 percent), productivity bonuses (17 percent), team performance awards (15 percent), and cash profit sharing (15 percent).[16] Among companies that give team performance awards, American Greetings Corp. even bases its cost-of-living increases on merit, and bonuses are based on each unit's results. Pacific Gas & Electric has a similar team award program for 8000 management-level workers.[25]

Incentive systems are certainly sound from a motivational standpoint. Rewards are tied directly to (i.e., made contingent upon) performance, and reinforcement (via the measurement of performance) is immediate. Yet incentive plans often generate conflict. *Work groups* may impose ceilings on output for the following reasons:

1. Employees may fear that if they earn too much, management will cut premium rates and/or increase workload standards.
2. As a result of excess inventory and production, employees will work themselves out of a job.
3. Unlimited incentives threaten status hierarchies within work groups. That is, older workers (higher status) may not be able to match the pace of their younger colleagues. So to protect their social position, work groups establish ceilings, or "bogeys," of what is safe or proper output.

Union attitudes

A unionized employer may establish an incentive system, but it is subject to negotiation through collective bargaining. Unions may also wish to participate in the day-to-day management of the incentive system, and management ought to consider that demand seriously. As noted earlier, employees often fear that management will manipulate the system to the disadvantage of employees. Joint participation helps reassure employees that the plan is fair.

Union attitudes toward incentives vary with the type of incentive offered. Unions tend to oppose individual piece-rate systems because they pit worker against worker, and they can create unfavorable intergroup conflict. However, unions tend to support organizationwide systems, such as profit sharing, because of the extra earnings they provide to their members. In fact, the 1987–1989 agreements between the United Auto Workers and Ford, and between the UAW and General Motors, both include profit sharing plans that give UAW members the opportunity to fatten their paychecks if their companies do well.

COMPANY EXAMPLE

Individual incentives at Lincoln Electric

From its earliest years, 90-year-old Lincoln Electric Company of Cleveland, Ohio, has charted a unique path in worker-management relations, featuring high wages, guaranteed employment, few supervisors, a lucrative bonus incentive system, and piecework compensation. The company is the world's largest maker of arc-welding equipment; it has 2650 U.S. employees, sales and distribution offices in Canada, France, and Australia, and no unions. Among the innovative management practices that set Lincoln apart are these:

- Guaranteed employment for all full-time workers with more than 2 years' service, and no mandatory retirement. No worker has been laid off for more than 40 years.
- High wages, including a substantial annual bonus (roughly 50 percent of base pay) based on the company's profits. Wages at Lincoln are roughly equivalent to wages for similar work elsewhere in the Cleveland area, but the bonuses the company pays make its compensation substantially higher. Lincoln has never had a strike and has not missed a bonus payment since the system was instituted in 1934. Individual bonuses are set by a formula that judges workers on four points: ideas and cooperation, output, ability to work without supervision, and work quality.
- Piecework—more than half of Lincoln's workers are paid according to what they produce, rather than an hourly or weekly wage. If a worker is sick, he or she does not get paid.
- Promotion is almost exclusively from within, according to merit, not seniority.
- Few supervisors, with a supervisor-to-worker ratio of 1 to 100, far lower than in much of the industry.

■ No break periods, and mandatory overtime. Workers must work overtime, if ordered, during peak production periods and must agree to job transfers to meet production schedules or to maintain the company's guaranteed employment program.

While the company insists on individual initiative—and pays according to individual effort—it works diligently to foster the notion of teamwork. And it did so long before the Japanese became known for emphasizing such concepts. If a worker is overly competitive with fellow employees, the worker is rated poorly in terms of cooperation and team play on his or her semiannual rating reports. Thus that worker's bonus will be smaller. Says one company official: "This is not an easy style to manage; it takes a lot of time and a willingness to work with people."[51]

Group and Organizationwide Incentives

To provide broader motivation than is furnished by incentive plans geared to individual employees, several other approaches have been tried. Their aim is twofold: to increase productivity and to improve morale by giving employees a feeling of participation in and identification with the company. These include group incentives, profit sharing, and the Scanlon plan. Briefly, let's consider the advantages and disadvantages of each of these.

Group incentives

Group incentives provide an opportunity for each group member to receive a bonus based on the output of the group as a whole. Groups may be as small as 4 to 7 employees, or as large as 35 to 40 employees. _Group incentives are most appropriate when jobs are highly interrelated._ They have the following advantages:

1. Group incentives make it possible to reward workers who provide essential services to line workers (so-called indirect labor) yet who are paid only their regular base pay. These employees do things like transport supplies and materials, maintain equipment, or inspect work output.
2. Group incentives encourage cooperation, not competition, among workers.

On the other hand, group incentives also have their disadvantages:

1. Fear that management will cut rates if employees produce too much.
2. Competition between groups.
3. Inability of workers to see their individual contributions to the output of the group. Since they do not see the link between their individual effort and increased rewards, they are not motivated to produce more.

To overcome the first two disadvantages of group incentives, many firms have introduced profit sharing plans. However, the third disadvantage remains.

Profit sharing

In the United States, profit sharing is the most common method that companies use to provide retirement income for their employees. Firms use it for any one or more of the following reasons: to provide a group incentive for increased productivity, to institute a flexible reward structure that reflects a company's actual economic position, to enhance employees' security and identification with the company, to attract and retain workers more easily, and/or to educate individuals about the factors that underlie business success and the capitalistic system.[14]

Employees receive a bonus that is normally based on some percentage (e.g., 10 to 30 percent) of the company's profits beyond some minimum level. Profit shares may be paid directly to employees at the end of the fiscal year (as is done by about 40 percent of all plans), but more often they are *deferred*; that is, they are placed in a managed stock and bond fund or a guaranteed investment contract with an insurance company. Increasingly, however, both small and large businesses are offering employees more alternatives with their profit sharing and savings accounts. In fact, one survey of 812 employers found that 68 percent made more than one investment option available to employees.[17]

Two of the advantages claimed for profit sharing are:

1. It strengthens employees' sense of involvement with the enterprise, cuts waste, and motivates employees to work harder.
2. The firm can provide pensions and other benefits without increasing fixed costs since contributions are made *only* in profitable years.

On the other hand, profit sharing also has the following disadvantages:

1. The relationship between performance and reward is weaker than even group incentives provide.
2. There is a long delay between effort and reward since employees do not receive their share of company profits until a year after they earn them. This need not always be the case—Cummins Engine of Columbus, Indiana, pays out quarterly profit shares to employees.[30]
3. Many employees do not understand how profits are computed. Even worse, if labor-management relations are poor, employees may suspect that profits are being underreported. (To avoid this problem, the plan might be applied both to workers and managers equally.)
4. Finally, from the employee's perspective, benefits and pensions are insecure under deferred profit sharing plans since the company pays only if it makes a profit.

Certainly the success of profit sharing plans depends on the company's overall human resource management policy and on the state of labor-management relations. This is even more true of the Scanlon plan.

The Scanlon plan

During the mid-1930s, Joseph N. Scanlon, then president of a steelworkers union local in Mansfield, Ohio, developed a plan for union-management cooperation. Under Scanlon's plan, the union agreed to work with the company on production committees to reduce costs *if* management would reopen its doors during a plant shutdown brought about by the Great Depression.[31] In 1944, at the Adamson Company in Ohio, Scanlon refined his original plan by developing a ratio of *total payroll to sales value of production* as a measure of performance. Today the Scanlon plan takes many different forms, but all include four basic elements: the ratio, the bonus, the production committee, and the screening committee.

The ratio, total payroll to sales value of production, ideally varies from 37 to 42 percent, although in practice it may vary considerably. The size of the *bonus* depends on the reduction in costs below the present ratio. Normally 75 percent of the bonus goes to employees, and 25 percent to the company, with 25 percent of 75 percent (or 18.75 percent) held in reserve for possible deficits. The basis for each employee's share of the bonus is his or her monthly earnings as a percentage of the monthly total labor costs.

A production committee consisting of two to five workers plus a supervisor is formed in each major department. It meets twice a month to discuss employee suggestions for increasing productivity, improving quality, and cutting waste. The committee works to develop an understanding of *all* production costs, and it publicizes this information throughout the business.

Finally a *screening committee* consisting of 8 to 12 members (workers plus members of top management) meets once a month to do three things:

1. Review all suggestions submitted from the production committees.
2. Review the monthly bonus and all aspects of business trends relative to the company.
3. Discuss current production problems.

When the Scanlon plan works, it works well. For example, in the Dana Corporation, a Toledo, Ohio, producer of parts for cars and trucks, the plan has worked remarkably well with its 24,000 employees. In 1979 absenteeism stood at an all-time low of 3 percent, sales were at a record high since the plan was adopted, and bonuses were running 25 percent of gross monthly pay.[44] Nevertheless, in the 50 years since the plan's inception, it has been abandoned by firms about as often as it has been retained. Here are some reasons why:

1. Generally it does not work well in piecework operations.
2. Some firms are uncomfortable about bringing unions into business planning.
3. Some managers feel that they may be giving up their prerogatives.[39, 54]

Neither the size of a company nor the type of technology it employs seems to be related to Scanlon plan success.[57] However, employee participation, positive managerial attitudes, the number of years a company has had a Scanlon plan, favorable and realistic employee attitudes, and involvement by a high-level executive are strongly related to the success of a Scanlon plan.[57] To develop an organizationwide incentive plan that has a chance to survive, let alone succeed, careful and in-depth planning must precede implementation. It is true of all incentive plans, though, that *none will work well except in a climate of trustworthy labor-management relations and sound human resource management practices.*

Policy Issues in Pay Planning and Administration

The effect of inflation

All organizations must make some allowances for inflation in their salary programs. Given an inflation rate of 8 percent, for example, the firm that fails to increase its salary ranges at all over a 2-year period will be 16 percent behind its competitors. Needless to say, it becomes difficult to recruit new employees under these circumstances, and it becomes difficult to motivate present employees to remain or to produce.

How do firms cope? One survey of 183 human resource executives indicated that most firms grant regular wage increases across the board for all employee groups. On top of this, some employees may get special pay supplements and incentives. These include pay for performance (provided by 39 percent of the companies), productivity or profit sharing bonuses (35 percent), and special bonuses for supervisors (11 percent).[49] Other surveys indicate that automatic pay raises for nonunion employees have almost disappeared at most major concerns. Companies are tying pay more to performance. For example, at Commercial Metals Co. of Dallas, cost-of-living adjustments will not be resumed even if inflation zooms. The company found that its employees—*including average performers*—prefer to be paid on the basis of their performance. However, other firms that have adopted this approach, such as Armco and B. F. Goodrich, note that the switch from automatic to merit increases does not necessarily lower labor costs.[33]

Pay compression

Pay compression is related to the general problem of inflation. It exists in many forms, including: (1) higher starting salaries for new hires, thereby leading long-term employees to see only a slight difference between their current pay and that of new hires; (2) hourly pay increases for unionized employees that exceed those of salaried and nonunion employees; (3) recruitment of new college graduates for management or professional jobs at salaries above those of current job holders; and (4) excessive overtime payme, some employees, or payment of different overtime rates (e.g., time and o, half for some and double time for others). However, first-line supervisors, unlike middle managers, may actually *benefit* from pay inflation among non-management employees since companies generally maintain a differential between the pay of supervisors and the pay of their highest-paid subordinates.[49] These differentials typically range from 15 to 25 percent.[22]

One solution to the problem of pay compression is to institute *equity adjustments;* that is, increases in pay are given to employees to maintain differences in job worth between their jobs and those of others. Some companies provide for equity adjustments through a constantly changing pay scale. Thus Aluminum Company of America (ALCOA) surveys its competitors' pay every 3 months and adjusts its pay rates accordingly. ALCOA strives to maintain at least a 20 percent differential between employees and their supervisors.[4]

Another approach is to grant benefits that increase gradually to more senior employees. Thus, although the difference between the *direct pay* of this group and that of their shorter-service coworkers may be slim, senior employees have a distinct advantage when the *entire* compensation package is considered.

Overtime as a cause of compression can be dealt with in two ways. First, it can be *rotated* among employees so that all share overtime equally. However, in situations where this kind of arrangement is not feasible, firms might consider establishing an overtime pay policy for management employees; for example, a supervisor may be paid an overtime rate after he or she works a minimum number of overtime hours. Such a practice does not violate the Fair Labor Standards Act, for under the law overtime pay is not *required* for exempt jobs, although it may be adopted voluntarily. Finally, a recent survey indicated that one of the most favored solutions by companies is to provide aids to upward mobility, such as training and rapid advancement; strategies of this type keep the pay structure intact while helping individuals to move within it.[22]

Pay compression is certainly a difficult problem—but not so difficult that it cannot be managed. Indeed it *must* be managed if companies are to achieve their goal of providing pay that is perceived as fair.[4]

Pay raises

Coping with inflation is the biggest hurdle to overcome in a merit-pay plan. On the other hand, *the only measure of a raise is how much it exceeds the increase in the cost of living:* 12.4 percent inflation in 1980 more than wiped out the average raise. However, the average 6 percent raise that employees received in 1987 provided a *real* increase since inflation was only about 4 percent.[29]

The simplest and most effective method for dealing with inflation in a merit-pay system is to increase salary ranges.[50] By raising salary ranges (e.g., based on a survey of average increases in starting salaries for the coming year) without giving general increases, a firm can maintain competitive hiring rates and at the same time maintain the merit concept surrounding salary increases.

Since a raise in minimum pay for each salary range creates an employee group that falls below the new minimum, it is necessary to raise these employees to the new minimum. Such adjustments technically violate the merit philosophy, but the advantages gained by keeping employees in the salary range and at a rate that is sufficient to retain them clearly outweigh the disadvantages.[50]

The size of the merit increase for a given level of performance should decrease as the employee moves farther up the salary range. Merit guide charts provide a means for doing this. Guide charts identify (1) an employee's current performance rating and (2) his or her location in a pay grade. The intersection of these two dimensions identifies a percentage of pay increase based on the performance level and location of the employee in the pay grade. Figure 12-8 shows an example of such a chart. The rationale for the merit guide chart approach is that a person at the top of the range is already making more than the "going rate" for that job. Hence she or he should have to demonstrate *more* than satisfactory performance in order to continue moving farther above the going rate.

A final aspect of the program is to give increases more than once a year (e.g., every 6 months). By getting a raise every 6 months, employees tend to feel that they are keeping up with inflation. The organization also benefits since the increases will cost less. This is so because rather than giving the entire increase for a full year, employees receive half the increase for 6 months and the rest for the other 6 months. For example, if an employee making $15,000 per year gets a 15 percent increase, that increase will cost the employer $2250 for the year. If, instead, the employee gets two 7.5 percent increases, the total

FIGURE 12-8

Example of a merit guide chart.

EMPLOYEE PERFORMANCE	PERCENT INCREASE				
Distinguished	14%	12%	11%	10%	9%
Commendable	11%	10%	9%	8%	Ceiling
Competent	9%	8%	7%	Ceiling	
Adequate	5%	0	Ceiling		
Provisional	0	Ceiling			
SALARY (as % of midpoint) IS:	80%	88%	96%	104%	112%	120%

cost for the year is only $1167.[50] Despite this fact, the vast majority of companies continue to award annual raises, either on an employee's anniversary date or on a common review date for all employees.[53] The proposal just outlined will not solve all the compensation problems caused by inflation, but it is important to remember that *it is not an organization's responsibility to pay wages that keep pace with inflation*. The responsibility is merely to pay wages that are competitive. What this merit compensation system will do is to allow most employees to stay close until the economy settles down.

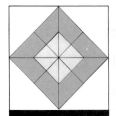

Impact of Incentives on Productivity, Quality of Work Life, and the Bottom Line

In this area, perhaps more than any other, there is a closer relationship between effective human resource management practice and the three major themes of this book: productivity, quality of work life, and profits. When employees can see a clear link between an increase in their efforts and an increase in rewards that they personally value, they are motivated to perform "above and beyond the call of duty." Increased motivation to perform well leads to increased productivity. And increased productivity should be rewarded in the form of incentives that can be earned *on top of* base pay. When work has high incentive value to employees, their quality of work life improves significantly. Actually employees benefit in two ways: (1) from the rewards they receive and (2) from the intrinsic satisfaction that results from a job well done. Organizations also benefit because rewards are granted *only* for increases in productivity, and increases in productivity mean improved bottom-line performance. As we have seen, individual incentive plans typically increase performance an average of 30 percent, while group incentive plans typically increase performance an average of 18 percent. In addition, individual incentives promote greater concern and ego-involvement with one's job than do group-based incentives.[34] In short, if the deep well of employee motivation can be tapped through an imaginative incentive plan (such as the "100 Club"), everybody wins.

**CASE 12-1
Conclusion**

The 100 Club: a million-dollar incentive plan

By 1983, productivity at the Diamond International plant was up 16.5 percent, and quality-related errors were down 40 percent. Worker grievances decreased 72 percent, and lost time due to industrial accidents decreased 43.7 percent. The turnaround meant more than $1 million in gross financial benefits for Diamond's parent company.

Remember how negative employee attitudes were in 1981 when the program began? When the survey was repeated in 1983, 86 percent of the employees said that management considered them important or very important, 81 percent felt that their work was recognized, and 79 percent reported that their work and the products of their work were of much greater concern to them.

Not surprisingly, labor relations also improved. Even though employees were due a 58-cent-per-hour wage hike in July 1983, they agreed to forgo it because of concerns about competition. Labor leaders credited the 100 Club with keeping the company afloat and fostering a new atmosphere of cooperation with management. As the director of human resources noted, "I'm a little tired of all those Japanese success stories. What we've done here shows that you can have American success stories as well." As a sign of that success, the 100 Club has been phased in at Diamond's three other fiber-product plants in Mississippi, California, and New York.

Summary

To enhance employees' motivation to work, the various elements of human resource management must be coordinated into a unified program. To do this, managers need to focus on three key areas of responsibility: (1) *performance definition* (describing what is expected of employees, plus the continuous orientation of employees toward effective job performance); (2) *performance facilitation* (eliminating roadblocks to performance, providing adequate resources, and careful personnel selection); and (3) *performance encouragement* (providing a sufficient amount of highly valued rewards in a fair, timely manner).

The most effective incentive programs are simple, specific, attainable, and measurable. One of the most popular is merit pay, and merit pay works best when the following guidelines are followed: (1) establish high standards of performance; (2) develop appraisal systems that focus on job-specific, results-oriented criteria; (3) train supervisors in the mechanics of performance ap-

---

TOMORROW'S FORECAST

If present trends continue, we can expect to see more organizations moving to performance-based pay plans, with a gradual phasing out of automatic cost-of-living adjustments. To the extent possible, more firms will adopt individually oriented incentive plans since the average payoff to be expected from them is higher than under group or organizationwide incentive plans. In effect, firms will be asking workers at all levels to put more of their pay "at risk," in return for potentially much higher rewards. To reassure workers who are vulnerable to layoff in the event of a corporate takeover, more firms will grant "silver" and "tin" parachutes to middle- and lower-level employees.[2] Finally, a wider *range* of pay increases will be used in an effort to make meaningful distinctions in performance. While recognition is certainly important, few firms will abandon the use of money as a motivator.

praisal and in the art of giving constructive feedback; (4) tie rewards closely to performance; and (5) provide a wide range of possible pay increases. The many different forms of individual, group, and organizationwide incentives differ along only two basic dimensions: how the premium rates are determined and how the extra payments are made. Long-term incentives for executives, for example, fall into two broad categories: those which tie executive gain to stock price growth and those which relate gains to predefined levels of company performance. Finally, we examined the following pay policy issues: the effect of inflation on pay planning and administration, pay compression, and pay raises.

Discussion Questions

12-1 What can managers do to motivate subordinates?

12-2 Critique the approach to managing people used by North American Tool and Die.

12-3 What key issues need to be taken into account in the development of an incentive-program budget?

12-4 Why do merit-pay plans fail so often?

12-5 Describe the operation of a Scanlon plan.

12-6 What are the causes, consequences, and cures for pay compression?

References

1. Belcher, D. W. (1979, Second Quarter). Pay equity or pay fairness? *Compensation Review*, **2**, 31–37.
2. Bennett, A. (1986, Apr. 3). Merger boom, deregulation cause pay problems at many companies. *Wall Street Journal*, p. 27.
3. Bennett, A. (1987, Apr. 10). Firms trim annual pay increases and focus on long term. *Wall Street Journal*, p. 29.
4. Bergmann, T. J., Hills, F. S., & Priefert, L. (1983, Second Quarter). Pay compression: Causes, results, and possible solutions. *Compensation Review*, **6**, 17–26.
5. Berkowitz, L., Fraser, C., Treasure, F. P., & Cochran, S. (1987). Pay equity, job gratifications, and comparisons in pay satisfaction. *Journal of Applied Psychology*, **72**, 544–551.
6. Bettner, J. (1986, Oct. 28). Executive dreams: What benefits to request under the new tax law. *Wall Street Journal*, p. 35.
7. Bettner, J. (1987, July 28). Executives get bonus for swap in stock options. *Wall Street Journal*, p. 25.
8. Bigger bonuses (1987, Sep. 17). *Wall Street Journal*, p. 37.
9. Campbell, J. P., Dunnette, M. D., Lawler, E. E., III, & Weick, K. E., Jr. (1970). *Managerial behavior, performance, and effectiveness*. New York: McGraw-Hill.
10. Cherrington, D. J. (1980). *The work ethic: Working values and values that work*. New York: AMACOM.

11. Cherrington, D. J., & Wixom, B. J., Jr. (1983). Recognition is still a top motivator. *Personnel Administrator*, **28**(5), 87–91.
12. Cook, F. W. (1980, Second Quarter). Long-term incentives for management, part I: An overview. *Compensation Review*, **3**, 15–25.
13. Dwortzan, B. (1982, June). The ABCs of incentive programs. *Personnel Journal*, pp. 436–442.
14. Florkowski, G. W. (1987). The organizational impact of profit sharing. *Academy of Management Review*, **12**, 622–636.
15. Gomez-Mejia, L. R., Tosi, H., & Hinkin, T. (1987). Managerial control, performance, and executive compensation. *Academy of Management Journal*, **30**, 51–70.
16. Good job (1986, Oct. 24). *Wall Street Journal*, p. 27.
17. Gottschalk, E. C. (1987, Apr. 16). Self-control: Firms let workers manage own profit-sharing funds. *Wall Street Journal*, p. 27.
18. Herzberg, F. (1966). *Work and the nature of man.* New York: Mentor Executive Library.
19. Hills, F. S., Madigan, R. M., Scott, K. D., & Markham, S. E. (1987). Tracking the merit of merit pay. *Personnel Administrator*, **32**(3), 50–57.
20. House, R. J., & Mitchell, T. R. (1974). Path-goal theory of leadership. *Journal of Contemporary Business*, **3**, 81–97.
21. Huseman, R. C., Hatfield, J. D., & Miles, E. W. (1987). A new perspective on equity theory: The equity sensitivity construct. *Academy of Management Review*, **12**, 222–234.
22. Kanter, R. M. (1987, March–April). The attack on pay. *Harvard Business Review*, pp. 60–67.
23. Katz, D., & Kahn, R. L. (1978). *The social psychology of organizations* (2d ed.). New York: Wiley.
24. Kopelman, R. E., & Reinharth, L. (1982, Fourth Quarter). Research results: The effect of merit-pay practices on white-collar performance. *Compensation Review*, **5**, 30–40.
25. Labor letter (1987, Mar. 31). *Wall Street Journal*, p. 1.
26. Labor letter (1986, June 10). *Wall Street Journal*, p. 1.
27. Labor letter (1987, June 23). *Wall Street Journal*, p. 1.
28. Labor letter (1987, July 7). *Wall Street Journal*, p. 1.
29. Labor letter (1987, Sep. 15). *Wall Street Journal*, p. 1.
30. Leefeldt, E. (1984, Nov. 5). Profit-sharing plans reward productivity. *Wall Street Journal*, p. 27.
31. Lesieur, F. (1958). *The Scanlon plan: A frontier in labor-management cooperation.* Cambridge, MA: MIT Press.
32. Locke, E. A., Shaw, K. N., Saari, L. M., & Latham, G. P. (1981). Goal-setting and task performance: 1969–1980. *Psychological Bulletin*, **90**, 125–152.
33. Lublin, J. (1984, Mar. 13). Labor letter. *Wall Street Journal*, p. 1.
34. Mannheim, B., & Angel, O. (1986). Pay systems and work-role centrality of industrial workers. *Personnel Psychology*, **39**, 359–377.
35. Maslow, A. H. (1954). *Motivation and personality.* New York: Harper.
36. McClelland, D. C. (1961). *The achieving society.* New York: Van Nostrand Reinhold.
37. McFillen, J., & Podsakoff, P. M. (1983). A coordinated approach to motivation can increase productivity. *Personnel Administrator*, **29**(7), 45–53.

38. Meyer, P. (1983). Executive compensation must promote long-term commitment. *Personnel Administrator,* 28(5), 37–42.
39. Moore, B., & Ross, T. (1978). *The Scanlon way to improved productivity.* New York: Wiley.
40. Perceptions of pay (1986, July 7). *Wall Street Journal,* p. 13.
41. Perham, J. (1987, July). Stock incentive backlash. *Business Month,* pp. 28–29.
42. Perry, N. J. (1984, Jan. 9). America's most admired corporations. *Fortune,* pp. 50–62.
43. Piamonte, J. S. (1979, September). In praise of monetary motivation. *Personnel Journal,* pp. 597–624.
44. Quick, T. (1979, January). Increasing productivity with the Scanlon plan. *Training HRD,* pp. 32–33.
45. Redling, E. T. (1982, March–April). The 1981 Tax Act: Boon to managerial compensation. *Personnel,* pp. 52–59.
46. Reibstein, L. (1987, Apr. 10). More employers link incentives to unit results. *Wall Street Journal,* p. 29.
47. Robbins, C. B. (1983). Design effective incentive plans. *Personnel Administrator,* 28(5), 8–10.
48. Rollins, T. (1987, June). Pay for performance: The pros and cons. *Personnel Journal,* pp. 104–107.
49. Roundup (1981, November–December). The impact of inflation on wage and salary administration. *Personnel,* pp. 53–56.
50. Schwartz, J. D. (1982, February). Maintaining merit compensation in a high-inflation economy. *Personnel Journal,* pp. 147–152.
51. Serrin, W. (1984, Jan. 15). The way that works at Lincoln. *New York Times,* p. D1.
52. Skinner, B. F. (1957). *Science and human behavior.* East Norwalk, CT: Appleton-Century-Crofts.
53. Time for a raise? (1986, July 31). *Wall Street Journal,* p. 25.
54. Tyler, L. S., & Fisher, B. (1983). The Scanlon concept: A philosophy as much as a system. *Personnel Administrator,* 29(7), 33–37.
55. Vough, C. F. (1979). *Productivity: A practical program for improving efficiency.* New York: AMACOM.
56. Vroom, V. H. (1964). *Work and motivation.* New York: Wiley.
57. White, J. K. (1979). The Scanlon plan: Causes and consequences of success. *Academy of Management Journal,* 22, 292–312.
58. Wickenden, D. (1983, Nov. 7). Merit pay won't work. *The New Republic,* pp. 12–15.

day was separate meetings to discuss the content and implications of the other group's descriptions of the actual relationship.

The managers' discussion

Management's discussion of the union's description of actual conditions centered on the union's contention of "hopelessness." The plant manager had warned of a possible strike, but it was apparent that management had been blind to the depth of the union's despair at achieving a turnaround prior to the expiration of the contract. In an effort to evaluate the implications of these circumstances, management concluded that (1) the union president had the backing of the employees and (2) he had the power to call a strike even though the union meetings routinely had poor attendance. The management group ended its discussion on the sobering note that a strike was a realistic possibility. They committed themselves to asking open-ended and honest questions in a search for genuine understanding and avoidance of further polarization.

The union's discussion

The union's discussion of management's description of actual conditions was "more of the same old stuff." Their feeling was that management was deaf and blind to union efforts to deal with management constructively.

The joint discussion

In the joint discussion of actual conditions, the union was astonished to learn that management saw their joint relationship as a game of win or lose. In fact, the union vice president felt that during the past 6 to 8 months management had tried to bypass the union and to go directly to the employees.

Overtime was an example. Employees had been told that many situations were emergencies and that the company therefore needed them to work overtime. It was only when employees would *not* work overtime that management came to the union. Members of the management group responded that they were responsible for getting the work out and needed people to do it. Nevertheless, the union was firm on the matter: Management had no credibility and no right to expect respect from people who were dehumanized and depersonalized in every possible way.

As the session continued, the beginnings of a reversal in the attitude of the management group became evident. Group members became less intent on defending their own positions and more interested in obtaining genuine understanding of the union perspective. They raised a series of questions about each of the union's points.

What past and current actions led the union to conclude that management was concerned only with production? The managers admitted that they were not perfect, but they also stressed that they were not responsible for *every* problem in the plant. They pointed out that they had inherited a number of problems, and they expressed the need to have the union's help to solve them.

The union group explained that its feeling of hopelessness was based on the constraints of the present system. Once they were locked into a contract, their only relief was the grievance procedure. They felt hopeless because management forced them to resolve grievances through arbitration by a third party. Since arbitration incurred expenses for their members, the union could not afford to pursue every grievance.

Other issues raised by the union included concrete examples of inconsistent enforcement of rules, of unwarranted suspensions, and of "unnecessary" grievances. After this exchange, there were no further questions between the two groups. Each returned to its own separate session for further deliberation on the issues.

QUESTIONS

1. How might the approach used at the Hillside plant contribute to an improvement in quality of work life?
2. Based on the information presented, how did management contribute to the problems? How did the union contribute?
3. Do you see any possibility for long-term resolution of the problems facing the Hillside plant? Why?

What's Ahead

Case 13-1 illustrates an important trend in the evolution of labor-management relations—a trend toward cooperation rather than conflict, a trend toward accommodation to each other's needs. This is a slow evolutionary process, and in this chapter and the next we shall see that it has not proceeded smoothly. Nevertheless, in the internationally competitive business environment in which we live, both sides must cooperate to survive. This chapter and the next focus on the legal, social, and economic contexts of labor-management relations, both in union and in nonunion work settings. As future managers, it is important that you understand some of the key factors that have shaped these relations over time: historical events, the passage of labor laws by Congress, and interpretations of the laws by the National Labor Relations Board and the federal courts.

In addition to these issues, Chapter 13 examines the internal organizational structures of unions, why employees join unions, the unionization process, and the current status of the labor movement. Chapter 14 deals with specific interactions between labor and management, such as collective bargaining and contract administration issues, and also the special concerns of nonunion employees, such as employment-at-will. Chapter 14 concludes with a discussion of problems facing the American labor movement.

Union Membership in the United States

During the 1980s, U.S. union membership dropped off dramatically, as Table 13-1 indicates. Between 1979 and 1987, there was a 20 percent plunge in the number of union jobs, largely due to plant closings and layoffs. Many of those jobs are gone for good. Overall, the percentage of workers who do not belong to unions has risen steadily from 71.6 percent in 1965 to 83 percent in 1987. Yet these overall figures may mask underlying trends. One of every four union members is a woman now, and while total union membership dropped in 1987, the number of female union members increased by 40,000.[58] The women tend to work in *service industries* represented by such unions as: the Retail Clerks; the Service Employees International Union; the American Federation of State, County, and Municipal Employees; and the United Federation of Teachers.

Several economic and demographic forces favor a resurgence of unions. Corporate cost cutting has rattled many workers; a recent survey showed them to be more receptive to unions than at any time since 1979. In addition, labor shortages in certain markets have emboldened workers who no longer fear losing their jobs. And both women and minority-group members, who are

TABLE 13-1 *Changes in union membership (in thousands), 1955–1985*

	1955	1965	1975	1985
United Steel Workers	980	876	1062	572
International Ladies' Garment Workers Union	383	363	363	210
United Rubber Workers of America	163	153	173	106
International Typographical Union	78	87	81	38
International Association of Machinists and Aerospace Workers	627	663	780	520
Communications Workers of America	249	288	476	524
United Automobile Workers	1260	1150	—	974
Service Employees International Union	205	305	480	688
American Federation of State, County, and Municipal Employees	99	237	647	997

Source: Unionism struggles through middle age, *New York Times*, Oct. 27, 1985, p. 4E. Copyright © 1985 by The New York Times Company. Reprinted by permission.

expected to continue entering the work force at a high rate, tend to favor unions.[32] However, these same workers are also sympathetic to business. Many came of age during the oil shocks of the mid-1970s, the back-to-back recessions that followed, and then the trade wars. This has led them to appreciate the importance of business in creating jobs and has made them want unions that cooperate with management rather than confront it.[21]

What complicates organizing efforts is that many in this new generation are white-collar workers—in fields as diverse as insurance and electronics.[20] Their goals and desires are different from those of labor's traditional blue-collar stalwarts, who seemed to want little more than high wages and steady work. And because so many young workers are highly mobile (workers under 35 stay on a job a median of 2.5 years, compared to 12 years for those over 45), they might not be willing to support a 6-month unionization drive that might culminate in a strike to win a first contract.[21] Finally, many young workers are taking jobs in the rapidly growing service sector—banking, computer programming, financial services—jobs that unions traditionally have not penetrated.

Although only about 17 percent of nonfarm workers in the United States belong to unions, unions are a powerful social, political, and organizational force. In the unionized firm, managers must deal with the union rather than directly with employees on many issues. Indeed, the "rules of the game" regarding wages, hours, and conditions of employment are described in a collective bargaining agreement (or contract) between management and labor. As we saw in the Hillside case, adversarial "us" and "them" feelings are frequently an unfortunate by-product of this process.

Economic and working conditions in unionized firms directly affect those in nonunionized firms, as management strives to keep unions out. As we shall see, managers have been much more successful at doing this in the 1980s than they were in the 1930s, 1940s, and 1950s. But first let's put the labor movement into historical perspective.

The Genesis of Labor Unions

The labor movement has had a long, colorful, and turbulent history in the United States. It began with the industrial revolution of the nineteenth century. Economically the industrial revolution was a great boon to productive output and to capital accumulation by business owners. Not so for the average worker. Wages were generally low, and working conditions were often hazardous. Labor was considered a commodity to be bought and sold, and the prevailing political philosophy of laissez-faire (leave things alone) resulted in little action by governments to protect the lot of the workers.[18] Against this backdrop, it was inevitable that workers would organize collectively to improve their wages and working conditions.

The first overt union activity in the United States took place in 1794 when the Philadelphia cordwainers (shoemakers) attempted to raise their wages, in reaction to a wage cut by their employers. The employers sued the union, arguing that the combination of workers to raise their wages constituted an illegal conspiracy in restraint of trade. In 1806, a federal court ruled in favor of the employers and fined the employees involved. Until this *conspiracy doctrine* was overturned in the 1842 *Commonwealth of Massachusetts v. Hunt* case, workers were discouraged from forming unions.[12] In that case the court ruled that labor unions were not criminal per se, for they could have honorable as well as destructive objectives. In short, a union's conduct would determine whether the union is legal or illegal.[11]

Early national unions

Following the *Commonwealth v. Hunt* decision, several national unions of skilled workers emerged, such as the National Molders Union and the National Typographical Union. The latter, formed in 1852, collected membership dues, maintained a strike fund, bargained with employers, and called strikes when demands were not met. In 1986 this 38,000-member organization merged with the Communications Workers of America.[43]

The first labor federation truly national in scope was the Knights of Labor, organized first in Philadelphia in 1869. The Knights accepted into membership both skilled and unskilled workers on a city-by-city basis rather than by craft, for they emphasized the solidarity of labor. Tactically, the Knights disavowed the use of strikes as a means of settling disputes; instead, they preferred to use arbitration and conciliation. Their early constitution identified goals pertaining to workers' cooperatives, the 8-hour day, the prohibition of child labor, equal pay for the sexes, the establishment of a bureau of labor statistics, government ownership of railroads and telegraphs, and the graduated income tax. Ironically, the Knights achieved their greatest membership gains as a result of a strike against several railroads in 1882 and 1883. However, the union failed to manage its growth constructively, and consequently it lost control of its members. Sabotage and unauthorized strikes occurred, only to be countered by strike breakers hired by the business owners. Although the leaders of the Knights of Labor publicly repudiated these strikes, the public and a hostile press associated them with much of the labor strife that was occurring. These forces, together with the Knights' failure to win consistent, practical gains for workers, led to its rapid decline after 1886. Many of its member unions that were comprised of skilled craftspeople joined a movement that was soon to become known as the American Federation of Labor (AFL).[13]

Emergence of the American Federation of Labor

The AFL was organized in 1886 as a group (technically, an amalgamation) of national craft unions. Some of these unions were: the Metal Workers, Carpenters, Cigar Makers, Iron Molders, Miners and Mine Laborers, Granite

Cutters, Bakers, Furniture Workers, Tailors, and Typographers. The AFL differed from its predecessors in two respects. One, it emphasized *craft* (i.e., employees in a single occupation) rather than *industrial* (i.e., all employees in a given industry) organization. Second, it espoused no particular political philosophy or set of broad social goals, for its objectives were more pragmatic. It sought immediate benefits for its craftspeople in the companies where they were employed. In the words of Samuel Gompers, the AFL's first president, the goals of the AFL were: "More, more, more; now, now, now."[13]

The Congress of Industrial Organizations

A combination of factors in the 1930s made industrial unionism attractive:

1. The Great Depression, which engendered such general gloom and pessimism in the entire economic system that it inevitably increased the propensity of workers to join unions[1]
2. The passage of federal labor laws that made it easier to organize workers
3. The emergence of rebel leaders within the AFL who wanted to organize unskilled workers into industrial unions [these included John L. Lewis (mine workers), Sidney Hillman (clothing workers), and Walter Reuther (auto workers)]

This worker took hers lying down when the United Electrical Workers union local called a sit-down strike at the National Fastener plant. Some of the vacant sewing machines can be seen in the background.

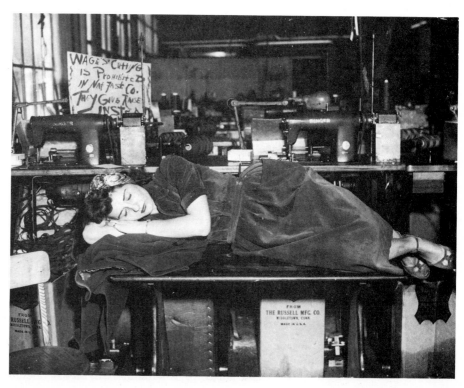

The rebels formed their own Congress of Industrial Organizations (CIO) in 1935 and intended to work within the AFL. However, the craft unionism versus industrial unionism issue, together with power rivalries within the AFL, led to an open break. The CIO's strategy was to organize *all* the workers in a given plant or company rather than to focus on certain crafts. They were quite successful, principally through use of the sit-down strike, in which workers refused to leave the premises until employers met their demands for recognition. Even before the formal AFL-CIO break in 1937, membership in CIO unions had reached 3.7 million, exceeding AFL membership by 300,000 workers.[13]

Merger of the AFL-CIO

By the early 1950s, both the AFL and the CIO realized that they were sacrificing power and efficiency by fighting on two fronts simultaneously: against employers and against each other. In 1954, therefore, the federations agreed not to attempt to organize workers who belonged to an affiliated union of the other. In 1955, they merged into the AFL-CIO under the leadership of George Meany, new president of the AFL, *and* Walter Reuther, former head of the United Auto Workers and new president of the CIO. In 1967, however, Meany and Reuther became bitter enemies when Reuther withdrew his United Auto Workers from the federation in a policy dispute. Meany became the first president of the AFL-CIO. Integrity was his hallmark, and he vigorously fought union corruption, most notably by expelling Jimmy Hoffa's Teamsters Union from the AFL-CIO in 1957. (In an attempt to unify the divided ranks of American unions, the AFL-CIO readmitted this 1.5 million member organization in 1987.)[26] Throughout his career, Meany said that *the wages and working conditions of the laborer, not economic philosophy, were his primary concerns.* But he elevated the labor movement beyond wages and hours to unprecedented standing in Washington, particularly with Democratic presidents. In fact, Meany played the game of power politics so well that by 1979 (when Meany retired), organized labor, in the words of a noted labor lawyer, "became a middle class movement of people earning $25,000, $30,000 a year, supplemented by federal benefits" (ref. 38, p. 5E). It certainly was different when Meany first appeared on the national scene in 1934. Then there was no Social Security to provide for aging workers, no National Labor Relations Act, public employee unions were unheard of, and the first national minimum wage—25 cents per hour for a 48-hour workweek—was still 4 years away.

Labor violence

Throughout the American labor movement, even until today, violence has occurred periodically.[55] For example, during the Civil War the "Molly Maguires," a secret society of Irish miners in the coal fields, beat, murdered, and generally terrorized employers. Their activities did not stop until 10 of their leaders were executed in 1876.[13]

Listen now as a retired union official describes what it was like to organize workers during the Great Depression:

Shaun McGillin Maloney—Jack to his friends—remembers vividly the day long ago when he ran full tilt around a Minneapolis street corner and into the American class struggle, Depression-style. It greeted him with flying buckshot and bullets.

It was 1934 and life was tough for the men who drove trucks and, even then, teams of horses for the huge distribution center based in Minneapolis. When you could get it, work was long, hard, and poorly paid; most of the time you couldn't get it. With drivers plentiful and loads scarce, employers didn't worry about workers' problems.

So Mr. Maloney and other drivers decided that they needed a labor union. When the Minneapolis business community resisted, the drivers sought to close down the trucking industry. Warfare broke out in the streets.

"We ran up the alley when we saw a truck being escorted by about 25 police cars," recalls Mr. Maloney. "And there was a cop, kneeling down with some sort of riot weapon, not 30 feet away."

According to Mr. Maloney, the officer "let fly" at him and two companions. In the shooting, Mr. Maloney says, "Harry DeBoer got it in the leg. Ben Koski was hit in the arm, and blood was spurting out all over the place. I was lucky; I got it in the stomach area but wasn't hurt bad."

Two men were killed, and dozens more sent to hospitals in that battle, which followed an earlier skirmish in which two antiunion businessmen were bludgeoned to death. Organizing unions wasn't easy in those times. (ref. 1, p. 1)

Have things really changed that much in the 1980s? Consider what happened in Dakota City, Nebraska, as a result of a contract dispute between Iowa Beef Processors, Inc., and Local 222 of the United Food and Commercial Workers Union.

In one confrontation, as union workers hurled railroad spikes and ball bearings at state troopers and strikebreakers, stinging clouds of teargas and chemical spray swirled into the protesters' eyes. Earlier, enraged members of the union had spread nails across the highway. Then, screaming "Scab! Scab!" they threw rocks and bricks at newly hired workers trying to enter the plant. The governor was finally forced to summon 160 National Guardsmen to aid the 100 besieged state police. The strike cost Dakota City and other towns that rely on the plant's $58 million payroll about $1 million a week in lost revenues. Moreover, the conflict turned local opinion against the workers. Said one citizen, "Every time there's violence, public opinion always swings behind the company."[3]

While we cannot condone violence, either by union or by management, it is not surprising that it sometimes occurs, especially in towns that are dominated by a single company. For example, when a strike occurs and management exercises its right to hire replacements for the striking workers, the strikers become resentful as they see the real possibility that their jobs are gone for good.[14] Backed into a corner, they often lash out to protect their hard-won gains and their way of life. Such violence can turn brother against brother, friend against friend. Few would deny management's social responsibility in these situations, coupled with the need to treat workers with dignity. Few also would deny that violence is no way for either side to achieve its long-term goals.

Understanding trade unionism

Whatever trade unions may or may not be, they are not pro-socialist institutions. Indeed, one of the most striking facts of the twentieth century is that trade unions do not fit comfortably *either* into a socialist (left) or a capitalist (right) political ideology. What we call "militancy" is as characteristic of an American union (e.g., the Teamsters) whose leadership may endorse Republican candidates as it is of a British union (e.g., the coal miners) whose leadership is openly socialist.

Nor does it matter whether the industries in which unions operate are nationalized or privately owned, public or private sector. The ways unions behave (as distinct from what their leaders say) are pretty much the same in either case. *Trade unions seem to be engaged in a peculiar kind of class struggle that is immune to conventional political preferences.*[33]

At a general level, the goal of unions is to increase their membership through improvement of economic and other conditions of employment. Increased membership and economic improvement are not independent of one another, as a study by the National Bureau of Economic Research shows. The study encompassed *all* manufacturing industries and indicated that union wages rise about 10 percentage points, on average, as the proportion of union members in an industry rises to 80 percent from 20 percent. One reason for the increase in wages is that unions in highly organized industries need not worry so much about losing jobs to nonunion companies when they demand higher wages. The bottom line is that *high unionization in an industry tends to increase the pay gap between union and nonunion workers.*[56]

The Legal Framework for Labor-Management Relations

The 1880s to 1926: the era of antiunion legislation and court rulings

The tone of the early legislative and court history of U.S. labor relations was distinctly antiunion. For example, from the 1880s until the early 1930s, the *injunction,* or restraining order, was widely used to control union activity. Power in the injunction stemmed from the courts' interpretation of the term "property." They held that an employer's property included the right to operate a business to make a profit. The expectation of profit thus became an intangible property. By this logic, *any* strike might be injurious to property and thus could be stopped by an injunction. Injunctions were generally granted by the courts upon request, and for years they effectively controlled union activity.

A landmark U.S. Supreme Court decision in 1908, frequently called the *Danbury Hatters* case, also curtailed union activity. The United Hatters Union, in an attempt to organize Loewe & Co. of Danbury, Connecticut, had promoted a successful national boycott against the company's products. The Court ruled that the boycott was an illegal restraint of trade under the Sherman Antitrust Act of 1890 and ordered the union and its members to pay treble damages of $252,000.[2]

Although unions rejoiced at the passage of the Clayton Act of 1914 (which exempted them from the provisions of the Sherman Antitrust Act, limited the use of injunctions, and made picketing legal), court rulings tended to negate these provisions and continued to limit union activities. An example of this was the Supreme Court's 1917 decision in *Hitchman Coal & Coke Co. v. Mitchell* that upheld the legality of the "yellow-dog contract." Such a contract was an oral or written agreement between a worker and management that, as a condition of employment, the worker would not join a labor union. Until they were outlawed in 1932, yellow-dog contracts were prime antiunion weapons.

1926 to 1947: the era of pro-union legislation

The first significant national pro-labor legislation that legitimized the right of employees to choose whether or not to be represented by a union and to engage in union activities was the Railway Labor Act of 1926. The act established the National Mediation Board to conduct representation elections, and it legitimized collective bargaining for railway (and through a later amendment, airline) employees. It outlawed yellow-dog contracts for these employees, and it established procedures for the mediation and arbitration of industrial disputes. The major reason for the creation of such procedures was to avoid interruptions in the manufacture of products or in the delivery of services. This has led often to the creation of emergency boards and settlements legislated by Congress to avoid strikes that might paralyze the railroad and airline industries.

Norris-La Guardia Act of 1932 In the depths of the Great Depression, Congress passed this act to promote collective bargaining and to balance the power of labor and management. The act covers all private-sector employers and labor organizations, and it affirms the right of all workers to organize and to bargain with employers. Workers can join labor organizations, unions can pay strike benefits to their members and aid them in litigation, publicize labor disputes, notify workers that union activity will take place, and assemble for the purpose of organizing. Further, the act outlaws the use of the yellow-dog contract as a condition of employment, and it limits federal judges' use of injunctions to instances where there is a clear and imminent danger to life or property. For all of its pro-labor provisions, the Norris-La Guardia Act had one glaring weakness: It did not *require* management to recognize or to bargain with unions, nor did it *forbid* them from discriminating against employees for union activity.

The Wagner, or National Labor Relations, Act of 1935   This act was another piece of distinctly pro-labor legislation that accorded management and labor roughly equal rights and obligations. It had three major provisions:

1. It affirmed the right of all employees to engage in union activities, to organize, and to bargain collectively without interference or coercion from management.
2. It corrected the weakness of the Norris-La Guardia Act by *requiring* management to bargain collectively with duly elected employee organizations regarding wages, hours, and conditions of employment.
3. It created the National Labor Relations Board to supervise representation elections and to investigate charges of unfair labor practices by management. Examples of unfair labor practices by management, as outlined in the National Labor Relations Act, include:
   a. Interference with, restraint of, or coercion of employees in the exercise of their rights to self-organize; to form, join, or assist labor organizations; to bargain collectively through representatives of their own choosing; and to engage in concerted activities for the purpose of collective bargaining or other mutual aid or protection
   b. Discrimination in hiring, firing, or any term or condition of employment on the basis of membership in a labor organization
   c. Discharge or other form of discrimination against an employee because he or she has filed charges or testified against management under this act
   d. Refusal to bargain collectively with employee representatives

Initially, employers strongly resisted the implementation of the National Labor Relations Act, for it clearly encouraged the growth of labor unions. Grow they did, for in the 12 years following passage of the act, union membership grew from roughly 3.5 million (6 percent of the workforce) to 15.7 million (23 percent).[57] Despite the act's pro-labor orientation, there is one controversial management practice that the courts have ruled fair: declaration of bankruptcy to void a labor contract. For example, the U.S. Supreme Court's 1984 ruling in the *Bildisco* case dealt a severe blow to organized labor. The Court ruled that once a firm has *filed* for reorganization under Chapter 11 of the Bankruptcy Code, it can void its "burdensome" labor contracts even before a bankruptcy judge has acted. In doing so, a company cannot be accused of engaging in an unfair labor practice. However, the Court's ruling did not specifically address whether labor costs can be used as the *principal* reason for a bankruptcy filing.[34]

It is no longer unusual to see bankruptcy used as a sword against unions instead of as a shield against creditors. What happens to an old union when a new company buys a failed business? The Supreme Court was asked to decide this issue in *Fall River Dyeing and Finishing Corp. v. National Labor Relations Board* (1987).[15] The Court's ruling has broad implications for corporate acquisitions.

The dispute began when an unprofitable Massachusetts textile company called Sterlingwale was closed and liquidated by the family that had owned it for more than 30 years. A customer and a former executive of Sterlingwale opened a slimmed-down version of the old business after a 7-month hiatus and renamed it the Fall River Dyeing and Finishing Corporation.

The new company did not buy all the assets of Sterlingwale, such as its trade name, goodwill, or customer lists. Nor did it assume any of its liabilities. Within 6 months, however, 51 of the 105 people working at Fall River were former employees of the defunct company. After its first month of operation, Fall River's owners heard from the union that had represented Sterlingwale workers for nearly three decades. The union asked the company to negotiate a collective bargaining agreement. Management refused to talk, claiming that the local no longer represented the employees. The union charged that management violated the National Labor Relations Act by refusing to bargain.

A divided National Labor Relations Board (NLRB), and later a divided U.S. Court of Appeals, held that Fall River's management had to recognize the union. The court reasoned that the union had satisfied the NLRB standards for showing that Fall River was a "successor" to Sterlingwale.

A pro-management decision by the Supreme Court would encourage acquisitions, since a new corporation would not be encumbered with any agreements that had been made by the liquidated company. Unions would be forced to start from scratch in organizing the workplace, and this would undermine the stability of collective bargaining agreements.[10]

In determining whether one company is a successor to another, the NLRB uses the following criteria:

- Has there been a substantial continuity of the same business operations?
- Does the new employer use the same plant?
- Does the alleged successor have the same or substantially the same workforce?
- Do the same jobs exist under the same working conditions?
- Does the new owner employ the same supervisors?
- Does the new employer use the same machinery, equipment, and methods of production?
- Does the new employer manufacture the same product or offer the same services?

In a 6-3 decision, the Supreme Court ruled that Fall River had a duty to bargain with the old union. It was a successor to Sterlingwale and had demonstrated a substantial continuity with the old company. An analysis of this and related cases revealed the following guiding principles in the context of a merger or an acquisition:[16]

1. A new employer, even if it is found to be a "successor," is not legally required to *adopt* its predecessor's collective bargaining agreement, although it may do so voluntarily.
2. A new employer need not hire its predecessor's employees and need not arbitrate its duty to do so.
3. A new employer may unilaterally alter the terms and conditions of employment in the unit or restructure the workplace, even in the face of unexpired collective bargaining contracts, as long as it does not adopt the unexpired contracts and alters the terms and conditions of employment *before* hiring new employees.
4. If the majority of a new employer's workforce is comprised of previously represented employees, and if the new employer does not make structural changes that alter the basic nature of the business, the new employer will be bound to bargain with the predecessor's union.

1947 to the present: attempts to balance the rights and obligations of unions and management

Between 1932 and 1947, most laws had been pro-union. Unions, in turn, became much more militant. Strikes were called frequently, and they affected millions of workers. In 1946, for example, a record 4.6 million workers participated in strikes. A nationwide steel strike, an auto strike, two coal strikes, and a railroad strike indirectly affected numerous other industries, causing shortages and layoffs.[6] Corruption, racketeering, and communist involvement in a few unions fueled negative public opinion toward unions and bolstered the view that unbridled union power had to be restrained. The Taft-Hartley Act of 1947 attempted to do just that.

The Taft-Hartley Act of 1947 This act covers most private-sector employers and nonmanagerial employees, except for those covered by the Railway Labor Act. Professional employees cannot be forced into a bargaining unit with nonprofessionals without their majority consent. Employees in the public sector are not covered by the Taft-Hartley Act, but its provisions are the basis for many public-sector laws.

Under the act, when 30 percent or more of employees desire union representation, the National Labor Relations Board is responsible for determining an appropriate bargaining unit and for conducting a representation election. If elected, the union has the right and the responsibility for *exclusive representation* and is the *bargaining agent* for *all* employees in the unit. Further provisions specify that unions are required to give 60 days' notice for the modification or termination of an agreement, and they can be sued for breach of contract.

The act expanded the National Labor Relations Board from three to five members and created the Office of General Counsel to the board. This office has the authority to investigate and issue complaints of unfair labor practices. In addition, the act established the Federal Mediation and Conciliation Service and gave it two major responsibilities. First, after being notified of contract expirations, it offers to assist the parties in settling new contracts without work stoppages. To dramatize this role, the service recently started issuing matchbooks whose inside covers read, "Call us before striking." The second major responsibility of the Federal Mediation and Conciliation Service is to maintain a list of arbitrators who are qualified to decide problems of contract interpretation that the parties are unable to resolve themselves.

A final provision of the act empowered the President of the United States to impose an 80-day "cooling-off" period to postpone strikes or lockouts (plant shutdowns by management) when the national health or safety is threatened.

Under the Taft-Hartley Act, employees have the right to organize a union, to bargain collectively with an employer, and to engage in other union activities for the purpose of collective bargaining. These rights are identical to those described in the Wagner Act. However, a so-called free-speech clause in the act specified that management has the right to express its opinion about unions or unionism to employees, provided that it does not threaten or promise favors to employees to obtain antiunion actions.

One especially controversial section of the Taft-Hartley Act, Section 14b, enables states to enact "right-to-work" laws that *prohibit* compulsory union membership (after a probationary period) as a condition of continued employment. Table 13-2 indicates that most types of such union security provisions are illegal in the 21 states that have passed right-to-work laws.

In 1984, the Supreme Court ruled in a suit by Western Airlines employees (covered by a union shop under the Railway Labor Act) over payments they were forced to make to the Railway Clerks Union. The Court upheld the use of dues to finance collective bargaining activities from workers who oppose the union but who must pay dues because their contracts require it. However, the Court ruled that the union cannot finance its own organizing expenses with such dues.[60] Finally, the Taft-Hartley Act specifies unfair labor practices *both* for unions and for management. These are shown in Table 13-3.

The Landrum-Griffin, or Labor-Management Reporting and Disclosure, Act of 1959 Complaints of union corruption and labor racketeering continued even after the Taft-Hartley Act was passed. As a remedy, Congress passed the Landrum-Griffin Act to regulate internal union affairs and to protect the rights of individual members. Title I of the act established a "Bill of Rights" for union members. These rights are shown in Table 13-4.

Other sections of the act: (1) require union constitutions, bylaws, and financial reports to be filed with the Department of Labor; (2) specify formal

TABLE 13-2 *Forms of union security and their legal status in right-to-work states*

	Legal	Illegal
Closed shop Individual must join the union that represents employees in order to be considered for employment.		X
Union shop As a condition of continued employment, an individual must join the union that represents employees after a probationary period (typically a minimum of 30 days).		X
Preferential shop Union members are given preference in hiring.		X
Agency shop Employees need not join the union that represents them, but, in lieu of dues, they must pay a service charge for representation.		X
Maintenance of membership Employee must remain a member of the union once he or she joins.		X
Checkoff Employee may request that union dues be deducted from his or her pay and be sent directly to the union.	X	

procedures to be followed in electing union officials; and (3) specify bonding (insurance) requirements for union officers to protect the members against embezzlement of union funds. Penalties are provided for any union officer or

TABLE 13-3 *Unfair labor practices for management and unions under the Taft-Hartley Act of 1947*

Management
1. Interference with, coercion of, or restraint of employees in their right to organize
2. Domination of, interference with, or illegal assistance of a labor organization
3. Discrimination in employment because of union activities
4. Discrimination because the employee has filed charges or given testimony under the act
5. Refusal to bargain in good faith
6. "Hot cargo" agreements: refusals to handle another employer's products because of that employer's relationship with the union

Union
1. Restraint or coercion of employees who do not want to participate in union activities
2. Any attempt to influence an employer to discriminate against an employee
3. Refusal to bargain in good faith
4. Excessive, discriminatory membership fees
5. Make-work or featherbedding provisions in labor contracts that require employers to pay for services that are not performed
6. Use of pickets to force an organization to bargain with a union, when the organization already has a lawfully recognized union
7. "Hot cargo" agreements: that is, refusals to handle, use, sell, transport, or otherwise deal in another employer's products[9]

TABLE 13-4 *Rights of union members under the Landrum-Griffin Act*

1. Members must be given equal rights and privileges in nominating candidates for union office, voting in union elections, and attending and participating in membership meetings.
2. Members must be assured of their rights to freedom of speech and assembly: i.e., the right to meet with other members to express views or opinions and to present these at union meetings.
3. A majority vote of members on a secret ballot is required before dues can be increased.
4. Members can sue their union or its officers.
5. Discipline or expulsion from the union (except for nonpayment of dues) is prohibited unless a member is served first with written, specific charges, given a reasonable time to prepare a defense, and afforded a full and fair hearing.
6. Every employee (whether or not a union member) is entitled to receive from a local union a copy of every collective bargaining agreement that affects his or her rights as an employee.
7. Members are free from discipline and from the threat of force or violence for exercising any of the preceding rights.

employee who misuses union funds, and union and management officials must report any financial dealings with each other that might potentially affect the interests of union members. Finally, trusteeships that allow national or international unions (discussed later in this chapter) to take over the management of a local union can be established only under conditions specified in the union's constitution and only to combat corruption or financial malpractice.

Landrum-Griffin also amended the Taft-Hartley Act to add the secondary boycott as an unfair labor practice. A *secondary boycott* occurs when a union appeals to firms or other unions to stop doing business with an employer who sells or handles a struck product.

Understandably, unions resented this law because they felt that it represented government intrusion into their day-to-day operations. However, research indicates that during its first three decades this has not been the case.[4, 5, 53]

The Civil Service Reform Act of 1978   Prior to 1978, labor-management relations within the federal government were administered through presidential executive orders. Thus in 1961 President Kennedy issued Executive Order 10988 that established the right of government employees to be represented by labor organizations and to bargain over working conditions. There was no right to strike, to demand that unresolved grievances be taken to arbitration, or to make wage or job-security demands, although government unions could lobby Congress for wage changes.[41] In 1978 the Civil Service Reform Act enacted into law the measures that had been adopted previously under presidential executive orders. The section of the act that deals with the conduct of labor relations in the federal government includes the following provisions:

1. Establishment of the Federal Labor Relations Authority to administer the act (the authority is a neutral, independent, and bipartisan body whose executives have no other positions within the federal government)
2. Establishment of unfair labor practices for both management and unions
3. Creation of the Office of General Counsel within the Federal Labor Relations Authority to investigate and prosecute charges of unfair labor practices
4. Restriction of the issues that unions and federal agency management may bargain over
5. Authorization of the Federal Services Impasse Panel to take whatever action is necessary to resolve impasses in collective bargaining
6. Requirement of binding arbitration for all unresolved grievances
7. Prohibition of strikes in the federal sector

The first major test of the law occurred during the summer of 1981 when the Professional Air Traffic Controller's Organization (PATCO) went on strike, in violation of the Civil Service Reform Act. President Reagan refused to negotiate with the union while it remained on strike, and he ordered its members to return to work within 48 hours or lose their federal jobs. The 11,301 who failed to return were terminated, as was PATCO's right to represent government employees since the act forbids either the advocacy of or the

TABLE 13-5 *Summary of major laws*

Law	Coverage	Trend
Sherman Antitrust Act (1890)	Employers and employees in any business affecting interstate commerce	Antiunion
Clayton Act (1914)	Same as Sherman Act	Pro-union
Railway Labor Act (1926)	Nonmanagerial rail and airline employees	Pro-union
Norris-La Guardia Act (1932)	Private-sector employers and labor organizations	Pro-union
Wagner Act (1935), the National Labor Relations Act	Private-sector employers and nonmanagerial employees not covered by Railway Labor Act	Pro-union
Taft-Hartley Act (1947)	Same as Wagner Act	Balanced the rights of management and of the union
Landrum-Griffin Act (1959)	Private-sector employers and labor organizations	Balanced the rights of management and of the union
Civil Service Reform Act (1978)	Nonmanagerial, nonuniformed federal civil service employees and agencies	Balanced the rights of management and of the union

Public-sector state and local employees are covered by the laws of the states.

implementation of work stoppages.[45] In 1987, dogged by low morale and friction with the Federal Aviation Administration, the controllers voted overwhelmingly to form a new union, designating the National Air Traffic Controllers Association as their official bargaining agent. Members took a no-strike pledge and promised to resolve disputes with the FAA in a nonconfrontational manner.[37]

A brief summary of the coverages and trends of the labor laws that have been discussed above is presented in Table 13-5.

The historical and legal frameworks of the labor movement are critical to understanding the environment of labor-management relations. Furthermore, it also is important to understand the organizational structures of unions.

Levels of Union Representation

To put this issue into perspective, it is important to review the objectives of unions. The overriding objective, of course, is to promote the interests of workers. At the same time, there are three more specific union objectives:

1. To provide a collective approach to negotiating workplace rules
2. To negotiate with employers over the terms and conditions of employment
3. To administer the resulting agreement jointly with management

While the union takes a *proactive* role in organizing and negotiating, it takes a *reactive* role in contract administration. That is, it acts as a police force to identify situations in which it believes management has exceeded its authority as defined in the contract. If management refuses to correct the situation, the union acts as a prosecutor on behalf of the worker(s) affected. To achieve these objectives, unions provide multiple "levels" of representation: (1) the local union, (2) the national or international union, and (3) the federations of local, national, and international unions (e.g., the AFL-CIO). Let's examine each of these in detail.

Local unions

Local unions represent employees within a particular geographical area. In the industrial sector, local representation may take different forms, as shown in Figure 13-1.

Most local unions operate under the constitution of the national or international union with which they are affiliated. However, a number of local unions are independent, operating without such national affiliation, or else they may affiliate directly with the AFL-CIO.

Most activities that affect union members directly are carried out at the local level. These include:

■ Negotiation of the collective bargaining agreement with the employer
■ Administration of the collective bargaining agreement

FIGURE 13-1

Alternative local union structures in the industrial sector.

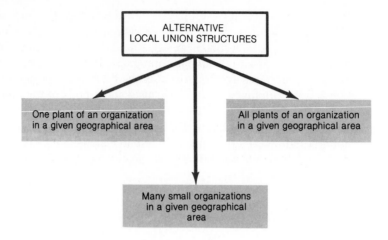

- Pursuit of grievances alleging management's violation of contract provisions
- Organizing unorganized workers in the local area
- Operation of union hiring halls
- Social, community, and public relations activities

These activities are carried out by representatives elected by the membership. However, the particular form of representation depends on whether the local membership is concentrated in a single organization or is dispersed across employers. Figure 13-2 illustrates these alternative types of local union representation.

When membership of the local is concentrated in a single organization

FIGURE 13-2

Forms of local union representation.

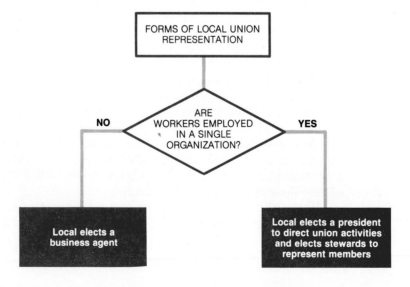

(e.g., the United Auto Workers' local representing Fisher Body plant workers in Lansing, Michigan), a president, vice president, and secretary-treasurer are elected. Also, a bargaining committee and a grievance committee are formed. The latter is generally composed of a chief steward and several departmental stewards. Stewards are responsible for:

- Recruiting new employees into the union
- Listening to worker complaints
- Handling grievances on behalf of the membership
- Observing management's administration of the collective bargaining contract

COMPANY EXAMPLE

New technology and payroll cuts: the frustrating job of a shop steward

Alan Moseley, still sweating from his workday in the steel mill, lumbers into the office of United Steelworkers Local 1010 and slams his briefcase down in frustration. Mr. Mosely is a shop steward, or "griever," handling union members' complaints against his employer, Inland Steel Industries, Inc. His frustration at the moment results from a year of sometimes rancorous talks with Inland over whether eight new jobs in its plant should go to union or salaried workers. As the face and voice of the union on the shop floor, Mr. Moseley combats the loss of jobs amid a rising backlog of increasingly complex grievances. As the bridge across the widening gulf between labor and management, he frequently draws attacks from both.

Acknowledging the growing demands of the job, unions have intensified their training of stewards. The United Auto Workers Union now holds winter and summer shop steward classes in northern Maine. The International Association of Machinists now conducts special classes on new technology for stewards and other union representatives.

Work as a steward today is a totally different ball game. Imports, high labor costs, and weak demand thrust Inland's results into the red for four consecutive years. At the same time, an ambitious modernization program earned Inland a reputation as one of the most efficient domestic steel producers.

Inside the mill's rumbling buildings, the lives of workers and their union representatives have changed irrevocably. Employment plunged 40 percent over 8 years to 11,100; the inspection workers Mr. Moseley represents have dwindled to 350 from 500. The older workforce—the average age is 40—is fighting furiously to hold on to every job. Many complain that although the members accepted temporary 9 percent wage cuts in 1983, the union still lost 3100 jobs by 1987. As a result, people are scared, and they don't trust the company. They are victims of the "post-concession blues." As one expert noted, "What we're looking at could be a slow-burning fuse that has explosive power somewhere down the road" (ref. 31, p. 1).

Generally, local officials work at regular jobs, but they are allowed to conduct union business during work time. In large locals, however, most union officials are full-time, paid employees of the union. If the local union needs assistance in handling contract negotiations, strikes, grievances, or arbitration hearings, it calls upon the *field representative* of its national or international union.

In industries where the membership is dispersed among several employers, local unions are often represented by a full-time paid official known as a *business agent*. The agent's job is to manage internal union activities, to negotiate contracts, to meet with members of management to resolve contract interpretation issues or grievances, and to represent workers at arbitration hearings.

National and international unions

These unions are generally governed by a constitution and have a national convention with each affiliated local union represented in proportion to its membership. Usually an executive council (consisting of a president, several vice presidents, and a secretary-treasurer) is elected at the convention. The president, in turn, appoints and manages a staff for handling matters such as organizing activities, research, and legal issues.

The field organization of a national or international union typically has regional or district offices headed by a regional director. *Field representatives*, who serve as liaisons to the local unions, report to the regional director. Some of the services and activities provided by the national or international union are:

- Organizing workers in unorganized areas or industries
- Assistance to local bargainers and/or industrywide bargaining
- Strike assistance, including economic benefits to members through union "war chests"
- Legislative, legal, and lobbying activities
- Contract interpretation and grievance assistance
- Benefit and pension plan administration
- Research, education, and communication to members

The national and international unions derive their power from the following sources:

- Chartering new locals and directing existing ones
- Approving or disapproving locally negotiated settlements
- Determining the legitimacy of strikes
- Requiring dues payments to the national or international union
- Supervising local elections and auditing local financial affairs
- Removing local officers and placing the local under *trusteeship* if rules of the national union are violated

<table>
<tr><td>

COMPANY EXAMPLE

Local versus international unions at Hormel

</td></tr>
</table>

Sometimes local and national unions disagree, as illustrated by the extremely bitter fight between meatpackers' Local P-9 at the Hormel plant in Austin, Minnesota, and its parent union, the United Food and Commercial Workers International.[52] During the course of a year-long strike against the company, the local and international unions were embroiled in a dispute over the handling of concessions. The parent union wanted to focus attention on raising wages at the low end of the pay scale and on establishing a strong industry wage rate. While the local union agreed that its parent union should pursue those goals, the local wanted to raise wages at the high end of the pay scale, like those at Austin, and believed that the company could afford it.

In the end, the local's intransigence proved suicidal. When the local refused to end its strike against Hormel, the international union placed the local under trusteeship, reached a contract agreement with Hormel, declared the strike settled, decertified the local, and approved the formation of a new local. After 14 months of trusteeship, a president for the new local was elected.[25, 39]

Federations

There are two types of federations: city and state federations and federations of local, national, and international unions. Since city and state federations are concerned primarily with political rather than with employment issues, they will not be discussed here.

The largest organizational unit within the union movement is the AFL-CIO. Recall that the AFL is comprised primarily of skilled craft workers (e.g., the International Brotherhood of Electrical Workers), while the CIO is comprised of both skilled and unskilled workers in a particular industry or group of industries (e.g., the Steelworkers or the Auto Workers). The organizational structure of the AFL-CIO is shown in Figure 13-3.

The AFL-CIO is comprised of affiliated national and international unions, affiliated state and local bodies, local unions affiliated directly with the AFL-CIO, and eight trade and industrial departments. The latter serve primarily to coordinate the activities of unions whose interests overlap (jurisdictional matters) and to promote cooperation among unions in collective bargaining. To deal with specific concerns and to provide services to the union membership, the AFL-CIO president appoints *standing committees*. However, several major national and international unions do not belong to the AFL-CIO; these include the National Education Association and the United Mine Workers.

Now that we understand the multiple levels of union representation available to employees, it seems appropriate to ask, "Why do employees want union representation?"

STRUCTURAL ORGANIZATION
of the

AMERICAN FEDERATION OF LABOR AND CONGRESS OF INDUSTRIAL ORGANIZATIONS

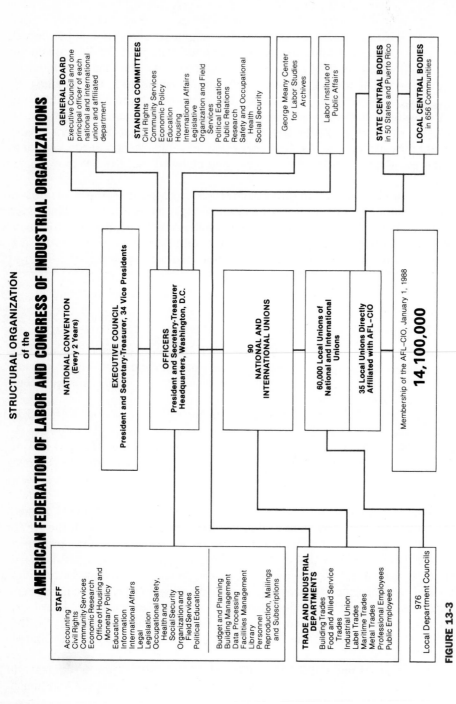

STAFF

Accounting
Civil Rights
Community Services
Economic Research
    Office of Housing and
    Monetary Policy
Education
Information
International Affairs
Legal
Legislation
Occupational Safety,
    Health and
    Social Security
Organization and
    Field Services
Political Education

Budget and Planning
Building Management
Data Processing
Facilities Management
Library
Personnel
Reproduction, Mailings
    and Subscriptions

**TRADE AND INDUSTRIAL
DEPARTMENTS**

Building Trades
Food and Allied Service
    Trades
Industrial Union
Label Trades
Maritime Trades
Metal Trades
Professional Employees
Public Employees

976
Local Department Councils

NATIONAL CONVENTION
(Every 2 Years)

EXECUTIVE COUNCIL
President and Secretary-Treasurer, 34 Vice Presidents

OFFICERS
President and Secretary-Treasurer
Headquarters, Washington, D.C.

90
**NATIONAL AND
INTERNATIONAL UNIONS**

60,000 Local Unions of
National and International
Unions

35 Local Unions Directly
Affiliated with AFL-CIO

Membership of the AFL-CIO, January 1, 1988

14,100,000

GENERAL BOARD
Executive Council and one
principal officer of each
national and international
union and affiliated
department

STANDING COMMITTEES
Civil Rights
Community Services
Economic Policy
Education
Housing
International Affairs
Legislative
Organization and Field
    Services
Political Education
Public Relations
Research
Safety and Occupational
    Health
Social Security

George Meany Center
for Labor Studies
Archives

Labor Institute of
Public Affairs

STATE CENTRAL BODIES
in 50 States and Puerto Rico

LOCAL CENTRAL BODIES
in 656 Communities

FIGURE 13-3

Organizational structure of the AFL-CIO. (Source: AFL-CIO, 1988.)

Why Employees Join Unions

More than 20 years of research has indicated consistently that unions form as a result of frustration by employees over their inability to gain important rewards.[2] More specifically, there seem to be two main factors underlying employees' interest in unions.[8] The first of these is *dissatisfaction with working conditions and a perception by employees that they cannot change those conditions.*

One study of over 87,000 salaried clerical, sales, and technical employees representing 250 units of a national retailing firm found that attitude measures taken 3 to 15 months *prior* to any organizing activity predicted the level of *later* organizing. Consistent with the maxim that "the best union organizer is the boss," this study found that the best predictors of the severity of unionization activity were items dealing with the supervision the workers receive.[23]

Another study of over 1200 employees who voted in 31 union representation elections supported these findings. Correlations between job satisfaction and votes for or against union representation are shown in Table 13-6.

Dissatisfaction with wages, job security, fringe benefits, treatment by supervisors, and chances for promotion was significantly related to a vote *for* union representation. However, dissatisfaction with the *kind* of work being done did not correlate strongly with a vote for union representation. Hence, *employee interest in unionization was triggered by working conditions, not by the work itself.*

The second factor that seems to underlie employee interest in unionization

TABLE 13-6 *Correlations between job satisfaction and votes for or against union representation*

Item	Correlation with vote*
1. Are you satisfied with your wages?	− .40
2. Do supervisors in this company play favorites?	− .34
3. Are you satisfied with the type or work you are doing?	− .14
4. Does your supervisor show appreciation when you do a good job?	− .30
5. Are you satisfied with your fringe benefits?	− .31
6. Do you think there is a good chance for you to get promoted in this company?	− .30
7. Are you satisfied with your job security at this company?	− .42
8. Taking everything into consideration, are you satisfied with this company as a place to work?	− .36

*The negative correlations indicate that satisfied employees tended to vote against union representation.

Source: Adapted from: J. M. Brett, Why employees want unions. Reprinted, by permission of the publisher, from *Organizational Dynamics,* **8**(4), Spring 1980, p. 51, © 1980 American Management Association, New York. All rights reserved.

is *the degree to which employees accept the concept of collective action and whether they believe unionization will yield positive rather than negative outcomes for them.* Thus, in the study shown in Table 13-6, dissatisfied employees tended *not* to vote for unionization if they believed the union was unlikely to improve the working conditions that dissatisfied them.[8] In addition, employees who hold a negative image of labor unions (i.e., those who feel that unions have too much political influence, abuse their power by calling strikes, cause high prices, misuse union dues and pension funds, and have leaders who promote their own self-interests) tend to vote *against* union representation.[29] In fact, knowing an employee's opinion on these issues allowed researchers to predict with 79 percent accuracy how he or she would vote on the issue of union representation.[8]

On the other hand, it is pure folly to assume that pro-union attitudes are based simply on expected economic gains; much deeper values are at stake. As one author noted:

> If one talks to any worker long enough, and candidly enough, one discovers that his loyalty to the union is not simply economic. One may even be able to show him that, on a strictly cost-benefit analysis, measuring income lost from strikes, and jobs lost as a result of contract terms, the cumulative economic benefits are delusions. It won't matter. In the end, he will tell you, the union is the only institution that insures and protects his "dignity" as a worker, that prevents him from losing his personal identity, and from being transformed into an infinitesimal unit in one huge and abstract "factor of production." (ref. 33, p. 28)

This conclusion that deeper values than money are at stake was illustrated in the 11-year battle to organize workers at the J. P. Stevens plant in North Carolina. The organizing drive was much publicized—the award-winning movie *Norma Rae* was based on it—and the settlement was heralded widely as a historic breakthrough in a decades-old attempt to organize southern industry. Even though the wages at the unionized Stevens plants are not substantially higher now than at the company's nonunionized plants or than the wages at other nonunion textile plants in the south, the wage level was never the biggest issue. The union contract has meant expanded benefits, a seniority system to protect workers when jobs are lost and to provide opportunities when jobs open, and a grievance procedure with access to binding arbitration. For the company, the settlement allowed it to put its past squabbles with the workers behind and to concentrate on battling foreign textile imports. Among union members, however, worker after worker echoes the same sentiment: The collective bargaining agreement has meant that they are treated with new dignity on the job.[51]

Finally, it appears that the intensity of a preelection campaign (and such campaigns are indeed intense) does not sway employee voting preferences one way or the other. Since employees' attitudes toward their jobs and toward unions in general are quite stable and well formed, their opinions tend not to be influenced much by campaign slogans and electioneering tactics.[19]

The Unionization Process

The organizing drive

There are three ways to kick off an organizing campaign: (1) Employees themselves may begin it, (2) employees may request that a union begin one for them, or (3) in some instances, national and international unions contact employees in organizations that have been *targeted* for organizing. In all three cases, employees are asked to sign *authorization cards* that designate the union as the employees' exclusive representative in bargaining with management.

Well-defined rules govern organizing activities:

1. Employee organizers may solicit fellow employees to sign authorization cards on company premises but not during working time.
2. Outside organizers cannot solicit on premises *if* a company has an existing policy of prohibiting all forms of solicitation and if that policy has been enforced consistently.[42]
3. Management representatives can express their views about unions through speeches to employees on company premises. However, they are legally prohibited from interfering with an employee's freedom of choice concerning union membership.

The organizing drive usually continues until the union obtains signed authorization cards from 30 percent of the employees. At that point it can petition the National Labor Relations Board (NLRB) for a representation election. If the union secures authorization cards from more than 50 percent of the employees, however, it may ask management *directly* for the right to exclusive representation. Usually the employer refuses, and then the union petitions the NLRB to conduct an election.

The bargaining unit

When the petition for election is received, the NLRB conducts a hearing to determine the appropriate (collective) bargaining unit; that is, *the group of employees eligible to vote in the representation election.* Sometimes labor and management agree jointly on the appropriate bargaining unit. When they do not, then the NLRB must determine the unit. The NLRB is guided in its decision, especially if there is no previous history of bargaining between the parties, by a concept called "community of interest." That is, the NLRB will define a unit that reflects the shared interests of the employees involved. Such elements include: similar wages, hours, and working conditions; the physical proximity of employees to each other; common supervision; the amount of interchange of employees within the proposed unit; and the degree of integration of the employer's production process or operation.[27]

The *size* of the bargaining unit is critical both for the union and for the employer because it is strongly related to the outcome of the representation election. The larger the bargaining unit, the more difficult it is for the union to win. In fact, if a bargaining unit contains several hundred employees, it is almost invulnerable.[28]

The election campaign

Emotions on both sides run high during a representation election campaign. However, management typically is unaware that a union campaign is underway until most or all of the cards have been signed. At that point, management has some tactical advantages over the union. It can use company time and premises to stress the positive aspects of the current situation, and it can emphasize the costs of unionization and the loss of individual freedom that may result from collective representation. Supervisors may hold informal meetings to emphasize these antiunion themes. However, certain practices by management are prohibited by law, such as:

1. Physical interference, threats, or violent behavior toward union organizers
2. Interference with employees involved with the organizing drive
3. Discipline or discharge of employees for pro-union activities
4. Promises to provide or withhold future benefits depending on the outcome of the representation election

Unions are also prohibited from unfair labor practices (see Table 13-3), such as coercing or threatening employees if they fail to join the union. In addition, the union can picket the employer *only* if (1) the employer is not presently unionized, (2) the petition for election has been filed with the NLRB in the past 30 days, and (3) a representation election has not been held during the previous year. Unions tend to emphasize two themes during organizing campaigns:

■ The union's ability to help employees satisfy their economic and personal needs
■ The union's ability to improve working conditions

The campaign tactics of management and the union are monitored by the NLRB. If the NLRB finds that either party engaged in unfair labor practices during the campaign, the election results may be invalidated and a new election conducted. However, a federal appeals court has ruled that the NLRB cannot *force* a company to bargain with a union that is not recognized by a majority of the workers, even if the company has made "outrageous" attempts to thwart unionization.[59] Earlier court rulings did allow the NLRB automatically to certify the union as the sole representative of the bargaining unit if evidence showed that management had interfered directly with the representation election process. This ruling may therefore indicate a change in sentiment toward labor by the courts.

The representation election and certification

If management and the union jointly agree on the size and composition of the bargaining unit, then a representation election occurs shortly thereafter. However, if management does not agree, then a long delay may ensue. Since such delays often erode rank-and-file union support, they work to management's advantage.[49] Not surprisingly, therefore, few organizations agree with unions on the size and composition of the bargaining unit. In 1983, for example, the NLRB had a backlog of 1336 cases that resulted in delays of up to 2 years before representation elections could be held. This situation led one union representative to describe such tactics by management as the "ultimate antiunion weapon."[36]

When a date for the representation election is finally established, the NLRB conducts a *secret ballot* election. If the union receives a majority of the ballots *cast* (not a majority of votes from members of the bargaining unit), then the union becomes certified as the exclusive bargaining representative of all employees in the unit. Once a representation election is held, regardless of the outcome, no further elections can be held in that bargaining unit for *1 year*. The entire process is shown graphically in Figure 13-4.

The records of elections won and lost by unions and management have changed drastically from the 1950s to the 1980s. In the 1950s, unions won over 70 percent of representation elections. By the late 1980s, that figure had slipped to 45 percent.[35]

The decertification of a union

If a representation election results in union certification, the first thing many employers want to know is when and how they can *decertify* the union. Under NLRB rules, an incumbent union can be decertified if a majority of employees within the bargaining unit vote to rescind the union's status as their collective bargaining agent in another representation election conducted by the NLRB.[54]

Since decertification is most likely to occur the first year or so after certification, unions will often insist on multiyear contracts to insulate themselves against decertification. Once the terms and duration of the labor contract are agreed to by both parties, the employer is obligated to recognize the union and to follow the provisions of the contract for the stipulated contract period. The AFL-CIO estimates that even after winning a certification election, unions are unable to sign contracts a third of the time. For example, after the Service Employees International Union won a 1981 election at the Hyatt Regency Hotel in New Orleans, it took the union 5 years to negotiate its first contract. By then, most of the original workers had left the hotel, and the union was decertified within 7 months.[31]

A petition for decertification must be supported by evidence that at least 30 percent of employees in the bargaining unit *want* a decertification election. NLRB cases indicate that two or more of the following types of evidence are necessary:

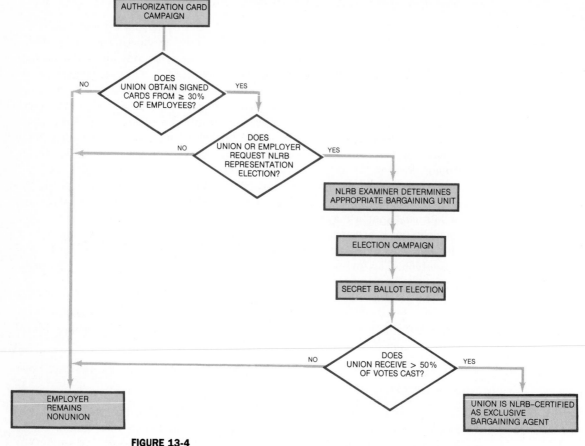

FIGURE 13-4

Steps involved and decisions to be made in a union organizing campaign.

- Employees have verbally repudiated the union.
- There is a marked decline in the number of employees who subscribe to union dues checkoff, and hence a minority of employees remain on checkoff.
- A majority of employees did not support the union during a strike.
- The union has become less and less active as a representative of employees.
- There was substantial turnover among employees subsequent to certification.
- The union has admitted a lack of majority support.

As with certification elections, once a decertification election is held, a full year must elapse before another representation election can take place. In keeping with the adage "An ounce of prevention is worth a pound of cure," some companies have gone to considerable effort to avoid union certification in the first place, thus making decertification unnecessary. Here is how one company did it.

INTERNATIONAL APPLICATION	**Avoiding Unionization at a Canadian ALCAN Plant**

In the 3 years since production began at the Grande Bai aluminum smelter, touted as one of the world's most modern, the facility's 500 employees have resisted repeated union attempts to organize them. What makes this situation noteworthy is that the plant sits in the heart of Quebec's Saguenay–Lac St. Jean region, where over half of all private-sector workers belong to unions, including almost all of ALCAN's 8500 employees. To stay nonunion, ALCAN has worked hard to keep its workers happy:

- It made parking space available on a first-come, first-served basis, even for managers.
- It encouraged a sense of responsibility and improved quality control by taking workers on trips to plants that turn Grande Bai ingots into aluminum sheets, and to a brewery that uses aluminum beer cans.
- It reduced the number of separate job descriptions from 150 (in unionized ALCAN smelters) to 5; that translates into improved job variety for the workers.
- It paid Grande Bai workers 10 percent more than their unionized colleagues.
- It improved working conditions by providing a gymnasium, a first-rate cafeteria, and a spotless production operation.

The union charged that the plant was *planned* as an antiunion bastion. The company owns 2400 acres around the smelter, which it says acts as a pollution buffer. But that also means that the union has to set up its recruiting trailer on a farmer's field some distance from the plant. Said one executive of another plant in the area, "It's pretty hard to hand out pamphlets when guys are driving by at 45 miles per hour."

Faced with rejection by the Grande Bai workers in two separate recruiting drives, the union took its case to a Quebec labor court, arguing that the Grande Bai plant was simply an extension of ALCAN's other smelters. It should therefore be unionized *automatically*. That angered the Grande Bai workers, who chipped in $20 each to hire a lawyer and fight the request, as did ALCAN.

"What got us mad is that the union tried to force us to join through the back door," said one Grande Bai worker. "We're adult enough to decide for ourselves whether or not we want to join the union." The labor court turned down the union's request.[17]

Survival tactics of unions

To respond to the conditions facing them, many unions have adopted a device long used by businesses to combat harsh economic conditions: *the merger*. There have been 23 mergers within the AFL-CIO within the last decade, and more than 60 such combinations since the grand merger that united the AFL-CIO in 1955. This does not include cases in which internationals absorbed local unions, a trend that is also accelerating. As the AFL-CIO's chief organizer noted, "In this tough climate, it's hard to imagine that a national organization with fewer than 50,000 members can really do much more than hold its own."[43]

By linking operations, unions that previously negotiated separate contracts with the same employer now negotiate as one and thereby increase their bargaining leverage. For unions that seek to sign up the same workers, a merger ends organizing competition, allowing wider deployment of recruiters and more efficient use of scarce funds. Bigger unions also have in-house research staffs capable of figuring out the costs of both their own and employer contract proposals. This tool is vital in building a case publicly and also at the bargaining table.[40]

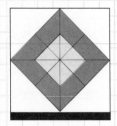

Impact of Unions on Productivity, Quality of Work Life, and the Bottom Line

There *are* situations in which companies benefit from unionization, particularly those in which (1) access to a union-operated hiring hall is important, (2) unions are important political allies, or (3) there are one or more established unions with whom an employer has a sound working relationship. In such cases, the cost of keeping the established union out is the risk of being organized by a less acceptable union.[27]

On the other hand, differences in the cost of labor between union and nonunion companies can be substantial, particularly in the deregulated airline and trucking industries; there, wage and benefit differences may be as high as 30 to 40 percent.[22] Among meatpackers, nonunion workers were paid roughly $6 per hour in 1987, compared to over $9 per hour at some unionized firms.[44]

Differences in wages have further effects on the industry. Nonunion meatpackers use their savings in labor costs to compete much more aggressively for livestock by paying higher prices. Since the points at which they break even are lower, this tactic helps maintain profits even when sales are slow.

A similar situation is found in the steel industry, among so-called minimills that use scrap steel and nonunion labor. By linking pay to productivity rather than to union wage scales, the minimills gain tremendous production efficiency, which they then use in bidding for customers. As a result, they are taking more and more business from bigger steel producers. For example, consider Nucor Corporation, headquartered in Charlotte, North Carolina.

Nonunion Nucor is the nation's largest and most profitable builder and operator of minimills. In fact, this Fortune 500 company is doing the improbable—making money producing steel. While U.S. steel mills average 347 tons of steel produced per employee per year, and while the top five integrated steel mills in Japan average 480 tons, Nucor's employees average 950 tons! Since pay is tied to productivity at Nucor, its employees averaged $30,000 in pay in 1986, versus $27,000 for the average unionized steelworker.[47] Said Nucor's president, "If the company were unionized, we'd still be able to compete—but not as effectively. It would increase our costs—not just because of high wage rates, but because of union work rules that would discourage productivity."[22]

General Motors showed a film called *A Battle for Survival* to over 400,000 unionized workers in an attempt to encourage them to hold down demands. The message was effective. GM workers accepted a 3 percent base-wage raise in 1987, and for 1988 and 1989 they accepted lump-sum payments equal to 3 percent of the base wage.[50]

Experts both inside and outside of the union movement generally agree that although the labor movement has been weakened, it still remains a mighty social force in American society. It has provided improvements in wages, hours, and working conditions, protection for workers through court and government action, and a kind of trickle-down effect. That is, many employers have improved the lot of their workers so that union organizers will remain at bay.[51]

Unions are also trying to broaden their base. Thus only about 11 percent of the 1.3 million members of the Teamsters union actually drive trucks. The remainder includes workers as diverse as pilots, zookeepers, and Disney World's Mickey Mouse.

Another tactic is the *corporate campaign*. This is a system under which pressure is placed not only on the employer but also on stockholders, on boards of directors, on financial institutions that deal with a company, on customers, and on legislators to pressure the company either to recognize unions or to agree to union demands. Thus unions are attempting to achieve their ends by applying secondary pressure—pressure on others to induce them to compel the company management to agree to union demands.[48] Have unions been successful? A recent study of 10 corporate campaigns concluded that union-sponsored boycotts and attempts to influence companies through bankers, investors, and Wall Street have not been very effective—yet. But unions have succeeded in pressuring companies through a variety of other groups—religious professionals, community and consumer activists, and politicians.[48] The lesson? Corporations may choose to ignore this new tactic, but they do so at their peril.[46]

**CASE 13-1
Conclusion**

*Improvement of
QWL through
positive union-
management
relations*

One of the members of the management group began the discussion by suggesting that the parties examine what kind of relationship they wanted and what they might do to shift away from win-lose. The plant manager asked what the union would do if management tried to change, and the union said it felt safer with win-lose.

At this point the consultant intervened to suggest that the parties were not using confrontation in a problem-solving way. It appeared as though management had been trying to resolve the conflict with the union in an arbitrary manner and via suppression. She pointed out that management seems to have discovered that "hard" does not work. People become angry, frustrated, and negatively motivated. But "soft" does not work either—the union does not respect it.

The plant manager responded that they wanted to do what was best; the "ideal" relationship that had seemed so remote before now seemed indispensable. He asked the others if they were willing to invest the time and effort necessary to achieve this kind of relationship. The employee relations director assured them that they had corporate support. They were convinced that they had no other option. So they listed five summary statements of their current thoughts and feelings and presented them to the union the next day:

1. We recognize that we have a deep win-lose orientation toward the union.
2. We want to change!
3. Barriers to overcome: Convince the union that we want to change; convince ourselves that we have the patience, skill, and convictions to change.
4. We are responsible to bring the rest of management on board.
5. We recognize the risk, but we want to resist the temptation of reverting to win-lose when things get tough.

As a suggestion for action, management recorded: "Identify concrete problems that require cooperation to solve, and develop strategies for solution of them with the union."

Members of the union group saw management's self-description as a giant step forward from its previous attitudes. They recognized that it must have been hard to initiate such drastic change, and they could not indicate strongly enough how pleased they were with that kind of shift. Members of the union group emphasized their sincere attempt to cooperate in any way in order to be able to assist in the change. Both parties realized that they would not be saying the same thing all the time, but the key was to remember the basic lessons of the seminar. This positive attitude on the part of both groups led to a desire to deal with specific details and to develop a list of outstanding issues between them that could be worked out jointly in the near future.

Five and a half years have elapsed since the seminar. Immediately after the seminar, 10 task forces were appointed to grapple with and solve problems. Each task force brought proposed solutions to the plant manager. He considered their recommendations and either approved them, modified them, or provided a full explanation for why he could not adopt them. This put the union and management on a sound basis and has led to continuing improvements at Hillside. At the time of the seminar, Hillside was eleventh in economic performance of 11 plants owned by the company. Today, Hillside is first.

| TOMORROW'S FORECAST | A combination of economic and demographic factors may be work-ing in favor of unions. Labor shortages, the growing disaffection of many workers as a result of corporate cost cutting in recent |

A combination of economic and demographic factors may be work-ing in favor of unions. Labor shortages, the growing disaffection of many workers as a result of corporate cost cutting in recent years, and the increasing numbers of women and minorities entering the workforce all favor a union resurgence. As one pollster noted, "The issues are there if unions want to organize" (ref. 32, p. 14).

However, problems remain. Several unions, such as the Teamsters and the International Longshoreman's Association, are believed to be dominated still by organized crime.[51] Some union leaders are perceived as being more interested in taking care of themselves than in taking care of their members, and the interests of minorities have often been served poorly.[7] Can unions accommodate debate? Can they become relevant to postindustrial workers—service and high-technology employees? Can they carry on the scorching reappraisal necessary to build imaginative institutions?[51] These are the real tests that will determine the long-term fate of the labor movement.

Summary

The U.S. labor movement has had a long and turbulent history, from the Philadelphia cordwainers' strike in 1794, to the founding of the Knights of Labor in 1869, the AFL in 1886, the CIO in 1935, to the merger of the AFL-CIO in 1955, and to the unions' struggle for survival today. At a general level, the goal of unions is to improve economic and other conditions of employment. Although they have been successful over the years in achieving these goals, more recently they have been confronted with challenges that have led to some loss of membership.

The labor-management relations of private-sector employers and workers are governed by the Railway Labor Act, the Norris-LaGuardia Act, the National Labor Relations Act, the Taft-Hartley Act, and the Landrum-Griffin Act. Federal employees are covered under the Civil Service Reform Act of 1978, and state and local workers are covered under the laws of the 50 states. Once an appropriate bargaining unit is determined and a representation election sanctioned by the National Labor Relations Board is held, no further elections (including decertification elections) can be held for at least 1 full year. If elected, a union is the *sole* bargaining agent for employees.

With the exception of public-sector unions, union membership has decreased significantly in the 1980s, such that now fewer than one in five workers belongs to a union. To respond, many unions have merged, have engaged in corporate campaigns, and have agreed to significant wage and benefit reductions in an effort to help their companies compete in worldwide markets.

Discussion Questions

13-1 If unions know that violence turns public sentiment against them, why does labor violence continue today?

13-2 Discuss the rights and obligations of unions and management during a union organizing drive.

13-3 Explain why you agree or disagree with the following statement: "Given today's economic and legislative climates, unions are obsolete."

13-4 What is meant by the saying "The most effective union organizer is the boss"?

13-5 What kind of evidence is required for a decertification election to take place?

References

1. After the fall: How depression gave a boost to big labor, changed its strategy (1979, Sep. 20). *Wall Street Journal*, pp. 1, 23.
2. Allen, R. E., & Keaveny, T. J. (1988). *Contemporary labor relations* (2d ed.). Reading, MA: Addison-Wesley, 1988.
3. Bad old days (1982, Aug. 9). *Time*, pp. 47, 48.
4. Bellace, J. R. (1987, Dec. 7). Personal communication.
5. Bellace, J. R., & Berkowitz, A. D. (1979). The Landrum-Griffin Act: Twenty years of federal protection of union members' rights. Philadelphia: Industrial Research Unit, Study 19, The Wharton School, University of Pennsylvania.
6. Big labor's first big defeat: The Taft-Hartley Act (1978, October). *Dun's Review*, pp. 35, 38.
7. Blood, sweat, and steel (1984, May). *Black Enterprise*, pp. 40–46.
8. Brett, J. M. (1980). Why employees want unions. *Organizational Dynamics*, 8(4), 47–59.
9. Brinker, P. A. (1971, November). Hot cargo cases in the construction industry since 1958. *Labor Law Journal*, **22**, 690–707.
10. Business and the law (1987, Mar. 30). *New York Times*, p. D2.
11. Cohen, S. (1960). *Labor in the United States*. Columbus, OH: Merrill.
12. Commons, J. R., & Filmore, E. A. (eds.) (1958). Labor conspiracy cases, 1806–1942, vol. 3 of *A documentary history of American industrial society*. New York: Russell & Russell.
13. Dulles, F. R. (1960). *Labor in America: A history* (2d rev. ed.). New York: Crowell.
14. Eshleman, R. E., Jr. (1988, Feb. 21). In a strike-torn town, even a hero firefighter is a "scab." *Philadelphia Inquirer*, pp. 1A, 12A.
15. *Fall River Dyeing and Finishing Corp. v. N. L. R. B.* (1987). *Labor Law Reports*, Sn. 12, 333.
16. Fasman, Z. D., & Fischler, K. (1987). Labor relations consequences of mergers and acquisitions. *Employee Relations Law Journal*, **13**, 14–42.

17. Freeman, A. (1983, Nov. 16). In a pro-labor area of Canada, ALCAN plant resists repeated attempts at unionization. *Wall Street Journal*, p. 29.

18. French, W. L. (1982). *The personnel management process* (5th ed.). Boston: Houghton Mifflin.

19. Getman, J. G., Goldberg, S. B., & Herman, J. B. (1976). *Union representation elections: Law and reality*. New York: Russell Sage Foundation.

20. Gifford, C. (1986). *Directory of U. S. labor organizations: 1986–87 edition*. Washington, DC: Bureau of National Affairs.

21. Greenhouse, S. (1985, Sep. 1). Reshaping labor to woo the young. *New York Times*, pp. 1F, 6F.

22. Growing inroads of non-union workers (1983, Sep. 19). *U. S. News & World Report*, pp. 77, 78.

23. Hamner, W. C., & Smith, F. J. (1978). Work attitudes as predictors of unionization activity. *Journal of Applied Psychology*, **63**, 415–421.

24. Hard times ahead for labor (1982, Jan. 4). *Time*, pp. 68, 69.

25. Johnson, D. (1987, Nov. 10). The home of Hormel: A town still divided. *New York Times*, p. A18.

26. Karr, A. R. (1987, Oct. 26). AFL-CIO, in bid to shore up movement, will let Teamsters rejoin federation. *Wall Street Journal*, p. 3.

27. Kilgour, J. G. (1978, April). Before the union knocks. *Personnel Journal*, pp. 186–192, 212, 213.

28. Kilgour, J. G. (1983, March–April). Union organizing activity among white-collar employees. *Personnel*, pp. 18–27.

29. Kochan, T. A. (1979). How American workers view labor unions. *Monthly Labor Review*, **103**(4), 23–31.

30. Kotlowitz, A. (1986, Oct. 13). Labor's ultimate weapon, the strike, is mostly failing. *Wall Street Journal*, p. 6.

31. Kotlowitz, A. (1987, Apr. 1). Grievous work. *Wall Street Journal*, pp. 1, 12.

32. Kotlowitz, A. (1987, Aug. 28). Labor's turn. *Wall Street Journal*, pp. 1, 14.

33. Kristol, I. (1978, Oct. 23). Understanding trade unionism. *Wall Street Journal*, p. 27.

34. Labor's pain: Unionists are alarmed by high court ruling in a bankruptcy filing (1984, Feb. 24). *Wall Street Journal*, pp. 1, 14.

35. Lipset, S. M. (1986, Dec. 18). Why do Canada's unions prosper? *Wall Street Journal*, p. 24.

36. Lublin, J. S. (1983, Nov. 3). NLRB record backlog is said to hamper union drives, prove costly to some firms. *Wall Street Journal*, p. 10.

37. McGinley, L. (1987, June 12). Air controllers, pressed by low morale, FAA friction, will form a new union. *Wall Street Journal*, p. 5.

38. Meany's legacy (1980, Jan. 13). *Miami Herald*, pp. 1E, 5E.

39. Meatpacker who crossed picket lines elected head of Hormel UFCW local (1987, July 22). *Daily Labor Report*, pp. A2–A3.

40. Merger mania spreads to organized labor (1983, Oct. 31). *U. S. News & World Report*, pp. 87, 88.

41. Nesbitt, M. A. (1976). *Labor relations in the federal government service*. Washington, DC: Bureau of National Affairs.

42. *NLRB v. Babcock & Wilcox* (1956). 105 U.S. 351.

43. Noble, K. B. (1986, Nov. 2). Once-mighty U.M.W. is seeking more muscle. *New York Times*, p. E5.

44. Noble, K. B. (1987, Jan. 18). Strikes are getting fewer but longer. *New York Times*, p. E4.

45. Northrup, H. R., & Thornton, A. D. (1987). *The federal government as employer: The Federal Labor Relations Authority and the PATCO challenge*. Philadelphia: Industrial Research Unit, Study 32, The Wharton School, University of Pennsylvania.

46. Novack, J. (1987, July 13). Publish and be damned. *Forbes*, pp. 380–381.

47. NUCOR's Ken Iverson on productivity and pay (1986). *Personnel Administrator*, 31(10), 46–52, 106–108.

48. Perry, C. R. (1987). *Union corporate campaigns*. Philadelphia: Industrial Research Unit, Study 66, The Wharton School, University of Pennsylvania.

49. Prosten, W. (1979). The rise in NLRB election delays: Measuring business's new resistance. *Monthly Labor Review*, 103(2), 39–41.

50. Schlesinger, J. M., & Lamphier, G. (1987, Oct. 26). GM labor contracts get wide approval from union members in U.S., Canada. *Wall Street Journal*, p. 3.

51. Serrin, W. (1985, Dec. 5). Union at Stevens, yes; upheaval, no. *New York Times*, p. A18.

52. Serrin, W. (1986, Feb. 15). Local and national union clash over tactics in Hormel strike. *New York Times*, p. A6.

53. Smith, B. A. (1980, May). Landrum-Griffin after twenty-one years: Mature legislation or childish fantasy? *Labor Law Journal*, pp. 273–282.

54. Swann, J. P., Jr. (1983). The decertification of a union. *Personnel Administrator*, 28(1), 47–51.

55. Thieblot, A. J., Jr., & Haggard, T. R. (1984). *Union violence: The record and the response by courts, legislatures, and the NLRB*. Philadelphia: Industrial Research Unit, Study 25, The Wharton School, University of Pennsylvania.

56. Troubles of U.S. labor unions eased in 1986 (1987, Feb. 15). *New York Times*, p. 31.

57. U.S. Department of Labor (1981). *Directory of national unions and employee associations*. Washington, DC: Department of Labor.

58. U.S. union membership shrank again in 1987 (1988, Jan. 25). *Daily Labor Report*, DLR No. 15, p. A1. Also, Union membership down, wages up (1988, Jan. 23). *Philadelphia Inquirer*, p. 5A.

59. Wermiel, S. (1983, Nov. 16). NLRB can't force companies to bargain with minority unions, U.S. court rules. *Wall Street Journal*, p. 12.

60. Wermiel, S. (1984, Apr. 26). Justice's restrict some unions' spending of the dues dissenting workers must pay. *Wall Street Journal*, p. 8.

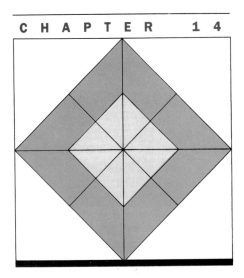

Contemporary Issues in Labor-Management Relations

"Are you crazy?" people in General Electric and in other industrial relations organizations ask when they first hear about the new Grievance Review Panel at GE's Appliance Park-East in Columbia, Maryland. They wonder how and why this nonunion facility—one of the largest in the GE chain—allows a rotating panel of three hourly employees to decide the fate of grievances. Yes, it is true that hourly employees, with a 3-to-2 majority over management, can control the results of most grievances submitted by their peers at the facility.

Why did GE undertake such a radical experiment? To answer this question, it is necessary to consider the previous decade of employee relations at the plant. As the second-largest nonunion plant in GE, located in the highly unionized Baltimore area, the plant had been a constant target of union organizers throughout the 1970s.

The production and quality of electric ranges and microwave ovens, as well as sound human relations programs, were severely hampered by extensive time devoted to union campaigns. During the first 8 years of the plant's op-

*Adapted from: R. T. Boisseau & H. Caras, A radical experiment cuts deep into the attractiveness of unions, *Personnel Administrator*, **28**(10), 1983, 76–79. Copyright, 1983, The American Society for Personnel Administration, Alexandria, VA.

erations, there were nine campaigns leading to six representation elections. GE's winning majorities were consistently under 60 percent.

More important, each election divided employees into pro- and antiunion camps, causing major morale problems from which it took months to recover. Finally management decided that the best way to put an end to the constant union battles was to make Columbia the best possible place to work.

Background on grievances

For years, the Columbia plant had used a formal, written grievance procedure that allowed employees to go immediately to higher levels of management with their grievances. Even though the company had a success rate of over 40 percent (considerably higher than at most union plants), each year there was a steady decline in the use of the formal process. To some extent the decline was due to improved supervision and more consistent application of policies, but some of it also resulted from employees' lack of faith in the process. Many employees admitted honestly that they had a low regard for GE's procedure.

Management brainstormed many different ideas but finally settled on the one recommended by the plant manager at Columbia. At the time, he was the final decision maker in the grievance review process. The plant manager recommended the use of a panel of hourly employees to help him make the best possible decisions. This was the framework:

- Each of five panelists has an equal vote.
- The two management panelists can be outvoted by the three hourly members of the grievance review panel.
- Review-panel decisions are final and binding.

Skeptical responses

The idea was presented to groups of managers, to first-line supervisors, and to employees. Their responses were all about the same—positive about the concept but skeptical that GE was really serious. Even more skepticism came from personnel managers at local companies and other GE plants: "How can you let yourselves be outnumbered and still maintain your right to run the business? they invariably asked.

To that question management had a standard response: "If we have a major issue that truly divides the management and hourly members of the panel—and if we cannot convince one of the hourly people that we are right—then we must be wrong."

To explain the new concept to employees and to solicit volunteer panelists, GE scheduled an after-work review of the new procedure. Employees came and listened on their own time. They contributed to the development of the concept, and unofficially they endorsed the plan. Thirty-nine of them volunteered to join an 8-hour program to train panelists. The training was held during off-duty hours, and it emphasized the legal and ethical elements of grievance handling, problem-solving techniques, and effective listening skills. It ended with a role play of an actual grievance.

The response from the panelists was overwhelming. Even some of the most skeptical among them had a totally different perception by the end of the sessions. All were geared up and ready for the first grievance.

Additional publicity

To explain the process further, a special edition of the GE News—with full details and comments from a panel of employees who had prior knowledge of the project—announced the grievance-panel idea. Second, the Management Hotline, a 60-second daily telephone commentary on items of interest in the business, encouraged people to take the training. Third, the GE News covered the first panel case at the plant. Fourth, a slide-tape program, developed for use at employee roundtable meetings with their supervisors, provided testimonials of how people felt after they had taken the panel training. The panel was then ready to receive its first grievant.

QUESTIONS
1. Discuss two advantages and two disadvantages of the GE grievance review panel.
2. What else needs to be done to improve the overall industrial relations system at the GE plant?
3. The grievance review process at the GE plant is important for what it is and for what it symbolizes. We know what it is and how it works, but what does it symbolize and what does it say about management's assumptions about workers?

What's Ahead

Case 14-1 illustrates another facet of labor-management accommodation: control of a grievance review panel by hourly workers rather than by management. It is another attempt to enhance the productivity and QWL of employees, although (as the case points out) it evolved only after constant union organizing campaigns. In the unionized organization, collective bargaining sets the basic framework within which labor and management operate. Chapter 14 examines this process, along with what happens when both sides cannot agree—strikes, lockouts, and mediation. It discusses trends in collective bargaining, especially two-tier wage structures, as well as contract administration issues: grievances, arbitration, and discipline. It also considers the special concerns of nonunion employees—employment-at-will, disclosure of trade secrets, and nonunion grievance procedures—and it concludes with a discussion of problems facing the American labor movement.

Collective Bargaining: Cornerstone of American Labor Relations

Origins of negotiation in America

The first American strike occurred in the late eighteenth century (the Philadelphia cordwainers), and many other "turnouts" followed during the first half of the nineteenth century. These disputes were neither preceded by nor settled by negotiation. *Negotiation* is a two-party transaction whereby both parties intend to resolve a conflict.[32] Employers unilaterally established a scale of wages. If the wages were unacceptable, journeymen drew up a higher scale, sometimes inserting it into a Bible on which each swore that he or she would not work for less. The scale was presented to the employer, and if he or she did not agree, the workers "turned out" and stayed out until one side or the other caved in. There was no counterproposal, no discussion, no negotiation.

Horace Greeley, who was simultaneously a union sympathizer and an employer, found a better way. In 1850 he told a workers' mass meeting in Tammany Hall, "I do not agree that the journeymen should dictate a scale, but they should get the employers to agree to some scale." A few years later Greeley proposed that workers come to negotiations with statistics and arguments supporting the fairness of their cause. He set the United States on the course known to the twentieth century as collective bargaining.[71]

The art of negotiation

When individuals bargain as consumers or to fix the terms of their employment, they usually act for themselves. Today, however, many agreements are negotiated by bargaining agents. The process is surrounded by ethical ambiguities. It does not necessarily involve dishonesty, but it is seldom open and candid. Even in commonplace negotiations (e.g., buying a car) buyers do not candidly disclose their eagerness to sellers; nor are they under any moral obligation to do so. Patterns of commercial bargaining—anciently established—allow, and sometimes require, negotiators to practice what in other contexts would amount to immoral deceit.

One negotiator may react to another's proposal by pretending more indignation than he feels. He may bluff. He may assert with every appearance of sincerity that he is unchangeably committed to a price beyond which he will not budge—and then budge.[71]

Yet bargaining is not a process in which anything goes. Some negotiators get a reputation for trickery that destroys their effectiveness. Others negotiate successfully for years and enjoy among their opponents and their sponsors a reputation for dealing fairly and squarely. Certainly a negotiator has no right to lie about objective facts. For example, if an employer in negotiation decides to produce figures showing that her business is in bad shape, she must not produce false figures. But she does not owe the union a candid exposure of *her own* view of what the figures imply for the future of the company; she may be less depressed by her accounts than she seems to be. Routinely the union representatives will test her attitude by continuing to insist on their demands and by pretending to be less depressed by the employer's figures than in fact they are. Through such well-worn and twisting—not necessarily immoral—paths, negotiators frequently reach a "striking point" where each is convinced the other will make no further concessions. At that point, it is best to settle.

But what constitutes a "good" settlement? To be sure, the best outcome of negotiations occurs when both parties win. Sometimes negotiations fall short of this ideal. A really bad bargain is when both lose, yet this is a risk that is inherent in the process. Despite its limitations, abuses, and hazards, negotiation has become an indispensable process in free societies in general and in the American labor movement in particular. The fact is that negotiation is the most effective device thus far invented for realizing common interests while compromising conflicting interests.[71] Any practice that threatens the process of collective bargaining will be resisted vigorously by organized labor.

Preparation for negotiations

Like any other competitive activity, physical or mental, the outcome of collective bargaining is influenced significantly by the preparation that precedes actual negotiations. What's worse, mistakes made during union-management negotiations are not easily corrected. Although there is no single "best" set of

FIGURE 14-1

Activities and lead times involved in preparation for negotiations.

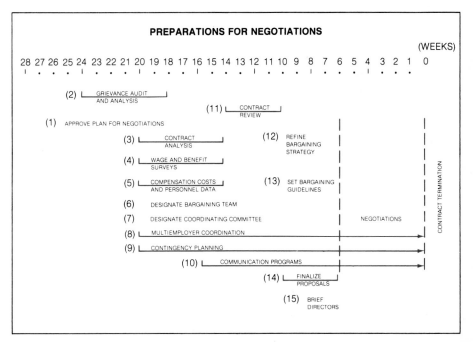

prebargaining activities or an optimum lead time to conduct them, the model shown in Figure 14-1 may provide a useful guide for planning.

In a general sense, planning for subsequent negotiations begins when the previous round of bargaining ends. However, as Figure 14-1 indicates, the formal process begins about 6 months (roughly 24 weeks) prior to the expiration of the current labor agreement. It includes the following 15 activities:[49]

1. *Approve the plan for negotiation* with top management, identifying management's objectives, intermediate and long-term plans, significant changes in the production mix, major technological innovations, and so forth.

2. *Conduct an audit and analysis of grievances* under the existing contract to provide such information as the number of grievances by section of the contract, interpretations of contract provisions through grievance settlements and arbitration awards, and weaknesses in contract language or provisions. One such analysis is shown in Table 14-1.

3. *Contract analysis* includes a section-by-section comparison with other benchmark collective bargaining agreements. This is particularly important if the agreements tend to establish patterns in an industry. In addition, a review of union demands during prior negotiations may help identify areas of mounting interest.

TABLE 14-1 *Analysis of 2 years of grievances in one company*

Type of grievance	Total
Temporary layoff benefits	98
Transfer clause	64
Supervisor working	60
Noncontractual and local agreement	32
Discharge and discipline	27
Discrimination for union activities	26
Overtime pay	20
Overtime equalization	13
Call-out pay	11
Safety and welfare (safety shoes)	9
Contractor doing bargaining-unit work	9
Pension, supplemental unemployment benefits, and insurance	7
New job rate	6
Daily upgrade	5
Holiday pay	4
Schedule change	3
Report pay	3
Timeliness of grievance	2
Seniority	1
Total grievances during contract	400

4. *Wage and benefit surveys of competitors,* both union and nonunion, are essential. Data on changes in the cost of living should be included, along with an assessment of the structure and operation of employee benefits. These data should be interpreted with respect to the current and projected composition of the workforce: for example, by age and sex.

5. *Compensation costs and personnel data* should be presented in a form that allows management to determine changes in costs. For example:

- Demographic profile of the workforce by sex, age, race, seniority group, shift, and job classification.
- Wage payments and premiums: current rates, overtime premiums, shift differential payments, report-in and call-in payments.
- Benefit payments: pay for sickness, vacations, holidays, and civic duties, and premiums for pensions, medical, and disability insurance coverage. (An example of one such calculation, costing out a holiday, is shown in Figure 14-2.)
- The costs of benefits that are required by law: unemployment insurance, workers' compensation, Social Security.
- Data on worker performance, including absenteeism, layoffs, promotions, transfers, paid time for union activities, and leaves of absence. (For more detailed information on labor contract costing, see ref. 15.)

FIGURE 14-2

Costing out a holiday.

Average holiday workforce per plant:

8 first shift, 3 second shift, 3 third shift = 14 workers on, 106 off

14 <u>workers</u> × 13 plants × 8 hr × $22.00* = $32,032

106 <u>nonworkers</u> × 13 plants × 8 hr × $11 = $121,264

Total hours worked per year by workforce:

120 workers/plant × 13 plants × 2080 annual hours/worker = 3,244,800 hr/work year

Cost for holiday workers:

$$\frac{\$32,032}{3,244,800} = .010 \text{ cent}$$

Cost for nonworkers who are paid:

$$\frac{\$121,264}{3,244,800} = .037 \text{ cent}$$

Total cost of each holiday:

.010 + .037 = .047 cent/hr

---

*Normal $11/hr × double time.

6. *Designate a bargaining team* on the basis of technical knowledge, experience, and personality. Include members from line management (not the CEO), human resources-labor relations staff, and finance-accounting (to provide expertise in cost analysis). Unfortunately, evidence indicates that financial officers do *not* negotiate, evaluate, or even participate in major wage and benefit agreements.[26] This is a costly mistake.

7. *Designate coordinating committee* to develop bargaining guidelines for approval by top management and to monitor progress during negotiations.

8. *Provide multiemployer coordination* (as appropriate). This may range from a simple information exchange among loosely connected employers to close coordination among organizations (e.g., regional hospitals) that bargain individually with the same union.

9. *Contingency planning* is essential, for the possibility of a bargaining impasse that may lead to a strike is always present. In the event of a strike, here are the items that one company is prepared to deal with:

Benefits (strikers)	Customer service
Notification of company attorneys	Plant contacts
Continuation of operations	Media communication
Staffing (continuation of production)	Security
Notification responsibilities	Photographic record
General picket report	Strike incident report
Poststrike instructions	Reinstatement of strikers
Treatment of nonstrikers	Vendors
Strike preparation (sales, production)	

10. *Communication programs* designed to facilitate two-way communication between the bargaining team and supervisors help bring supervisors' interests into the planning process. During negotiations, informed supervisors can be an effective means of communication to nonsupervisory personnel.

11. *Contract review*, by the coordinating committee, based on all the data assembled thus far, results in an assessment of contract provisions. Particular attention should be paid to:

- Identification of important differences among contract provisions, workplace practices, and personnel policies.
- Identification of contract provisions to be revised, added, or eliminated. (Examples of ambiguous contract language that can lead to different interpretations are shown in Table 14-2. We might consider these "words to grieve by.")

12. *Refine the bargaining strategy*, once the preparatory activities are completed. The strategy established at the beginning of the planning process

TABLE 14-2 *Words to grieve by*

Ability	Fully	Possible
Absolutely	Habitually	Practical
Adequate	High degree	Properly
Almost	Immediately	Qualification
Capacity	Minimal	Reasonable
Completely	Minimum	Regular
Day	Necessary	Substantially equal
Equal	Normal	Sufficient number
Forthwith	Periodic	With all dispatch
Frequent		

should be modified to reflect such factors as union demands and strategy, management's objectives, experience with multiemployer coordination, and the likelihood of a work stoppage.

13. *Set bargaining guidelines* for top management's approval. Ensure that the chief negotiator has the authority to reach a settlement within the guidelines. A procedure should also be established to modify the guidelines as needed once negotiations are underway.

14. *Finalize proposals* in writing, along with acceptable variations, to provide flexibility. Recheck the data bank for accuracy, comprehensiveness, and ease of access. Assure that notices required by contract or by labor law have been issued and acknowledged. Compile bargaining aids (e.g., a bargaining book, data reference sheets, and work sheets), and finalize arrangements for note taking and record keeping.

15. *Brief directors*, as necessary, on the planning process, guidelines, and bargaining strategy. Establish a procedure for additional briefings during negotiations and reinforce the principle that governing board members should stay out of the bargaining process.

Bargaining "pros" say flatly that there is really only one way to become good at the process—through actual bargaining experience. Yet everybody has to start somewhere, and in recent years advances in technology have helped to ease the transition from inexperienced novice to seasoned professional. Both role playing[32] and computer simulation[14] make such a transition possible and provide insight into the human dynamics of the bargaining process. Certainly the optimum outcome, as noted earlier, is when both parties cooperate and compromise to the extent that both "win." Unfortunately this is not always the case. Contract negotiations sometimes fail because the parties are not able to reach a timely and mutually acceptable settlement of the issues—economic, noneconomic, or a combination of both. When this happens, the union may strike, management may shut down operations (a lockout), or both parties may ask for help from the Federal Mediation and Conciliation Service. Let's examine these processes in detail.

Bargaining Impasses: Strikes, Lockouts, or Mediation?

In every labor negotiation there exists the possibility of a strike. The right of employees to strike in support of their bargainable demands is protected by the Landrum-Griffin Act. However, there is no *unqualified* right to strike. A work stoppage by employees must be the result of a lawful labor dispute and not in violation of an existing agreement between management and the union. Strikers engaged in activities protected by law may not be discharged, but they may be replaced during the strike. Strikers engaged in activities that are not protected by law need not be rehired after the strike.[4]

Types of strikes

As you might suspect by now, there are several different types of strikes. Let's consider the major types:

Unfair-labor-practice strikes. These are caused or prolonged by unfair labor practices of the employer. Employees engaged in this type of strike are afforded the highest degree of protection under the act, and under most circumstances they are entitled to reinstatement once the strike ends. Management must exercise great caution in handling unfair-labor-practice strikes because the National Labor Relations Board will become involved and company liability can be substantial.

An economic strike. This is an action by the union of withdrawing its labor in support of bargaining demands, including those for recognition or organization. Economic strikers have limited rights to reinstatement.

Unprotected strikes. All remaining types of work stoppages, both lawful and unlawful, are included. These include sit-down strikes, strikes in violation of federal laws (e.g., the air traffic controllers), slowdowns, wildcat strikes, and partial walkouts. Participants in unprotected strikes may be discharged by their employers.

Sympathy strikes. These are refusals by employees of one bargaining unit to cross a picket line of a different bargaining unit (e.g., when more than one union is functioning at an employer's plant). Although the National Labor Relations Board and the courts have recognized the right of the sympathy striker to stand in the shoes of the primary striker, the facts of any particular situation will ultimately determine the legal status of a sympathy strike.[3]

During a strike, certain rules of conduct apply to *both* parties; these are summarized in Table 14-3. In addition, certain special rules apply to management; *do not:*

- Offer extra rewards to nonstrikers or attempt to withhold the "extras" from strikers once the strike has ended and some or all strikers are reinstated.

TABLE 14-3 *Rules of conduct during a strike*

- People working in or having any business with the organization have a right to pass freely in and out.
- Pickets must not block a door, passageway, driveway, crosswalk, or other entrance or exit.
- Profanity on streets and sidewalks may be a violation of state law or local ordinances.
- Company officials, with the assistance of local law enforcement agents, should make every effort to permit individuals and vehicles to move in and out of the facility in a normal manner.
- Union officials or pickets have a right to talk to people going in or out. Intimidation, threats, and coercion are not permitted, either by verbal remarks or by physical action.
- The use of sound trucks may be regulated by state law or local ordinance with respect to noise level, location, and permit requirements.
- If acts of violence or trespassing occur on the premises, officials should file complaints or seek injunctions. If you are the object of violence, sign a warrant for the arrest of the person(s) causing the violence.
- Fighting, assault, battery, violence, threats, or intimidation are not permissible under the law. The carrying of knives, firearms, clubs, or other dangerous weapons may be prohibited by state law or local ordinance.

- Threaten nonstrikers or strikers.
- Promise benefits to strikers in an attempt to end the strike or to undermine the union.
- Threaten employees with discharge for taking part in a lawful strike.
- Discharge nonstrikers who refuse to take over a striker's job.

When the strike is over

The period of time immediately after a strike is critical, since an organization's problems are not over when the strike is settled. There is the problem of conflict between strikers and their replacements (if replacements were hired) and the accommodation of strikers to the workplace. After an economic strike is settled, the method of reinstatement is best protected by a written *memorandum of agreement* with the union that outlines the intended procedure. A key point of consideration in any strike aftermath is misconduct by some strikers. To refuse reinstatement for such strikers following an economic strike, management must be able to present evidence (e.g., photographs) to prove the misconduct.

The most important human aspect at the end of the strike is the restoration of harmonious working relations as soon as possible so that full operations can be resumed. A letter or a speech to employees welcoming them back to work can help this process along, as can meetings with supervisors indicating that no resentment or ill will is to be shown toward returning strikers. In practice, this may be difficult to do. However, keep this in mind:

Nothing is gained by allowing vindictiveness of any type in any echelon of management.

The burden of maintaining healthy industrial relations now lies with the organization.

There is always another negotiation ahead and rancor has no place at any bargaining table. (ref. 3, p. 22)

COMPANY PRACTICES

More Firms Keep Operating in Spite of Strikes

To an increasing number of companies, "strike" is no longer a frightening word, for they are prepared to continue operating right through a labor walkout. Highly automated firms like American Telephone & Telegraph Company have been operating through strikes for years, but in today's economic climate, where many labor-intensive firms such as Magic Chef, Inc., and Whirlpool Corporation truly believe that their survival depends on not giving in to union demands, such a strategy is revolutionary. Although union officials criticize these management tactics, such actions are producing a flourishing business for security firms. The security firms provide companies with armored cars, vans, and guards to protect nonstriking workers during labor disputes. For example, one security firm helped Dannon Company, the yogurt maker, maintain operations at several New York area plants during a series of strikes by members of the Teamsters union. The security firm provided about 100 guards to escort company trucks. The guards do not carry weapons, but they are armed with cameras. When strikers know that they will be photographed, there tends to be a lot less violence. The cost for the 14-week security service: over $1 million.

Even small companies that cannot afford outside security services are beginning to take on strikers. Extrusion Technology, a Randolph, Massachusetts, manufacturer of aluminum extrusions, caved in to union demands for a dozen years. "When we had our first negotiations with the Teamsters 12 years ago, they stood up and stormed out of the room," said the company's president. "We rushed after them to come back in and give us a contract. That set the tempo for a dozen years. We felt a strike would be deadly" (ref. 27, p. 1).

However, 2 years of losses strengthened the company's resolve. When the company insisted on a wage-scale plan tied to job classifications and the right to assign mandatory overtime, a 6-week strike ensued. Initially the company tried to operate its plant with about 20 nonunion office workers. But after 3 weeks the company hired 15 workers through newspaper ads. The plant began running at about 50 percent of capacity.

The company president drove a truck through the picket line himself to deliver products and to pick up supplies. "I wasn't going to ask my people to do that," he says. After 3 more weeks, the union settled. The company won the overtime issue, and it reached a compromise on the wage scale.

"I wasn't out to break the union; I was out to settle the dispute," the president says. "But I wanted to keep my customers while I was resolving it." He adds, "If the union says 'strike' three years from now, they better be prepared to stay out for a long time" (ref. 27, p. 18).

Unions are pondering what to do about the tougher management reaction to strikes. Says the Machinists Union's president, William Winpisinger, "It's part of a disease that's running amuck in the country, and it's going to get worse unless picket lines start to mean something again" (ref. 27, p. 18).

Labor's ultimate weapon, the strike, is mostly failing. Automation, recent court decisions, growing antiunion sentiment, and a pool of unemployed workers willing to break a strike make it easier for employers to defeat a walkout.[36] As a result, the number of strikes and lockouts has decreased from an average of 285 per year in the 1960s and 1970s to an average of 62 in 1984–1986. When jobs are tight, such a decrease is not surprising. Thus when 100 workers at Ludington News Company, a magazine and book distributor, went on strike, 500 people mobbed the plant. They taunted picketers with the chant, "We want your job," as they shoved and grabbed for job applications. The specter of losing jobs forced the union back to the bargaining table.[36]

Proposed alternatives to strikes, including corporate campaigns and in-plant slowdowns, have had mixed success. During a slowdown, while workers adhere to the minimums of their job requirements, they continue to get paid, thereby frustrating management, but such a "work-to-rule" strategy could backfire in the long run; if productivity suffers a prolonged decline and companies fail to meet production schedules, competitors will move in quickly. Then everybody loses. Companies are fighting back by retaliating in kind, firing activist employees and in some cases locking out the entire workforce. A recent NLRB decision that permits companies to replace locked-out workers with temporary employees has strengthened management's hand.[38]

Management's antiunion tactics have been quite successful, but this does not absolve management of the responsibility to treat workers with dignity and respect, to avoid arrogance, and to recognize that it is hard to give up gains that were so difficult to earn in the first place.

Mediation

Strikes and lockouts are expensive, in human as well as in monetary terms. Thus the 111-day coal strike in 1978 caused 25,500 layoffs of workers in *related* industries, and the 1979 Teamsters' strike and lockout caused 295,000 layoffs in other industries, primarily the auto industry.[41] For this reason, both union and management often turn to mediation by an outside party in a last-ditch effort to avoid a work stoppage.

The Federal Mediation and Conciliation Service that most people have to deal with dates back to the Taft-Hartley Act of 1947. It has roughly 260 mediators in 79 offices divided among seven regions. More than half of these government mediators are former union negotiators, about 40 percent worked for management, and the rest come from related agencies, such as the National Labor Relations Board.

There is no such thing as a "typical" mediator. "Two hundred and sixty prima donnas," says one. "Some are low key, some are flamboyant, some go for the jugular, real hit men and head knockers" (ref. 70, p. 7F).

There is no set time when a mediator will go in and attempt to resolve a dispute. By law the Federal Mediation and Conciliation Service must be notified 30 days prior to the expiration of all labor contracts. But some unions, such as the United Auto Workers, traditionally refuse mediation, and so many others manage to settle by themselves that the agency estimates that it is involved in only 8000 to 9000 of the country's 100,000 yearly labor negotiations. However, their public-sector caseload has been growing sharply.[48]

Mediators have two restrictions on their power: (1) They are involved by invitation only, and (2) their advice lacks even so much as the umpire's option of throwing someone out of the game. Some will do almost anything to get a settlement.

PRACTICAL EXAMPLE

Mediation tactics

During a Philadelphia teachers' strike, hundreds of strikers had been arrested, and the union leaders had been in jail for weeks. The first task facing Bill Usery, the mediator sent by the Federal Mediation and Conciliation Service, was to get the union leaders released under his recognizance so that negotiations could continue.

"One guy got to talking to me about what it's like in jail," Usery remembers. "He said when his wife came to visit, he had to sit behind a wire cage, he couldn't even touch her. 'You can't imagine,' he said, 'how that makes a man feel.'"

So Usery got the union leader released and immediately had the man's wife visit him in Usery's hotel suite. Usery had dinner with them, ordered wine, and afterward handed the man the key to his suite. Usery told him he'd be back later that evening.

"You never saw somebody so happy," Usery says. "I don't know what they did, but I'd proved myself to him, so he would listen to my suggestions." Two days later the strike was settled.

Bill Usery is considered the best mediator there is. As he says in his courtly southern drawl, "There is no finer profession than making peace among men" (ref. 70, p. 7F).

Trends in Collective Bargaining

Over the past decade, unions, especially those in the trucking, meatpacking, railroad, airline, construction, auto, steel, and mining industries, have made unprecedented concessions on wages and benefits.[33] Here are some reasons why:

1. The harsh realities of the 1981 to 1983 economic recession.
2. The highest unemployment rates since the Great Depression.
3. Fierce international and domestic competition, much of which has been fueled by deregulation in the airline, telecommunications, trucking, and railroad industries.[67] This has meant an end to bargaining in which union contracts negotiated at leading companies set the pattern for an industry.
4. Concern over job security.

Examples of these concessions during the 1979–1984 period are shown in Table 14-4.

Some viewed concessionary bargaining as a temporary phenomenon, just a blip on the time line of ever-increasing wages and benefits. Union leaders tried to put the best face on the wage and benefit cuts—calling them temporary measures to strengthen companies and, above all, to protect jobs. Time has told a different story, as cuts in wages and benefits have become a way of economic life in the "postconcessionary" era. Unions have found that getting back the "give-backs" has not been easy. Thus one-third of the members of unions that settled contracts during 1986 received either pay cuts or no raises.[53] Understandably, the granting of concessions represents a fundamental change. It is a grim but necessary recognition that labor costs have to be reduced if the United States is to remain competitive in the context of a global economy.

Although wage patterns throughout the United States have traditionally been influenced by the unions—consistent increases—employers are resisting more and more. They are changing the pattern of negotiations by tying wages to productivity through employee profit sharing or stock ownership plans. Recently, for example, workers at Safeway grocery stores in Denver approved a contract that included a 14 percent wage cut in return for a share of the net operating profits of *individual* stores. For example, if a store makes a 2 percent net operating profit amounting to $208,000 over a 12-week period, Safeway distributes $15,600—that's 15 percent of the $104,000 profit exceeding 1 percent—to the workers as profit sharing. The objective is to reduce costs and to improve profits. Workers can help by properly handling perishable goods, spotting shoplifters and bad-check writers, and preventing cash shortages at the cash register.[61] As we saw in Chapters 11 and 12, the trend toward putting more of one's pay "at risk" is gaining momentum throughout the economy. And as emphasized in Chapters 13 and 14, this kind of labor-management cooperation makes companies more competitive by boosting the employees' productivity and quality of work life.

TABLE 14-4 *Collective bargaining concessions in some key industries, 1979–1984*

Date	Company	Union	Concessions
1979	Chrysler	United Auto Workers	Wage cuts
1981	Armour Food	United Food and Commercial Workers	Wage and cost-of-living freezes
1982	Ford	United Auto Workers	Wage freeze
1982	General Motors	United Auto Workers	Wage freeze
1982	CF&I Steel	United Steel Workers	Wage and benefit cuts for profit sharing
1982	CONRAIL (Penn Central, others)	Railway Labor Executives (16 unions)	Wage concessions
1982	Trucking industry	Teamsters	Wage freeze, work-rule changes, and benefit concessions
1983	U.S. Steel, others	United Steel Workers	Wage cuts and reduced benefits
1983	Aluminum Co. of America	Aluminum, Brick, & Glass Workers	Wage freeze
1983	Kennecott, others	United Steel Workers	Wage freeze
1983	Kaiser Aluminum	United Steel Workers	Wage freeze
1983	Western Airlines	Airline Pilots, others	Wage and cost-of-living concessions for ESOP
1983	Pan Am Airlines	Airline Pilots, others	Wage cuts and wage freezes
1983	Republic Airlines	Airline Pilots, others	Wage cuts and work-rule changes
1984	Frontier Airlines	Airline Pilots, others	Wage and benefit concessions
1984	Eastern Airlines	Airline Pilots, others	Wage and benefit concessions

Sources: J. Taylor, Recession alters face of labor, *The Denver Post*, Oct. 2, 1983, p. 1D; Frontier union backs 20% cut in pay, benefits, *Wall Street Journal*, Mar. 29, 1984, p. 16. Reprinted by permission of The Wall Street Journal, © Dow Jones & Company, Inc. 1984. All Rights Reserved.

COMPANY EXAMPLE

Ford gets tough in extracting give-backs

Ford's unprofitable Rouge mill in Dearborn, Michigan, was built in the 1920s. It is part of a sprawling complex that was once the model integrated manufacturing facility. Iron ore and coal were unloaded from a fleet of Ford ships in the Detroit River at one end of the complex, and completed cars rolled off the assembly line at the other.

In the past, the Rouge mill provided the majority of the sheet steel that Ford used to make cars. But over the years the company's investment in the operation failed to keep pace with those of other U.S. and foreign steel makers, and the quality of its products began to slip. By 1981 the mill provided only 40 percent of Ford's steel needs, which accounted for 25 percent of the mill's output. The remainder was sold to outside customers, often at deep discounts from list prices.

After several months of negotiations, Ford and the United Auto Workers reached an impasse over wage and other concessions. Ford said the mill was unprofitable because its total labor costs (wages and benefits) were running $28 per hour, or about $5 per hour higher than competing U.S. steel plants. Without the concessions, Ford said it would not make the investments necessary to improve the mill's productivity and quality. The steel operation was losing $10 million per month.

The union felt that Ford was not being completely candid about its intentions. It charged that Ford was trying to get lower labor costs so that it could sell the Rouge mill to a Japanese firm. Many workers were averse to any more give-backs for three reasons: (1) They had enough seniority to bump other lower-seniority workers out of jobs elsewhere in the 12,500-employee manufacturing complex connected to the mill; (2) rules regarding the dumping of steel assured them of jobs elsewhere in the Rouge complex; and (3) others felt that Ford would close the mill anyway even if they did give up more.

After extended negotiations, Ford and the United Auto Workers reached an agreement. Ford's labor costs were cut by $4.15 per hour as a result of reductions in incentive pay, cost-of-living payments, and vacations. In return, the agreement specified that if the steel operation were sold, the buyer would have to honor the agreement. Ford also agreed to recall some of the 860 workers laid off indefinitely from the Rouge mill.

In an unusual step, all 15,000 workers throughout the integrated complex were allowed to vote on the contract. More than 66 percent of them endorsed it.[10, 11, 12, 23]

Two-tier wage structures

Two-tier wage structures (one for current workers, one for future hires) take a variety of forms. In some, wages are reduced for almost all job categories; others apply only to a few specialties. In some agreements new workers can catch up eventually to the wages that older employees earn. In others, parity between new and old workers is ruled out forever. This ensures that a disadvantaged class of employees will be working side by side with a privileged one until all the higher-paid employees retire.[22] Examples of some two-tier wage agreements are shown in Table 14-5.

Two-tier wage structures are not new. A Roman emperor's use of a two-tier pay system for his army in A.D. 217 resulted in his assassination.[45] Among all the concessions proposed by management, two-tier agreements seem to be

TABLE 14-5 *Examples of two-tier wage agreements*

Company	Union (number of workers covered by contract)	Entry-level wage differential	
		New contract	Old contract
Boeing	International Association of Machinists & Aerospace Workers (26,000)	$6.70 per hour	$11.38 per hour
Lockheed	International Association of Machinists & Aerospace Workers (23,000)	$6 per hour	$8.64 per hour
McDonnell Douglas	International Association of Machinists & Aerospace Workers (3400)	$6.73 per hour	$9.36 per hour
Giant Food	United Food & Commercial Workers International (12,000)	$5 per hour	$6.95 per hour
Safeway Stores	United Food & Commercial Workers International (6300)	$5 per hour	$6.95 per hour
American Airlines	Allied Pilots Association (4000)	$18,000 per year	$36,000 per year
Briggs & Stratton	Allied Industrial Workers of America (8000)	$5.50 per hour	$8 per hour
Dow Chemical	United Steelworkers of America (2600)	$6.895 per hour	$7.08 per hour

Note: Except for the pilots at American Airlines, all wage rates are for the companies' lowest job category or labor grade.
Source: S. Flax, Pay cuts before the job even starts, *Fortune*, Jan. 9, 1984, p. 75.

the most agreeable to rank-and-file union members, in part because their own incomes are not on the line. By 1987, for example, American Airlines had about 15,000 employees, or about 20 percent of its unionized workforce, on its lower pay scale. Labor costs dropped to 30 percent of operating costs, from 38 percent in 1983. American needs the savings in order to compete with nonunion carriers like Continental, where labor makes up about 25 percent of operating costs. However, *the risk of two-tier contracts is that the sense of unfairness among workers could hurt productivity*. Events have justified that concern, as more companies are finding that two-tier wages often cause more trouble than they are worth.[9]

The system has produced a resentful class of workers who, in some cases, are taking their hostility out on customers. It has generated friction between lower- and higher-paid employees. At some companies it has caused turnover to soar and made recruitment more difficult. And at a time when unions have been on the defensive, the system has sparked a new wave of militancy.[60, 65] As a result, the percentage of new labor contracts with two-tier structures declined to 10 percent in 1986, after rising from 5 to 11 percent from 1982 to 1985.[45]

Paying new workers less once sounded like an easy way out to many people in both labor and management. What they forgot is that new employees soon become old ones. And after a few years, those workers can see no reason why they should be paid less than other people doing the same job.[9]

Emerging trends

A 5-year study of the financial economics of basic industries in the United States—steel, meat packing, railroads, and trucking—concluded that management and labor have bargained their way into an economic corner. They have set wages and benefits at levels far beyond the ability of many companies to pay. Had the escalation not occurred, many mature industries would not suffer as they now do, and they would have access to the capital necessary to modernize. In the words of the study's author:

> I believe that bargaining decisions that have resulted in a rising standard of living and economic health for employees—and that have satisfied the short-term concerns of managers—have also destroyed the economic structures of many mature industries. In labor contracts, managers have bargained away their competitiveness on the assumption that if every domestic company faced the same wage structure, none would suffer a competitive disadvantage. The consumer would pay for the consequences—not labor, management, or the shareholders. But the consumer has not paid. (ref. 26, p. 131)

This is a grim prospect for union members, some of whom earn total compensation that is 60 percent higher than that of nonunion employees for roughly comparable work. However, those who are most threatened are not labor's elite, such as tool-and-die makers and electronics specialists, but rather machine operators and other less skilled production workers in big plants in large cities. TRW Inc.'s strategy is typical: If possible, cut pay and benefits. If that does not work, then buy overseas or from lower-wage domestic suppliers those items which the company once made in high-wage plants. Meanwhile, make new products in smaller plants and in smaller, less unionized cities, and phase out the big old plants.[72]

Whether companies are responding to domestic or international competition, of one thing we can be certain: Over the long term, changes in the makeup of the American labor movement seem inevitable. As John R. Opel, former president of IBM, has noted, "Everybody knows that you're in a world market. You better be prepared to compete as a world-class competitor."[35]

Contract Administration

In both the public and private sectors, once an agreement has been reached, the tentative contract must be ratified by the union. Actually, ratification takes place at two levels: the international union and the local union. The international union must approve the agreement negotiated by the local to ensure that it includes terms and conditions comparable to those negotiated by other unions. Members of the local union also have an opportunity to voice their opinion of the settlement reached by the members of their negotiating team. If both the international and the local union ratify the contract, it becomes legally binding.

Once the contract has been ratified, labor and management return to their everyday roles. The emphasis then shifts to contract administration.

Grievances

Occasionally during the life of the contract, disputes about interpretation require that the parties resolve their differences through a formal process known as the *grievance procedure*. A typical grievance procedure in a unionized firm works as shown in Figure 14-3. As the figure indicates, unresolved grievances proceed progressively to higher and higher levels of management and union representation and culminate in voluntary, binding arbitration. While the number of steps and the time required to proceed through each step vary across contracts, the grievance process is expensive.

Costing a grievance   One study found that to process 500 grievances (the actual number filed in a single West Coast union local over a 1-year period), a total of 4580 work hours were required, or an average of 9.1 hours per grievance. Assume that the average total compensation (wages plus benefits) for the grievant, union, and management representatives is $65 per hour, or more than $590 per grievance. This translates into an annual cost of almost $300,000 to resolve 500 grievances. However, this figure is conservative, for it reflects only the *direct* time used for formal meetings on grievances. It does not include such other factors as preparation time, informal meetings, clerical time, and administrative overhead for management and the union.[18] In complex grievance cases that proceed all the way to arbitration (Step 6 in Figure 14-3), the cost to the company or union may exceed $5000 per grievance.[37, 39]

FIGURE 14-3

Example of a formal grievance procedure in a unionized firm.

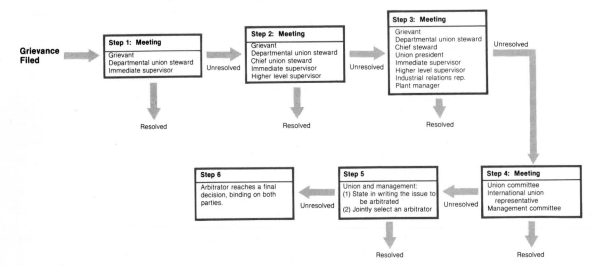

TABLE 14-6 *Percentage of grievances filed by category*

Grievance category	Percentage
Suspension	20.8
Seniority	10.4
Miscellaneous	8.6
Transfer	7.4
Termination	6.6
Disciplinary memoranda	6.6
Scheduling	6.4
Vacation	5.8
Grievance process	4.4
Management performing production work	4.0
Safety	3.4
Discrimination	3.4
Performance evaluations	3.0
Union representation	2.0
Sick benefits denial	2.0
Pay (differentials, travel, etc.)	1.8
Excused and complimentary time	1.6
Work out of classification	1.2
Training	0.6

Source: D. R. Dalton & W. D. Todor, Win, lose, draw: The grievance process in practice, *Personnel Administrator,* **26**(3), 1981, 27. Copyright, 1981, The American Society for Personnel Administration, Alexandria, VA.

Common grievances and their resolution   For the West Coast local just mentioned, the percentage of grievances filed by category is shown in Table 14-6. The majority of grievances were filed over disciplinary issues: the introductory disciplinary memorandum, suspensions, and termination. Seniority, the basis of many individual work rights for union employees, is grieved frequently. Beyond that, no single category accounts for a large proportion of the grievances filed.

Of the grievances that were submitted to binding arbitration in 1983, unions lost more than half, according to a random sample of 1789 cases by the American Arbitration Association. Unions won in 29 percent of the cases, and in about 18 percent of the cases the union and the company won partial victories.[42] However, the majority of grievances filed are resolved without resorting to arbitration. Of these, *unions* tend to win more grievances related to such issues as the denial of sick benefits, termination, transfer, suspension, and disciplinary memoranda. Ordinarily the burden of proof in a grievance proceeding is on the union. Since fewer issues of interpretation are involved in the areas that unions usually win, this pattern of grievance resolution is not surprising.[18]

Arbitration

Binding arbitration is used by management and labor to settle disputes arising out of and during the term of a labor contract. As Figure 14-3 indicates, compulsory, binding arbitration is the final stage of the grievance process. It is also used as an alternative to a work stoppage, and it is used to ensure labor peace for the duration of a labor contract. Arbitrators may be chosen from a list of qualified people supplied by the American Arbitration Association or the Federal Mediation and Conciliation Service.

Arbitration hearings are quasi-judicial proceedings. Prehearing briefs may be filed by both parties, along with lists of witnesses to be called. Witnesses are cross-examined, and documentary evidence may be introduced. However, *arbitrators are not bound by the formal rules of evidence*, as they would be in a court of law.

Following the hearing, the parties may each submit briefs to reiterate their positions, evidence supporting them, and proposed decisions. The arbitrator then considers the evidence, the contract clause in dispute, and the powers granted the arbitrator under the labor agreement, and finally issues a decision. In rare instances where a losing party refuses to honor the arbitrator's decision, the decision can be enforced by taking that party to federal court.[30]

Grievance arbitration has generally worked well, and this is why many companies have extended it as an option to their nonunion employees. For example, Federal Express Corporation's "guaranteed fair-treatment process" lets employees appeal problems to a peer review board chosen by the worker involved and management. The board rules for employees about half the time. Bosses cannot appeal decisions, but employees can, to a panel of top executives. TWA employees take disputes to a panel comprised of an arbitrator, a representative from the human resources staff, and another employee. One reason for the growing popularity of these programs is that they tend to reduce lawsuits. At Aetna Life & Casualty Company, for example, only one of the almost 300 complaints handled by Aetna's program has gone to litigation.[69]

Discipline

Make no mistake about it: Most employees want to conduct themselves in a manner acceptable to the company and to their fellow employees. Occasionally problems of absenteeism, poor work performance, or rule violations arise. When informal conversations or coaching sessions fail to resolve these problems, formal disciplinary action is called for.

Employee discipline is the final area of contract administration that we shall consider. Typically the "management rights" clause of the collective bargaining agreement retains for management the authority to impose *reasonable* rules for workplace conduct and to discipline employees for *just cause*. Management is expected to administer discipline fairly and consistently across people and offenses. In a unionized firm, employees who feel that they have been disciplined unjustly may appeal to higher management or else use the grievance procedure. As we have seen, such appeals are common. Unions rarely object to employee discipline, *provided that* (1) it is applied consistently, (2) the rules are publicized clearly, and (3) the rules are considered reasonable.

Discipline is indispensable to management control. Ideally it should serve as a corrective mechanism to prevent serious harm to the organization.[7] Unfortunately, some managers go to great lengths to avoid using discipline. To some extent this is understandable, for discipline is one of the hardest personnel actions to face. Managers may avoid imposing discipline because of (1) ignorance of organizational rules, (2) fear of formal grievances, or (3) fear of losing the friendship of employees. Yet failure to administer discipline can result in implied acceptance or approval of the offense. Thereafter, problems may become more frequent or severe, and discipline becomes that much more difficult to administer.[54]

Let us begin by outlining the negative effects of punishment. These include:

- Punishment indicates only that the behavior being punished is *not* desired by the organization; it does not indicate what behavior *is* desired.
- Punishment serves only to eliminate the undesirable behavior as long as the person enforcing the punishment is present. If that individual is not present, the punished behavior reappears.
- Punishment may create feelings of anger and resentment, which may then be manifested as aggressive behavior, sabotage, and similar undesirable conduct.[4]

These arguments for not imposing punishment are persuasive. But evidence also indicates that discipline (that is, punishment) may be beneficial.[56] Consider that:

- Discipline may alert the marginal employee to his or her low performance and result in a change in behavior.
- Discipline may signal other employees regarding expected levels of performance and standards of behavior.
- If the discipline is perceived as legitimate by other employees, it may increase motivation, morale, and performance.

In fact, a statistical reanalysis of the original Hawthorne experiments concluded that managerial discipline was the major factor in increased rates of output.[25] A subsequent study supports these conclusions.[56] Department managers in a retail store chain who used informal warnings, formal warnings, and dismissals more frequently than their peers had higher departmental performance ratings (in terms of annual cost and sales data and ratings by higher-level managers). This relationship held even when length of service was taken into account. More frequent use of sanctions was associated with improved performance. Why is this so?

First, the performance ratings used reflected *departmental* performance, not *individual* performance. Supervisors must deal with the behavior of individuals in a *social* context, not with the isolated behavior of a single person.

Hence, generalizations based on reinforcement theory (a theory of individual behavior) may not hold true when applied in a social context.[63]

A more powerful explanation for these results may lie in social learning theory.[6] *Individuals in groups look to others to learn appropriate behaviors and attitudes.* They learn them by modeling the behavior of others, by adopting standard operating procedures, and by following group norms. Individuals whose attitudes or behaviors violate these norms may cause problems. Tolerance of such behavior by the supervisor may *threaten* the group by causing feelings of uncertainty and unfairness. On the other hand, management actions that are seen as maintaining legitimate group standards may instill feelings of fairness and result in improved performance. Failure to invoke sanctions may lead to a loss of management control and unproductive employee behavior. Finally, do not underestimate the *symbolic* value of disciplinary actions, especially since punitive behavior tends to make a lasting impression on employees.[16, 58]

Progressive discipline   Many firms, both unionized and nonunionized, follow a procedure of progressive discipline that proceeds from an oral warning to a written warning to a suspension to dismissal. However, to administer discipline without at the same time engendering resentment by the disciplined employee, managers should follow what Douglas McGregor called the "Red Hot Stove Rule." Discipline should be:

Immediate. Just like touching a hot stove, where feedback is immediate, there should be no misunderstanding about why discipline was imposed. People are disciplined not because of who they are (personality) but because of what they did (behavior).

With warning. A small child knows that, if he touches a hot stove, he will be burned. Likewise, employees must know very clearly what the consequences will be of undesirable work behavior. They must be given adequate warning.

Consistent. Every time a person touches a red hot stove, she gets burned. Likewise, if discipline is to be perceived as fair, it must be administered consistently, given similar circumstances surrounding the undesirable behavior. Consistency *among* individual managers across the organization is essential.

Impersonal. A hot stove is blind to who touches it. So also, managers cannot play favorites by disciplining subordinates they do not like, while allowing the same behavior to go unpunished for those they do like.

Documenting performance-related incidents   Documentation is a fact of organizational life for most managers. While such paperwork is never pleasant, it should conform to the following guidelines:

- Describe what led up to the incident—the problem and the setting. Is this a first offense or part of a pattern?
- Describe what actually happened, and be specific: i.e., include names, dates, times, witnesses, and other pertinent facts.

FIGURE 14-4

Sample written warning of disciplinary action.

DATE: April 14, 1988

TO: J. Hartwig

FROM: D. Curtis

SUBJECT: Written Warning

    On this date you were 30 minutes late to work with no justification for your tardiness. A similar offense occurred last Friday. At that time you were told that failure to report for work on schedule will not be condoned. I now find it necessary to tell you in writing that you must report to work on time. Failure to do so will result in your dismissal from employment. Please sign below that you have read and that you understand this warning.

[Name]   [Date]

- Describe what must be done to correct the situation.
- State the consequences of further violations.

Conclude the warning by obtaining the employee's signature that he or she has read and understands the warning. A sample written warning is shown in Figure 14-4. Note how it includes each of the ingredients just described.

The disciplinary interview Generally such interviews are held for one of two reasons: (1) over issues of *workplace conduct,* such as attendance or punctuality, or (2) over issues of *job performance,* such as low productivity.[56] They tend to be very legalistic. As an example, consider the following scenario:

    You are a first-line supervisor at a nonunion facility. You suspect that one of your subordinates, Susan Fox, has been distorting her time reports to misrepresent her daily starting time. While some of the evidence is sketchy, you know that Fox's time reports are false. Accompanied by an industrial relations representative, you decide to confront Fox directly in a disciplinary interview. However, before you can begin the meeting, Fox announces, "I'd appreciate it if a coworker of mine could be present during this meeting. If a coworker cannot be present, I refuse to participate." Your reaction to this startling request is to:

A Ask Fox which coworker she desires and reconvene the meeting once the employee is present.

B   Deny her request and order her to participate or face immediate discipline for insubordination.
C   Terminate the meeting with no further discussion.
D   Ignore the request and proceed with the meeting, hoping that Fox will participate anyway.
E   Inform Fox that, as her supervisor, you are a coworker and attempt to proceed with the meeting.

Unless your reaction was A or C, you have probably committed a violation of the National Labor Relations Act.[34]

In *NLRB v. J. Weingarten, Inc.*, the Supreme Court ruled that a *union* employee has the right to demand that a union representative be present at an investigatory interview that the employee reasonably believes may result in disciplinary action.[51] However, in *NLRB v. Sears, Roebuck and Co.* (1985), the court overturned an earlier decision, ruling that *Weingarten* rights do not extend to nonunion employees.[50] To summarize the Weingarten mandate:

1. The employee must *request* representation; the employer has no obligation to offer it voluntarily.
2. The employee must reasonably believe that the investigation may result in disciplinary action taken against him or her.
3. The employer is not obligated to carry on the interview or to justify its refusal to do so. The employer may simply cancel the interview and thus effectively disallow union or coworker representation.
4. The employer has no duty to bargain with any union representative during the interview.

If the National Labor Relations Board determines that these rights were violated and that an employee was subsequently disciplined for conduct that was the subject of the unlawful interview, the board will issue a "make-whole" remedy. This may include (1) back pay, (2) an order expunging from the employee's personnel records any notation of related discipline, or (3) a cease-and-desist order. To avoid these kinds of problems, top management must decide what company policy will be in such cases, communicate that policy to first-line supervisors, and give first-line supervisors clear and concise instructions regarding their responsibilities should an employee request representation at an investigatory interview.[34]

Having satisfied their legal burden, how should supervisors actually conduct the disciplinary interview? They must do *nine* things well:

1. Come to the interview with as many facts as possible. Check the employee's personnel file for previous offenses as well as for evidence of exemplary behavior and performance.
2. Conduct the interview in a quiet, private place. "Praise in public, discipline in private" is a good rule to remember. Whether the employee's attitude is truculent or contrite, recognize that he or she will be apprehensive. In

contrast to other interviews, where your first objective is to dispel any fears and help the person relax, a "light touch" is inappropriate here.

3. Avoid aggressive accusations. State the facts in a simple, straightforward way. Be sure that any fact you use is accurate, and never rely on hearsay, rumor, or unconfirmed guesswork.

4. Be sure that the employee understands the rule in question and the reason it exists.

5. Allow the employee to make a full defense, even if you think he or she has none. If any point the employee makes has merit, tell him or her so and take it into consideration in your final decision.

6. Stay cool and calm; treat the subordinate as an adult. Never use foul language or touch the subordinate. Such behaviors may be misinterpreted or grossly distorted at a later date.

7. If you made a mistake, be big enough to admit it.

8. Consider extenuating circumstances and allow for honest mistakes on the part of the subordinate.

9. Even when corrective discipline is required, try to express confidence in the subordinate's worth as a person and ability to perform acceptably in the future. Rather than dwelling on the past, which you *cannot* change, focus on the future, which you *can.*

Special Concerns of Nonunion Employees

Employment-at-will

For the more than 70 percent of American workers who are not covered by a collective bargaining agreement or an individual employment contract, dismissal is an ever-present possibility. An *employment-at-will* is created when an employee agrees to work for an employer but there is no specification of how long the parties expect the agreement to last. Under a century-old common law in America, employment relationships of indefinite duration can, in general, be terminated at the whim of either party.[47] However, unlike the winners of most sex- or race-bias cases, who generally collect back pay only, successful victims of unjust dismissal can collect sizable punitive and compensatory damages from their former employers. Thus an analysis of 40 jury verdicts in employment-at-will cases in California showed that former employees won 75 percent of the cases and received a median award of $548,000.[21]

Those who stand to gain the most tend to be lower- and middle-level professionals and managers not covered by collective bargaining agreements or the individual employment contracts frequently given to senior executives. As one labor lawyer noted, "It's the white male manager's discrimination law."[1] Here is a company example.

COMPANY EXAMPLE *Bissell, Inc.*	At Bissell, Inc., a maker of carpet sweepers and other home-care products, the performance of a manufacturing executive with 23 years' experience with Bissell began to slip after he was passed over for a promotion to vice president. Officials told him of their vague dissatisfaction, but he received neither dismissal warnings nor an opportunity to improve before he was fired.

He accused Bissell of negligence. A federal judge partly agreed, saying that Bissell had a duty to inform him more fully. The judge initially awarded the former manager over $360,000 in lost wages, pension benefits, and damages due to mental distress. Then he reduced the award to $61,000 because the man's poor performance made him "largely responsible for his discharge."

This decision has led Bissell to put greater emphasis on tough, honest performance appraisals. Before dismissals can occur now, supervisors must be able to demonstrate that employees have been properly warned and notified and that their personnel files reflect proper justification.[21]

In recent years, several important exceptions to the "at-will" doctrine have emerged. These exceptions provide important protections for workers. The first—and most important—is legislative. Federal laws limit an employer's right to terminate at-will employees for such reasons as age, race, sex, religion, national origin, union activity, reporting of unsafe working conditions, or physical handicap.[68] However, employment-at-will is primarily a matter of state law.[40]

State courts have carved out three judicial exceptions. The first is a *public policy exception*. That is, an employee may not be fired because he or she refuses to commit an illegal act, such as perjury or price-fixing. Second, when an employer has promised not to terminate an employee except for unsatisfactory job performance or other good cause, the courts will insist that the employer carry out that promise. This includes *implied* promises (such as oral promises and implied covenants of good faith and fair dealing) as well as explicit ones.[29] For example, in *Fortune v. National Cash Register Company*, a salesperson (Mr. Fortune) was fired after he sold a large quantity of cash registers. Under the terms of his contract, Mr. Fortune would not receive a portion of his commission until the cash registers were delivered. He claimed he was fired before delivery was made to avoid payment of the full $92,000 commission on the order. The court held that terminating Mr. Fortune solely to deprive him of his commissions would breach the covenant of good faith implied in every contract.[5]

The third exception allows employees to seek damages for outrageous acts related to termination, including character defamation. For example, in *Rulon-Miller v. IBM* an employee was fired for dating the manager of a competing firm. A California court ruled that the supervisor's actions in demanding that the employee choose between her job or her beau were severe enough to support an action for outrageous conduct.[40]

To avoid potential charges of unjust dismissal, managers should scrutinize each facet of the human resource management system. For example:

Recruitment. Beware of creating implicit or explicit contracts in recruitment advertisements. Ensure that no job duration is implied and that employment is not guaranteed or "permanent."

Interviewing. Phrases intended to entice a candidate into accepting a position, such as "employment security," "lifelong relationship" with the company, "permanent" hiring, and so forth, can create future problems.

Applications. Include a statement that describes the rights of the at-will employee, as well as those of the employer. However, do not be so strident that you scare off applicants.

Handbooks and manuals. A major source of company policy statements regarding "permanent" employment and discharge for "just cause" is the employee handbook. Courts in most states have refused to bind employers to statements made in these handbooks on the grounds that they are only unilateral expressions of company policy and procedure for which the parties could not have bargained. But according to a growing number of state laws, such handbook language constitutes an *implied contract* for employment.

Performance appraisals. Include training and written instructions for all raters, and use systems that minimize subjectivity to the greatest extent possible. Give employees the right to read and comment on their appraisals, and require them to sign an acknowledgment that they have done so whether or not they agree with the contents of the appraisal.[46] Encourage managers to give "honest" appraisals; if an employee is not meeting minimum standards of performance, "tell it like it is" rather than leading the employee to believe that his or her performance is satisfactory.

Document employee misconduct and poor performance, and provide for a progressive disciplinary policy, thereby building a record establishing "good cause."[20]

Disclosure of trade secrets

The employment contracts given to top-level executives protect the company by requiring them to promise not to divulge secrets if they leave. In many cases, executives cannot even accept employment with a competitor, sometimes for years. Among the top 100 U.S. industrial companies, about one-third require contracts. The practice is most common in such highly competitive industries as computers, pharmaceuticals, toys, defense equipment, and electronics. However, whether or not a contract has been signed, executives are still required to maintain all trade secrets with which their employers have entrusted them. This obligation, often called a "fiduciary duty of loyalty," cannot keep the executive out of the job market, but it does provide the employer with legal recourse if an executive joins a competitor and tells all.

Indeed, this is precisely what McDonald's claimed when it succeeded in muzzling a former market researcher.[57]

COMPANY EXAMPLE

McLitigation

The former employee (we'll call him McEx) was an expert in market research. He quit to join a competitor a few years ago, taking with him a large batch of papers. McDonald's filed suit, alleging that he walked away with company secrets.

Before filing suit and within a few days of his leaving, McDonald's sent a letter to McEx warning him not to divulge any "confidential information" regarding activities such as marketing, advertising, training methods, profit margins, raw materials prices, selling prices, and operating procedures.

The letter further requested a meeting with McEx, during which he would be asked to return any written materials he had taken from McDonald's and also to sign an agreement not to divulge any company trade secrets to his new employer.

When McEx declined to attend the meeting, McDonald's promptly filed suit in McEx's new home state. The company managed to win a temporary restraining order that McEx says effectively meant he could not perform *any* market research for his new employer. He was thereafter relegated to less important work.

Finally, about 6 months after the suit was filed, the case was settled out of court. McEx agreed not to use information gained on the job with McDonald's in his new job. But the issue had become academic. Disenchanted with his new nonjob and aware that his new employer was viewing him more as a problem than as an asset, McEx left his new job. He is now employed by another food chain, not involving fast-food restaurants.[57] In short, companies are now playing hard ball when it comes to the disclosure of trade secrets. For both parties, the stakes are high.

Nonunion grievance procedures

To avoid the kinds of industrial relations problems just described, nearly two-thirds of nonunion firms have established formal grievance procedures.

Figure 14-5 illustrates how they work in one company. This procedure emphasizes the supervisor as a key figure in the resolution of grievances. As a second step, the employee is encouraged to see the department head, a human resources department representative, or any other member of management. Alternatively, the employee may proceed directly to the roundtable, a body of employee and management representatives who meet biweekly to resolve grievances. Management immediately answers those questions which it can and researches those requiring an in-depth review. The minutes of roundtable

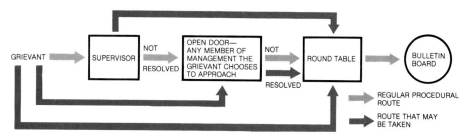

FIGURE 14-5

Example of a nonunion grievance procedure. This diagram indicates the possible routes a grievant may take to resolve a complaint. The regular procedural route is designed to resolve the grievance at the lowest possible level—the supervisor. However, if the grievant feels uncomfortable approaching the supervisor, the grievance may be presented directly to any level of management via the open-door policy or via the roundtable. (Source: Reprinted from D. A. Drost & F. P. O'Brien, Are there grievances against your non-union grievance procedure? Personnel Administrator, 28(1), 1983, 37. Copyright, 1983, The American Society for Personnel Administration, Alexandria, VA.)

meetings, plus the answers to the questions presented, are posted conspicuously on bulletin boards in work areas.[19]

To work effectively, a nonunion grievance procedure should meet three requirements:

1. All employees must know about the procedure and exactly how it operates.
2. They must believe that there will be no reprisals taken against them for using it.
3. Management must respond quickly and thoroughly to all grievances.[19]

About 100 companies, including Control Data, Digital Equipment, and Borg-Warner, now use peer review panels (the roundtable in Figure 14-5) to resolve disputes over firings, promotions, and disciplinary actions. A panel typically consists of three peers and two management representatives. Most companies do not permit grievants to have outside representation; instead, they provide a human resource staff member if help is needed in preparing the case. The panel's decisions are binding on both sides.

This peer-review trend represents an effort by companies to broaden employees' rights in disciplinary matters. Companies also say that peer review panels build an open, trusting atmosphere, help deter union organizing, and stem the rising number of costly lawsuits claiming wrongful discharge and discrimination.

Do peers routinely overrule management decisions? Surprisingly not; in fact, peer review panels side with management's decision 60 to 70 percent of the time.[55, 62]

Problems Facing the American Labor Movement

The following problems are well known: the severe economic recession of the early 1980s that crippled manufacturing, labor's traditional base; the rapid growth of service jobs, 90 percent of which are not organized; a changing workforce with far more women and minorities; the movement of industry to Sun Belt areas, where unions have never been strong; and union leaders ignoring the needs of their membership.[8, 28, 52] Less well known problems facing labor include plant-level bargaining tactics, productivity challenges, and coordinated company efforts to remain nonunion. Briefly, let's consider each of these.

Plant-level bargaining

The era of big-time national labor talks—in which union and management leaders haggle over pennies an hour—is fading fast. Years ago, industrial unions rose to power mostly by shifting the most important issues to national contract talks, so-called pattern bargaining. But unprecedented competition in the economy is making it harder for unions to preserve that concentration of power.

Wages, the main focus of national negotiations, are becoming less important than work rules and productivity, which usually are handled in local contracts. It is in these latter two areas that U.S. companies are the farthest behind their international competitors and can make the most progress. Although the subsistence-level pay of developing countries (such as Mexico and South Korea) still poses a threat to U.S. industrial workers, the dramatic plunge in the value of the dollar has put Americans roughly on an even footing with their Japanese and West German competitors.

Deregulation and the resulting breakup of AT&T destroyed national wage bargaining in the telecommunications industry. In 1983 the Communications Workers of America negotiated one wage contract for 525,000 workers with AT&T. In 1986, however, the union negotiated 22 different contracts with AT&T, the Bell operating companies, and their various subsidiaries.[66] Unions are increasingly afraid that the emphasis on local talks is threatening their power—that separate local negotiations will force equal concessions at other plants. This tactic is called whipsawing. As we shall see below, the unions' concerns are well founded.

Productivity challenges

Whipsawing This is the tactic of pitting workers in one production facility against fellow union workers in another production facility. It is devastatingly simple. Here is an example of how it works. To get General Motors to reverse its decision to close two of six Fisher Body plants, the United Auto Workers (UAW) agreed to boost output among hourly workers at the two plants by 20 percent. Soon GM demanded matching gains at the four other plants and threatened to close at least one of them if the union did not go along. Worried about big job losses, the UAW reluctantly agreed. Although whipsawing incenses the union, it nevertheless represents one of a company's best hopes for cutting labor costs in the near future. In fact, one industry cost expert estimated that automakers could cut $50 to $200 off the cost of building each car from work-rule changes alone.[13]

Outsourcing This tactic, which shifts work to lower-wage, nonunion contractors in the United States and abroad, is a tactic related to whipsawing. In the union view, outsourcing is (1) an attempt by companies to abrogate their collective bargaining contracts and (2) a variation of plant closings. In some cases, the union is right. Milwaukee Spring Co., a manufacturing firm, shifted its assembly operations to a nonunion plant in the middle of a union contract period in order to cut labor costs. In a controversial 1984 decision, the National Labor Relations Board ruled that an employer has no duty to bargain with a union before moving its operations from a union to a nonunion shop unless its contract with the union specifically provides for bargaining in such a situation. In 1985 a federal appeals court upheld that decision.[2]

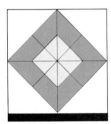

Impact of Labor-Management Relations on Productivity, Quality of Work Life, and the Bottom Line

As U.S. organizations confront change, the tensions, inherent or created, among productivity, QWL, and the bottom line seem to escalate. The practice of whipsawing is a prime example of this. While it is true that "necessity is the mother of invention," must productivity improvements emerge *only* out of fear of job loss? Certainly not.

The QWL process developed jointly by the Communication Workers of America and Bell System companies is a case in point. The heart of the process is the *workforce team* composed of 5 to 10 employees. Team members are responsible for defining problems they see at work, proposing solutions, and keeping other workers informed of their actions. More than 1000 such teams have been established since the program began in 1980. Since then, management and the workers have *jointly* resolved workplace problems ranging from such minor, but important, matters as the proper office temperature to complicated problems involving performance measurement systems.

Such QWL efforts that focus on cooperation rather than on confrontation provide great hope for labor peace. Certainly they are preferable to strikes that can cost both a company and its workers dearly. For instance, at Sunset Slacks in Tampa, Florida, 200 workers went out on strike for 6 months. When the strike ended, the workers won a 10-cent-an-hour wage increase; however, it will take each worker 4 years and 46 weeks to recover all the wages lost during the strike. Was it worth it?

Coordinated company efforts to remain nonunion

In the mid-1960s, unions won more than 60 percent of representation elections; by 1983 that figure had declined to 45 percent. Although several factors may account for this decline, increased aggressiveness on the part of management, coupled with the growing practice of using labor lawyers and consultants to undermine union organizing efforts and to weaken unions, has played an im-

TOMORROW'S FORECAST

In 1986, on the 100th anniversary of the founding of the AFL, the AFL-CIO issued a report entitled "The Changing Situation of Workers and Their Unions," a statement designed to reorient organized labor. The real significance of the report was its recognition that organized labor must convince people of the justice of its cause.[8]

To be more attractive to today's mobile, better-educated, and often white-collar young workers, unions are changing their tactics. Many are pushing for "portable" pensions and other benefits that workers can take from job to job. They are bringing in more organizers who are young and female, reflecting the important role that women now play in the workforce. They are beginning to understand that although young workers care about wages, many care even more about issues like day care, job security, quality of work life, developing new skills, and having some say about how their jobs are done. Finally, labor is pushing hard to change management's view of labor from a variable cost to a fixed one, through guarantees of job security.

Is this the wave of the future? You bet. Consider the 1987–1989 agreement between Ford Motor Company and the United Auto Workers. The company agreed, among other things, (1) not to close any U.S. assembly plants, (2) to replace one worker for every two lost through attrition, and (3) to "lock in" 1987 employment levels at each of its 89 U.S. facilities (workers were protected against layoffs except during industrywide sales slumps). The agreement did not end outsourcing, although Ford agreed to extend the required notification period before outsourcing work. In addition, the UAW agreed to encourage local unions to alter work rules to enhance productivity.[67]

A revitalized labor movement may look very different from the old one. Cooperation may replace conflict.[43] The number of unions will probably decline, as more of them merge. White-collar members may outnumber blue-collar members. And increasingly sophisticated unions may play an even bigger role in corporate mergers and restructurings.[39] If this is to happen, then labor, management, and government must be willing to acknowledge that conflict is counterproductive in the face of the mobility of capital and relentless international competition.[17] Indeed, increased competition provides a good reason to reduce the conflict. If they can do this, then an economic pressure will have produced a positive social gain.[64]

portant role. In fact, an AFL-CIO survey found that 95 percent of all employers actively resist unions.[44]

The literature on union avoidance emphasizes that maintenance of nonunion status depends on four distinct types of employer practices:[24, 31]

1. Fair human resource management practices
2. Defensive tactics to make union organizing efforts more difficult
3. Early detection of union organizing activities
4. A well-orchestrated election campaign

One study that related these specific practices to union election outcomes found that *only certain practices* were related to victories by employers. These were (1) the hiring of employees who had never been represented by a union, (2) the detection of union organizing activities relatively early, (3) the restriction of employee solicitation activities, and (4) influence on the composition of the bargaining unit and the date of the election. Finally, employers that won tended to use many channels of communication (e.g., speeches, posters, personal letters, and payroll messages) to convey the negative aspects of unionism and the positive treatment by the employer.[59]

In response to these tactics, unions have taken several specific actions. For example, some unions simply avoid the NLRB through so-called top-down organizing. They organize workers by pressuring companies and sometimes by embarrassing them through picketing and public appeals. In 1986, for example, 87 percent of the United Food and Commercial Workers' 82,000 new members were involved in elections that circumvented the NLRB.

The organizing tactics of unions are becoming more sophisticated as well. Unions such as the Clothing and Textile Workers are using surveys before undertaking expensive organizing campaigns. Unions such as the Airline Pilots Association and the Steelworkers are hiring investment bankers for projects ranging from examining an employer's balance sheet to buying a company, as United Airlines' pilots tried to do. Finally, unions are lobbying hard for pro-labor legislation; for example, legislation that would outlaw "double-breasting," in which unionized construction firms legally transfer work to nonunion subsidiaries.[39] As these few examples demonstrate, it will be a long time before organized labor's obituary is written.

**CASE 14-1
Conclusion**

A radical experiment at GE: hourly workers control a grievance review panel*

Shortly after the procedure went into effect, a grievant took the first case to the panel. By policy, he was allowed to choose the names of four panelists of hourly workers at random and to put one name back, leaving three panelists of hourly workers to hear the case with the two managers.

The case was an intriguing one. It involved a job promotion that had been denied because of a rule prohibiting a person from downgrading to a lower-level job and then upgrading back to the same previous job within 6 months. The grievant felt that extenuating circumstances should have allowed him to bypass the 6-month rule.

After hearing all the evidence and investigating precedents, the panel ruled against the grievant. One of the hourly members of the panel said, "We sympathize with the guy, but a rule is a rule and it's the same for everyone." The message in that statement is that the panelists have taken their responsibility seriously.

Is the expanded grievance procedure with the review panel a cure-all for GE's employee relations concerns? Certainly not. But the company has proven itself correct in its belief that employees can be trusted to make wise decisions. As a result, both management and employees agree, the Columbia plant is now a better place in which to work.

Summary

Collective bargaining is the cornerstone of the American labor movement. Anything that even remotely threatens its continued viability will be resisted vigorously by organized labor. Both sides typically prepare about 6 months in advance for the next round of negotiations. This preparation involves an analysis of grievances, current wage and benefits costs, and the cost of proposed settlements. Sometimes negotiations reach an impasse, at which point the union may strike, management may lock out workers, or both parties may ask for a federal mediator. The trend today, however, is for firms to continue operating in spite of strikes. Other trends include (1) changes by employers in the pattern of collective bargaining by tying wages to productivity improvements through profit sharing or stock ownership plans, (2) plant-level bargaining, and (3) demands by employers for permanent wage and benefit concessions.

Once a contract has been ratified, the emphasis shifts to contract administration. Often this involves the processing of grievances, the majority of which are filed over disciplinary and seniority issues. It may also involve arbitration and discipline. Unions rarely object to discipline provided that it is applied consistently, that the rules are publicized clearly, and that the rules are considered reasonable.

Employment-at-will is a special concern of all employees not covered by collective bargaining agreements or individual employment contracts. To avoid charges of wrongful discharge, employers must examine each facet of the human resource management system to ensure that no employment contracts are expressed or implied. Also, it is wise for the nonunion company to establish a formal grievance procedure. Many challenges face labor in the coming years. To overcome them, cooperation rather than confrontation is critical.

Discussion Questions

14-1 "Management gets the kind of union it deserves." Do you agree or disagree?

14-2 Are the roles of labor and management inherently adversarial?

14-3 What are the major advantages and disadvantages of two-tier wage contracts?

14-4 What specific steps can unions take to remain viable and relevant in the late twentieth century?

14-5 Discuss the advantages and disadvantages of employment-at-will.

14-6 Should employees be disciplined for *what* they do or fail to do (e.g., in caring for a postsurgical patient, a nurse leaves the bed railing down), or for the *consequences* of what they do or fail to do (in one case the patient falls out of bed; in another, the patient does not fall out of bed)?

14-7 Difficult social, political, and economic changes confront labor and management. Discuss the impact of three of these changes on labor-management relations.

References

1. A fight over the freedom to fire (1982, Sep. 20). *Business Week*, p. 116.
2. Apcar, L. (1985, June 19). NLRB ruling on moving union jobs to nonunion plant upheld on appeal. *Wall Street Journal*, p. 14.
3. American Society for Personnel Administration (1983). *Strike preparation manual* (rev. ed.). Berea, OH: ASPA.
4. Arnold, H. J., & Feldman, D. C. (1986). *Organizational behavior*. New York: McGraw-Hill.
5. Bakaly, C. G., Jr., & Grossman, J. M. (1984, August). How to avoid wrongful discharge suits. *Management Review*, pp. 41–46.
6. Bandura, A. (1986). *Social foundations of thought and action: A social cognitive theory*. Englewood Cliffs, NJ: Prentice-Hall.
7. Belohlav, J. (1983). Realities of successful employee discipline. *Personnel Administrator*, 28(3), 74–77, 92.
8. Benson, H. (1986, Dec. 18). America's labor federation turns 100—Leaders must let fresh air in. *Wall Street Journal*, p. 24.
9. Bernstein, A. (1987, Mar. 16). Why two-tier wage scales are starting to self-destruct. *Business Week*, p. 41.
10. Buss, D. D., & Nag, A. (1983, Sep. 14). Ford to close its unprofitable Rouge plant after failing to obtain labor concessions. *Wall Street Journal*, p. 3.
11. Buss, D. D. (1983, Sep. 15). UAW hopes Ford plan to close Rouge mill will spur workers to agree to givebacks. *Wall Street Journal*, p. 4.
12. Buss, D. D. (1983, Sep. 19). UAW endorses Rouge steel pact on concessions. *Wall Street Journal*, p. 2.
13. Buss, D. D. (1983, Nov. 7). GM vs. GM. *Wall Street Journal*, pp. 1, 8.
14. Cantrell, D. O. (1984, September). Computers come to the bargaining table. *Personnel Journal*, pp. 27–30.
15. Cascio, W. F. (1987). *Costing human resources: The financial impact of behavior in organizations* (2d ed.). Boston: PWS-Kent.
16. Curtis, W., Smith, R., & Smoll, F. (1979). Scrutinizing the skipper: A study of leadership behaviors in the dugout. *Journal of Applied Psychology*, **64**, 391–400.
17. Dale, R. (1983). Work in the 21st century: International forces will prevail, but will unions be able to change with the new global work place? *Personnel Administrator*, 28(12), 100–104.

18. Dalton, D. R., & Todor, W. D. (1981). Win, lose, draw: The grievance process in practice. *Personnel Administrator*, **26**(3), 25–29.

19. Drost, D. A., & O'Brien, F. P. (1983). Are there grievances against your non-union grievance procedure? *Personnel Administrator*, **28**(1), 36–42.

20. Engel, P. G. (1985, Mar. 18). Preserving the right to fire. *Industry Week*, pp. 39–40.

21. Firing line: Legal challenges force firms to revamp ways they dismiss workers (1983, Sep. 13). *Wall Street Journal*, pp. 1, 15, 16.

22. Flax, S. (1984, Jan. 9). Pay cuts before the job even starts. *Fortune*, pp. 75–77.

23. Ford Rouge workers vote concessions to keep plant open (1983, Sep. 26). *Wall Street Journal*, p. 7.

24. Foulkes, F. K. (1980). *Personnel policies in large nonunion companies*. Englewood Cliffs, NJ: Prentice-Hall.

25. Franke, R., & Karl, J. (1978). The Hawthorne experiments: First statistical interpretation. *American Sociological Review*, **43**, 623–643.

26. Fruhan, W. E., Jr. (1985). Management, labor, and the golden goose. *Harvard Business Review*, **63**(5), 131–141.

27. Greenberger, D. (1983, Oct. 11). Striking back. *Wall Street Journal*, pp. 1, 18.

28. Greenhouse, S. (1985, Sep. 1). Reshaping labor to woo the young. *New York Times*, pp. 1F, 6F.

29. Heshizer, B. (1984). The implied contract exception to at-will employment. *Labor Law Journal*, **35**, 131–141.

30. Hill, M., Jr., & Sinicropi, A. V. (1980). *Evidence in arbitration*. Washington, DC: Bureau of National Affairs.

31. Hughes, C. (1976). *Making unions unnecessary*. New York: Executive Enterprises.

32. Hunsaker, J. S., Hunsaker, P. L., & Chase, N. (1981). Guidelines for productive negotiating relationships. *Personnel Administrator*, **26**(3), 37–40, 88.

33. Hymowitz, C. (1983, Dec. 7). More USW benefits will be reduced under labor ruling. *Wall Street Journal*, p. 2.

34. Israel, D. (1983). The Weingarten case sets precedent for co-employee representation. *Personnel Administrator*, **28**(2), 23–26.

35. Jacobsen, S. (1984, Mar. 20). Business sees tougher labor stance. *Rocky Mountain News*, p. 1F.

36. Kotlowitz, A. (1986, Oct. 13). Labor's ultimate weapon, the strike, is mostly failing. *Wall Street Journal*, p. 6.

37. Kotlowitz, A. (1987, Apr. 1). Grievous work. *Wall Street Journal*, pp. 1, 12.

38. Kotlowitz, A. (1987, May 22). Labor's shift: Finding strikes harder to win, more unions turn to slowdowns. *Wall Street Journal*, pp. 1, 7.

39. Kotlowitz, A. (1987, Aug. 28). Labor's turn? *Wall Street Journal*, pp. 1, 14.

40. Koys, D. J., Briggs, S., & Grenig, J. (1987). State court disparity on employment-at-will. *Personnel Psychology*, **40**, 565–577.

41. Labor letter (1979, Apr. 17). *Wall Street Journal*, p. 1.

42. Labor letter (1984, Feb. 7). *Wall Street Journal*, p. 1.

43. Labor letter (1988, Apr. 26). *Wall Street Journal*, p. 1.

44. Labor letter (1985, Mar. 1). *Wall Street Journal*, p. 1.

45. Labor letter (1987, June 16). *Wall Street Journal*, p. 1.

46. Lorber, L. Z. (1984). Basic advice on avoiding employment-at-will troubles. *Personnel Administrator*, **29**(1), 59–62.

47. Lorber, L. Z., Kirk, J. R., Kirschner, K. H., & Handorf, C. R. (1984). *Fear of firing: A legal and personnel analysis of employment-at-will.* Alexandria, VA: ASPA.

48. Merry, R. W. (1979, Jan. 30). Federal mediators find their public-sector caseload growing sharply. *Wall Street Journal*, p. 1.

49. Miller, R. L. (1978, January). Preparations for negotiations. *Personnel Journal*, pp. 36–39, 44.

50. *NLRB v. Sears Roebuck and Co.* (1985, Feb. 27). *Daily Labor Report*, 39, D1–D5.

51. *NLRB v. Weingarten* (1974). 420 U.S. 251, 95 S. Ct. 959.

52. Noble, K. B. (1986, Nov. 2). Once-mighty U.M.W. is seeking more muscle. *New York Times*, p. E5.

53. Noble, K. B. (1987, Jan. 18). Strikes are getting fewer but longer. *New York Times*, p. E4.

54. Oberle, R. L. (1978, January). Administering disciplinary actions. *Personnel Journal*, pp. 29–31.

55. Olson, F. C. (1984). How peer review works at Control Data. *Harvard Business Review*, 62(6), 58–61.

56. O'Reilly, C. A., III, & Weitz, B. A. (1980). Managing marginal employees: The use of warnings and dismissals. *Administrative Science Quarterly*, 25, 467–484.

57. Personal affairs (1983, June 6). *Forbes*, pp. 174, 178.

58. Pfeffer, J. (1981). Management as symbolic action: The creation and maintenance of meaning. In L. Cummings & B. Staw (eds.), *Research in Organizational Behavior*, vol. 3. Greenwich, CT: JAI Press.

59. Porter, A. A., & Murman, K. F. (1983). A survey of employer union-avoidance practices. *Personnel Administrator*, 28(11), 66–71, 102.

60. Premeaux, S. R., Mondy, R. W., & Bethke, A. L. (1986). The two-tier wage system. *Personnel Administrator*, 31(11), 92–100.

61. Purdy, P. (1987, July 8). Worker input key to Safeway experiment. *Denver Post*, pp. 1C, 6C.

62. Reibstein, L. (1986, Dec. 3). More firms use peer review panel to resolve employees' grievances. *Wall Street Journal*, p. 33.

63. Roberts, K., Hulin, C., & Rousseau, D. (1978). *Developing an interdisciplinary science of organizations.* San Francisco: Jossey-Bass.

64. Roderick, D. M. (1983). Work in the 21st century: Basic industries won't die away; technology will strengthen them, despite socio-political problems. *Personnel Administrator*, 28(12), 72–74.

65. Salpukas, A. (1987, July 21). Two-tier wage system: For many it leads to a second-class status. *New York Times*, pp. A1, D22.

66. Schlesinger, J. M. (1987, Mar. 16). Going local. *Wall Street Journal*, pp. 1–20.

67. Schlesinger, J. M., & White, J. B. (1987, Sep. 18). Ford and UAW agree on 3-year pact that grants broad job guarantees except during industry slump. *Wall Street Journal*, pp. 3, 9.

68. Spurgeon, Haney, & Howbert, P. A. (1985). *Ready, fire! (aim): A manager's primer in the law of terminations.* Colorado Springs, CO: Author.

69. Taking it to arbitration (1985, July 16). *Wall Street Journal*, p. 1.

70. Turan, K. (1974, Nov. 10). The mediators. *Miami Herald*, pp. 1F, 7F.

71. Ways, M. (1979, Jan. 15). The virtues, limits, and dangers of negotiation. *Fortune*, pp. 86–90.

72. Winter, R. E. (1984, Mar. 6). New givebacks: Even profitable firms press workers to take permanent pay cuts. *Wall Street Journal*, pp. 1, 16.

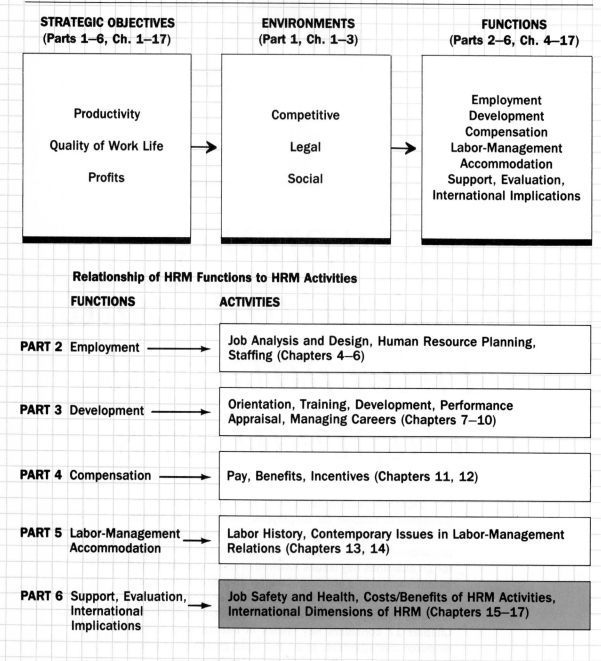

A Conceptual View of Human Resource Management:
Strategic Objectives, Environments, Functions

STRATEGIC OBJECTIVES
(Parts 1–6, Ch. 1–17)

Productivity

Quality of Work Life

Profits

ENVIRONMENTS
(Part 1, Ch. 1–3)

Competitive

Legal

Social

FUNCTIONS
(Parts 2–6, Ch. 4–17)

Employment
Development
Compensation
Labor-Management
Accommodation
Support, Evaluation,
International Implications

Relationship of HRM Functions to HRM Activities

FUNCTIONS

ACTIVITIES

PART 2 Employment → Job Analysis and Design, Human Resource Planning, Staffing (Chapters 4–6)

PART 3 Development → Orientation, Training, Development, Performance Appraisal, Managing Careers (Chapters 7–10)

PART 4 Compensation → Pay, Benefits, Incentives (Chapters 11, 12)

PART 5 Labor-Management Accommodation → Labor History, Contemporary Issues in Labor-Management Relations (Chapters 13, 14)

PART 6 Support, Evaluation, International Implications → Job Safety and Health, Costs/Benefits of HRM Activities, International Dimensions of HRM (Chapters 15–17)

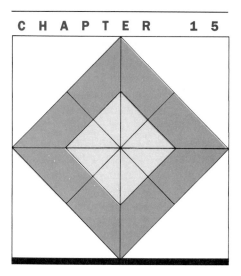

Safety, Health, and Employee Assistance Programs

CASE 15-1

The Supreme Court's benzene decision*

In 1980 the U.S. Supreme Court ruled on the fundamental question of how much a regulatory agency must weigh the costs of a regulation against its potential benefits. At issue was a new workplace standard for benzene, a widely used and highly toxic chemical, issued by the Occupational Safety and Health Administration (OSHA). In 1977 OSHA ordered a sharp reduction in the amount of benzene to which workers may be exposed. Three years later, the reduction still had not taken place; it had been immediately challenged by the oil, rubber, and other industries that produce benzene or use it to make solvents, pesticides, detergents, and other products.

In 1978, a federal appeals court set aside the ordered reduction. It ruled that OSHA cannot legally regulate occupational health hazards without first using a cost-benefit analysis to "determine whether the benefits expected from the standard bear a reasonable relationship to the costs imposed." OSHA then appealed to the Supreme Court.

The Supreme Court's decision has had far-reaching economic and legal implications. OSHA estimated that over 30,000 workers are exposed to unacceptable concentrations of benzene. To comply with the new standard, how-

*Adapted from: Regulatory balancing act, *Wall Street Journal*, Jan. 9, 1980, p. 44.

ever, employers would have to spend hundreds of millions, perhaps even billions, of dollars.

The controversy began in early 1977 when Eula Bingham, an occupational health expert, took command of OSHA. She was outraged to learn that the agency had been allowing workers to be exposed to concentrations of benzene as high as 10 parts per million parts of air, or 10 ppm. On the basis of recent studies that had confirmed a link between benzene and leukemia, OSHA reduced the allowable exposure level to 1 ppm.

There was not, as Bingham knew, any direct evidence that benzene exposure below 10 ppm causes leukemia. All the workers studied had been exposed to much higher concentrations, many to concentrations above 400 ppm. Because the 10-ppm standard had been in effect for only a few years (before that, higher levels of exposure were allowed), and because there can be a lag of decades between exposure to a toxic substance and resulting ill effects, Bingham also knew that it might be years before there were any studies of exposure below 10 ppm. The law says OSHA must base its standards for toxic substances on "the best available evidence." What was OSHA to do when there was no direct evidence available? How to answer that question is the heart of the dispute between benzene-producing and benzene-consuming industries.

In their written argument to the Supreme Court, the industries maintained that a risk curve drawn by a Harvard University scientist "showed that the leukemia risk from benzene exposure at 10 ppm is exceedingly small—indeed it is comparable to the cancer risk associated with such everyday activities as air travel or eating or drinking normal amounts of foods and liquids." Further, a risk study done by the Environmental Protection Agency suggested that reducing the exposure level to 1 ppm "would prevent, at most, only one case of leukemia every 15 to 38 years." To install and operate the equipment needed to reduce exposures to 1 ppm would cost the industries from $500 million to $5 billion, depending on whose estimate is accepted—OSHA's or the industries'.

OSHA categorically rejected the industries' approach. The agency argued that too little is known about the quantity of benzene the studied workers were exposed to. The data were "too imprecise" to establish reliable risk relationships, the agency maintained. But if a risk curve could not be drawn, then cost-benefit analysis would be impossible.

Lacking direct evidence, OSHA took a different tack. First, it argued that the law does not *require* cost-benefit analyses, especially in cases like benzene where benefits are hard to estimate. Second, the law does not even *permit* cost-benefit analyses. The costs of regulation, OSHA conceded, are relevant if they are so onerous as to make compliance infeasible. But to balance costs and benefits "squarely violates" the law's requirement to prevent impairment of health, OSHA contended.

The industries read the law differently. They noted, for example, that the law defines a standard as a regulation "reasonably necessary or appropriate" to protect workers' health and safety. A standard that fails a cost-benefit test is not "reasonably necessary or appropriate," the industries argued.

How the high court will interpret the law is uncertain. However, people on both sides of the issue are anxiously awaiting the benzene decision.

QUESTIONS
1. "What price safety and health?" is an issue that has been debated for a long time. Is cost relevant?
2. Do you think that cost-benefit analyses should be required of all agencies before they issue new regulations?
3. How do you think the Supreme Court actually ruled?

What's Ahead

Some managers feel that the costs of improving job safety and health must be justified by the benefits. Case 15-1 shows how difficult these cost-benefit relationships are to demonstrate. Yet organizations bear social and ethical obligations for the safety and health of their employees.

Chapter 15 begins by examining how social and legal policies on the federal and state levels have evolved on this issue, beginning with workers' compensation laws and culminating with the passage of the Occupational Safety and Health Act. The chapter then considers enforcement of the act, with special emphasis on the rights and obligations of management. It also examines prevailing approaches to job safety and health in other countries. Finally it considers the problems of AIDS and business, employee assistance programs, and corporate "wellness" programs. Underlying all these efforts is a conviction on the part of many firms that it is morally right to improve job safety and health—and that doing so will enhance the productivity and quality of work life of employees at all levels.

Extent and Cost of Safety and Health Problems

Consider these startling facts. Every year in U.S. workplaces:[1]

■ Roughly 1 of every 12 workers is injured or becomes ill on the job.[37]
■ 11,000 workers die in workplace accidents.
■ 2 million workers are disabled.
■ 400,000 new cases of disabling illness occur.
■ 2.5 million workers suffer injuries involving lost workdays.
■ 40 million workdays are lost.

The cost? A staggering $33 billion in lost wages, medical costs, insurance administration costs, and indirect costs. At the level of the individual firm, a

Du Pont safety engineer determined that a disabling injury costs an average of $18,650. A company with 1000 employees could expect to have 27 lost-workday injuries per year. With a 4.5 percent profit margin, the company would need $11.3 million of sales to offset that cost.[46]

Regardless of one's perspective, social or economic, these are disturbing figures. In response, public policy has focused on two types of actions: *monetary compensation* for job-related injuries and *preventive measures* to enhance job safety and health. State-run workers' compensation programs and the federal Occupational Safety and Health Administration are responsible for implementing public policy in these areas. Let's examine each of them.

Workers' Compensation: A Historical Perspective

In the late nineteenth and early twentieth centuries, employers were relatively free to run their operations as they saw fit, whether or not the operations were safe. Employees injured on the job had to file lawsuits against their employers in order to receive *any* compensation for their injuries. Employers lost only when it could be proven that their negligence resulted in the injury. This rarely happened, and, in fact, workers rarely brought suit because it cost money to do so. Under common law the firm had certain defenses. It could not be held liable if it could show either (1) that an employee in accepting the job knew of the hazards or (2) that the worker, or even a fellow worker, had been negligent and in any way contributed to the accident.[56]

These views began to change only after major disasters in which many workers lost their lives. For example, state inspection of mines in Pennsylvania was first authorized in 1870 after a fire in an anthracite mine killed 109 miners. Mandatory safety regulations concerning fire escapes were instituted after the 1911 Triangle Shirtwaist Company fire, in which over 100 women in a crowded sweatshop died trying to escape the flames when the exit doors were locked.

Another new development was the introduction of workers' compensation laws by state governments in the early 1900s. Such laws are based on the principle of *liability without fault*, under which employers contribute to a fund providing compensation to employees involved in work-related accidents and injuries. The scale of benefits is related to the nature of the injury. The benefits are not provided because of liability or negligence on the part of the employer; rather, they are provided simply as a matter of social policy.[2] Since the premiums paid reflected the accident rate of the particular employer, states hoped to provide an incentive for firms to lower their premium costs by improving work conditions. The Supreme Court upheld the constitutionality of such laws in 1917, and by 1948 all states had adopted them in one form or another.[16]

For the more than 75 million workers, or 88 percent of the nation's workforce, who are covered, workers' compensation provides three types of benefits: (1) payments to replace lost wages while an employee is unable to work, (2) payments to cover medical bills, and (3) if an individual is unable to return to his or her former occupation, financial support for retraining.[90] To replace lost wages, the legislation typically allows for some percentage of regular wages (60 to 67 percent) up to a maximum amount. However, the benefits actually received are often less than half of regular wages.[80]

By the 1960s it was becoming apparent that neither the workers' compensation laws nor state safety standards were acting to reduce occupational hazards. Evidence began to accumulate that there were health hazards (so-called silent killers) in the modern work environment that either had not been fully recognized previously or were not fully understood. Research on industrial disease was beginning to discover that even brief exposure to certain toxic materials in a work environment could produce disease, sterility, and high mortality rates. This new concern was dramatized by revelations of "black lung" (pneumoconiosis) among coal miners, of "brown lung" (byssinosis) among textile workers, and of the toxic and carcinogenic (cancer-causing) effects of substances such as vinyl chloride and asbestos in other work environments. In addition to *compensation* for work-related injuries, it became clear that a federally administered program of *prevention* of workplace health and safety hazards was essential. This concern culminated in the passage of the Williams-Steiger Occupational Safety and Health Act of 1970.

The Occupational Safety and Health Act

Purpose and coverage

The purpose of the act is an ambitious one: "To assure so far as possible every working man and woman in the Nation safe and healthful working conditions and to preserve our human resources." Its coverage is equally ambitious, for the law extends to any business (regardless of size) that *affects* interstate commerce. Since almost any business affects interstate commerce, almost all businesses are included, for a total of about 75 million workers in 5 million workplaces.[87] Federal, state, and local government workers are excluded since the government cannot easily proceed against itself in the event of violations.

Administration

The 1970 act established three government agencies to administer and enforce the law:

- *The Occupational Safety and Health Administration* to establish and enforce the necessary safety and health standards
- *The Occupational Safety and Health Review Commission* (a three-member board appointed by the President) to rule on the appropriateness of OSHA's enforcement actions when they are contested by employers, employees, or unions

■ *The National Institute for Occupational Safety and Health* to conduct research on the causes and prevention of occupational injury and illness, to recommend new standards (based on this research) to the Secretary of Labor, and to develop educational programs

Safety and health standards

Under the law, each employer has a "general duty" to provide a place of employment "free from recognized hazards." Employers also have the "special duty" to comply with all standards of safety and health established under the act.

In setting safety and health standards, OSHA is required by Congress to adopt existing "consensus standards." Some of these were existing federal standards in industries such as mining, construction, and longshoring. Others had been developed over the years by organizations such as the American National Standards Institute and the National Fire Protection Association and by various trade associations such as the Associated General Contractors and the Manufacturing Chemists Association. Finally, labor unions, public interest groups, various states, and the National Institute for Occupational Safety and Health (NIOSH) have suggested new or revised OSHA standards. NIOSH, for example, has identified over 15,000 toxic substances based on its research.

To date, OSHA has issued a large number of detailed standards covering numerous environmental hazards. These include power tools, machine guards, compressed gas, materials handling and storage, and toxic substances such as asbestos, cotton dust, silica, lead, and carbon monoxide. While the majority of such standards were acknowledged as helpful and important, employers found some of them infuriatingly niggling. For example:

> (In a portable toilet) The building shall be of fly-tight construction, doors shall be self-closing. . . . The seat top shall be not less than 12 inches nor more than 16 inches above the floor.
>
> In response to numerous complaints, and in compliance with President Carter's orders that regulatory agencies get rid of their nuisance rules and standards, OSHA dropped 928 of its least important.[30, 84]

Record-keeping requirements

A good deal of paperwork is required of employers under the act. Specifically:

■ A general log of each injury or illness (OSHA Form 200), shown in Figure 15-1
■ Supplementary records of each injury or illness (OSHA Form 101)

Employees are guaranteed access, on request, to Form 200 at their workplace, and the records must be retained for 5 years following the calendar year they cover.[84] The purpose of these reports is to identify where safety and health problems have been occurring (if at all). Such information helps call manage-

U.S. Department of Labor

For Calendar Year 19 ______ Page ___ of ___

Form Approved
O.M.B. No. 1220-0029

Company Name

Establishment Name

Establishment Address

Extent of and Outcome of INJURY						Type, Extent of, and Outcome of ILLNESS												
Fatalities	Nonfatal Injuries					Type of Illness							Fatalities	Nonfatal Illnesses				
Injury Related	Injuries With Lost Workdays				Injuries Without Lost Workdays	**CHECK Only One Column for Each Illness** ***(See other side of form for terminations or permanent transfers.)***							Illness Related	Illnesses With Lost Workdays				Illnesses Without Lost Workdays
Enter **DATE** of death. Mo./day/yr.	Enter a **CHECK** if injury involves days away from work, or days of restricted work activity, or both.	Enter a **CHECK** if injury involves days away from work.	Enter number of **DAYS** ***away from work.***	Enter number of **DAYS** of ***restricted work activity.***	Enter a **CHECK** if no entry was made in columns 1 or 2 but the injury is recordable as defined above.	Occupational skin diseases or disorders	Dust diseases of the lungs	Respiratory conditions due to toxic agents	Poisoning (systemic effects of toxic materials)	Disorders due to physical agents	Disorders associated with repeated trauma	All other occupational illnesses	Enter **DATE** of death. Mo./day/yr.	Enter a **CHECK** if illness involves days away from work, or days of restricted work activity, or both.	Enter a **CHECK** if illness involves days away from work.	Enter number of **DAYS** ***away from work.***	Enter number of **DAYS** of ***restricted work activity.***	Enter a **CHECK** if no entry was made in columns 8 or 9.
(1)	(2)	(3)	(4)	(5)	(6)	(7) (a)	(b)	(c)	(d)	(e)	(f)	(g)	(8)	(9)	(10)	(11)	(12)	(13)

INJURIES ILLNESSES

Certification of Annual Summary Totals By ______________ Title ______________ Date ______________

OSHA No. 200

POST ONLY THIS PORTION OF THE LAST PAGE NO LATER THAN FEBRUARY 1.

FIGURE 15-1

OSHA Form 200, log and summary of occupational injuries and illnesses.

ment's attention to the problems, as well as that of an OSHA inspector, should he or she visit the workplace. The annual summary must be sent to OSHA directly, to help the agency determine which workplaces should receive priority for inspections.

OSHA enforcement

In administering the act, OSHA inspectors have the right to enter a workplace and to conduct a compliance inspection. However, in the 1978 *Marshall v. Barlow's, Inc.* decision, the Supreme Court ruled that employers could require a search warrant before allowing the inspector onto company premises.[51] In practice, only about 3 percent of employers go that far, perhaps because the resulting inspection is likely to be especially "close."[21]

Since it is impossible for the roughly 1100 agency inspectors, or "coshos" (compliance safety and health officers), to visit the nation's 5 million workplaces, a system of priorities has been established. Coshos, most of whom are either safety engineers or industrial hygienists, assign top priority to workplaces where there is an imminent danger to worker health and safety or where a disaster involving deaths or accidents hospitalizing five or more employees has already occurred.

Second priority goes to investigating employee complaints that safety or health standards have been violated. Employers are prohibited from discriminating against employees who file such complaints, and an employee representative is entitled to accompany the cosho during the inspection.

Special inspection attention is also given to highly hazardous industries, such as marine cargo handling, roof and sheetmetal work, meat and meat products, lumber and wood products, and miscellaneous transportation equipment (such as mobile homes).[16] Finally, random inspections of workplaces of all sizes that do not fit into one of the preceding categories are common.[86] Such a prospect is an effective motivator for most employers to provide safe and healthful working environments.

Considerable emphasis has been given to OSHA's role of *enforcement*, but not much to its role of *consultation*. Employers in nearly every state who want help in recognizing and correcting safety and health hazards can get it from a free, on-site consultation service funded by OSHA. The service is delivered by state governments or private-sector contractors using well-trained safety and/or health professionals (e.g., industrial hygienists). Primarily targeted for smaller businesses, this program is penalty-free and completely separate from the OSHA inspection effort. An employer's only obligation is a commitment to correct serious job safety and health hazards.

Penalties   Fines are mandatory where serious violations are found. If a violation is willful (one in which an employer either knew that what was being done constituted a violation of federal regulations or was aware that a hazardous condition existed and made no reasonable effort to eliminate it), employers can be assessed a civil penalty of up to $10,000 for each violation. An employer who fails to correct a violation (within the allowed time limit) for which a citation has been issued can be fined up to $1000 for each day that the violation continues. Finally, a willful first violation involving the death of a worker can carry a criminal penalty as high as $10,000 and 6 months in prison. A second such conviction can mean up to $20,000 and a full year behind bars.[78] Needless to say, the legislators who enacted OSHA put real teeth into the law.

Appeals   Employers can appeal citations, proposed penalties, and corrections they have been ordered to make through multiple levels of the agency, culminating with the Occupational Safety and Health Review Commission. The commission presumes the employer to be free of violations and puts the burden of proof on OSHA.[87] Further appeals can be pursued through the federal court system.

Role of the states

Although OSHA is a federally run program, the act allows states to develop and to administer their own programs if they are approved by the Secretary of Labor. There are many criteria for approval, but the most important is that the state program must be judged "at least as effective" as the federal program. Between 1970 and 1987, 25 states and territories put approved plans into operation.[64]

Workers' rights to health and safety

Both unionized and nonunionized workers have walked off the job when subjected to unsafe working conditions.[89] In unionized firms, walkouts have occurred during the term of valid collective bargaining agreements that contained no-strike and grievance and/or arbitration clauses.[28] Are such walkouts legal? Yes, the Supreme Court has ruled, under certain circumstances. Consider the case of *Gateway Coal Co. v. United Mine Workers of America.*

COMPANY EXAMPLE

Unsafe conditions at Gateway Coal

As a result of line supervisors' making false entries in their logs, the accumulation of gas significantly increased the probability of an explosion in the mine. The union called a meeting, during which members voted unanimously to refuse to work under those supervisors. That day the supervisors in question were suspended, but they subsequently returned to work despite the fact that criminal charges were pending against them.

The miners immediately walked off their jobs. When the company offered to submit the dispute to arbitration, the union refused. An injunction was issued, ordering the miners to return to work and to submit the dispute to arbitration. The employees honored the injunction and the case was submitted. The arbitrator ruled that retention of the supervisors did not present a health hazard.

The union appealed the issuance of the injunction to the Third Circuit Court of Appeals, which sided with the union. The court reasoned that if employees *believe* dangerous conditions exist, there is no reason to subordinate their judgment to that of an arbitrator. Regardless of how impartial the arbitrator is, he or she is not staking his or her life on the outcome of the decision.

Gateway Coal appealed to the Supreme Court, which found that a work stoppage that is called to protect workers from "immediate danger" is authorized by Section 502 of the Taft-Hartley Act. The walkout cannot be stopped by an injunction, even when employees have agreed to a comprehensive no-strike clause.

Reviews of case law in this area found the following precedents currently in force:[34, 80]

- Objective evidence must be presented to support the claim that abnormally dangerous working conditions exist.
- If such evidence is presented, a walkout under Section 502 is legal *regardless* of the existence of a no-strike or arbitration clause.
- It is an unfair labor practice for an employer to interfere with activity protected under Section 502. This is true whether a firm is unionized or nonunionized.
- Expert testimony (e.g., by an industrial hygienist) is critically important in establishing the presence of abnormally dangerous working conditions.
- If a good-faith belief is not supported by objective evidence, then employees who walk off the job are subject to disciplinary action.

OSHA's impact

From its inception, OSHA has been both cussed and discussed, and its effectiveness in improving workplace safety and health has been questioned by the very firms it regulates.[31] Controversy has ranged from disagreements over the setting of health standards to inspection procedures.[75] Employers complain of excessively detailed and costly regulations ($25 billion in the agency's first 10 years), which, they believe, ignore workplace realities. OSHA has even been satirized in a video game called "Hard Hat Mack."

OSHA versus Hard Hat Mack. The blue-collar blip, called Mack, is described as a "bona fide working-class hero" striving to build a high-rise building. Another blip, which spends the game going after the blue-collar blip, is described as a representative from OSHA. The game package says that the OSHA blip has a "crew cut, clipboard, and absolutely no sense of humor. The government sends a generous supply of these guys to cite you into oblivion."

Mack faces a lot of other obstacles, of course—falling rivets, runaway jackhammers, and exposed wires. At advanced levels, a misstep on a girder can even send Mack tumbling into a portable toilet. But the OSHA blip is just as dangerous; if it catches him, Mack dies. Although the game has outraged some public officials, OSHA took it in stride. In fact, the head of the agency wrote to the game's developer: "Let's be fair; Hard Hat Mack is a lot safer on the job with OSHA around."[57]

It is one thing for employers to cite the total cost of compliance, but a fair evaluation requires that we put this figure into perspective. Over a 10-year period, a $25 billion expenditure averages out to $2.5 billion per year in a trillion-dollar-per-year economy. This is about 7.5 percent of what workplace accidents have recently cost the nation annually.[1] Such "preventive" expenditures do not seem unreasonable.

Organized labor has generally praised OSHA for identifying and restricting exposure to health hazards that 10 years ago were considered "part of the job" and for imposing safety protections and participatory rights for workers.[42] While not criticizing OSHA directly, unions have objected that employers often force standards to be modified to such a point that they become ineffective. Unions also believe that the transfer of some administrative authority to state governments, as urged by some employers, will weaken the enforcement process.[16]

Small businesses have praised OSHA for delivering on its regulatory reform promises. Thus one survey of small business showed that 42.6 percent believed OSHA had shown the most positive change of all regulatory agencies. No other agency received more than 6 percent of the vote from this survey.[62]

OSHA's ability to improve workplace safety and health continues to be debated. On the one hand, investigations by Congress[15] and by outside researchers[52] have found that OSHA has made no significant, lasting reductions in lost workdays or injury rates; thus, after declining for 4 straight years, the rates of work-related injuries, illnesses, and deaths began rising across a broad front in 1984. On the other hand, these rising rates were largely beyond OSHA's control. During the recession of the early 1980s, companies sharply reduced their spending on health and safety. Then, with the recovery, many employers hired a significant number of inexperienced workers, which further contributed to the increase in mishaps. Moreover, the Reagan administration de-emphasized the writing and enforcement of safety rules, while some employers tried to improve their competitiveness at the expense of safety.[76] Here's an example.

COMPANY EXAMPLE

Maintaining productivity at the expense of safety

Such a cost-benefit attitude may have contributed to the deaths of two pipe fitters at McDonnell Douglas Corporation's fighter-plane plant in St. Louis. The two died of chemical burns after a 6000-gallon tank they were filling with hydrofluoric acid overflowed. Said an official of the International Association of Machinists: "The safety rules weren't being enforced; sometimes it cuts into the profit" (ref. 76, p. 18).

The tank had no quantity indicator, and because a safety valve had been blowing out frequently, a solid rubber plug had been inserted "to avoid shutdowns." The men were not wearing chemical-proof suits or respirators, as safety rules require. OSHA cited the company for eight safety violations and proposed fines totalling $44,200. The company said it was reemphasizing safety practices.[76]

Despite these problems, even OSHA's critics have agreed that simply by calling attention to the problems of workplace safety and health, OSHA has caused a lot more *awareness* of these dangers than would otherwise have been the case. Management's willingness to correct hazards and to improve such vital environmental conditions as ventilation, noise levels, and machine safety is much greater now than it was before OSHA. Critics also agree that, because of OSHA and the National Institute for Occupational Safety and Health, we now know far more about such dangerous substances as vinyl chloride, PCBs, asbestos, cotton dust, and a host of other carcinogens. As a result, management has taken at least the initial actions needed to protect workers from them.[78]

Finally, any analysis of OSHA's impact must consider the fundamental issue of the *causes* of workplace accidents. OSHA standards govern potentially unsafe *work conditions* that employees may be exposed to. There are no standards that govern potentially unsafe *employee behaviors*. And while employers may be penalized for failure to comply with safety and health standards, employees are subject to no such threat. Research suggests that the enforcement of OSHA standards, directed as it is to environmental accidents and illnesses, can hope *at best* to affect 25 percent of on-the-job accidents.[20] The remaining 75 percent require *behavioral* rather than *technical* modifications.

In short, a company's response to enforcement plays as important a role as the nature of the enforcement activities themselves. Simple examination of the frequency or severity of accidents reportable to OSHA over time fails to take into account the *process* of compliance, that is, what happened between inspections and subsequent accidents.[31] Shortly we will examine the kinds of preventive safety and health activities that do work, but first let's consider an approach to assessing the costs and benefits of occupational safety and health programs.

Assessing the Costs and Benefits of Occupational Safety and Health Programs

Employers frequently complain that there is no systematic method of quantifying costs and benefits when dealing with employee safety and health conditions. Technically that is true, but here is a behavior costing model that may provide a useful start.[29]

Let's begin by distinguishing *nondiscretionary* from *discretionary* safety and health expenditures. Federal, state, and local agencies require firms to comply with safety and health regulations. To comply, firms may have to purchase and install special equipment, such as machine guards, safety switch interlocks, and treaded, nonslip flooring. These costs are nondiscretionary. To do otherwise is to risk heavy fines and losses from liability and damage suits.

Beyond mere compliance, however, companies have a number of options regarding the degree to which they invest in employee safety and health. A motivational poster program (e.g., "Think Safety") is a token effort that requires minimal expense. Creation of a safety committee to encourage active employee involvement through meetings, plant inspections, and evaluation of employee complaints is more expensive. The highest-cost option includes regular safety training for all employees. The training may involve films, lectures by safety experts, or hands-on drills and demonstrations with safety and emergency apparatus. For each of these levels of safety and health programs, investment *costs* are measurable. They include the salaries and wages of employees participating in the program, the costs of outside services used, and the costs to implement the programs.

Unfortunately, the *benefits* to be derived from such programs cannot be traced as easily to the bottom line. Certainly the most quantifiable benefit resulting from the successful introduction of a safety and health program is a reduction in casualty and workers' compensation insurance rates. Less measurable benefits involve the *avoidance* of the "indirect" costs of an accident, including:

1. Cost of wages paid for time lost
2. Cost of damage to material or equipment
3. Cost of overtime work required by the accident
4. Cost of wages paid to supervisors while their time is required for activities resulting from the accident
5. Costs of decreased output of the injured worker after she or he returns to work
6. Costs associated with the time it takes for a new worker to learn the job
7. Uninsured medical costs borne by the company
8. Cost of time spent by higher management and clerical workers to investigate or to process workers' compensation forms

Prediction of these costs, and identification of trends in them, is very difficult. It must be done on the basis of historical information (to gauge trends) and judgment by managers (to assess the seriousness of accidents *avoided*). These concepts may be incorporated into a cost/benefit curve of the sort shown in Figure 15-2.

The shape of the curve will depend on the range of factors just discussed, and it may well be that cost/benefit relationships can be plotted for various hazard classifications in a particular plant or industry. As each preventive cost is added, additional savings or benefits accrue to some point of diminishing (economic) return. The word "economic" is in parentheses because there should be no limit to efforts to eliminate accident and health hazards. Like many other problems of the marketplace, safety and health programs involve what econ-

FIGURE 15-2

Safety cost/benefit curve.

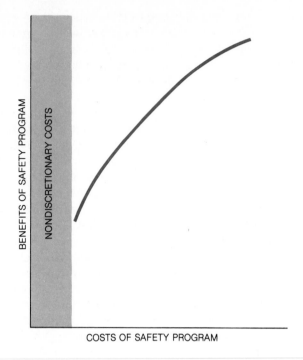

COSTS OF SAFETY PROGRAM

omists call "externalities"—the fact that all the social costs of production are not necessarily included on a firm's profit and loss statement. The employer does not suffer the worker's injury or disease and therefore lacks the full incentive to reduce it. As long as the outlays required for preventive measures are less than the social costs of disability among workers, higher fatality rates, and the diversion of medical resources, then the enforcement of safety and health standards is well worth it and society will benefit.[6, 16]

Organizational Safety and Health Programs

As noted earlier, accidents result from two broad causes: *unsafe work conditions* (physical and environmental) and *unsafe work behaviors*. Unsafe physical conditions include defective equipment, inadequate machine guards, and lack of protective equipment. Examples of unsafe environmental conditions are noise, radiation, dust, fumes, and stress. In one study of work injuries, 50 percent resulted from unsafe work conditions, 45 percent resulted from unsafe work behaviors, and 5 percent were of indeterminate origin.[23] However, accidents often result from an *interaction* of unsafe conditions and unsafe acts. Thus if a particular operation forces a worker to lift a heavy part and twist to set it on a bench, then the operation itself forces the worker to perform the unsafe act. Telling the worker not to lift and twist at the same time will not solve the problem. The *unsafe condition itself* must be corrected, either by redesigning the flow of material or by providing the worker with a mechanical device for lifting.[38]

To eliminate, or at least to reduce, the number and severity of workplace accidents, a combination of management and engineering controls is essential. These are shown in Figure 15-3.

Engineering controls attempt to eliminate unsafe work conditions and to neutralize unsafe worker behaviors; management controls attempt to increase safe behaviors. Engineering controls involve some modification of the work environment: for example, installing a metal cover over the blades of a lawn-mower to make it almost impossible for a member of a grounds crew to catch his or her foot in the blades.

Management's first duty is to formulate a safety policy. Its second duty is to implement and sustain this policy through a *loss control program*. Such a program has four components: a safety budget, safety records, management's personal concern, and management's good example.[39]

To reduce the frequency of accidents, management must be willing to spend money and to budget for safety. As we have seen, accidents involve *direct* as well as *indirect* costs. Since the national average for indirect costs is 4 times higher than the average for direct costs, it is clear that money spent to improve safety is returned many times over through the control of accidents. Detailed analysis of accident reports, as well as management's personal concern (e.g., meeting with department heads over safety issues, on-site visits by top executives to discuss the need for safety, and publication of the company's accident record), keeps employees aware constantly of the need for safety.

Study after study has shown the crucial role that management plays in

FIGURE 15-3

Causes of and responses to workplace accidents.

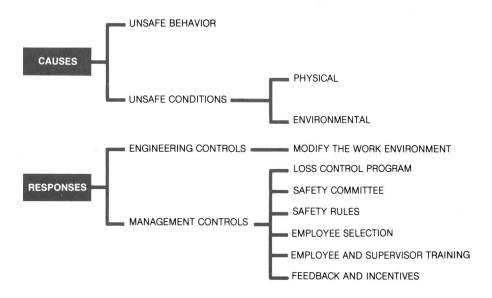

effective safety programs.[19, 79] Such concern is manifest in a number of ways: appointment of a high-level safety officer, rewards to supervisors on the basis of the safety records of their subordinates, and comparison of safety results against preset objectives. Management's good example completes a loss control program. If hard hats are required at a particular operation, then executives should wear hard hats even if they are in business suits. If employees see executives disregarding safety rules or treating hazardous situations lightly by not conforming with regulations, then they will feel that they, too, have the right to violate the rules. In short, organizations show their concern for loss control by establishing a clear safety policy and by assuming the responsibility for its implementation.

Here are two examples, one illustrating management's concern for safety, the other illustrating management's lack of concern.

PRACTICAL EXAMPLE

Management concern affects mine safety

In a recent study, a National Academy of Sciences panel examined each of almost 40,000 coal mine injuries and deaths which occurred over a 2-year period and which involved the 19 largest underground coal producers. The panel also visited mines and interviewed safety experts, managers, and laborers. It found large and persistent differences in safety rates among the firms. Why? "We found the most important of these factors to be management's commitment, as reflected by the attention and resources it devotes to improving safety," said the panel. Other important factors, according to the panel, are *cooperation* between management and labor in safety programs, and the *quality* of safety training provided to employees and supervisors. Not to be overlooked, however, are *better laws and stricter enforcement*, especially by the federal government; *better safety technology*, such as roof supports and ventilation systems; and *improved knowledge of geological conditions* in underground mines.

Mines are safer today than even 10 years ago, and injuries tend to be less severe than they used to be, but still there are about 100 fatalities annually. This evidence indicates clearly that there should be no dilution or compromise to the safety effort.[48]

COMPANY EXAMPLE

Cutting corners in the meatpacking industry

IBP, formerly known as Iowa Beef Processors, is the largest meatpacker in the United States. It operates 12 plants that employ 17,000 workers. In 1987 OSHA levied a $2.59 million fine against the company for failing willfully to report more than 1000 job-related injuries and illnesses over a 2-year period. Among the unreported injuries and illnesses cited by the agency were knife cuts and wounds, concussions, burns, hernias, and fractures.

OSHA determined that 1 week before it subpoenaed IBP's records, the company assembled 50 people to "revise" injury and illness logs.

According to OSHA, IBP added more than 800 injuries and illnesses that had not been recorded when they occurred. How did OSHA know this to be true? Company workers had previously obtained the unrevised logs and had given them to agency investigators.[75]

Role of the safety committee

Representation on the committee by employees, managers, and safety specialists can lead to much higher commitment to safety than might otherwise be the case. Indeed, merely establishing the committee indicates management's concern. Beyond that, however, the committee has important work to do:

- Recommend (or critique) safety policies issued by top management.
- Develop in-house safety standards and ensure compliance with OSHA standards.
- Provide safety training for employees and supervisors.
- Conduct safety inspections.
- Continually promote the theme of job safety through the elimination of unsafe conditions and unsafe behaviors.

Safety rules

Safety rules are important refinements of the general safety policies issued by top management. To be effective, they should make clear the consequences of not following the rules: for example, progressive discipline. Evidence indicates, unfortunately, that in many cases the rules are not obeyed. Take protective equipment, for example. OSHA standards require that employers *furnish* and that employees *use* suitable protective equipment (e.g., hard hats, goggles, face shields, earplugs, respirators) where there is a "reasonable probability" that injuries can be prevented by such equipment. However, as the following data show, "You can lead a horse to water, but you can't make him drink":[87]

- Hard hats were worn by only 16 percent of those workers who sustained head injuries, although 40 percent were required to wear them.
- Only 1 percent of workers suffering facial injuries were wearing facial protection.
- Only 23 percent of workers with foot injuries were wearing safety shoes or boots.
- Only 40 percent of workers with eye injuries were wearing protective equipment.

Perhaps the rules are not being obeyed because they are not being enforced. But it is also possible that they are not being obeyed because of flaws in employee selection practices, inadequate training, or because there is simply no incentive for doing so.

Employee selection

To the extent that keen vision, dexterity, hearing, balance, and other physical or psychological characteristics make a critical difference between success and failure on a job, they should be used to screen applicants. However, there are two other factors that also relate strongly to accident rates among workers: *age* and *length of service*.[72, 77] Regardless of length of service, the younger the employee, the higher the accident rate. In fact, accident rates are substantially higher during the *first month* of employment than in all subsequent time periods, regardless of age. And when workers of the same age are studied, accident rates decrease as length of service increases. Thus in mining, the disabling injury rate for miners 18 to 24 years of age is about 3 times that of miners over 45, and it is about twice that of miners between the ages of 25 and 45.[48] The same general pattern holds true in industries as diverse as retail trade, transportation and public utilities, and services. The lesson for managers is clear: *New worker equals high risk!*

Training for employees and supervisors

Accidents often occur because workers lack one vital tool to protect themselves: *information*. Consider the following data collected by the Bureau of Labor Statistics:[87]

- Nearly one out of every five workers injured while operating power saws received no safety training on the equipment.
- Of 724 workers hurt while using scaffolds, 27 percent had received no information on safety requirements for installing the kind of scaffold on which they were injured.
- Of 554 workers hurt while servicing equipment, 61 percent were not told about lockout procedures that prevent the equipment from being turned on inadvertently while it is being serviced.

In nearly every type of injury that researchers have studied, the same story is repeated over and over. Workers often do not receive the kind of safety information they need, *even on jobs that require them to use dangerous equipment*. This is unfortunate, but a problem that is just as serious occurs when safety practices that are taught in training are not reinforced back on the job. Regular feedback and incentives for compliance are essential.

Feedback and incentives

Previous chapters have underscored the positive impact on the motivation of employees when they are given feedback and incentives to improve productivity. The same principles can also be used to improve safe behavior. Thus in one study of a wholesale bakery that was experiencing a sharp increase in work accidents, researchers developed a detailed coding sheet for observing safe and unsafe behaviors. Observers then used the sheets to record systematically both safe and unsafe employee behaviors over a 25-week period before, during, and after a safety training program. Slides were used to illustrate both safe and unsafe behaviors. Trainees were also shown data on the percentage of safe behaviors in their departments, and a goal of 90 percent safe behaviors was established. Following all of this, the actual percentage of safe behaviors was posted in each department. Supervisors were trained to use positive re-inforcement (praise) when they observed safe behaviors. In comparison to departments that received no training, workers in the trained departments averaged almost 24 percent more safe behaviors. Not only did employees react favorably to the program, but the company was able to maintain it. One year prior to the program, the number of lost-time injuries per million hours worked was 53.8. Even in highly hazardous industries, this figure rarely exceeds 35. One year after the program, it was less than 10.[44]

Similar results were found in a farm machinery manufacturing firm.[69] Be-havioral safety rules were obeyed more when employees received frequent feedback concerning their performance in relation to an accepted standard. Although the implementation of a training session to teach employees exactly what was expected of them also resulted in a significant increase in perfor-mance, it did not produce optimum performance. Assigning employees specific, difficult, yet acceptable safety goals, and providing information concerning their performance in relation to these goals, produced the maximum reduction in lost-time injuries. The results of these studies suggest that training, goal setting, and feedback provide useful alternatives to disciplinary sanctions or extrinsic incentives (safety awards) to encourage compliance with the rules.

Promoting Job Safety and Health: Approaches that Work

An in-depth study of 27 heavy manufacturers within the foundry industry revealed four general types of responses to OSHA regulations:[31]

1. *Technical responses* include replacing or fixing equipment, modifying physical workspaces, and providing worker protection (engineering controls).
2. *Information responses* refer to changes in the way that health and safety information is transmitted within the organization.
3. *Administrative responses* include changes in the authority structure or in policies and procedures with respect to safety and health (e.g., upgrading the safety function and shifting it from the engineering to the human resources department).
4. *External responses* refer to legal or political actions to change the enforcement of safety and health regulations.

When the types of responses to OSHA between 1971 and 1978 were related statistically to the number of accidents in 1982, the results indicated that OSHA was successful in generating all four types of responses through its inspection

improve the conditions that caused the explosion. After years of neglect and rampant pollution at Pemex facilities, the government was loathe to clamp down because that would focus attention on the main culprit: the Mexican government itself.[25]

Neither the Bhopal nor the Pemex incidents had any noticeable effect on multinational investment in Mexico. In fact, all the developing countries in one survey seem to rely on the multinationals, rather than on draconic new regulations, to prevent a repeat of Bhopal. This is true in South Korea, Taiwan, and Egypt, for example. Like Mexico, the biggest polluters in Egypt are government-owned. Many pesticide, fertilizer, dye, cement, and steel plants are in the suburbs of Cairo and Alexandria, the biggest population centers of overcrowded Egypt. Most of the factories are old and poorly maintained by the government, which owns them and has more pressing problems.[25] As these few examples make clear, in many of the less developed countries around the world, foreign investment is a political and economic issue, not a safety issue.

Health Hazards at Work

The National Institute of Occupational Safety and Health has identified over 15,000 toxic substances, of which some 500 might require regulation as carcinogens (cancer-causing substances). The list of harmful chemical, physical, and biological hazards is a long one. It includes carbon monoxide, vinyl chloride, dusts, particulates, gases and vapors, radiation, excessive noise and vibration, and extreme temperatures. When present in high concentrations, these agents can lead to respiratory, kidney, liver, skin, neurological, and other disorders. Scary, isn't it?

OSHA is making headway in these areas. Thus in late 1987 it began drafting regulations to protect workers against blood-borne biological hazards such as AIDS and hepatitis B. Workers with the highest risk of contracting these diseases include health-care professionals, blood-bank technicians, firefighters, law enforcement officials, and laundry workers who might come into contact with contaminated blood in the course of their work. Possible modes of protection might include special clothing and equipment, vaccination programs, training and education, and management of needle-puncture, cut, and splash injuries.[63]

There have been some well-publicized lawsuits against employers for causing occupational illnesses as a result of lack of proper safeguards or technical controls. In a 1987 decision, for example, a jury in Cleveland awarded $520,000 to a former government employee who sued the maker of a fire-proofing material that contained asbestos after she was diagnosed as having an asbestos-related disease. The woman had worked in the building for 12 years and sued the original seller of the material 3 years after that.[91] Nevertheless, some of the criticism against employers is not fair. To prove negligence, it must be shown that management *knew* of the connection between exposure to the hazards and negative health consequences and that management *chose* to do nothing to reduce worker exposure. Yet few such connections were made until recent years. Even now, alternative explanations for the causes of disease or illness cannot be ruled out in many cases. Responsibility for regulation has been left to OSHA.

To date, OSHA has issued 10 major health standards that deal with 22 toxic substances and cover 7.5 million workers. The primary emphasis has been on installing engineering controls that *prevent* exposure to harmful substances. As an example, consider the agreement between OSHA and Asarco to control the exposure of steelworkers to lead.

COMPANY EXAMPLE

Controlling lead exposure at Asarco

The agreement between OSHA and Asarco was designed to control worker exposure to lead through "feasible" controls and workplace practices at three Asarco smelters and a refinery. It resulted from lengthy discussions between the government, the company, and the United Steelworkers union.

OSHA's lead standard calls for, among other things, an air concentration of 50 micrograms (i.e., 50 millionths of a gram) per cubic meter. Under the agreement, Asarco will improve ventilation and provide filtered air for mobile equipment and certain rooms. The parties agreed that when the agreement expires, they will renew it and incorporate technological improvements in the monitoring of exposure to lead. In the meantime, OSHA retains its authority to inspect the facilities in response to serious accidents or complaints from employees.

The union strongly backed the whole idea; in fact, an industrial hygienist for the Steelworkers commented, "We get better control a whole lot faster than when we have to fight it out in a government review procedure. Frequently a judge winds up making a decision about how to control hazardous substances, and the judge probably hasn't been in the plant or isn't familiar with procedures and technical equipment used to control exposure levels."[5]

It might seem surprising that OSHA has issued only 10 major health standards, especially in view of the results of a government study showing that between 20 and 38 percent of the cancer contracted in the United States is occupationally related.[4] Policy development in this area can best be described as "rough sledding" for two reasons: (1) identification of carcinogenic substances and (2) development of regulatory standards once such substances are identified.

Since cancer can take from 20 to 40 years to manifest itself, records of industrial exposure are generally unavailable. Yet industry has sharply opposed the use of data based on experiments with animals. In fact, there has been little agreement among scientists, labor, and industry regarding what types of data are appropriate, and this has led to disagreements over the validity of the data that are available.

Management representatives object to the omission of cost considerations, but labor representatives argue that any determination of the cost effectiveness of achieving compliance should emphasize human safety rather than the dollar cost to employers.[81] Management also argues that animal tests cannot be relied on completely to determine whether substances cause cancer, that a safe level of exposure exists, and that substances should be ranked in terms of their suspected potency in causing cancer. Is it any surprise that there is no consensus among the parties concerned, given that they begin with such different assumptions?

The risks of doing nothing

In assessing the consequences of the problem, one is reminded of the TV ad that says, "You can pay me now, or pay me later." One study concluded that compliance with OSHA's proposed regulations will cost between $9 billion and $88 billion.[65] Yet an estimated $25 billion is spent annually to *treat* preventable cancer. If some portion of this money were spent instead to *prevent* the exposure of workers to carcinogenic substances, employers might well recoup their costs in 3 to 5 years or even less. But is cost-benefit analysis appropriate when lives are literally at stake?

The Supreme Court recognized this problem in its 1981 "Cotton Dust" decision. It held that OSHA need not balance the costs of implementing standards against the benefits expected. OSHA has to show only that it is *economically feasible* to implement the standards. The decision held that Congress had already decided the balance between costs and benefits in favor of the worker when it passed the law.[81] On one issue all parties agree: *The nature of cancer itself makes it virtually impossible for workers to protect themselves from exposure to cancer-causing substances.* In the absence of government-mandated exposure regulations, a few firms have instituted genetic screening for job applicants and genetic monitoring for employees.

Legal implications of genetic screening and monitoring

Genetic screening is a one-time test (via a blood or urine count) to determine whether a job applicant carries genetic traits that might predispose her or him to adverse health effects when exposed to certain chemicals. Genetic monitoring is the routine testing of employees who work with potentially toxic substances, to detect evidence of genetic impairment.[61] With today's technology, it is possible to screen individuals for very few diseases—emphysema, heart disease, hemophilia, and sickle-cell anemia.[66] Moreover, scientists have not yet been able to screen out such "confounders" as the age of the workers, prior illnesses, and above-average smoking or drinking. Hence it is impractical for businesses to begin widespread testing.[49]

Unfortunately, it appears that there is a potential contradiction between OSHA and Title VII of the 1964 Civil Rights Act with regard to genetic screening. Such screening may trigger lawsuits under Title VII because there is considerable evidence showing that genetic impairments differ as a function of ethnicity. If a charge of racial discrimination is filed against an employer based on the results of genetic screening, it is necessary to show the validity, or "business necessity," of such screening. However, given the present state of the science, validity evidence is unavailable. Furthermore, the demonstration of business necessity to support unequal hiring or promotion rates has been upheld *only on the basis of expected differences in job performance, not on the basis of the probability of contracting disease.*[61] To date, there are no legal precedents in this area.

On the other hand, the "general duty" clause of OSHA and specific standards that deal with the removal of employees from environments that are potentially damaging to them can be interpreted as sanctioning *any* practice that contributes to improvements in the health of workers. Consequently, if employers *fail* to take genetic-screening and genetic-monitoring information into account, they may be violating the spirit of OSHA. What can firms do? Policies similar to that of Dow Chemical are typical: "No employee, male or female, will knowingly be exposed to hazardous levels of material known to cause cancer or genetic mutations in humans." And further, "We will not place women capable of reproduction in any work situation involving exposure to materials that can harm the fetus." In limited legal tests, courts have ruled that fetal-protection policies are discriminatory—unless a company makes a strong scientific showing that workplace hazards pose a particular risk to unborn children.[53]

Unfortunately, many hazardous jobs are high-paying. This situation is "unfortunate" because workers are understandably reluctant to transfer out of these jobs to avoid occupational exposures unless they are protected against loss of income. Both AT&T and Digital Equipment have provided just such income protection for pregnant production workers who might be exposed to the toxic gases and liquids used to etch microscopic circuits onto silicon wafers.[7] Some workers have even gone so far as to have themselves sterilized to protect their jobs.[12] It seems, then, that companies have two choices: Either guarantee transferees no loss of income, or else obtain signed, voluntary consent agreements from employees who choose to stay on hazardous jobs. While consent agreements will not absolve employers from liability under workers' compensation laws and civil disability suits, they may minimize the amount of punitive damages that employees are awarded.[59] Better yet, if at all possible, alter the workplace rather than the workforce. Eliminate the *causes* of biological impairment.

AIDS and business

AIDS (acquired immune deficiency syndrome) is a medical time bomb. With 40,000 confirmed cases of AIDS now and 324,000 cases expected by the end of 1991, employers are fast having to deal with increasing numbers of AIDS victims in the workplace.[18] Consider these prognoses about the disease:

- Hospital charges will rise by 20 percent per year through 1990, in part because of AIDS.
- Non-AIDS public-health programs will be curtailed in cities hit hard by the epidemic.
- With no cure in sight for at least 20 years, the Public Health Service estimates that the AIDS medical bill may be as much as $16 billion by 1991. The U.S. Centers for Disease Control (CDC) estimates that 215,000 Americans will have died of the disease by the end of 1991.[13]
- The cost of treating an AIDS patient from diagnosis to death was $94,000 in 1987. This is higher than the average cost of treating leukemia, cancer of the digestive system, a heart attack, or paraplegia from an auto crash.[32]
- By 1991 AIDS is expected to be the leading cause of death for those aged 25 to 44. These are people whose historically low rates of sickness and death help keep at least a loose lid on health-care and insurance costs and whose tax dollars subsidize government programs for children and the elderly.
- The cumulative costs of long-term disability payments to people with AIDS through 1995 are expected to exceed $2 billion.
- Life insurance policies already in force will generate AIDS-related life insurance claims of $50 billion through the end of the century—up from $200 million in 1986.
- Of all the economic costs of AIDS, the greatest by far is the productivity drain—$7 billion in 1986 and an estimated $56 billion in 1991, representing 12 percent of the economic costs of all illness.[32]
- Jobs held by AIDS-afflicted persons are protected by laws in 45 states, prohibiting discrimination against people with disabilities.[55]

Bank of America has developed a model corporate policy to deal with the AIDS problem at work. Its basic features include the following:

Assumption 1. AIDS is not a casually contagious disease, and there is little risk of transmission in the workplace. But given the irrational fear that AIDS often inspires, the best way to avoid a difficult and disruptive situation is to prepare and educate both management and employees before the first employee gets AIDS.

Assumption 2. An employee's health condition is personal and confidential. At Bank of America employees are not required to tell their managers that they have AIDS or other life-threatening illnesses. But they are assured that they can work with the human resources department to facilitate benefits and to discuss other illness-related concerns. (Human resources department personnel receive extensive training about AIDS.) Providing a supportive work environment for people with life-threatening illnesses not only helps them financially; it can even prolong their lives.

Policy. As long as employees with AIDS are able to meet acceptable performance standards—and their condition is not a threat to themselves or others—they should be treated like other employees. If warranted, the bank makes reasonable accommodations for the employee (such as flexible hours), as long as these do not hamper the business needs of the work unit.

Policy. Coworkers who wish to transfer may do so, although Bank of America found that such apprehension is usually based on lack of information. Since publishing its policy, the bank has not had any requests for transfer based on fear of a coworker's illness.

Policy. An employee who contracts AIDS should be encouraged to seek assistance from established community support groups for medical treatment and counseling. The bank has found that the best and most cost-effective way to treat employees with AIDS is through "case management" programs that provide for home or hospice care. Such flexible benefits coverage is a fairly recent development, but Bank of America has worked with its third-party insurers to provide it.

In short, Bank of America is playing an important role in AIDS-related education, support, and benefits for *all* its employees. In fact, its board and top-management committee's main concern is "Are we doing enough?"[54]

Employee Assistance Programs

Another (brighter) side of the employee health issue is reflected in employee assistance programs (EAPs). Such programs represent an expansion of traditional work in occupational alcoholism treatment programs. From a handful of such programs begun in the 1940s (led by Du Pont), different schools of thought have emerged regarding the best way to treat alcoholism in industry, along with a diversity of treatment programs. As recently as 1959, only about 50 American companies were operating such programs.[74] By 1987, more than 10,000 companies had implemented these programs in public and private work environments.[26]

Management's concern over the issue is understandable, for alcohol misuse by employees is costly in terms of productivity, time lost from work, and treatment. How prevalent is alcoholism and how costly is it? Unfortunately, while many figures are bandied about, a critical review of the development and reporting of knowledge about employee alcoholism treatment programs showed these estimates to be supported by limited empirical data.[88] Specifically, three problems remain. One, no study yet reported has determined whether employees diagnosed as alcoholic on the basis of job performance problems (e.g., absenteeism, poor judgment, erratic performance) are indeed alcoholics. Two, the impact of "constructive coercion" ("shape up or ship out") on *drinking behavior*—rather than on *work behavior*—has not been assessed adequately. Three, it is not at all clear that the diagnosis and treatment of

EAP program were studied over a period of $3\frac{1}{2}$ years, the results are likely to be quite reliable.

Corporate Health Promotion: The Concept of "Wellness"

Consider these sobering facts:

- In 1960, per capita expenditures for medical care were $146. By 1987, as noted in Chapter 11, they averaged over $1500 per person. This is a record that promises to be broken every year.
- Business today pays half the nation's health-care bill. Common backaches alone cause a loss of 91 million workdays per year, for a total cost of more than $9 billion in lost productivity, disability payments, and lawsuits.[71]
- Business spends some $700 million per year to replace the 200,000 employees aged 45 to 65 who are killed or disabled by heart disease.

All of this means rising costs for health benefits, which now account for about 10 percent of total compensation.[35] Keep in mind that health plans do not promise good health. They simply pay for the cost of ill health and the associated rehabilitation.

Because 8 of the 10 leading causes of death are largely preventable, managers are beginning to look to *disease prevention* as one way to reduce health-care spending. The old saying "an ounce of prevention is worth a pound of cure" is certainly true when one compares the costs of a workshop to help employees stop smoking with the price tag on an average coronary bypass operation.[10]

Is it possible that health-care costs can be tamed through on-the-job exercise programs and health promotion efforts? Convinced that if people were healthier, they would be sick less often, over 500 corporations (including IBM, Control Data, Xerox, and Kimberly-Clark) are building jogging tracks, providing personalized risk-factor calculations, and improving workers' ways of handling stress. Do such programs work? In a moment we will consider that question, but first let's define our terms and look at the overall concept.

The process of corporate health promotion begins by promoting *health awareness*, that is, knowledge of the present and future consequences of behaviors and lifestyles and the risks they may present.[14] The objective of "wellness programs" is not to eliminate symptoms and disease; it is to help employees build lifestyles that will enable them to achieve their full physical and mental potential.[45] Wellness programs differ from EAPs in that *wellness focuses on prevention, while EAPs focus on rehabilitation.* Health promotion is a four-step process:[70]

1. Educate employees about health-risk factors—life habits or body characteristics that may increase the chances of developing a serious illness. For heart disease (the leading cause of death), some of these risk factors are: high blood pressure, cigarette smoking, high cholesterol levels, diabetes, a sedentary lifestyle, and obesity. Some factors, such as smoking, stress, and poor nutrition, are associated with many diseases.
2. Identify the health-risk factors that each employee faces.
3. Help employees eliminate or reduce these risks through healthier lifestyles and habits.
4. Help employees maintain their new, healthier lifestyles through self-monitoring and evaluation. The central theme of health promotion is "No one takes better care of you than you do."

To date, the most popular programs are smoking cessation, blood pressure control, cholesterol reduction, weight control and fitness, and stress management. In well-designed programs, 40 to 50 percent of employees can be expected to participate.[50] Here is a company example.

COMPANY EXAMPLE

Control Data's "Stay Well" program

Control Data Corporation, with over $4 billion in annual sales, has an ambitious health promotion program. It is called "Stay Well," and it reaches 22,000 employees and their families in 14 cities. A key ingredient of the program is the recruitment of informal "opinion leaders" to promote the program at each plant. Stay Well includes physiological tests, computerized health-risk profiles, wellness education classes, and courses in lifestyle change. The lifestyle courses cover such areas as stress, fitness, weight control, nutrition, and smoking cessation.

Stay Well also features follow-up worker support groups to help make the lifestyle changes stick and employee task forces to promote health-enhancing changes in the workplace. Such task forces have won stretch breaks, showers, no-smoking areas, and fresh fruit in vending machines. Said the director of the company's health-care services division, "We want to produce cultural changes in the workplace. We want to change the norms of health-related behavior."[3]

A 4-year study of 15,000 Control Data employees showed dramatic relationships between employees' health habits and insurance claim costs. For example, people whose weekly exercise was equivalent to climbing fewer than five flights of stairs, or walking less than half a mile, spent 114 percent more on health claims than those who climbed at least 15 flights of stairs or walked 1.5 miles weekly. Health-care costs for obese people were 11 percent higher than those for thin ones. And workers who routinely failed to use seat belts spent 54 percent more days in the hospital than those who usually buckled up. Finally, people who smoked an average of one or more packs of cigarettes

documentation of this conclusion, nor any evidence that OSHA weighed the relevant considerations. The agency simply announced its finding of cost-justification without explaining the method by which it determines that the benefits justify the costs and their economic effects. No rational system of administration can permit its administrators to make policy judgments without explaining how their decisions [further] the purposes of the governing law, and nothing in the [OSHA act] authorizes such laxity in this case."[36]

Summary

Public policy regarding occupational safety and health has focused on state-run workers' compensation programs for job-related injuries and federally mandated preventive measures to enhance job safety and health. OSHA enforces the provisions of the 1970 Occupational Safety and Health Act, under which employers have a "general duty" to provide a place of employment "free from recognized hazards." Employers also have the special duty to comply with all standards of safety and health established under the act. OSHA's effectiveness has been debated for over a decade, but it is important to note that workplace accidents can result either from *unsafe work conditions* or from *unsafe work behaviors*. OSHA can affect only unsafe work conditions. There are no standards that govern potentially unsafe employee behaviors. To date, OSHA has issued only 10 major health standards. Two reasons account for this: It is difficult to identify carcinogenic substances, and it is difficult to determine regulatory standards once they are identified. Management's first duty in this area is to develop a safety and health policy. Management's second duty is to implement and sustain the policy through a loss control program.

TOMORROW'S FORECAST

In the coming years, we can expect to see four developments in occupational safety and health. One, there is likely to be more widespread promotion of OSHA's consultative role, particularly as small businesses recognize that this is a no-cost, no-penalty option available to them. Two, we can expect to see the elimination of regulatory standards for each toxic substance. The fact that OSHA has issued only 10 such standards, when in fact hundreds of toxic substances threaten worker health, will stimulate this effort. Three, we can expect to see wider use of cost-benefit analysis by regulatory agencies. Industry is demanding it, and top government officials have endorsed it (via Executive Order 12291 issued by President Reagan). Four, we can expect to see the target group for EAPs broadened to include dependents and retirees. Together, these trends suggest that occupational safety and health issues will command greater attention by management in the coming years.

Employee assistance programs represent a brighter side of the health issue. Such programs offer assistance to all "troubled" employees. Under an EAP, supervisors need be concerned only with identifying declining work performance, not with involvement in employee problems. Treatment is left to professionals. Finally, health promotion, or "wellness," programs differ from EAPs in that their primary focus is on prevention, not rehabilitation. Like EAPs there is controversy over their relative worth, and like EAPs they hold considerable promise.

Discussion Questions

15-1 Should OSHA's enforcement activities be expanded? Why or why not?

15-2 What advantages and disadvantages do you see with workers' compensation?

15-3 Discuss the relative effectiveness of engineering versus management controls to improve job safety and health.

15-4 You have just been named CEO of a company that manufactures athletic shoes. Outline a job safety and health program.

15-5 If the benefits of EAPs cannot be demonstrated to exceed their costs, should EAPs be discontinued?

15-6 Should organizations be willing to invest more money in employee wellness? Why or why not?

References

1. *Accident facts* (1983). Chicago: National Safety Council.
2. Allen, R. E., & Keaveny, T. J. (1988). *Contemporary labor relations* (2d ed.). Reading, MA: Addison-Wesley.
3. American business is bullish on "Wellness" (1982, Mar. 29). *Medical World News*, pp. 33–39.
4. Anderson, M. C., Isom, R. N., Williams, K., & Zimmerman, L. J. (eds.) (1979, Mar. 30). *Proceedings of a conference for workers on job-related cancer*. Houston, Texas.
5. Apcar, L. M. (1984, Feb. 1). OSHA signs union-backed Asarco plan to control steelworker exposure to lead. *Wall Street Journal*, p. 7.
6. Ashford, N. A. (1976). *Crisis in the workplace: Occupational disease and injury*. Cambridge, MA: MIT Press.
7. AT&T bans pregnant from toxic area. (1987, Jan. 14). *Denver Post*, p. 1E.
8. Balgopal, P. R., Ramanathan, C. S., & Patchner, M. A. (1987, December). *Employee assistance programs: A cross-cultural perspective*. Paper presented at the Conference on International Personnel and Human Resource Management, Singapore.
9. Berg, N. R., & Moe, J. P. (1979). Assistance for troubled employees. In D. Yoder & H. G. Heneman, Jr. (eds.), *ASPA handbook of personnel and industrial relations*. Washington, DC: BNA, pp. 1.59–1.77.

10. Bernstein, J. E. (1983, November). Handling health costs by reducing health risks. *Personnel Journal*, pp. 882–887.

11. Bhopal judge orders Union Carbide to pay $270 million in interim relief. (1987, Dec. 18). *Wall Street Journal*, p. 4.

12. Bitter reaction (1979, Feb. 9). *Wall Street Journal*, pp. 1, 33.

13. Blustein, P. (1987, May 18). The nation comes to grips with the widening problem of AIDS. *Wall Street Journal*, p. 20.

14. Brennan, A. J. (1983). Worksite health promotion can be cost-effective. *Personnel Administrator*, 28(4), 39–42.

15. Brooks, J. (1977). *Failure to meet commitments made in the Occupational Safety and Health Act.* Committee on government operations, 95th Congress of the United States, Washington, DC: USGPO.

16. Burtt, E. J. (1979). *Labor in the American economy.* New York: St. Martin's Press.

17. Carbide to pay gas victims $350 million (1986, Mar. 23). *Honolulu Star Bulletin*, p. A-18.

18. Chase, M. (1987, May 18). AIDS costs. *Wall Street Journal*, pp. 1, 20.

19. Cohen, A. (1977). Factors in successful occupational safety programs. *Journal of Safety Research*, **9**, 168–178.

20. Cook, W. N., & Gautschi, F. H. (1981). OSHA plant safety programs and injury reduction. *Industrial Relations*, 20(3), 245–257.

21. Elliott, S. (1984, June 27). OSHA Region III Area Director, personal communication.

22. Falkenberg, L. E. (1987). Employee fitness programs: Their impact on the employee and the organization. *Academy of Management Review*, **12**, 511–522.

23. Follmann, J. F., Jr. (1978). *The economics of industrial health.* New York: AMA-COM.

24. Foote, A., & Erfurt, J. (1981, September–October). Evaluating an employee assistance program. *EAP Digest*, pp. 14–25.

25. Foreign firms feel the impact of Bhopal most (1985, Nov. 26). *Wall Street Journal*, p. 24.

26. French, H. W. (1987, Mar. 26). Helping the addicted worker. *New York Times*, pp. 29, 34.

27. Gaeta, E., Lynn, R., & Grey, L. (1982, May–June). AT&T looks at program evaluation. *EAP Digest*, pp. 22–31.

28. *Gateway Coal Co. v. United Mine Workers of America* (1974). 1974 OSHD, Sn. 17,085. Chicago: Commerce Clearing House.

29. Ginter, E. M. (1979, May). Communications and cost-benefit aspects of employee safety. *Management Accounting*, pp. 24–32.

30. Gobbledygook out (1977, Dec. 6). *Miami Herald*, p. 17A.

31. Gricar, B. G., & Hopkins, H. D. (1983). How does your company respond to OSHA? *Personnel Administrator*, 28(4), 53–57.

32. Harris, D. (1987, November). AIDS: We'll all pay. *Money*, pp. 109–134.

33. Hays, L. (1986, July 8). New rules on workplace hazards prompt intensified on-the-job training programs. *Wall Street Journal*, p. 31.

34. Hoover, J. J. (1983). Workers have new rights to health and safety. *Personnel Administrator*, 28(4), 47–51.

35. Howard, J. S. (1987, May–June). Employee wellness: It's good business. *D&B Reports*, pp. 34–37.

36. *Industrial Union Dept., AFL-CIO, American Petroleum Institute, et al., v. Marshall* (1980). 1980 OSHD, Sn. 30,613. Chicago: Commerce Clearing House.

37. Injuries on the job (1984, Mar. 30). *USA Today*, p. 1B.
38. *Inside OSHA: Supervisory participation in safety* (1975, Sep. 1). New York: Man and Manager, Inc.
39. *Inside OSHA: The role of management in safety* (1975, Nov. 1). New York: Man and Manager, Inc.
40. James, F. B. (1987, Apr. 14). Study lays groundwork for tying health costs to workers' behavior. *Wall Street Journal*, p. 37.
41. Karr, A. R. (1987, July 7). Chrysler agrees to pay $1.6 million fine to settle OSHA health, safety charges. *Wall Street Journal*, p. 3.
42. Kirkland, L. (1980, July). OSHA: A 10-year success story. *AFL-CIO American Federationist*, pp. 1–4.
43. Klarreich, S. H., DiGiuseppe, R., & DiMattia, D. J. (1987). EAPs: Mind over myth. *Personnel Administrator*, 32(2), 119–121.
44. Komaki, J., Barwick, K. D., & Scott, L. R. (1978). A behavioral approach to occupational safety: Pinpointing and reinforcing safe performance in a food manufacturing plant. *Journal of Applied Psychology*, **63**, 434–445.
45. Kreitner, R. (1982, May–June). Personal wellness: It's just good business. *Business Horizons*, pp. 28–35.
46. Labor letter (1987, Apr. 14). *Wall Street Journal*, p. 1.
47. LaVan, H., Mathys, N., & Drehmer, D. (1983). A look at the counseling practices of major U.S. corporations. *Personnel Administrator*, 28(6), 76–81, 143–146.
48. Leary, W. E. (1982, Aug. 2). Management concern affects mine safety. *Denver Post*, p. 1C.
49. Leib, J. (1987, July 6). Screening for genetic ills threatens to rile workplace. *Denver Post*, p. 1B.
50. List, W. (1987, May 15). Employee fitness pays dividends. *Toronto Globe and Mail*, p. D18.
51. *Marshall v. Barlow's, Inc.* (1978). 1978 OSHD, Sn. 22,735. Chicago: Commerce Clearing House.
52. McCaffrey, D. P. (1983). An assessment of OSHA's recent effects on injury rates. *Journal of Human Resources*, 18(1), 131–146.
53. Meier, B. (1987, Feb. 5). Companies wrestle with threats to workers' reproductive health. *Wall Street Journal*, p. 25.
54. Merritt, N. L. (1987, Mar. 23). Bank of America's blueprint for a policy on AIDS. *Business Week*, p. 127.
55. Micheli, R. (1987, November). When AIDS hits home. *Money*, pp. 137–150.
56. Milkovich, G. T., & Newman, J. M. (1987). *Compensation* (2d ed.). Plano, TX: Business Publications.
57. Miller, J. (1983, Nov. 17). Is-nothing-sacred dept.: OSHA is the bad guy in this video game. *Wall Street Journal*, p. 33.
58. Miller, M. (1985, Nov. 26). Words still speak louder than deeds: India hasn't come to grips with plant safety. *Wall Street Journal*, p. 24.
59. Nothstein, G., & Ayres, J. (1981). Sex-based considerations of differentiation in the workplace: Exploring the biomedical interface between OSHA and Title VII. *Villanova Law Review*, **26**(2), 239–321.
60. Olian, J. (1987, December). *Employee wellness: Managerial, governmental, and legal reactions in the U.S. and internationally*. Paper presented at the Conference on International Personnel and Human Resource Management, Singapore.
61. Olian, J. D., & Snyder, T. C. (1984). The implications of genetic testing. *Personnel Administrator*, 29(1), 19–27.

62. OSHA chief leaves agency in limbo (1984, April–May). *NFIB Mandate*, p. 6.

63. OSHA is weighing disease measures (1987, Nov. 27). *New York Times*, p. B19.

64. OSHA Regional Office, Philadelphia (1987, Dec. 21). Personal communication.

65. OSHA rules will speed carcinogen regulation (1980, Jan. 29). *Chemical and Engineering News*, p. 30.

66. Otten, A. L. (1986, Feb. 24). Probing the cell. *Wall Street Journal*, pp. 1, 41.

67. Parkes, K. R. (1987). Relative weight, smoking, and mental health as predictors of sickness and absence from work. *Journal of Applied Psychology*, **72**, 275–286.

68. Ray, J. S. (1982). Having problems with worker performance? Try an EAP. *Administrative Management*, **43**(5), 47–49.

69. Reber, R. A., & Wallin, J. A. (1984). The effects of training, goal setting, and knowledge of results on safe behavior: A component analysis. *Academy of Management Journal*, **27**, 544–560.

70. Reed, R. W. (1984, January). Is education the key to lower health care costs? *Personnel Journal*, pp. 40–46.

71. Renner, J. F. (1987, March–April). Wellness programs: An investment in cost containment. *EAP Digest*, pp. 49–53.

72. Root, N. (1981). Injuries at work are fewer among older employees. *Monthly Labor Review*, **104**(3), 30–34.

73. Saddler, J. (1987, July 30). OSHA seeks to fine General Dynamics $615,000 for alleged records violations. *Wall Street Journal*, p. 10. See also: K. Noble, Chrysler will pay $295,000 fine for violations on injury records, *New York Times*, Jan. 31, 1987, p. 7; A. Karr, OSHA cites plant of Caterpillar, Inc. on safety breaches, *Wall Street Journal*, May 21, 1987, p. 7.

74. Scanlon, W. (1983, May–June). Trends in EAPs: Then and now. *EAP Digest*, pp. 38–41.

75. Shabecoff, P. (1987, Oct. 11). Industry is split over disclosure of job dangers. *New York Times*, p. 28.

76. Simison, R. L. (1986, Mar. 18). Safety last. *Wall Street Journal*, pp. 1, 18.

77. Siskind, F. (1982). Another look at the link between work injuries and job experience. *Monthly Labor Review*, **105**(2), 38–41.

78. Sloane, A. A. (1983). *Personnel: Managing human resources*. Englewood Cliffs, NJ: Prentice-Hall.

79. Smith, M. J., Cohen, H. H., Cohen, A., & Cleveland, R. J. (1978). Characteristics of successful safety programs. *Journal of Safety Research*, **10**, 5–15.

80. Sovereign, K. L. (1984). *Personnel law*. Reston, VA: Reston.

81. Stead, W. E., & Stead, J. G. (1983, January). OSHA's cancer prevention policy: Where did it come from and where is it going? *Personnel Journal*, pp. 54–60.

82. Substance abuse in the workplace (1987, June 20). *Hospitals*, pp. 68–73.

83. Taking drugs on the job (1983, Aug. 22). *Newsweek*, pp. 52–58.

84. Thanks, Dr. Bingham (1978, Nov. 29). *Wall Street Journal*, p. 22.

85. Trice, H. M., & Roman, P. M. (1978). *Spirits and demons at work* (2d ed.). Ithaca, NY: New York State School of Industrial and Labor Relations.

86. Trost, C. (1986, Jan. 8). OSHA to check safety at more firms in an expansion of inspection policy. *Wall Street Journal*, p. 50.

87. U.S. Department of Labor (1983, March). *Program Highlights: Job safety and health*. Washington, DC: USGPO, Fact Sheet No. OSHA-83-01 (revised).

88. Weiss, R. M. (1987). Writing under the influence: Science versus fiction in the analysis of corporate alcoholism programs. *Personnel Psychology*, **40**, 341–356.

89. *Whirlpool Corporation v. Marshall* (1981, Feb. 26). *Daily Labor Report*, Washington, DC: Bureau of National Affairs, pp. D3–D10.
90. Worker insurance evolution (1983, Dec. 6). *New York Times*, pp. D1, D17.
91. $520,000 awarded in an asbestos-related illness (1987, Oct. 8). *New York Times*, p. A21.

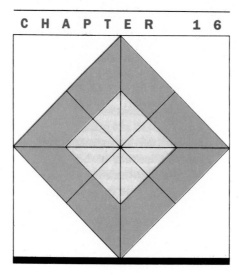

Assessing the Costs and Benefits of Human Resource Management Activities

CASE 16-1

Attitude survey results: catalyst for management action*

Attitude surveys can yield far more than a measure of morale. By relating specific management actions and styles to high employee turnover and lowered profitability, the results of an attitude survey in one company led to concrete directions for change. The changes implied improved productivity, quality of work life, and bottom-line financial gain.

The company is a nationwide retail operation with an exceptional record of growth and profitability. To staff its rapidly expanding management positions, the company hires large numbers of men and women as trainees in store management. However, despite attractive salaries and promotion opportunities, the company was having trouble retaining the new hires. Top management was at a loss to explain why. Turnover among store managers accelerated beyond the most recent hires; managers in whom the company invested considerable time and money were also quitting. Moreover, there was no apparent pattern to the turnover—some locations were experiencing a great deal, others very little.

Despite continued profitability, there was growing concern among top man-

*Adapted from: B. Goldberg and G. G. Gordon, Designing attitude surveys for management action, *Personnel Journal*, October 1978, pp. 546–549.

agement that the level of turnover might be detrimental to the company's long-term success. The actual dollar outlay for the cost of turnover was only one aspect of the problem. An additional consideration was the possibility of poor public relations resulting from unhappy former employees. As a consumer-oriented company, the firm was concerned about its public image and the effect that a "bad employer" reputation could have on the patronage of its stores.

The problem: turnover versus profitability

As turnover worsened, the company conducted various statistical analyses and reviewed reports from field managers in an attempt to locate the source of the problem. Several theories were proposed, such as low pay and inconvenient scheduling of work, but none was supported by sufficient evidence to produce change. Indeed, most of the proposed solutions to the turnover problem (e.g., hire more employees to work fewer hours) were rejected because their anticipated costs would reduce company profitability.

Top management initially felt that high turnover was acceptable because it did not have much of an adverse effect on profits. In fact, many managers believed that turnover actually increased profitability because it kept overall salary costs down. Vacancies caused stores to operate understaffed until replacements were hired, and these new hires were paid lower salaries than their predecessors.

Why an attitude survey?

Despite attempts to find it, the root cause of the turnover of store managers remained elusive. The problem could lie anywhere in the management system, in the types of employees hired, in how they were trained, in how they were managed, or in how their performance was rewarded.

Top management decided to conduct a broad survey among the store managers themselves to determine the cause of the high turnover. The survey's intent was not to determine how to improve morale and thereby to reduce turnover. It was to help management discover the factors contributing to turnover and the concrete and constructive actions that might reduce it. And, because top management believed that high turnover had a positive effect on profitability, another objective of the survey was to determine what could be done to reduce turnover without reducing profitability! This part of the survey yielded some very enlightening results.

Designing the survey

The company first rank-ordered its profit centers in two ways—(1) according to turnover and (2) according to profitability—based on results for the most recent 12-month period. A questionnaire was developed through personal interviews with a number of store managers, and hypotheses were advanced concerning the relationship between the attitudes of store managers and turnover. The hypotheses produced further guides for questionnaire design; they also yielded an outline for subsequent data analyses.

The resulting questionnaire covered a broad range of management issues, including:

- Store characteristics (location and volume)
- Biographical characteristics of the store managers
- Recruitment and selection practices
- Training activities
- Working conditions
- Management climate
- Rewards system

The questionnaire was sent to every store manager then working in one of the profit centers identified earlier.

Survey results

The survey revealed significant differences in the ways store managers were selected, managed, and treated. It also identified a number of fundamental management practices that were counterproductive. For example, some higher-level supervisors never made field visits to work with their store managers.

However, the most revealing part of the survey results had to do with turnover and profitability. Many factors contributing to high turnover were also contributing to lower profitability. The survey revealed six critical areas of human resource management, all interrelated and each related to turnover and profitability.

QUESTIONS

1. What are some of the advantages and disadvantages of a low turnover rate?
2. How can attitude surveys help orient managers toward more effective performance?
3. In the survey design phase, why do you think the company first ranked each store in terms of its profitability and turnover rate?

What's Ahead

In business settings, it is hard to be convincing without data. If the data are developed systematically and comprehensively and are analyzed in terms of their strategic implications for the business or business unit, they are more convincing. Case 16-1 demonstrates how a systematic procedure (an attitude survey) designed to collect data on a broad range of management issues could be used to improve management practices. This chapter presents tools to help you "cost out" five key areas of human resource management: employee absenteeism, employee turnover, employee assistance programs, employee selection programs, and employee training programs. Finally, it considers the general issue of personnel research—what it is, major topics that have been investigated, and how it can be used to improve human resource management.

Orientation

As emphasized earlier, the focus of this book is *not* on training personnel specialists. Rather, the focus is on training line managers who must, by the very nature of their jobs, manage people and work with them to accomplish organizational objectives. Consequently, the purpose of this chapter is not how to measure the effectiveness of the human resources department; the purpose is how to assess the costs and benefits of key human resource management activities. The methods can and should be used in cooperation with the human resources department. But they are not the exclusive domain of that department. They are general enough to be used by any manager in any department to measure the costs and benefits of employee behavior.

This is not to imply that dollars are the only barometer of the effectiveness of human resource activities. The payoffs from some activities, such as affirmative action and child care, must be viewed in a broader social context. Further, the firm's strategy and goals must guide the work of each business unit *and* of that unit's human resource management activities. For example, to emphasize its outreach efforts to the disadvantaged, a firm might adopt a conscious strategy to *train* workers for entry-level jobs, while *selecting* workers who already have the skills to perform higher-level jobs. To make the most effective use of the tools that follow, it is important always to keep these points in mind.

Accounting for the Costs Invested in Managers

In the mid-1960s the first attempts were made to account for the costs of human resource management activities. This accounting has come to be known generally as human resource accounting (HRA).

The first firm to report HRA results was the R. G. Barry Corporation of Columbus, Ohio, which did so in its 1967 annual report.[31] The company's objective was to report accurate estimates of the worth of the human assets in its employ. For each manager, costs were accumulated in five subsidiary accounts: (1) recruiting and acquisition, (2) formal orientation and training, (3) informal orientation and training, (4) experience, and (5) development. The costs for each manager were amortized over his or her expected working lifetime; unamortized costs (such as for a manager who leaves the company) were written off.

Valuing managers in this way is what accountants call the "asset model of accounting," which uses the historical cost of the asset. That is, the organization's investment in each manager—the asset—is measured by the expenses actually incurred—the historical cost—in developing each manager as an asset.

Such an approach considers only the investments made in managers and not the returns on those investments. This is one reason why asset models of HRA never caught on widely.[1, 29]

A newer approach focuses on dollar estimates of the behaviors, such as the absenteeism, turnover, and job performance of managers. This approach does not measure the value of a manager as an asset, but rather the economic consequences of his or her behavior. This is an *expense model* of HRA.[19] It is the approach taken in this chapter to assessing the costs and benefits of the activities of all personnel, managerial as well as nonmanagerial. We will apply standard cost accounting procedures to employee behavior. To do this, we must first identify each of the elements of behavior to which we can assign a cost; each behavioral cost element must be separate and mutually exclusive from another. To begin, let's define some key terms.

The behavior costing approach

Contrary to popular belief, there are methods for determining the costs of employee behavior in *all* human resource management activities—behaviors associated with the attraction, selection, retention, development, and utilization of people in organizations. These costing methods are based on several definitions and a few necessary assumptions.

To begin, there are, as in any costing situation, controllable and uncontrollable costs, and there are direct and indirect measures of these costs.

Direct measures refer to actual costs, such as the accumulated, direct cost of recruiting.

TABLE 16-1 *Direct and indirect costs associated with mismanaged stress*

Direct costs	Indirect costs
Participation and membership	**Loss of vitality**
Absenteeism	Low morale
Tardiness	Low motivation
Strikes and work stoppages	Dissatisfaction
Turnover	
	Communication breakdowns
Performance on the job	Decline in frequency of contact
Quality of productivity	Distortions of messages
Quantity of productivity	
Grievances	**Faulty decision making**
Accidents	
Unscheduled machine downtime and repair	**Quality of work relations**
Material and supply overutilization	Distrust
Inventory shrinkages	Disrespect
	Animosity
Compensation awards	**Opportunity costs**

Source: B. A. Macy & P. H. Mirvis, *Evaluation Review*, **6**(3), 1982, Figure 4-5.

FIGURE 16-1

The costs of accidents and grievances.

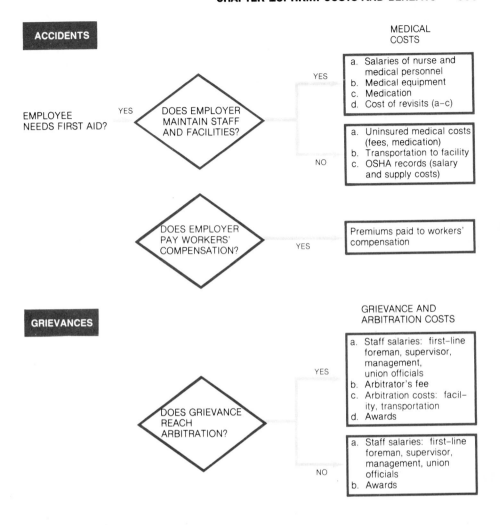

Indirect measures do not deal directly with cost; they are usually expressed in terms of time, quantity, or quality.[11] In many cases indirect measures can be converted to direct measures. For example, if we know the length of time per preemployment interview plus the interviewer's hourly pay, it is a simple matter to convert time per interview into cost per interview.

Indirect measures have value in and of themselves, and they also supply part of the data needed to develop a direct measure. As a further example, consider the direct and indirect costs associated with mismanaged organizational stress, as shown in Table 16-1. The direct costs listed in the left column of Table 16-1 can all be expressed in terms of dollars. To see this, consider just two items: the costs associated with work accidents and grievances (Figure 16-1). Figure 16-1 presents just some of the direct costs associated with accidents; it is not meant to be exhaustive, and it does not include such items as lost time, replacement costs, "work to rule" by coworkers if they feel that the firm is responsible, the cost of the safety committee's investigation, and the costs associated with changing technology or job design to prevent future accidents. Items shown in the right column of Table 16-1 cannot be expressed as easily in dollar terms, but they are no less important, and the cost of these indirect items may in fact be far larger than the direct costs. Both direct and indirect costs, as well as benefits, must be considered in order to apply behavior costing methodology properly.

Controllable versus uncontrollable costs   In any area of behavior costing, some types of costs are controllable through prudent personnel decision making, while other costs are simply beyond the control of the organization. Consider employee turnover as an example. To the extent that people leave for reasons of "better salary," "more opportunity for promotion and career development," or "greater job challenge," the costs associated with turnover are somewhat controllable. That is, the firm can alter its human resource management practices to reduce the voluntary turnover. However, if the turnover is due to such factors as death, poor health, or spouse transfer, the costs are uncontrollable.

The point is that in human resource costing, our objective is not simply to *measure* costs but also to *reduce* the costs of human resources by devoting resources to the more "controllable" factors. To do this, we must do two things well:

1. Identify, for each personnel decision, which costs are controllable and which are not.
2. Measure these costs at Time 1 (prior to some intervention designed to reduce controllable costs) and then again at Time 2 (after the intervention).

Hence the real payoff from determining the cost of employee behaviors lies in being able to demonstrate a financial gain from the wise application of human resource management methods.

The following five sections present both hypothetical and actual company examples of behavior costing in the areas of absenteeism, turnover, employee assistance programs, selection, and training. Our focus will be limited *only* to behavior costing methods and practical examples of each. We will not deal with alternative human resource management approaches that might be used to reduce costs in each area: for example, to reduce the costs of employee absenteeism or turnover. These have been discussed elsewhere in the book.

Costing Employee Absenteeism

In any human resource costing application, it is important first to define exactly what is being measured. From a business standpoint, *absenteeism is any failure of an employee to report for or to remain at work as scheduled, regardless of reason.* The term "as scheduled" is very significant, for this automatically excludes vacations, holidays, jury duty, and the like. It also eliminates the problem of determining whether an absence is "excusable" or not. Medically verified illness is a good example of this. From a business perspective, the employee is absent and is simply not available to perform his or her job; that absence will cost money. How much money? At General Motors, the annual tab is $1 billion.[20]

A flowchart (based on ref. 15) that shows how to estimate the total cost of employee absenteeism over any period is shown in Figure 16-2. To illustrate

FIGURE 16-2

Total estimated cost of employee absenteeism. (Source: Wayne F. Cascio, Costing Human Resources: The Financial Impact of Behavior in Organizations, 2d ed. Boston: PWS-Kent Publishing Co. © by PWS-Kent Publishing Co. Reprinted by permission of PWS-Kent Publishing Co., a division of Wadsworth, Inc.)

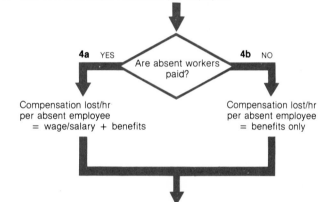

1. Compute total employee hours lost to absenteeism for the period.

2. Compute weighted average wage or salary/hr per absent employee.

3. Compute cost of employee benefits/hr per employee.

4a YES / **4b** NO

Are absent workers paid?

Compensation lost/hr per absent employee = wage/salary + benefits

Compensation lost/hr per absent employee = benefits only

5. Compute total compensation lost to absent employees [(1) × (4a) or (4b) as applicable].

6. Estimate total supervisory hours lost to employee absenteeism.

7. Compute average hourly supervisory salary + benefits.

8. Estimate total supervisory salaries lost to managing absenteeism problems [(6) × (7)].

9. Estimate all other costs incidental to absenteeism.

10. Estimate total cost of absenteeism [(5) + (8) + (9)].

11. Estimate total cost of absenteeism/employee [(10) ÷ Total no. of employees].

the computation of each cost element in Figure 16-2, let us use as an example a hypothetical 1800-employee firm called Mini-Mini-Micro Electronics; dollar figures are shown in Table 16-2. An item-by-item explanation of each of them follows.

Item 1: Total hours lost. If we assume a 2.1 percent monthly absenteeism rate (about average for manufacturing firms in 1987),[6] we can apply this figure to *total scheduled work hours*. Hours of *scheduled work time* per employee may be determined as follows:

2080 hours of work per year
−80 hours of vacation (2 weeks)
−40 hours (5 days) paid holidays

This equals 1960 hours of scheduled work time per employee × 1800 employees = 3,528,000 total scheduled work hours per year. If 2.1 percent of total scheduled work hours are lost to absenteeism, then a total of 3,528,000 × 0.021, or 74,088, hours are lost.

Item 2: Weighted average wage or salary per hour per absent employee. If a computerized system is available for employees to phone in a report of

TABLE 16-2 *Cost of employee absenteeism at Mini-Mini-Micro Electronics*

Item	Mini-Mini-Micro Electronics
1. Total hours lost to employee absenteeism for the period	74,088 hours
2. Weighted average wage or salary per hour per employee	$10.159 per hour
3. Cost of employee benefits per hour per employee	$3.556 per hour
4. Total compensation lost per hour per absent employee (a) If absent workers are paid (wage or salary plus benefits)	$13.715 per hour
(b) If absent workers are not paid (benefits only)	—
5. Total compensation lost to absent employees [total hours lost × 4(a) or 4(b), whichever applies]	$1,016,116.92
6. Total supervisory hours lost on employee absenteeism	8,820 hours
7. Average hourly supervisory wage, including benefits	$18.225 per hour
8. Total supervisory salaries lost to managing problems of absenteeism (hours lost × average hourly supervisory wage—item 6 × item 7)	$160,744.50
9. All other costs incidental to absenteeism not included in the preceding items	$50,000
10. Total estimated cost of absenteeism—summation of items 5, 8, and 9	$1,226,861.42
11. Total estimated cost of absenteeism per employee: Total estimated costs ÷ total number of employees	$681.59 per employee absence

their absence, then the exact wage or salary per hour per absent employee can be determined. If not, then the following procedure may be used:

Occupational group	Approx. percent of total absenteeism	Average hourly wage	Weighted average wage
Blue collar	0.55	$10.45	$ 5.747
Clerical	0.35	8.15	2.852
Management	0.10	15.60	1.560
Total weighted average pay per employee per hour			$10.159

Item 3: Cost of employee benefits per hour. We include the cost of benefits in our calculations because benefits consume, on average, more than a third of total compensation (see Chapter 11). Ultimately we want to be able to calculate the total compensation lost due to absenteeism. Since our primary interest is in the cost of benefits per absentee, we take the weighted average hourly wage multiplied by benefits as a percentage of base pay. (If benefits differ as a function of union-nonunion or exempt-nonexempt status, then a weighted average benefit should be computed in the same manner as was done to compute a weighted average wage.) For Mini-Mini-Micro, this figure is

$10.159 × 35% = $3.556 per hour

Item 4: Total compensation lost per hour per absent employee. This equals the weighted average hourly wage plus hourly cost of benefits (assuming that absent workers are paid). Some firms do not pay absentees: "No work, no pay." In such instances, only the cost of benefits should be included in the estimate of total compensation lost per hour per absent employee. For Mini-Mini-Micro, the compensation lost per hour for each absent employee is

$10.159 + $3.556 = $13.715

Item 5: Total compensation lost to absent employees. This is simply total hours lost multiplied by total compensation lost per hour:

74,088 hr × $13.715/hr = $1,016,116.92

Note that the first five items shown in Figure 16-2 refer to the costs associated with absentees themselves. The next three items refer to the firm's costs of *managing* employee absenteeism.

Item 6: Total supervisory hours lost in dealing with employee absenteeism. Three factors determine this lost time, which is the product of $A × B × C$, where:

A = Estimated average number of hours lost per supervisor per day managing absenteeism problems

The supervisor's time is "lost" because, instead of planning, scheduling, and troubleshooting productivity problems, he or she must devote time to non-productive activities associated with managing absenteeism problems. The actual amount of time lost can be determined by having supervisors keep diaries indicating how they spend their time or by conducting structured interviews with experienced supervisors.

B = Total number of supervisors who deal with absenteeism problems

C = Total number of working days in the period for which absentee costs are being analyzed (including all shifts and weekend work).

For Mini-Mini-Micro Electronics, the data needed for this calculation are:

Estimate of A = 30 min, or .50 hr, per day

Estimate of B = 1800 employees (10%, or 180, are supervisors, and 40% of the 180, or 72, of the supervisors deal regularly with absenteeism problems)

Estimate of C = 245 days per year

Supervisory hours lost
in dealing with   = .50 hr/day × 72 supervisors × 245 days/year
absensteeism

                         = 8820 supervisory hours lost per year

Item 7: Average hourly supervisory salary plus benefits. For those supervisors who deal regularly with absenteeism problems, assume that their average hourly salary is $13.50 plus 35 percent benefits ($4.725), or $18.225 per hour.

Item 8: Total cost of supervisory salaries lost to managing problems of absenteeism. To determine this cost, multiply the total supervisory hours lost by the total hourly supervisory salary:

     8820 hr lost × $18.225/hr = $160,744.50

Item 9: All other absenteeism-related costs not included in items 1 through 8. Assume that Mini-Mini-Micro spends $50,000 per year in absenteeism-related costs that are not associated either with absentees or with supervisors. These costs are associated with elements such as overtime premiums, wages for temporary help, machine downtime, production losses, inefficient materials usage by temporary substitute employees, and, for very large organizations, permanent labor pools to "fill in" for absent workers.

Item 10: Total cost of employee absenteeism. This is the sum of the three costs determined thus far: costs associated with absent employees (item 5) plus costs associated with the management of absenteeism problems (item 8)

plus other absenteeism-related costs (item 9). For Mini-Mini-Micro Electronics, this figure is

$$\$1,016,116.92 \ + \ \$160,744.50 \ + \ \$50,000 \ = \ \$1,226,861.42$$

Item 11: Per-employee cost of absenteeism. This is the total cost divided by 1800 employees, or $681.59.

Perhaps the first question management will ask upon seeing absenteeism cost figures is "What do they mean? Are we average, above average, or what?" Unfortunately, there are no industrywide figures on the costs of employee absenteeism. Certainly these costs will vary depending on the type of firm, the industry, and the level of employee that is absent (unskilled versus skilled or professional workers). Remember that the dollar figure just determined (we will call this the "Time 1" figure) becomes meaningful as a *baseline* from which to measure the financial gains realized as a result of a strategy to reduce absenteeism. At some later time (we will call this "Time 2"), the total cost of absenteeism should be measured again. The difference between the Time 2 figure and the Time 1 figure, minus the cost of implementing the strategy to reduce absenteeism, represents *net gain*.

Another question that often arises at this point is "Are these dollars real? Since supervisors are drawing their salaries anyway, what difference does it make if they have to manage absenteeism problems?" True, but what is the best possible gain from them for that pay? Let's compare two firms, A and B, identical in regard to all resources and costs—supervisors get paid the same, work the same hours, manage the same size staff, and produce the same kind of product. *But* absenteeism in A is very low, and in B it is very high. The paymasters' records show the same pay to supervisors, but the accountants show higher profits in A than in B. Why? Because the supervisors in firm A spend less time managing absenteeism problems. They are more productive because they devote their energies to planning, scheduling, and troubleshooting. Instead of putting in a 10- or 12-hour day (that the supervisors in firm B consider "normal"), they wrap things up after only 8 hours. In short, reducing the hours that supervisors must spend managing absenteeism problems has two advantages: (1) It allows supervisors to maximize their productivity, and (2) it reduces the stress and wear and tear associated with repeated 10- to 12-hour days, which in turn enhances the quality of work life of supervisors.

Costing Employee Turnover

Turnover may be defined as *any permanent departure beyond organizational boundaries*[17]—a broad and admittedly ponderous definition. Not included as turnover within this definition, therefore, are transfers within an organization

FIGURE 16-3

Types of employee turnover.

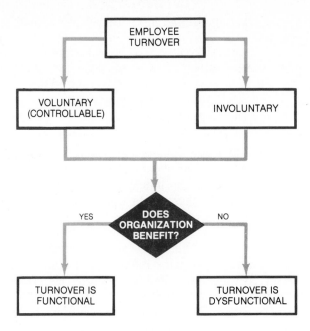

and temporary layoffs. The rate of turnover in percent over any period can be calculated by the formula:

$$\frac{\text{Number of turnover incidents per period}}{\text{Average workforce size}} \times 100\%$$

Nationwide in 1987, for example, monthly turnover rates averaged about 1 percent, or 12 percent annually.[6] However, this figure most likely represents both controllable turnover (controllable by the organization) and uncontrollable turnover. Controllable turnover is "voluntary" by the employee, while uncontrollable turnover is "involuntary" (e.g., retirement, death, or spouse transfer). Furthermore, turnover may be *functional*, where the employee's departure produces a benefit for the organization, or *dysfunctional*, where the departing employee is someone the organization would like to retain. These ideas are illustrated in Figure 16-3.

In costing employee turnover, first we determine the total cost of all turnover, and then we estimate the percentage of that amount representing controllable, dysfunctional turnover—resignations which represent a net loss to the firm and which the firm could have prevented. Thus, if total turnover costs $1 million, and 50 percent is controllable and dysfunctional, then $500,000 is our Time 1 baseline measure. To demonstrate the net financial gain associated with the strategy adopted prior to Time 2, the total gain at Time 2, say $700,000, minus the cost of implementing the strategy to reduce turnover, say $50,000, must be compared to the cost of turnover at Time 1 ($500,000). In this example, the net gain to the firm is $150,000. Now let's see how the total cost figure is derived.

Computational formulas

There are three components to the basic turnover costing model: separation costs, replacement costs, and training costs. Formulas used to estimate each component are shown in Figures 16-4 through 16-6.

Separation costs Figure 16-4 indicates that there are four cost elements in separation costs. These are:

Exit interview, including the cost of the interviewer's time and the cost of the terminating employee's time.

Administative functions related to termination: for example, removal of the employee from payroll, termination of benefits, and turn-in of company equipment.

‹ **FIGURE 16-4**

Measuring separation costs.

Exit interview (S_1)

$$\begin{pmatrix} \text{Cost of} \\ \text{interviewer's} \\ \text{time} \end{pmatrix} = \begin{pmatrix} \text{time required} \\ \text{prior to} \\ \text{interview} \end{pmatrix} + \begin{pmatrix} \text{time required} \\ \text{for interview} \end{pmatrix} \times \begin{pmatrix} \text{interviewer's} \\ \text{pay rate} \\ \text{during period} \end{pmatrix} \times \begin{pmatrix} \text{number of} \\ \text{turnovers} \\ \text{during period} \end{pmatrix}$$

$$\begin{pmatrix} \text{Cost of} \\ \text{terminating} \\ \text{employee's time} \end{pmatrix} = \begin{pmatrix} \text{time required} \\ \text{for the} \\ \text{interview} \end{pmatrix} \times \begin{pmatrix} \text{weighted average} \\ \text{pay rate for} \\ \text{terminated employees} \end{pmatrix} \times \begin{pmatrix} \text{number of} \\ \text{turnovers} \\ \text{during period} \end{pmatrix}$$

Administrative functions related to termination (S_2)

$$S_2 = \begin{pmatrix} \text{time required by personnel} \\ \text{department for administrative} \\ \text{functions related to termination} \end{pmatrix} \times \begin{pmatrix} \text{average personnel} \\ \text{department employee's} \\ \text{pay rate} \end{pmatrix} \times \begin{pmatrix} \text{number of turnovers} \\ \text{during period} \end{pmatrix}$$

Separation pay (S_3)

$$S_3 = \begin{pmatrix} \text{amount of separation pay} \\ \text{per employee terminated} \end{pmatrix} \times \text{number of turnovers}$$

Unemployment tax (S_4)

$$S_4 = \begin{pmatrix} \text{unemployment} \\ \text{tax rate} \end{pmatrix} - \begin{pmatrix} \text{base} \\ \text{rate} \end{pmatrix} \times \left[\begin{pmatrix} \$7{,}000 \times \begin{pmatrix} \text{number of} \\ \text{employees earning} \\ \text{at least } \$7{,}000 \end{pmatrix} \end{pmatrix} + \begin{pmatrix} \text{weighted average} \\ \text{earnings if} \\ \text{less than } \$7{,}000 \end{pmatrix} \begin{pmatrix} \text{number of} \\ \text{employees earning} \\ \text{less than } \$7{,}000 \end{pmatrix} \right]$$

$$+ \begin{pmatrix} \text{unemployment} \\ \text{tax rate} \end{pmatrix} \times \begin{pmatrix} \$7{,}000 \text{ or weighted} \\ \text{average earnings} \\ \text{if less than } \$7{,}000 \end{pmatrix} \times \begin{pmatrix} \text{number of} \\ \text{turnovers} \\ \text{during period} \end{pmatrix}$$

Separation pay, if applicable.

Increased unemployment tax. Such an increase may come from either or both of two sources. First, in states that base unemployment tax rates on each company's turnover rate, high turnover will lead to a higher unemployment tax rate. Suppose a company with a 10 percent annual turnover rate was paying unemployment tax at a rate of 3 percent on the first $7000 of each employee's wages in 1987. But in 1988, because its turnover rate jumped to 15 percent, the company's unemployment tax rate may increase to 3.5 percent. Second, replacements for those who leave will result in extra unemployment tax being paid. Thus a 500-employee firm with no turnover during the year will pay the tax on the first $7000 (or whatever the state maximum is) of each employee's wages. The same firm with a 20 percent annual turnover rate will pay the tax on the first $7000 of the wages of 600 employees.

The sum of these four cost elements represents the total separation costs for the firm.

Replacement costs   The eight cost elements associated with replacing employees who leave are shown in Figure 16-5. These include:

Communicating job availability

Preemployment administrative functions: for example, accepting applications and checking references

Entrance interview, or perhaps multiple interviews

Testing and/or other types of assessment procedures

Staff meetings, if applicable, to determine if replacements are needed, to recheck job analyses and job specifications, to pool information on candidates, and to reach final hiring decisions

Travel and moving expenses: travel for all applicants and travel plus moving expenses for all new hires

Postemployment acquisition and dissemination of information: for example, all the activities associated with in-processing new employees

Medical examinations, if applicable, either performed in-house or contracted out

The sum of these eight cost elements represents the total cost of replacing those who leave.

Training costs   This third component of turnover costs is shown in Figure 16-6. Two points should be noted: First, if there is a formal orientation program, the per-person costs associated with replacements for those who left should be included in the first cost element, *informational literature*. This cost should reflect the per-person, amortized cost of developing the literature, not just its

$$\text{Communicating job availability } (R_1) = \left[\begin{array}{l} \text{advertising and} \\ \text{employment agency} \\ \text{fees per termination} \end{array} + \left(\begin{array}{l} \text{time required for} \\ \text{communicating} \\ \text{job availability} \end{array} \times \begin{array}{l} \text{personnel department} \\ \text{employee's} \\ \text{pay rate} \end{array} \right) \right] \times \begin{array}{l} \text{number of} \\ \text{turnovers replaced} \\ \text{during period} \end{array}$$

$$\text{Preemployment administrative functions } (R_2) = \begin{array}{l} \text{time required by} \\ \text{personnel department} \\ \text{for preemployment} \\ \text{administrative functions} \end{array} \times \begin{array}{l} \text{average} \\ \text{personnel department} \\ \text{employee's pay rate} \end{array} \times \begin{array}{l} \text{number of} \\ \text{applicants} \\ \text{during period} \end{array}$$

$$\text{Entrance interview } (R_3) = \begin{array}{l} \text{time required} \\ \text{for interview} \end{array} \times \begin{array}{l} \text{interviewer's} \\ \text{rate} \end{array} \times \begin{array}{l} \text{number of} \\ \text{interviews during period} \end{array}$$

$$\text{Testing } (R_4) = \left(\begin{array}{l} \text{cost of materials} \\ \text{per person} \end{array} + \begin{array}{l} \text{cost of scoring} \\ \text{per person} \end{array} \right) \times \begin{array}{l} \text{number of tests} \\ \text{given during period} \end{array}$$

$$\text{Staff meeting } (R_5) = \begin{array}{l} \text{time required} \\ \text{for meeting} \end{array} \times \left(\begin{array}{l} \text{personnel department} \\ \text{employee's} \\ \text{pay rate} \end{array} + \begin{array}{l} \text{department} \\ \text{representatives'} \\ \text{pay rate} \end{array} \right) \times \begin{array}{l} \text{number of} \\ \text{meetings} \\ \text{during period} \end{array}$$

$$\text{Travel/moving expenses } (R_6) = \left(\begin{array}{l} \text{average} \\ \text{travel cost} \\ \text{per applicant} \end{array} \times \begin{array}{l} \text{number of} \\ \text{applicants} \end{array} \right) + \left(\begin{array}{l} \text{average} \\ \text{moving cost} \\ \text{per new hire} \end{array} \times \begin{array}{l} \text{number of} \\ \text{new hires} \end{array} \right)$$

$$\text{Postemployment acquisition and dissemination of information } (R_7) = \begin{array}{l} \text{time required for} \\ \text{acquiring and} \\ \text{disseminating} \\ \text{information} \end{array} \times \begin{array}{l} \text{average} \\ \text{personnel department} \\ \text{employee's} \\ \text{pay rate} \end{array} \times \begin{array}{l} \text{number of} \\ \text{turnovers replaced} \\ \text{during period} \end{array}$$

$$\text{In-house medical examinations } (R_8) = \left[\left(\begin{array}{l} \text{time} \\ \text{required for} \\ \text{examination} \end{array} \times \begin{array}{l} \text{examiner's} \\ \text{pay rate} \end{array} \right) + \begin{array}{l} \text{cost of} \\ \text{supplies} \\ \text{used} \end{array} \right] \times \begin{array}{l} \text{number of} \\ \text{turnovers replaced} \\ \text{during period} \end{array}$$

OR

$$\text{Contracted medical examinations } (R_9) = \begin{array}{l} \text{rate per} \\ \text{examination} \end{array} \times \begin{array}{l} \text{number of} \\ \text{turnovers replaced} \\ \text{during period} \end{array}$$

FIGURE 16-5

Measuring replacement costs.

delivery. Do not include the total cost of the orientation program unless 100 percent of the costs can be attributed to employee turnover.

Second, probably the major cost associated with employee turnover, *reduced productivity during the learning period*, has not been included along with the cost elements *instruction in a formal training program* and *instruction by employee assignment*. The reason for this is that formal work-mea-

$$\begin{matrix} \text{Informational} \\ \text{literature} \\ (T_1) \end{matrix} = \begin{matrix} \text{cost of} \\ \text{informational} \\ \text{package} \end{matrix} \times \begin{matrix} \text{number of} \\ \text{replacements} \\ \text{during period} \end{matrix}$$

$$\begin{matrix} \text{Instruction in a} \\ \text{formal training} \\ \text{program } (T_2) \end{matrix} = \left[\begin{matrix} \text{length of} \\ \text{training} \\ \text{program} \end{matrix} \times \begin{matrix} \text{average} \\ \text{pay rate} \\ \text{of trainer(s)} \end{matrix} \times \begin{matrix} \text{number of} \\ \text{programs} \\ \text{conducted} \end{matrix} \times \begin{matrix} \text{proportion of training} \\ \text{costs attributed} \\ \text{to replacements} \end{matrix} \right]$$

$$+ \left[\begin{matrix} \text{average} \\ \text{pay rate} \\ \text{per trainee} \end{matrix} \times \begin{matrix} \text{total number of} \\ \text{replacements trained} \\ \text{during period} \end{matrix} \times \begin{matrix} \text{length of} \\ \text{training} \\ \text{program} \end{matrix} \right]$$

$$\begin{matrix} \text{Instruction by} \\ \text{employee assignment} \\ (T_3) \end{matrix} = \begin{matrix} \text{number of} \\ \text{hours required} \\ \text{for instruction} \end{matrix} \times \left[\left(\begin{matrix} \text{average pay rate} \\ \text{of experienced} \\ \text{employee} \end{matrix} \times \begin{matrix} \text{proportional reduction} \\ \text{in productivity} \\ \text{due to training} \end{matrix} \right) + \left(\begin{matrix} \text{new} \\ \text{employee's} \\ \text{pay rate} \end{matrix} \times \begin{matrix} \text{number of} \\ \text{instructions} \\ \text{during period} \end{matrix} \right) \right]$$

FIGURE 16-6

Measuring orientation and training costs.

surement programs are not often found in employment situations. Thus it is not possible to calculate accurately the dollar value of the loss in productivity during the learning period. If such a program does exist, then by all means include this cost. For example, a major brokerage firm did a formal work-measurement study of this problem and reported the results shown in Table 16-3.

The bottom line in all of this is that we want to be conservative in our training cost figures so that we can defend every number we generate. As before, the sum of the cost elements represents the total cost of orientation and training.

TABLE 16-3 *Productivity loss over each third of the learning period for four job classifications*

Classification	Weeks in learning period	Productivity loss during learning		
		1	2	3
Management and partners	24	75%	40%	15%
Professionals and technicians	16	70	40	15
Office and clerical	10	60	40	15
Broker trainees	104	85	75	50

Note: The learning period for the average broker trainee is 2 years, although the cost to the firm is generally incurred only in the first year. It is not until the end of the second year that the average broker trainee is fully productive.

The sum of the three component costs—separation, replacement, and training—represents the total cost of employee turnover for the period in question. Other factors could also be included in our tally, such as the uncompensated performance differential between leavers and their replacements, but that is beyond the scope of this book. For more on this, see ref. 9. Now for a practical example.

PRACTICAL EXAMPLE

Costing turnover at Justus Security

Justus Security is a 500-employee firm with a 30 percent annual turnover rate (controllable + uncontrollable). Management decides that this rate is too high. As a first step toward dealing with the problem, management decides to compute the annual cost to the company of this 30 percent turnover. Human resources staff members collect the following data. Explanatory notes are contained within braces.

Weighted average pay rate per terminated employee

Occupational group	Percent of total turnover (in decimal form)	Average hourly wage	Weighted average hourly wage
Security guards	0.55	$14.40	$ 7.92
Clericals	0.25	13.80	3.45
Managers	0.20	25.50	5.10
Total			$16.47

Separation costs

Exit interview (S_1)

Cost of interviewer's time = (15 min + 45 min) × $17/hr per turnover × 150 turnovers
= $2550

{15-min preparation, 45-min interview, $17 human resource specialist's hourly pay rate, 150 turnovers}

Cost of terminating employees' time = (45 min, or .75 hr) × $16.47 average hourly pay rate × 150 turnovers
= $1853

Administrative functions related to terminations (S_2)

S_2 = (90 min, or 1.5 hr) × $17/hr × 150 turnovers
= $3825

Separation pay (S_3)

$$S_3 = (80 \text{ hr} \times \$16.47/\text{hr}) \times (150 \times .50)$$
$$= \$98,820$$

{All employees with more than 6 months' service get 2 weeks' severance pay, and 50 percent of those who leave qualify.}

Unemployment tax (S_4)

$$S_4 = \left(\begin{array}{c} 0.003 \text{ increase} \\ \text{in tax rate} \end{array}\right) \times \left[\begin{array}{c} \$7000 \\ \text{wages taxed} \end{array} \times \left(\begin{array}{c} 500 \text{ regular} \\ \text{employees} \end{array} + \begin{array}{c} 150 \\ \text{turnovers} \end{array}\right)\right]$$

$$= \begin{array}{c} \$13,650 \\ \text{penalty} \end{array} + \left[\left(\begin{array}{c} 0.03 \text{ regular} \\ \text{tax rate} \end{array}\right) \times \left(\$7000 \times 150\right)\right]$$

$$= \$13,650 \text{ penalty} + \$31,500 \text{ additional cost} = \$45,150$$

{Due to its high turnover, Justus must pay 0.003 more in unemployment tax both for the 150 replacements and for the 500 regular workers. It also must pay regular unemployment tax of 0.03 on the first $7000 of wages for the 150 additional workers it hired during the year.}

Total separation costs

$$S_1 + S_2 + S_3 + S_4$$
$$= \$2550 + \$1853 + \$3825 + \$98,820 + \$45,150$$
$$= \$152,198$$

Replacement costs

Communicating job availability (R_1)

$$R_1 =$$

$$\left[\begin{array}{c} \$200 \\ \text{advertisements} \end{array} + \left(5 \text{ hr} \times \begin{array}{c} \$17/\text{hr personnel} \\ \text{representative's pay} \end{array}\right)\right]$$
$$\times 150 \text{ turnovers} = \$42,750$$

{For each employee who leaves, Justus spends $200 in ads, and a personnel representative spends an average of 5 more hours communicating job availability.}

Preemployment administrative functions (R_2)

$$R_2 = (2 \text{ hr per turnover}) \times (\$17/\text{hr}) \times 150 \text{ turnovers}$$
$$= \$5100$$

Entrance interview (R_3)

$$R_3 = (1 \text{ hr}) \times (\$17/\text{hr}) \times (4 \text{ applicants} \times 150 \text{ jobs to fill})$$
$$= \$10,200$$

{Justus hires, on average, one of every four applicants who apply.}

Testing (R_4)

$$R_4 = (\$3 + \$7) \times 600 \text{ applicants}$$
$$= \$6000$$

{Per-applicant cost of testing materials = \$3; per-applicant cost of scoring = \$7; tests are administered to 4 × 150, or 600, applicants.}

Staff meeting (R_5)

$$R_5 = (90 \text{ min, or } 1.5 \text{ hr}) \times (\$17/\text{hr} + \$25.50/\text{hr}) \times 15 \text{ meetings}$$
$$= \$956.25$$

{Departmental representative's pay rate averages \$25.50 per hour, and 15 meetings are held annually.}

Travel and/or moving expenses (R_6)

$$R_6 = (\$50 \text{ travel cost} \times 600 \text{ applicants})$$
$$+ (\$2000 \text{ moving cost} \times 150 \text{ replacements hired})$$
$$= \$330,000$$

{Average per-applicant travel cost is \$50, and average per-hire moving cost is \$2000.}

Postemployment acquisition and dissemination of information (R_7)

$$R_7 = (75 \text{ min, or } 1.25 \text{ hr}) \times (\$17 \text{ hr}) \times (150 \text{ replacements hired})$$
$$= \$3187.50$$

Contracted medical examinations (R_9)

$$R_9 = \$75 \times 150 = \$11,250$$

Total replacement costs

$$R_1 + R_2 + R_3 + R_4 + R_5 + R_6 + R_7 + R_9$$

$$= \$42{,}750 + \$5100 + \$10{,}200 + \$6000$$
$$+ \$956.25 + \$330{,}000 + \$3187.50 + \$11{,}250$$
$$= \$409{,}443.75$$

Training costs

Informational literature (T_1)

$$T_1 = \$12/\text{unit} \times 150 \text{ units} = \$1800$$

Instruction in a formal training program (T_2)

$$T_2 = (80 \text{ hr} \times \$25/\text{hr} \times 10 \text{ programs} \times 0.60 \text{ of expenses to train}$$
$$\text{replacements}) + (\$10/\text{hr} \times 150 \text{ replacements}$$
$$\times 80 \text{ hr of training})$$
$$= \$12{,}000 + \$120{,}000 = \$132{,}000$$

{Training lasts ten 8-hour days, trainers earn $25 per hour, the program is run 10 times per year, 60 percent of training costs can be attributed to those who leave, and trainees earn $10 per hour.}

Instruction by employee assignment (T_3)

$$T_3 = (14 \text{ days} \times 8 \text{ hr/day, or } 112 \text{ hr})$$
$$\times [(\$25/\text{hr} \times 0.50 \text{ loss in productivity}) +$$
$$(\$10/\text{hr} \times 150 \text{ replacements})]$$
$$= \$169{,}400$$

{There are 14 days of on-the-job training, and we assume that the trainer's own productivity decreases 50 percent while he or she is training others.}

Total training costs

$$T_1 + T_2 + T_3 = \$1800 + \$132{,}000 + \$169{,}400$$
$$= \$303{,}200$$

Total turnover costs

Separation costs + replacement costs + training costs
$$= \$152,198 + \$409,444 + \$303,200$$
$$= \$864,842 \text{ or } \$5,765.61 \text{ for each}$$
employee who left Justus Security

Remember, *the purpose of measuring turnover costs is to improve management decision making.* Once turnover figures are known, managers have a sound basis for choosing between current turnover costs and instituting some type of turnover reduction program (e.g., job enrichment, realistic job previews). If we assume that 50 percent of the turnover is controllable (and dysfunctional for the organization), then the total cost to Justus Security is still over $430,000. The cost per terminating employee, however, remains at $5765.61. If controllable turnover could be reduced by only 10 percent, net gains to the company will still be over $43,000 *per year.* How does the cost per terminated employee at Justus compare to figures in other industries? At a major brokerage firm the cost per terminating employee was almost $7000,[8] and the cost per terminating store manager at a large retail department store chain was $10,000.[30] Obviously, there are opportunities in this area for enterprising managers to make significant bottom-line contributions to their organizations.

The Costs and Benefits of an Employee Assistance Program

As noted in Chapter 15, AT&T examined the impact of its EAP for 110 employees 22 months pre- and postinvolvement.[12] Unfortunately, many of the variables associated with cost savings either are difficult to measure in terms of dollars saved (e.g., the impact on productivity and morale) or are not accessible to researchers. At AT&T, savings formulas could not be developed in all areas where behavioral changes were reported. To be conservative, *estimates were not used.* In areas where savings formulas could be developed, cost figures on *actual* company expenditures were used. This process resulted in a cost analysis of five variables: on-the-job accidents, incidental absences (1 to 7 days), disability absences, employee visits to the medical department, and "anticipated" losses that did not occur. The study did not include the cost of creating the EAP or training the supervisors and staff personnel. Despite the fact that the study is old, it remains one of the best-controlled evaluations to date. Dollar costs have been updated to account for inflation (using the average annual change in the Consumer Price Index from 1978 to 1987). There is, of course, no guarantee that the figures below reflect *actual* cost savings in 1988.

On-the-job accidents

The only accidents considered were those which involved lost work time. The cost per accident, $4698, is the actual company cost for expenses, including administrative costs, medical expenses, replacement costs, and disability expenses under law. Lost-productivity costs and lost-time costs are not included in this figure. As the following data indicate, the reduction in the cost of accidents for EAP clients following their involvement in the program was $98,658.

	No. of accidents	Cost per accident	Total cost	Difference
Before EAP	26	$4698	$122,148	
After EAP	5	$4698	23,490	$98,658

Incidental absences

The data used in this analysis were supplied by the corporate controller's department. The costs represent the average daily amount charged to departments based on gender and on management or nonmanagement status. The costs were then multiplied by the number of days absent for each category. The actual savings to AT&T, $37,981, is the difference between the cost of pre- and post-EAP incidental absenteeism for the employees studied.

	Pre-EAP			Post-EAP		
Category	Days	Average salary	Cost	Days	Average salary	Cost
Male management	101	$219	$22,119	35	$219	$ 7,665
Male nonmanagement	209	79	16,511	31	79	2,449
Female management	50	141	7,050	5	141	705
Female nonmanagement	61	78	4,758	21	78	1,638
Totals	421		$50,438	92		$12,457

Difference in cost pre- and post-EAP: $50,438 − $12,457 = $37,981.

Disability absence

Disability absences do not include incidental absence days. The average daily amount charged to each department for disability absence was $129. This figure does not include hospital, medical, or surgical costs; replacement costs; or lost productivity resulting from absence.

	Pre-EAP	Post-EAP
Total days	1531	192
Cost @ $129 per day:	$197,499	$24,768
Difference pre- and post-EAP: $172,731		

Savings of $173,000 were realized as a result of a reduction in disability absence from before to after program participation. However, the cost for disability days incurred as a result of EAP hospitalizations (980 days × $129 per day, or $126,420) must also be taken into account. Subtracting out these costs ($173,000 − $126,020) still yields a net savings of $47,000 in disability absences.

Visits to the medical department

Costs in this category were based on all recorded visits as indicated by the medical file of each client. In 1988 dollars, it cost $85, on average, per visit to the medical department. This figure included only the actual costs of operating the medical department and not the cost of time away from the job. As the figures below indicate, $32,215 was saved following the EAP as a result of fewer visits to the medical department.

	Number of visits	Average cost per visit	Total cost	Cost savings
Pre-EAP	818	$85	$69,530	
Post-EAP	439	85	37,315	$32,215

Anticipated losses

There were 44 employees referred to the EAP who were in danger of losing their jobs. In all cases, progressive discipline leading toward dismissal had been initiated by management. Of the 44 referred to the EAP, four employees were actually dismissed. The other 40 were retained, and their job performance improved significantly. In fact, 41 percent of them were promoted during the postinvestigation period.

The human resources department reported that the average replacement cost to the company for each employee lost was $3300. This figure, multiplied by the 40 employees retained, yielded a savings of $132,000. These are not really out-of-pocket costs to the firm. Nevertheless, they represent savings because they are costs not incurred—given the success of the EAP with respect to the retention of the 40 employees who were not dismissed because their performance improved.

In addition, the training organization reported average training costs of $466 for 2 days of training per year for each nonmanagement employee, and $700 for 3 days of training per year for each management employee. The 40 employees retained represented a cumulative total of 113 years of service for nonmanagement employees and 421 years of service for management employees. Savings as a result of training investments were $347,358. These calculations are shown as follows:

$$\begin{array}{l} \text{44 Potentially lost employees} \\ \text{referred to EAP} \end{array} - \text{4 actually lost} = \begin{array}{l} \text{40 remaining} \\ \text{on payroll} \end{array}$$

Average company investment in employment and training

$3300 replacement cost $\times$ 40 = $132,000

$466/year training cost
per nonmanagement employee $\times$ 113 total years of service = $52,658

$700/year training cost
per management employee $\times$ 421 total years of service = $294,700

Total savings = $479,358

This amount does not include administrative time, lost productivity, or reduced morale.

Summary of savings

The costs and benefits associated with improved performance on five key variables indicated a substantial financial gain associated with EAP treatment of employee medical and/or behavioral problems. Net savings are shown below.

On-the-job accidents	$ 99,000
Incidental absence	38,000
Disability absence	47,000
Visits to medical	32,000
Anticipated losses	480,000
Total savings	$696,000

Clearly the program was worth the effort financially as well as socially. Costing out net benefits associated with an EAP also illustrates the point that the economic consequences of employee behavior can be determined for any human resource management activity.

The Costs and Benefits of Employee Selection Programs

Of all the aspects of human resource management, the opportunity for the greatest cost-benefit payoff will come from hiring the best available candidates and not hiring less than the best available candidates. By using accurate (that is, valid) predictors of actual job performance, a firm can have meaningful

TABLE 16-4 *Factors that determine dollar payoffs from selection procedures*

Factor	Dimension	Technical name
1. Total gain in dollars over random selection	Dollars	Utility (ΔU)
2. How many people are hired	Number of employees	Number of selectees (N_s)
3. How accurately the procedure(s) forecast which applicants will be the most productive employees	Correlation coefficient (varies from -1 to $+1$)	Validity (r_{xy})
4. How much individual applicants differ in productivity (that is, the variability in job performance in dollars)	Dollars per year	Standard deviation of job performance (SD_y)
5. The percentage of applicants selected	Percent in decimal form	Selection ratio (SR)
6. The average score on the predictor(s) achieved by selectees	A scale from -3 to $+3$	$\bar{Z}_x$
7. The cost of the selection procedure(s)	Dollars	C

measures of candidates who will perform well as employees and candidates who are unlikely to perform well. Further, candidates who are predicted to be "high-caliber" employees and are hired will derive more from a training program.

Benefits also accrue to the candidates selected as a result of accurate matching of their abilities and interests with job requirements. Hence valid employee selection programs enhance the quality of their work lives. Placing a skilled electronics worker into an unskilled production job is just one example of such a mismatch. We do no favors to any applicant by mismatching his or her individual capabilities and interests with job requirements.

Unfortunately, the dollar payoffs associated with valid selection programs are unknown in many firms because the firms simply do not know how to assess them. This issue was discussed briefly in Chapter 6; a fuller treatment now follows. Let us begin by reviewing the factors that determine the dollar gain in productivity associated with any selection procedure, as shown in Table 16-4.

The net payoff (utility), in dollars, expected to result from the use of any selection procedure(s) can be determined from the following formula:

$$\Delta U = (2) \times (3) \times (4) \times (6) - [(2) \times (7)/(5)]$$

In words, the formula is:

$$\begin{matrix} \text{Dollar} \\ \text{gain in} \\ \text{productivity} \end{matrix} = \begin{matrix} \text{number} \\ \text{of} \\ \text{selectees} \end{matrix} \times \begin{matrix} \text{validity of} \\ \text{the selection} \\ \text{procedure} \end{matrix} \times \begin{matrix} \text{variability in} \\ \text{job performance} \\ \text{in dollars per year} \end{matrix} \times \begin{matrix} \text{average score} \\ \text{of selectees on} \\ \text{the selection} \\ \text{procedure} \end{matrix}$$

$$- \left(\begin{matrix} \text{number of} \\ \text{selectees} \end{matrix} \times \begin{matrix} \text{cost to fill} \\ \text{one vacancy} \end{matrix} \right)$$

In technical notation, the formula is:

$$\Delta U = N_s r_{xy} \text{SD}_y \overline{Z}_x - N_s \frac{C}{\text{SR}} \tag{16-1}$$

This general utility formula has been around for almost 40 years,[5] and although its derivation is straightforward (see ref. 9), it is too lengthy to illustrate here. Perhaps the major reason that the formula has not been used widely is the difficulty with estimating SD_y, for until the late 1970s it was thought that detailed cost accounting procedures were necessary to do this. Now, however, we know that simpler, faster, behavioral estimation methods work just as well, if not better.[9, 13, 22] As a result of lots of personnel research, we now know that SD_y is roughly 40 percent of annual salary.[14] Let's consider the role that each term in the general utility formula plays in determining financial gain.

The number of people selected (N_s)

The larger the number of new hires, the larger the *total* financial gain to the firm, all other things being equal. However, to focus strictly on total financial gain to the firm can be misleading. The gain per selectee is the important consideration, especially in a small business. To determine the gain per selectee, divide the total gain resulting from Equation 16-1 by the number of selectees. Thus if the total gain is $1,000,000 and 100 candidates are selected, then the gain per selectee is $1,000,000 divided by 100, or $10,000.

Validity of the selection procedure(s) (r_{xy})

Football, basketball, or cigar? As Figure 16-7a suggests, the relationship (correlation or validity r_{xy}) between the selection procedure(s) and dollar-valued job performance may vary from zero (a basketball), in which case knowledge of how the applicant did on the predictor(s) tells us nothing about how well he or she will do on the job, to 1.0 (a perfect relationship). When the correlation is 1.0, knowledge of predictor performance tells us *without error* how well each applicant will do in terms of actual job performance. In practice, correlations of 1.0 do not exist.

When a moderately strong relationship (e.g., .30) is scatterplotted, it looks like a football. When a strong relationship (e.g., .70) is scatterplotted, it looks like a cigar. So, the fatter the football, the weaker the predictor–job performance relationship; the skinnier the football, the stronger the relationship.

In practice, our objective is to search for cigar-shaped predictor–job performance relationships because, other things being equal, the higher the validity, the higher the payoff (utility) to the firm.

FIGURE 16-7

Three parameters that affect utility: (a) Validity; (b) the selection ratio, or SR; and (c) the standard deviation of job performance in dollars, or SD_y.

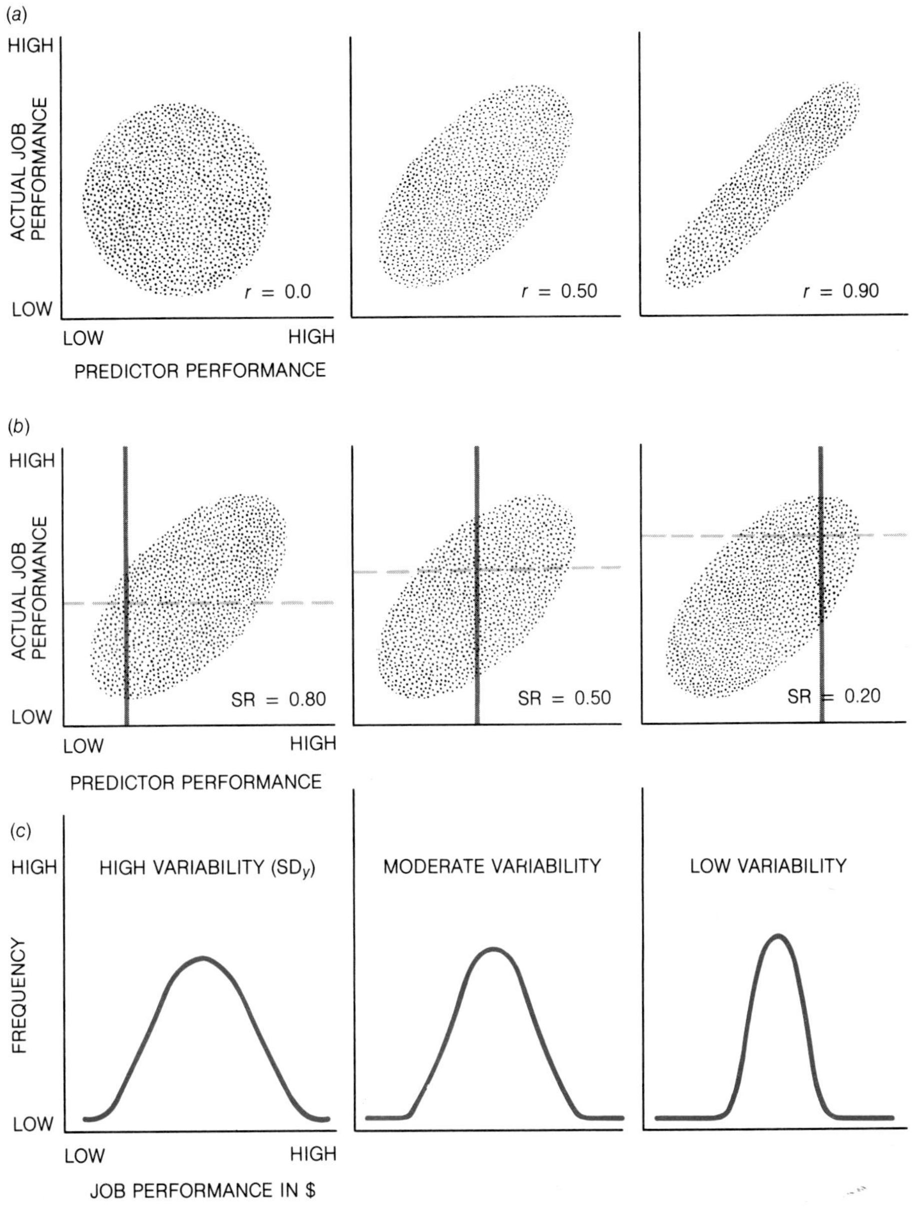

(a)

ACTUAL JOB PERFORMANCE — HIGH / LOW

PREDICTOR PERFORMANCE — LOW / HIGH

r = 0.0   r = 0.50   r = 0.90

(b)

ACTUAL JOB PERFORMANCE — HIGH / LOW

PREDICTOR PERFORMANCE — LOW / HIGH

SR = 0.80   SR = 0.50   SR = 0.20

(c)

FREQUENCY — HIGH / LOW

HIGH VARIABILITY (SD_y)   MODERATE VARIABILITY   LOW VARIABILITY

JOB PERFORMANCE IN $ — LOW / HIGH

The selection ratio (SR), or percentage of applicants hired

An organization that has a selection ratio (SR) approaching 1.0 is selecting all candidates who apply—not a very favorable situation. Of course, the converse is an SR approaching zero, which means that the firm is selecting very few applicants, or, in other words, it is able to be quite selective. This is a very favorable situation for the firm. As Figure 16-7*b* illustrates, the SR can have a wide-ranging effect on a predictor with a given validity. Note the dashed horizontal line in each scatterplot of Figure 16-7*b*. It represents the average level of job performance of the candidates selected. Note how the average level of job performance increases as the SR decreases. Even predictors with low validity can be useful if the SR is also low and the organization needs to choose only the "cream of the crop." However, if the SR is high and therefore many applicants must be selected, then a highly valid predictor is necessary in order to choose the best applicants.

The variability of job performance in dollars per year (SD$_y$)

This term is a critical component of the general utility equation. To appreciate this, consider Figure 16-7*c*. If the variability in expected productivity among job applicants is very small (as in the graph on the right, where all are predicted to be about equally productive), then it really does not matter who we select. On the other hand, when the variability in expected productivity among applicants is large, as in the graph on the left of Figure 16-7*c*, that is precisely the situation in which valid predictors can make an important, practical difference. The more valid the predictor(s), as demonstrated through prior research, the less likely it is that an applicant of expected low performance will get through the selection process. A key consideration, then, is "How much will it cost us if we make a mistake by selecting the wrong person?" The larger the cost of such a downside risk, the greater the need for highly valid predictors.

The average predictor score of those hired ($\overline{Z}_x$)

This score, expressed in Z-score or standard-score units (where the Z score for any applicant equals the applicant's predictor score minus the average predictor score of all applicants divided by the SD of applicants' predictor scores), varies from about $+3.0$ to -3.0. The average predictor score of those hired ($\overline{Z}_x$) depends on how selective the organization is—that is, the more selective, the higher the average score.*

To summarize the presentation thus far: Validity, the variability of job performance in dollars, and the average predictor score of those hired combine to determine the *gross* dollar payoff from the use of some selection procedure. The payoff will be the greatest when the validity is high, few applicants are selected, and the variability in job performance is large. To determine the *net* dollar payoff, however, we need to subtract out the total cost of the selection procedure(s) used.

---

*Not surprisingly, $\overline{Z}_x$ is related to the SR. Thus, if applicants' predictor scores are distributed as a bell-shaped curve, the more selective the organization is in choosing candidates, that is, the lower the selection ratio, the higher will be the average predictor score of those who are selected.

The per-person cost of the selection procedure(s) (C)

The cost of selection can vary from about $20 per applicant (e.g., the cost of purchasing, administering, and scoring a paper-and-pencil test of clerical aptitude) to several thousand dollars per applicant (e.g., high-level management assessment). While such costs are not insignificant, they are less important considerations than the downside cost of a mistake in selection. Notice in the right-hand term of the general utility equation that the per-person cost of administering the selection procedure, C, is divided by the percentage of applicants selected, SR. We do this to include the actual cost of filling one vacancy. Thus, if C = $25 and SR = .25 (1 in 4 applicants is selected), the cost to fill one vacancy is $100. This figure is then multiplied by N_s to determine the total cost of the selection procedure. When this total cost is subtracted from the gross dollar gain (the left-hand side of the general utility equation), we are left with the net dollar gain in productivity, ΔU, per year over *random* selection. "But no organization selects people for jobs randomly," you argue. OK, that means current selection procedures must have a validity greater than zero. It's easy to modify the general utility equation to reflect this:

$$\Delta U = N_s(r_1 - r_2)(\text{SD}_y)(\overline{Z}_x) - N_s \frac{C_1 - C_2}{\text{SR}} \tag{16-2}$$

where all terms are as defined earlier, except that r_1 = validity of the new procedure, r_2 = validity of the old procedure, C_1 = cost of the new procedure, and C_2 = cost of the old procedure. Now let's consider an actual company effort to cost out the value of its selection system.

COMPANY EXAMPLE

The dollar value of JEPS at Life of Georgia

The Life Office Management Association undertook a research project to determine the dollar value in improved worker productivity obtained from a new test (JEPS) to select claims approvers.[16] From actual work-measurement records, the standard deviation of claims processed per year (SD_y) was found to be 1679.29 claims processed at a cost of $4.30 per claim. Using Equation 16-2, the expanded version of the general utility formula, Life of Georgia determined the following values (where all dollar amounts are expressed in terms of 1988 dollars):

N_s = 10 claims approvers hired in Year 1, and 10 hired in Year 2
r_1 = validity of the new test, .36
r_2 = validity of the old procedure (interviewer decision), .14
SD_y = 1679.29 × $4.30 = $7220.95 per year
$\overline{Z}_x$ = 1.428 in Year 1 (SR = .19), and 1.918 in Year 2 (SR = .07)
$N_s \dfrac{C_1 - C_2}{\text{SR}}$ = $1437.26

Substituting these values into Equation 16-2, Life of Georgia determined the *yearly* dollar value of improved worker productivity obtained by selecting 10 claims approvers by each of three methods: (1) using interviewer decisions only, (2) using the new test only, and (3) using a combination of the two procedures. Here are the results:

Yearly dollar value in improved worker productivity

Year	Interviewer decision only	New test only	Interviewer decision and new test
1	$15,077	$22,190	$37,267
2	19,378	29,014	48,392

Note that in this example the combined effects of the interview and test are additive. This will occur to the extent that there is a 0.0 correlation between the two predictors. The greater the correlation, the more redundant the information that is being collected, and therefore the combined payoff will be less than the sum of the two individual payoffs.

The differences in the figures for years 1 and 2 are due to the fact that the company selected 19 percent of the applicants for jobs as claims approvers in Year 1, but only 7 percent in Year 2. These are substantial gains in productivity that will continue to accrue to the company over the entire tenure of these claims approvers. The total payoff of the new test over, say, a 10-year period can also be determined.[4] To do so, however, we must discount future dollars to present dollars, and we must take taxes and variable costs into account.[39] As noted at the outset of this section, the payoffs associated with the use of valid selection procedures may far exceed those associated with any other personnel activity. The technology is now available for an organization of any size to demonstrate this.

Costing the Effects of Training Activities

As noted in Chapter 7, we assess the results of training to determine whether it is worth the cost. Training valuation (meaning in financial terms) is not easy, but the technology to do it is available and well developed. A manager may have to value training in two types of situations: one in which only *indirect* measures of dollar outcomes are available, and one in which *direct* measures of dollar outcomes are available. We will consider both.

Situation 1: indirect measures available

It was noted at the beginning of this chapter that indirect measures often can be converted into estimates of dollar impact on outcomes; this is often the case with training outcomes. The formula[23] for assessing the utility of training outcomes builds directly on the general utility formula (Equation 16-1) for assessing the utility of selection programs:

$$\Delta U = T \times N \times d_t \times SD_y - (N \times C) \qquad (16\text{-}3)$$

where ΔU = dollar value of the training program

$\quad T$ = number of years duration of the training effect on performance

$\quad N$ = the number of persons trained

$\quad d_t$ = the true difference in job performance between the average trained and untrained worker in standard Z-score units (see equation 16-4)

$\quad SD_y$ = the variability (standard deviation) of job performance in dollars of the untrained group

$\quad C$ = the per-person cost of the training

Note 1. If the training is not held during working hours, then C should include only direct training costs. If the training is held during working hours, then C should include, in addition to direct costs, all costs associated with having employees away from their jobs during the training. Also, specific procedures are available that account for the effects of employee attrition in subsequent periods on the payoffs from training programs.[4, 9]

Note 2. The term d_t is called the *effect size*. We begin with the assumption that there is no difference in job performance between trained workers (those in the experimental group) and untrained workers (those in the control group). The effect size tells us (1) whether there is a difference between the two groups and, if so, (2) how large it is. The formula for effect size is:

$$d_t = \frac{\overline{X}_e - \overline{X}_c}{SD(\sqrt{r_{yy}})} \qquad (16\text{-}4)$$

where $\overline{X}_e$ = average job performance of the trained workers (those in the experimental group)

$\quad \overline{X}_c$ = average job performance of the untrained workers (those in the control group)

$\quad SD$ = dollar-valued standard deviation of the untrained group

$\quad \sqrt{r_{yy}}$ = the reliability of the job performance measures (e.g., the degree of interrater agreement, expressed as a correlation coefficient)

Now let's consider a practical example.

PRACTICAL EXAMPLE

Apogee Aerospace

Apogee, a manufacturer of electronic components for the space program, instituted a new type of training program for its quality control inspectors at plant A. The new program stresses visual aids plus a programmed troubleshooting guide. Plant B, geographically separate but equal to plant A in number of inspectors, their average

age, seniority, education, and pay ($20,000 per year, on average), serves as a control group. Six months after training, both groups are given a test. Each worker is given a standard part with a known number of defects, and, in a given amount of time, is told to inspect the part and to identify as many defects as possible. The results are as follows:

	Plant A	Plant B
Number of workers	125	125
Average number of defects identified	9.5	6.0
Standard deviation	1.85	2.5
Cost per trainee	$800.00	
Interrater agreement	0.90	

Assuming that the duration of the training effect is 3 years, what is the dollar value of improved job performance that Apogee can expect to receive?

Solution

Remember, we begin with the assumption that there is no difference in job performance between the trained workers at plant A and the untrained workers at plant B. Then we compute the value of d_t:

$$d_t = \frac{9.5 - 6.0}{(2.5)(\sqrt{.90})}$$

$$= \frac{3.5}{2.37}$$

$$= +1.48 \text{ (on a scale from } -3 \text{ to } +3)$$

Substituting this value into Equation 16-3, along with the other values given (remember, the variability of job performance in dollars may be expressed as $SD_y = \$20,000 \times 40\%$, or $8000):

$$\Delta U = T \times N \times d_t \times SD_y - (N \times C)$$

$$= 3(125)(1.48)(\$8000) - 125(\$800)$$

$$= \$4,440,000 - \$100,000$$

$$= \$4,340,000$$

Assuming an annual inflation rate of 4.5 percent over 3 years, a corporate tax rate of 40 percent, and variable costs of −5 percent, the adjusted payoff may be computed. (See ref. 9 for computing formulas.) It is $2,259,056—48 percent smaller than the unadjusted payoff, but arguably more realistic. This payoff averages out to $18,072 per trainee over 3 years, or about $6000 per year in improved job performance. That's a return of $7.50 for every $1 invested—not bad for an $800 investment per trainee!

Situation 2: direct measures available

When direct measures of the dollar outcomes of training are available, then standard valuation methods are appropriate. The following study valued the results of a behavior-modeling training program (see Chapter 7 for a fuller description of behavior modeling) for sales representatives in relation to the program's effects on sales performance.[18]

Study design   A large retailer conducted a behavior-modeling program in two departments, Large Appliances and Radio/TV, within 14 of its stores in one large metropolitan area. The 14 stores were matched into seven pairs in terms of size, location, and market characteristics. Stores with unusual characteristics that could affect their overall performance, such as declining sales or recent changes in management, were not included in the study.

The training program was then introduced in seven stores, one in each of the matched pairs, and not in the other seven stores. Other kinds of ongoing sales training programs were provided in the control group stores, but the behavior-modeling approach was used only in the seven experimental-group stores. In the experimental-group stores, 58 sales associates received the training, and their job performance was compared to that of 64 sales associates in the same departments in the control-group stores.

As in most sales organizations, detailed sales records for each individual were kept on a continuous basis. These records included total sales as well as hours worked on the sales floor. Since all individuals received commissions on their sales and since the value of the various products sold varied greatly, it was possible to compute a job performance measure for each individual in terms of average commissions per hour worked.

There was considerable variation in the month-to-month sales performance of each individual, but sales performance over 6-month periods was more stable. In fact, the average correlation between consecutive sales periods of 6 months each was about .80 (where 1.00 equals perfect agreement). Hence the researchers decided to compare the sales records of participants for 6 months before the training program was introduced with the results achieved during the same 6 months the following year, after the training was concluded. All sales promotions and other programs in the stores were identical, since these were administered on an areawide basis.

The training program itself   The program focused on specific aspects of sales situations, such as "approaching the customer," "explaining features, advantages, and benefits," and "closing the sale." The usual behavior-modeling procedure was followed. First the trainers presented *guidelines* (or "learning points") for handling each aspect of a sales interaction. Then the trainees *viewed a videotaped situation* in which a "model" sales associate followed the guidelines in carrying out that aspect of the sales interaction with a customer. The trainees then *practiced* the same situation in role-playing rehearsals. Their performance was *reinforced* and shaped by their supervisors, who had been trained as their instructors.

Study results   Of the original 58 trainees in the experimental group, 50 were still working as sales associates 1 year later. Four others had been promoted during the interim, and 4 others had left the company. In the control group stores, only 49 of the original 64 were still working as sales associates 1 year later. Only 1 had been promoted, and 14 others had left the company. Thus the behavior-modeling program may have had a substantial positive effect on turnover since only about 7 percent of the trained group left during the ensuing year, in comparison to 22 percent of those in the control group. (This result had not been predicted.)

Figure 16-8 presents the changes in average per-hour commissions for participants in both the trained and untrained groups from the 6-month period before the training was conducted to the 6-month period following the training. Note in Figure 16-8 that the trained and untrained groups did not have equal per-hour commissions at the start of the study. While the *stores* that members of the two groups worked in were matched at the start of the study, *sales commissions* were not. Sales associates in the trained group started at a lower point than did sales associates in the untrained group. Average per-hour commissions for the trained group increased over the year from $9.27 to $9.95; average per-hour commissions for the untrained group declined over the year

FIGURE 16-8

Changes in per-hour commissions before and after the behavior modeling training program.

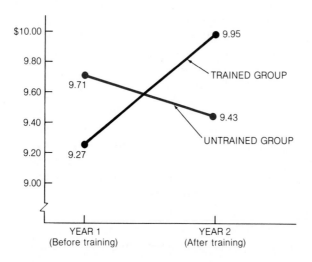

from $9.71 to $9.43. In other words, the trained sales associates increased their average earnings by about 7 percent, whereas those who did not receive the behavior-modeling training experienced a 3 percent decline in average earnings. This difference was statistically significant. Other training outcomes were also assessed (e.g., trainee attitudes, supervisory behaviors), but, for our purposes, the most important lesson was that the study provided objective evidence to indicate the dollar impact of the training on increased sales.

The program also had an important secondary effect on turnover. Since all sales associates are given considerable training (which represents an extensive investment of time and money), it appears that the behavior modeling contributed to *cost savings* in addition to *increased sales*. As noted in the previous discussion of turnover costs, an accurate estimate of these cost savings requires that the turnovers be separated into controllable and uncontrollable because training can affect only controllable turnover.

Finally, the use of objective data as criterion measures in a study of this kind does entail some problems. As pointed out earlier, the researchers found that a 6-month period was required to balance out the month-to-month variations in sales performance resulting from changing work schedules, sales promotions, and similar influences that affected individual results. It also took some vigilance to ensure that the records needed for the study were kept in a consistent and conscientious manner in each store. According to the researchers, however, these problems were not great in relation to the usefulness of the study results. "The evidence that the training program had a measurable effect on sales was certainly more convincing in demonstrating the value of the program than would be merely the opinions of participants that the training was worthwhile" (ref. 18, p. 761).

Personnel Research

Assessing the costs and benefits of human resource management is just one aspect of personnel research. Most managers recognize the need for research and development in the technical areas of their businesses. However, few managers recognize the value of research and development related to the management of people at work.

Why the neglect?

Acquiring and developing the right talents for a business as it changes strategy, technology, and products requires more shrewd, wise, long-range planning than any other corporate endeavor. Companies can usually replace or rebuild technology, physical facilities, products, markets, or business systems in 3 to 5 years. But how long does it take to change the attitudes of 1000 employees with an average age, say, of 40 and with 10 years of seniority?[26]

Effective people management requires long-term thinking and consistency.

Unfortunately, short-range pressures, such as budgets and annual plans, force short-term reactions to human resource management needs. Furthermore, successful managers seldom stay put long enough to see their investments in people pay off. Moreover, executive compensation systems seldom reward a manager for 5 years' investment in human resource policies and activities.[26]

The problems of workforce apathy, poor morale, and low productivity persist. Unfortunately, managers whose "quick fix" efforts fail to resolve these problems blame the government, unions, the "vanishing work ethic," or the "new breed" of worker instead of their own piecemeal, reactive approaches to the management of people. Changing the habits, skills, attitudes, or beliefs of employees takes years. Such efforts need to be guided and reinforced by the kinds of information that personnel research can provide. In short, to get at fundamental rather than superficial symptoms, managers need to develop a "spirit of inquiry" coupled with a long-range (e.g., 5- to 7-year) strategy for the management of people. Reward systems, in turn, need to recognize these investments by managers in their people. For example, IBM's philosophy that people are the corporation's most important asset has permeated the organization both by word and deed ever since the company was founded. The same is true at Hewlett-Packard. To this day, these values persist with great benefit to both companies.

What is personnel research?

In 1923, L. L. Thurstone, speaking before the American Political Science Association in Columbus, Ohio, described personnel research primarily as *the study of the relationship between working and living*. Its objective is *to understand the conditions under which the opportunities for self-expression, self-assertion, self-respect, self-advancement, and social approval may be provided in ways that are consistent with productive work*.[28]

These ideas persist even to today. In many organizations, the general objective of personnel research is to contribute to the development and application of improved solutions to employee relations problems and to the more effective use of the company's human resources. In large companies, a special unit may be designated to conduct personnel research; in small companies, it is left to individual managers. To avoid "reinventing the wheel," therefore, it is important that managers have some familiarity with established research findings in the human resource management area. Many of these findings have been presented in this book. Let's now put them into historical perspective.

Dominant issues in the history of personnel research

An analysis of over 6000 articles published in practitioner-oriented human resource management journals from 1927 to 1980 indicated that the important issues of the past are still important today.[24] While the percentage of coverage

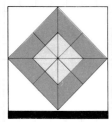

Impact of Human Resource Management Activities on Productivity, Quality of Work Life, and the Bottom Line

There is a rapidly growing awareness in the business community of the need for personnel research. Indeed, there is a growing consensus among managers in many industries that the future success of their firms may depend more on the skill with which human problems are handled than on the degree to which their firms maintain leadership in technical areas. Awareness alone will not improve productivity. Rather, to quote Thomas A. Edison, it will be a matter of "99 percent perspiration and 1 percent inspiration." There are no quick-fix solutions; as General Motors found in the gradual turnaround of its problem plants at Tarrytown and Lordstown, when personnel research results get translated into operating management practices, everybody wins. Labor-management relations improve, productivity goes up, quality goes up, profitability goes up, reworks go down, and the quality of work life becomes more tolerable. Quoting from Thurstone's 1923 speech again, "opportunities for self-expression, self-assertion, self-respect, self-advancement, and social approval [are] provided in ways that are consistent with productive work."[28]

of certain issues and topics has changed, the overall rankings are quite similar, even when viewed across three separate time periods: 1927 to 1940, 1941 to 1960, and 1961 to 1980. In order of popularity, these topics are:

1. Career planning and development (1545 articles)
2. Staffing (852 articles)
3. Compensation (783 articles)
4. Job satisfaction (727 articles)
5. Union-management relations (583 articles)
6. Equal employment opportunity (315 articles)
7. Occupational safety and health (298 articles)
8. Outplacement (170 articles)
9. Human resource planning (169 articles)

In sum, personnel research is still struggling to understand and predict the factors that underlie the attraction, retention, and motivation (ARM) of employees.

Where do research ideas come from?

Among academicians, research ideas may spring from:[7, 27]

1. Personal values or assumptions regarding the interests of managers
2. Topics that can be investigated through the scientific method or through a "pet" methodological technique

3. Outright convenience (that is, data just happen to be available)
4. Behavioral science literature that identifies problems that need to be studied

Among managers, however, personnel research often begins only when an organizational problem occurs.[2] This may be changing as more organizations undertake personnel research even when there is no problem. Specifically, attitude surveys—one form of personnel research—are becoming much more popular. To a large extent this is due to an idea stressed in many popular books on management: that it is important to listen to employees. This idea has taken on added significance as more companies endure the organizational trauma of mergers and restructurings or adopt more participative management styles.

As employee surveys become more common, the range of issues on which opinions are solicited is expanding considerably. At Wells Fargo & Co. in San Francisco, for instance, employees have been asked about such things as the effectiveness of the bank's advertising, the quality of innovation of its products, and its responsibility to the community.

It is one thing to ask employees for their opinions—it shows that management is willing to listen. But surveys can backfire; employees become angry and resentful if their expectations are raised but management fails to react to their comments or complaints. When facing employees who feel that they are underpaid, for example, one manager noted that firms "had better be prepared with facts to tell them that their perception is incorrect or perhaps that there are reasons. That can get very sensitive."[21] As a result of its own survey, Hewlett-Packard found out that engineers were concerned about their lack of communication with peers in other units. After listening to the engineers at a postsurvey meeting, the company accelerated development of an electronic mail system.

After mergers and acquisitions, many companies try to move quickly to evaluate the morale of the evaluated company and to discover any differences in operating styles. Just 2 months after it acquired Crocker National Corporation, for example, Wells Fargo surveyed 1500 Crocker employees. As a Wells Fargo vice president noted: "There's a lot of organizational change going on. . . . Wells Fargo was in a major downsizing, and now [there is] the acquisition. This helps us know what's going on . . . we really didn't know what the silent majority felt."[21]

Attitude surveys represent just one type of personnel research tool. In addition, the wide availability of computerized employee databases makes it possible to answer a variety of other questions, such as factors that relate consistently to the retention of engineers, the productivity and turnover of salespeople, and the personal characteristics of employees who accept offers of early retirement. Finally, detailed, sophisticated research is being conducted on issues as diverse as the impact of plant shutdowns, worker participation in management decisions, worker ownership, and the social costs of unemployment and concession bargaining.[25] As these few examples show, the range of personnel research topics, and the methods used to investigate them, are limited only by the imagination and ingenuity of the managers and researchers involved.

<table>
<tr>
<td>

CASE 16-1
Conclusion

Attitude survey
results: catalyst for
management action

</td>
<td>

The survey highlighted six areas of human resource management that were related to effective company performance in terms of turnover and profitability:

</td>
</tr>
</table>

1. *Recruitment and selection.* High-profit locations were recruiting many more management trainees from among the non-management employees already working for the company. Hence the high-profit locations were getting store manager trainees who already had experience and an understanding of what the job entailed.

2. *Training.* Classroom instruction was rated favorably by everyone and was not a factor in turnover. The training that did make a difference was *on-the-job training*. Store managers in high-profit, low-turnover areas reported that they received better in-store training than did their counterparts in lower profitability areas.

3. *Staffing.* Keeping management staff at a minimum was not producing greater profits. It was producing overworked and disenchanted managers who could neither run their stores effectively nor provide the training found to be so important for new store managers. Less effective profit centers had fewer managers, who worked many more hours, had fewer days off, and were bothered more frequently at home about work-related matters when they had a scheduled day off.

4. *Performance management.* Managers in the high-profit, low-turnover areas received performance reviews on a quarterly basis. Store managers throughout the system who received performance reviews less than quarterly wanted to see them conducted more often. In addition, everyone expressed a desire for more informal feedback from superiors about their performance.

A second aspect of performance management and control was regular store visits by higher-level supervisors. Supervisors in high-profit areas visited their stores more frequently than did their counterparts in low-profit areas.

5. *Climate.* Job security in this company's environment was not associated with compensation or with promotion opportunities. However, it was associated with the needs of the store managers to be treated fairly, to be kept informed, and to have superiors available when needed to help the store managers solve their problems. In less effective profit centers, store managers saw their superiors as less competent at handling problems, they had less confidence that their superiors would back them up in their actions, and they felt that their superiors neglected them in terms of the frequency of store visits and formal performance reviews. They also indicated that they were more apt to hear things first through the grapevine rather than directly from their superiors.

6. *Management style.* The areas described thus far all point to some basic

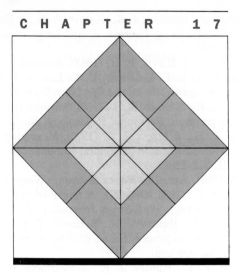

International Dimensions of Human Resource Management

CASE 17-1

Costs of a cross-culturally naive employee*

A cross-culturally naive employee can do great damage by running up costs unnecessarily or by failing to accomplish the purpose of the travel. As an example, consider the American company, eager to do business in Saudi Arabia, that sent a sales manager to Riyadh to "get something going." His flight and expenses for a week were expected to cost $3700. The salesperson arrived on a Monday, checked into a hotel, and began making phone calls to the obvious points of contact. To his surprise, he could not track down anyone to see regarding his business. After three exasperating days, he discovered that most offices were closed on Thursday and Friday. There was nothing to do but to extend his stay and hope for better luck the next week. Eventually, he made contact with several of the officials with whom he would have to work, but in each case he was frustrated by hour or longer waits, lack of privacy during appointments, endless cups of coffee, and being told to "come back another day." He was particularly unsettled by the Arab habit of getting off the subject and rambling on about issues unrelated to the business at hand. No one seemed impressed by his company's credentials and products, which he so enthusiastically described. After a month, he ran into an old Army buddy

*Adapted from: L. Copeland and L. Griggs, *Going international: how to make friends and deal effectively in the global marketplace*, San Francisco: Copeland Griggs Productions.

who gave him an introduction to some basic rules of Saudi etiquette and a pep talk on how to do business with Arabs. He was horrified to learn that he had repeatedly insulted his contacts by his thinly disguised impatience, refusal of coffee, rush to talk business, aggressive (boastful) selling, handing papers with his left hand, use of an occasional mild swearword, exposing the sole of his shoe when sitting on the floor, and even by asking, in the course of a conversation, about a Saudi official's wife. By now his trip had cost over $13,000, and he had established himself as an arrogant, rude, and untrustworthy American. He learned too late the three secrets to successful business in Saudi Arabia: patience, relationship building, and respect for the Arabs' ways.

QUESTIONS
1. Describe some of the indirect costs associated with cross-cultural naiveté.
2. As a top manager in the American company, what lessons did you learn from this disastrous experience?
3. How can this kind of situation be avoided in the future, and whose organizational responsibility should it be to see that such situations do not arise?

What's Ahead

Case 17-1 illustrates the fact that ignorance of cultures with whom one does business can be costly. Yet it is a cost that can and should be avoided as the world increasingly becomes a "global village" and as multinational investment continues to grow. All the human resource management issues that have been discussed to this point are interrelated conceptually and operationally and are particularly relevant in the international context: human resource planning, recruitment, selection, orientation, training and development, career management, compensation, and labor relations. In examining all these issues, as well as considering the special problems of repatriation (the process of reentering one's native culture after being absent from it), this chapter thus provides a capstone to the book. As usual, numerous practical examples will illustrate important issues.

The Multinational Company: A Fact of Modern Organizational Life

In order to maintain a leadership position in any one developed country, any business, whether large or small, increasingly has to attain and hold leadership positions in all developed markets worldwide. It has to be able to do research, to design, to develop, to engineer, to manufacture in any part of the developed world, and to export from any developed country to any other. It has to go transnational.[13]

The vehicle for doing this is often not an acquisition or a financial transaction, but what the Germans call a "community of interest": a joint venture, research pooling, joint marketing, or a cross-licensing agreement. Such arrangements are becoming more and more common in manufacturing as well as in service industries. To illustrate, a highly specialized, medium-size American asset-management firm recently formed a partnership with an equally specialized, medium-size Japanese asset management firm and a somewhat larger financial house in London. Each firm remains independent, but the American firm manages all U.S. investments for the three partners, the Tokyo firm manages all Japanese investments, and the British firm manages all investments in Europe.

One reason that leadership in any one developed market increasingly requires leadership in all is that the developed world has become one in terms of technology. All developed countries are equally capable of doing everything, doing it equally well, and doing it equally fast. All developed countries also share instant information. Companies can therefore compete just about everywhere the moment that economic conditions give them a substantial price advantage. In an age of sharp and violent currency fluctuations, this means that a leader must be able to innovate, to produce, and to market in every area of the developed world—or else be defenseless against foreign competition should currency exchange rates shift sharply.[13]

In this emerging economic order, foreign investment by the world's leading corporations is a fact of modern organizational life. Today foreign investment is viewed not just as an opportunity for U.S. companies investing abroad but also as an opportunity for other countries to develop subsidiaries in the United States and elsewhere. Before proceeding further, let's define some terms that will be used throughout the chapter:[18]

A *multinational company* (*MNC*) is a firm with substantial investment outside its home country in plant (as a rule, 20 percent or more of its total plant investment) and management. Such a company operates across national borders and claims its legitimacy from its effective use of assets to serve its far-flung customers.

An *expatriate* or *foreign-service employee* is a generic term applied to anyone working outside her or his home country with a planned return to that or a third country.

Home country is the expatriate's country of residence.

Host country is the country in which the expatriate is working.

A *third-country national* is an expatriate who has transferred to an additional country while working abroad. A German working for a U.S. firm in Spain is a third-country national.

One of the most important determinants of a company's success in an international venture is *the quality of its executives*. In the words of one international executive, "Virtually any type of international problem, in the final analysis, is either created by people or must be solved by people. Hence, having the right people in the right place at the right time emerges as the key to a company's international growth. If we are successful in solving that problem, I am confident we can cope with all others" (Dueer, in ref. 19, p. 61).

Growth of MNCs

Do you recognize these firms? More than 46 percent of their total revenue comes from overseas operations: Exxon, Mobil, IBM, Dow Chemical, Coca-Cola, National Cash Register, Pan Am, Gillette, Citicorp, and Chase Manhattan.[46] Notice how the firms include major sectors of the economy—oil, computers, chemicals, electronics, consumer goods, airlines, and banking. This is no accident. Since World War II there has been a major increase in the number of American executives and technical specialists employed outside the United States, a trend that has accompanied the growth of the MNC. At present, about 100,000 companies do business overseas, including 25,000 firms with foreign office affiliates, and 3500 major multinational companies. One-third of U.S. profits come from international business, and one-sixth of the nation's jobs are created by foreign trade.[47]

Foreigners hold top management positions in one-third of large U.S. firms and in one-fourth of European-based firms. They are even more conspicuous in third-world, developing countries. Thus a study of four large European MNCs (among the 60 largest in Europe) revealed that 80 percent of all international transfers were into developing countries, and only 20 percent into Europe or North America. In 60 to 70 percent of all transfers, the companies were not able to find qualified local individuals. Most of the executives transferred had specific technical expertise in fields such as engineering, agriculture, medicine, or accounting and finance.[16]

It should be clear by now that today's world economy is governed by an entirely new set of rules, and that to compete effectively U.S. firms must abandon such outdated assumptions and behaviors as these:

- Believing that there is "one best way" to approach all problems or that for each problem there is only "one best answer"
- Attending only to immediate short-term problems and issues, focusing on details, seeing only the parts and not the whole, ignoring the long-term, failing to put problems in a context, and losing sight of the objectives of the overall organization and the entire economy
- Failing to be aware of the implicit and unstated assumptions that have guided individual behavior and organizational policies in the past, and failing to change them when they are no longer appropriate in the current environment[30]

To take an example of the "one best way" approach, many American executives were surprised to find out how well Japanese ways worked at Nissan's car and truck plant in Smyrna, Tennessee. The plant features Japanese-style quality controls (small work groups with a big say in problem solving, job rotation every 2 hours, and statistical quality control techniques), just-in-time delivery of parts, and widespread use of industrial robots. Painting is done with West German technology, using robots from Norway. Fiber-optic communications, developed by U.S. aerospace firms, monitor 3000 points in the paint process. The result? After producing 500,000 vehicles, the plant showed two things: (1) U.S. workers are just as productive and skilled as the Japanese, and (2) the plant is one of the most efficient, highest-quality plants in the world.[20]

As the United States lost market share and jobs in important industries like steel, autos, and electronics, both labor and management in many firms grudgingly acknowledged that they had to change, that they could not continue doing business as usual. They had to "reach out" to the broader world at large. Reaching out involves more than just an occasional trip overseas. In the words of one exporter, "If you want the competitive edge, you've got to get over there frequently and let your foreign partners know you care about them" (ref. 11, p. 47). As Case 17-1 demonstrated, however, mere company presence on foreign soil is no guarantee of success. In fact, it may be a prescription for failure if the company representative is ill-equipped culturally, socially, or politically.

Costs of overseas executives

One of the first lessons that MNCs learn is that it is far cheaper to hire competent host-country nationals (if they are available) than to send their own executives overseas, for foreign-service employees typically cost *3 times* their annual home-country salaries.[27] Table 17-1 illustrates some of these costs.

TABLE 17-1 *Typical U.S. expatriate compensation package (annual expense): married and one child*

Category	U.S. compensation	Overseas compensation
Base salary	$70,000	$70,000
Overseas incentive		7,500
Hardship		5,000
Housing differential		25,000
Furniture		8,000
Utilities differential		12,000
Car and driver		10,000
Cost-of-living adjustment		2,000
Club memberhip		500
Education		5,000
Total	$70,000	$145,000
U.S. tax	15,000	15,000
Net annual compensation	$55,000	$130,000

Note: A complete expatriate package also includes the following: (1) annual transportation to the United States for home leave, (2) storage of U.S. household goods, (3) shipment of some goods to the foreign location, (4) U.S. auto disposal, (5) U.S. house management, (6) interim living, (7) travel to new assignment and return, and (8) annual tax equalization.

Source: M. A. Conway, Manage expatriate expenses for capital returns, *Personnel Journal*, July 1987, p. 69.

Even for executives who do not relocate overseas, daily allowances (in 1988 dollars) are high: $330 in Abu Dhabi, $265 in Tokyo, $295 in Lagos, and $235 in London.[11] Of course, these costs fluctuate with international exchange rates relative to the U.S. dollar. From 1985 to 1987 the dollar lost 50 percent or more of its value relative to most major foreign currencies—and the costs to maintain executives in foreign cities climbed accordingly.

On top of the high costs, there is a high failure rate among overseas personnel—an average of 30 percent over all locations and even higher in developing countries.[48] For all levels of employees, the costs of mistaken expatriation include the costs of initial recruitment, relocation expenses, premium compensation, repatriation costs (i.e., costs associated with resettling the expatriate), replacement costs, and the tangible costs of poor job performance.[10] When an overseas assignment does not work out, it *still* costs a company, on average, 2.5 times the employee's base salary.[7]

It is senseless to send people abroad who do not know what they are doing overseas and cannot be effective in the foreign culture. As the manager of international human resources at Hewlett-Packard remarked, "When you are sending someone abroad to work on an important agreement, it is terribly important that they have as much information as possible about how to do business in that country. The cost of training is inconsequential compared to the risk of sending inexperienced or untrained people" (ref. 11, p. 47).

For all these reasons, companies need to consider the impact of culture on international human resource management. But as noted at the outset, there are two aspects to this problem: U.S. MNCs operating overseas and foreign MNCs operating in the United States. This chapter emphasizes the special problems of U.S. MNCs operating overseas, although it also provides examples of how foreign MNCs have adapted to the United States.

Human Resource Management Practices as a Cultural Variable

Particularly when business does not go well, Americans returning from overseas assignments tend to blame the local people, calling them irresponsible, unmotivated, or downright dishonest.[11] Such judgments are pointless, for many of the problems are a matter of fundamental cultural differences that profoundly affect how different people view the world and operate in business. This section explores nine of these cultural differences.

Legal constraints

U.S. MNCs must contend with a bewildering web of labor laws that are specific to each country. As examples, we will consider a French labor law, a German labor law, and a Malaysian labor law.

In 1978 the French passed a law requiring the head of each firm with more than 300 employees to submit annually to employees and to the government a *social audit*. The purpose of the social audit, as with financial accounts, is to provide an account of the past year, except that a social audit focuses on the social situation of the employees of the firm. The social audit must contain information on:

- Employment.
- Remuneration and fringe benefits.
- Health and security conditions.
- Work organization and hours of work.
- Training.
- Industrial relations.
- Conditions of life of employees and their families that are related to the firm. These include housing, travel to work, rehabilitation, and leisure— where organized by the firm—as well as complementary social services relating to illness, death, preretirement, and so forth.

The long-range goal is to require each covered firm to formulate a balance sheet comparing what it has received with what it has given—financially as well as socially. This legislation also requires each firm to evaluate the consequences of its activities on retailers, subcontractors, consumers, and the environment.[37]

In West Germany, the Works Constitution Act provides a legal framework for the principle of codetermination, under which a works council (comprised of representatives of a plant's manual and nonmanual labor force) may be formed in each establishment with at least five employees. The council's duty is to safeguard the interests of employees relative to those of the employer. The works council is obliged to work with management in a spirit of mutual trust and in cooperation with the trade unions and employer's associations represented in a company.[39]

The works council has *enforceable codetermination rights* in social matters, such as: (1) the determination of working hours; (2) determination of the date, place, and manner of the payment of wages; (3) the introduction and use of technical devices serving to monitor the conduct or performance of the workforce; and (4) the fixing of job and bonus rates and other performance-related compensation.

The council also has far-reaching participation rights in personnel matters, such as recruitment, transfers, dismissals, human resource planning, and vocational training. Finally, the council has informational and consultation rights regarding changes in a plant that might impact employees, such as a shutdown, relocation, merger, or significant reorganization, including the institution of new work methods.[39]

As our third example, we will consider one part of the Malaysian Employment Act of 1955 (amended in 1981). This act prescribes the minimum terms and conditions of employment for employees in the private sector, whether they are unionized or not. It protects employees in such matters as the payment of wages, hours of work, sick leave, annual leave, and maternity benefits.

Malaysia is a Moslem country, and its labor laws regarding the employment of females are worthy of note. The section of the law that relates to the employment of women makes it illegal, under most circumstances, for a female employee to work between 10 P.M. and 5 A.M. in an "industrial undertaking." Electronics factories that employ three shifts around the clock are exempted. Another section of the law recognizes that although it is socially unjust, it is not illegal for an employer to pay a female a lower wage just because she is a woman. The labor laws are silent on the issue of equal pay for equal work for both sexes. Finally, depending on the nature of the job, and consistent with prehire agreements, females may be fired if they marry or become pregnant.[41]

Clearly it is imperative that a firm know and adhere strictly to the labor laws of the countries in which it does business.

Pace and process

To Americans, time is money. We live by schedules, deadlines, and agendas; we hate to be kept waiting, and we like to "get down to business" quickly. In many countries, however, people simply will not be rushed. They arrive late for appointments, and business is preceded by hours of social rapport. People in a rush are thought to be arrogant and untrustworthy.[11]

In America, the most important issues are generally discussed first when making a business deal. In Ethiopia, however, the most important things are taken up last. While being late seems to be the norm for business meetings in Latin America, the reverse is true in Sweden, where prompt efficiency is the watchword.[47] The lesson for Americans doing business overseas is clear: *Be flexible about time and realistic about what can be accomplished.* Adapt to the process of doing business in any particular country.

Local customs

Local customs are related closely to issues of pace and process; they vary all over the globe. Here is a sampling:

- A businessperson's inquiry about the spouse and family of a client would be well received in Mexico, but such a question would be highly improper in Saudi Arabia.
- In China it is considered socially unacceptable to give gifts to individuals in business situations. In similar situations in Japan, however, small gifts are almost obligatory.
- The bottom of the heel is considered to be the most unclean part of the

body in some Arab nations. Hence it is a social offense to turn up one's shoe or foot to a companion.

Communication: verbal and nonverbal

The axiom "Words mean different things to different people" is especially true in cross-cultural communication. When an American says she is "tabling" a proposition, it is generally accepted that it will be put off. In England, "tabling" means to discuss something now. Translations from one language to another can generate even more confusion as a result of differences in style and context. Coca-Cola found this out when it began marketing its soft-drink products in China.

The traditional Coca-Cola trademark took on an unintended translation when shopkeepers added their own calligraphy to the company name. "Coca-Cola," pronounced "ke kou ke la" in one Chinese dialect, translates as "bite the wax tadpole." Reshuffling the pronunciation to "ko kou ko le" is roughly translated to mean "may the mouth rejoice."[47]

In many cultures, directness and openness are not appreciated. An open person may be seen as weak and untrustworthy, and directness can be interpreted as abrupt and hostile behavior. Providing specific details may be seen as insulting to one's intelligence. Written contracts may suggest that a person's word is not good.

Nonverbal cues may also mean different things. In America, one who does

not look someone in the eye arouses suspicion and is called "shifty-eyed." In some other countries, however, looking one in the eye is perceived as aggression.[11] Just as communication skills are key ingredients for success in American business, such skills are also basic to success in international business. There is no compromise on this issue; ignorance of local customs and communications protocol is a high-risk strategy.

Work motivation and values

Knowledge of what motivates foreign workers, combined with (or based on) a knowledge of what they think matters in life, is critical to the success of the MNC manager. Europeans pay particular attention to *power and status*, which results in more formal management and operating styles in comparison to the *informality* found in the United States. In the United States individual *initiative and achievement* are rewarded, but in Japan managers are encouraged to seek *consensus* before acting, and employees work as teams. In one comparison of the values of middle-aged Japanese and American business managers, the Japanese showed more interest in advancement, money, and forward striving. Since these characteristics tend to be closely associated with success, it may be that achievement and advancement motivation are driving forces behind Japanese productivity, and "team" action only their method for disciplining and rewarding it.[22]

The determinants of work motivation may not be all that different in developing countries. In Zambia, for example, work motivation seems to be determined by six factors: the nature of the work itself, opportunities for growth and advancement, material and physical provisions (i.e., pay, benefits, job security, favorable physical work conditions), relations with others, fairness or unfairness in organizational practices, and personal problems. The effect of personal problems is totally negative. That is, *their presence impairs motivation, but their absence does not enhance it.*[23]

Finally, the issue of nepotism is viewed very differently in different parts of the world. While most U.S. firms frown upon the practice of hiring or contracting to work directly with family members, in Latin America or the Arab countries, it only makes sense to hire someone you can trust.[11]

Outlook

T. Fujisawa, cofounder of Honda Motor Company, once remarked, "Japanese and American management is 95 percent the same, and differs in all important respects." In other words, while organizations are becoming more similar in terms of structure and technology, people's behavior within those organizations continues to reveal culturally based dissimilarities.[1] One area where this is apparent is in outlook. The Japanese and Europeans look to long-term accomplishments; Americans tend to stress short-term results. Each has its advantages and disadvantages. The U.S. approach translates into management styles that can be very exciting and dynamic but narrow in range and shallow in strategy. On the other hand, since Japanese and European managers tend to be less opportunistic, they sometimes miss out on fast-breaking opportunities.[17]

Mobility

Europeans tend to be less mobile than Americans. Unlike Americans, who sometimes move their families 6 to 10 times for the sake of their careers, most Europeans stay close to their original homes and to their roots.[17]

Role of the corporation

Many American managers see the corporation as a vehicle for attaining their individual goals. To the Japanese and the Europeans, however, the corporation is a mechanism for attaining certain social objectives: full employment, prestige, a lifetime job, as well as various social benefits.[17]

National policies

Among European firms, managers are preoccupied with the politics and policies of their national governments. In the United States, despite much complaining about government's role, managers operate more independently. To them, the government is just one more obstacle on the road to profitability.[17] In Japan, government ministries that set national economic priorities can exert substantial pressure on companies, but their influence is much less than is believed outside Japan. According to the president of the Japan Federation of Employers, "The amount of government interference or the role of government in private business is very small as compared with the U.S. or the European Community." Adds a Western economist in Tokyo, "There is no Japan, Inc.— if there ever was one" (ref. 21, p. 60).

There are three important lessons to be learned from this brief overview of cross-cultural differences.[18] One, it is critically important that managers of MNCs *guard against exportation of headquarters-country bias.* As we have seen, the human resource management approach that works well in the headquarters country might be totally out of step in another country. It is the responsibility of the manager of international human resources to understand the cultural differences inherent in the management systems of the countries in which his or her firm does business. Two, *think in global terms.* We live in a world where a worldwide allocation of physical and human resources is necessary for continued survival. Three, *recognize that no country has all the answers.* Flexible work hours, quality circles, and various innovative approaches to productivity have arisen outside the United States. Effective multinational managers must not only think in global terms but must also be able to synthesize the best management approaches to deal with the complex problems at hand.

PRACTICAL EXAMPLE
*Bargaining with the Japanese**

The knot tightens in the Western businessman's stomach as he peers glumly at the Japanese negotiating team across the table. The executive's flight leaves early tomorrow. His home office has been pressing him to complete a deal quickly. But although the talks have dragged on for days, the key issues have barely been discussed. "What is this?" the frustrated businessman wonders. "Don't these people know that time is money?"

Such questions arise frequently when Western executives confront the Japanese. Foreigners eager to do business must often endure endless rounds of what seem to be aimless talks, dinners, and drinks. Still, they have little choice but to put up with the ceremony if they hope to gain access to Japan's vast domestic market.

The exotic set of rituals seen during negotiations is the face Japan presents to the world of business. Japanese negotiators are exquisitely polite and agonizingly vague, yet at the same time they are determined to win the best possible deal. Perhaps the most striking feature of this system of bargaining is the huge amount of time it consumes. One Australian attorney offers the following rule of thumb: *allow 5 times as long as usual when doing business in Japan.*

Japanese companies negotiate slowly because everyone from junior management to major shareholders must approve a deal, in keeping with the national tradition of consensus. Startled Western executives may therefore find themselves confronting negotiating teams of 10 to 15 Japanese. Moreover, this may be only the beginning. The faces can change from session to session as new experts are added for different topics.

The Japanese are usually minutely well informed about their prospective partners. Said one former official of British Leyland who worked on a joint agreement with Honda, "The Japanese negotiators seemed to know more about our labor and managerial problems than we did."

At first the Japanese seem to have remarkably little interest in the business at hand. Their conversation is likely to dwell at length on social and family concerns rather than on products and prices. They stress personal relations because they are interested in the long-term implications of an agreement. Western executives, on the other hand, may tend to look more at the shorter term. Said one expert, "The American feeling is that it's the horse buyer's fault if he fails to ask whether a horse is blind; . . . for the Japanese, however, a deal is more of a discussion of where mutual interests lie" (ref. 32, p. 42).

Guidelines for negotiating with the Japanese

Experts on Japanese business methods offer the following guidelines for foreign negotiators:[32]

*Adapted from: The negotiation waltz, *Time*, Aug. 1, 1983, pp. 41, 42.

1. Women should not be part of any formal talks. Japanese women are all but barred from the management of big companies, and the important after-hours socializing in Japan is exclusively stag. (Understandably, this is difficult for American professional women to accept.)

2. Do not send anyone under 35 to conduct negotiations. Said an American manager with a high-tech firm, "You are insulting the Japanese by sending a young man to deal with a senior executive, who is likely to be 65."

3. Be wary of mistaking Japanese politeness for agreement. A Japanese negotiator may frequently nod and say "hai" (yes) during talks. But the word also is used to let the listener know that the conversation is being followed, as with the English "uh-huh" or "I see." In short, "yes" does not always mean "yes."

4. Japanese negotiators may confuse outsiders by lapsing into silence to mull a point. Western businesspeople may then jump into that pool of silence, much to their regret. Thus the head of a Japanese firm did nothing when a contract from International Telephone and Telegraph (ITT) was presented for his signature. The ITT manager then hastily sweetened the deal by $250,000. If he had waited just a few more minutes, he would have saved the company a quarter of a million dollars.

5. Evasiveness is another characteristic of Japanese negotiators. They hate to be pinned down, and they often suppress their views out of deference to their seniors. Add to this the Japanese tendency to tell listeners what they seem to want to hear, and a foreign negotiator can easily go astray.[32]

To be successful, a visiting executive never lets on what he is really thinking, he has unending patience, and he is unfailingly polite. In short, he acts very Japanese.

Human Resource Management Activities of MNCs

Before we consider recruitment, selection, training, and other international human resource management issues, it is important that we address a fundamental question: Is this subject worthy of study in its own right? The answer is yes, for two reasons—scope and risk exposure.[31] In terms of scope, there are at least five important differences between domestic and international operations. International operations have:

1. More functions, such as taxation and coordination of dependents
2. More heterogeneous functions, such as coordination of multiple-salary currencies
3. More involvement in the employee's personal life, such as housing, health, education, and recreation

4. Different approaches to management, since the population of expatriates and locals varies
5. More complex external influences, such as from societies and governments

Heightened risk exposure is a second distinguishing characteristic of international human resource management. Companies are vulnerable to a variety of legal issues in each country, and the human and financial consequences of a mistake in the international arena are much more severe. On top of that, terrorism is now an ever-present risk for Americans overseas. This has had an important effect on how people are prepared for and moved to and from international assignment locations. In light of these considerations, it seems reasonable to ask, "Why do people accept overseas assignments?" Why do they go? When people agree to uproot themselves from their native lands, permanently or temporarily, more than finances have to be taken into account. Psychological and social issues must also be considered. A study of 135 middle-level American expatriate managers revealed two primary underlying factors in their decisions to accept a foreign assignment: increased pay and career mobility.[29]

As we have seen, companies often "sweeten the pot" considerably for their overseas personnel. But what about career mobility? Many companies say that, in making international assignments, they are trying to develop an internal cadre of sophisticated executives. Yet data on the degree to which such assignments actually enhance one's chances for success seem to be mixed. In one study, for example, 80 percent of repatriated American middle managers felt that they had more authority *before* serving abroad than they did upon reentry.[50] Results like these should serve as a red flag to companies, indicating a need for careful attention to the repatriation process as well as to long-term career planning.

Organizational structure

Successful expatriate managers must be able to balance local conditions and cultures with home-office desires. These problems are compounded, of course, in international joint ventures, characterized by multiple ownership and multinational affiliations.[43] Research indicates that organizational structure can facilitate communications in this environment, thus increasing the expatriate's effectiveness. An effective structure is one that is decentralized and has few formal rules instead of rigid rules and policies originating in one environment (the home office) and applied in a very different one.[34] Lloyd's Bank International has established procedures to address this need specifically. Branch offices must operate within broad policies, and home-office personnel must make regular inspections to ensure that these policies are being followed; at the same time, there has been an effort to build a high degree of flexibility into the system.[42]

Human resource planning

This issue is particularly critical for MNCs, for they need to analyze both the local *and* international external labor markets as well as their own internal labor markets in order to estimate the supply of people with the skills required at some time in the future. In North America and Europe, national labor markets can usually supply the skilled technical and professional people needed. However, developing countries are characterized by severe shortages of qualified managers and skilled workers and by great surpluses of people with little or no skill, training, or education.[38] The bottom line for MNCs operating in developing countries is that they must be prepared to develop required skills among their own employees.

Recruitment

Broadly speaking, MNCs follow three basic models in the recruitment of executives: (1) They may select from the national group of the parent company only, (2) they may recruit only from within their own country and the country where the branch is located, or (3) they may adopt an international perspective and emphasize the unrestricted use of all nationalities.[42] Each of these strategies has both advantages and disadvantages.

Ethnocentrism: home-country executives only

This strategy may be appropriate during the early phases of international expansion, because firms at this stage are concerned with transplanting a part of the business that has worked in their home country. Hence, detailed knowledge of that part is critical to success. On the other hand, a policy of ethnocentrism, of necessity, implies blocked promotional paths for local executives. And if there are many subsidiaries, home-country nationals must recognize that their foreign service may not lead to faster career progress. Finally, there are cost disadvantages to ethnocentrism as well as increased tendencies to *impose* the management style of the parent company.[19]

Limiting recruitment to home- and host-country nationals only

This may result from acquisition of local companies. In Japan, for instance, where the labor market is tight, most people are reluctant to switch firms. Thus, use of a local partner may be extremely important. Hiring nationals has other advantages as well. It eliminates language barriers, expensive training periods, and cross-cultural adjustment problems of managers and their families. It also allows MNCs to take advantage of (lower) local salary levels while still paying a premium to attract high-quality employees.

Yet these advantages are not without cost. Local managers may have difficulty bridging the gap between the subsidiary and the parent company, for the business experience to which they have been exposed may not have prepared them to work as part of a multinational enterprise.[19] Finally, consideration of *only* home- and host-country nationals may result in the exclusion of some very able executives.

Geocentrism: seek the best person for the job regardless of nationality   At first glance it may appear that this strategy is optimal and most consistent with the underlying MNC philosophy. Yet there are potential problems. Such a policy can be *very* expensive, it would take a long time to implement, and it requires a great deal of centralized control over managers and their career patterns. To implement such a policy effectively, MNCs must make it very clear that cross-national service is important to the firm and that it will be rewarded. They also must foster actively a policy of open career opportunities for top management positions. In view of these requirements, is it really any surprise that so few MNCs have developed a truly international executive cadre? Let's now consider a very serious problem that confronts many executives offered overseas assignments.

PRACTICAL EXAMPLE

Job aid for spouses of overseas executives*

In half of all U.S. families, both husband and wife hold jobs. By 1995, according to the U.S. Department of Labor, more than 81 percent of married women aged 35 to 44 will be employed or seeking work. Here is a scenario likely to become more and more common in the future. A company offers a promotion overseas to a promising executive. But the executive's spouse has a flourishing career in the United States. What should the company—and the couple—do?

Employers and employees are wrestling with this dilemma more often these days. As noted in Chapter 10, job aid for the so-called trailing spouse is already a popular benefit for domestic transfers. Now, on a limited basis, some employers are also providing informal job help to the spouses of international transferees.

Personnel officers may try to find a job for the spouse within the company, press a spouse's current employer for a foreign post, provide job leads through customers and suppliers, or plow through costly government red tape to get work permits. This kind of aid usually occurs in industries like banking, financial services, pharmaceuticals, and computers, all of which have significant numbers of high-level women executives.

Despite company efforts, it is often very difficult to place spouses abroad. Where there are language barriers or barriers of labor laws, tradition, or underemployment, it can be almost impossible. Certain Mideast nations frown on women working or even driving. Moreover, an international assignment can slow a spouse's professional progress and sometimes stir resentment. And when both husband and wife work for the same employer, nepotism rules can

---

*Adapted from: J. S. Lublin, More spouses receive help in job searches when executives take positions overseas, *Wall Street Journal*, Jan. 26, 1984, p. 29.

interfere with the pursuit of their careers overseas because one is more likely to have to supervise the other. For example, a Citibank lending officer decided to get married just before the bank moved him to a small, 40-person office in Maracaibo, Venezuela. His wife, also a Citibank lending officer, had to go on unpaid leave.

Sensitive about the employment of more women, a few companies are considering expansion of their informal job assistance for spouses of employees transferred abroad. Consultants and spouses of executives who have lived abroad are convinced that employers *could* provide additional guidance. They also say that businesses should not penalize aspiring managers who reject foreign transfers because of their mate's career needs.

Despite all the obstacles, overseas assignments for dual-career couples can work out—but it may require some "creative juggling" by both employers and employees. Thus an electronics company sought to recruit a marketing executive for a Hong Kong post, but his wife, a financial services corporation executive, lacked any job prospects. At the urging of an executive recruiter, the electronics company hired the woman for a 4-month project to promote a new product. It also helped start her career as a marketing consultant with introductions to the Hong Kong business community.

International personnel selection

There are two important guidelines in this area: (1) Do not assume that a job requires the same skills from one location to another, and (2) do not underestimate the effect of the local culture and physical environment on the candidate.[51] In many cultures, tribal and family norms take precedence over technical qualifications in hiring employees. African managers often hire relatives and members of their tribes.[38] Likewise, in India, Korea, and Latin America, family connections are frequently more important than technical expertise. For an expatriate, technical competence along with other factors, such as the ability to relate well to others, may increase her or his chances of successful performance abroad.[49]

Selection criteria for international jobs cover five areas: *personality, skills, attitudes, motivation, and behavior.*[51] Personality traits related to success include: perseverance and patience (for when everything falls apart); initiative (because no one will be there to indicate what one should try next); and flexibility (to accept and to try new ways).

Highly developed technical skills, of course, provide the basic rationale for selecting a person to work overseas. In addition, however, candidates should possess skills in communication (oral and written); interpersonal relations (in developing countries, native people will simply walk off the job rather than continue to work with disagreeable outsiders); and stress management (to overcome the inevitable "culture shock"—frustration, conflict, anxiety, and feelings of alienation—that accompanies overseas assignments).

Tolerant attitudes toward people who may differ significantly in race, creed, color, values, personal habits, and customs are essential for success in overseas work. People who look down smugly upon other cultures as inferior to their own simply will not make it overseas.

High motivation has long been acknowledged as a key ingredient for success in missionary work. Who, for example, can forget the zeal of the Protestant missionaries in the book *Hawaii*, by James Michener, as they set out from their native New England? While motivation is often difficult to assess reliably, at the very least, firms should try to eliminate from consideration those who are only looking to get out of their own country for a change in scenery.

The last criterion is behavior—especially concern for other members of a group, tolerance for ambiguity, displays of respect, and nonjudgmental behavior. These characteristics may be determined from tests or interviews. Research indicates that U.S. psychological tests can be used by MNCs in many countries, but the content as well as the administration of the tests may need to be adapted to the culture in which they are to be used.[3, 24]

With regard to interviews, Table 17-2 provides a checklist of areas to probe in selecting candidates for international assignments. Note the section on "language ability." In a recent survey, almost two-thirds of 100 top managers of MNCs indicated that in their future selection decisions for international assignments, a command of foreign languages would be prized. As one manager noted: "We wonder how a manager can assess business opportunities in a foreign country if he does not speak the language and has little knowledge of the culture. . . . Management by walking around, visiting foreign operations, and keeping in touch by telephone is not enough."[14]

A final issue involves government regulation of personnel selection in foreign countries. In several western European countries, for example, employment offices are operated by the government, and private agencies are not permitted. And in countries such as Holland, Poland, and Sweden, prospective employees have the right to prior knowledge of psychological tests. If they so choose, they can insist that test results not be reported to an employer. In fact, in Sweden, employer, union, peers, and subordinates all participate in the entire selection process for managers—from job analysis to the hiring or promotion decision.[12] These kinds of personnel practices and regulations may require that U.S. MNCs radically modify their human resource and industrial relations policies to operate successfully overseas.

Orientation

Orientation is particularly important in overseas assignments, both before departure and after arrival. Formalized orientation efforts—for example, elaborate audiovisual presentations for the entire family, supplemented by presentations by representatives of the country and former expatriates who have since returned to the United States—are fine, to a point. Such approaches try to provide a comprehensive picture of the new environment, its opportunities, inconveniences, and essential differences. However, unless firms recognize that

TABLE 17-2 *Interview worksheet for international candidates*

Motivation

- Investigate reasons and degree of interest in wanting to be considered.
- Determine desire to work abroad, verified by previous concerns such as personal travel, language training, reading, and association with foreign employees or students.
- Determine whether the candidate has a realistic understanding of what working and living abroad requires.
- Determine the basic attitudes of the spouse toward an overseas assignment.

Health

- Determine whether any medical problems of the candidate or his or her family might be critical to the success of the assignment.
- Determine whether he or she is in good physical and mental health, without any foreseeable change.

Language ability

- Determine potential for learning a new language.
- Determine any previous language(s) studied or oral ability (judge against language needed on the overseas assignment).
- Determine the ability of the spouse to meet the language requirements.

Family considerations

- How many moves has the family made in the past among different cities or parts of the United States?
- What problems were encountered?
- How recent was the last move?
- What is the spouse's goal in this move?
- What are the number of children and the ages of each?
- Has divorce or its potential, death of a family member, etc., weakened family solidarity?
- Will all the children move? Why or why not?
- What are the location, health, and living arrangements of grandparents and the number of trips normally made to their home each year?
- Are there any special adjustment problems that you would expect?
- How is each member of the family reacting to this possible move?
- Do special educational problems exist within the family?

Resourcefulness and initiative

- Is the candidate independent; can he or she make and stand by his or her decisions and judgments?
- Does he or she have the intellectual capacity to deal with several dimensions simultaneously?

Resourcefulness and initiative (continued)

- Is he or she able to reach objectives and produce results with whatever personnel and facilities are available, regardless of the limitations and barriers that might arise?
- Can the candidate operate without a clear definition of responsibility and authority on a foreign assignment?
- Will the candidate be able to explain the aims and company philosophy to the local managers and workers?
- Does he or she possess sufficient self-discipline, and self-confidence to overcome difficulties or handle complex problems?
- Can the candidate work without supervision?
- Can the candidate operate effectively in a foreign environment without normal communications and supporting services?

Adaptability

- Is the candidate sensitive to others, open to the opinions of others, cooperative, and able to compromise?
- What are his or her reactions to new situations, and efforts to understand and appreciate differences?
- Is he or she culturally sensitive, aware, and able to relate across the culture?
- Does the candidate understand his or her own culturally derived values?
- How does the candidate react to criticism?
- What is his or her understanding of the U.S. government system?
- Will he or she be able to make and develop contacts with his or her peers in the foreign country?
- Does he or she have patience when dealing with problems?
- Is he or she resilient; can he or she bounce back after setbacks?

Career planning

- Does the candidate consider the assignment anything other than a temporary overseas trip?
- Is the move consistent with his or her progression and that planned by the company?
- Is his or her career planning realistic?
- What is the candidate's basic attitude toward the company?
- Is there any history or indication of personnel problems with this employee?

Financial

- Are there any current financial and/or legal considerations which might affect the assignment, e.g., house purchase, children and college expenses, car purchases?
- Are financial considerations negative factors, i.e., will undue pressures be brought to bear on the employee or his or her family as a result of the assignment?

Source: D. M. Noer, *Multinational People Management*, Washington, DC: Bureau of National Affairs, 1975, pp. 55–57.

these "differences" are not the same for everybody in the audience of prospective expatriates, their orientation efforts are doomed.[10] Instead of trying to convey the "truth about Tokyo," overseas orientation programs should make quite clear that employees and family members will each experience their *own* Tokyos. No matter what they may have heard or read, each of their experiences will be unique.

Another important aspect of overseas orientation that is sometimes overlooked is the company's culture at the overseas site.[10] Its ways of doing things, its expectations from employees and their families, and its differences in the ways jobs are done may all differ from U.S. practices. Failure to include such information only exacerbates the ensuing culture shock upon arrival.

In fact, there may be three separate phases to orientation:[10] The first is called *initial orientation*, and it may last as long as 2 full days. Key components are:

- *Cultural briefing.* Traditions, history, government, economy, living conditions, clothing and housing requirements, health requirements, and visa applications. (Drugs get a lot of coverage, both for adults and for teenagers—whether they use drugs or not. Special emphasis is given to the different drug laws in foreign countries. Alcohol use also gets special attention when candidates are going to Moslem countries, such as Saudi Arabia.)
- *Assignment briefing.* Length of assignment, vacations, salary and allowances, tax consequences, and repatriation policy.
- *Relocation requirements.* Shipping, packing, or storage; and home sale, rental, or acquisition.

During this time, it is important that employees and their families understand that there is no penalty attached to changing their minds about accepting the proposed assignment. It is better to bail out early than reluctantly to accept an assignment to be regretted later.

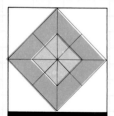

Impact of MNC Human Resource Management on Productivity, Quality of Work Life, and the Bottom Line

The impact of effective (or ineffective) recruitment, selection, orientation, training and development, compensation, and industrial relations practices are magnified when overseas assignments are involved. The *downside* risk associated with poor performance (regardless of cause) and reduced morale of subordinates is huge, given the costs (roughly 3 times annual salary) associated with sending managers abroad. On the other hand, there is potential for great gains in productivity and QWL, the incumbent's as well as her or his subordinates', and, consequently, bottom-line profits when the processes discussed in this chapter are implemented properly.

The second phase is *predeparture orientation*, which may last another 2 or 3 days. Its purpose is to make a more lasting impression on employees and their families and to remind them of material that may have been covered months earlier. Topics covered at this stage include:

- Introduction to the language
- Further reinforcement of important values, especially open-mindedness
- Enroute, emergency, and arrival information

The introduction to the language is important, for facility with the host country's language sets up an immediate rapport. Indeed, many foreign business people consider it a compliment for an expatriate to be able to converse in their language. Yet it often takes months, sometimes years, to master a foreign language. As is often the case, U.S. multinationals can learn from the practices of their overseas counterparts. British Petroleum uses outside facilities, such as Berlitz, for this purpose. For senior-level appointments to exotic locations, the duration of the language training is generally 6 weeks, followed by further tutoring upon arrival in the destination country. Spouses are also encouraged to take language training, to facilitate faster adaptation overseas.[49]

The final aspect of overseas orientation is *arrival orientation*. Upon arrival, employees and their families should be met by assigned company sponsors. This phase of orientation usually takes place on three levels:

- *Orientation toward the environment.* Language, transportation, shopping, and other subjects that—depending on the country—may be understandable only through actual experience.
- *Orientation toward the work unit and fellow employees.* Often a supervisor or a delegate from the work unit will introduce the new employee to his or her fellow workers, discuss expectations of the job, and share his or her own initial experiences as an expatriate. The ultimate objective, of course, is to relieve the feelings of strangeness or tension that the new expatriate feels.
- *Orientation to the actual job.* This may be an extended process that focuses on cultural differences in the way a job is done. Only when this process is complete, however, can we begin to assess the accuracy and wisdom of the original selection decision.

Cross-cultural training and development

In a recent study of MNCs, 68 percent of American firms that responded had no training programs *at all* for expatriate managers. Yet the same study found that rigorous selection and training procedures predicted success as an expatriate in American, western European, and Japanese multinationals! In the U.S. sample, the most important reasons for expatriate failure were: inability of the manager's spouse to adjust abroad and the manager's own failure to adjust to the different physical and cultural environment. Furthermore, U.S. expatriates had a higher failure rate than either Japanese or Europeans.[49]

To provide a deeper understanding of the relationship between lack of training and expatriate failure, consider the results of a recent survey on training needs for expatriate managers of U.S. companies doing business in Beijing. The results were clear. First, the formal aspects of the business and economic systems in China were viewed as less important than the behavioral factors—the "intangibles." Chinese language ability ranked very high. People with the greatest business experience—not necessarily those with the best Chinese language skills—all said that knowledge of the language was essential. Chinese negotiating style and Chinese social practices also received high marks. In short, China training should deal specifically with the interaction of Chinese cultural, political, and economic forces with the practicalities of the business environment. It should also aim to develop "creative" survival skills. Indeed, there really are only three tasks set out for the executive headed for a foreign country: surviving, coping, and, finally, succeeding.[15] Sending a manager overseas without training is like sending David to meet Goliath without even a sling shot.

To a very great extent, expatriate failure rates can be attributed to the culture shock that usually occurs 4 to 6 months after arrival in the foreign country. The symptoms are not pleasant: homesickness, boredom, withdrawal, a need for excessive amounts of sleep, compulsive eating or drinking, irritability, exaggerated cleanliness, marital stress, family tension and conflict (involving children), hostility toward host-country nationals, loss of ability to work effectively, and physical ailments of a psychosomatic nature.[7]

To be sure, many of the common stresses of everyday living become amplified when a couple is living overseas with no support other than from a spouse. To deal with these potential problems, spouses are taught to recognize stress symptoms in one another, and they are counseled to be supportive. One exercise, for example, is for the couples periodically to list what they believe causes stress in their mates, what the other person does to relieve it, and what they themselves do to relieve it. Then they compare lists.[7]

A model of multinational training and development Figure 17-1 provides a "road map" for the kinds of training and development activities that MNCs might undertake. This kind of guidance is essential, because in the glitter and glow of the many training techniques available, it is easy to lose sight of the forest for the trees.

Regardless of the specific method used, cross-cultural training may be conducted on two levels: academic and interpersonal.[18] Academic training uses books, maps, films, and discussions of the history, culture, and socioeconomic patterns of the host country. Interpersonal training is more direct, for it is

FIGURE 17-1

A model for the development of multinational management.

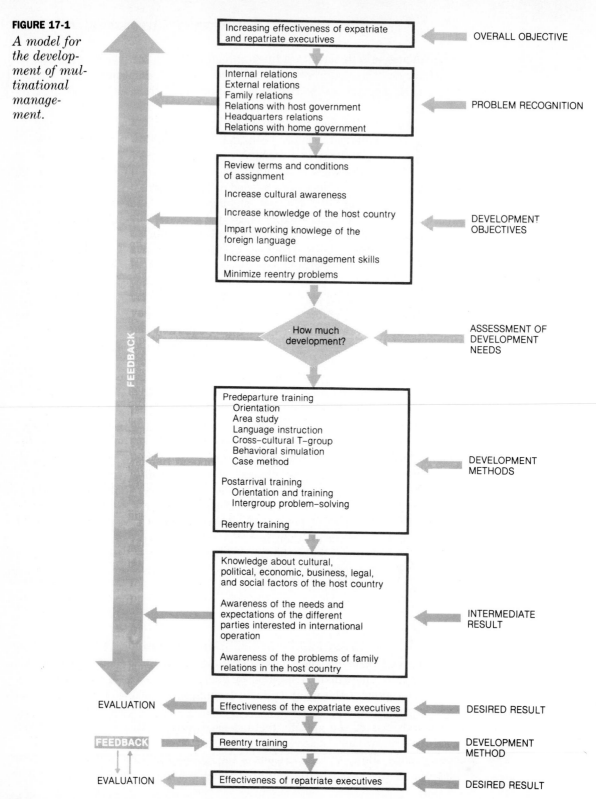

Increasing effectiveness of expatriate and repatriate executives — OVERALL OBJECTIVE

Internal relations
External relations
Family relations
Relations with host government
Headquarters relations
Relations with home government
— PROBLEM RECOGNITION

Review terms and conditions of assignment

Increase cultural awareness

Increase knowledge of the host country

Impart working knowlege of the foreign language

Increase conflict management skills

Minimize reentry problems
— DEVELOPMENT OBJECTIVES

How much development? — ASSESSMENT OF DEVELOPMENT NEEDS

Predeparture training
  Orientation
  Area study
  Language instruction
  Cross-cultural T-group
  Behavioral simulation
  Case method

Postarrival training
  Orientation and training
  Intergroup problem-solving

Reentry training
— DEVELOPMENT METHODS

Knowledge about cultural, political, economic, business, legal, and social factors of the host country

Awareness of the needs and expectations of the different parties interested in international operation

Awareness of the problems of family relations in the host country
— INTERMEDIATE RESULT

EVALUATION — Effectiveness of the expatriate executives — DESIRED RESULT

FEEDBACK — Reentry training — DEVELOPMENT METHOD

EVALUATION — Effectiveness of repatriate executives — DESIRED RESULT

FEEDBACK

the actual (or simulated) *experience* of living in the host country. Here is how one company does it.

<table>
<tr>
<td>

COMPANY EXAMPLE

Job swaps at Molex enhance international understanding*

</td>
<td>

Eighteen shop-floor employees of a manufacturer of electrical components, Molex, Inc., in Ireland, Japan, and the United States recently swapped jobs; they discovered quickly that their way of doing things is not necessarily best or easiest. The 18 employees, 6 from each country, were given 10-day working holidays in a foreign country to see how similar operations are being done elsewhere.

</td>
</tr>
</table>

The employees performed the same job in the foreign plant as they did in their own country, and they were each paid their regular wages. All expenses were paid by the sponsoring plant. Participants were chosen by draw. However, to be considered, they must have been with the company at least 3 years. Participation was voluntary.

U.S. employees who visited Molex Japan came home with much admiration for their Japanese colleagues. They were particularly impressed with their dedication and attention to quality. Visitors to Molex Shannon in Ireland were impressed with the plant layout and the appearance of the machines and the facility. They were also impressed with the speed and efficiency of the work performed by their Irish colleagues.

The U.S. workers also came back with an idea for redesigning one of the U.S. plant's work areas to reduce the need for continual bending. The Japanese picked up several useful tips from the Americans on how to operate their machines more efficiently. The employees also exchanged ideas and little tricks on stocking materials, loading machines, loading hoppers, and sorting runners.

Said one executive, "Employees are more willing to accept new ideas and accept hard facts from other shop-floor employees than from management, we found." The $48,000 exercise also gives the employees a greater feeling of pride. "They now feel they are part of a much larger, worldwide organization. They have also come to understand that by having subsidiary companies overseas we are not taking jobs from Americans, as they previously argued, but rather [we] are creating jobs. They now recognize that we do things here in the United States in support of our manufacturing operations overseas to serve overseas markets. And that we are becoming a stronger company and protecting U.S. jobs as a result."

Integration of training and business strategy   The multinational firm must have a continuing, long-range program of management development that is integrated with its global strategy and business planning. It needs to work constantly toward broadening the experience and outlook of all of its executives.[19] These ideas are best illustrated by an example.

*Adapted from: How Molex swaps jobs for international understanding, *Management Review*, July 1985, p. 35.

COMPANY EXAMPLE

Industrial relations for an MNC operating in Taiwan*

This example focuses on the industrial relations strategy involved in the recent expansion of a joint-venture Taiwanese and American company—Ford Lio Ho Motor Company, Ltd. All the company's 2000 hourly paid employees and 20 percent of the 465 salaried employees are unionized. All are becoming increasingly interested in the improvement of working conditions and an overall upgrading of their quality of work life.

To provide adequate management control during the company's expansion and to establish a base for orderly future growth of the company, a comprehensive personnel and organizational plan was developed. The following actions were taken:

- The position of industrial relations advisor was created.
- Managerial and technical staff were recruited from among Ford's foreign-service employees to fill key management positions. All were assigned specific training and development objectives, and their performance was measured on these and other objectives.
- A training specialist with experience in new-plant training was brought in from one of Ford's U.S. divisions to devote 9 months full time to the development of training programs related to expansion. This person was also assigned the specific responsibility of developing training expertise among Taiwanese employees.

Chinese employees view educational and training opportunities as a very important benefit. The Chinese have a proverb: "Give a man a fish and you feed him for a day. Teach him to fish and you feed him for the rest of his life." Company employees were eager to learn and were highly motivated to take advantage of company training programs.

A comprehensive list of training needs related to expansion was identified and programs were developed. At the same time, a program was established to improve replacement strength by at least 75 percent. Four key positions were identified, and management development plans were formulated to qualify employees as potential replacements for these positions. As proof of how well Chinese employees respond to training and development opportunities, the company experienced over 90 percent improvement in replacement strength when the end of one year was compared to the end of the previous year. In addition, 20 employees had been promoted to positions just below the key positions. Finally, three Taiwanese nationals replaced management and foreign-service employees.

The company's objectives were to keep fixed costs down while training a competent workforce, to pay competitively, to anticipate emerging employee needs, and to demonstrate that the company was conscious of the desires of employees for an improved quality of work life. This example has focused only on the first of these objectives, but if the company does as well with the other

*Adapted from: D. T. McKee, Industrial relations for an MNC operating in Taiwan, *Personnel Journal*, **60**(9), 1981, 672–674.

three, it will be well on its way toward long-term success in this joint venture overseas.

International compensation

Compensation policies can produce some of the most intense internal conflicts within an MNC. They can also influence the pattern of promotion that executives seek within the firm. Overpaid posts in peripheral foreign activities, for example, might attract executive talent away from more important, but lower-paid, posts in the mainstream of the firm's development. Few other areas in international human resource management demand as much top-management attention as does compensation.

The principal problem is straightforward: *Salary levels for the same job differ among countries in which an MNC operates.* Compounding this problem is the fact that fluctuating exchange rates require constant attention in order to maintain constant salary rates in U.S. dollars.

Ideally, an effective international compensation policy should meet the following objectives:

■ Attract and retain employees who are qualified for overseas service.
■ Facilitate transfers between foreign affiliates and between home-country and foreign locations.
■ Establish and maintain a consistent relationship between the compensation of employees of all affiliates, both at home and abroad.
■ Maintain compensation that is reasonable in relation to the practices of leading competitors.[19]

It is important that a worldwide compensation system be established within each MNC so that cultural variables can be dealt with systematically. The following two principles have helped establish such systems in many MNCs:

Home-country concept. All expatriates are tied to their respective home-country payrolls regardless of where they are working. Doing so provides, in essence, a cultural frame of reference within which to make compensation decisions. Also, it keeps the overseas employee thinking in terms of her or his home-country compensation values. This can help make repatriation less traumatic.

Modular approach. This approach breaks the compensation package down into its separate elements, and, relative to home-country and host-country laws, modifies those elements so that the expatriate neither loses nor gains. Specific "modules" of the compensation package are therefore set up to balance out the total package. The philosophy underlying this approach is to keep the employee "whole" in terms of home-country purchasing power.[18]

In analyzing the international compensation package, there are two major components: direct salary payments (with their associated tax consequences) and indirect payments in the form of (1) benefits and (2) adjustments and incentives. Let's consider each of these.

Salaries   To be competitive, MNCs normally follow local salary patterns in each country. Is there any other alternative? A firm that tried to maintain the same salary levels in all countries would "cost itself out" of markets where lower salary levels prevail, and it would be unable to attract managers in high-salary countries. To deal with this problem, one approach is to establish base salaries relative to those of the home country (this is the *home-country concept*) and then to add to these various types of premiums (See Table 17-1). One of the most common is the *expatriation premium*, which may range from 10 to 30 percent or more of base pay.[45] Some companies offer this premium tax-free. Its purpose also varies. In MNCs that take a modular approach to international compensation, it represents a combination of compensation for living away from the home country plus an inducement to accept an overseas assignment. In this case, the percentage is usually low. However, in MNCs that intend the expatriation premium to compensate for *all* overseas problems, it is much higher.

Another adjustment usually made in international compensation is *income tax equalization* with the home country. Its objective is to ensure that when the expatriate is assigned overseas, she pays neither more nor less tax than she would have paid had she remained in her home country. This is an important part of the compensation package, for under the Tax Reform Act of 1986, U.S. citizens working abroad can exclude up to $70,000 per year of foreign income from U.S. taxes. Tax liability for income above $70,000 (salary, bonuses, and allowances) is largely academic for U.S. residents covered by a company tax equalization program.[35]

In addition, Americans are allowed to deduct from their income the amount they pay for housing overseas above a base housing cost—currently $7322.[44] This is a big break, considering, for example, that apartments designed for expatriates in Hong Kong can cost as much as $5000 to $6000 per month![45]

Benefits   These may vary drastically from one country to another. For example, in Europe it is common for employees to get added compensation in proportion to the number of family members or unpleasant working conditions. In Japan, a supervisor whose weekly salary is only $350 may also get benefits that include family income allowances, housing or housing loans, subsidized vacations, year-end bonuses that can equal 3 months' pay, and profit sharing.[19]

MNCs commonly handle benefits coverages in terms of the "best of both worlds" benefits model.[18] Figure 17-2 illustrates the approach. Wherever possible, the expatriate is given home-country benefits coverages. However, in areas such as disability insurance, where there may be no home-country plan, the employee may join the host-country plan.

Another benefit provided by most U.S. multinationals is the *cost-of-living*

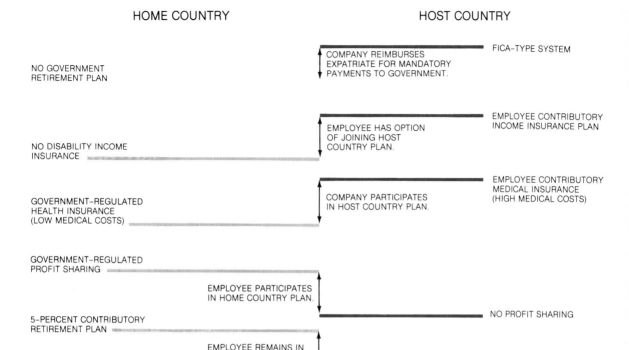

HOME COUNTRY   HOST COUNTRY

NO GOVERNMENT RETIREMENT PLAN — COMPANY REIMBURSES EXPATRIATE FOR MANDATORY PAYMENTS TO GOVERNMENT. — FICA-TYPE SYSTEM

NO DISABILITY INCOME INSURANCE — EMPLOYEE HAS OPTION OF JOINING HOST COUNTRY PLAN. — EMPLOYEE CONTRIBUTORY INCOME INSURANCE PLAN

GOVERNMENT-REGULATED HEALTH INSURANCE (LOW MEDICAL COSTS) — COMPANY PARTICIPATES IN HOST COUNTRY PLAN. — EMPLOYEE CONTRIBUTORY MEDICAL INSURANCE (HIGH MEDICAL COSTS)

GOVERNMENT-REGULATED PROFIT SHARING — EMPLOYEE PARTICIPATES IN HOME COUNTRY PLAN. — NO PROFIT SHARING

5-PERCENT CONTRIBUTORY RETIREMENT PLAN — EMPLOYEE REMAINS IN HOME COUNTRY PLAN. — NO RETIREMENT PLAN

FIGURE 17-2

Best-of-both-worlds benefits model.

allowance (COLA). Its purpose is to provide for the difference in living costs (that is, the costs of goods, services, and currency realignments) between the home country and the host country. COLAs may include any one or more of the following components:

- *Housing allowance*
- *Education allowance* to pay for schools, uniforms, and other educational expenses that would not have been incurred had the expatriate remained in the United States
- *Income tax equalization allowance* (as described earlier)
- *Remote-site pay*, which is usually a percentage of base pay provided as compensation for living in a culturally deprived area—one with no schools, transportation, or entertainment[45]
- *Hazardous-duty pay* to compensate for living in an area where physical danger is present, such as a war zone

Finally, it is common practice for companies to pay for security guards in many overseas locations, such as the Middle East, the Philippines, and Indonesia.

Pay adjustments and incentives   In the United States adjustments in individual pay levels are based, to a great extent, on how well people do their jobs, as reflected in a performance appraisal. In most areas of the third world, however, objective measures for rating employee or managerial performance are uncommon. Social status is based on characteristics such as age, religion, ethnic origin, and social class. Pay differentials that do not reflect these characteristics will not motivate workers. For example, consider Japan. Rewards are based less on the nature of the work performed or individual competence than on seniority and personal characteristics such as age, education, or family background. A pay system based on individual job performance would not be acceptable since group performance is emphasized, and the effect of individual appraisal would be to divide the group.[40] Needless to say, exportation of American performance appraisal practices to these kinds of cultures can have disastrous effects.

When implementing performance appraisal overseas, therefore, first determine the *purpose* of the appraisal. Second, whenever possible, set standards of performance against quantifiable assignments, tasks, or objectives. Third, allow more time to achieve results abroad than is customary in the domestic market. Fourth, keep the objectives flexible and responsive to potential market and environmental contingencies.[23] More and more U.S. MNCs that are exploring strategic compensation approaches at home are beginning to adopt similar approaches for their senior executives worldwide. They are beginning to introduce local and regional performance criteria into these plans, and they are attempting to qualify the plans under local tax laws. Why are they doing this? To create stronger linkages between executives' performance and long-term business goals and strategies, to extend equity ownership to key executives (through stock options), and in many instances to provide tax benefits.[4]

Multinational Collective Bargaining

Labor relations structures, laws, and practices vary considerably among countries. Unions may or may not exist. Management or government may dictate terms and conditions of employment. Labor agreements may or may not be contractual obligations. Management may conclude agreements with unions that have little or no membership in a plant, or with nonunion groups that wield more bargaining power than the established unions. And principles and issues that are relevant in one context may not be in others: for example, seniority in layoff decisions, or even the concept of a layoff.[26]

One of the most intriguing aspects of international labor relations is multinational collective bargaining. Unions have found MNCs particularly difficult to deal with in terms of union power and difficult to penetrate in terms of union representation.[36] Here are some of the special problems that MNCs present to unions:

1. While national unions tend to follow the development of national companies, union expansion typically cannot follow the expansion of a company across national boundaries, with the exception of Canada. Legal differences, feelings of nationalism, and differences in union structure and industrial relations practices are effective barriers to such expansion.[2]

2. The nature of foreign investment by MNCs has changed. In the past, MNCs tended to invest in foreign sources of raw materials. As a result, the number of processing and manufacturing jobs in the home country may actually have increased. However, in recent years there has been a shift toward the development of parallel, or nearly parallel, operations in other countries. Foreign investment of this type threatens union members in the home country with loss of jobs or with a slower rate of growth of jobs, especially if their wages are higher than those of workers in the host country. This threat is especially serious to American union members, whose wages may be higher than those of workers in other countries.[2]

3. When an MNC has parallel operations in other locations, the firm's ability to switch production from one location shut down by a labor dispute to another location is increased. This, of course, assumes that the same union does not represent workers at each plant or that, if different unions are involved, they do not coordinate their efforts and strike at the same time. Another assumption is that the various plants are sufficiently parallel that their products are interchangeable.

One solution to the problems that MNCs pose for union members is multinational collective bargaining. For this to work, though, requires coordination of efforts and the cooperation of unions. What is called for is an "international union" with the centralization of authority characteristic of American national unions. Yet two persistent problems stand in the way of such an international union movement:[2]

1. National and local labor leaders would have to be willing to relinquish their autonomy to an international level. This is a major stumbling block because the local union or enterprise union is essentially an autonomous organization.

2. Political and philosophical differences pose a further barrier to any international union movement. For example, a French labor leader committed to a communist form of economic organization is unlikely to yield authority willingly to an international union patterned after the United Auto Workers or any other union committed to the capitalist economic system. Conversely, the leaders of the United Auto Workers are unlikely to relinquish their autonomy to a communist international labor union.

How have multinational collective bargaining efforts worked? Research indicates that such bargaining efforts have typically placed little pressure on management. When labor has been successful in attaining its objectives, this has usually been due to some action by a critical national union. However, that union would probably have engaged in the same action without multinational union coordination and cooperation.[2]

Alternative union strategies

Since the prospects for effective multinational collective bargaining by unions are not very promising, unions must consider alternative strategies. These include:

- Independent bargaining by unions with an MNC within each country
- Securing legislation to protect union members' jobs within each country
- Attempting to coordinate multinational collective bargaining

In 1976, the adoption of a set of voluntary guidelines by the Organization for Economic Cooperation and Development (OECD) regarding a "code of conduct" for MNCs provided a skeletal structure on which unions could base claims for, and enhance the credibility of, multinational collective bargaining.[6] OECD member countries (most of Europe plus the United States, Canada, Japan, Australia, and New Zealand) account for 20 percent of the world's population, 60 percent of its industrial output, and 70 percent of its trade.[6] The voluntary guidelines cover the following areas: disclosure of information, competition, financing, taxation, employment and industrial relations, and science and technology. Business interests are represented before the OECD through the Business and Industry Advisory Committee, and labor's interests are represented by the Trade Union Advisory Committee (TUAC). The TUAC consists of national trade union centers, such as the AFL-CIO in the United States, the Federation of German Trade Unions in West Germany, and the Trade Union Congress in the United Kingdom. Certainly the OECD guidelines provide a good start toward the development of an international framework for industrial relations. But they are no panacea, as the following company example illustrates.

COMPANY EXAMPLE

Power tactics in multinational union-management relations

On arriving for work one Valentine's Day, the 500 employees of Hyster Company's forklift truck factory in Irvine, Scotland, were taken to a meeting run by Hyster's chief executive, William Kilkenny. He was fresh in from the head office in Portland, Oregon, bearing big new plans for Irvine. With a British government grant, he disclosed, Hyster was set to invest $60 million in the plant. It was prepared to reorganize and expand. It was willing to close two production lines at its Dutch factory and move them to Scotland. Irvine would gain 1000 jobs.

In return, Hyster wanted a sacrifice. Workers would have to take a pay cut of 14 percent, managers 18 percent. They had, Kilkenny told them, 48 hours to decide.

On the following morning, each employee received a letter from the company. "Hyster," it said, "is not convinced at this time that Irvine is the best of the many alternatives open to it. It has not made up its mind. The location of the plant to lead Europe is still open."

At the bottom of the page there was a ballot. A yes or a no was called for. Only 11 people voted no.

Workers complained that they had no warning, no consultation. Said one, "It was industrial rape—do or else." Hyster's workers in Irvine have no union, but the vote might have been no different if they did. The most powerful union in Europe is no match for a company run out of Portland. A union is concerned with the workers in its country; a multinational corporation knows no bounds.

Plant managers within an MNC could easily tell their Swiss workers, as the managers of one reputedly did, that new work was going to the lower-paid British, tell the British that production was being passed to the more efficient French, and tell the French that the MNC was creating jobs for the highly cooperative Swiss. MNCs rarely tell their scattered workers everything. Workers of different nationalities rarely tell each other anything. In an age when information is power, they lack both.

A day after its Scottish staff accepted a pay cut, Hyster telexed the news to its plant manager in Holland. It was his first official word of Hyster's "decision," which turned out to include the firing of a number of Dutch workers and his own early retirement.

Dutch law calls for consultation about such things, and the plant union took Hyster to court. There, a judge ordered Hyster to discuss its strategy with members of the factory works council. It did, revealing the sliver of its corporate plan that applied to them. The union did not like it and went to court again.

A long legal battle could have cost dearly, so Hyster struck a deal: The workers would drop the suit, and the company would not transfer production before 1986. Now the Scottish workforce is off balance again, despite Hyster's assurance that its expansion will go through.

Company view

Hyster's managing director in Europe is an American. But he is fighting a different war. "We're battling the Japanese," he says. "They've captured an alarmingly large share of the European market. To counter them, we have to produce a cost-effective forklift truck, and to do that, we've implemented a worldwide restructuring program. That required some very tough decisions. Given the circumstances, we've made every effort to communicate effectively with our employees."

Union view

Said one union leader, "What they call decentralized industrial relations means isolation for us. Without a multinational union you're at the mercy of a company like this." International unions have set up about 50 worker groups representing the car makers, the electronics companies, and the oil and chemicals industries. Their aim is to collect and exchange information. To date, however, not one MNC has agreed to meet with any of them. The MNCs are playing "hard ball," and they wield considerable power in international labor relations.[33]

Repatriation

The problems of repatriation, for those who succeed abroad as well as for those who do not, have been well documented. *All* repatriates experience some degree of anxiety in three areas: personal finances, reacclimation to the U.S. lifestyle, and readjustment to the corporate structure.[8] They also worry about the future of their careers and the location of their U.S. assignments.[9] Precisely the same issues were found in a study of Japanese expatriates who returned to Japan.[5]

Financially, repatriates face the loss of the expatriate premium and the effect of inflation on home purchases. Having become accustomed to foreign ways, upon reentry they often find home-country customs strange and, at the extreme, even annoying. Finally, many repatriates complain that their assignments upon return to their home country were mundane and lacked status and authority, in comparison to their overseas positions.[8] Possible solutions to these problems fall into three areas: planning, career management, and compensation.

Planning   Both the expatriation assignment and the repatriation move should be examined as parts of an integrated whole—not as unrelated events in the individual's career.[8] To do this, a firm agreement must be reached *prior* to expatriation about the specific job assignment overseas, the term of the assignment, the compensation package for the assignment, and the position, level, and location to which the employee will return.[25] Increasingly, MNCs are seeking to improve their human resource planning and also to implement it on a worldwide basis. Careful inclusion of expatriation and repatriation moves in this planning will help reduce uncertainty and the fear that accompanies it.[8]

Career management   Some MNCs appoint a "career sponsor" to look out for the expatriate's career interests while she or he is abroad and to ensure that a suitable assignment is available when the expatriate returns. This person must be sensitive to the "job shock" the expatriate may suffer when she or he gets back and must be trained to counsel the returning employee (and her or his family as well) until resettlement is deemed complete.[25]

Compensation   Loss of a monthly premium to which the expatriate has been accustomed is a severe shock financially, whatever the rationale. To overcome this problem, some firms have replaced the monthly foreign-service premium with a one-time "mobility premium" (e.g., 3 months' pay) for each move— overseas, back home, or to another overseas assignment. MNCs are also providing low-cost loans or other financial assistance so that expatriates can get back into their hometown housing markets at a level at least equivalent to what they left. Finally, there is a strong need for financial counseling for repatriates. Such counseling has the psychological advantage of demonstrating to repatriates that the company is willing to help with the financial problems that they may encounter in uprooting their families once again to bring them home.[8]

**CASE 17-1
Conclusion**

Costs of a cross-culturally naive employee

Many popular management books contain a fatal flaw. They focus on *style* and very little on *culture*. At Honeywell, managers have found that one of the most dangerous—and futile—corporate practices is to apply the management style of another country without first understanding its cultural foundation. This is because there are sharp cultural differences among countries, even among European nations, that generate vastly different management styles.

The relationship between cultural heritage and managerial style has been examined carefully by Dr. Andre Laurent at the European Institute of Business Administration. He asked managers from different countries a series of questions about how they would respond or react to certain situations in their own companies. The data show marked differences among countries on such concepts as authority, hierarchy, and politics, as well as everyday social conventions.

To operate effectively in a foreign culture, Laurent suggests, a manager must first understand his or her own culture. Then he or she must understand the culture of the country of which he or she is a temporary resident and the differences in management style that spring not from schooling or training, but from the culture itself.

Honeywell views such diversity as a source of vitality. Rather than *force* its foreign managers into an American mold, Honeywell draws on their unique cultural characteristics to strengthen its market position and its worldwide organization. Instead of imposing the management style of the parent company on foreign affiliates, the company focuses instead on the strengths of each.

The management group in Great Britain, for example, excels in interpersonal relationships, so much so that Honeywell has begun to look to its British affiliate as a testing ground for new human resource programs.

The Italian management team is known for its flexibility, for responding rapidly to change, so it has responsibility for Honeywell's business in the Middle East, Mediterranean countries, and Africa.

The discipline and creativity of the company's German and Swiss organizations are frequently the basis for major new product developments.

Honeywell has chosen Belgium and The Netherlands for its European headquarters, its European distribution center, and its Process Automation Center for Europe because of the international skills of the management groups in those countries.

Honeywell's Japanese organization has provided leadership in innovative, cost-effective designs. Finally, the company looks to the United States for strategic guidance, marketing skills, and basic technology.

No one has discovered a single best way to manage. But before a company can build an effective management team, it must understand thoroughly its own culture, the other cultures in which it does business, and the challenges and rewards of blending the best of each.

Summary

Foreign investment by the world's leading corporations is a fact of modern organizational life. For American executives transferred overseas, the opportunities are great, but the risks of failure (roughly 3 in 10) are considerable. This is because there are fundamental cultural differences that affect how different people view the world and operate in business. The lesson for MNCs is clear: Guard against the exportation of home-country bias, think in global terms, and recognize that no country has all the answers.

Recruitment for overseas assignments is typically based on one of the three basic models: (1) ethnocentrism, (2) limiting recruitment to home- and

---

TOMORROW'S FORECAST

MNCs dominate today's global economy, yet they are not without sin.[18] They have displayed some arrogance of power and selfish interests (e.g., the tactics used to gain MNC management power over labor). At the same time, however, they have brought technology and capital to the far reaches of the world, and they have made possible advances in the standards of living of many people. Above all, perhaps, they have made visible the emerging global economy—the interdependence of nations on raw materials and sources of energy. MNCs are the forerunners of business enterprises of the future, and their management teams have great challenges and great opportunities before them.

In the immediate future, there will certainly be international opportunities for managers at all levels, particularly those with the technical skills needed by developing countries. In the longer run, each MNC may have its own "foreign legion," a cadre of sophisticated international executives drawn from many countries.[42] There is a bright future for managers with the cultural flexibility to be sensitive to the values and aspirations of foreign countries.

Finally, there is one thing of which we can be certain. Talent—social, managerial, and technical—is needed to make MNCs go. Competent human resource management practices can find that talent, recruit it, select it, train and develop it, motivate it, reward it, and profit from it. This will be the greatest challenge of all in the years to come.

host-country nationals, or (3) geocentrism. Selection is based on five criteria: personality, skills, attitudes, motivation, and behavior. Orientation for expatriates and their families often takes place in three stages: initial, predeparture, and postarrival. Cross-cultural training may be academic (books, films, discussions) or interpersonal (the actual or simulated experience of living in the host country), but to be most effective it should be integrated with the firm's long-range global strategy and business planning. International compensation presents special problems since salary levels differ among countries. To be competitive, MNCs normally follow local salary patterns in each country. Expatriates, however, receive various types of premiums (expatriation, tax equalization, and COLAs) in addition to their base salaries. Benefits are handled in terms of the best-of-both-worlds model. An overseas assignment is not complete until repatriation problems have been resolved; these fall into three areas: personal finances, reacclimation to the U.S. lifestyle, and readjustment to the corporate structure. Finally, since MNCs operate across national boundaries while unions typically do not, the balance of power clearly rests with management in the multinational arena.

Discussion Questions

17-1 What advice would you give to a prospective expatriate regarding the application of his management style in Japan?

17-2 Discuss the special problems that women face in overseas assignments.

17-3 How can the balance of power between management and labor be restored in international labor relations?

17-4 Describe the conditions necessary in order for a geocentric recruitment policy to work effectively.

17-5 What are some key cultural differences that need to be addressed by MNCs operating across national boundaries?

17-6 Should foreign language proficiency be required for executives assigned overseas? Why or why not?

References

1. Adler, N. J., Doktor, R., & Redding, S. G. (1986). From the Atlantic to the Pacific century: Cross-cultural management reviewed. *Journal of Management, 12,* 295–318.
2. Allen, R., & Keaveny, T. (1988). *Contemporary labor relations* (2d ed.). Reading, MA: Addison-Wesley.
3. Birnbaum, P. H., Farh, J. L., & Wong, G. Y. Y. (1986). The job characteristics model in Hong Kong. *Journal of Applied Psychology, 71,* 598–605.
4. Brooks, B. J. (1987, May). Trends in international executive compensation. *Personnel,* pp. 67–70.